P9-CMF-526

THE PULPIT COMMENTARY

EDITED BY THE

VERY REV. H. D. M. SPENCE, D.D.

DEAN OF GLOUCESTER

AND BY THE

REV. JOSEPH S. EXELL, M.A.

ST. LUKE

Exposition

BY VERY REV. H. D. M. SPENCE, D.D.

DEAN OF GLOUCESTER

Homiletics

BY REV. J. MARSHALL LANG, D.D.

THE BARONY PARISH, GLASGOW

Homilies by Various Authors

REV. W. CLARKSON, B.A. REV. R. M. EDGAR, M.A.

VOL. II

NEW EDITION

FUNK & WAGNALLS COMPANY

LONDON AND NEW YORK

THE

GOSPEL ACCORDING TO ST. LUKE.

EXPOSITION.

CHAPTER XIII.

Vers. 1—9.—*Signs of the times. The Lord continues his solemn warnings. Israel pictured in the parable of the barren fig tree.*

Ver. 1.—**There were present at that season some that told him of the Galilæans, whose blood Pilate had mingled with their sacrifices;** better rendered, *now there were present at that particular time;* namely, when the Master was discoursing of the threatening signs of the times, and urging men to repent and to turn and make their peace with God while there was yet time, for a terrible crisis was impending on that doomed land. Some of those then present, probably Jerusalem Jews, specially told off to watch the great Teacher, struck with his grave foreboding tone, when he spoke of the present aspect of affairs, quoted to him a recent bloody fray which had taken place in the temple courts. "Yes, Master," these seemed to say, "we see there is a fierce hatred which is ever growing more intense between Jew and Roman. You know, for instance, what has just taken place in the city, only the victims in this case were Galilæans, not scrupulous, righteous Jews. Is it not possible that these bloody deeds are simply punishments of men who are great sinners, as *these* doubtless were?" Such-like incidents were often now occurring under the Roman rule. This, likely enough, had taken place at some crowded Passover gathering, when a detachment of soldiers came down from the Castle of Antonia and had dealt a red-handed "justice" among the turbulent mob. Josephus relates several of the more formidable of such collisions between the Romans and the Jews. At one Passover he relates how three thousand Jews were butchered, and the temple courts were filled with dead corpses; at another of these feasts two thousand perished in like manner (see 'Ant.,' xvii. 9. 3; xx. 5. 3; and 'Bell. Jud.,' ii. 5; v. 1). On another occasion disguised legionaries were sent by Pilate the governor with daggers among the Passover crowds (see 'Ant.,' xviii. 31). These wild and terrible collisions were of frequent occurrence in these sad days.

Vers. 2, 3.—**And Jesus answering said unto them, Suppose ye that these Galilæans were sinners above all the Galilæans, because they suffered such things? I tell you, Nay: but, except ye repent, ye shall all likewise perish.** "Yes," answered the Master, "these, you are right, are among the dread signs of the times I spoke of; but do not dream that the doom fell on those poor victims because they were *special* sinners. What happened to *them* will soon be the doom of the *whole nation*, unless a great change in the life of Israel takes place."

Ver. 4.—**Or those eighteen, upon whom the tower in Siloam fell, and slew them, think ye that they were sinners above all men that dwelt in Jerusalem?** "You remember," goes on the Master, "the catastrophe of the fall of the tower in Siloam; the poor sufferers who were crushed there were not specially wicked men." The Lord used these occasions, we see, for something more than the great national lesson. Men are too ready, now as then, to give way to the unloving error of looking at individual misfortune as the consequence of individual crime. Such human uncharitable judgments the Lord bitterly condemns. Ewald's conjecture in connection with this Siloam accident is ingenious. He supposes that the rigid Jews looked on the catastrophe as a retribution because the workmen who perished were paid by Pilate out of the sacred corban money (see Josephus, 'Bell. Jud.,' ii. 9. 4). The works were no doubt in connection with the aqueduct to the Pool of Siloam.

Ver. 5.—**Except ye repent, ye shall all likewise perish.** The words were indeed prophetic to the letter. Thousands of Jews perished in the last terrible war by the swords of the Roman legionaries, like the Galilæans of ver. 1; not a few met their death in the capital among the ruins of the burning fallen houses. We know that Jerusalem in its entirety was destroyed, and the loss of life in the siege, and especially in its dread closing scenes, was simply incalculable. Within forty years all this happened.

Ver. 6.—**He spake also this parable; A certain man had a fig tree planted in his vineyard.** And then, without any further prelude, Jesus spoke this parable of the barren fig tree, which contained, in language scarcely veiled at all, warnings to Israel as a nation—the most sombre and threatening he had yet given utterance to "Hear, O people," said the Master. "In the vineyard of the Lord of hosts is a fig tree, long planted there, but utterly unfruitful. It is now on its last trial; indeed, were it not for the intercession of the Gardener, the Lord of the vineyard had already pronounced its final doom." "The very intercession, though, is ominous; the Vinedresser shows his mercifulness by deprecating immediate cutting down, but the careful specification of conditions, and the limitation of the period within which experiments are to be made, intimate that peril is imminent. . . . The restriction of the intercession of the Vinedresser for a single year's grace indicates Christ's own sympathy with this Divine rigour. . . . The Vinedresser knows that, though God is long-suffering, yet his patience as exhibited in the history of his dealings with men is exhaustible, and that in Israel's case it is now all but worn out. And he sympathizes with the Divine impatience with chronic and incurable sterility" (Professor Bruce). **A fig tree planted in his vineyard; and he came and sought fruit thereon, and found none.** It is not an uncommon practice to plant fig trees at the corners of vineyards, thus utilizing every available spot of ground. Still the Lord's choice of a fig tree as the symbol of Israel, the chosen people, is at first sight strange. This image was no doubt selected to show those Pharisees and other Jews, proud of what they considered their unassailable position as the elect of the Eternal, that, after all, the position they occupied was but that of a fig tree in the corner of the vineyard of the world—planted there and watched over so long as it promised to serve the Lord of the vineyard's purpose; if it ceased to do that, if it gave no further promise of fruit, then it would be ruthlessly cut down.

Ver. 7.—**Behold, these three years I come seeking fruit on this fig tree, and find none.** Some expositors see in this period of three years an allusion to the storied past of Hebrew life, and in the number 3 discern the three marked epochs, each lasting several centuries, of the high priests, judges, and kings. This, however, is a very doubtful reference, owing to the impossibility of separating the first two periods of the rule of high priests and judges, as these interchange and overlap each other. Another school of interpreters sees a reference to the three years of the public ministry of Jesus. A better reference would be God's successive calls to Israel by the Law, the prophets, and by Christ. It is, however, safer, in this and in many of the Lord's parables, not to press every little detail which was necessary for the completion of the picture. Here the period of three years in which the Lord of the vineyard came seeking fruit, represents by the number 3 the symbol of completeness—a period of full opportunity given to the tree to have become fruitful and productive. **Cut it down; why cumbereth it the ground?** better rendered, *why doth it make the ground useless?* It is an unproductive tree, and occupies the place which another and a fertile tree might fill.

Ver. 8.—**And he answering said unto him, Lord, let it alone this year also, till I shall dig about it, and dung it.** The last year—the year of grace *they* who listened to him then were living in. It was the last summons to repentance, the final reminder to the old covenant people that to their high privileges as the chosen race there were duties attached. They prided themselves on the privileges, they utterly forgot the duties. The period represented by this last year included the preaching of John the Baptist, the public ministry of Jesus Christ, and the forty years of apostolic teaching which followed the Crucifixion and Resurrection. The last chance was given, but in the Vinedresser's prayer to the Lord of the vineyard there is scarcely a ray of hope. The history of the world supplies the sequel to this parable-story.

Vers. 10—17.—*A miracle of mercy. The Lord's teaching on certain strict observances of the sabbath day then practised by the more rigid Jews.*

Ver. 10.—**And he was teaching in one of the synagogues on the sabbath.** We hear little of our Lord's public teaching in the synagogues of the towns and villages through which he was then passing in this his last long journey. In the earlier months of the ministry of Jesus he seems to have taught frequently in these houses of prayer, very possibly every sabbath day. It has been suggested, with considerable probability, that owing to the persistent enmity of the hierarchy and dominant class at Jerusalem, he was excluded from some at least of the synagogues by what was termed the "lesser excommunication."

Ver. 11.—**And, behold, there was a woman which had a spirit of infirmity eighteen years, and was bowed together, and could in no wise lift up herself.** The description of the sufferer, so accurate in its details, marks the medical training of the compiler here. The malady was evidently a curvature of the spine of a very grave character. Her presence in the synagogue that day gives us a hint, at least, that this poor afflicted one loved communion with her God. Doubtless the faith and trust on her side necessary to the cure were there. Her first act, after she was sensible of the blessed change wrought in her poor diseased frame, was an outpouring of devout thanks to God.

Ver. 14.—**And the ruler of the synagogue answered with indignation, because that Jesus had healed on the sabbath day.** The people, as usual, were stirred to enthusiasm by this glorious act of power and mercy. Afraid, before the congregation of the synagogue, to attack the Master personally, the "ruler," no doubt influenced by members of the Pharisee party who were present, attempted to represent the great Physician as a deliberate scorner of the sacred Law. The sabbath regulations at this time were excessively burdensome and childishly rigorous. The Law, as expounded in the schools of the rabbis, allowed physicians to act in cases of emergency, but not in chronic diseases such as this. How deep an interest must such a memory of the Master's as this sabbath day's healing have had for that beloved physician who has given his name to these memoirs we call the Third Gospel! Often in later years, in Syrian Antioch, in the great cities of Italy and Greece, would he, as he plied his blessed craft among the sick on the sabbath day, be attacked by rigid Jews as one who profaned the day. To such would he relate this incident, and draw *his* lessons of mercy and of love.

Ver. 15.—**The Lord then answered him, and said, Thou hypocrite, doth not each one of you on the sabbath loose his ox or his ass from the stall, and lead him away to watering?** The older authorities here read "hypocrites," and thus join the cavilling synagogue ruler with the whole sect of men who taught an elaborate ritual in place of a high, pure life. The Lord, in a few master-touches, exposes the hollowness of such sabbath-keeping. Every possible indulgence was to be shown in cases where their own interests were involved; no mercy or indulgence was to be thought of, though, where the sick poor only were concerned. He vividly draws a contrast between the animal and the human being. The ox and the ass, though, were personal property; the afflicted daughter of Abraham was but a woman, friendless and poor.

Vers. 18—21.—*The Lord, in two little prophetic parables tells the people how strangely and mightily his religion would spread over the earth.*

Ver. 18.—**Then said he, Unto what is the kingdom of God like? and whereunto shall I resemble it?** In the seventeenth verse—after the Lord's words spoken to his enemies, who took exception at his miracle of healing worked for the poor woman who had been bent for eighteen years, because he had done it on the sabbath day—we read how "all his adversaries were ashamed; and all the people rejoiced for all the glorious things that were done by him." This discomfiture of the hypocrites, and the honest joy of the simple folk over a noble and Divine deed of mercy, accompanied by brave, kind words, seem to have suggested to the Master the subject of the two little parables of the mustard seed and the leaven, in which parables the growth of his glorious kingdom was foreshadowed from very small beginnings. The very small beginning he could discern in what then surrounded him.

Ver. 19.—**It is like a grain of mustard seed, which a man took, and cast into his garden; and it grew, and waxed a great tree; and the fowls of the air lodged in the branches of it.** The simile was a well-known one in the Jewish world. "As small as a grain of mustard seed" was a proverb current among the people in those days. In Eastern countries this little seed often becomes a tree, and stories are even told of mustard trees so tall that a man could climb up into their branches or ride beneath them on horseback. Such instances are possibly very rare, but it is a common sight to see a mustard plant, raised from one of these minute grains, grown to the height of a fruit tree, putting forth branches on which birds build their nests. It was with sorrowful irony that the great Teacher compared the kingdom of God in those days to this small grain. The kingdom of God on earth then was composed of Jesus and his few wavering followers. To the eye of sense it seemed impossible that this little movement could ever stir the world, could ever become a society of mighty dimensions. "See," said the Master, taking up a little mustard seed; "does *this* seem as though it would ever become a tree with spreading branches on which the birds might rest? The kingdom of God is like this seed."

Ver. 21.—**It is like leaven, which a woman took and hid in three measures of meal, till** the whole was leavened. The *first* of these two little parables of the kingdom, "the mustard seed," portrayed its strangely rapid growth. The *second*, "the leaven," treats of the mighty inward transformation which the kingdom of God will effect in the hearts of men and women. Chemically speaking, leaven is a lump of sour dough in which putrefaction has begun, and, on being introduced into a far greater mass of fresh dough, produces by contagion a similar condition into the greater bulk with which it comes in contact. The result of the contact, however, is that the mass of dough, acted upon by the little lump of leaven, becomes a wholesome, agreeable food for men. It was a singularly striking and powerful simile, this little commonplace comparison, and exactly imaged the future progress of "the kingdom." Quietly, silently, the doctrine of the Master made its way into the hearts and homes of men. "He shall not strive, nor cry; neither shall any man hear his voice in the streets" (Matt. xii. 19). None on earth would have dared hint at the future success of the doctrine of the Master during the Master's life, and his death seemed as though it would effectually crush out the last feeble spark of life. The apparent result of his work was the devotion of a few simple hearts, mostly of fishermen, artisans, and the like, and yet, though men suspected it not, the secret and powerful influence was already at work among men. The story of the years succeeding the cross and the Resurrection, on a broader stage and with more actors, was a story of similar silent, quiet working. In a century and a half after the strange leaven-parable had been spoken, the whole civilized world knew something of the Master's history and doctrine. His disciples then were counted by tens of thousands. No city, scarcely a village, but contained some into whose hearts the teaching had sunk, whose lives the teaching had changed. *In three measures of meal.* Perhaps referring here to the well-known division of man into body, soul, and spirit. More likely, however, the number 3 is used as the symbol of completeness, signifying that the Divine purpose was then influencing the whole mass of mankind. *Till the whole was leavened.* It would seem as though the Master looked on to a definite time when all nations should come and worship him, and acknowledge his glorious sovereignty. If this be the case, then a very long period still remains to be lived through by the world; many kingdoms must rise and fall, new civilizations spring up, before that day of joy and gladness dawns upon the globe—that is, reasoning on the analogy of the past. Be this, however, as it may, the drift of both these parables of the kingdom distinctly points to a slow yet a progressive development of true religion. Very different, indeed, was the Jewish conception of Messiah's kingdom. They expected a rapid and brilliant metamorphosis of the then unhappy state of things. They never dreamed of the slow and quiet movement Messiah's coming was to inaugurate. One thing is perfectly clear—the Speaker of these two parable-stories never contemplated a speedy return to earth. With strange exactness the last eighteen hundred and fifty years have been fulfilling the conditions of the two similes, and as yet, as far as man can see, they are not nearly complete.

Ver. 22.—**And he went through the cities and villages, teaching, and journeying toward Jerusalem.** This note of the evangelist simply calls attention that the last solemn progress in the direction of the capital was still going on. The question has been discussed at length above. St. Luke, by these little notes of time and place, wishes to direct attention to the fact that all this part of the Gospel relates to one great division of the public ministry—to that which immediately preceded the last Passover.

Vers. 23—30.—*Jesus replies to the question of "Are there few that be saved?"*

Ver. 23.—**Then said one unto him, Lord, are there few that be saved?** The immediate circumstance which called out this question is not recorded, but the general tone of the Master's later teaching, especially on the subject of his kingdom of the future, had disturbed the vision of many in Israel, who loved to dwell on the exclusion of all save the chosen race from the glories of the world to come. The words of the Second Book of Esdras, written perhaps forty or fifty years after this time, well reflect this selfish spirit of harsh exclusiveness, peculiarly a characteristic of the Jew in the days of our Lord. "The Most High hath made this world for many, but the world to come for few" (2 Esdr. viii. 1). "There be many more of them which perish, than of them which shall be saved: like as a wave is greater than a drop" (2 Esdr. ix. 15, 16). Other passages breathing a similar spirit might be quoted. What relics we possess of Jewish literature of this period all reflect the same stern, jealous, exclusive spirit. The questioner here either hoped to get from the popular Master some statement which might be construed into an approval of this national spirit of hatred of everything that was not Jewish, or, if Jesus chose to combat these selfish hopes, the Master's words might then be quoted to the people as unpatriotic.

Ver. 24.—**Strive to enter in at the strait**

gate: for many, I say unto you, will seek to enter in, and shall not be able. The Master, as was frequently his custom, gave no direct answer to his questioner, but his teaching which immediately follows contained the answer to the query. The older authorities, in place of "at the strait gate," read "through the narrow door." The meaning of the image, however, is the same, whichever reading be adopted. The image was not a new one. It had been used before by the Lord, perhaps more than once (see Matt. vii. 13, 14), and not improbably had been suggested by some town or fortress hard by the spot where he was teaching—a fort on a hill with a narrow road winding up to a narrow door. In the rabbinical schools he frequented in his youth, he might, too, have heard some adaptation of the beautiful allegory known as the 'Tablet' of Cebes, the disciple of Socrates: "Dost thou not perceive a narrow door, and a pathway before the door, in no way crowded, but few, very few, go in thereat?" The teaching of the Master here is, that the door of salvation is a narrow one, and, to pass through it, the man must *strive* in real earnest. "See," he seems to say; "if only few are saved, it will not be because the Jews are few and the Gentile nations many, but because, of the Jews and Gentiles, only *a few* really strive. Something different from race or national privileges will be the test at that narrow door which leads to life. "Many will seek to enter in, and shall not be able." The reason for the exclusion of these many is to be sought in themselves. They *wished* to enter in, but confined themselves to wishes. They made no strong, vigorous efforts. Theirs was no life of stern self-surrender, of painful self-sacrifice. To wish to pass through that narrow door is not enough.

Ver. 25.—**When once the master of the house is risen up, and hath shut to the door, and ye begin to stand without, and to knock at the door, saying, Lord, Lord, open unto us; and he shall answer and say unto you, I know you not whence ye are.** The great Teacher here slightly changes the imagery. The narrow door no longer is the centre of the picture; one, called the "master of the house," becomes the principal figure. The door now shut may still be, most probably is, the narrow fort or hill-city entrance, and the one called the master is the governor of the Place of Arms, into which the door or gate led. It is now too late even for the earnest striver to enter in. Sunset probably—the shades of night, had the Divine Painter furnished the imagery—would have been the signal for the final closing of the door of the fortress. Death is the period when the door of salvation is shut to the children of men. It has been asked—To what time does the Master refer in the words "when once"? It cannot be the epoch of the ruin of Jerusalem and the breaking up of the Jewish nationality, for then there was nothing in the attitude of the doomed people to answer to the standing without, to the knocking at the door, and to the imploring cries, "Lord, Lord, open unto us," portrayed here. It cannot be the second coming of the Lord; surely then his people will not call on him in vain. It refers, without doubt, to the day of judgment, when the dread award will be pronounced upon the unbelieving, the selfish, and the evil-liver.

Vers. 26, 27.—**Then shall ye begin to say, We have eaten and drunk in thy presence, and thou hast taught in our streets. But he shall say, I tell you, I know you not whence ye are; depart from me, all ye workers of iniquity.** A very stern declaration on the part of Jesus that in the day of judgment no special favour would be granted to the souls of the chosen people. It was part of the reply to the question respecting the "fewness of the saved." The inquirer wished to know the opinion of the great Teacher on the exclusive right of Israel to salvation in the world to come, and this statement, describing salvation as something independent of all questions as to race, was the Master's reply.

Ver. 28.—**There shall be weeping and gnashing of teeth, when ye shall see Abraham, and Isaac, and Jacob, and all the prophets, in the kingdom of God, and you yourselves thrust out.** No less than six times is this terrible formula, which expresses the intensest form of anguish, found in St. Matthew's Gospel. St. Luke only gives us the account of one occasion on which they were spoken. They indicate, as far as merely earthly words and symbols can, the utter misery of those unhappy ones who find themselves shut out from the kingdom in the world to come. "Abraham, and Isaac, and Jacob." In his revision of St. Luke's Gospel, Marcion, the famous Gnostic heretic, in place of these names, which he strikes out, inserts "all the just." He did this with a view to lower the value of the Old Testament records.

Ver. 29.—**And they shall come from the east, and from the west, and from the north, and from the south, and shall sit down in the kingdom of God.** Instead of "shall sit down," a clearer and more accurate rendering would be, *shall recline as at a banquet.* This image of the heaven-life as a banquet, at which the great Hebrew patriarchs were present, was a well-known one in popular Hebrew teaching. There is an unmistakable reference to Isa. xlv. 6 and xlix. 12

in this announcement of comers to the great banquet of heaven from all the four quarters of the globe. This completes the answer to the question. It forbids any limitation to the numbers of the saved. It distinctly includes in those blessed ranks men from all parts of the far isles of the Gentiles.

Ver. 30.—**And, behold, there are last which shall be first, and there are first which shall be last.** This expression, which apparently was more than once used by the Lord, in this place clearly has an historical reference, and sadly predicts the rejection of Israel, not only in this present world.

"There above (on earth)
How many hold themselves for mighty kings,
Who here like swine shall wallow in the mire,
Leaving behind them horrible dispraise!"
(Dante, 'Inferno.')

Vers. 31—35.—*The message of Jesus to Herod Antipas, and the lament over the loved city of Jerusalem, the destined place of his own death.*

Ver. 31.—**The same day there came certain of the Pharisees, saying unto him, Get thee out, and depart hence: for Herod will kill thee.** Very many of the older authorities read here, instead of "the same day," "in that very hour." This incident connected with Herod Antipas, which is only related by St. Luke, not improbably was communicated to Luke and Paul by Manaen, who was intimately connected with that prince, and who was a prominent member of the primitive Church of Antioch in those days when Paul was beginning his work for the cause (see Acts xiii. 1). This curious message probably emanated from Herod and Herodias. The tetrarch was disturbed and uneasy at the Lord's continued presence in his dominions, and the crowds who thronged to hear the great Teacher occasioned the jealous and timorous prince grave disquietude. Herod shrank from laying hands on him, though, for the memory of the murdered friend of Jesus was a terrible one, we know, to the superstitious tetrarch, and he dreaded being forced into a repetition of the judicial murder of John the Baptist. It is likely enough that the enemies of the Lord were now anxious for him to go to Jerusalem and its neighbourhood, where he would be in the power of the Sadducean hierarchy, and away from the protection of the Galilæan multitudes, with whom his influence was still very great. The Pharisees, who as a party hated the Master, willingly entered into the design, and under the mask of a pretended friendship warned him of Herod's intentions.

Ver. 32.—**And he said unto them, Go ye, and tell that fox;** literally, *that she-fox.* The Lord saw through the shallow device, and, in reply to his false friends, bade them go to that intriguing and false court with a message which he would give them. The epithet "she-fox" is perhaps the bitterest and most contemptuous name ever given by the pitiful Master to any of the sons of men. It is possible it might have been intended for Herodias, the influence of that wicked princess being at that time all-powerful at court. **Behold, I cast out devils, and I do cures to-day and to-morrow, and the third day I shall be perfected.** "Tell Herod or Herodias that I have a work still to work here; a few more evil spirits to cast out, a few more sick folk to heal. I am going on as I have begun; no message, friendly or unfriendly, will turn me from my purpose. I have no fears of his royal power, but I shall not trouble him long; just to-day and to-morrow—this was merely (as in Hos. vi. 2) a proverbial expression for a short time—and on the third day I complete my work." This completion some have understood by the crowning miracle on dead Lazarus at Bethany, but it is far better to understand it as referring to the Passion, as including the last sufferings, the cross, and the resurrection. The τελειοῦμαι here was supplemented by the utterance with which the blessed life came to its close on the cross—Τετελέσται! Τελείωσις became a recognized term for martyrdom.

Ver. 33.—**Nevertheless I must walk to-day, and to-morrow, and the day following: for it cannot be that a prophet perish out of Jerusalem.** He reflects, "Yes, I must go on with my journey for the little space yet left to me;" and then turning to the false Pharisee friends, with the saddest irony bids them not be afraid. Priest and Sanhedrin, the unholy alliance against him of Sadducee and Pharisee, would not be balked of the Victim whose blood they were all thirsting after. Their loved city had ever had one melancholy prerogative. It had ever been the place of death for the prophets of the Lord. That sad privilege would not be taken from it in his case.

Ver. 34.—**O Jerusalem, Jerusalem, which killest the prophets, and stonest them that are sent unto thee!** This exquisite and moving apostrophe was uttered in similar language in the Passion-week, just as Jesus was leaving the temple for the last time. It was spoken here with rare appropriateness in the first instance after the promise of sad irony that the holy city should not be deprived of the spectacle of the Teacher-Prophet's death. "O Jerusalem, Jerusalem!" It was a farewell to the holy city. It was the sorrowful summing-up of the tenderest love of centuries. Never had earthly city been loved like this. There the anointed of the Eternal were to fix their home. There the stately shrine for the service of the invisible King of Israel was to keep watch and ward over the favoured capital of the chosen race. There the visible presence of the Lord God Almighty, the Glory and the Pride of the people, was ever and anon to rest. And in this solemn last farewell, the Master looked back through the vista of the past ages of Jerusalem's history. It was a dark and gloomy contemplation. It had been all along the wicked chief city of a wicked people, of a people who had thrown away the fairest chances ever offered to men—the city of a people whose annals were memorable for deeds of blood, for the most striking ingratitude, for incapacity, for folly shading into crime. Not once nor twice in that dark story of Israel chosen messengers of the invisible King had visited the city he loved so well. These were invested with the high credentials which belong to envoys from the King of kings, with a voice sweeter and more persuasive, with a power grander and more far-reaching than were the common heritage of men; and these envoys, his prophets, they had maltreated, persecuted, murdered. **How often would I have gathered thy children together, as a hen doth gather her brood under her wings!** God's great love to Israel had been imaged in the far back days of the people, when Moses judged them, under a similar metaphor. *Then* it was the eagle fluttering over her young and bearing them on her wings; now it is slightly altered to one if possible more tender and loving, certainly more homely. How often in bygone days would the almighty wings, indeed, had Israel only wished it, have been spread out over them a sure shelter! Now the time of grace was over, and the almighty wings were folded. **And ye would not!** Sad privilege, specially mentioned here by the Divine Teacher, this freedom of man's will to resist the grace of God. "Ye would not," says the Master, thus joining the generation who heard his voice to the stiffnecked Israel of the days of the wicked kings.

Ver. 35.—**Behold, your house is left unto you desolate.** The older authorities omit "desolate." The sentence will then read, "your house is left unto you." *Their* house from henceforth, not *his*. **Ye shall not see me, until the time come when ye shall say, Blessed is he that cometh in the Name of the Lord.** "Ye shall not see me." Van Oosterzee comments here: "Their senses are still blinded. The veil of the Talmud that hangs over their eyes is twice as heavy as the veil of Moses." The promise which concludes this saying of the Master can only refer to the far future, to the day of the penitence of Israel. It harmonizes with the voice of the older prophets, and tells us that the day will surely come when the people shall look on him whom they pierced, and shall mourn. But *that* mourning will be turned speedily into joy.

HOMILETICS.

Vers. 1—9.—*The barren fig tree.* "At that season," or "at that particular time"—whilst the pleading, warning words which follow from the forty-ninth verse of the previous chapter are ringing in the ears of those around the Lord—some bystanders tell him of judgments which had actually been fulfilled, of Galilæans whose blood Pilate had mingled with their sacrifices. We have no information as to the particular event referred to. Riots, small insurrections, revolts from Roman authority, were by no means uncommon, and we know that Pilate was cruel in his repression of them. Probably these Galilæans had been rioting, and the procurator had profaned the holy things of the sanctuary by casting their blood over the offering made by fire. And the thought simmering in the minds of the superstitious speakers was, "These wretched people had not given the diligence which had been spoken of. They died unreconciled and impenitent. They were great offenders, therefore they endured great punishment." It was a prevalent belief among the Jews that signal calamity to individuals was the token of signal Divine displeasure. This was the inference of Job's companions when they saw him in the day of his sore grief. This was the inference of the men near Christ as to the victims of the dark catastrophe. And he who knows what is in man at once finds the place of their thought, rebukes their hasty reasoning, and summons them, instead of reflecting on others, to try their own ways and remember, "Except ye repent, ye shall all likewise perish." The parable which follows enforces this appeal to the conscience. It is a short but wonderfully expressive parable. "Everything is involved in it," says Stier, "which a mission of repentance to a people demands."

I. Observe, the truth on which Jesus insists is THE NEED OF PERSONAL REPENTANCE

ON THE PART OF ALL. In contrast with his audience, this was the application of the calamities related which he made. These were to him the prophecy of the doom awaiting every one who continued in his sins. Archbishop Trench emphasizes the "likewise." "Ye shall all *likewise* perish, *i.e.* in a manner similar to that in which both the Galilæans and the eighteen on whom the tower in Siloam fell perished. So, in the destruction of Jerusalem years afterwards, multitudes of the inhabitants were crushed beneath the ruins of their temple and their city, and, during the last siege and assault, numbers were pierced through by the Roman darts, or, more miserably yet, by those of their own frantic factions in the courts of the temple, in the very act of preparing their sacrifices. So that, literally, their blood, like that of the Galilæans, was mingled with their sacrifices, one blood with another." All befallings of judgment which men witness should be, not occasions of criticism or of harsh stricture on others, but voices bidding to humility and self-examination. The sin which I can trace in my neighbour should chiefly remind me of the sin which has dominion over myself. If I have been kept from his transgression, let me thank the grace which has kept me, recall how great perhaps was the difference between his circumstances and mine, and ask whether, in some other form, I may not have been a transgressor as great as he. Reflections such as these will save from all Pharisaic exaltation, will send us to our knees for the erring brother, ay, and send us to our knees for ourselves—the word of the Lord sounding within, "Thinkest thou that he is a sinner above thee, because he suffers such things? I tell thee, Nay: except thou repent, thou shalt likewise perish."

II. Now see in the parable BOTH THE GOODNESS AND THE SEVERITY WHICH LEAD TO REPENTANCE. The details—who owns the vineyard? what the vineyard represents? who is the Dresser or the Gardener? for what the three years and the one year of grace stand?—need not here be discussed. The parable is a picture of Almighty God in his dealings with his Church, Jewish or Gentile, in the desire of his love, in the responsiveness of his heart to the intercession of the Mediator whom he has appointed, in the deferring of his judgment so that a fuller opportunity may be given to men to confess his presence and seek him with their whole heart, and flee from the wrath to come. Notice three of the salient features. 1 *The fruit which is sought*—sought year by year with increasing disappointment: fruit, the legitimate product of the tree, growing out of its life, marking its use and value. We hear the astonished "What more could I do to my vineyard that I have not done?" And nothing—"nothing but leaves." Herein we recognize the longing of the love of God. He gives to men that men may give of his, one to another. As his own goodness is "a flowing life-fountain," so is the goodness which is the expression of the new heart and the right spirit. The fruitless tree keeps a certain energy to itself. There is a power in it which remains undeveloped. It draws the moisture away from the surrounding soil, it receives the rain and sunshine of heaven; it is all an *in*-come, there is no *out*-come. Is it not the type of the kind of person who is a stranger and foreigner to the life of the Eternal—a person who is fed, but does not feed; who claims to be ministered to, but does not seek the bliss of ministering; whose character has no distinct influence for good; who is not what, in his place and according to his opportunity, the Lord of the vineyard expects him to be? God comes to men for his harvest. Is he receiving it from us? "Herein," says Christ, "is my Father glorified, that ye bear much fruit." Remember, "*much* fruit"—the well-matured, well-ripened godliness of the one in whose heart are God's ways. Resemblances cannot impose on him whose eyes are as a flame of fire. Why did he curse the tree which he beheld on his way to Bethany? Not because it was barren, but because it was false. In the fig tree the fruit should appear before the leaves. He saw leaves where there had been no fruit. Profession is nothing. A routine of religious offices is nothing. Appearance before God is nothing. All this may be only an extra assumed for an occasion, and then taken off. The tree which produces is the tree that is sound at the core. The conscience right produces the life right. Repentance, the way of making the tree good; holiness, the life of repentance—for this God comes to each of us, seeking, expecting. 2. *What as to the intercession?* There appears on the scene the one who has been charged with the care of the vineyard. The first reference, no doubt, is to the Lord Jesus Christ himself, into whose hand the Father has given all things, and in whom is substantiated the craving of the old patriarch for the Interpreter—"the one among a thousand to whom the Eternal is gracious, and saith, Deliver from going down into the pit: I have found a ransom." It is he who ever liveth, the God-Man, to make intercession. "Yet not," as has been remarked, "as though the Father and the Son had different minds concerning sinners, not as though the counsels of the Father were wrath, and of the Son mercy: for righteousness and love are not qualities in him who *is* Righteousness and who *is* Love; they cannot, therefore, be set the one against the other, since they are his essential Being." Yes, "if any man sin, we have an Advocate with the Father, Jesus Christ the Righteous." But there is a secondary reference not to be overlooked. Before Jesus left the world to go to the Father, he promised to send the Holy Ghost as another Advocate; not another in the sense that he would be a different Person, but in the sense that he would be his other self—a Divine presence inhabiting the Church which is his body, and revealing and glorifying him. All faithful souls, anointed with the sevenfold gifts of this Paraclete, are joined with him in intercession for the unfaithful and unfruitful. The prayer of the Church is the voice of the Holy Ghost—Christ's voice echoing from human hearts. And the whole Bible is charged with the thought that, for the sake of the elect, because of their life and work and cry to heaven, judgments impending over the earth are stayed. Intercession is not a merely beautiful and becoming function; it is the power which binds "the whole round earth by golden chains about the feet of God." "Cut it down; why mischieveth it the ground? . . . Lord, let it alone this year also." 3. Finally, *God's times and spaces—what are they?* "These three years I come." The three years have been supposed to signify the epoch of the natural law, the epoch of the written Law, and, finally, the epoch of grace; Moses, the prophets, the acceptable year of the Lord's coming; the three years of Christ's ministry; childhood, manhood, old age. Whatever may be the value we attach to these explanations, the fact denoted is the long-suffering of God. Notice the two aspects of the waiting: to judge, but be gracious, and to judge and condemn. The latter is the "strange work." In grace, God comes silently; for condemnation, he comes, first crying aloud by his threatenings, "I am coming quickly," that the opportunity for the Intercessor may be given. First, the axe is laid at the root of the tree; there it lies, ready, yet the blow is deferred. "Cut it down;" yet a little longer—"this year also."

Vers. 22—30.—*The question and the answer.* "He went through the cities and villages." The circuits into which the ministry of Jesus was divided are most interesting. "He went about doing good." One feature is suggested by the evangelist's sentence. The *village* is not overlooked. If the desire had been merely to gain influence, he would have limited the teaching to the city. "Win the great centres of the populations; thus you will establish your reputation; thence the light will radiate to the obscurer places;"—this would have described the method of the action. Christ had another method. The small hamlet, no less than the crowded town, was the scene of his labour. It was the passion for souls which inspired him. The human soul, under all outward conditions, was one and the same to him. "The Son of man came to seek and to save that which was lost." Note *the direction of the face.* He is "journeying *towards* Jerusalem." The shadows of Gethsemane and Golgotha are lengthening. Ever before him, and now pressing on his heart, is the thought of the decease that he should accomplish. It is the occasion at once of the Saviour's sorrow and the Saviour's joy. The teaching would have been little without the forecast of the sacrifice; apart from the sacrifice, it loses its power. Jerusalem and its cross is the reference ever present to the Christian minister, whether in city or in village. In one of the places visited, the Lord is accosted by a person of whom the only notice is, "Then said one unto him." But the incident is instructive. It reminds us of (1) *a kind of question that is to be discountenanced*; and (2) *a kind of practical exhortation that is to be enforced.*

I. A KIND OF QUESTION THAT IS TO BE DISCOUNTENANCED. There is no reason to doubt the good faith of the interrogator. He is reverent in his inquiry, "Lord." There is nothing captious in his tone. He is the type of many earnest minds, puzzled over the problems of human life and destiny—minds that feel the pressure of the things which circumscribe the opportunity of multitudes, the bars which seem to interpose between men's souls and salvation, the limitations arising from imperfect knowledge and untoward condition; and, looking far and near over the ever-pouring throng, ask,

"Lord, what will this man and that man do? What is the extent to which the purpose to save will be realized?" He answers by not answering. The absence of a direct reply is itself a reply. It intimates that speculations and inquiries in the line of the word addressed to him are not to be encouraged. There was the wisdom which he emphasizes in the response once given by a child of quietness to the question, "What are the decrees of God?" "He knows that best himself," was the response. There are secrets which belong to the Lord our God, and these we must be content to leave with him. The things revealed belong to us; and these are expressed in the assurances that God loved the world, that whosoever believeth in the only begotten Son shall not perish, that him who comes to Christ he will in no wise cast out. They forget Christ's silence on the occasion before us who dogmatize either Calvinistically or Arminianistically. What can poor human nature do, in view of all that relates to the ultimate state of men, but simply trust him who is absolute Righteousness and Infinite Love? We may "faintly trust" larger hopes; we can, not faintly, but fully, trust him who will do what is best for all, who "hateth nothing that he hath made."

"Wait till he shall himself disclose
Things now beyond thy reach,
And be not thou meanwhile of those
Who the Lord's secrets teach.

"Who teach thee more than he has taught,
Tell more than he revealed,
Preach tidings which he never brought,
And read what he left sealed."

II. A KIND OF PRACTICAL EXHORTATION THAT IS TO BE ENFORCED. Withdrawing the mind of the inquirer from vague speculations, the matter which the Lord places next before him is this, "*Agonize* to enter in at the strait gate." How urgent, how solemn is the entreaty! The strait gate! Is it not a wide and ever-open one? Yes, in one sense it is. None who come with a true heart, in full assurance of faith, will be, can be, excluded. There is room for the east, and for the west, and for the north, and for the south; all nations, kindreds, peoples, and tongues. Christ's aim is, a universal religion. He throws his arms wide to all who labour and are heavy laden. But, in another sense, it is a strait gate. It is too narrow to admit any one in his sins. It is too narrow to admit the Pharisee in his Pharisaism, or the Sadducee in his Sadduceeism, or the Herodian in his Herodianism; too narrow to admit any one in his "*-ism*," in his self-righteousness, in anything on which he rests with satisfaction as a ground of distinction or superiority. All who enter, enter as sinners looking for the mercy of God, and desiring to be cleansed from all unrighteousness.

"Nothing in my hand I bring,
Simply to thy cross I cling."

The entrance into the strait gate is the first of all interests, is the most pressing of all concerns. Instead of scattering energy over secondary issues, energy is to be concentrated on this. Put your whole strength into the accomplishment of the one end. Christ insists, "Strive [or, 'agonize'] to enter." "Faith is a very simple thing." Yet there is a discipline which is not a very simple thing. Evangelical, especially the phase which is called evangelistic, preaching too often overlooks the discipline. It is frequently an exclusive repetition of the cry, "Believe, and you receive; believe, and you shall live." It forgets that the beginning of the gospel of Christ was "Repent!" It has not a distinct enough place for repentance. It is so occupied with the endeavour to make the way easy, that it fails to urge, with the intensity of Jesus' preaching, the necessity of a thorough self-repression, of a real taking of the cross, of the fighting of the good fight of faith. Let none overlook the *agonistic* side of the Christian life. Let the preacher echo and illustrate the sharp, stern, "Agonize to enter in"—not, indeed, a joyless and weary, but always, to flesh and blood, a real *agony*. There are three enforcements of the exhortation. 1. *Many are unable to enter:* unable when the desire becomes active. The door was open when the desire was torpid, when the heart was listless. They might have heard the beseechings of grace, but there was only a feeble response. Perhaps they intended, at some time, to enter; like Augustine, who prayed for his conversion, and added, "But not yet." Anyhow, the hour is coming when the impotence of unfulfilled intentions will be made manifest. Jesus' language passes (ver. 25) into the familiar form of parable. He imagines the Master of the house allowing the door to stand open—the invitation to all free and full. But at length he rises and shuts the door, and then those who had thought that any time would do, that there was no call to make haste, rush forward, clamouring for the entrance of which they had thought little—their clamour to be met only with the retort, "I know you not whence ye are." "My sheep hear my voice, and I know them." These had not heard his voice. It is not the attraction of his voice to which they confess; it is only the sense of their danger. And the word goes forth for judgment: "I know you not; you are not mine." The parable is not to be unduly strained; but the point which it tends to illustrate is the necessity of *instant*, as well as *earnest*, agonizing. There is a "too late, too late!" From its unutterable darkness may the good Lord deliver us! 2. *Enjoyment of privilege will not avail as a plea.* (Vers. 26, 27.) To have had the teaching of the Lord in street and house, to have lived in the marvellous light of his gospel, to have realized his fellowship and the influences of his grace,—this is much. But the vital matter is, what is the use which has been made of privilege, of opportunity, of instruction, of means of grace? That the Lord displayed his tokens in our midst may only add to our condemnation. Negligence, hardness of heart, the contempt of his Word and commandments, which is evidenced in the refusal to yield ourselves wholly to him who speaks from heaven, is iniquity; and most solemn is the protestation, "Depart from me, all ye workers of iniquity." 3. *Grace unavailed of is blessing lost.* (Vers. 28—30.) The Jew assured himself that in the kingdom of God, when declared, he would share the everlasting banquet with Abraham and Isaac and Jacob, and that part of the zest of this feast would be the consciousness that the hated Gentiles were excluded. The Lord warns his audience that the picture might be, would be, reversed. The grace which they would not use would be transferred to others, coming from the east, and the west, and the north, and the south. And he concludes with the sentence, which at other times also he utters, "There are last which shall be first, and there are first which shall be last." Verily it may here be added, "He that hath an ear, let him hear."

Vers. 31—35.—*The composure and the emotion of Jesus.* I. THE COMPOSURE IN THE FACE OF A MESSAGE WHICH MIGHT HAVE AGITATED. The message may have been a concoction of the Pharisees, who, wishing to have him removed from the district, used the name of Herod to alarm him; or it may have been inspired by Herod himself, who, although desiring to see Jesus, was jealous of his popularity, and was fearful lest in some way an uproar might be excited among the people. The latter seems the more likely supposition. The circumstance that Jesus sends his reply to the king, and that in so doing he singles him out as crafty and subtle, trying to do by intrigue what he could not do openly—"that fox"—gives weight to the view that, in saying what is recorded, certain of the Pharisees obeyed the command of the human tyrant. Be that as it may, the message was calculated to disturb the mind with secret terrors. For, of all the persons who pass before us in the life of our Lord, none was more capable of doing "the hellish thing" by mean ways than this petty ruler of Peræa. His character has been thus described: "He was false to his religion, false to his nation, false to his friends, false to his brethren, false to his wife—the meanest thing the world had ever seen." What could not such a man do? Would it not be well at once to take the hint, "Get thee out and depart thence"? But how perfectly calm is Jesus! No word like that could throw his soul off from its centre. The only phrase expressive of sheer scorn and contempt which ever fell from his lips belongs to this occasion (ver. 32). "Go tell that fox"—that human embodiment of deceit and cunning—"I shall take my time; *he* cannot frighten me; he cannot hasten me. My work in his country will be done. I must work to-day, and to-morrow, and the day following; for it cannot be that a prophet perish out of Jerusalem." Notice some characteristic points in this reply. 1. *The three days.* Is it a definite space of time that is marked out? If so, does it point to the remaining portion of the Galilæan ministry? or to the time which would elapse before his departure from Herod's territory? I incline to the latter view. But it may be better to accept the saying as an intimation that, deliberately and without hurry, he would accomplish his task—"not to-day nor to-morrow, but on a third day he would be perfected, or finished." 2. *The clause, "it cannot be that a prophet perish out of Jerusalem."* Ah! there is a sad irony in it. "Herod kill me here? No; I must reach the holy city. That is the slaughter-house of the prophets. It would never do that I, the Prophet of Galilee, should perish elsewhere." Sublime, serene, we have the sentences, "Behold, I cast out devils, and do cures" (ver. 32); "I must walk to-day and to-morrow, and the day following" (ver. 33). A good man's mission is a concern of God; God will take care of it and of him, so far as he is essential to it. It may be said that no person is indispensable; yet, to a certain extent, persons are indispensable. And every one who is consciously striving after the best and noblest, and who is giving himself to some labour of love, may be sure that there is a Divinity hedging him around through which no fox can break. The Herods of the world, with all their scheming, cannot shorten the times of God. As he wills, and while he wills, we must walk. Until he wills that we walk no longer, we are immortal. Reposing in his heavenly Father's love, straitened until his baptism of blood is accomplished, "journeying towards Jerusalem," the Christ of the Eternal is lifted above the region of selfish fears. Tyrant cannot harm him, threat cannot ruffle him: "Walk and work to-day and to-morrow, and a third day to boot, I must and shall."

II. BUT OBSERVE HOW AND WHY THE EMOTION OF "THAT SAME HOUR" BURSTS FORTH. These Pharisees could not scare him from his purpose, but they touched the fountain of a Divine sensibility in his breast. And now, as at a later stage, a cry of intense sorrow escapes him—the sorrow of wounded, but agonizing love. The feeling of patriotism combines with the tenderness of Saviour-longing in the wail, more than wail, which begins (vers. 34, 35), "O Jerusalem, Jerusalem, that killest the prophets, and stonest them that are sent to thee!" The cry naturally follows the sadly ironical reference to Jerusalem as the slaughter-house of the prophets! What are the thoughts which fill the mind of Christ as he utters it? 1. *The conscious opposition between a love that would save and an obstinate dulness that will not be saved.* Note the figure, so often employed in the Psalms and prophetical books of the Old Testament—the wings stretched out for the shelter and warmth, the peace and safety, of the brood (see Deut. xxxii. 11, 12). "How often," says the Lord Jesus (ver. 34), "would I have gathered thy children together, as a hen gathereth her brood under her wings, and ye would not!" Is this, "How often would I!" merely a reference to previous visits to the capital and ministrations in it? Nay, it is the Lord of the prophets who is speaking; the allusion, in its full meaning, is to the often-made effort to gather the children together through the prophets whom Jerusalem killed, the messengers whom Jerusalem stoned. It is the truth afterwards brought out in the parable of the wicked husbandmen (see ch. xx). The protest is wrung from the patient, seeking, yet often baffled will to save and bless. It is the protest which reverberates through infinite space concerning men—the protest whose subject-matter is, slighted overtures, unheeded calls, grace resisted, gifts sent away, knocks heard yet doors unopened; the "I would" of God defied by the "I will not" of men. 2. *The knowledge of opportunity for ever gone.* "If thou hadst known even in this thy day the things that belong to thy peace! but now they are hid from thine eyes." This is spoken on the same day, at the same hour, as that in which the warnings connected with the entering in at the strait gate were uttered. Observe the connection with ver. 25. Solemn, awful words! The things were open to the eyes during the day, the time of Divine visitation; then the eye would not regard them. It was fixed on other things—the black dust of earthly care, or the glittering dust of earthly vanity. Now the story is reversed. The eye would fain behold. Oh for a day of the Son of man! Oh for the moments that have been thrown away! But the Master of the house has risen up, and has shut to the door. The vision now (ver. 35) is a desolate house—a house left to itself, God-forsaken. "O Jerusalem, Jerusalem, all thy palaces swallowed up, thy strongholds destroyed, thy solemn feasts and sabbaths forgotten, thine altar cast off, thy sanctuary abhorred, thy gates sunk, thy bars broken; thou that wast called the perfection of beauty, the joy of the whole earth, abandoned, as it might seem, by him who sought to gather thee, and thou wouldst not! O Jerusalem, Jerusalem, bleak-

bare, stripped! dost thou not sit in thy lonely place among the silent lonely hills, spreading forth thy hands, but there is none to comfort thee, yet ever in thy desolation witnessing, 'The Lord is righteous, for I have rebelled against his commandments'?" Jesus weeps! My soul, are these tears wept over thee? Dost thou know the things that belong to thy peace? Hast thou received the One who seeks to gather thee, and whose goodness and severity urge thee to repentance? O my soul, remember that he who shed tears, from the same fountain of love and mercy shed blood also. Let the tears of compassion and remonstrance send thee to the blood of cleansing.

"Foul, I to the fountain fly;
Wash me, Saviour, or I die."

HOMILIES BY VARIOUS AUTHORS.

Vers. 1—5.—*The significance of suffering.* What does it mean, that all men suffer? and what is signified by the great calamities which some men endure? The Jews of our Lord's time were drawing inferences which were common and natural enough; but they were not the safest nor the wisest that might have been drawn. In the light of the Master's teaching, we conclude—

I. THAT SUFFERING IS ALWAYS SIGNIFICANT OF SIN. Whenever we see any kind of suffering, whether it be ordinary sickness and pain, or whether it be of such an extraordinary character as that referred to here (vers. 1—4), we safely conclude that there has been sin. And this for two reasons. 1. That all sin tends toward suffering; it has the seeds of weakness, of decline, of dissolution, in it. Give time enough, and sin is certain, "when it is finished, to bring forth death." It carries an appropriate penalty in its own nature, and, except there be some merciful and mighty interposition to prevent it, the consequences will be felt in due time. 2. That it is certain there would have been no suffering had there been no sin. A good and holy man may be experiencing the results of other men's iniquity, and his troubles not be directly traceable to any wrong or even any imprudence in himself. Yet were he not a sinful man, to whom some penalty for some guilt is due, he would not have been allowed to be the victim of the wrong-doing of others. We bear the burden of one another's penalty; and there is no injustice in this, because, though we all suffer on account of other men's actions, we suffer no more than is due to our own delinquency. The fact that a man is suffering some evil thing is therefore a proof that, whether or not he brought this particular trial on himself, he has offended, he has broken Divine law, he has come under righteous condemnation.

II. THAT GREAT CALAMITY IS SUGGESTIVE OF GREAT GUILT. There are two considerations which suggest this conclusion. 1. One is a logical inference. We argue that if sinners suffer on account of their guilt, the greater sinners will be the greater sufferers. 2. The other is the result of observation. We do often see that men who have been guilty of flagitious crimes are compelled to endure signal sorrows; the tempest of human indignation bursts upon them, or the fires of a terrible remorse consume them, or the retribution of a righteous Providence overtakes and overwhelms them.

III. THAT WE ARE BOUND TO TAKE CARE LEST WE DO OUR NEIGHBOUR WRONG in this conclusion of ours. 1. For the heinousness of individual guilt and the measurable magnitude of present punishment do not always correspond with one another. We do not always know how much men are suffering; they may be experiencing inward miseries we know not of; and it is most likely that they are undergoing inward and spiritual deterioration which we cannot estimate—a consequence of sin which is immeasurably more pitiful than any loss of property or of health. 2. And the calamities that have overtaken a man may be due to the fault of others, and they may be *disciplinary* rather than *punitive* in their bearing upon him. They may rather indicate that God is cleansing his heart and preparing his spirit for higher work, than that God is visiting him with penalty for past iniquity. We must therefore be slow to act on the principle on which the Jews based the conclusion of the text. There is one thing which it is always right to do. We may be sure—

II. THAT NOTHING BETTER BEFITS THE DAY OF THE LORD than doing the distinctive work of the Lord. Jesus Christ completely disposed of the carping and censorious criticism of the ruler. If it was right, on the sabbath day, to discharge a kindly office of no very great value and at some considerable trouble to a brute beast, how much more must it be right to render an invaluable service, by the momentary exercise of a strong will, to a poor suffering sister-woman who was one of the children of Abraham, and one of the people of God? And how can we better spend the hours which are sacred, not only to bodily rest, but to spiritual advancement, than by doing work which is peculiarly and emphatically Divine—by helping the helpless; by relieving the suffering; by enriching the poor; by enlightening those who are in darkness; by extricating those who are in trouble; by lifting up them that are bowed down? When, on the sabbath day, we forget our own exertions in our earnest desire to comfort, or to relieve, or to deliver, we may be quite sure that the Lord of the sabbath will not remember them against us, but only to say to us, "Well done."

III. THAT A FORMAL PIETY WILL NOT PRESERVE US FROM THE SADDEST SINS. This ruler was probably regarded as a very devout man, because his ceremonialism was complete. But his routine observances did not save him from making a cowardly, because indirect, attack upon a beneficent Healer; nor from committing an act of gross inhumanity—assailing the woman he should have been the first to rejoice with; nor from falling into an utter misconception of the mind of God, thinking that evil which was divinely good. We may hold high positions in the Church of Christ, may habitually take very sacred words into our lips, may flash out into great indignation against supposed religious enormities, and yet may be obnoxious to the severe rebuke of the final Judge, and may stand quite outside and even far off the kingdom of heaven. Let us be sure of our own position before we undertake the office of the accuser; let us beware lest over our outward righteousness Divine Truth will at last inscribe that terrible word "hypocrisy." Formal piety proves nothing; the only thing we can be sure about is the love of God in the heart manifesting itself in the love of men.—C.

Vers. 18, 19.—*The growth of the kingdom of God.* When we think of it we cannot fail to be impressed with the confidence, amounting even to the sublime, which Jesus Christ cherished in the triumph of his sacred cause. For consider—

I. THE UTTER INSIGNIFICANCE of "the kingdom" at its commencement. At first it was represented by one Jewish Carpenter, a young Man born of very humble parents, unlearned and untravelled, without any pecuniary resources whatever, regarded with disfavour by the social and the ecclesiastical authorities of his time, teaching doctrines that were either above popular apprehension or that ran counter to popular prejudices, unable to find a single man who thoroughly sympathized with him in his great design, moving steadily and fearlessly on toward persecution, betrayal, an ignominious and early death. Here was *a grain* indeed, something which, to the eye of man, was utterly insignificant and destined to perish in a very short time. Had we lived then and exercised our judgment upon the prospects of the nascent faith called by its Founder "the kingdom of God," we should certainly have concluded that in fifty years at the utmost it would have disappeared as a living power, and would only have remained, if it survived in any form at all, as a tradition of the past. But let us glance at—

II. ITS MARVELLOUS GROWTH. Truly the least of all seeds has become the greatest of all herbs; the grain has grown and become a "great tree." In spite of (1) the determined opposition of other faiths, which resented and resisted its claim to supplant them; (2) the sanguinary violence of the civil power, which almost everywhere strove to drown it in the blood of its adherents; (3) the hostility of the human heart, which has opposed itself continually to its purity, its spirituality, its unselfishness; (4) the deadly injury done to it by the inconsistency, the unfaithfulness, the dissensions of its own disciples;—it spread with wonderful rapidity. In three centuries it triumphed over the paganism of the known world; it has become the accepted faith of Europe and of (the greater part of) America, and of many "islands of the sea;" it has gained a firm foothold in the other continents, in the midst of the most venerable systems of religious error. Since the purification of its creed and the awakening of its members to their high privileges, it has made an immense advance toward the goal of a complete triumph; it has proved itself to be a benign and elevating power wherever it has been planted; it is the refuge, the strength, the hope, of the human world. What are—

III. Its prospects? 1. It has numerous enemies who predict that it will decline and die. They regard it as a spent force that must give place to other powers. But this prediction has been often made before, and it has been falsified by the event. 2. Its friends are more numerous, and they are more intelligent, and they are more energetic and self-denying than they ever were at any former period in its history. 3. It holds truth which ministers to the wants of the human world—its sorrows, its sins, its aspirations—such as no other doctrine can pretend to. There is but one Jesus Christ in the history of the human race; but one Saviour from sin, one unfailing Refuge and Friend in life and in death. 4. God is with us in our work of faith and our labour of love. The crucified Lord will "draw all men unto him," and his salvation shall cover the earth, because the power which prevails against all finite forces is on its side. "All power is given unto me in heaven and in earth. Go ye *therefore*, and teach all nations," etc. (Matt. xxviii. 18, 19).—C.

Vers. 20, 21.—*The peaceableness and diffusiveness of Christian truth.* The words of Christ may properly suggest to us—

I. The quiet peaceableness of the Christian method. The starting and the spreading of "the kingdom of God" is like a woman taking and hiding leaven in some meal. How impossible to imagine any of the founders of the kingdoms or empires of this world thus describing the course of their procedure! The forces they employed were forces that shone, dazzled, smote, shattered; that excited wonder and struck terror; that crushed and clanged and conquered. Those which the Son of man employed were such as fittingly reminded of a *woman hiding leaven in some meal*—silently but effectually penetrating to the depth; quietly, peaceably spreading on every hand. He did not "strive nor cry," etc.; his gospel "came not with observation," with beat of drum, with dramatic display; shunning rather than seeking celebrity, he lived, taught, suffered, witnessed, died, leaving behind a penetrating power for good that should renew and regenerate the race. There may be occasion, now and then, to say and do that which astonishes or alarms or otherwise arouses; but that is not *the* Christian method. The influence which steals into the soul, which insinuates itself into the whole body, which noiselessly communicates a right spirit and diffuses itself without ostentation or pretence from centre to circumference,—that is the method of the Master.

II. The diffusiveness of Divine truth from within outwards. "Leaven, which a woman . . . *hid;*" not spread over the surface, but put into, placed in the heart of it, there to spread, to permeate, working from the centre towards the surface. This is the method of the gospel as distinguished from that of the Law. The Law exerts its power in the opposite direction—*from without inwards;* it acts directly on behaviour, leaving behaviour to become habit and habit to become principle. 1. Jesus Christ places the leaven of Divine truth in the *mind*, in the understanding, teaching us how *to think* of God and of ourselves, of sin and of righteousness, of the present and the future. 2. Then Divine truth affects our *feelings*, producing awe, reverence, fear, hope, trust, love. 3. Thence it determines the desires and convictions, leading to choice, decision, full and final determination. 4. And thence, moving towards the surface, it decides behaviour and ends in rectitude of action, excellency of life; so "the whole man," the complete nature, is leavened. Similarly, Divine truth is placed in the heart of the community, and, once there, it communicates itself from man to man, from home to home, from circle to circle, until "the whole" nation is leavened. But a man may ask, How is my entire nature to be thoroughly leavened with Christian principle—perfectly sweetened, purified, renovated, as it is not now? *Have we enough of the sacred leaven hidden within us?* It is true that "a little leaven leaveneth the whole lump," but there is a quantity, less than which is insufficient for the work. Have we enough of the truth of Christ lodged in our minds for this great and high purpose? Are we thinking, as Christ meant us to think, of our Divine Father, of our human spirit, of our human life, of the needs and claims of our neighbour, about giving and about forgiving, and about eternal life? Is our Master's thought on these great, decisive, determining themes *hidden in our hearts*, doing its sweetening and renewing work within us? Christ says, "Come to me;" he also says, "*Learn of me.*" Are we diligently, meekly, devoutly learning of Christ, receiving more and more of his hallowing and transforming truth into our mind, to stir our feeling, to regulate our choice, to beautify and to ennoble our life?—C.

Vers. 23, 24.—*Vain inquiry and spiritual strenuousness.* There is all the difference in the world between the question that is general and speculative and that which is personal and practical; between asking, "Are there few that be saved?" and asking, "What must I do to be saved?" A great many unspiritual people show no small concern respecting matters that pertain to religion. It may be that they are curious, or that they are imaginative, or that they are visionary, and that religion provides a wide field for investigation, or for romance, or for mysticism. This speculative and unpractical piety may be: 1. A vain and unrewarded curiosity. It was so in this instance; the applicant was moved by nothing more than a mere passing whim, and he received no gratification from Christ (see ch. xxiii. 8, 9; John xxi. 21, 22). It will be found that, on the one hand, Jesus always answered the questions of those who were in earnest, however humble might be the applicant; and, on the other hand, that he never answered the questions of the irreverent, however distinguished the inquirer might be. And it is found now by us that if we go to his Word or to his sanctuary to inquire his will, we shall not go away unblessed; but that if we go to either for mere gratification, we shall be unrewarded. 2. The retreat of irreligion and unworthiness (see John iv. 18—20). It is convenient to pass from personal and practical considerations to those of theological controversy. 3. The act of mistaken religiousness (see John xiv. 8). We act thus when we want to see the *Divine side* of God's dealings with us, or are anxious to know "the times and seasons which the Father hath put in his own power." Our Lord's reply suggests—

I. THE SUPREME IMPORTANCE OF PERSONAL RELIGION. "Are there few that be saved? . . . Strive to enter in," etc.; *i.e.* the question for you to be concerned to answer is, whether you yourself are in the kingdom of God; that is preliminary to all others; that is the thing of primary importance; *that* is worth your caring for, your seeking after, your diligent searching, your strenuous pursuit. Surely the most inconsistent, self-condemning, contradictory thing of all is for men to be thinking, planning, discussing, expending, in order to put other people into the right way when they themselves are taking the downward road. Shall we not say to such, "Go and learn what *this* meaneth, 'Let every man prove his own work, then shall he have rejoicing in himself alone, and not in another; for every man shall bear his own burden' of responsibility to God"? The first duty a man owes to God and to his neighbour is the duty he owes to himself—to become right with the living God by faith in Jesus Christ his Saviour.

II. The fact that ENTRANCE INTO THE KINGDOM OF GOD DEMANDS GREAT STRENUOUSNESS OF SOUL. 1. It is the great crisis of a man's career, and may well be attended with much spiritual disturbance. When a human soul first hears and heeds his Father's call and rises to return to his true spiritual home, he may well be affected with profound spiritual solicitude, and may well count that the goal he is seeking is worth all the labour and all the patience he expends to reach it. 2. There are occasions when special strenuousness of soul is demanded. Such are these: (1) When a man by long neglect has lost nearly all his sensibility. (2) When the earnest seeker cannot find the consciousness of acceptance which he yearns to attain. (3) When a man finds himself opposed by adverse forces; when "a man's foes are they of his own household;" when he has to act as if he positively "hated" father and mother, in order to be loyal to his Lord; when downright earnestness and unflinching fidelity bring him into serious conflict with the prejudices and the practices of the home, or the mart, or the social circle; and when to follow the lead of his convictions means to suffer, to lose, to endure much at the hands of man. Then comes the message of the Master—Strive, wrestle, agonize to enter in; put forth the effort, however arduous; make the sacrifice, however great; go through the struggle, however severe it may prove to be. *Strive* to enter in; it will not be long before you will have your reward in a pure and priceless peace, in a profound and abiding joy, in a heritage which no man and no time can take from you.—C

Ver. 30. *First and last.* There are many beside those to whom these words were first applied by Jesus Christ to whom they are applicable enough. They were originally intended to denote the positions of—

I. THE JEW AND THE GENTILE. The Jew, who prided himself on being the first favourite of Heaven, was to become the very last in God's esteem; he was to bear the penalty due to the guilty race that "knew not the day of its visitation," but imbrued its hands in the blood of its own Messiah. The scenes witnessed in the destruction of Jerusalem are commentary enough on these words of Christ. But this truth has a far wider meaning; it is continually receiving illumination and illustration. It applies to—

II. THE OUTWARDLY CORRECT AND THE ILL-BEHAVED. The Pharisee of every age and land is first in his own esteem, but he stands, in sullen refusal, far off the kingdom, while "the publican and the sinner" are found at the feet of Christ, asking for the way of life, for the waters of cleansing, for the mercy of God.

III. THE LEARNED AND THE IGNORANT; the astute and the simple-minded. Still we ask, "Where is the wise? where is the scribe? where is the disputer of this world?" Still may we, after the Master himself, give God thanks that he has "hidden these things from the wise and prudent, and revealed them unto babes." Human learning, in its unholy and foolish pride, still closes its ear to the voice that speaks from heaven. Lowly minded simplicity still listens to the truth and enters the open gate of the kingdom of God.

IV. THE PRIVILEGED AND THE UNPRIVILEGED. The children of privilege may be said to be among "the first." We congratulate them sincerely and rightly enough; yet are they too often found among the last to serve and to shine. For they build upon their privileges, or they reckon confidently on turning them some day to account, and they fail to use them as they should; and the end of their presumption is indifference, hardness of heart, insensibility, death. The first has become the last. On the other hand, the ear that never before heard "the music of the gospel" is ravished by the sound of it; the heart that never knew of the grace of God in Jesus Christ is touched by the sweet story of a Saviour's dying love, and is won to penitence and faith and purity; the last is first. Let presumption everywhere tremble; it stands on perilous ground. Again and again is it made to humble itself in the dust, while simplicity of spirit is lifted up by the hand of God.—C.

Ver. 34.—*Divine emotion, etc.* These words are full of—

I. DIVINE EMOTION. They are charged with sacred feeling. The heart of Jesus Christ was evidently filled with a profound and tender regret as he contemplated the guilt and the doom of the sacred city. Strong emotion breathes in every word of this pathetic and powerful lament. And manifesting to us the Divine Father as Jesus did, we gather therefrom that our God is not one who is unaffected by what he witnesses in his universe, by what he sees in his human children. The infinite Spirit is one in whom is not only that which answers to our intelligence, but that also which answers to our emotion; and this, of course, in a manner answering to his Divinity. He rejoices in our return to his side and his service; he is gladdened by our spiritual growth, by our obedience and activity; he is pleased with our silence and submissiveness when we do not understand his way but bow to his holy will; and he is pained by our spiritual distance from him, is grieved by our slackness and our lukewarmness and our withdrawal, is saddened by our sin. He looks with a deep, Divine regret on a Church or on a child of his that is rejecting his grace as Jerusalem did, and over whom, as over it, there impends a lamentable doom.

II. DIVINE PERSISTENCY. "How often would I have gathered," etc.! The Saviour desired and endeavoured to gather the children of Jerusalem under his gracious guardianship, not once, nor twice, nor thrice; his effort was a frequent act of mercy; it was repeated and prolonged. God "bears long" with us, forbearing to strike though the stroke be due and overdue; he is "slow to anger and of great mercy." But he does more than that, and *is* more than that; he continues to seek us that he may save us. He follows us, in his Divine patience, through childhood, through youth, through early manhood, through the days of prime, or unto declining years, with his teaching and his influence. He speaks to us by his Word, by his ministry, by his providence, by his Spirit. He seeks to win us, to warn us, to alarm us, to humble, and thus to save us. At how many times and in how many ways does our Saviour seek us! *How often* does he endeavour to gather us under the shadow of his love!

III. HUMAN FREEDOM. "How often would I!" "Ye would not!" It is quite vain for us to attempt to reconcile God's omnipotence with our freedom, his right and power over us with our power to act according to our own will. The subject is beyond our comprehension, and it is true wisdom to leave it alone, as an inaccessible mountain peak which we cannot climb; there is danger, if not death, in the attempt. But the *facts* are before us, visible as the mountain itself. God has power over us, and exercises that power benignantly and patiently. But he does not interfere with our freedom; that, indeed, would be to unman us, to put us down from the level of children into that of irresponsible creaturedom. He leaves us free; and we are free to oppose his sovereign will, to resist his Divine grace, to be deaf to his pleading voice, to shake off his arresting hand. He "would" that we should be reclaimed, be raised, be enlarged, be ennobled; and too often we "will not." A solemn, awful thing it is to share a human heritage, to live a human life, to incur human responsibility.

IV. HUMAN OBDURACY. Jerusalem "often" refused to be drawn to its Redeemer. Not only can we and do we resist the grace of God; we can continue to do so; and we *do* continue. We can spend our life in a long contest with redeeming love; we can repel the overtures of mercy and go on rejecting our Father's offer of eternal life through all the years and periods of a long life of privilege. Men do this, and to them the words of Jesus are applicable in all their force; over them, also, his lament has to be uttered. 1. It is well for those to whom it may apply to awake and to return before he says to them, "Your house is left unto you desolate." 2. It is better, for it is safer for us all to heed his inviting voice and place ourselves under the wings of his blessed friendship long before such words as those of our text are anywise applicable to us.—C.

Vers. 1—21.—*The grace and progress of God's kingdom.* We saw at the close of last chapter how urgent a matter it is to get reconciled to God. Luke, in constructing his Gospel, introduces us next to a cognate thought—the necessity of repentance if judgment is to be escaped. Let us take up the orderly thoughts as they are laid before us in this passage.

I. JUDGMENT EXECUTED UPON OTHERS IS A CALL TO REPENTANCE ADDRESSED TO US. (Vers. 1—5.) There was a disposition then, as there is still, to set down special judgment as the consequence of some special sin. Job's comforters simply expressed the fallacy to be found in every heart. When Christ's attention was, therefore, directed to the Galilæan *émeute*, and to the bloody way in which Pilate had put it down, he directed his hearers to discern in it a providential warning and call to repentance. The accident at the tower of Siloam had the same significance. It was a call to survivors to repent lest a judgment as severe should overtake them. The fate of the dead was no proof of special sin, but it was a clear call to repentance addressed to the survivors.[1] The warning was singularly appropriate. The cruelty of Pilate and the overturning of the tower of Siloam had their counterparts in the siege of Jerusalem forty years after, when the people had demonstrated their impenitence. Hence we should learn the practical lesson from every judgment of the imperative necessity of personal repentance. These terrible calamities are allowed to occur, not that we may uncharitably criticize the conduct of the dead, but that we may carefully review the conduct of ourselves who survive, and repent before God.[2]

II. BEFORE MEN BECOME FINALLY IMPENITENT AND INCORRIGIBLE THEY GET A LAST CHANCE OF AMENDMENT AND REFORM. (Vers. 6—9.) The siege of Jerusalem has been before the prophetic eye of Christ, and, to impress the necessity of personal amendment and reform upon the people, he tells the parable of the fig tree. It is a history of care without any return. Orientals dig about their fruit-trees, and manure the roots, and encourage fruitfulness in every way.[3] Fruitless trees they burn, after a three-years' probation. Now, the Jews were as a nation represented by this fig tree.

[1] Cf. Geikie's 'Life and Words of Christ,' vol. i. p. 279; also Wolfe's 'Remains,' 6th edit., pp. 318—329.

[2] Cf. Gerok's 'Pilgerbrod,' s. 764; Gerok's 'Aus Ernster Zeit,' s. 687; and Saurin's 'Sermons,' tome i. p. 375.

[3] Cf. Van Lennep, p. 136.

Through long years the heavenly Husbandman had given it every chance of bearing fruit. His long-suffering is nearly exhausted, and but for the dresser of the vineyard—by whom Jesus means himself—it would have been cut down as a cumberer of the ground. His intercessions saved the nation for other forty years. And what tender care was expended on it in the closing ministry of Christ, and in the ministry of the apostles! Truly the tears of our Lord over Jerusalem, the self-sacrificing zeal of Paul and Peter and the rest for the conversion of their own countrymen, and the series of significant providences with which the forty years were filled, unite to show that the national annihilation was deserved. A fruitless nation must make way for others. Let this last chance of the Jewish nation, the forty years of respite between Christ's death and Jerusalem's doom, admonish sinners of their solemn responsibility amid similar respites still. The Lord's long-suffering, though great, is not infinite; upon it sinners need not eternally presume; a day comes round in every case, when he who will be filthy and unholy is allowed to be so still (Rev. xxii. 11).

III. THE SABBATH SHOULD BE THE SEASON OF SPECIAL UPLIFTING TO INFIRM SOULS. (Vers. 10—17.) How should a Divine day be spent? This was the controversy Christ had with the chief priests and Jewish rulers. The rabbinical idea was that it should be a day of purely physical rest, and that even healing should be postponed to the succeeding and secular days. Our Lord, on the contrary, held that the sabbath was a day for special philanthropies, a day of opportunities such as the other days, with their secular routine, cannot afford. Hence the sabbaths were days of special miracle. Meeting a poor woman whose infirmities had been of eighteen years' standing, he took her, laid his hands upon her, and healed her. It was a glorious uplifting which the poor bent woman received. But the ruler of the synagogue, where this happened, indignantly objected to such a work being done on the sabbath day; only to draw upon him, however, the rebuke of Jesus, "Ye hypocrites, doth not each one of you on the sabbath loose his ox or his ass from the stall, and lead him away to watering? And ought not this woman," etc.? (Revised Version). His argument is unanswerable. They were accustomed to deal mercifully with their own beasts, but were ready most inconsistently to deal unmercifully with human beings, who should have been more valued, but are often, alas! less cared for than dumb animals. Such hypocrisy found in Jesus a constant foe. His adversaries were thus put to shame, and the common people rejoiced and praised God for the glorious sabbath services which Jesus rendered to the poor and needy. Ought we not, then, to look for special upliftings of our infirm souls on the holy days? Jesus is waiting to heal us, and to raise us up to spiritual power.[1] As Gerok daintily puts it, we should expect to pass from work-day worry to sabbath rest; from earthly grief to heavenly joy; from the yoke of sin to the service of the Lord. We do not utilize our Lord's days aright, if such experiences are not enjoyed.

IV. THE KINGDOM OF GOD IS A WIDENING PHILANTHROPY. (Vers. 18, 19.) After the philanthropy extended to the infirm woman, it was natural for our Lord to pass to the parable of the mustard seed. This represents an insignificant beginning, followed by growth to such an extent, that under the branches of the mustard tree the birds of heaven find fitting shelter. In the same way the kingdom of God began around Jesus, apparently an insignificant Person, and eventually passed on to afford shade to many. In a word, the kingdom of God is an extending philanthropy. It widens its arms and embraces more and more in its shadow. In the same way, we may be sure that it has no true lodgment within us, unless it is making our philanthropy a growing and extending power. We are not Christ's unless we have his beautiful and philanthropic spirit.

V. THE KINGDOM OF GOD IS A THOROUGHLY TRANSFORMING POWER. (Vers. 20, 21.) From mustard seed and its growth, Christ proceeds to speak of leaven. It is hid in the three measures of meal, and works its way onwards until the whole mass is leavened. There is thus indicated how thorough and gradual the work of Christianity is. We are not true Christians unless every portion of our nature feels its transforming power; nor will Christianity pause until it has penetrated to the utmost extent the population of the world. The great idea of the parable is *thoroughness*. Let this characterize us always in our connection with the kingdom.—R. M. E.

[1] Cf. Gerok's 'Evangelien Predigten,' s. 582.

Vers. 22—35.—*Christ's farewell words to the theocracy.* As Jesus was journeying steadily towards Jerusalem, the people saw that a crisis was at hand. Hence their anxiety to know how many would be saved in the new kingdom. They consequently inquire if the number of the saved shall be few. To this speculation the Lord returns a very significant answer; he tells them that many shall strive to enter in on false grounds, and that they should strive to enter in on true ones.

I. THOSE WHO SPECULATE ABOUT NUMBERS ARE USUALLY PEOPLE WHO PLUME THEMSELVES UPON THEIR PRIVILEGES. (Ver. 26.) It is wonderful how men deceive themselves. Here we find our Saviour asserting that at the last people shall come maintaining that because they have eaten and drunk in his presence, and because he has taught in their streets, they should be accepted and saved. We should naturally imagine that these privileges should lead souls to inquire anxiously how they have profited by them, whereas they are made the ground of claim and the hope of salvation. The Jews thought that, because they were possessed of privileges beyond other nations, they should be accepted before God; and self-righteous people to-day think that, because they have regularly gone to church and sacrament, and the various privileges of the sanctuary, they should for this reason be accepted and saved at last. So far from privileges constituting a ground of salvation, they are certain to prove a ground of increasing condemnation, if not faithfully used. People may be sinners all the time that they are associating with saints. They may be sitting at groaning tables provided by God, they may be listening to the lessons which he has furnished in his holy gospel, and yet their hearts may be homes of vanity, waywardness, and sin.

II. OUR LORD DIRECTS THEM TO STRIVE TO ENTER IN AT THE STRAIT GATE INSTEAD OF SPECULATING ABOUT NUMBERS. (Ver. 24.) Many are more addicted to speculation and religious controversy than to decision of character. They would rather argue a point than make sure of their personal salvation. Now, what was the strait gate in our Lord's time? It was attachment to himself as the humiliated Messiah, just as the wide gate and broad way were the expectation of a glorious and worldly Messiah (cf. Godet, *in loc.*). It is easy to attach one's self to a winning, worldly cause; it needs no spiritual preparation. But it was not easy, but took an effort of self-denial, to stick to the despised Saviour through all his sad and humiliating experience. And the same struggle is still needed. The cause of Christ is not a winning, worldly cause. You might do better in a worldly sense without identifying yourself with Jesus. But no man will ever have reason to regret identifying himself with the Saviour. No matter what self-denial it entails, it is worth all the struggle.

III. THE LAST JUDGMENT SHALL BE A REVERSAL OF HUMAN JUDGMENTS. (Vers. 25—30.) The current notions of Christ's time accorded to the Pharisees and religious formalists the chief seats in the new order of things which Messiah was to introduce. But Christ showed plainly that the Pharisaism and formalism of sinners will not save them or their sins in the day of the revelation of the righteous judgment of God. The first shall then be last; while the last in the world's estimation shall be the first in God's.[1] Abraham, Isaac, and Jacob would have received scanty recognition from the Pharisees of Christ's time; the patriarchs were men of a meek and quiet spirit, who did not seek to exalt themselves. Hence our Lord represents the despised ones getting to their bosom at the last, while the bustling Pharisees shall find themselves cast out.

IV. WE HAVE NEXT TO NOTICE CHRIST'S CONTEMPT FOR HEROD. (Vers. 31, 32.) It was thought by some of the poor spirits in the crowd that Christ would quail before the murderous king Herod, and that the sooner he got out of his jurisdiction the better. But no sooner do they suggest this to Christ, than he bursts into contemptuous terms about the cunning king. He calls him fox, and tells them to tell him, if they like, "Behold, I cast out devils, and I do cures to-day and to-morrow, and the third day I shall be perfected." The perfection of which he speaks is that which is reached through experience. Christ was sinless, but he had to go through the whole gamut of human trial, including death itself. He had to experience all the "undertones" of human experience before he could be perfect. Hence he was "made perfect through suffering." Contempt of others may be the very finest proof of our healthy moral state. It is the antipodes of that despicable flattery which is generally extended to kings.

[1] Cf. Mozley's 'University Sermons,' No. iv.

V. Lastly, we must notice his lament over Jerusalem, because the murderer of the prophets. (Vers. 33—35.) Our Lord was going to perish at Jerusalem. The reason was that there the policy of the nation was carried out, and all the prophets had found there their fate, and yet Christ had offered his protection to the doomed city. As easily as ever hen gathered her tiny brood beneath her wings could he gather the whole cityful under his wings. It is a beautiful and indirect proof of his Divinity. No mere man would have expressed himself thus.[1] But Jerusalem would not accept his protection. Instead thereof, it resolved to murder him, as the last in the line of the prophets. No wonder, therefore, that their house was left desolate, and that the murdered Messiah would withdraw himself until better times! He takes his "adieu of the theocracy," to use the words of Godet, and speaks of a welcome being his when the new views of a better time shall prevail. How important that we all should accept the proffered protection of the Saviour, and not imitate Jerusalem in her obstinacy and her doom!—R. M. E.

EXPOSITION.

CHAPTER XIV.

Vers. 1—6.—*The Pharisee's feast on a sabbath day. The healing of the sick with dropsy.*

Ver. 1.—**And it came to pass, as he went into the house of one of the chief Pharisees to eat bread on the sabbath day.** Still on the same journey; the Lord was approaching gradually nearer Jerusalem. The house into which he entered this sabbath belonged to one who was a leading member of the Pharisee party, probably an influential rabbi, a man of great wealth, or a member of the Sanhedrin. "To eat bread on the sabbath day," as a guest, was a usual practice; such entertainments on the sabbath day were very usual; they were often luxurious and costly. The only rule observed was that all the viands provided were cold, everything having been cooked on a previous day. Augustine alludes to these sabbath feasts as including at times singing and dancing. **They watched him.** This explains the reason of the invitation to the great Teacher, on the part of a leading Pharisee, after the Master's bitter denunciation of the party (see ch. xi. 39—52). The feast and its attendant circumstances were all arranged, and Jesus' watchful enemies waited to see what he would do.

Ver. 2.—**And, behold, there was a certain man before him which had the dropsy.** This was the scheme of the Pharisee host. The sick man was not one of the invited guests; with the freedom which attends a feast in a large Oriental house, the afflicted man was introduced, as though by chance, with other lookers-on. The skilful plotters stationed him in a prominent position, where the eyes of the strange Guest would at once fall on him. The situation is described by the evangelist with dramatic clearness: "And, behold, there was a certain man before him which," etc. In an instant Jesus grasped the whole situation. It was the sabbath, and there before him was one grievously sick with a deadly chronic malady. Would he pass by—contrary to his wont—such a sufferer? Would he heal him on the sabbath day? *Could* he? perhaps thought the crafty foes of the great Physician-Teacher. The disease was a deadly one, utterly *incurable*, as they thought, by earthly means.

Ver. 3.—**And Jesus answering spake unto the lawyers and Pharisees, saying, Is it lawful to heal on the sabbath day?** And the Heart-reader read their thoughts, and in a moment he saw all and understood all, and answered the unasked question of his host and the assembled guests by putting to them another query, which went to the root of the whole matter which they were pondering in their evil hearts.

Ver. 4.—**And they held their peace.** What could they say? If they had pressed the absurd restrictions with which they hedged round the sabbath day, they felt they would be crushed by one of the Master's deep and powerful arguments. They had hoped he would have acted on the impulse of the moment, and healed the sufferer or else failed; but his calm question confused them. **And he took him, and healed him, and let him go.** With one of his majestic exercises of Divine power—so slight a task to Christ—the deadly disease was cured in a moment, and then, with quiet crushing contempt, the Physician passed into the Rabbi, and to the awe-struck guests he put a question; it was his apology for the late infringement of the traditions of the sabbath day. What had they to say?

Ver. 5.—**And answered them, saying,**

[1] Cf. Brown's 'Divine Glory of Christ,' pp. 9, 10.

Which of you shall have an ass or an ox fallen into a pit, and will not straightway pull him out on the sabbath day? Most of the older authorities here, instead of "an ass or an ox," read "a *son* or an ox." The difference here in the reading without doubt arises from the perplexity which was felt in very early days over the strangeness of the collocation of "a son and an ox." This is the reading, however, which, according to all the acknowledged principles of criticism, we must consider the true one. The meaning is clear. "If thy son, or even, to take a very different comparison, thy ox, were to fall into a pit, wouldn't you," etc.? How the sophistries of the scribes and the perplexing traditions of the Jerusalem rabbis on their sabbath restrictions must have been torn asunder by the act of mercy and power performed, and the words of Divine wisdom spoken by the Physician-Teacher of Galilee! The noble instincts even of the jealous Pharisees must have been for a moment stirred. Even they, at times, rose above the dreary, lightless teaching with which the rabbinical schools had so marred the old Divine Law. Dr. Farrar quotes a traditional instance of this. "When Hillel"—afterwards the great rabbi and head of the famous school which bore his name—"then a poor porter, had been found half-frozen under masses of snow in the window of the lecture-room of Shemaiah and Abtalion, where he had hidden himself, to profit by their wisdom, because he had been unable to earn the small fee for entrance, they had rubbed and resuscitated him, *though it was the sabbath day*, and had said that he was one for whose sake it was well worth while to break the sabbath."

Vers. 7—14.—*At the Pharisee's feast. The Master's teaching on the subject of seeking the most honourable places. Who ought to be the guests at such feasts.*

Ver. 7.—**And he put forth a parable to those which were bidden, when he marked how they chose out the chief rooms; saying unto them.** The scene with the sufferer who had been healed of his dropsy was now over. The Master was silent, and the guests proceeded to take their places at the banquet. Jesus remained still, watching the manœuvring on the part of scribes and doctors and wealthy guests to secure the higher and more honourable seats. "The chief rooms;" better rendered "first places."

Vers. 8, 9.—**When thou art bidden of any man to a wedding, sit not down in the highest room.** The pretensions and conceit of the Jewish doctors of the Law had been for a long period intolerable. We have repeated examples in the Talmud of the exaggerated estimate these, the scholars and doctors of the Law, formed of themselves, and of the respect they exacted from all classes of the community. One can well imagine the grave displeasure with which the Divine Teacher looked upon this unholy frame of mind, and upon the miserable petty struggles which constantly were resulting from it. The expositors of the Law of God, the religious guides of the people, were setting an example of self-seeking, were showing what was their estimate of a fitting reward, what was the crown of learning which they coveted—the first seats at a banquet, the title of respect and honour! How the Lord—the very essence of whose teaching was self-surrender and self-sacrifice—must have mourned over such pitiful exhibitions of weakness shown by the men who claimed to sit in Moses' seat! **Lest a more honourable man than thou be bidden of him; and he that bade thee and him come and say to thee, Give this man place.** As an instance of such unseemly contention, Dr. Farrar quotes from the Talmud how, "at a banquet of King Alexander Jannæus, the rabbi Simeon ben Shetach, in spite of the presence of some great Persian satraps, had thrust himself at table between the king and queen, and when rebuked for his intrusion quoted in his defence Ecclus. xv. 5, 'Exalt wisdom, and she . . . shall make thee sit among princes.'"

Ver. 12.—**Then said he also to him that bade him, When thou makest a dinner or a supper, call not thy friends, nor thy brethren, neither thy kinsmen, nor thy rich neighbours; lest they also bid thee again, and a recompense be made thee.** This remark of Jesus took place somewhat later in the course of the feast. Those present were evidently mostly, if not all, drawn from the upper ranks of Jewish society, and the banquet was no doubt a luxurious and costly entertainment. Godet's comment is singularly interesting, and well brings out the half-sorrowful, half-playful sarcasm of the Master. He was the rich Pharisee's Guest; he was partaking of his hospitality, although, it is true, no friendly feelings had dictated the invitation to the feast, but still he was partaking of the man's bread and salt; and then, too, the miserable society tradition which then as now dictates such conventional hospitality, all contributed to soften the Master's stern condemnation of the pompous hollow entertainments; so he "addresses to his host a lesson on charity, which he clothes, like the preceding, in the graceful form of a recommendation of intelligent self-interest." The μήποτε, *lest* (ver. 12), carries a tone of liveliness and almost of pleasantry. "Beware of it; it is a misfortune to be avoided. For, once thou shalt have received human requital, it is all over with Divine recompense." Jesus did not mean to forbid our entertaining those whom we love. He means simply, "In view of the life to come, thou canst do better still."

Vers. 13, 14.—**But when thou makest a feast, call the poor, the maimed, the lame, the blind: and thou shalt be blessed; for they cannot recompense thee.** Great pagan moralists, sick at heart at these dreary, selfish society conventionalities, have condemned this system of entertaining those who would be likely to make an equivalent return for the interested hospitality. So Martial, writing of such an incident, says, "You are asking for gifts, Sextus, not for friends." Nehemiah gives a somewhat similar charge to the Jews of his day: "Eat the fat, and drink the sweet, and send portions unto them for whom nothing is prepared" (viii. 10). **Thou shalt be recompensed at the resurrection of the just.** There is no doubt that Jesus here was alluding to that first resurrection which would consist of the "just" only; of that resurrection which St. John speaks of in rapt and glowing terms: "Blessed and holy is he that hath part in the first resurrection" (Rev. xx. 6). This was a doctrine evidently much insisted on by the early teachers of Christianity (see John v. 25; Acts xxiv. 15; 1 Cor. xv. 23; 1 Thess. iv. 16; Phil. iii. 11; and compare our Lord's words again in ch. xx. 35).

Vers. 15—24.—*In reply to an observation of one of the guests, Jesus relates the parable of the great supper, in which he shows how few really cared for the joys of God's kingdom in the world to come.*

Ver. 15.—**And when one of them that sat at meat with him heard these things, he said unto him, Blessed is he that shall eat bread in the kingdom of God.** One of those who were partaking of the banquet, and had witnessed the whole scene, now speaks to the Stranger Guest. He had looked on the miracle performed for the afflicted man; he had heard the wise words spoken by the Galilæan Rabbi; he had listened to the gentle and yet pungent rebuke to the Pharisee for his ostentatious hospitality to the rich and great; he had marked the quiet reminder as to the many sufferers who really stood in need of the viands so plentifully spread for those who wanted them not; he had been specially struck by the mention of the recompense which the just who remembered the poor would receive at the resurrection. This quiet observer, noticing that the Master's remarks were touching upon the recompense of the just in the world to come, now breaks in with a remark on the blessedness of him who should eat bread in the kingdom of God. The words do not seem to have been spoken in a mocking spirit, but to have been the genuine outcome of the speaker's admiration of the Guest so hated and yet so wondered at. There is, no doubt, lurking in the words a certain Pharisaic self-congratulation—a something which seems to imply, "Yes, that blessedness to which you, O Master, are alluding, I am looking forward confidently to share in. How happy will it be for us, Jews as we are, when the time comes for us to sit down at that banquet in the kingdom of heaven!"

Ver. 16.—**Then said he unto him.** The parable with which the great Teacher answered the guest's remark contains much and varied teaching for all ages of the Church, but in the first instance it replies to the speaker's words. "Yes," said the Master, "blessed indeed are they who sit down at the heavenly feast. You think you are one of those whom the King of heaven has invited to the banquet; what have you done, though, with the invitation? I know many who have received it who have simply tossed it aside; *are you of that number?* Listen now to my story of the Divine banquet and of the invited thereto." **A certain man made a great supper, and bade many.** The kingdom of heaven, under the imagery of a great banquet, was a picture well known to the Jews of that age. The guests in the Pharisee's house for the greater part were probably highly cultured men. At once they would grasp the meaning of the parable. They knew that the supper was heaven, and the Giver of the feast was God. The many—these were Israel, the long line of generations of the chosen people. So far strictly true, they thought; the Galilæan Teacher here is one with the rabbis of our Jerusalem schools. But, as Jesus proceeded, a puzzled, angry look would come upon the self-satisfied faces of Pharisee, scribe, and doctor; whispers would run round, "What means the Galilæan here?"

Vers. 17—20.—**Come; for all things are now ready. And they all with one consent began to make excuse.** The excuses, viewed as a whole, are paltry, and "if," as it has been well said, "as a mere story of natural life it seems highly improbable, it is because men's conduct with regard to the Divine kingdom is not according to right reason. . . . The excuses are all of the nature of pretexts, not one of them being a valid reason for non-attendance at the feast." The fact was, the invited were pleased to be invited, but there the matter ended with them. The banquet, which they were proud to have been asked to share in, had no influence upon their everyday lives. They made their engagements for pleasure and for business without the least regard to the day or the hour of the banquet; indeed, they treated it with perfect indifference. The key to the parable is easily found. The Jews were "solemn triflers in the matter of religion. They were under invitation to enter the kingdom, and they did not assume the attitude of men who avowedly cared nothing for it. On the contrary, they were pleased to think that its privileges were theirs in offer, and even gave themselves credit for setting a high value on them. But in truth they did not. The kingdom of God had not by any means the first place in their esteem. . . . They were men who talked much about the kingdom of heaven, yet cared little for it; who were very religious, yet very worldly—a class of which too many specimens exist in every age" (Professor Bruce, 'Parabolic Teaching'). **I have bought a piece of ground. . . . I have bought five yoke of oxen. . . . I have married a wife, etc.** These excuses, of course, by no means exhaust all possible cases. They simply represent examples of usual everyday causes of indifference to the kingdom of God. To all these excuses one thing is common—in each a present good is esteemed above the heavenly offer; in other words, temporal good is valued higher than spiritual. The three excuses may be classed under the following heads. (1) The attraction of property of different kinds, the absorbing delight of possessing earthly goods. (2) The occupations of business, the pleasure of increasing the store, of adding coin to coin, or field to field. (3) Social ties, whether at home or abroad, whether in general society or in the home circle; for even in the latter case it is too possible for family and domestic interests so completely to fill the heart as to leave no room there for higher and more unselfish aims, no place for any grander hopes than the poor narrow home-life affords. The primary application of all this was to the Jews of the Lord's own time. It was spoken, we must remember, to a gathering of the *élite* of the Israel of his day. In the report of the servant detailing to the master the above-recorded excuses, it has been beautifully said, "we may hear the echo of the sorrowful lamentation uttered by Jesus over the hardening of the Jews during his long nights of prayer." The invitation to the feast was neglected by the learned and the powerful among the people.

Ver. 21.—**Then the master of the house being angry said to his servant, Go out quickly into the streets and lanes of the city, and bring in hither the poor, and the maimed, and the halt, and the blind.** The invitations to the great feast, seeing that those first bidden were indifferent, were then sent out far and wide—through broad streets and narrow lanes, among wealthy publicans (tax-collectors) and poor artisans. The invitations were distributed broadcast among a rougher and less cultured class, but still the invitations to the banquet were confined to dwellers *in the city;* we hear as yet of no going *without the walls*. Here the invitation seems generally to have been accepted. All this in the first instance referred to the Galilæan peasants, to the Jewish publicans, to the mass of the people, who heard him, on the whole, gladly.

Ver. 22.—**And the servant said, Lord, it is done as thou hast commanded, and yet there is room.** While these words are necessary to complete the picture, still in them we have a hint of the vast size of the kingdom of God. The realms of the blessed are practically boundless. Here, again, in the first instance, there was a Jewish instruction intended to correct the false current notion that that kingdom was narrow in extent, and intended to be confined to the chosen race of Israel. It is very different in the Lord's picture.

Ver. 23.—**And the lord said unto the servant, Go out into the highways and hedges.** Hitherto the parable-story has been dealing with the past and the present of Israel; it now becomes prophetic, and speaks of a state of things to be. The third series of invitations is not addressed to inhabitants of a city. No walls hem in these far-scattered dwellers among the highways and hedges of the world. This time the master of the house asks to his great banquet those who live in the isles of the Gentiles. **And compel them to come in.** A greater pressure is put on *this* class of outsiders than was tried upon the favoured first invited. The indifferent ones were left to themselves. *They* knew, or professed to know and to appreciate, the nature of that feast in heaven, the invitation to which they treated *apparently* with so much honour, and *really* with such contempt. But *these* outsiders the Divine Host would treat differently. To them the notion of a pitying, loving God was quite a strange thought; *these* must be compelled—must be brought to him with the gentle force which the angels used when they laid hold of the hand of lingering Lot, and brought him out of the doomed city of the plain. Thus faithful men, intensely convinced of the truth of their message, *compel* others, by the bright earnestness of their words and life, to join the company of those who are going up to the feast above. Anselm thinks that God may be also said to *compel* men to come in when he drives them by calamities to seek and find refuge with him and in his Church. **That my house may be filled.** In ver. 22 the servant, who knew well his master's mind and his master's house too, and its capabilities, tells his lord how, after many had accepted the invitation and were gone in to the banquet, "yet there was room." The master of the house, approving his servant's words, confirms them by repeating, "Bring in more and yet more, that my house may be filled." Bengel comments here with his quaint grace in words to which no translation can do justice: "Nec natura nec gratia patitur vacuum." Our God, with his burning love for souls, will never bear to contemplate a half-empty heaven. "Messiah will see of the travail of his soul, and be satisfied." "The love of God," says Godet, "is great; it requires a multitude of guests; it will not have a seat empty. The number of the elect is, as it were, determined beforehand by the riches of the Divine glory, which cannot find complete reflection without a certain number of human beings. The invitation will, therefore, be continued, and consequently the history of our race prolonged, until that number be reached."

Ver. 24.—**For I say unto you, That none of those men which were bidden shall taste of my supper.** Whose words are these? Are they spoken by the host of the parable-story; and if so, to whom does he address them? For in the original Greek it is not "I say unto *thee*" (singular), the servant with whom throughout he has been holding a colloquy, but "I say unto you" (plural). Who does he mean by "you"? The assembled guests? or especially the already introduced poor of ver. 21 (so Bengel)? But what conceivable purpose, as Stier well asks, would be served by addressing these stern words to the guests admitted? Would *their* bliss be increased by a side-glance at those who had lost what they were to enjoy? How inharmonious a close would this be of a parable constructed with such tender graciousness throughout! It is better, therefore, to understand it as spoken with deep solemnity by the Master himself to the assembled guests in the Pharisee's house, with whom he was then sitting at meat, and for whose special instruction he had spoken the foregoing parable of the great supper. "I say unto you, that none of *those* who were bidden in the parable-story (and ye know full well that you yourselves are included in that number) shall sit at my table in heaven." This identification of himself as the Host of the great heavenly banquet was quite in accordance with the lofty and unveiled claims of the Master during the last period of his public ministry. Throughout this exposition of the great supper parable, the idea of the primary reference to the Jewish people has been steadily kept in view. It was a distinct piece of teaching, historic and prophetic, addressed to the Jew of the days of our Lord. As years passed on, it became a saying of the deepest interest to the Gentile missionaries and to the rapidly growing Gentile congregations of the first Christian centuries. In time it ceased to be used as a piece of warning history and of instructive prophecy, and the Church in every succeeding age has recognized its deep practical wisdom, and is ever discovering in it fresh lessons which belong to the life of the day, and which seemingly were drawn from it and intended for its special instruction, for its warning and for its comfort.

Vers. 25—35.—*The qualifications of his real disciples. Two short parables illustrative of the high price such a real disciple must pay if he would indeed be his. The half-hearted disciple is compared to flavourless salt.*

Ver. 25.—**And there went great multitudes with him.** These great multitudes were made up now of enemies as well as friends. Curiosity doubtless attracted many; the fame of the Teacher had gone through the length and breadth of the land. The end, the Master well knew, was very near, and, in the full view of his own self-sacrifice, the higher and the more ideal were the claims he made upon those who professed to be his followers. He was anxious now, at the end, clearly to make it known to all these multitudes what *serving him* really signified—entire self-renunciation; a real, not a poetic or sentimental, taking up the cross (ver. 27). Even his own chosen disciples were yet a long way from apprehending the terrible meaning of this cross he spoke of, and which to him now bore so ghastly a significance.

Ver. 26.—**If any man come to me, and hate not his father, and mother, and wife, and children, and brethren, and sisters, yea, and his own life also, he cannot be my disciple.** The Lord's teaching throughout, in parable and in direct saying, pressed home to his followers that no home love, no earthly affection, must ever come into competition with the love of God. If home and his cause came ever into collision, home and all belonging to it must gently be put aside, and everything must be sacrificed to the cause. Farrar quotes here from Lovelace—

> "I could not love thee, dear, so much,
> Loved I not honour *more*."

Vers. 28—30.—**For which of you, intending to build a tower, sitteth not down first, and counteth the cost, whether he have sufficient to finish it? Lest haply, after he hath laid the foundation, and is not able to finish it, all that behold it begin to mock him, saying, This man began to build, and was not able to finish.** The imagery was not an unfamiliar one in those days. The magnificent Herodian house had a passion for erecting great buildings, sacred and profane, in the varied cities under their sway. They would doubtless be often imitated, and no doubt many an unfinished edifice testified to the foolish emulation of some would-be imitator of the extravagant royal house. Now, such incomplete piles of masonry and brickwork simply excite a contemptuous pity for the builder, who has so falsely calculated his resources when he drew the plan of the palace or villa he was never able to finish. So in the spiritual life, the would-be professor finds such living harder than he supposed, and so gives up trying after the nobler way of living altogether; and the world, who watched his feeble efforts and listened with an incredulous smile when he proclaimed his intentions, now ridicules him, and pours scorn upon what it considers an unattainable ideal. Such an attempt and failure injure the cause of God.

Vers. 31, 32.—**Or what king, going to make war against another king, sitteth not down first, and consulteth whether he be able with ten thousand to meet him that cometh against him with twenty thousand? Or else, while the other is yet a great way off, he sendeth an ambassage, and desireth conditions of peace.** It is not improbable that this simile was derived from the history of the time. The unhappy connection of the tetrarch Herod with Herodias had brought about the divorce of that sovereign's first wife, who was daughter of Aretas, a powerful Arabian prince. This involved Herod in an Arabian war, the result of which was disastrous to the tetrarch. Josephus points out that this ill-omened incident was the commencement of Herod Antipas's subsequent misfortunes. Our Lord not improbably used this simile, foreseeing what would be the ultimate end of this unhappy war of Herod. The first of these two little similes rather points to the *building* up of the Christian life in the heart and life. The second is an image of the warfare which every Christian man must wage against the world, its passions, and its lusts. If we cannot brace ourselves up to the sacrifice necessary for the completion of the building up of the life we know the Master loves; if we shrink from the cost involved in the warfare against sin and evil—a warfare which will only end with life—better for us not to begin the building or risk the war. It will be a wretched alternative, but still it will be best for us to make our submission at once to the world and its prince; at least, by so doing we shall avoid the scandal and the shame of injuring a cause which we adopted only to forsake. The Swiss commentator Godet very naturally uses here a simile taken from his own nationality: "Would not a little nation like the Swiss bring down ridicule on itself by declaring war with France, if it were not determined to die nobly on the field of battle?" He was thinking of the splendid patriotism of his own brave ancestors who had determined so to die, and who carried out their gallant purpose. He was thinking of stricken fields like Morgarten and Sempach, and of brave hearts like those of Rudolph of Erlach, and Arnold of Winkelried, who loved their country better than their lives. This was the spirit with which Christ's warriors must undertake the hard stern warfare against an evil and corrupt world, otherwise better let his cause alone. The sombre shadow of the cross lay heavy and dark across all the Redeemer's words spoken at this time.

Ver. 33.—**So likewise, whosoever he be of you that forsaketh not all that he hath, he cannot be my disciple.** "We must live in this world as though the soul was already in heaven and the body mouldering in the grave" (St. Francis de Sales). There was much unreasoning, possibly not a little sentimental enthusiasm, among the people who crowded round Jesus in these last months of his work. The stern, uncompromising picture of what ought to be the life of his real followers was painted especially with a view of getting rid of these useless, purposeless enthusiasts. The way of the cross, which he was about to tread, was no pathway for such light-hearted triflers.

Vers. 34, 35.—**Salt is good: but if the salt have lost his savour, wherewith shall it be seasoned? It is neither fit for the land, nor yet for the dunghill; but men cast it out.** Here "salt" stands for the spirit of self-sacrifice, self-renunciation. When in a man, or in a nation, or in a Church, that salt is savourless, then that spirit is dead; there is no hope remaining for the man, for the people, or the Chnrch. The lesson was a general one—it was meant to sink into each listener's heart; but the Master's sad gaze was fixed, as he spoke the sombre truth, on the people of Israel whom he loved, and on the temple of Jerusalem where his glory-presence used to dwell. *Men cast it out.* Jesus could hear the armed tramp of the Roman legions of the year 70 as they cast out his people from their holy land.

HOMILETICS.

Vers. 1—24.—*The great supper.* The feast of which Christ was partaking had been carefully prepared, and was an event of some consequence in the town. This may be inferred not only from the tone of the Lord's remarks, but also from the intimations of the evangelists. Thus from ver. 12 it appears that the Pharisee had gathered together the *élite* of the place, along with his more intimate friends and his kinsmen. From ver. 7 we learn that there had been an eager scramble on the part of the guests for the chief places, the precedencies, and dignities. It was the observation of this which called forth the saying (ver. 11), "Whosoever exalteth himself shall be abased; and he that humbleth himself shall be exalted." Notice, too, as proving the care which had been bestowed on the entertainment, that there was an understanding among the more prominent guests that the movements and words of the invited Prophet should be closely watched. In fact, the supper was a trap laid. To complete the scheme, a man was introduced (ver. 2) who laboured under a severe illness—dropsy; a man whose presence might be a temptation to the loving-hearted Healer to violate the sacredness of the sabbath. Jesus, we are told (ver. 3), "answering," *i.e.* knowing the intention of the lawyers and Pharisees, put a question to them which revealed the thoughts of the heart, whilst it so vindicated his work of mercy that it reduced his hypocritical friends to silence: "they could not answer him again to these things" (ver. 6). This great supper is the text of one of the most beautiful of our Lord's parables. The introduction of the parable is very simple. He had taught his host a lesson of charity (vers. 12—14), when one of the company, catching at the last clause, "recompensed at the resurrection of the just," and giving this the accepted Pharisee-meaning—a banquet at which the elect of the nation would sit down with Abraham, Isaac, and Jacob (presuming, of course, that he would have a place at that banquet)—exclaims, "Blessed is he that shall eat bread in the kingdom of God" (ver. 15). "Yes," virtually replies the Prophet, "only recollect that this kingdom of God is not the blessedness which you imagine; nay, since the call to it has been rejected by those who were bidden—*i.e.* the covenant-people—that call will be extended, in the fulness of its glory, to the publicans and sinners whom you reject—the people of the streets and lanes; it will be extended further still, even to the ignorant heathen—the people of the highways and hedges. For (representing in these words the giver of the festival) "None of those men that were bidden shall taste of my supper" (ver. 24). Such was the primary application of the parable. In its details it is entirely within the circle of prophetic ideas. The supper is an Old Testament symbol of the day of Christ, the Messiah (see Isa. xxv. 6). The "many bidden" were those who, having Moses and the prophets, were possessors both of the Word heard outwardly with the ear, and of the grace through which it is grafted inwardly in the heart. The servant at the supper-time denotes that preaching of the kingdom which began with John the Baptist, and was carried on by our Lord and those whom "he sent before his face into every city and place, whither he himself would come." The excuses intimate the pleas on which the invited, with one consent, turned away from the call. And the further missions of the servant, first keeping within the city, to the streets and lanes, and, secondly, quitting the precincts of the city, to the highways and hedges, denote, as has been said, the inclusion of the excluded classes of the Jews, along with the Samaritans, and the bidding of the Gentiles to the light of the gospel. "I said," thus ancient prophecy expressed it (Isa. lxv. 1), "Behold me, behold me, unto a nation that was not called by my Name." Passing from the first relations of the parable to those which more directly concern us, every part of it is suggestive of some aspect of Christian truth or life. Notice three points—

I. The hospitality of God. God is the Presence shadowed forth in the "man who makes the great supper." In the notion of such a supper we see the Divine hospitality. A supper carries with it the thought of an abundant provision, of satisfaction for all want, of an infinite and various fulness. And is not this associated in the Scriptures with the very name of God? Take, *e.g.*, one of the most beautiful utterances of the Psalter, Ps. xxxvi. 5—9. Indeed, the manifold revelation of God in nature, providence, grace, in the firmament above us, the earth around us, the great and wide sea, our own consciousness, the Word who in the beginning was with God and was God—God himself in every form of his communication, is the exceeding joy of the pure in heart. His greatness is so hospitable. It makes room for all our littleness and weakness "in its lap to lie." As Faber, in verses of sweetest music, has sung—

"Thus doth thy grandeur make us grand ourselves;
'Tis goodness makes us fear;
Thy greatness makes us brave, as children are
When those they love are near.

"Great God! our lowliness takes heart to play
Beneath the shadow of thy state;
The only comfort of our littleness
Is that thou art so great.

"Then on thy grandeur I will lay me down;
Already life is heaven for me;
No cradled child more softly lies than I:
'Come soon, Eternity.'"

It is this hospitality that is declared in the Son of the Eternal Love. Christ is the Great Supper. In him God has "abounded towards us in wisdom and prudence." St. Paul speaks of "the love of Christ which passeth knowledge," of Christ "the All in all;" and, more particularly defining the supper-making, he says, "Christ, of God made to us Wisdom, Righteousness, Sanctification, Redemption." All that we need as men, all that is salvation for sinners, is ours in him. And how is it ours? "If any man hear my voice, and open the door, I will come in to him, and will sup with him, and he with me."

II. THE CHURLISHNESS OF MEN. This is God, with the door thrown wide open, the table prepared, the life eternal given, the grand, ever-urgent "Come!" "Ho, every one that thirsteth, . . . and he that hath no money, come!" But what is the reception? Strange, wonderful, but still too true, "They all with one consent began to make excuse" (ver. 18). Look at the excuses. They are pictures of states of mind, of attitudes of thought, as real now as at any time. Three such pictures are sketched. The first (ver. 18), a mind which rejoices in a good realized. The man has the desire of his heart. He is the lord of broad acres. "Soul, take thine ease; what need for thee of the supper?" The second (ver. 19), a mind still immersed in business, with its cares and anxieties. The man has just concluded an important purchase; before all else he must prove it. The third (ver. 20), a mind absorbed in earthly delights and social relationships—he "cannot come." We can trace, in the three pictures, a climax like that of the parable reported in Matt. xxii., which closely resembles this. There is an ascending scale in the rejection. The first is covetous to a degree; he would go with all his heart—only that little estate; he must needs "pray let me be excused." The second is polite, but more abrupt; there is a graceful wave of the hand, a gentlemanly "Pray let me be excused;" but there is no "I must needs." The third is rude and flat in his denial; there is a quick "No, I cannot." Is it not the climax of worldliness in every period? And what is worldliness? The celebrated Robert Hall one day wrote the word "God" on a slip of paper. "You can read that?" he said, as he passed the slip to a friend. "Yes." He covered the name on the slip with a sovereign. "Can you read it now?" The sovereign was above, was nearer the gaze than *God*. That is worldliness. It is not the having, not the purchasing, of the ground or the oxen. It is the having the earthly thing in the first place, the setting of the "must needs" over against it. And it is the mind which does this, to which the heavenly kingdom is second to the earthly good, which is fruitful of excuses. Oh, how often it puts off! how often there comes even the rude "I cannot"! Has the Giver of the supper found such a mind in any of us?

III. THE COMMISSION OF THE SERVANT. It is to bear the Master's call, to declare that "all things are ready;" that salvation is full and is present; life now, life for ever, given with God's "yea" and "amen" to even the chief of sinners. The word of the reconciliation is "Come!" the ministry of reconciliation implies, "Go, ever out and out." The house of the Lord must be filled; he is bent on the winning of souls. A supper, and none to eat; a great supper, and only a few guests!

"Salvation! O salvation!
The joyful sound proclaim,
Till earth's remotest nation
Has learnt Messiah's Name."

"Compel them" is the voice of the Everlasting Love. Use, *i.e.*, all means of moral suasion; circle around their wills; plead, beseech, entreat, persuade, "instant in season and out of season;" draw them, watch over them; establish such links between the messenger and them that they shall feel that they must come with you, since God is with you of a truth. "Now then we are ambassadors for Christ, as though God did beseech you by us: we pray you in Christ's stead, be ye reconciled to God."

HOMILIES BY VARIOUS AUTHORS.

Vers. 7—11.—*Christ's word on modesty.* The remark which the conduct of these guests called forth from Christ suggests to us—

I. OUR LORD'S INTEREST IN THE HUMBLER DETAILS OF OUR DAILY LIFE. We might have imagined, judging antecedently, that the great Teacher would not concern himself with a matter so trivial as this; or that, if he did, we should not find a record of his remark in a narrative so brief as are our evangels. We know that he had occasion to rebuke the Pharisees for letting religious faith lose itself altogether in minute and infinitesimal prescriptions (ch. xi. 42; Mark vii. 4). And there is a very remarkable absence from our Master's teaching of petty regulations. He sought not to prescribe particulars of behaviour, but to convey Divine principles and to impart a holy and a loving spirit; he knew that these would spontaneously and invariably issue in appropriate conduct. But Jesus Christ would not have us think that he is indifferent to the way in which we act on small occasions. He could be "much displeased" by an act of small officiousness (Mark x. 13, 14); and he could be deeply moved by an act of simple generosity (ch. xxi. 2, 3). And we may learn from this incident that it is not a matter of indifference how we behave in the common occurrences of our daily life: to what homes we go, what place in the house we take, how we act at the table (1 Cor. x. 31), what is the tone of our conversation (Matt. xii. 37), with what raiment we are clothed (1 Pet. iii. 3), whether we encourage or discourage the weak and timid disciple (Matt. x. 42; xviii. 6). These things, and such things as these, are occasions when, by manifesting a kindly and humble spirit, we may greatly please our Divine Lord, or when, by an opposite spirit, we may seriously offend him.

II. THE PREFERENCE OF MODESTY TO SELF-ASSERTION. Jesus Christ here plainly and emphatically commends modesty of spirit and behaviour, and as decidedly condemns an immodest self-assertion. To take a lower place than we might claim to do is often found to be the prudent and remunerative course. Self-assertion frequently goes too far for its own ends, and is discomfited and dishonoured. Every one is pleased when the presumptuous person is humiliated. But modesty is frequently recognized and honoured, and every one is gratified when the man who "does not think more highly of himself than he ought to think" is the object of esteem. But when, in a more worldly and diplomatic sense, such modesty does not answer; when a strong complacency and a vigorous self-assertion do, as they often will, pass it in the race of life, and snatch the fading laurel of "success;"—still is it the becoming, the beautiful thing; still is it worth possessing for its own sake. To *be lowly-minded* is a far better portion than to *have* all the honours and all the gains which an ugly assertiveness may command.

III. THE VITAL VALUE OF HUMILITY. (Ver. 11.) Lowliness of mind, penitence, may be of small account in the eyes of men, but, on the part of those as guilty as we are, it is everything in the sight of God: "Blessed are the poor in spirit: for theirs is the kingdom of heaven." Spiritual pride is utterly offensive to God, and draws down his most serious condemnation; if we exalt ourselves we shall be abased by him. But a sense of our own unworthiness is what he looks to see in children that have forgotten their Father, in subjects that have been disloyal to their King; and when he sees it he is prepared to pardon and to restore. If we humble ourselves before him and plead his promise of life in Jesus Christ, he will exalt us; he will treat us as his children; he will make us his heirs; he will raise us up to "heavenly places in Christ Jesus."—C.

Vers. 12—14.—*Moderation; disinterestedness; patience.* We find in these words of our Lord—

I. THE CORRECTION OF A COMMON FAULT. Jesus Christ did not, indeed, intend to condemn outright all family or social gatherings of a festive character. He had already sanctioned these by his own presence. The idiomatic language, "do not, but," signifies, not a positive interdiction of the one thing, but the superiority of the other. Yet may we not find here a correction of social, festive extravagance; the expenditure of an undue measure of our resources on mutual indulgences? It is a very easy and a very common thing for hospitality to pass into extravagance, and even into selfish indulgence. Those who invite neighbours to their house in the full expectation of being invited in return may seem to themselves to be open-handed and generous, when they are only pursuing a system of well-understood mutual ministry to the lower tastes and gratifications. And it is a fact that both then and now, both there and here, men are under a great temptation to expend upon mere enjoyment of this kind a degree of time and of income which seriously cripples and enfeebles them. Thus that is given to display and indulgence which might be reserved for benevolence and for piety; thus life is lowered, and its whole service is reduced; thus we fail to reach the stature to which we might attain, and to render to our Master and his cause the service we might bring. In the matter of indulgence, direct or (as here) indirect, while we should keep away from asceticism, it is of still greater consequence that we do not approach a faulty and incapacitating selfishness.

II. AN INVITATION TO A NOBLE HABIT. "Call the poor . . . and thou shalt be blessed; for they cannot recompense thee." An act of disinterested kindness carries its blessing with it. 1. It is an intrinsically excellent thing. "To do good and to communicate" is honourable and admirable; and to do this with no thought of return from those who are benefited, is an act of peculiar and exceptional worth. It takes very high rank in the scale of spiritual nobleness. 2. It allies us with the highest and the best in all the universe; with the noblest men and women that ever lived in any land or age; with the angels of God (Heb. i. 14); with our Divine Exemplar (Mark x. 45); with the eternal Father himself (Matt. v. 45). 3. It leaves a benign and elevating influence on our own spirit. Every man is something the better, is so much the worthier and more Christ-like, for every humblest deed of disinterested benevolence.

III. THE PROMISE OF A PURE REWARD. If the idea of recompense is admitted, everything turns upon the character of the reward, so far as the virtue of the action is concerned. To do something for an immediate and sensible reward is unmeritorious; to act in the hope of some pure and distant recompense is an estimable because a spiritual procedure. Our life is, then, based upon faith, upon hope, and especially upon patience. To do good and to be content to wait for our recompense until "the resurrection of the just," when we shall reap the approval of the Divine Master and the gratitude of those whom we have served below,—this is conduct which our Lord approves; it bears the best mark it can bear—that of his Divine benediction.—C.

Ver. 18.—*Excusing ourselves.* There are two things which seem as if they could not exist together, but which we continually confront. One is the felt obligation and value of religion, and the other is the mournful commonness of irreligion. Where shall we find an explanation of the coexistence of these two things? We find it in *the habit of self-excuse.* With one consent men excuse themselves. Now, an excuse is one of two things.

I. A PRETEXT which men invent, so as to shun, without self-reproach, a plain but painful duty. A tradesman is not prospering in business; he is aware that he is losing money; he feels sure that an examination of his books will show a serious deficit at the end of the year; he knows that he ought to acquaint himself with his actual financial position; but he is reluctant to see how far he is behind; he would much rather escape that scrutiny, and he consequently looks about for a reason that he can place before his own mind for postponing it. He easily discovers one. He could make better use of the time; he ought not to neglect an opportunity that offers of making a good bargain—or anything else. What does it matter? Anything will serve; one pretext is as good as another. Here is a human soul that owes much to its Creator; has received everything, and has paid nothing or scarcely anything—owes "ten thousand talents," and "has nothing to pay." One comes to him from God, and says, "See how things stand between you and your Maker; 'acquaint thyself with him, and be at peace.'" But the man shrinks from the scrutiny; he is in debt, and knows that he is; he would much rather enter into any other account than that. So he searches for some plausible reason for putting it off to another time. And he easily finds one. Excuses are in the air, at every one's command. He has no time for religious inquiry; so many people speak in God's Name, he is not sure who holds the truth; he will be under more favourable spiritual conditions further on—or something else. What does it matter? One excuse serves as well as another. It is nothing but a screen put up between the eye and the object. This is a course of action to be ashamed of. It is not manly; it is not right; it is perilous; it is delusive, and leads down to destruction.

II. A PREFERENCE of that which is second-rate to that which is of supreme importance. Here the particular illustrations of the parable serve us. These men are invited to be present at that which they ought to attend; but they allow something of inferior urgency to detain them. God is inviting us to partake of a most glorious spiritual provision; he is offering eternal life to his human children. He is sending his servants to say, "Come, for all things are ready!" But how many decline! and they decline because they "make excuse;" they put into the first place that which should come second. It is the demands of business; or it is the cares of the household; or it is the sweets of literature, of art, of family affection; or it is the claims of human friendship; or it is the hope of political influence or renown. It is something human, earthly, finite, on the ground of which the soul is saying, "Ambassador of Christ, I pray thee have me excused!" But it is wrong and it is ruinous to act thus. 1. Nothing will ever justify a man in placing first in his esteem that which God has placed second, in keeping behind that which has such sovereign claims to stand in front. The claims of God the eternal Father of spirits, of Jesus Christ our Divine Saviour, of our own priceless spirit, of those whom we love and for whose immortal well-being we are held responsible by God,—these cannot be relegated to a secondary and inferior position without serious *guilt*. 2. Nothing will make it other than *foolish* for a man to leave unappropriated the immeasurable blessings of godliness; to prefer any passing earthly good to the service of Jesus Christ, the service which hallows all joy, sanctifies all sorrow, ennobles all life, prepares for death, and makes ready for judgment and eternity. How can such folly be surpassed?—C.

Ver. 23.—*Spiritual breadth.* The parable presents the gospel as a sacred feast prepared by the Divine Lord for the hungering hearts of men. The invitation is declined by one and another, who have inclinations for other and lower good than that which is thus provided. Hence the measures taken to supply their room. The text suggests—

I. THE LARGENESS OF GOD'S LOVING PURPOSE. God wills that his house "shall be filled." This house of his grace is built on a large scale; in it are "many mansions," many rooms. The magnitude of it answers to the greatness of his power and to the boundlessness of his love. The number of the ultimately redeemed will be vast indeed. To this point: 1. The hopes of all holy and generous souls. 2. The terms of predictive Scripture. 3. The attributes of the wise, strong, benignant Father of men. 4. The duration of the redemptive scheme. 5. The character of the redemptive work—the Incarnation, the sorrow, the shame, the death, of the Son of God. God's loving purpose is to gather a multitude which no man can number into the heavenly home, into the eternal mansions.

II. THE FULNESS OF THE DIVINE COMMISSION. Those who represent the Lord of the feast are to "go into the highways and hedges, and *compel* men to come in." No people are to be excluded; no efforts are to be spared; no "stone is to be left unturned" to win men to the feast. There is to be a sacred compulsion used rather than the efforts of the "servants" should be unsuccessful. Here is no warrant for persecution. No two things can conceivably be further apart from one another than the use of violence and the spirit of Christ. To employ cruelty in order to compel men into Christianity is worse than a senseless solecism; it is a flagrant and guilty contradiction. There are other and nobler ways of "compelling men to come in" to the kingdom and the Church of Christ—ways which are not discordant but harmonious with the spirit and the teaching of the Lord of love. They are such as these: 1. The constant and irresistible beauty of our daily life. The "waters" of spiritual loveliness "wear" the hardest stones of spiritual obduracy. 2. Occasional magnanimity of Christian conduct. Men are often *compelled* to bow down in admiration and even in reverence before some deed of noble self-sacrifice, of lofty heroism. 3. Convincing presentation of the Christian argument. The truth of Christ may be presented so cumulatively, so forcibly, so directly, so practically, so winningly, so affectionately, that the most defiant are abashed, the most prejudiced are convinced, the most impervious are penetrated, the most insensible are moved and won; they are compelled to come in. 4. Earnest persistency of Christian zeal. There is a blind, imprudent zeal, which is worse than worthless, which only teases and torments, which does not allure but drives to a greater distance. But there is also a wise, holy, Divine persistency, which will not be refused, which employs every weapon in the sacred armoury, which knows how to wait in patience as well as how to work in ardour, which, like the patient Saviour himself, "stands at the door, and knocks." This is the zeal which continues to plead with men for God, and ceases not to plead with God for men, until the barriers are broken down, until the indifference is broken up, until the heart looks up to heaven and cries, "What shall I do that I may inherit eternal life?"—C.

Vers. 25—33.—*The time and the room for calculation in religion.* What room is there in the religion of Jesus Christ for calculation? What amount of reckoning before acting is permissible to the disciple of our Lord? When and in what way should he ask of himself—Can I afford to do this? Have I strength enough to undertake it?

I. THE CIRCUMSTANCE WHICH SUGGESTED THE IDEA. It was the temporary popularity of Christ that led him to the strain of remark we have in the text. "There went great multitudes with him" (ver. 25), fascinated by his presence and bearing, or struck by his teaching, or marvelling at his mighty works. And these men and women were far from entering into his spirit or sharing his high purpose; it was necessary that they should understand what discipleship to Jesus meant, what absolute self-surrender it involved. So the Master gave utterance to the strong and trenchant words recorded in the context (vers. 26, 27). And the words of the text itself are explanatory of this utterance. Their import is this: "I say this because it is much better you should know what you are doing by following me than that you should enter upon a course which you will find yourselves obliged to abandon, than that you should undertake a duty to which you will find yourselves unequal. All wise people, before they definitely commit themselves to any policy carefully consider whether they can carry it through. Every wise builder calculates the cost before he begins to build; every wise king estimates his military strength before he declares war. So do you consider whether you are prepared to make a full surrender of your will to my will, of your life to my service, before you attach yourselves to my side; for whoever is not able to 'forsake all that he hath' at my bidding, 'cannot be my disciple.' Ponder the matter, therefore; weigh everything before you act, count the cost, decide deliberately and with a full understanding of what it is you are doing."

II. THE PLACE THERE IS FOR CALCULATION IN PERSONAL RELIGION. 1. At the entrance upon a Christian life. It would seem as if there could be no room for reckoning here. We may well ask—When God calls us to himself, when Christ invites us to come unto him, what time should we allow ourselves before responding to his summons? Should not our response be immediate, instantaneous? We reply—Time enough to understand what we are undertaking to be and to do; time enough to take the Divine message into our full and intelligent consideration; so that our choice may be not the impulse of an hour, but the fixed and final purpose of our soul. God would not have us act in ignorance, in misconception. In malice we may well be children, but in understanding we should be men. There is no step any man can take which is comparable in importance with that which is taken when a human soul enters the kingdom of God: on that hang everlasting issues. Let men, therefore, diligently and reverently inquire until they understand what it means to have a living faith in Jesus Christ, to enter his spiritual kingdom, and become one of his subjects; let them understand, among other things, that it means the cheerful and full surrender of themselves to the Saviour himself, with all that such surrender involves (ver. 33). 2. At the entrance on a public profession of personal religion. Here is a visible "Church" which we are invited to join, taking upon ourselves the Christian name, and openly avowing our attachment to our Lord; thus honouring him before men. This is a step to be taken deliberately. Before taking it, a man should certainly ask himself whether he is prepared to act in accordance with his profession *everywhere*, in all circles and in every sphere; not only where he will be encouraged to do the right, but where he will be solicited to do the wrong thing; not only in the midst of genial influences, but in the throng of perilous temptations. But while these things are to be carefully taken into account, there must be reckoned, on the other side, the assurance which genuine piety may always cherish of *needed Divine succour*. If we go forth in the Name and in the strength of our Lord to do that which is his own command, we may confidently count on his support; and with him at our right hand we shall not be moved from the path of integrity and consistency. Look the facts in the face, but include *all* the facts; and do not forget that among these are the promises of the faithful Friend. 3. Before undertaking any post of sacred service. It would be worse than foolish for a Christian man to go forth to any enterprise requiring an amount of physical strength, or of intellectual capacity, or of educational advantages, which he knows well he does not possess. That would be to begin to build and to be unable to finish, to declare war with the certainty of defeat. At all times, when we are thinking of Christian work, we must carefully consider our qualifications. A wise and modest refusal is a truer sacrifice than an indiscreet and unwarrantable acceptance. But, again, let our judgment include the great factor of the Divine presence and aid, and also the valid consideration that competency comes with exercise, that to him that hath (uses his capacities) is given, and he has abundance (of power and of success).—C.

Ver. 26.—*Christ and kindred.* The circumstances under which these words were spoken will explain the strength of the language used. Jesus Christ said that he came "not to send peace on earth, but a sword," by which he meant that the first effect of the introduction of his Divine truth would be (as he said) to set the members of the same family "at variance" against one another, and to make a man's foes to be "they of his own household" (Matt. x. 34—36). By honouring and acknowledging him as the Messiah of the Jews and as the Redeemer of mankind, his disciples would excite the bitterest enmity in the minds of their own kindred; they would be obliged to act *as if they hated them*, causing them the keenest disappointment and the severest sorrow. They would be compelled to act as if they *hated their own life* also, for they would take a step which would remove all comfort and enjoyment from it, and make it valueless if not miserable. On the relation of Jesus Christ and his gospel to human kindred, it may be said that Christianity—

I. Disallows parental tyranny. Such unmitigated authority as the Roman law gave to the parent over the child is not sanctioned, but implicitly condemned, by Jesus Christ. No human being is wise enough or good enough to exercise such prerogative; and to yield such deference is to cede the responsibility which our Creator has laid upon us, and which cannot be devolved.

II. Disallows filial worship. Such idolatrous homage as the children of the Chinese render to their parents is also distinctly unchristian; it is giving to the creature what is due only to the Creator. It is to elevate the human above its lawful level.

III. Sanctions and enjoins filial devotedness. Our Lord himself severely condemned the perversity of the Pharisees, who contrived to evade filial obligations by sacred subtleties (Mark vii. 9—13). And amid the physical agonies and the spiritual struggles and sufferings of the cross he found time to commend his mother to the care of "the beloved disciple." His apostles explicitly enjoined filial obedience (Eph. vi. 1). And entering into the profounder spirit of our Lord's teaching, we are sure that he desires of children that they should not only be formally obedient to their parents' word, but that they should be careful to render to them all filial respect in manner; should have regard to their known will, whether uttered or unexpressed; should render the service of love and of cheerfulness rather than of constraint; should make their filial ministry to abound as parental health and strength decline.

IV. RESERVES ABSOLUTE OBEDIENCE FOR THE DIVINE REDEEMER. When Christianity is assailing a false faith, as in the first century, as in heathen lands to-day, it very frequently happens that disciples have to choose between their attachment to the earthly parent and their obligations to Christ. Then the words of Jesus Christ have a literal application; then the convert has to pass through the most severe and trying of all conflicts; he has to weigh one authority against another; he has to make a decision which will cause grief and wrath to one whom he would fain please and honour. But much as the human parent may have been to him, and strong as are his claims, the Divine Redeemer is more, and his claims are stronger still and stronger far. The Lord who created him (John i. 3; Col. i. 16); who redeemed him with his own blood; who sought and found and restored him; who has made him an heir of eternal life;—this Lord, who has been upholding him by his power, and who is the one Hope and Refuge of his soul, has claims upon his obedience to which even those of a human parent are utterly unequal. And when the choice has to be made, as it sometimes has even here and now, there can be but one course which he recognizes as right; it is to choose the side and the service of the holy Saviour; *meekly bearing* the heavy cross of domestic severance; *earnestly praying* for the time when the human authority will be reconciled to the Divine; *faithfully believing* that the sacrifice which is thus entailed will bring with it, in Christ's own time and way, a large and abundant recompense (Mark x. 28—30).—C.

Vers. 34, 35.—*Ourselves as salt.* It is hardly possible to mistake the meaning of Christ here. We know that salt is the great preservative of animal nature, the antidote of putrefaction and decay. We know also that the great Teacher intended that his disciples should *be* the salt of the earth, doing in the human the same purifying work which salt does in the animal world.

I. THE PRESERVING POWER OF THE GOOD IN THE SOCIETY IN WHICH THEY ARE FOUND. 1. As those who act directly on God, and so on behalf of men. Had there been ten righteous men in Sodom, they would have preserved it from destruction. Similarly, the presence of a few righteous men would have saved the cities of Canaan. Is it not the presence of the righteous men and women in our modern cities which averts the retribution of God? 2. As those that act directly on man, and thus on God. As there is a tendency in animal nature, when life is extinct, towards putrefaction, so is there a tendency in human nature, when spiritual life is extinct, towards degeneracy and corruption. It is the function of salt in the economy of nature to prevent this result, to preserve sweetness and wholesomeness; it is the part of moral goodness to prevent corruption in society and to preserve purity and excellency there. And this it does. Purity, sobriety, uprightness, reverence, self-control,—these are powers for subduing, for restraining; they are powers that permeate, that sweeten, that preserve. This is eminently true of *Christian discipleship*: for it has (1) *truth* to *propound* which is most cleansing in its character; and it has (2) a *life* to *live* which is eminently purifying in its influence—the distinctive truth of the gospel of Jesus Christ, and the life of the great Exemplar, which every follower of his is charged and is empowered to live again.

II. THE DANGER THAT THIS POWER WILL BE LOST. "Salt is good: but *if the salt have lost its savour!*" It may do so. The salt, by exposure to sun and rain, may lose its pungency and its virtue while retaining its appearance. 1. And so Christian truth may lose its distinguishing force. Men may use Christian forms of speech in their teaching, and yet the doctrine they declare may be an enfeebled and emasculated Christianity, from which all that is distinctive and all that is redeeming is extracted: it is salt without its savour. 2. And so Christian life may lose its excellency and its virtue. These may be blurred and blemished lives, or they may be spotted and stained lives, or they may be lives with nothing in them beyond mere conventional propriety —lives not animated by the love of Christ, not filled with the Spirit of Christ, not governed by the principles of Christ; not blamable, but not beautiful; not wicked, but worldly; not criminal, but not Christian: the salt has lost its savour.

III. THE EXTREME UNLIKELIHOOD OF RESTORATION. "If the salt have lost . . .

wherewith shall it be seasoned?" That is an impossibility. Salt that has lost its virtue is useless for all ordinary purposes, and is "cast out." It is not *absolutely* impossible for the soul that has lost its Christian spirit and character to regain its worth, but it is very difficult and it is very rare. The recovery of lost feeling is a spiritual marvel. 1. It is so improbable that no man who loves his soul will expose himself to the peril; if he does, he most seriously endangers his spiritual life, he most gravely imperils his eternal future. 2. It is not *so* impossible that any unfaithful soul need despair. True penitence and genuine faith will bring back the wanderer from the fold to the shelter of the good Shepherd's love.—C.

Vers. 1—24.—*Table-talk of Jesus.* We have now brought before us an interesting conversation which Jesus had with certain guests at an entertainment in the house of "one of the chief Pharisees." It was a sabbath-day feast, indicating that sociality was not incompatible even with Jewish sabbath-keeping. Into the guest-chamber had come a poor man afflicted with the dropsy, and, to the compassionate eye of our Lord, he afforded an opportunity for a miracle of mercy. But, before performing it, he tests their ideas about sabbath-observance. They were sufficiently merciful to approve of sociality among themselves, but the healing of neighbours was another matter. They could even be merciful to cattle if they were their own; but to be merciful to a brother-man would have shown too much breadth of sympathy. The sick man might wait till Monday, but an ass or an ox might die if not delivered out of its difficulty, which would be so much personal loss. In spite of their narrow-mindedness, our Lord took the poor man and healed him, and then proceeded to give the guests very wholesome advice.

I. LET US LOOK AT THE PARABLE ABOUT THE WEDDING. (Vers. 7—11.) To the Lord's eye the feast became the symbol of what is spiritual. The wedding of the parable is the consummation of the union between God and his people. The invitation is what is given in the gospel. Hence the advice is not instructive as to the prudential temper, but as to our spirit in coming before God. Shall it be the spirit which claims as right the highest room, or that which accepts as more than we deserve the lowest room? In other words, shall we come before God in a spirit of self-righteousness or in a spirit of self-abasement? Now, our Lord points out, from the collisions of social life, the absolute certainty of the self-important and self-righteous being abased among men: how much more in the righteous administration of God! The self-righteous under his administration shall be abased, how deeply and terribly we cannot conceive. On the other hand, those who have learned to humble themselves under the mighty hand of God shall be exalted in due season, and have glory in the presence of the celestial guests! Jesus thus attacked the self-righteousness of the Pharisees, not as a social, but as a spiritual question. God would at last cast it away from his presence and society with loathing and contempt.[1] On the other hand, self-abasement is the sure sign of grace and the sure earnest of glory. He who takes with gratitude the lowest room in God's house is certain of speedy promotion!

II. OUR HOSPITALITY SHOULD BE DIVINE IN ITS SPIRIT AND CHARACTER. (Vers. 12—14.) Having improved the conduct of the guests, and shown its spiritual bearings, he next turns to the host, and gives him an idea of what hospitality should be. It should not be *speculative*, but disinterested—something, in fact, which can only be recompensed at the resurrection of the just. In no clearer way could our Lord indicate that hospitality should be exercised in the light of eternity; and the bearing of it upon spiritual interests should constantly be regarded. And here we surely should learn: 1. How important it is to be social. God is social. His Trinity guarantees the sociality of his nature. We are to be God-like in our sociality. 2. It may be most helpful to lonely spirits upon earth. Many a lonely heart may be saved for better things by a timely social attention. 3. There is great blessing in giving attention to people who cannot return it. It is a great field of delight that those with large hearts may have. "It is more blessed to give than to receive." We are following

[1] Suggestive discourses on this passage may be found in Gerok's 'Pilgerbrod,' s. 669; Gerok's 'Aus Ernster Zeit,' s. 574; Hofacher's 'Predigten,' s. 670; Beck's 'Christliche Reden,' i. s. 290.

God's plan in the attentions we bestow. 4. At the final arrangement of God's kingdom, all such disinterested hospitality shall be recompensed. How? Surely by opportunity being afforded of doing the like again! The hospitable heart, which keeps eternity in view in all its hospitality, shall have eternity to be still more hospitable in.

III. THE PARABLE OF THE GREAT SUPPER. (Vers. 15—24.) Jesus proceeds from the question of hospitalities to present the gospel in the light of a supper provided by the great Father above, and to which he invites sinners as his guests. And here we have to notice: 1. The *greatness of the supper.* The preparations were long and elaborate. How many centuries were consumed in preparing the feast which we have in the gospel! It was to be the greatest "feast of reason and flow of soul" the world has seen. And so it is. Nowhere else does man get such food for his mind and heart as in the gospel of Christ. 2. The *freedom of the invitations.* Many were bidden. No niggardliness about the invitations. They are scattered so freely that, alas! they are not by many sufficiently prized. 3. The *supplementary summons by the faithful servant.* It is not an invitation by ink and pen merely that God sends, but he backs the written revelation by personal persuasion by the mouth of faithful servants. Here is the sphere of the gospel ministry. These true ministers tell what a feast is ready in the gospel, and what their own experience of it has been. 4. The *triviality of the excuses.* To the invitations sent out by God men make excuses. There is something peculiarly sad and significant in refusals upon insufficient grounds. Our Lord gives us three examples of the excuses men make for refusing salvation and the gospel. (1) The first man puts a *piece of ground* before salvation. "Real property" keeps many a man out of the kingdom of heaven. (2) The second puts *cattle* before salvation. Many men are so interested in good "stock," and all the mysteries of breeding and work, as to have no time for their eternal interests. A few chattels keep multitudes out of God's kingdom. (3) The third puts *social concerns* before spiritual. He has married a wife, and so cannot attend to the claims of God. Society, its attractions and allurements, is keeping multitudes out of the kingdom above. These are but specimens of the trivialities which are monopolizing men's attention, and preventing their giving good heed to the things of the gospel. 5. The extension of the invitation to *those who are sure to accept it.* The poor, maimed, halt, and blind represent the souls who feel their spiritual poverty and defects, and who are sure to appreciate God's gracious invitation. When the self-righteous spurn it, the abased and humiliated greedily receive it. 6. The *abundant room, and the difficulty in getting the places filled.* There is no possibility of any one coming and being refused admittance. There is room for all who care to come. Those who will not taste of the supper are those who thought themselves better employed. In compelling men to come in, we must do our best in persuading them to accept the gospel. May we leave nothing undone that the Divine table may be filled.[1]—R. M. E.

Vers. 25—35.—*The cost of discipleship.* The Pharisee's banquet being over, our Lord continues his journey towards Jerusalem, and, as a crisis is evidently at hand, he has a goodly multitude of expectant followers. Have they any notion of the cost of discipleship? Are they prepared for all which it involves? Jesus determines to make this unmistakable, and so he gives them the admonition contained in the present section. He gives point to his advice by mentioning the folly of beginning to build a tower without calculating the cost of finishing it, or of beginning a war without calculating the reasonable chances of success. Each follower would have a costly tower to build in the devoted life he must lead, and a costly war to wage in the contest for the faith. It was every way desirable, therefore, that they should go carefully into the meaning of discipleship, and undertake it intelligently.

I. NOTHING LESS THAN THE FIRST PLACE IN THE HEART MUST BE OFFERED UNTO JESUS. (Ver. 26.) He insists on being put before father and mother, before wife and children, before brothers and sisters. All relations are to be put below him. He must be more than them all. It is a great demand, and yet a most reasonable one. For: 1. The love of Jesus anticipated all *parental* love. In fact, the love of our parents is only the latest expression of his far-seeing and foreseeing love. The generations to whom we owe so much have only mediated for us the love of Jesus. 2. The unity of

[1] Cf. Gerok's 'Evangelien-Predigten,' s. 806.

marriage only feebly illustrates the *intensity* of Christ's love. Husband owes much to wife, and wife to husband. The marriage union is a close and intimate one; but Jesus comes closer to our hearts than husband or wife can. He is nearer, and should be dearer, than either. 3. The *rising generation* does not lay so much love and hope at our feet as Jesus. Children are dear; the promise of their young lives and hearts is precious; they come as pledges for the future; they are prophecies of the world about to be; but "the holy Child Jesus" comes closer to our hearts than even they. He is the prophecy of all coming time, the goal and ideal at which, not the rising generation only, but generations yet unborn, are to aim. 4. He gives us a more profound *brotherhood* than brothers or sisters can. The brotherhood of Jesus, "the elder Brother born for all adversity, and who can never die," is an experience which brothers and sisters can only help us to understand.[1] Jesus consequently claims first place, because in his manifold relations he is not only more than each, but more than all combined.

II. WE MUST PRIZE CHRIST MORE THAN LIFE ITSELF. (Ver. 26.) Life is another precious benefit which we naturally prize. Satan, in the trial of Job, imagined that Job would give all that he had rather than lose his life (Job ii. 4). He fancied that the patriarch, who would not curse God under the loss of children and property, would break down if God touched his bone or his flesh. But Job was so spiritually minded as to be ready to trust God, even should he, for some mysterious and hidden reason, slay him (Job xiii. 15). Now, Jesus comes and insists on being put before life itself. When the two come into competition there must be no question about yielding the palm to Christ. Jesus is more to us than physical life, because he is our spiritual life (John xiv. 6). We can never forfeit blessed existence so long as we trust in Christ, and the mere existence of the body is but a bagatelle in comparison.

III. SELF-SACRIFICE IS THE MARCHING ORDER OF THE REDEEMED. (Ver. 27.) The idea of cross-bearing is often interpreted as if it simply meant enduring those "crosses" to which life is heir. But much more is meant than this. In the Revised Version it is put, "Whosoever doth not bear *his own* cross." Now, as Christ carried his cross to to die upon, so must we take our lives in our hands, and be ready at any moment to sacrifice them for Jesus. He was crucified for us: are we ready to be crucified for him, or to die in any other way he wishes? It is the *martyr-spirit* which Christ here insists upon. He is surely worthy of such self-sacrifice.

IV. WE MUST FORSAKE ALL AS A GROUND OF CONFIDENCE IF WE WOULD FOLLOW JESUS. (Ver. 33.) Christ, having insisted on disposing of our lives as he pleases, nexts insists on disposing of our property. He comes in with his *right* to tell us, as he told the rich young ruler, that we must give up our all for his sake. Not, of course, that he exercises this right often. Voluntary poverty has been an *exceptional* way of serving him. But we may all show plainly that our property is his, and that, when Christ and our possessions come into competition, all must give way to him. If we prize property more than Jesus, then he is nothing to us. We must be ready to put him before everything which we have, and to sacrifice everything when he claims it from us. In this way we make Christ first and all in all.

V. THE WORLD NEEDS SUCH PRINCIPLES IN PRACTICE TO KEEP IT FROM CORRUPTION. (Vers. 34, 35.) Were it not for the self-sacrifice of souls, the world would become utterly corrupt. Now, it is this heroic element which Christ's cause has *par excellence* supplied. Only by the martyr-band, whose pure self-sacrifice was unmistakable, has the world been kept from utter selfishness and corresponding corruption. It was mindful of this martyr-spirit which his gospel ensures, that Jesus told his servants they were "the salt of the earth" (Matt. v. 13). Unless this wholesome antidote to natural selfishness be supplied, society must go to pieces. It cannot be built on selfishness. The economics which assume no higher ethical element than each man looking after himself, may give expression to tendencies; but they must be overpassed by realities if the world is to keep moderately sweet and habitable.[2] But suppose that Christ's servants make a mere profession of self-sacrifice, and do not carry out the spirit of their Master, then they become but insipid salt, which can only be trodden underfoot of men on the highway, where nothing is meant to grow. In other words,

[1] Cf. Hull's sermon at King's Lynn, on "The Christian Brotherhood of Man:" 'Sermons,' i. p. 121.

[2] Cf. Cairnes's 'Logical Method of Political Economy.'

the Christians who are not genuine are sure to be despised. They are trodden down by a world whom they have vainly tried to deceive. A *false* professor is the most contemptible of all men.—R. M. E.

EXPOSITION.

CHAPTER XV.

Vers. 1—32.—*The Lord speaks his three parable-stories of the "lost," in which he explains his reason for loving and receiving the sinful.*

Vers. 1, 2.—**Then drew near unto him all the publicans and sinners for to hear him. And the Pharisees and scribes murmured, saying, This Man receiveth sinners, and eateth with them;** more accurately rendered, *there were drawing near to him.* This was now, in the last stage of the final journey, the usual state of things. The great outside class came in crowds to listen to Jesus. These were men and women who, through home and family associations, through their occupations, which were looked upon with disfavour by the more rigid Jews, often no doubt through their own careless, indifferent character, had little or nothing to do with their religious and orthodox countrymen. Poor wanderers, sinners, thoughtless ones, no one cared for them, their present or their future. Do not these in every age make up the majority? The religious, so often Pharisees in heart, despising them, refusing to make allowances for them, looking on them as hopelessly lost ones. But at no time was this state of things so accentuated as when Jesus lived among men. Now, among such careless irreligious men and women, are many whose hearts are very tender, very ready to listen if the teacher of religion has any kind, wise words for them. The grave and severe, yet intensely pitiful and loving, doctrines of the Galilæan Master *found* such. His words were words of stern rebuke, and yet were full of hope, even for the hopeless. No man had ever spoken to them like this Man. Hence the crowds of publicans and sinners who were now ever pressing round the Master. But the teachers of Israel, the priestly order, the learned and rigid scribes, the honoured doctors of the holy Law,—*these* were indignant, and on first thoughts not without reason, at the apparent preference felt for and special tenderness shown by Jesus to this great outside class of sinners. The three parables of this fifteenth chapter were the *apologia* of the Galilæan Master to orthodox Israel, but they appeal to an audience far greater than any enclosed in the coasts of the Holy Land, or living in that restless age.

Vers. 3—5.—**And he spake this parable unto them, saying, What man of you, having an hundred sheep, if he lose one of them, doth not leave the ninety and nine in the wilderness?** Now, there are two leading ideas in the three stories—one on the side of the Speaker; one on the side of those to whom the parable-stories were spoken. (1) *On the side of the speaker.* God's anxiety for sinners is shown; he pities with a great pity their wretchedness; he sets, besides, a high value on their souls, as part of a treasure belonging to him. (2) *On the side of the listeners.* Their sympathy with him in his anxiety for sinners is claimed. He has sought it hitherto in vain. The imagery of the first story is very homely—easy, too, to understand. A small sheep-master pastures his little flock of a hundred sheep in one of those wide uncultivated plains which fringe portions of the land of promise. This is what we must understand by "the wilderness." The hundred sheep represent the people of Israel. The lost sheep, one who had broken with Jewish respectability. *One* only is mentioned as lost, not by any means as representing the small number of the outcast class—the contrary is the case—but as indicative of the value in the eyes of the All-Father of *one* immortal soul. **And go after that which is lost, until he find it? And when he hath found it, he layeth it on his shoulders, rejoicing.** This diligent search after the lost one, the tender care shown by the shepherd when the object of his search was found, and the subsequent joy, pictured in a humble everyday figure the mode of acting of which the orthodox Jews complained. They said, "He receiveth sinners, and eateth with them."

Ver. 6.—**And when he cometh home, he calleth together his friends and neighbours, saying unto them, Rejoice with me; for I have found my sheep which was lost.** And here the shepherd craves for *sympathy* from his fellows; he would have others share in his joy in finding the perishing, suffering sheep. This sympathy with his effort to win the lost the Galilæan Master had looked for among the rulers and teachers of Israel in vain. Now, sympathy, it must be remembered, is not merely sentiment or courtesy. True sympathy with a cause means working in good earnest for the cause. This, however, the ruling spirits in Israel, in every sect, coldly refused. They not only declined their sympathy with the acts of Jesus; they positively condemned his works, his efforts, his teaching.

Ver. 7.—**I say unto you, that likewise joy shall be in heaven over one sinner that repenteth, more than over ninety and nine just persons, which need no repentance.** "But," the Master went on to say, "what I looked for in vain on earth, see, I have found in heaven. What men coldly refused me, the celestials have joyfully given. These understand *me*. *They* love both *me* and *my* work, do the holy angels." This coldness, even opposition, on the part of the Pharisees and the religious men of Israel to himself and his works, to his teachings of mercy and love, seems certainly to be the reason why Jesus emphasizes, both here and in the next parable, the sympathy which he receives, not on earth from men, but in heaven from beings, inhabitants of another world. Men, have, however, asked—Why do these heavenly beings rejoice over the one more than over the ninety and nine? It is utterly insufficient to say that this joy is occasioned by the getting back something that was lost. Such a feeling is conceivable among men, though even here it would be an exaggerated sentiment, but in heaven, among the immortals, no such feeling *could* exist; it partakes too much of the sentimental, almost of the hysterical. This higher joy must be due to another cause. Now, the shepherd, when he found the wanderer, did not bring it back to the old fold, or replace it with the rest of the flock, but apparently (ver. 6) brought it to his own home. This would seem to indicate that sinners whom Jesus has come to save, and whom *he has saved*, are placed in a better position than that from which they originally wandered. This gives us the clue to the angels' joy over the "found one" more than over those who were safe in the old fold. The Talmudists have taught—and their teaching, no doubt, is but the reflection of what was taught in the great rabbinical schools of Jerusalem before its ruin—that a man who had been guilty of many sins might, by repentance, raise himself to a higher degree of virtue than the perfectly righteous man who had never experienced his temptations. If this were so, well argues Professor Bruce, "surely it was reasonable to occupy one's self in endeavouring to get sinners to start on this noble career of self-elevation, and to rejoice when in any instance he had succeeded. But it is one thing to have correct theories, and another to put them into practice. . . . So they found fault with One (Jesus) who not only held this view as an abstract doctrine, but acted on it, and sought to bring those who had strayed furthest from the paths of righteousness to repentance, believing that, though last, they might yet be first."

Ver. 8.—**Either what woman having ten pieces of silver, if she lose one piece, doth not light a candle, and sweep the house, and seek diligently till she find it?** Another and very homely picture is painted in this parable. This time the chief figure is a woman, a dweller in a poor Syrian village, to whom the loss of a coin of small value out of her little store is a serious matter. In the story of the lost sheep the point of the parable turns upon the suffering and the sin of man, under the image of a lost sheep searched for and restored by the Divine pity. Here, in the second parable-story, the ruined soul is represented as a lost coin, and we learn from it that God positively misses each lost soul, and longs for its restoration to its true sphere and place in the heaven life and work for which it was created. In other words, in the first parable the lost soul is viewed from man's standpoint; in the second, from God's. If, then, a soul be missed, the result will be, not only missing for itself, but something lost for God.

Vers. 9, 10.—**And when she hath found it, she calleth her friends and her neighbours together, saying, Rejoice with me; for I have found the piece which I had lost. Likewise, I say unto you, there is joy in the presence of the angels of God over one sinner that repenteth.** Again, as in the parable of the lost sheep, we find this longing for sympathy; again the finding of this sympathy in heavenly places, among heavenly beings, is especially recorded. There is a slight difference in the language of rejoicing here. In the first parable it was, "Rejoice with me; for I have found my sheep *which was* lost;" here, ". . . for I have found the piece *which I had* lost." In the first it was the anguish of the sheep which was the central point of the story; in the second it was the distress of the woman who had lost something; hence this difference in the wording. "What grandeur belongs to the picture of this humble rejoicing which this poor woman celebrates with her neighbours, when it becomes the transparency through which we get a glimpse of God himself, rejoicing with his elect and his angels over the salvation of a single sinner!" (Godet).

Ver. 11.—**And he said, A certain man had two sons.** It seems probable that this and the two preceding shorter parables were spoken by the Lord on the same occasion, towards the latter part of this slow solemn journeying to the holy city to keep his last Passover. The mention of the publicans and sinners in ver. 1 seems to point to some considerable city, or its immediate vicinity, as the place where these famous parables were spoken. This parable, as it is termed, of the prodigal son completes the trilogy. Without it the Master's formal *apologia* for his life and work would be incomplete, and the rebuke of the Pharisaic selfishness and censoriousness would have been left unfinished. In the *apologia* much had still to be said concerning the limitless love and the boundless pity of God. In the *rebuke* the two first parables had shown the Pharisee party and the rulers of Israel how they ought to have acted; this third story shows them how they did act. But the Church of Christ—as each successive generation read this exquisite and true story—soon lost sight of all the temporal and national signification at first connected with it. The dweller in the cold and misty North feels that it belongs to him as it does to the Syrian, revelling in his almost perpetual summer, to whom it was first spoken. It is a story of the nineteenth century just as it was a story of the first. We may, with all reverence, think of the Divine Master, as he unfolded each successive scene which portrayed human sin and suffering, and heavenly pity and forgiveness, man's selfish pride and God's all-embracing love, passing into another and broader sphere than that bounded by the Arabian deserts to the south and the Syrian mountains to the north, forgetting for a moment the little Church of the Hebrews, and speaking to the great Church of the future—the Church of the world, to which, without doubt, this Catholic parable of the prodigal, in all its sublime beauty and exquisite pathos, with all its exhaustless wealth of comfort, belongs.

Vers. 12, 13.—**And the younger of them said to his father, Father, give me the portion of goods that falleth to me. And he divided unto them his living. And not many days after the younger son gathered all together.** The subject of the story this time is not derived from humble life. The family pictured is evidently one belonging to the wealthy class. There was money to be distributed; there were estates to be cultivated; means existed to defray the cost of feasting on a large scale; mention, too, is made incidentally of costly clothing and even of gems. Like other of the Lord's parable-teachings, the framework of the story was most likely founded upon fact. The family of the father and the two sons no doubt had been personally known to the Galilæan Teacher. This imperious demand of the younger seems strange to us. Such a division, however, in the lifetime of the father was not uncommon in the East. So Abraham in his lifetime bestowed the main body of his possessions on Isaac, having previously allotted portions to his other sons. There was, however, no Jewish law which required any such bestowal of property in the parent's lifetime. It was a free gift on the part of the father. But to the young son it was a hapless boon.

"God answers sharp and sudden on some
prayers;
And flings the thing we have asked in our
face,
A gauntlet—with a gift in it."
(E. B. Browning.)

And took his journey into a far country. The youth, who probably in the Master's experience had suggested this part of the story, after receiving his share of money, started with unformed purposes of pleasure, perhaps of trade. The man, who was a Jew, left his home for one of the great world's marts, such as Carthage or Alexandria, Antioch or Rome. **And there wasted his substance with riotous living.** This is an extreme case. Few probably of the publicans and sinners whose hearts the Lord touched so deeply, and who are examples of the great class in every age to whom his gospel appeals so lovingly, had sinned so deeply as the young man of the story. Indecent haste to be free from the orderly quiet home-life, ingratitude, utter forgetfulness of all duty, the wildest profligacy,—these were the sins of the prodigal. It has been well remarked that the line runs out widely to embrace such a profligate, that every sinner may be encouraged to return to God and live. There is a grave reticence in sparing all details of the wicked life—a veil which the elder son with pitiless hand would snatch away (ver. 30).

Ver. 14.—**And when he had spent all.** True of many a soul in all times, but especially in that age of excessive luxury and splendour and of unbridled passions.

"On that hard Roman world, disgust
And secret loathing fell;
Deep weariness and sated lust
Made human life a hell."
(Matthew Arnold.)

There arose a mighty famine in that land; and he began to be in want. The "mighty famine" may be understood to represent difficult times. War or political convulsions, so common in those days, may have speedily brought about the ruin of many like the prodigal of our story, and his comparatively small fortune would quickly have been swallowed up. Selfish evil-living, excesses of various kinds, had gained him no real friends, but had left him to meet the ruin of his fortune with enfeebled powers, homeless and friendless: hence the depth of the degradation in which we speedily find him. Not an unusual figure in the great world-drama, this of the younger son—the man who had sacrificed everything for selfish pleasure, and soon found he had absolutely nothing left but suffering. Very touchingly the greatest, perhaps, of our English poets writes of this awful soul-famine. In *his* case fortune and rank still remained to him, but everything that can really make life precious and beautiful had been wasted.

"My days are in the yellow leaf;
 The flowers and fruits of love are gone;
The worm, the anguish, and the grief,
 Are mine alone.

"The fire that on my bosom preys
 Is lone as some volcanic isle;
No torch is kindled at its blaze—
 A funeral pile!"
 (Byron.)

Ver. 15.—**And he went and joined himself to a citizen of that country.** "That citizen," says St. Bernard, quoted by Archbishop Trench, "I cannot understand as other than one of the malignant spirits, who in that they sin with an irremediable obstinacy, and have passed into a permanent disposition of malice and wickedness, are no longer guests and strangers, but citizens and abiders in the land of sin." This is a true picture of the state of such a lost soul, which in despair has yielded itself up to the evil one and his angels and their awful promptings and suggestions; but the heathen citizen is well represented by the ordinary sordid man of the world, who engages in any infamous calling, and in the carrying on of which he employs his poor degraded ruined brothers and sisters. **To feed swine.** What a shudder must have passed through the auditory when the Master reached this climax of the prodigal's degradation! For a young Israelite noble, delicately nurtured and trained in the worship of the chosen people, to be reduced to the position of a herdsman of those unclean creatures for which they entertained such a loathing and abhorrence that they would not even name them, but spoke of a pig as *the other thing!*

Ver. 16.—**And he would fain have filled his belly with the husks that the swine did eat: and no man gave unto him.** So low was this poor lost man reduced, that in his bitter hunger he even came to long for the coarse but nutritious bean with which the herd was fed. These swine were of some value when fattened for the market; but he, the swineherd, was valueless—he might starve. The husks in question were the long bean-shaped pods of the carob tree (*Caratonia siliqua*), commonly used for fattening swine in Syria and Egypt. They contain a proportion of sugar. The very poorest of the population occasionally use them as food.

Ver. 17.—**And when he came to himself.** This tardy repentance in the famous parable has been the occasion of many a sneer from the world. Even satiety, even soul-hunger, did not bring the prodigal to penitence; nothing but absolute bodily suffering, cruel hunger, drove him to take the step which in the end saved him. There is no doubt it would have been far more noble on the young man's part if, in the midst of his downhill career, he had suddenly paused, and, with a mighty and continued effort of self-control, had turned to purity, to duty, and to God. Certainly this had been heroic conduct—a term no one would think of applying to anything belonging to the life of the younger son of our story. But though not heroic, is not the conduct of the prodigal just what is of daily occurrence in common life? The world may sneer; but is not *such* a repentance, after all, a blessed thing? It is a poor mean way, some would tell us, of creeping into heaven; but is it not better to enter into God's city even thus, with bowed head, than not at all? Is it not better to consecrate a few months, or perhaps years, of a wasted life to God's service, to noble generous deeds, to brave attempts to undo past mischief and neglect, than to go sinning on to the bitter end? There is something intensely sorrowful in this consecrating to the Master the end of a sin-worn life; but there is what is infinitely worse. What a deep well, too, of comfort has the Church-taught teacher here to draw from in his weary life-experiences! **How many hired servants of my father's have bread enough and to spare, and I perish with hunger!** Among the bitternesses of his present degradation, not the least was the memory of his happy childhood and boyhood in his old home.

"For a sorrow's crown of sorrows
 Is remembering happier things."

The family of the prodigal, as we have already remarked, was certainly possessed of wealth, and was probably one of high rank. In the old home there was nothing wanting.

Vers. 18, 19.—**I will arise and go to my father . . . make me as one of thy hired servants.** The repentance of the prodigal was real. It was no mere sentimental regret, no momentary flash of sorrow for a bad past. There was before him a long and weary journey to be undertaken, and he—brought up in luxury—had to face it without means. There was the shame of confession before dependents and relatives and friends, and, as the crown of all, there was the position of a servant to be filled in the home where once he had been a son, for that was all he hoped to gain even from his father's pitying love.

Ver. 20.—**And he arose, and came to his father.** And so he came safe home; sad, suffering, ragged, destitute, but still safe. But, in spite of this, the parable gives scant encouragement indeed to sin, poor hope indeed to wanderers from the right way, like the hero of our story; for we feel that, though he escaped, yet many were left behind in that sad country. We dimly see many other figures in the picture. The employer of the prodigal was a citizen, but only one of many citizens. The prodigal himself was a servant—one, though, of a great crowd of others; and of all these unhappy dwellers in that land of sin, we only read of *one coming out.* Not an encouraging picture at best to any soul purposing deliberately to adventure into that country, with the idea of enjoying the pleasant licence of sin for a season and then coming home again. Such a home-coming is, of course, possible—the beautiful story of Jesus tells us this; but, alas! how many stay behind! how few come out thence! **But when he was yet a great way off, his father saw him, and had compassion, and ran, and fell on his neck, and kissed him.** But although many who wander never escape from that sad country, it is not because they would be unwelcomed should they choose to return. The whole imagery of this part of the parable tells us how gladly the eternal Father welcomes the sorrowful penitent. The father does not wait for the poor wanderer, but, as though he had been watching for him, sights him afar off, and at once takes compassion, and even hastens to meet him, and all is forgiven.

Ver. 21.—**Father, I have sinned against heaven, and in thy sight, and am no more worthy to be called thy son.** Many, though not all, of the older authorities add here (apparently taking them from ver. 19) the words, "make me as one of thy hired (servants)." The selfsame words of the original resolution are repeated. They had been stamped deep into the sad heart which so intensely desired a return to the old quiet, pure home-life; but now in his father's presence he feels all is forgiven and forgotten, therefore he no longer asks to be made as one of the servants. He feels that great love will be satisfied with nothing less than restoring him, the erring one, to all the glories and happiness of the old life.

Ver. 22.—**But the father said to his servants, Bring forth the best robe, and put it on him; and put a ring on his hand, and shoes on his feet.** The older authorities add "quickly" after the words "bring forth." Everything is done by the father to assure the wanderer of full and entire forgiveness. Not only is a welcome given to the tired, ragged son, but he is invested at once, with all speed, with the insignia of his old rank as one of the house. But it is observable not a word is spoken of reply to the confession; in grave and solemn silence the story of the guilty past is received. Nothing can excuse it. He forgives, but forgives in silence.

Vers. 23, 24.—**And bring hither the fatted calf.** There was a custom in the large Palestinian farms that always a calf should be fattening ready for festal occasions. **And let us eat. . . . And they began to be merry.** Who are intended by these plurals, *us* and *they*? We must not forget that the parable-story under the mortal imagery is telling of heavenly as well as of earthly things. The sharers in their joy over the lost, the servants of the prodigal's father on earth, are doubtless the angels of whom we hear (vers. 7, 10), in the two former parables of the lost sheep and of the lost drachma, as rejoicing over the recovery of a lost soul.

Ver. 25.—**Now his elder son was in the field.** The broad universal interest of the parable here ceases. Whereas the story of the sin and the punishment, the repentance and the restoration, of the prodigal belongs to the Church of the wide world, and has its special message of warning and comfort for thousands and thousands of world-workers in every age, *this* division of the story, which tells of the sour discontent of the prodigal's elder brother, was spoken especially to the Pharisees and rulers of the Jews, who were bitterly incensed with Jesus being the Friend of publicans and sinners. They could not bear the thought of sharing the joys of the world to come with men whom they had despised as hopeless sinners here. This second chapter of the great parable has its practical lessons for everyday common life; but its chief interest lay in the striking picture which it drew of that powerful class to whom the teaching of Jesus, in its broad and massive character, was utterly repulsive. Now, while the events just related were taking place, and the lost younger son was being received again into his father's heart and home, the elder, a hard and selfish man, stern, and yet careful of his duties as far as his narrow mind grasped them, was in the field at his work. The rejoicing in the house over the prodigal's return evidently took him by surprise. If he ever thought of that poor wandering brother of his at all, he pictured him to himself as a hopelessly lost and ruined soul. The Pharisees and rulers could not fail at once to catch the drift of the Master's parable. They too, when the

Lord came and gathered in that great harvest of sinners, those firstfruits of his mighty work—they too were "in the field" at work with their tithings and observances, making hedge after hedge round the old sacred Hebrew Law, uselessly fretting their lives away in a dull round of meaningless ritual observances. They—the Pharisee party—when they became aware of the great crowds of men, whom they looked on as lost sinners, listening to the new famous Teacher, who was showing them how men who had lived their lives too could win eternal life—they, the Pharisees, flamed out with bitter wrath against the bold and daring Preacher of glad tidings to such a worthless crew. In the vivid parable-story these indignant Pharisees and rulers saw themselves clearly imaged.

Ver. 28.—**Therefore came his father out, and entreated him.** The disapprobation of Jesus for Pharisee opinions was very marked, yet here and elsewhere his treatment of them, with a few exceptional cases, was generally very gentle and loving. There was something in their excessive devotion to the letter of the Divine Law, to the holy temple, to the proud traditions of their race, that was admirable. It was a love to God, but a love all marred and blurred. It was a patriotism, but a patriotism utterly mistaken. The elder brother here was a representative of the great and famous sect, both in its fair and repulsive aspect, in its moral severity and correctness, in its harshness and exclusive pride. The father condescended to entreat this angry elder son; and Jesus longed to win these proud mistaken Pharisees.

Vers. 29—32.—**Lo, these many years do I serve thee.** Bengel quaintly comments here, "Servus erat." This was the true nature of this later Jewish service of the Eternal. To them the eternal God was simply a Master. They were *slaves* who had a hard and difficult task to perform, and for which they looked for a definite payment. **Neither transgressed I at any time thy commandment.** We have here reproduced the spirit, almost the very words, of the well-known answer of the young man in the gospel story, who was no doubt a promising scion of the Pharisee party: "All these things have I kept from my youth up." The same thought was in the mind, too, of him who thus prayed in the temple: "God, I thank thee that I am not as other men are," etc. (ch. xviii. 11, 12). **Yet thou never gavest me a kid. . . . All that I have is thine.** Thy brother has the shoes, the ring, the robe, the banquet; thou the *inheritance*, for all that I have is thine. Why grudge to thy brother an hour of the gladness which has been thine these many years? **As soon as this thy son was come, . . . For this thy brother was dead.** The angry elder son will not even acknowledge the prodigal as *his* brother; with bitter scorn and some disrespect he speaks of him to his father as "*thy* son." The father throughout the scene is never incensed. He pleads rather than reproaches, and to this insolence he simply retorts, "*Thy* brother was dead to us, but now—It was meet that we should make merry, and be glad." What was the end of this strange scene? The last words, breathing forgiveness and joy, leave a sweet sense of hope upon the reader that all would yet be well in that divided household, and that the brothers, friends again, would clasp hands before the loving father's eyes. But when Jesus told the parable to the crowds, the story was not yet played out. It depended on the Pharisees and rulers how the scene was to end. What happened at Jerusalem a *few weeks later*, when the Passion-drama was acted, and some *forty years later*, when the city was sacked, tells *us* something of what subsequently happened to the elder son of the Lord's parable. But the end has yet to come. We shall yet see the brothers, Jew and Gentile, clasp hands in loving friendship before the father, when the long-lost elder son comes home. There will be joy then indeed in the presence of the angels of God.

HOMILETICS.

Vers. 11—32.—*The parable of the prodigal son.* This parable is at once a history, a poem, and a prophecy. A history of man in innocence, in sin, in redemption, in glory. A poem—the song of salvation, whose refrain, "My son was dead, and is alive again, was lost, and is found," is ringing through the courts of the Zion of God. A prophecy, speaking most directly and solemnly, in warning and meditation, emphasis of reproof or of encouragement, to each of us. It is beyond the reach of the scalpel of criticism. Its thoughts, its very words, have enriched every speech and language in which its voice has been heard. It stands before us "the pearl of parables," "the gospel in the gospel" of our Lord and Saviour Jesus Christ. It is the last of three stories, illustrative of Divine grace, which were spoken especially to the Pharisees, and to them with reference to their cavil as expressed in ver. 2. Without minutely analyzing the three, the progress of the teaching may be indicated. Bengel has, with his usual felicitousness of touch, indicated this progress. The silly sheep represents the sinner in his foolishness. The sinner lying in the dust, yet still with the stamp of Divinity on him, is figured by the piece of money. Finally, the younger of the two sons is the representation of the sinner left to the freedom of his own will, and falling into an estate of sin and misery. We can trace, too, a progress in the setting forth of the Divine love. The journey of the shepherd into the far wilderness speaks to us of the infinite compassion of highest God; for the sheep's own sake he goes after it until he finds it; and the recovery is the occasion of the joy of heaven. The aspect specially illustrated by the search for the piece of silver is the infinite value to God of every soul. Not one will he lose; for his righteousness' sake he will seek until he finds. The last of the parables combines the two former, with a glory superadded: Infinite Compassion recognizing the infinite preciousness of the human life, but this, now, in the higher region of Fatherhood and sonship. Let us discard all stiffening exposition of Christ's words; *e.g.* that which takes as its key-thought that the younger son is the Gentile world, the elder son the Jewish Church. Let us regard it in the width of its generosity, as the picture of him whose love is reflected in the "Man who receiveth sinners, and eateth with them." The two words of the parable are "lost" and "found." Let us try to open up the wealth of meaning in them.

I. LOST. 1. *Whence?* There is a glimpse into the sweet home-life—the father with the two sons. The joy of the father's home is the communion of his children. It was what he saw in the Father which moved the prayer of Jesus, "That they whom thou gavest me may be with me where I am." The joy of the child's home is the communion of the Father, and is realized when the Father's life—not the Father's living—is the desire, and the word of the psalm is fulfilled, "In thy presence is fulness of joy, and in thy right hand are pleasures for evermore." So we think of the days speeding on—musical, blessed days, such as we recollect, perhaps, in the home of our childhood, when, as we look back, the sun seemed to shine far more brightly than now, and the day was longer, and all was peace. Parents and children together! For it is man's home to abide with God as Father. By-and-by there comes the far country, because there is no Father. 2. *How?* The younger son demands the portion of goods that falleth to him. Mark how the tone has lowered, how the eye has drooped. "Father, give me!" is the cry of the filial heart. "Give me my daily bread!" is a true prayer, because it waits on God; it sees the living in the life which he gives. But "my portion of goods" is the voice of a sinful independence. It separates "what is mine" from what is "my Father's;" it conceives of his as being, by some right or title, mine. Himself, as the good, is no longer the all. This is the serpent's lie. "Ye shall not surely die, for God doth know that in the day ye eat thereof your eyes shall be opened, and ye shall be as gods, knowing good and evil." Such was the seductive whisper in the beginning. As if (1) God was keeping to himself a God-dom, in jealousy preventing the enjoyment of a blessedness which was the man's right. And as if (2) the way to know good is through the experience of evil—good discerned as the opposite of that which we have tasted, instead of evil being felt only as the darkness seeking to overtake the light in which we are abiding. The serpent's lie repeats itself in many forms, not the least familiar that which insinuates, "Let the young man sow his wild oats; the good oats will come afterwards. Let him take his fill of enjoyment; there will come the sober days and the quiet time." It works in us all; it is the tendency of the sinful mind to withdraw from the authority of Heaven, from the rule of duteous love, to appropriate for self, and in mere self-will, the living of God. The father does not deny the son. He respects the sovereignty in the son which is derived from himself. "He who suffers us to go our way takes care indeed that it be hedged with thorns." But a son cannot be forced as a slave. If go he will, go he must. The father divides the living. 3. *Whither?* Not at once, possibly, does the separation in will show itself. It is not always easy to trace the first moment of the apostasy. Many a one continues, for a time, in the semblance of piety, even after he has ceased to desire spiritual things. But "not many days after" the rift in the lute appears. "He gathers all together." Now the purpose of the will is active; no advice will stand in the man's path. The father's tear, the father's smile, avails not;

not the sight of the old roof-tree, or the remembrance of the sweet life that lies behind. There is an eager "farewell;" he rushes forward—*Whither?* "To a far country." Yes; yield to appetite, to fleshly lust, it will take the soul on and on, away from the fences of religion, away to the far-off Nod, bidding it, as Cain did, build there the city of habitation, yet bidding only to mock, since he who would put miles between him and the face of his Father in heaven must be a sorry fugitive and vagabond. "A far country!" That is wherever God is forgotten, is dishonoured as the Father. No ship is needed to bear one to the uttermost parts of the earth; the distance is measured not by oceans or continents, but by tracts of affection and sympathy. "Alienated from the life of God"—this is the far country. Observe the two stages of the existence in the far country—the *fulness* and the *famine.* (1) There is *fulness*—a season of apparently inexhaustible happiness: "riotous living." The life of the youth is like a mountain-torrent that has been pent up and bursts forth. The Greek word has the force of "prodigally." And prodigal the wanderer is in the earlier period. Fill high the bowl; loud let the revel swell; eat, drink; there is more to follow, there is more behind.

> "Such is the world's gay garish feast
> In her first charming bowl,
> Infusing all that fires the breast,
> And cheats th' unstable soul."

But—what? "The substance is wasting;" literally, is "scattering abroad;" for so it is. As has well been said, "All creaturely possession consumes itself in the using; all wealth must turn itself into poverty, either by its actual dissipation or in consequence of the folly of covetousness, which the more mammon increases is the less satisfied by it. Thus man, in his sin, consumes first of all his earthly goods, so that he can no more find comfort or satisfaction in them; and then, alas! the true and real possessions which his heavenly Father communicated to him are also consumed." What a description of substance scattered (Prov. v. 7—14)! (2) Then comes in the second stage. All which had been gathered together spent; then arises the *famine.* For one who has nothing there is always a famine in that land. The world will give you so long as you have to give it; when you can bring nothing, when you are used up; ah, the fields which seemed golden become the bleakest of moors. There is no sight more pitiful than a worn-out, used-up worldling.

> "The fire that on my bosom preys
> Is lone as some volcanic isle;
> No torch is kindled at its blaze—
> A funeral pile!"

Alas! the pleasure has died out; the soul, the immortal self, not yet dead, is in want in a famine-stricken land. How is this want to be met? 4. *Wherein?* It is an evil and bitter thing to forsake the Lord. The son's own wickedness is correcting him, and his backslidings are reproving him. In want, but not yet in poverty blessed with desire. Here is the witness. Hitherto the son has been the son, wicked, reckless, but still not naturalized in that far country. The day of this separation has passed; and, oh! the double degradation! "He *joins* himself"—"*pins* himself" is the word—becomes wholly, abjectly dependent on, "a citizen of that country." He began by being his own master; he ends by being the slave of the citizen. The world uses for its pleasure the one who uses the world for his pleasure. A man's passion is his minister for a time; by-and-by it becomes his tyrant. A very hard tyrant! The devil has no respect for the freedom of the will: "I was your companion, your Mephistopheles, your slave. Now I have you, you are mine; get out and feed these swine." It was an employment which conveyed the idea of utter wretchedness to a Jew. Strong, thickly laid, is the colouring; it is not one whit too strong or too thickly laid for fact. How do we behold this prince, this son of the Father? Toiling in the fields, with no shelter except the rude hut which he makes, and his only companions—the herd of swine! And all the while the hunger gnawing! Were not these swine, wallowing in the mire, picking the carobs, eating the scanty grass, happy as compared with him? They got what they wanted; he provided their food for them, but there is none to give him. He had rejected his father's hand, and there is no hand in all the world outstretched to him. In Oriental lands there grows a tree whose fruit is like the bean-pod, though larger than it, with a dull, sweet taste; the swine would take of it; and the longing eye of the swineherd is cast on it. It is all he can get, for there is no food in that far country suited to him. The soul starves, whether in riotous living or in want, until it looks upwards and learns the old home-cry, "Father, give me!"

II. Found. Consider the return, the welcome, the supper. "It is meet," says the father, "that we should make merry and be glad." 1. Mark *the steps of the return.* The hopeful feature about the poor swineherd is that, although *pinned* to the citizen of the country, he is yet a person distinct. He has sold himself; but himself is more than, other than, the citizen. There is an inalienable nobility which even "riotous living" cannot stamp out. There are "obstinate questionings," "blank misgivings," "fugitive recollections of the imperial palace whence he came." Ponder the record of the finding of the conscience, and the Litany first, and the Jubilate afterwards, which followed the finding. "He comes to himself." He has never been the right true self from the moment when he demanded the portion. The right self is sonship. This wallowing in the sty with swine, this bound-overness to tyrant appetite and earthliness ah! as one awaking from a horrid dream he recognizes the *reality*. And wherein does the conscience, now awakened, become articulate? (1) There is the sense of an awful discord and wrong. The menial of that citizen left to starve. How different are the menials in his father's house! *They* have bread enough and to spare. "Whatever is orderly is blest. I, the disorderly, the one out of place, out of my right mind, am the unblest, the one perishing with hunger." It was this feeling which came over the wild student when, in the solemn sweet moonlight, he gazed from the height on one of the fairest scenes of nature. And the cry was evoked, "All lovely, all peaceful, except myself!"—a cry that bade him back to another and nobler life. Who is there that in calmer moments does not understand the inward glance of the vision—the peaceful father's house, and the misrule, unrule, of the self-willed and undutiful? (2) There succeeds a higher thought: "The menial in that house, and I, the son!" Gradually there emerges the feeling of the heaven—the authority from which the soul has broken, the order it has contravened, and more still, "against heaven, and *before thee.*" The recollection of the father rushes in, bringing tides of holy ardour. *His* eye, the son feels, has been following him in the journey, in the wasting of the substance; it has been all "*before him.*" "O my father, my father! to have grieved and wounded thee! I will weep no longer. I will arise and go. I will throw myself on thee. I will ask for a place anywhere, if only it is near thee; if I may be again in thy sight, and no longer *the* sinner!" It is a repentance not to be repented of. The matter of it is not, "I have played the fool exceedingly;" it is ever and throughout "I have sinned." What causes the will to arise is the longing to be again with the father, to pour out the broken and contrite spirit on his bosom. And he arises and goes. "The best and most blessed said and done" that can be in heaven or on earth. 2. And now for *the welcome.* The love that descends is always greater than the love that ascends. The love of the child is only a response to the love of the parent. And as to this father! Most touchingly explicit is the word of Jesus. "When yet a great way off, the father saw him." A very great way off! Even in the far country he had been near. The seeing expresses the knowing all about the misery, and the earnestness of the return—a seeing that is a drawing also, a drawing through the need, and all along the journey forming an atmosphere of love that compassed him about. To come to the love of God is to realize that he was first; it is to find that which found us when yet a great way apart. What more? A reproach? A reproof? The arms are at once thrown around the neck, and the kiss of reconciling fatherliness is printed on the cheek. The forgiveness, observe, comes before all confession. In confessing the sin we meet the blessing that has already covered us. But there is a confession. "The truest and best repentance," as it has been said, "follows, and does not precede, the sense of forgiveness; and thus too, repentance will be a thing of the whole life long, for every new insight into that forgiving love is as a new reason why the sinner should mourn that he ever sinned against it." Only, note, beneath the pressure of that fatherly heart there is no mention of the hired servant's place. The "Father, I have sinned," is sobbed forth on the father's heart, and the son leaves himself to the father's will. And how the expression of the welcome rises! The best robe is ordered out; a sonship higher than that of mere birth. "The adoption of children by Jesus Christ to the Father" is the best robe. And the ring is to be put on the hand—the ring with the seal of the spirit of adoption. And shoes are provided for the torn and weary feet, that henceforth they may walk up and down in the Name of the Lord. And hasten, complete the tokens of the rejoicing—make ready the supper in which the father can rejoice over his child with joy, and rest in his love. 3. The fulfilment of the welcome is *the supper*, with the slain fatted calf, and the dancing and music. It denotes the free festal joy of God, of heaven, in the found, repenting sinner. It denotes also the festal blessedness of the sinner himself when the great Object of all need and longing is found, when he is at home with his God. There is a representation of the supper in Rom. v. We hear the music and dancing in Rom. viii. They express the truth of the new existence. There had been, in the past, a living, but not a fellowship, with the Father; henceforth it is fellowship: God is the soul's Good, and the life is lived in and out of him. Oh the swellings of harmony, of poetic triumphant raptures, now! "My son was dead; and is alive again; was lost, and is found." So much for the younger son and the father. But we must not overlook the elder son. And we must not misjudge him. He was not bad; he is not a mere churl. He is faithful, if he is not free; he is just, if he is not generous. He had never transgressed a command; if his life had no heights, it had no depths; it had been even and calm. And he had been blessed, for he had been ever with the father, and all that was the father's had been his. We need not fix on any particular representation of the elder son. The Pharisee-heart is, no doubt, castigated in the picture. But it touches many who would resent being associated with the Pharisee. Krummacher was once asked his opinion of the elder son. He quietly said, "I well know now, for I learned it only yesterday." Being asked further, he laconically remarked, "Myself," and confessed that yesterday he had fretted his heart to find that a very ill-conditioned person had suddenly been enriched with a remarkable visitation of grace. The sketch supplies the foil to the love of God. It brings out, also, his patience and gentleness in the dealing with the elder son. How the father bears even with the foolish wrath! How he reasons and expostulates, and invites to a share in the joy! "Meet that *we* should make merry, and be glad—I over my son, thou over thy brother." Two things notice. 1. The one as *bearing on the elder son.* He comes *out of the fields,* punctual and orderly in all his ways. He cannot understand the merry-making; he never had received a kid. That son's life had been a wholesome one. The prodigal had his ecstasies; but the elder son had had his lifetime. He is the man of habit—habit which is to us better than instinct. The danger to the man of habit is that he becomes mechanical, doing his part steadily, but without the oil of gladness. 2. The other as *bearing on the younger son.* Let not Christ's teaching be misapplied. Do not think that it is a higher thing to be first irreligious and then religious; to spend the best part of the life in self-gratification, and give God only the remnants. Ah! years of godlessness leave their record. They write their impression on brain and heart; and, free and full as is God's forgiveness, the impression cannot be obliterated. What a man sows, he reaps.

HOMILIES BY VARIOUS AUTHORS.

Vers. 1, 2.—*A bitter charge the highest tribute.* The great Teacher himself said that the things which are highly esteemed among men may be abomination in the sight of God; and we may safely assume that the converse of this proposition is true also. Certainly, in this bitter charge brought against our Lord we now perceive the very highest tribute which could be paid him.

I. A BITTER CHARGE AGAINST THE SAVIOUR. It is not easy for us to realize the intensity of the feeling here expressed. The Jews, arguing from the general truth that holiness shrinks from contact with guilt, supposed that the holier any man was, the more scrupulously would he avoid the sinner; and they concluded that the very last thing the holiest man of all would do was to have such fellowship with sinners as to "eat with them." Their patriotic hatred of the publican, and their moral repugnance toward "the sinner," filled them with astonishment as they saw him, who claimed to be the Messiah himself, taking up a positively friendly attitude toward both of these intolerable characters. Their error was, as error usually is, a perversion of the truth. They did not understand that the same Being who has the utmost aversion to sin can have and does have the tenderest yearning of heart toward the sinner; that he who utterly repels the one is mercifully pitying and patiently seeking and magnanimously winning the other. So the men of acknowledged piety and purity in the time of our Lord failed completely to understand him, and they brought against him the charge which might well prove fatal to his claims—that he was having a guilty fellowship with the outcast among men and the abandoned among women.

II. THE HIGHEST TRIBUTE TO THE SAVIOUR. In that attitude and action of his which seemed to his contemporaries to be so unworthy of him we find the very thing which constitutes his glory and his crown. Of course, association with sinners, on the basis of spiritual sympathy with them, is simply shameful; and to break up their association with the intemperate, the licentious, the dishonest, the scornful, is the first duty of those who have been their companions and have shared their wrong-doings, but whose eyes have been opened to see the wickedness of their course. It is for such to say, "Depart from me, ye evil-doers; for I will keep the commandments of my God." But that is far from exhausting the whole truth of the subject. For Christ has taught us, by his life as well as and as much as by his Word, that to *mingle with the sinful* in order to *succour and save* them is the *supreme act of goodness*. When a man's character has been so well established that he can afford to do so without serious risk either to himself or to his reputation, and when, thus fortified, well armed with purity, he goes amongst the criminal and the vicious and the profane, that he may lift them up from the miry places in which they are wandering, and place their feet on the rock of righteousness, then does he the very noblest, the divinest thing he can do. It was this very thing which Jesus Christ came to do: "He came to seek and to save that which was lost." It was this principle which he was continually illustrating; and nothing could more truly indicate the moral grandeur of his spirit or the beautiful beneficence of his life than the words by which it was sought to dishonour him: "This Man receiveth sinners, and eateth with them." It is this which will constitute the best tribute that can be paid to any of his disciples now. "There is nothing of which any true minister of Jesus Christ, whether professional or not, ought to be so glad and so proud, as to be such that the enemies of the Lord shall say tauntingly, while his friends will say thankfully, 'This man receiveth sinners.'"

III. THE GREATEST POSSIBLE ENCOURAGEMENT TO OURSELVES. There are men who know they are sinners, but care not; there are those who do not know that they are guilty in the sight of God; and there are others who do know and who do care. It is to these last that the Saviour of mankind is especially addressing himself. To them all he is offering Divine mercy; restoration to the favour, the service, and the likeness of God; everlasting life. On their ear there may fall these words, intended for a grave accusation, but constituting to the enlightened soul the most welcome tidings—"This Man receiveth sinners."—C.

Vers. 3—7.—*The parable of the lost sheep.* Of these three parables, illustrative of the grace of Christ shown to lost human souls, the first brings into view—

I. THE GREAT FOOLISHNESS OF THE WANDERING SOUL. It goes from God as a foolish sheep strays from the fold. So doing, it leaves *security for peril.* In the fold is safety; in the wilderness are many and serious dangers. At home with God the soul is perfectly safe from harm; its life, its liberty, its happiness, is secure; but, apart and astray from God, all these are not only gravely imperilled, they are already forfeited. It also leaves *plenty for want.* In the fold is good pasture; in the wilderness is scarcity of food and water. With God is rich provision for the spirit's need, not only satisfying its wants, but ministering to its best and purest tastes; at a moral distance from him the spirit pines and withers. To go from God is an act of uttermost folly.

II. THE STRAITS TO WHICH IT IS REDUCED. 1. It is on the point of perishing. Without the interposition of the seeking Shepherd, it would inevitably perish. 2. It is reduced to such utter helplessness that it has to be carried home, "laid upon his shoulders." (1) Under the dominion of sin the soul draws nearer and nearer to spiritual destruction;

and (2) it is often found to be reduced to so low a state that it can put forth no effort of its own, and can only be carried in the strong arms of love.

III. The love of the Divine Shepherd. The strong and keen interest taken by the human shepherd in a lost sheep is indicative of the tender interest which the Father of our spirits takes in a lost human soul. The former is more occupied in his thought and care with the one that is lost than he is, for the time, with the others that are safe; the latter is really and deeply concerned for the restoration of his lost child. And as the shepherd's sorrow leads him to go forth and search, so does the Father's tender care lead him to seek for his absent son. Christ's love for us is not general, it is particular; it reaches every one of us. He cares much that each one of the souls for whom he suffered should enjoy his true heritage, and when that is being lost he desires and he "seeks" to restore it.

IV. His persistency in seeking. "Until he find it." The shepherd, in pursuit of the lost sheep, is not detained by difficulty or danger; nor does he allow distance to stop his search; he goes on seeking until he finds. With such gracious persistency does the Saviour follow the wandering soul; year after year, period after period in his life, through several spiritual stages, the good Shepherd pursues the erring soul with patient love, until he finds it.

V. His joy in finding it. The shepherd's joy in finding and in recovering, shown by calling his friends and neighbours together, saying, "Rejoice with me," etc., is pictorial of the Saviour's joy when a soul is redeemed from sin and enters into the life which is eternal. He rejoices not only, not chiefly, because therein does he "see of the travail of his soul," but because he knows well from what depth of evil that soul has been rescued, and to what height of blessedness it has been restored; he knows also how great is the influence, through all ages, which one loyal and loving human spirit will exert on other souls.—C.

Ver. 10.—*The joy of the angels.* Our first thought may be—What do the angels know about us? But our second thought should be—How likely it is that the angels would be deeply interested in us! For, granted that there are "heavenly hosts" who are in supreme sympathy with God, and who are therefore careful to watch the workings of his holy will in the broad realm he rules, what is there more likely than that they would be profoundly interested in the recovery of a lost world, in the restoration of a rebellious and ruined race? We could well believe that it would be *the* study of the angelic world, the practical problem that would engage their most earnest thought, if it did not occupy their most active labours. And this being so, we can understand the greatness of their joy "over one sinner that repenteth." For—

I. They know, better than we, the stern consequences of sin. Not, indeed, by experience. Experience is not the only teacher, and it does not at all necessarily follow that one who has had some experience of a course of conduct knows more about it than another who has had no experience at all; otherwise we should be driven to the absurd conclusion that guilty man knows more about sin than God does. Many of the inexperienced are a great deal wiser than many who have had "part and lot in the matter," because those learn from all they witness, and these do not learn from anything they do and suffer. The "angels of God" witness the commission and also the fruits of sin; they see what lengths and depths of wrong and wretchedness it brings about from year to year, from age to age; they see what evil it works within and without, in the sinner himself and on all with whom he has to do. As they live on through the centuries, and as they learn Divine wisdom from all that they behold in the universe of God, they must acquire a hatred of sin and a pity for sinners which is beyond our own emotion and which passes our reckoning. How great, then, their joy when they witness the emancipation of one human soul from spiritual bondage, the birth of a spirit into the life eternal!

II. They know, better than we, the blessed fruits of obedience. Here they have their own angelic experience to guide and to enlighten them. With added years of loyalty to the King of heaven; with the spiritual enlargement which (we can well believe) comes with a holy and stainless life, they rejoice in God and in his service with ever-deepening delight; their heritage becomes ampler, their prospects brighter, as the celestial periods pass away; and when they think what it means for one holy intelligence to be filled with the fulness of Divine life and of heavenly blessedness, we can comprehend that they would rejoice "over one sinner that repenteth."

III. THEY ARE DEEPLY INTERESTED IN THE PROGRESS OF THE KINGDOM OF GOD, and they know, better than we, how limitless is the influence one soul may exercise. 1. Because they earnestly, supremely desire the honour of God, the glory of Christ on the earth, they rejoice that one more spirit is brought into loyal subjection to his rule. 2. Because they desire that everything may be put under his feet, they rejoice that all that one man can do—which means more in their measurement than it means in ours—will be done to further his cause and exalt his Name.—C.

Ver. 11.—*The Father's home.* By the Father's home we commonly mean the heavenly home, the sphere where the nearer and more immediate presence of God is realized. But heaven once included earth—earth was once a district of heaven. God meant this world to be a part of his own home; this, but for the separating force of sin, it would be now; and this, when sin has been cast forth, it will be again. And it is properly regarded as a home because *the* relation in which God wished its inhabitants to stand toward himself was that (and *is* that) of children to a Father. The truest picture, the nearest statement, the least imperfect representation of that relationship, is not found in the words, "A certain king had subjects," or "A certain proprietor had servants (or slaves)," but in those of our text, "*A certain man had sons.*" Nothing *so* adequately represents God's position toward us as fatherhood, or our true position toward him as sonship, or the sphere in which we live before him as the Father's home. This family relationship means—

I. HIS DWELLING WITH US. God's dwelling with us or in us is very closely associated with his Fatherhood of us (see 2 Cor. vi. 16—18). The ideal human father is one who dwells under the roof where the family resides; who is at home with his children, maintaining a frequent and a close and intimate intercourse with them. Such is God our Father's desire concerning us. He wishes to be near us all and near us always; so near to us that we have constant access to him; that our free, full, happy, unconstrained "fellowship is with the Father;" that it is the natural and instinctive thing for us to go to him and make our appeal to him in all time of need.

II. HIS CONTROL OF OUR LIVES. God's purpose is to direct the lives we are living, to choose our way for us, even as a father for his children; so that we shall be going where he sends us, be doing his work, be filling up his outline, be walking in the path his own hand has traced.

III. HIS EDUCATION OF OUR SPIRITS. Our children come to our home with great capacities, but with no power. It is our parental privilege to educate them, so that their various faculties—physical, mental, spiritual—shall be developed, so that they shall gain knowledge, acquire wisdom, exert influence, be a blessing and a power in the world. God places us here, in this home of his, that he may educate us; that, by all we see and hear, by all we do and suffer, we may be taught and trained for noble character, for faithful service, for an ever-broadening sphere.

IV. HIS PARENTAL SATISFACTION WITH US. Perhaps the most exquisite satisfaction, the very keenest joy which fills and thrills the human heart, is that which is born of parental love; it is the intense and immeasurable delight with which the father and the mother behold their children as these manifest not merely the beauties of bodily form but the graces of Christian character, and as they bring forth the fruits of a holy and useful life. God meant and still means to have such parental joy in us; to look on us, the children of his home, and be gladdened in his heart more than when he looks on all the wonders of his hand in field and forest, in sea and sky. It is our docility, our affection, our obedience, our rectitude and beauty of character and of spirit, that constitute *the* source of his Divine satisfaction. The children of the Father's home are dearer and more precious far than any marvellous things in all the breadth of his universe. Thus God's thought concerning our race was to establish *a holy family*, himself the Divine Father; we his holy, loving, rejoicing, human children; this world a happy home. That *was* his thought in creation, that *is* his purpose in redemption. To its blissful realization the best contribution each one of us can make is to become his true and trustful child, reconciled to him in Jesus Christ, living before him every day in filial love and joy.—C.

Vers. 12, 13.—*Departure; the far country.* We all know only too well that God's gracious purpose concerning us (see previous homily) has been diverted by our sin; the holy and happy home-life which he designed and introduced has been broken up by our unfilial attitude and action. From the Father's home we have wandered away into "the far country." The strict parallel to this picture we find in the disobedience of our first parents and in the gradual departure of our race from God and from his righteousness to a great distance from him. As to ourselves, there never was a time when we were not outside the home; yet we may speak of—

I. The nearness of childhood. For not only does a great poet speak of "heaven lying about us in our infancy," but One from whom there is no appeal tells us that "of such [as the little child] is the kingdom of heaven." In childhood are those qualities which are most favourable to the reception of the truth and grace of God. And if in our childhood we did not stand actually within the door, we did stand *upon the threshold* of the Father's house. Then God spoke to us, whispered his promises in our ear, laid his hand upon us, touched the chords of our heart, drew forth our thought, our wonder, our hope, our yearning, our prayer. And well is it for us, blessed are we among the children of men, if, thus hearing that voice and feeling that hand Divine, we chose the good part, entered in at the open door, and have been thenceforth inmates of that home of faith and love! But perhaps it was not so; perhaps, like the prodigal son, we were dissatisfied with the heritage of the Father's favour, of a Saviour's love; perhaps we wanted a "portion of goods" quite different from this, and went away and astray from God. And there came—

II. A departure from this nearness of childhood. We opened the Bible with less interest and closed it with less profit; we neglected the throne of grace; we began to shun the sanctuary; we became less careful of our speech and our behaviour; God was less and still less in our thought; our hold upon Christian principle became relaxed, and the cords of the temporal and the material were wound around us. Then we dwelt in—

III. The far country of sin. For sin *is* a "far country." 1. *It is to be a long way off from God himself;* to be separated from him in spirit and in sympathy; to be willing to spend our time without his society; to be satisfied with his absence. The soul, instead of continually looking up for his guidance and his good pleasure, shuns his eye and tries to shake itself free from his hand; instead of placing itself under his elevating teaching and enlarging influence, the soul sinks into lower conditions, and loses its grasp of truth and power and goodness; instead of sharing his likeness, the soul goes down into folly and wrong. 2. *It is to be a long way from his home.* For God's home is the home of righteousness, of wisdom, and of blessedness; and to be living under the dominion of sin is to be dwelling in a sphere of unrighteousness; it is to be spending our days and our powers in an element of folly; it is to be cutting ourselves off from the sources of true joy, and to be where all the roots of sorrow are in the soil. Surely there is no epithet anywhere applied to sin which so truly and so powerfully characterizes it as this—it is *the far country of the soul;* under its sway the human spirit is separated by a measureless distance from all that is worthiest and best. Why should any soul continue there, when God is ever saying, "Return unto me, and I will return unto you;" when Christ is ever saying, "Come unto me, and I will give you rest"?—C.

Vers. 13—15.—*Life in the far country.* When the prodigal son had attained his wish and was free to do as he liked without the restraints of home, how did he fare? He found, as in our distance from God we shall find, that life there meant three evil things—

I. A twofold waste. He "wasted his substance in riotous living." He misspent his powers, devoting to frivolous and unremunerative enjoyment those bodily and mental faculties that might have been put to profitable use, and he scattered the material resources with which he started. Sin is spiritual waste. 1. *It is the waste of consumption.* The "substance" of the soul includes: (1) *Spiritual understanding;* a noble capacity to perceive Divine truths and heavenly realities—the thoughts, the wishes, the purposes of God. Under the dominion of sin this capacity becomes enfeebled; in disuse it rusts and is eaten away: "From him that hath not [uses not what he has] is taken away that [unused capacity] which he has." (2) *Spiritual sensibility*; the capacity of feeling the force of things Divine, of being sensibly and practically affected by them, of being moved and stirred by them to appropriate decision and action. No man can live on in conscious sin without continually losing this sacred and precious sensibility. Neglected and unapplied, it withers away, it wastes. 2. *It is the waste of perversion.* Man was made for the very highest ends—made for God; to study, to know, to love, to serve, to rejoice in God himself. And when he spends his powers on himself and on his own animal enjoyment, he is "wasting his substance," turning from their true Object to one immeasurably lower the faculties and the opportunities with which he came into the world.

II. PITIABLE WANT. "He began to be in want." Indulgence is expensive, and unfits for work; sinful companions are happy to share the treat, but they are slow to refill the purse. Sin leads down to destitution; it takes away a taste for all pure enjoyment, and provides nothing lasting in its stead. The man who yields himself to the power of sin loses all joy in God, all relish for spiritual enjoyments, all gratification in sacred service, all capacity for appreciating the fellowship of the good and great, all sense of the sacredness and spiritual worth of life. What has he left? He is beggared, ruined. "No man gives unto him;" no man *can* give unto him. You cannot give to a man what he is not capable of receiving; and until he is radically changed he cannot receive anything truly precious at your hands.

III. GRIEVOUS DEGRADATION. He was "sent into the fields to feed swine." This was bad enough; yet was there one thing worse—"he was fain to fill his belly with the husks the swine did eat." He went down to the lowest grade imaginable. The degradation of the soul is the very saddest thing under the sun. When we see a man who was made to find his heritage in God's likeness and service satisfying himself with that which is bestial, degrading himself to the drunkard's song, to the impure jest, to the part of astute roguery, and finding a horrible enjoyment in these shameful things, then we see a human heart satiating itself with "husks that the swine do eat," and then we witness the most lamentable of all degradations.

Such is life in the "far country." Distance from God means waste, want, degradation. Its full and final outworking may take time, or it may hasten with terrible rapidity. But it comes sooner or later. 1. There is a way of return even from that "strange land," that evil estate (see succeeding homilies). 2. How wise to place ourselves out of danger of these dire evils by connecting ourselves at once with Jesus Christ!—C.

Vers. 17—19.—*The soul's return.* Out in the far country, living a life of guilty waste, of dreary want, of shameful degradation, the prodigal son was in truth a man "beside himself;" he was lost to himself; he had taken leave of his own better self, of his understanding, of his reason; from his own true self he was afar off. But now there is—

I. A RETURN TO HIMSELF. 1. He regains his wisdom as he gains a sense of his folly. He returns to his right mind; he loses his infatuation as he perceives how great is his foolishness to be in such a state of destitution when he might "have all things and abound." What insensate folly to be starving among the swine when he might be sitting down at his father's table! The soul comes to itself and regains its wisdom when it perceives how foolish it is to be perishing with hunger in its separation from God when it might be "filled with all the fulness of God." Our reason returns to us when we refuse to be any longer misled by the infatuation, by "the deceitfulness of sin," and when we see that the pining and decay of our spiritual powers is a poor exchange indeed for the wealth and health of spiritual integrity. 2. He is restored to sanity of mind as he obtains a sense of his sinfulness. To be able to say, as he is now prepared to say, "I have sinned," is to come back into a right and sound spiritual condition. We are in a wholly unsound mental state when we can regard our disloyalty and disobedience to God with complacency and even with satisfaction. But when our ingratitude, our forgetfulness, our unfilial and rebellious behaviour towards God, is recognized by us as the "evil and bitter thing" it is, as the wrong and shameful thing it is, and when we are ready, with bowed head and humbled heart, to say, "Father, I have sinned," then are we in our right mind; then have we *returned to ourselves*.

II. A RESOLVE TO RETURN TO GOD. This return on the part of the prodigal: 1. Arose from a sense of the greatness of his need. 2. Was based on a sound confidence, viz. that the father, whose disposition he knew so well, would not reject but receive him. 3. Included a wise and right determination, viz. to make a frank confession of his sin and to accept the humblest position in the old home which the father might allot him. (1) Out of the greatness and soreness of our need we come to the conclusion that we will return unto God. Our state of guilt and shame is no longer tolerable; we must turn our back on the guilty past and the evil present; there is no refuge for our soul but in God—"in God, who is our home." (2) We may hold fast the firm conviction that we shall be graciously received. Of this we have the strongest assurance we could have in the character and the promises of God, and in the experience of our brethren. (3) Our resolution to return should include the wise and right determination: (*a*) To make the fullest confession of our sin; meaning by that not the use of the strongest words we can employ against ourselves, but the full outpouring of all that is in our heart; for, above all things, God "desires *truth* in the inward parts." (*b*) To accept whatever position in God's service he may appoint us. Not that we are expecting that he will make us "as a hired servant;" we may be sure (see next homily) that he will place us and count us among his own children; but so humble should our spirit be, such should be our sense of undeservedness, that we should be ready to be anything and to do anything, of however lowly a character it may be, which the Divine Father may assign us in his household.—C.

Vers. 20—24.—*The welcome home.* Having seen the younger son of this parable dissatisfied with his estate, having followed him into the far country of sin, having seen how there he frittered or flung everything away in his guilty folly and was reduced to utmost want and degradation, and having been with him in the hour of self-return and wise resolve, we now attend him on his way home to his father. We look at—

I. THE WISDOM OF IMMEDIATE ACTION. "He said, I will arise . . . *and he arose.*" "Most blessed said and done," as has been well remarked. What if he had lingered and given room for vain imaginations of things that would "turn up" on his behalf where he was, or for needless fears as to the reception he would have at home! How many more sons and daughters would there be now in the Father's home if all who said, "I will arise," had *at once* arisen, without parleying, without giving space for temptation and change of mind! Let there be no interval between saying and doing; let the hour of resolution to return be the hour of returning.

II. THE ABOUNDING GRACE OF HIS FATHER'S WELCOME. 1. He eagerly desired his son's return; he was looking out for it; when he was *yet a great way off* he saw him, and recognized him in all his rags and in all his shame. 2. He went forth to meet him; did not let his dignity stand in the way of his giving his son the very earliest assurance of his welcome home; he "put himself out," he "ran" to receive him back. 3. He welcomed him with every possible demonstration of parental love. He tenderly embraced him; he had him at once divested of his livery of shame and clad with the garments of self-respect and even honour; he ordered festivities to celebrate his return. As if he would say, "Take from him every sign and token of misery and want; remove every badge of servitude and disgrace; clothe him with all honour; enrich him with all gifts; ring the bells; spread the table; wreathe the garlands; make every possible demonstration of joy; we will have music in our hall to utter the melody in our hearts, 'for this my son,' etc." It all means one thing; every stroke in the picture is intended to bring out this most precious truth—the warm and joyous welcome which every penitent spirit receives from the heavenly Father. (1) We do not wonder at the misgivings of the guilty heart. It is natural enough that those who have long dwelt at a great distance from God should fear lest they should fail to find in God *all* the mercy and grace they need for full restoration. (2) Therefore we bless God for the fulness of the promises made to us in his Word—promises made by the lips of the psalmist, of the prophet, and of his Son our Saviour. (3) And therefore we thankfully accept this picture of the prodigal's return; for as we look at it and dwell upon it we gain a sense and a conviction, deeper than any verbal assurances can convey, of the readiness, the eagerness, the cordiality, the fulness, of the welcome with which the Father of our spirits takes back his erring but returning child If any wandering one comes to us and says, "Will God receive *me* if I ask his mercy?" we reply, "Look at that picture, and decide; it is a picture drawn by the eternal Son to indicate what the eternal Father will do when any one of his sons comes back to him from the far country of sin. Look there, and you will see that it is not enough to say, in reply to your question, 'He will not refuse you;' that is immeasurably short of the truth. It is not enough to say, 'He will forgive you;' *that* also is far short of the whole truth. That picture says, 'O children of men, who are seeking a place in the heart and the home of the heavenly Father, know this, that your Father's heart is yearning over you with a boundless and unquenchable affection, that he is far more anxious to enfold you in the arms of his mercy than you are to be thus embraced; he is not only willing, but waiting, ay, longing, to receive you to his side, to give you back all that you have lost, to reinstate you at once into his fatherly favour, to confer upon you all the dignity of sonship, to admit you to the full fellowship of his own family, to bestow upon you the pure and abiding joy of his own happy home.'"—C.

Ver. 31.—*Ungrateful recipiency and ample heritage.* The "elder brother" is by no means so unpopular out of the parable as he is in it. As he is seen in the picture every one is ready to throw a stone at him. In actual life there are many Christian people who pay him the high compliment of a very close imitation. We are in danger of setting up a certain type of Christian character as a model, and if one of our neighbours should show any serious departure from that type, we are disposed to be shy of him and to shun him. Is the returned penitent whom Christ has received into his love always cordially welcomed into our society and made to feel at home with us? But let us look at this young man as—

I. A TYPE OF THE UNGRATEFUL RECIPIENTS OF THE CONSTANT KINDNESS OF GOD. He complained of his father's partiality in that for his brother there had been killed a fatted calf, while not even a kid had been slain for himself and his friends. But the reply was that, without any intermission, he had been enjoying the comfort of the parental hearth and the bounty of the parental table; that one extraordinary feast granted to his brother was nothing in comparison with the constant and continued manifestations of fatherly love and care he had been receiving day by day for many years. "Thou art ever with me, and all that I have is thine." It is for us to remember that our Divine Father's continual loving-kindnesses are much more valuable than one interposition on our behalf. A miracle is a much more brilliant and imposing thing than an ordinary gift, but one miracle is not such evidence of fatherly love as we have in an innumerable series of daily and hourly blessings. A greater gift than the manna in the wilderness were the annual harvests which fed many generations of the people of God. A more valuable gift than the water that issued from the rock in the desert were the rains, the streams, and the rivers that fertilized the soil from year to year. Kinder than the providential rescue from threatening embarrassment or impending death is the goodness which preserves in peaceful competence and unbroken health through long periods of human life. It is a sad and serious mistake; it is indeed more and worse than a mistake when we allow the very constancy of God's kindness, the very regularity of his gifts, to hide from our hearts the fact that he is blessing us in largest measure and in fullest parental love. He is saying to us the while, "Children, ye are ever with me, and all that I have is yours."

II. A TYPE OF OUR COMMON SONSHIP. In the parable the father says to his son, "My property is thine—thine to use and to enjoy; there is nothing I have made that is within your view and your reach which you are not free to partake of and employ; all that I have is thine." Is not that our goodly estate as the sons of God? This world is God's property, and he shares it with us. He interdicts, indeed, that which would do us harm or do injury to others. Otherwise he says to us, "Take and partake, enrich your hearts with all that is before you." 1. And this applies not only to all material gifts, but to all spiritual good—to knowledge, wisdom, truth, love, goodness; to those great spiritual qualities which are the best and most precious of the Divine possessions. 2. It has also a far-reaching application; it is a promise as well as a declaration. Of "all that God has" we only see and touch a very small part now and here. Soon and yonder we shall know far more of what is included in his glorious estate, and still and ever will it be true that what is his is ours; for he lives to share with his children the blessedness and the bounty of his heavenly home.—C.

Vers. 1—10.—*Murmurs on earth, and joy in heaven.* Our blessed Lord, in his progress towards Jerusalem, had shown the same kindly interest in the outcast classes which had always characterized him, and his love was beginning to tell. Publicans and sinners gathered eagerly around him to hear his tender, saving words; while the reputable Pharisees and scribes eyed him from a distance with self-righteous suspicion. Their murmurs, however inaudible to mere man, were audible to him to whom all things are naked and open, and he exposes their criticisms by a *trinity* of parables which are without peers in literature. Stier thinks that the trinity of parables is intended to present the Persons of the adorable Trinity in their respective relations to our salvation. The first would thus represent the Son's shepherd-care; the second, the Spirit's maternal solicitude for the restoration of lost souls to the heavenly treasure; and the third, the Father's yearning that prodigal sons might come home.[1] This view is certainly commendable, and not too artistic for such a weighty Preacher as the Lord Jesus Christ, and such a reporter as St. Luke. Leaving the third and greatest of the parables for separate treatment, let us, in this homily, discuss the other two; and as they are so similar, we need not separate them in our treatment.

I. We are here taught by Christ what unfallen beings think about themselves. (Ver. 7.) A door is opened by these parables into heaven, and we have glimpses of the celestial world. Jesus is here testifying about heavenly things (John iii. 12). Now, we must know, in the first place, who are meant by the ninety and nine sheep which never went astray, and by the nine pieces of silver which were never lost. They cannot mean self-righteous souls such as the Pharisees and scribes. For they needed repentance, and over them no celestial ones would think of rejoicing. Hence they can only refer to *unfallen* beings.[2] Now, the parables imply that there is joy over the unfallen. Why should there not be? To us who are fallen it appears but right that the most intense joy should be taken in the unfallen and sinless. They are a new type of beings to us. We have only had one of them in this world. The sinless Saviour broke the law of continuity, and constitutes the marvel of human history.[3] Ninety and nine unfallen beings would seem to us a marvellously interesting group. A sinless city, such as the new Jerusalem is, appears to our comprehension such a novelty, such a new notion and thought amid the sad monotony of sin, that we almost wonder how those who have got within the city could ever think of aught beyond it. And yet to the unfallen ones themselves—sinlessness being the rule, and no exception being found within the celestial city—there must come over the joy with which they contemplate each other a certain monotony, which must keep the joy down to a certain uniform level. Where everything is exactly as it should be, and no tragedy is possible, the joy of contemplation must be so uniform as to partake almost of what is common. The sinless ones contemplate one another with rapture, doubtless, but the joy is not of the *intensest* type by reason of the monotony and sameness associated of necessity with it. We may make sure of this by simply contrasting the complacency of the self-righteous with the consciousness of the sinless that they never can be more than unprofitable servants, for they can never rise above the sphere of duty. Nothing corresponding to the self-satisfaction of the Pharisee, who thanks God that he is not as other men, can be entertained by the celestial world. They are not absorbed in self-admiration. That is only possible with lost men! So that the joy of unfallen beings over one another is modified by the thought that their sinlessness is nothing more than should be expected from those possessed of such privileges as they. Unlost sheep and money receive but moderate admiration.

II. We are here taught with what intense interest unfallen beings contemplate the career of lost souls. (Vers. 4, 8.) The problem of sin comes upon the sinless as an exception to the rule. They contemplate the career of the lost as a

[1] Cf. 'Words of the Lord Jesus' (Clark's edition of 1864), vol. iv. pp. 109, 110.

[2] Cf. Nettleton's 'Sermons and Remains,' p. 62; also Arndt's 'Gleichniss-Reden,' erster theil, s. 97; Gerok's 'Aus Ernster Zeit,' s. 400; and Beck's 'Christliche Reden,' band i. s. 128.

[3] Cf. Mozley's Essay 'Of Christ alone without Sin.'

tragedy added to the monotony of life. They hover over the lost ones with intense interest. They follow their career and study its issues. We must not regard the celestial world as walled out from the tragedies of this earth. All, according to Christ's idea, is open to the celestial side. We may not see with our dull eyes the city of the Apocalypse; but the celestials can follow our terrestrial careers and note the lessons of our different destinies. "The bourne from whence no traveller returns" is the celestial country. The lack of tidings is *here*, not there! The majority beyond the shadows may seem all silent, like the grave, to us; but the din of our voices reaches across the void to them, and constitutes a study of unfailing interest.

III. THE UNFALLEN ONES HAVE SENT FORTH MESSENGERS TO SAVE THE LOST. (Vers. 4—6, 8, 9.) Angels hover around us, and with intensest interest contemplate our sin-burdened, sin-stained careers. But the celestial world did not contemplate the problem from a distance, and allow the wanderers to die. Two, at all events, came forth from heaven in the interests of lost men—the shepherd Son of God, and the Spirit, with all womanly tenderness. The Second and Third Persons of the adorable Trinity have come forth as messengers to save lost men. In addition, there are multitudes of ministering angels who exercise a mysterious but real ministry, and aid the heirs of salvation in their pilgrimage home. To the celestial visitants, however, who are set before us in these parables, we must meanwhile give our attention. 1. *The good Shepherd.* He follows the lost sheep over the mountains into the wilderness, up the rocky steeps, wherever lost souls wander and are waiting to be found. It was arduous work. It involved the exchange of Paradise for this wilderness-world, and a life of privation and trouble of many kinds, and all that the lost sheep might be found and brought home. Christ's work was self-denial and self-sacrifice in the highest degree. He had to lay down his life for the rescue of the sheep. 2. *The painstaking Spirit.* Like the housewife who searched so thoroughly the dust of the house until she found the lost piece of money, so the Spirit comes down and searches in the dust of this world for lost souls, that he may restore them to the heavenly treasure. There is no work too severe or too searching for the Spirit to undertake in the rescue of our lost souls. As Gerok puts it, "No trouble is too great for God to undertake in seeking out a soul."

IV. THE JOY OF THE CELESTIAL WORLD OVER REPENTANT SOULS IS GREATER THAN THEIR JOY OVER THE UNFALLEN. (Vers. 7, 10.) Our Lord represents the joy of heaven over *one* repentant sinner as greater than the joy over even *ninety and nine* unfallen beings. No angel of light amid his sinless glory ever caused such rapture to the heavenly world as does a sinner repenting and returning to God. "Gabriel," says Nettleton, "who stands in the presence of God, never occasioned so much joy in heaven. We may number ninety and nine holy angels and then say, 'There is joy in heaven over one sinner that repenteth, more than over those ninety and nine just persons.' The creation of the world was a joyful event, when 'the morning stars sang together, and all the sons of God shouted for joy.' But this is not to be compared with the joy over one sinner that repenteth. . . . The joy of angels is most sensibly felt every time one more is added to the company of the redeemed. The ninety and nine already redeemed seem to be forgotten, when, with wonder and joy, they behold their new companion with whom they expect to dwell for ever. Could we know, as well as angels do, the reality of a sinner's repentance, we should know better how to rejoice." How important, consequently, should we regard the repentance of a sinner! Instead of our indulging in Pharisaic suspicion and murmuring, should we not join the joyful companies above in their ecstasy over the lost being found? And does it not further help us to understand why evil has been permitted, seeing that grace can translate it into so much joy? In all the assemblies of the saints we have reason to believe angels are present, watching with intense interest the exercises and noting what repentances result. The interest we take in such services is, we must believe, as nothing to the interest of the heavenly world. How they must wonder at so much indifference on our part! How they must wonder at the cool and matter-of-fact way we receive tidings of credible conversions to God! The joy of heaven over penitent sinners is a standing rebuke to our murmurings or apathy! May the thought of it lead to a better feeling and a better life!—R. M. E.

Vers. 11—32.—"*From home, and back.*" The two previous parables which our

Lord related in defence of his conduct are really but introductory to what has been with justice called "the pearl of parables," that of the prodigal son. To it we will now devote ourselves, under the title recently given to it as "From home, and back." It brings out in a most interesting way the attitude of God the Father towards lost souls. It is necessary before setting out, however, to notice that, according to the ancient Law, the division of the family inheritance was *not* conditioned by the parent's death. If a son insisted on his share, the father publicly declared to his household his testamentary intentions, and the son entered at once into possession.[1] What our Lord's parable supposes, therefore, is what constantly occurred. The father did not keep his testamentary intentions a secret to be revealed only at his death, but got up and declared publicly how the inheritance was to be allotted, and the impatient son entered at once into possession. Death, as a matter of fact, does not enter into the case at all. There is another preliminary point which we had better distinctly state, and that is that historically the younger son is intended to cover the case of the "publicans and sinners" Jesus was receiving into the kingdom of God; while the elder son covers the case of the "Pharisees and scribes" who murmured at Christ's policy. If we keep this clearly in view, it will help us greatly in our interpretation. We shall take up the two sons in the order presented in the parable.

I. THE PRODIGAL LEAVING HOME AND COMING BACK. (Vers. 11—24.) Imagining he could not enjoy life with his father and amid the restraints of home, he clamours for his share of the inheritance, turns it into money, and sets out. We cannot do better than take up the stages in the history one by one, and interpret them as we proceed. We have, then: 1. *The emigration.* (Ver. 13.) Now, if this younger son represents historically "the publicans and sinners," we must remember that they did not leave Palestine or even Jerusalem when separated from the Jewish Church. The emigration pictured in the parable was, therefore, not emigration to a *locally* distant land, but to a *morally* distant land; in other words, by the "far country" is not meant a foreign country, but the country of *forgetfulness of God.* The soul that lives at a distance from God, that never considers that he is near, has by that forgetfulness of him emigrated to the "far country," and gone from home. In strict accordance with this principle of interpretation, the "substance" which was gathered and wasted in the far country was *moral wealth,* not monetary. As a matter of fact, the publicans, or tax-gatherers, were in many cases careful, money-gathering men, and not spendthrifts in the vulgar sense. What was squandered, therefore, in the far-off land of forgetfulness of God was moral wealth, the wealth of the heart and mind. The waste was moral waste. And it is just here that we have to notice what may be called the *defamation of the prodigal,* in that painters and expositors have represented his "riotous living" as including actually the deepest immorality. This was the line adopted, too, by the elder brother, who represented his brother as having devoured the father's living with harlots (ver. 30), although, as a matter of fact, he had no evidence of such "excess of riot" in the case at all. The most careful expositor of this parable has accordingly pointed out that the prodigal did not reach the sphere of sensuality until he envied the swine, and then only entered it by the mental act.[2] It is when we note how carefully our Lord constructed the parable, that we can see how the moral character of the publicans was appreciated in the picture, and they were not confounded with sinners of the more sensual type. The far-off country, then, and the waste which took place there, represent the land of forgetfulness of God, and the waste of mind and heart that a God-forgetting life is certain to experience. 2. *The famine.* (Ver. 14.) This is the second stage. It represents the hunger of the heart and mind which comes over the soul that has forgotten God and taken to worldly courses. The famine is the utter vacancy of heart that settles down upon the moral emigrant. He begins to realize what he has lost by leaving God. 3. *The effort after recovery.* (Vers. 15, 16.) The famished worldling betakes himself to work; becomes a swineherd—an unlawful occupation for a Jew—our Lord touching thus gently on the question of the farming of the taxes for Rome by the publicans; and finds that there is no real regeneration to be found in work. He, in his utter want of satisfaction, wishes he could satisfy his soul

[1] Cf. Maine's 'Ancient Law,' 4th edit., pp. 198—214.
[2] 'La Parabole de l'Enfant Prodigue,' par D. Chantepie de la Saussaye, p. 48.

as the swine satisfy their nature, upon husks. Sensuality is seen by the famished one to be as unsatisfying as work. And then the last experience is the utter helplessness of man. "No man gave unto him;" no one could minister to his mental trouble. It is through a similar experience the soul comes. Self-recovery turns out to be a delusion, and man is found to be of no avail. 4. *The return of reason.* (Vers. 17—19.) In his isolation he begins to see that all the past forgetfulness of God was a mistake; that he was insane to take the course he did; and that in his right mind he must act differently. Accordingly he begins in sane moments to reflect on the Father's house, how good a Master God is, how his hirelings have always enough and to spare, and that the best thing for him to do is to return, confess his fault, and get what place in God's house he can. This is repentance—the remembrance of God and how we have sinned against him. 5. *Coming back.* (Ver. 20.) The resolution to come home must be put in practice. The hope may only be for a servant's place, yet it is well to begin the return journey and test the loving-kindness of God. 6. *The welcome home.* (Vers. 20, 21.) The father has been on the look-out for the son, and, the moment he begins the journey, the father's compassion becomes overpowering, and he runs and falls on the prodigal's neck and kisses him. And when the broken-hearted son pours forth his penitence, and that he is no more worthy to be called a son, he is met by the father's welcome and passionate embrace. In this most beautiful way does our Lord bring out God's yearning for lost souls, and his intense delight when they return to him. 7. *The feast of joy.* (Vers. 22—24.) Orders are given to the servants to take away his rags, and put upon him the best robe, and a ring on his hand, as signs of his rank as his father's son, and shoes on his feet, and to prepare the fatted calf and have a merry feast. In this way does our Lord indicate the joy which fills God's heart and that of the angels and that of the returned soul himself when he has come home to God. It is indeed "joy unspeakable and full of glory." These are the stages, then, in a soul's history as it passes into the far-off land of forgetfulness of God, and then gets back to his embrace.

II. THE ELDER SON STAYING AT HOME, BUT NEVER HAPPY. (Vers. 25—32.) We now turn to our Lord's picture of the Pharisees and scribes, under the guise of the elder brother. Although these men had not left the Church, although they put in their appearance at the temple, they never were happy in their religion. 1. *Nominally at home, the elder son is yet from home.* (Ver. 25.) The elder son was always at work in the fields, happiest away from the father. The self-righteous spirit is after all an isolating spirit. The elder son was really as forgetful of God as the younger, only the forgetfulness took a different form. 2. *The merry-making at home distresses him.* (Vers. 26—30.) He first asks an explanation of the unusual mirth, and then, when he gets it, bursts into a fit of censoriousness of the most exaggerated character, in which he accuses the father of favouritism in receiving his penitent child, and refuses to be any party to such merry-making. How it exposes the gloomy, Pharisaic spirit which with some passes for religion! 3. *The godless spirit manifests itself within him.* (Ver 29.) He has been a faithful and faultless servant, he believes, and yet he has never got even a kid to make merry with his friends. His whole idea of joy is away from the father. He is still in the first stage of the younger brother, from which he happily has escaped. 4. *He is unable to realize how meet it is to rejoice over the return of the lost.* (Vers. 31, 32.) The father's expostulations are vain, although they ought to have been convincing. Joy over the recovery of the lost is one of the necessities of an unwarped nature. It was this great sin of which the scribes and Pharisees were guilty, that they would not rejoice at the recovery of fallen fellows by the ministry of Christ. May the broken-heartedness of the prodigal be ours, and never the heartlessness and censoriousness of the elder brother!—R. M. E.

EXPOSITION.

CHAPTER XVI.

Vers. 1—31.—*The Lord's teaching on the right use of earthly possessions with regard to the prospect of another world, in the form of the two parables of the unjust steward, and Dives and Lazarus.*

Vers. 1, 2.—And he said also unto his

disciples. There is no doubt that this important teaching belongs to the last portion of our Lord's life, and it is probable that it is closely connected with the parable of the prodigal son just related. It is not likely that two such weighty sermons had been preached at the same time, but in the evening, or on the following day, or at least on the next sabbath, the same auditory that listened to the prodigal son we believe were startled and enthralled by the story of the unjust steward, and then, or very shortly after, by the awful and vivid picture of life beyond the grave in the parable of the rich man and Lazarus. There is a close link of thought between the parable of the unjust steward and that of the prodigal. The heroes of both these narratives, in the first instance, had a considerable share of this world's goods entrusted to their charge, and by both, in the early portions of the story, these goods were misused and wasted. The Greek words used of the "wasting" of the prodigal and of the steward were in both cases the same (ch. xv. 13; xvi. 1). No parable in the New Testament has been so copiously discussed or has received so many and such varying interpretations at the hands of expositors. We will at once put aside all the ingenious, but from our point of view mistaken, interpretations which see in "the steward" the Pharisees, the publicans, Judas Iscariot, or Satan. The parable has a broader, a more direct, a more universally interesting, meaning. It contains a deep and important teaching for *every* man or woman who would wish to rank among the followers of Jesus Christ. Now, our Lord would have all men look forward gravely and calmly to the certain event of their death, and, in view of that event, would have them make careful and thoughtful preparation for the life which was to come after death. To press this most important lesson home, the Master, as his custom was at this late period of his ministry, conveyed his instruction in the form of a parable. The sketch of a steward about to be dismissed from his office, and who thus would be stripped of his income, was a fit emblem of a man about to be removed from this world by death. The steward in the parable-story felt that, when dismissed, he would be as it were alone, stripped of all, and destitute. The soul of such a man, when dead, would be also stripped of everything, would be alone and destitute. The question here might be asked—Why take for the principal figure of the parable so immoral a character as an *unjust* steward? The answer is well suggested by Professor Bruce, "For the simple reason that his misbehaviour is the natural explanation of the impending dismissal. Why should a *faithful* steward be removed from office? To conceive such a case were to sacrifice probability to a moral scruple." Roughly, then, two things all-important to us are taught here: (1) that dismissal, death, will certainly come; (2) that some provision certainly ought to be made for the life that lies beyond—the life that comes *after* the dismissal, or death. **There was a certain rich man, which had a steward; and the same was accused unto him that he had wasted his goods. And he called him, and said unto him, How is it that I hear this of thee? give an account of thy stewardship; for thou mayest be no longer steward.** The story of the parable contains little incident. There is the rich man, clearly a noble of high rank, whose residence is at a distance from his estates, the scene of the little story. Over these he has placed, as administrator or factor, the one called here a steward; the revenues of the lands this official has wasted; he appears to have been generally a careless if not a dishonest servant. The owner of the estates, when he becomes aware of the facts of the case, at once gives notice of dismissal to the steward, desiring him, however, before yielding up his office, to give in his accounts. Appalled at the sudden and utter destitution which lay before him, the steward occupies the short time of office yet remaining to him in devising a plan by which he would secure the good offices of certain persons who were in debt to his master. He (the steward) had yet a little time of power remaining before he was turned adrift; he would turn this to account, and would do a good turn to these men, poor neighbours of his, and debtors to his lord, while he was in office, and so win their friendship, and, on the principle that one good turn deserves another, would be able to reckon on their gratitude when all else had failed him. With the immorality of the act by which he won the good will of these debtors of his master we have nothing to do; it is simply a detail of the picture, which is composed of figures and imagery chosen for their fitness to impress the lesson intended to be taught. ***Give an account of thy stewardship; for thou mayest be no longer steward.*** This taking away the position and privileges of the man represents the act of death, in which God takes away from us all the varied gifts, the possessions, and the powers large or small with which we are entrusted during our lifetime. Our day of dismissal will be the day of our passing away from this life.

Ver. 3.—**What shall I do? for my lord taketh away from me the stewardship.** This day of dismissal *must* be prepared for; very carefully, very anxiously, the man who has received the sentence of doom ponders over his future. The lesson of the Master is spoken to all; it is a solemn warning to each of us to see what we can do by way of providing for the inevitable day when we shall find ourselves alone and naked and perhaps friendless in the great, strange world to come. The hero of the parable seems suddenly, after a life of carelessness and thoughtlessness, to have awakened to a sense of his awful danger. So the voice of the *real Owner* of the goods, which we have so long deluded ourselves into thinking were our own, comes to us, bidding us make ready to give them back again to him, their Owner, and at the same time to render an account of our administration of them. The voice comes to us in the varied forms of conscience, sickness, misfortune, old age, sorrow, and the like; well for us if, when we hear it, we at once determine, as did the steward of the parable, to make a wise use of the goods in our power for the little time they are still left to us to dispose of as we will.

Ver. 4.—**I am resolved what to do.** The first part of the parable teaches, then, this great and all-important lesson to men—that they will do well to provide against the day of dismissal from life. The second part points out very vividly how kindness, charity, beneficence, towards those poorer, weaker, more helpless than ourselves is one way, and that a very sure and direct way, of so providing against the inevitable dismission, or death. Vers. 5, 6, and 7 simply paint in the details of the interesting picture of the parable. This singular plan of providing for himself by becoming a benefactor of the debtor, remarks Professor Bruce, was by no means the only possible one under the circumstances; but the Speaker of the parable made his hero make choice of it as the aim of the imaginary narrative was to teach the value of beneficence as a passport into the eternal habitations. Various explanations have been suggested to account for the difference in the gifts to the debtors. It is probable that when our Lord spoke the parable, reasons for these varied gifts were given, such as the circumstances of the debtors. It is scarcely now worth while to frame ingenious guesses respecting the details, which apparently do not affect the grand lessons which the story was intended to teach.

Ver. 8.—**And the lord commended the unjust steward, because he had done wisely.** This, again, is a detail which has little bearing on the main teaching. It is a graphic and sarcastic eulogy which a good-humoured man of the world would pronounce upon a brilliant and skilful, although unprincipled, action, and it completes the story as a story. It seems evident that the intentions of the steward in regard to the debtors were carried out, and that they were really indebted to him for the release of a part of their indebtedness, and that the owner of the property did not dispute the arrangement entered into by his steward when in office. **For the children of this world are in their generation wiser than the children of light.** This was a melancholy and sorrowful reflection. It seems to say, "I have been painting, indeed, from the life. See, the children of this world, men and women whose ends and aims are bounded by the horizon of this world, who only live for this life, how much more painstaking and skilful are *they* in their working for the perishable things of this world than are the children of light in their noble toiling after the things of the life to come. The former appear even more in earnest in their search after what they desire than do the latter. There is underlying the Lord's deep and sorrowful reflection here, a mournful regret over one feature that is, alas! characteristic of well-nigh all religious life—the unkindness which religious professors so often show to one another. One great division of Christianity despises, almost hates, the other; sect detests sect; a very slight difference in religious opinion bars the way to all friendship, often to even kindly feeling. With truth Godet remarks here "that the *children of this world* use every means for their own interest to strengthen the bonds which unite them to their contemporaries of the same stamp, but, on the other hand, the *children of light* neglect this natural measure of prudence; they forget to use God's goods to form bonds of love to the contemporaries who *might* one day give them a full recompense, when they themselves shall want everything, and these shall have abundance."

Ver. 9.—**And I say unto you, Make to yourselves friends of the mammon of unrighteousness.** Then, with his usual solemn formula, "I say unto you," the Lord gave out his moral interpretation of the parable. His words were addressed to possessors of various degrees of wealth. "You will soon have to give up all your worldly goods; be prudent in time, make some real friends out of the mammon of unrighteousness; by means of that money entrusted to your care, do good to others who are in need." *The mammon of unrighteousness.* This word "mammon" does not denote, as some have supposed, the name of a deity, the god of wealth or money, but it signifies "money" itself. It is a Syriac or Aramaic term. The words, "of unrighteousness," are added because in so many cases *the getting* of money is tainted with unrighteousness in some form or other; and, when possessed, it so often hardens the heart, as the Lord himself said in another place (ch. xviii. 25), that it was easier for a camel to pass through the eye of a needle than for a rich man to enter the kingdom of God. "What the steward of my story," said the Master, "did to men of *his* world, see that you with your money do toward those who belong to *your* world." **That, when ye fail, they may receive you into everlasting habitations.** So that when you shall be dismissed from being stewards of God's possessions, that is, when ye shall die, "when ye suffer the last eclipse and bankruptcy of life," that then others, your friends, may receive you (welcome you) into everlasting dwellings. The majority of the older authorities here, instead of "when ye fail," read, "when it (money) shall fail you" (by the event of your death). The sense of the passage, however, remains the same, whichever reading be adopted. But now a deeply interesting question arises—When the Lord speaks of *friends* receiving us after death into eternal homes, to what *friends* is he alluding? Great expositors, Ewald and Meyer, for instance, tell us that he means *the angels.* But the plain sense of the parable points, not to angels, but to poor, weak, suffering persons whom we have helped here; these, then, must be the friends who will receive us, or welcome us, in the world to come. A further query suggests itself—*How* will these be able to receive us? To such a question no definite reply can be given. We know too little of the awful mysteries of *that* world to be able even to hazard a surmise as to the help or the comfort which grateful, blessed spirits will be able to show to their brethren the newly arrived, when they receive them. His word here must suffice us; well will it be for us, if one day we practically discover the holy secret for ourselves. Godet has a weighty note with which he concludes his exposition of this difficult but most instructive parable: "There is no thought more fitted than that of this parable, on the one hand to undermine the idea of merit belonging to almsgiving (what merit could be got out of that which is another's? and is not all money, are not all goods out of which we bestow our alms, God's?); and on the other, to encourage us in the practice of that virtue which assures us of friends and protectors for the grave moment of our passing into the world to come." One beautiful and exquisitely comforting thought is shrined in this playful and yet intensely solemn utterance of Jesus. The eternal tents, the "many mansions," as John calls them, will have among their occupants, it is certain, many a one whose life on earth was hard and sorrowful. These are now enjoying bliss indescribable, these poor Lazaruses, to whom this world was so sad. so dreary a habitation. And perhaps a portion of their blessedness consists in this power, to which the Lord makes allusion here, of assisting others—*the helped here becoming the helpers there.* Although the teaching of Christ and his chosen servants here and elsewhere shows us distinctly that no *merit* can attach to almsgiving, seeing that our alms are only given out of property entrusted to us for a short time by God for this and other similar purposes, yet the same authoritative teaching informs us that God *has* regard to almsdeeds done in the true spirit of love, in determining our eternal destiny. Thus a message direct from heaven informs the Roman legionary Cornelius that his prayers and alms were come up for a memorial before God. Paul writes to Timothy to charge the Ephesus Christians "that they do good, that they be rich in good works, ready to distribute, willing to communicate; laying up in store for themselves a good foundation against the time to come, that they may lay hold on eternal life." In the parable of Lazarus and Dives we shall find this principle yet more clearly illustrated. These are only a few out of the many passages where this generosity and almsgiving is commended to the believer with peculiar earnestness.

Ver. 10.—**He that is faithful in that which is least is faithful also in much: and he that is unjust in the least is unjust also in much.** This and the next three verses are closely connected with the parable of the unjust steward. Our Lord no doubt continued speaking, and these four verses contain a general *résumé* of what may be called his reflections on the important piece of teaching he had just delivered. We have here the broad rule, upon which God will decide the soul's future, laid down. If the man has been faithful in his administration of the comparatively unimportant goods of earth, it is clear that he can be entrusted with the far more important things which belong to the world to come. There is, too, in these words a kind of limitation and explanation of the foregoing parable of the unjust steward. The conduct of that steward, regarded in one point of view, was held to be wise, and we, though in a very different way, were advised to imitate it; yet here we are distinctly told that it is fidelity, not unfaithfulness, which will be *eventually* rewarded—the just, not the unjust steward.

Ver. 11.—**The unrighteous mammon.** As above in the parable, "mammon" signifies money. The epithet "unrighteous" is used in the same sense as in ver. 9, where we read of the "mammon of unrighteousness."

Ver. 12.—**And if ye have not been faithful in that which is another man's.** Here we have our earthly possessions plainly spoken of as the goods of another, that is, of God, and of these goods we are but the temporary stewards. Who shall give you that which is your own? We have here a very magnificent promise. Although on earth man can possess nothing of his own — here he is but a steward for a time of property belonging to another—yet a prospect is held out to him that, if he be found faithful in the trust while on earth, in the world to come something will be given to him really and truly his own. There will be no dismissal or death there.

Ver. 13.—**No servant can serve two masters. . . . Ye cannot serve God and mammon.** Very vividly is this experience brought out in the great parable which immediately follows. There the rich man was evidently one who observed the sacred ritual of the Law of Moses: this we learn without doubt from his conversation after death with Abraham. Thus he tried, after his light, to serve God, but he also served mammon: this we learn, too, clearly from the description given to us of his life, from the mention of the gorgeous apparel and the sumptuous feeding. The service of the two was incompatible, and we know from the sombre sequel of the story to which master the rich man really held, and whom—alas for him!—in his heart he despised.

Ver. 14.—**And the Pharisees also, who were covetous, heard all these things: and they derided him.** This shows that many of the dominant sect had been present and had listened to the parable of the unjust steward. Although scrupulous, and in a way religious men, these Pharisees were notorious for their respect and regard for riches, and all that riches purchase, and they felt, no doubt deeply, the Lord's bitter reproach of covetousness. *They*, the rulers and leaders of Israel, the religious guides, were evidently attacked in such teaching as they had been lately listening to, not the common people whom they so despised. The scornful words alluded to in the expression, "they derided him," were no doubt directed against the outward poverty of the popular Galilæan Teacher. "It is all very well," they would say, "for one springing from the ranks of the people, landless, moneyless, to rail at wealth and the possessors of wealth; we can understand such teaching from one such as *you*."

Ver. 15.—**And he said unto them, Ye are they which justify yourselves before men; but God knoweth your hearts.** The part the Pharisees played in public imposed upon the people. The great influence which they exercised was in great measure due to the respect generally felt for their strict and religious lives. The hypocrisy of this famous sect—it was probably in many cases unconscious hypocrisy—and the false colouring which it gave religion, contributed not a little to the state of things which led to the final disruption of the Jewish nation as a nation some forty years after these words were spoken. It is only a student of the Talmud who can form any notion of the Pharisee mind; a superficial study even of parts of this strange, mighty collection will show why our Lord was so seemingly hard in his rebukes of these often earnest and religious men; it will show, too, why the same Divine Master at times seemed to change his words of bitter wrath into accents of the tenderest sympathy and love. **For that which is highly esteemed among men is abomination in the sight of God.** Especially alluding to that haughty pride of men in wealth and money, which, after all, is not theirs.

Ver. 16.—**The Law and the prophets were until John: since that time the kingdom of God is preached, and every man presseth into it.** Some expositors discern so little connection between the sayings contained in these verses which intervene between the two great parables of the unjust steward and the rich man and Lazarus, that they consider them as a number of sayings of the Master collected by Luke and inserted here. A clear thread, however, runs through the whole piece between the two parables. Probably, however, here, as in many parts of the Gospel, we only have just a bare sketch, or *précis*, of what the Lord said; hence its fragmentary character. Here (in the sixteenth verse), the Master went on speaking to the Pharisees who derided him (ver. 14). "Up to the period of John the Baptist," said the Master, "the old state of things may be said to have continued in force. With him began a new era; no longer were the old privileges to be confined to Israel exclusively; gradually the kingdom of God was to be enlarged, the old wall of separation was to be taken down. See, every man is pressing into it; the new state of things has already begun; you see it in the crowds of publicans, sinners, Samaritans, and others pressing round me when I speak of the kingdom of God."

Ver. 17.—**And it is easier for heaven and earth to pass, than one tittle of the Law to fail.** "Yet think not," went on the Master, "that, though things are changing, the Divine Law will ever fail. The mere temporary and transitory regulations will, of course, give place to a new order, but not the smallest part of one letter of the Divine moral Law will fail." "One tittle." This is the rendering of a Greek word the diminutive of "horn," which denoted the horn or extremity of a Hebrew letter, by the omission or addition of which—to give an instance —the letter *d* becomes the letter *r*; thus with the horn it is ד, daleth, *d*; without the horn ר, resh, *r*. The heresiarch Marcion (second century) here, in his recension of St. Luke, changes the text thus: "It is easier for heaven and earth to pass, than for one *tittle of my sayings* to fail." Marcion, who refused to allow the Divine origin of any part of the Old Testament, was afraid of the testimony which this assertion of our Lord would give to the Divine authority of the Pentateuch. In illustration of his saying that the moral Law given to the Jews was changeless, and while earth endured would never fail, the Master instances one grave chapter of the Law with which there had been much tampering—that of divorce. "See," he said, "the new state of things which I am now teaching, instead of loosening the cords with which the old Law regulated human society, will rather tighten them. Instead of a laxer code being substituted, I am preaching a yet severer one. My law of divorce is a severer one than that written down by Moses."

Ver. 18.—**Whosoever putteth away his wife, and marrieth another, committeth adultery: and whosoever marrieth her that is put away from her husband, committeth adultery.** The teaching of the rabbis in the time of our Lord on the question of the marriage tie was exceedingly lax, and tended to grave immorality in the family life. In the late unlawful marriage of Herod Antipas with Herodias, in which so many sacred and family ties were rudely torn asunder, no rabbi or doctor in Israel but one had raised his voice in indignant protest, and that one was the friend and connection of Jesus of Nazareth, the prophet John the Baptist. Divorce for the most trivial causes was sanctioned by the rabbis, and even such men as Hillel, the grandfather of that Gamaliel whom tradition speaks of as the rabbi whose lectures were listened to by the Boy Jesus, taught that a man might divorce his wife if in the cooking she burnt his dinner or even over-salted his soup (see Talmud, treatise 'Gittin,' ix. 10).

SS. Luke and Paul, different to the great masters of profane history, like Thucydides, or Livy, or Xenophon, were evidently at no pains to round off their narratives. They give us the account of the Lord's words and works very much as they had them from the first listeners and eye-witnesses. When the notes and memories were very scant and fragmentary, as appear to have been the case in the Lord's discourse which St. Luke interposes between the parable of the steward and that of Dives and Lazarus, the fragmentary notes are reproduced without any attempt to round off the condensed, and at first sight apparently disconnected, utterances. So here, directly after the fragmentary report of certain sayings of Jesus, the great parable of Lazarus and Dives is introduced with somewhat startling abruptness; nothing of St. Luke's is added—simply the original report as Luke or Paul received it is reproduced.

The following is probably the connection in which the famous parable was spoken.

When the Lord spoke the parable-story of the unjust steward, he pressed home to the listeners, as its great lesson, the necessity of providing against the day of death, and he showed how, by the practice of kindness here towards the poor, the weak, and the suffering, they would make to themselves friends who would in their turn be of use to them—who would, in their hour of sore need, when death swept them out of this life, receive them into everlasting habitations.

We believe that the Master, as he spoke these things, purposed—either on that very occasion, or very shortly after, when his listeners were again gathered together—supplementing this important teaching by another parable, in which the good of having friends in the world to come should be clearly shown. The parable of Lazarus and Dives, then, may be regarded as a piece of teaching following on to and closely connected with the parable of the unjust steward.

Nine verses, however, as we have seen are inserted between the two parables. Of these, vers. 10—13 are simply some reflections of the Master on the parable of the steward just spoken. Then comes ver. 14—a scornful interruption on the part of the Pharisee listeners. Our Lord replies to this (vers. 15—18), and then goes on, either then or very soon after, to the same auditory, with the parable of Lazarus and Dives, which is, in fact, a direct sequel to the parable of the unjust steward, and which St. Luke proceeds to relate without any further preamble.

Ver. 19.—**There was a certain rich man.** He is thus introduced by the Lord without any details respecting his age or place of residence—*nameless, too!* Seems he not to have been reading from that book where he found the name of the poor man written, but found not the name of the rich; for that book is the book of life?" (Sermon 178. 3 of St. Augustine). Tradition says his name was Nimeusis, but it is simply a baseless tradition. **Which was clothed in purple and fine linen.** The words which describe the life of Dives were chosen with rare skill; they are few, but enough to show us that the worldly hero of the story lived a life of royal magnificence and boundless luxury. His ordinary apparel seems to have been purple and fine linen. This purple, the true sea purple, was a most precious and rare dye, and the purple garment so dyed was a royal gift, and was scarcely used save by princes and nobles of very high degree. In it the idol-images were sometimes arrayed. The fine linen (byssus) was worth twice its weight in gold. It was in hue dazzlingly white. **And fared sumptuously every day.** With this princely rich man banquets were a matter of daily occurrence. Luther renders the Greek here, "lebte herrlich und in Freuden." Thus with all the accompaniments of grandeur this nameless mighty one lived, his halls ever filled with noble guests, his antechambers with servants. Everything with him that could make life splendid and joyous was in profusion. Some have suspected that our Lord took, as the model for his picture here, the life of the tetrarch Herod Antipas. The court of that magnificent and luxurious prince would certainly have well served as the original of the picture; but Herod was still living, and it is more likely that Jesus was describing the earth-life of one who had already been "dismissed" from his earthly stewardship, and who, when he spoke the parable, was in the world to come.

Vers. 20, 21.—**And there was a certain beggar named Lazarus, which was laid at his gate, full of sores, and desiring to be fed with the crumbs which fell from the rich man's table.** In striking contrast to the life of the rich man, the Master, with a few touches, paints the life of the beggar Lazarus. This giving a name to a personage in the parable occurs nowhere else in the evangelists' reports of our Lord's parabolic teaching. It probably was done in this case just to give us a hint, for it is nothing more, of the personal character of the poor sufferer who in the end was so blessed. The object of the parable, as we shall see, did not include any detailed account of the beggar-man's inner life; just *this* name is given him to show us why, when he died, he found himself at once in bliss. Among the Jews the name very often describes the character of him who bears it. The Greek name *Lazarus* is derived from two Hebrew words, *El-ēzer* ("God-help"), shortened by the rabbis into *Leazar*, whence *Lazarus*. He was, then, one of those happy ones whose confidence, in all his grief and misery, was in God alone. Well was his trust, as we shall see, justified. The gate at which he was daily laid was a stately portal (πυλῶν). Lazarus is represented as utterly unable to win his bread. He was a constant sufferer, covered with sores, wasting under the dominion of a loathsome, incurable disease. This representative of human suffering has taken a strange hold on the imagination of men. In many of the languages of Europe the name of the beggar of the parable appears in the terms "lazar," "lazar-house," and "lazaretto," "lazzaroni." Unable himself to walk, some pitying friend or friends among the poor—the poor are never backward in helping others poorer than themselves, thus setting a noble example to the rich—brought him and laid him daily close by the splendid gates of the palace of Dives. The crumbs signify the broken fragments which the servants of the rich man would contemptuously, perhaps pityingly, toss to the poor helpless beggar-man as he lay by the gate. **Moreover the dogs came and licked his sores.** These were the wild, homeless pariah dogs so common in all Eastern cities, who act as the street-scavengers, and are regarded as unclean. This mention of the dogs clustering round him does not suggest any contrast between the pitying animals and pitiless men, but simply adds additional colour to the picture of the utter helplessness of the diseased sufferer; there he lay, and as he lay, the rough homeless dogs would lick his unbandaged wounds as they passed on the forage.

Ver. 22.—**And it came to pass, that the beggar died, and was carried by the angels into Abraham's bosom.** At last kind death came, and relieved Lazarus of his sufferings. His *dismissal*, as might have been expected, preceded that of the rich man; for he was enfeebled by a deadly disease. We must not, of course, press too much the details we find in parables; still, from our Lord's way of speaking of the great change in the cases of both Lazarus and Dives, it would seem as though there was absolutely no pause between the two lives of this world and the world to come. The rich man evidently is pictured as closing his eyes upon his gorgeous surroundings *here*, and opening them directly again upon his cheerless surroundings *there*. Lazarus is described as being borne at once into Abraham's bosom. Indeed, some interpret the words as signifying that the body as well as the soul was carried by angels into Paradise. It is, however, better, with Calvin, to understand the expression as alluding only to Lazarus's soul; of the body of the pauper nothing was said, as *men* probably contemptuously, if not carelessly, buried it with the burial rites which such homeless, friendless ones too often receive. The place whither the blest Lazarus went is termed "Abraham's bosom." This term was used by the Jews indifferently, with "the garden of Eden," or "under the throne of glory," for the home of happy but waiting souls. **The rich man also died, and was buried.** There is a terrible irony here in this mention of burial. This human pageantry of woe was for the rich man what the carrying by the angels into Abraham's bosom was for Lazarus—it was *his* equivalent; but while these empty honours were being paid to his senseless, deserted body, the rich man was already gazing on the surroundings of his new and cheerless home. After the moment's sleep of death, what an awakening!

Ver. 23.—**And in hell he lift up his eyes, being in torments**; more accurately, *in Hades* (the unseen world of the dead) *he lift up his eyes.* The idea of *suffering* does not lie in these first words, but in the participle "being in torments," which immediately follows. It is noticeable that, in this Divine picture of unhappy life in the other world there is no coarse, vulgar word-painting such as we meet with so often in mediæval human works. The very fact of the man's being *unhappy* is gently represented. The graver aspect of the torments we learn from the hapless one's own words. Still, it is all very awful, though the facts are so gently told us. "Being in torments:" How could it be otherwise for such a one as Dives? The home of the loving, where Abraham was, would be no home for that selfish man who had never really loved or cared for any one save himself. What were the torments? men with hushed voices ask. A little further on the doomed one speaks of a flame and of his tongue apparently burning, owing to the scorching heat; but it would be a mistake to think of a material flame being intended here. There is nothing in the description of the situation to suggest this; it is rather the burning never to be satisfied, longing for something utterly beyond his reach, that the unhappy man describes as an inextinguishable flame. Were it desirable to dwell on these torments, we should remind men how lustful desires change rapidly into torture for the soul when the means for gratifying them exist not. In the case of Dives, his delight on earth seems to have been society, pleasant jovial company, the being surrounded by a crowd of admiring friends, the daily banquet, the gorgeous apparel, the stately house,—these details more than hint at the pleasure he found in the society of courtier-friends; but in the other world he seems to have been quite alone. Whereas among the blessed there appears to be a sweet companionship. Lazarus is in the company of Abraham, who, of course, only represents a great and goodly gathering. "Abraham's bosom" is simply the well-known expression for that feast or banquet of the happy souls judged worthy of an entrance into Paradise. But in that place where the rich man lifted up his eyes there seems a strange and awful solitariness. A total absence of everything, even of *external* causes of trouble, is very noticeable. He was *alone;* alone with his thoughts. **And seeth Abraham afar off, and Lazarus in his bosom.**

Ver. 24.—**And he cried and said, Father Abraham, have mercy on me, and send Lazarus, that he may dip the tip of his finger in water, and cool my tongue; for I am tormented in this flame.** His intense longing seems to be for companionship. "Oh for a friend," he seems to say, "who could speak to me, comfort me, give me the smallest alleviation of the pain I suffer!" What picture of a hell was ever painted by man comparable to this vision of eternal solitude, peopled alone by remorseful memories, described by Jesus? As the Divine Speaker advanced in his thrilling, melancholy description of the rich man's condition in the world to come, how vividly must the listeners have recalled the Master's earnest advice to them, in his former parable of the steward, to make to themselves *while here* friends who would receive them into everlasting habitations! They saw the meaning of that detail of the parable then. Were *they*, in their luxurious abundance, were *they* making friends here who would help them there in the eternal tents? Were they not, perhaps, making the same mistake as the rich man of the story? The question might be asked—Why is Abraham, the father of the chosen race, the centre of this blessed life in Hades? In reply, *firstly*, it must be remembered that the whole colouring of this parable is peculiarly rabbinic, and in the schools of the rabbis the life of the blessed in Paradise is represented as a banquet, over which, until Messiah come, Abraham is represented as presiding. And, *secondly*, when the parable was spoken, the Saviour was actually on earth; his great redemption work had still to be accomplished. There was truth as well as error mingled in that strange rabbinical teaching. Messiah, *as Messiah*, when the parable was being probably acted, had not entered that realm where Abraham and many another holy and humble man of heart were in the enjoyment of exquisite bliss.

Ver. 25.—**But Abraham said, Son, remember that thou in thy lifetime receivedst thy good things, and likewise Lazarus evil things: but now he is comforted, and thou art tormented.** Abraham here simply bids the tortured man to call to his memory the circumstances of the life he had lived on earth, telling him that in these circumstances he would find the reason for his present woeful state. It was no startling record of vice and crime, or even of folly, that the father of the faithful calls attention to. He quietly recalls to the rich man's memory that on earth he had lived a life of princely splendour and luxury, and that Lazarus, sick and utterly destitute, lay at his palace gate, and was allowed to lie there unpitied and unhelped. And because of the studied moderation of its language, and the everyday character of its hero Dives—for he, the rich man, not Lazarus, is the real hero, the central character of the great parable-lesson—the lesson of the parable goes home necessarily to many more hearts than it would have done had the hero been a monster of wickedness, a cold calculating or else a plausible villain, a man who shrank not from sacrificing the lives and happiness of his fellowmen if their lives or happiness stood in his way. Dives was merely a commonplace wealthy man of the world, with self-centred aims, and the sin for which he was condemned to outer darkness was only that everyday sin of neglecting out of the mammon of unrighteousness—in other words, out of his money—to make for himself friends who should receive him into the eternal tents.

Ver. 26.—**And beside all this, between us and you there is a great gulf fixed: so that they which would pass from hence to you cannot; neither can they pass to us, that would come from thence.** Although the whole thought which runs through this parable is new, and peculiar to Christ, yet the colouring of the picture is nearly all borrowed from the great rabbinic schools; one of the few exceptions to this rule being this chasm or gulf which separates the two regions of Hades. The rabbis represented the division as consisting only of a wall. "What is the distance between Paradise and Gehenna? According to R. Johanan, a wall; according to other teachers, a palm-breadth, or only a finger-breadth" ('Midrash on Koheleth'). What, asks the awestruck reader, is this dreadful chasm? why is it impassable? will it be for ever there? will no ages of sorrow, no tears, no bitter heartfelt repentance succeed in throwing a bridge across it? Many have written here, and kindly souls have tried to answer the stern question with the gentle, loving reply which their souls so longed to hear. What is impossible to the limitless love of God? Nothing, wistfully says the heart. But, when interrogated closely, the parable and, indeed, all the Master's teaching on this point preserves a silence complete, impenetrable.

Vers. 27, 28.—**Then he said, I pray thee therefore, father, that thou wouldest send him to my father's house: for I have five brethren; that he may testify unto them; lest they also come into this place of torment.** The condemned acquiesces in this dread fact; convinced of the utter impossibility of any interchange of sympathy between him and the dwellers in the realms of bliss, he ceases to pray for any alleviation of his own sad and wretched state. But another wail of woe quickly rises from the awful solitude. What means this second prayer of the doomed man? Are we to read in it the first signs of a new and noble purpose in the lost soul, the first dawning of loving thoughts and tender care for others? It seems, perhaps, unkind not to recognize this; but the Divine Speaker evidently had another purpose here when he put these words into the mouth of the lost rich man—he would teach the great lesson to the living that a selfish life is inexcusable. On first thoughts, the rich man's request to Abraham appears prompted alone by his anxiety for the future of his brothers who were still alive; but on examination it would seem, to use the striking words of Professor Bruce, that he wished rather to justify his own sad past by some such reflection as this: "Had only some one come from the dead with the calm, clear light of eternity shining in his eyes, to inform me that this life beyond is no fable, that Paradise is a place or state of unspeakable bliss, and Gehenna a place or state of unspeakable woe, I should have renounced my voluptuous, selfish ways, and entered on the path of piety and charity. If one had come to me from the dead, I had surely repented, and so should not have come to this place of torment."

Ver. 29.—**Abraham saith unto him, They have Moses and the prophets; let them hear them.** The reply of Abraham was especially addressed to those Jews who were standing round him and even asking for a sign. *They* had all read and heard again and again the Books of Moses and the records of the prophets; if these guides had failed to show them the right way, a special messenger sent to them would be quite useless.

Vers. 30, 31.—**And he said, Nay, father Abraham: but if one went unto them from the dead, they will repent. And he said unto him, If they hear not Moses and the prophets, neither will they be persuaded, though one rose from the dead.** The Master not only wished to drive home this momentous truth to the hearts of the group of varied ranks and orders listening to him then; his words were for a far larger auditory, so he prolongs the dialogue between Dives and Abraham. "If Lazarus from the dead would only go to them," pleaded the lost soul. "Even if I send," replied Abraham, "and Lazarus goes, they will not be persuaded." They would see him, listen to him, perhaps, and then, when the first feelings of amazement and fear were dying away, would find some plausible reasons for disregarding the messenger and his message. Criticism would discuss the appearance; it would be disposed of by attributing it to an hallucination, or others would suggest that the visitant from the other world had never been really dead, and these pleas would be readily taken up by others who cared not to examine the question for themselves, and so life, careless, selfish, thoughtless, would go on as it had done aforetime. A striking example of what the Lord asserted through the medium of the shade of Abraham took place within a few days from that time. *Another* Lazarus *did* come back again from the dead into the midst of that great company of friends and mourners and jealous watchers of Jesus gathered round the sepulchral cave of Bethany, and though some true, faithful hearts welcomed the mighty sign with awful joy, still it served not to touch the cold and calculating spirit of Pharisee, scribe, and Sadducee, thirsting for the blood of the Master, whom they feared and hated, and whose word had summoned back the dead into their midst. The mighty wonder wrought no change there. One went unto them from the dead, and yet their hard hearts only took counsel together how they might put Lazarus again to death.

And so the parable and this particular course of teaching came to a close. Perhaps it is the deepest, the most soul-stirring of all the utterances of the Master. Expositors for eighteen centuries have drawn out of its clear, fathomless depths new and ever new truths. It is by no means yet exhausted. This voice from the other side of the veil charms and yet appals, it terrifies and yet enthrals all ages, every class, each rank of men and women. There are many other important items of special teaching which have been scarcely touched on in the notes above. Among the more interesting of these is the brief notice of the life which the blessed lead in Paradise. The happy dead are represented as a wide family circle. Abraham is pictured with Lazarus in his bosom. The image is taken from the way guests used to sit at a banquet. John at the Last Supper occupied a similar position with regard to the Master (John xiii. 23, 25) to that occupied by Lazarus with regard to Abraham here. The two extremes of the social scale are thus represented as meeting in that blessed company on terms of the tenderest friendship. With these were Isaac and Jacob and all the prophets (ch. xiii. 28). "All the just," as Marcion gives it in his recension of St. Luke. And while the Paradise-life for the blessed dead is described as a holy communion of saints, there is evidently no corresponding communion in the case of the *unhappy* dead. The selfish rich man finds himself in an awful solitude. The suffering is rather represented by the image of the void; there are no external causes of pain apparently; hence his longing to speak a word with Lazarus, to feel the touch of a friendly sympathizing hand, if only for a moment, to distract his burning remorseful thoughts. There was nothing to live for *there*, nothing to hope for, but he felt he must go on living —*hopeless*. As no special crime, no glaring sin of lust or wanton excess or selfish ambition, is laid to the rich man's charge, and yet when dead he is represented as lifting up his eyes, being in torments, many, especially men belonging to those schools which are generally unfriendly to the religion of Jesus Christ, have endeavoured to show that the condemned was condemned on account of his riches, while the saved was saved because of his deep poverty. Nor is this error alone common to the Tübingen school, and to brilliant free-lances in religious literature like M. Renan. Some such mistaken notion doubtless materially aided the rise and the popularity of the mendicant orders, who played so important a part in the Christianity of the Middle Ages in so many lands. But the burden of our thrilling parable emphatically is not "*Woe to the rich! blessed are the poor!*" The crime of the life to which so awful a punishment was meted out as the guerdon, was *selfish inhumanity*, which Christ teaches us is the damning sin. (See his words in his great picture of the final judgment, Matt. xxv. 41—46.) Lazarus was no solitary individual; he was one of the many suffering poor who abound in this world, and to find whom the rich need not go far from their own gates. Lazarus represents here the *opportunity* for the exercise of Dives's humanity. Of this, and doubtless many like opportunities, Dives cared not to avail himself. He was apparently no ill-natured, cruel man, he was simply self-centred, delighting in soft living, generous wines, costly fare, sumptuous clothing, good society. He loved to be surrounded with applauding, pleasant guests; but the Lazaruses of the world, for him, might pine away and die in their nameless awful misery. Professor Bruce, with great force, puts the following words into the beggar Lazarus's mouth; these words tell us with startling clearness what was the sin of Dives: "I was laid at this man's gate; he knew me; he could not pass from his house into the street without seeing my condition, as a leprous beggar, yet as a beggar I died." Dives here was endowed richly with all the materials of human happiness, but he kept all his happiness to himself, he took no trouble whatever to diffuse his joy and gladness, his bright and many-coloured life among that great army of weak, poor, woe-begone brothers and sisters who go far to make up the population of every great city. That riches are not in themselves a ground for exclusion from the blessed life is plainly shown by the position occupied by Abraham in that happy family circle of the blessed. For Abraham, we know, was a sheik possessed of vast wealth. Then, too, in the latter part of the parable, when the imminent danger which the five brothers of the lost Dives ran of being similarly lost, was discussed, the danger is represented as springing from their careless disregard of the Law and the prophets, and not from the fact of their being rich men. When Ezekiel sought for examples of the most righteous men that had ever lived, he chose, it must be remembered, as exemplars of mortals living the fair, noble life loved of God, three men distinguished for their rank and riches—Noah, Daniel, and Job (Ezek. xiv. 14, 20).

HOMILETICS.

Vers. 1—13.—*The unjust steward.* Whereas the three preceding parables were spoken to the Pharisees, this is spoken to the disciples. It is not quite certain whether all the parables were uttered at or about the same time; but the use of the word "also" (ver. 1) suggests that they were. Anyhow, the saying before us has reference to a different kind of wasting from that of the younger son—a wasting against which the followers of Jesus are solemnly warned. We are called to listen to the Master as he indicates temptations and enforces duties within the special circle of discipleship. This parable is a saying hard to be understood. Many explanations have been given. A very learned commentator, appalled by the difficulties connected with the interpretation, abandoned the attempt, declaring that the solution of the problem is impossible. And truly, if we canvassed all the schemes of exposition which have been proposed, all the inferences which have been founded on clauses, and all the speculations which have been raised, we should find "no end in wandering mazes lost." Let our aim be less ambitious; let us try to get hold of some plain, practical instruction which shall help us to be better disciples of Jesus Christ. The outline of the story is simple. The *dramatis personæ* are not numerous. A wealthy landowner has a steward who, in the management of his estates, possesses a large discretionary power. He is informed that this steward has, not stolen or wrongfully applied, but by neglect or want of skill has squandered, the estate entrusted to him. He is called to account and is dismissed peremptorily. Now comes into view the adroitness of the man. He wishes to have some friends who can do him a good turn when he is out of a situation; and so, before news of his dismissal reaches any, while it is supposed that he has full power, he calls together those who are in arrears of rent or are otherwise indebted to his lord. We can imagine the trembling with which they obey the summons. How bland and smiling is the factor! What kind inquiries as to wife and children and belongings! And then, "By the way, what is the amount of your obligation?" Two specimens are given. One person owes a hundred measures of oil. "Take your pen," says the factor, "score out the hundred, and make it fifty." Another owes a hundred measures of wheat. "Take your pen, write down eighty." All retire charmed, loud in the steward's praise. Had he not secured a warm place in their regard? When told of his downfall, would not they all cry, "Shame!" and speak of him as the tenants' friend, and welcome him to their houses? The point of the lesson which Christ would teach is this—separate the energy from the dishonesty, the foresight from the fraud, and as he, for his own wrong ends, was wise and calculating, so, for your right ends, practise a wisdom like his, though nobler than his: "Make to yourselves friends of the mammon of unrighteousness, that when ye die, or fail, they may receive you into everlasting habitations." Now, without puzzling ourselves over the details of the parable, consider the lessons inculcated as to (1) *Christian responsibility;* (2) *Christian administration;* and (3) *Christian service.*

I. Christian responsibility. In the relation of the steward to the rich man we have a foreshadowing of the relation in which we stand to God. "Steward" is the word which indicates this relation. To every one of us is given a charge of goods whose Owner is God. Our own constitution—physical, mental, moral—is a trust; all our endowments—talents, powers of whatsoever kind—are a property of which we are farmers; and he who thinks that he can do as he likes with these, that he can dissipate his substance by intemperance, or alienate his strength from higher ends, is false to his Maker and false to himself. So with regard to all our influence—direct and indirect—it is a power delegated to us by the Almighty, and to be realized under the sense of the account to be rendered to him. Money, relationships, social positions,—all are items of the estate over which we are set. Do we all realize this as we should? Do we not sadly forget this fact of stewardship? Christ speaks of "the mammon of unrighteousness." Here is an explanation which has been given. "The ears of Jesus must have been repeatedly shocked by the kind of rashness by which men speak, without hesitation, of '*my* fortune,' '*my* land,' '*my* house.' He who felt keenly the dependence of man on God perceived that there was in this feeling of property a sort of usurpation, a forgetfulness of the real owner; in hearing such language he seemed to see the tenant changing into the master." Ah! does he not hear such language every day? Is it not in the air? Is it not in our own feeling? Are we not, in many ways, changing the tenant into the master, the steward into the owner? taking the goods, and using them without giving praise to him whose they are? Would that the answer given to the first question in an old Catechism were written into the texture of every life—"Man's chief end is to glorify God, and to enjoy him for ever."

II. Connected with Christian stewardship is THE TRUTH OF CHRISTIAN ADMINISTRATION. And may it not be said that this is a truth far too little studied and practised? When we hear of depressions of trade, of hard, dull times, we may well reflect on the saying of the Prophet Haggai (i. 5, 6), "Consider your ways. Ye have sown much, and bring in little; ye eat, but ye have not enough; ye drink, but ye are not filled with drink; ye clothe you, but there is none warm; and he that earneth wages, earneth wages to put it into a bag with holes." In regard to Christian objects, is there not much to learn from such tact and prudence as the steward's in the parable? Do we not need them much in the conduct of benevolent enterprises? Competition may be healthy; but a competition which, in a limited area, or on mere windmills, spends a force which should be far more diffusive, is not only not healthy, it is a loss and a scandal. Is not this the kind of competition which is too prevalent in ecclesiastical and in charitable spheres? Otherwise must we not confess that, through our want of inventiveness or wisdom in management, our want of skill to turn opportunities to the best advantage, of the sagacity which is exercised in worldly matters, we lay ourselves open to the reproach, "The children of this age are wiser in their generation than the children of light" (ver. 8)? Realize that, whether there is much or little, faithfulness is demanded of the steward—such a disposal or investment of all wealth as that the Lord's interests are furthered. To each of us is given the charge, "So allocate the mammon of unrighteousness, the uncertain, unstable wealth which you possess, that it shall not hinder, but help you to the everlasting habitations." How many does that mammon hinder! How few of us so use our money as to advance not only Christ's cause but our own holiness! But should it not be rendered a means of spiritual gain? It is concerning this fidelity to God in the laying out of the perishable riches that Christ hints that they in whom it abounds will not want the friendly welcome when the tent of this tabernacle is dissolved, and the spirit passes into the everlasting habitations.

III. A word as to CHRISTIAN SERVICE. This mammon, which was meant to be an instrument for the accomplishment of our stewardship, is apt to assume the bearing of a master. At first it is the slave, the most obedient, until, by constant trafficking with it and by taking it into the region of our affections, it becomes our love; and when it is the love of a man, the consideration which to him is first, the supreme point of his interest, then it ascends from the kitchen into the parlour, and claims the self as its own. This mammon-rule, mammon-worship, is one of the most distinct features of the day, and few of us know how deep is its mark in our souls. Here is the choice—this mammon, or Christ with the thorn-crowned brow; this mammon, or God himself. One or other we may serve; Christ insists we cannot serve both (ver. 13). "That usurping lord has a will so different from God's will, gives commands so opposite to his, that occasion must speedily arise when one or other will have to be slighted, despised, and disobeyed, if the other be regarded, honoured, and served. God, for instance, will command a scattering, when mammon will urge to a further keeping and gathering; God will require spending on others, when mammon or the world will urge a spending on one's own lusts. Therefore, the two Lords having characters so different and giving commands so opposite, it will be impossible to reconcile their services: one must be despised if the other is held to; the only faithfulness to the one is to break with the other; 'ye cannot serve God and mammon.'" "Choose ye this day whom ye will serve." There is to be no playing at religion. A saintly voice (Augustine) has thus interpreted the election: may the "amen" to his words arise from our souls! "O my God, thou sweetness ineffable, make bitter for me all carnal comfort which draws me away from the love of eternal things, and in evil manner allures me to itself by the view of some present delightsome good. Let me not be overcome, O Lord, by flesh and blood. Let not the world and the brief glory thereof deceive me. Let not the devil and his subtle fraud supplant me. Give me strength to resist, patience to endure, and constancy to persevere. Give me, instead of all the comforts of the world, the most sweet unction of thy Holy Spirit and the love of thy blessed Name."

Vers. 19—31.—*The rich man and Lazarus.* A parable so striking and solemn that, as has been said, "they must be fast asleep who are not startled by it." It is in several respects unique. Figure is so blended with reality, so rapidly passes into reality, that we are doubtful where and how far to separate between the form of truth and the truth itself. Indeed, it has been questioned whether the discourse is to be regarded as a parable at all; whether it is not to be regarded as the record of facts and experiences. Alone, too, of all the pictorial sayings of Jesus, it carries thought into the region behind the veil; it gives us a glimpse into the hidden economy. He who has access to the invisible takes us whither the eye of man has never pierced. And yet it is most difficult to settle on what principle we shall interpret the mysterious conversations reported, and what signification we are to attach to the words concerning the world of the dead. Let us not strain the sentences beyond the meanings which they are fairly entitled to bear; let us aim at a calm, truthful, practical application of Christ's teaching to heart and conscience.

I. Consider THE RELATION OF THE PARABLE TO THE WORDS WHICH PRECEDE, AND TO THE CIRCUMSTANCES WHICH SURROUND, IT. The Pharisees, we are told in ver. 16, had derided the teaching as to "the mammon of unrighteousness," their opposition having been intensified by the declaration, "Ye cannot serve God and mammon." The reply of Christ contains an indictment with two counts, in respect of which their mammon-worship was made apparent. 1. *Their self-justifying spirit before men.* Their piety was so disposed as to attract the observation and win the applause of men. It was the covering of covetousness, because it indicated a dependence on men, a wish to make gain of godliness. The parable which follows illustrates the same state of mind and heart under another phase of the same world-worship. Certainly the portrait of the rich man resembles the Sadducee rather than the more severe and abstemious Pharisee. But extremes often meet. Pharisee and Sadducee have this in common—man and the present are more than God and the future: to look well, to stand well with society, is really the horizon of the aim and the prize of the ambition. 2. *Their merely outward and legal righteousness.* In their casuistry (as, *e.g.*, about marriage, glanced at in ver. 19) they tampered with the eternally right and good; and their essential unbelief was proved by the failure to see that Moses and the prophets prepared men for that kingdom of God to which John had pointed, and into which he had called every one to press. They were so imbedded in their respectabilities that they felt no need of this kingdom, and did not receive it. The parable presents a man who, having Moses and the prophets, had never awakened out of a false, carnal security, had never seen his real poverty and wretchedness. And all, in the latter part of the tale, which brings out his awakenment when too late—the torments of his conscience, his appeal, his cry, his pleading for his brethren—is intended to vivify the worthlessness and worse than worthlessness of the trust on which the Pharisee was built up, and to declare that, before the judgment-seat of the Eternal, Moses and the prophets would witness against him for his rejection of the Light that had come into the world.

II. Now, having seen its root in moral conditions which Christ intended to lay bare, REGARD THE SALIENT FEATURES OF THE SKETCH BEFORE US. 1. There is *a rich man.* No particulars as to his estate are given; no judgment is passed on his character. It is not said that he had amassed his wealth by unfair means, or that he was unjust, or that he was harsh; he is simply presented as rich, fond of show and glitter and good living. Now and again a monarch might assume his robe of costly purple, but purple and fine linen are the ordinary dress of this Dives, and the appointments of his table are always splendid. A jovial, magnificent personage, to whom menials in gorgeous array do homage, and whom all the flunkeydom of his city silently reverences. There is only one drawback. At the entrance to his palace, a beggar—a miserable creature, full of sores—is laid; one so reduced that he is glad of the crumbs which fall from the table. Such crumbs are dainties to him. Clearly, no effort is made to relieve this beggar; none is employed to heal his diseases; his only guardians and mediciners are the curs which prowl about Eastern cities. The "inhumanity of man" is condemned by the action of these curs. 2. The rich man has no name, *the beggar has—Lazarus*, or Eleazar, "God's help." Beautifully Augustine asks, "Seems not Christ to you to have been reading from that book where he found the name of the poor man written, but found not the name of the rich; for that book is the book of life?" Thus day by day, the millionaire, reclining on his couch, his table groaning with delicacies, elegantly sipping at this, and taking that, and withal complaining of indigestion, occasionally sallying forth and dazzling all by his splendour, is yet offended by the loathsome thing at the gate, from which the eye is withdrawn. Day by day the gaunt form of haggard poverty obtrudes on the rights of wealth; squalor, in all its hideousness, stares into the face of wealth. Is it not the contrast which, instead of lessening, becomes more intense as the curious complexity which we call civilization develops?—civilization, with its heights separated only by hand-breadths from its depths. Day by day it is so, until—— 3. "*Died.*" Ah! a word which it is impossible to expunge, which gathers up the fears and tears, which crowns or crushes the hopes of men. First the beggar. To him death is a message of relief, bidding away from sores which dogs have licked to joys in which angels share, from the flagged pavement, hard and cold, of the palace of the rich man harder and colder still, to the embrace and warmth and fulness of Abraham's bosom. "It is well," says Dives, when he misses the bundle of rags and disease; "it is the best thing which could happen to that Lazarus!" But the clock moves on; the "purple and fine linen" begin to hang about the limbs; the viands come and go untasted; there is the sickness, the sick-bed, the muffled knocker, the bated breath of physicians and attendants. Oh, horror of horrors! it is *death!* All must be left. The hands which used to be so full are now still, starched, and empty! The poor to die,—that is good; but the rich man also to die! What is the difference between the two? Of the one the burial is noted; no doubt a grand affair, for which, possibly, he had himself arranged. I have heard of a Dives, who, afraid that he might not have a sufficiently splendid coffin, procured a sarcophagus from Egypt, and lay down in it to be sure that it would fit. The burial; yes, but something more! Beggar and millionaire are in Hades—the *sheôl* of the Old Testament—the unknown place, the unseen region which contains the departed until the coming of the Lord. What of the beggar? While he was on earth man in pity carried him to the palace gate, and laid him there to starve and rot unless the crumb was thrown to him. When he dies angels carry him to the place of bliss, though not yet heaven, which was signified sometimes by the word "paradise," sometimes by the phrase "under the throne," sometimes by "Abraham's bosom." For the millionaire there is only Hades; no purple robe and fine linen, no sumptuous feast; the robe and the linen are now only a garment of fire, the sumptuous feast only a reminiscence continued in torments. To him Hades is only the reservation to the judgment of the great day. 4. And *there is the awakenment.* The Lord describes it in sentences which it is better only to summarize. The eyes of Dives are lifted up, and lo! near, yet far off, is Abraham, and—can it be?—with him Lazarus; no rags now, no sores now; his now the "purple and fine linen" and the sumptuous living, for he is in the bosom of Abraham. And through these distances there rings a cry—no cry to the Father in heaven, no cry for repentance; only to "Father Abraham," and only a respite from the pain, even a moment's respite; a cry which is still charged with the old *hauteur*,

"Send that beggar to serve me." To this he has come; there is no thought of banquet or wines; only the tip of the erstwhile beggar's finger dipped in water and cooling the tongue. Alas! the reply sounds the knell of all hope; mild, yet awful, it is, "Son, remember!" What? The good things are exhausted. He had got all that he had lived for; he had, in the bygone existence, a choice of things, and he had made his choice. His reward was drained. Lazarus had no portion in the world which was gone from sight. His election had been outside of it. He has come to his choice; he has entered on his reward. "He is comforted, but thou art tormented." For the rest, even supposing the will to grant the request, it cannot be. "There is a great gulf fixed" (ver. 26), and no passage may be between the upper and lower sides of the Hades of the dead. "Without God, and without hope." Is it a touch of still surviving humanity, or is it lest the misery be aggravated, that the petition of Dives proceeds, "Then send him where there is no gulf fixed; send him to my father's house, to my five brethren" (vers. 27, 28). "They have Moses and the prophets" (ver. 29). "Nay, but if one went to them from the dead, they will repent" (ver. 30). "If they hear not Moses and the prophets, neither will they be persuaded, though one rose from the dead" (ver. 31).

CONCLUSION. What a variety of "instruction in righteousness" is suggested by this parable! It invites thought in the direction of the most awful questions which connect themselves with human destiny. 1. As to *the Hades*—the condition, or place, of the dead. Dean Alford proposes a good rule of interpretation: "Though it is unnatural to suppose that our Lord would, in such a parable, formally reveal any new truth respecting the fate of the dead, yet, in conforming himself to the ordinary language current on these subjects, it is impossible to suppose that he whose essence is truth could have assumed as existing anything which does not exist. It would destroy the truth of our Lord's sayings if we could conceive him to have used popular language which does not point at truth." What is that, then, in the figures, in the symbols employed, as to which we can say, "Here is matter to be pondered and believed in"? Christ seems to put the stamp of his approval on these things. (1) That there is a conscious personal life after death. If this is not true, he would have started from a falsehood. (2) That in this future life the identity of the self is preserved. All references imply this. The rich man lifts up his eyes. He sees Lazarus. He cries, "Father Abraham!" He recalls his father's house and his five brethren. The I who *was* is the essential *I* for ever. (3) That in the other world, the intermediate Hades, there is a separation between the evil and the good. We should not unduly strain the meaning of "the great gulf fixed." It is in Abraham's reply to a soul in which there is no sign of a turning to God; which is as far from the faith of the patriarch as hell is from heaven. Between a soul thus godless, and the holy dead who are at rest in the Lord, there is a great gulf fixed. But to press this into an argument for a hell of endless torment is to overstep the limits of parabolic interpretation. Yet, undoubtedly, a most solemn warning is conveyed—the warning that, in the world to come, the distinctions of character are sharp, clear, and fixed; that then the real tendencies of mind are manifested, and find their natural affinities. As to the torment of this Dives in Hades, Luther hit on the right explanation when, in one of his sermons, he exclaims, "It is not corporeal. All is transacted in the conscience as he perceives that he has acted against the gospel. Nothing was actually spoken by him, but only internally felt." It is in view of this that we apprehend the scope of the recorded conversation. That is the outward form in which the emotion, the terror, of the conscience is portrayed. For, the retribution, whose fire is not quenched, is pointed to in the saying, "Son, remember!" "It is not necessary to imagine anything beyond the stroke, stroke, stroke, ever repeating, of a scorpion-conscience," recalling, revivifying all the past, the real character of actions being made evident, as with the force of a fire from whose heat nothing can be hidden. To perceive the awful vengeance-taking on every soul of man that doeth evil, it is not necessary to suppose more than the quickening of conscience into full energy, than the continual accusation of the soul which forgets nothing, or finds all preserved, eternized for it, "when the roaring cataract of earthly things is still." 2. To return to the most pressing instruction of the parable; *life or death is the choice before every one of us.* Death; if to any one comforts are more than duties, if the plane of the existence is a merely worldly one—good things of one kind or another, and the kingdom of God left out of the reckoning. The rich man is not condemned because of his riches; the poor man is not carried into Abraham's bosom because of his poverty. The riches were the temptation, and the soul had been mastered; but one may be rich and yet simple in heart as a child, not trusting in the riches, willing to distribute, and recognizing the stewardship to God for all. One may be poor, yet greedy, showing covetousness by the fierceness with which the sense of want is expressed, by the bitter envying of the more fortunate, by the utter absence of poverty of spirit. But, "Son, remember!" if thou livest for good things, thou mayest have them; but then, the greater the prosperity, the greater the curse, the more fatal will the possession be to the true life—the life in God. By-and-by, for even the hardest and dullest there is an awakenment—to shame and everlasting contempt. Here, messages of love, the very pleading of the one risen from the dead may fail to reach the heart; there, where the ever-shifting scenes of this world disappear for ever, shall be heard the voice of conscience, speaking only for doom.

HOMILIES BY VARIOUS AUTHORS.

Vers. 1—9.—*Cleverness and sagacity.* There is a wide difference between worldly cleverness and spiritual sagacity; of these two acquisitions, the former is to be questioned if not avoided, the latter to be desired and attained. Christ's teaching here will be entirely misunderstood if we fail to discriminate between them.

I. THE EMPLOYER'S COMMENDATION OF HIS STEWARD'S CLEVERNESS. "*His* lord" (not *our* Lord) commended the unjust steward because he had acted "shrewdly" (not "wisely") (ver. 8). What does this commendation amount to? It cannot be a justification of his action upon the whole,—that idea cannot be entertained, for this action on the steward's part was wholly adverse to the employer's interests. It was simply a compliment paid to his keenness; it was equivalent to saying, "You are a very clever fellow, a very sharp man of the world; you know how to look after your own temporal affairs;" only that, and nothing more than that, is meant.

II. OUR LORD'S COMMENDATION OF SPIRITUAL SAGACITY. 1. Jesus Christ could not possibly praise cleverness *when devoid of honesty.* He could not do that for two reasons. (1) Because mere cleverness without honesty is a criminal and a shameful thing; no amount of imaginable "success" would compensate for the lack of principle; he who pays truthfulness for promotion, conscientiousness for comfort, purity for gratification, self-respect for honour or applause, pays much too high a price, does himself an irreparable wrong, sins against his own soul. (2) Because mere cleverness does not succeed in the end. It did not here. The steward of the text would have been better off if he had shown less sharpness and more fidelity; if he had been faithful he would not have been reduced to a dishonourable shift to secure a roof above his head. It does not anywhere. No one is more likely to outwit himself than a very clever man of the world. Unprincipled dexterity usually finds its way to desertion and disgrace. Success begets confidence, confidence runs into rashness, and rashness ends in ruin. No wise man would bind up even his earthly fortunes with those of his clever, unscrupulous neighbour. 2. Jesus does praise sagacity *in connection with integrity.* He would like the "children of light" to show as much forethought, ingenuity, capacity, in their sphere as the "children of this world" show in theirs. He counsels them, for instance, to put out their money to good purpose, so as to secure much better results than it is often made to yield. *Make friends with it,* he suggests. What better thing can we buy than friendship? Not, indeed, that the very best fellowship is to be bought like goods over the counter or like shares in the market; but by interesting ourselves in our fellow-men, by knowing their necessities and by generously ministering to them, we can win the gratitude, the blessing, the benediction, the prayers of those we have served and succoured. And how good is this! What will personal comforts, bodily gratifications, luxuries in dress and furniture, any visible grandeurs, weigh against this? Nay, more, our Lord suggests, we may make even money go further than this; it may yield results that will pass the border. It, itself, and all the worldly advantages it secures, we know that we must leave behind; but if by its means we make friends with those who are "of the household of faith," we relieve them in their distress, help them in their emergencies, strengthen them as they pass along the rough road of life, —then even poor perishable gold and silver will be the means of helping us to a fuller, sweeter, gladder welcome when our feet touch the other shore of the river that runs between earth and heaven. This is true sagacity as compared with a shallow shrewdness. It is to make such of our possessions, and of all our resources of every kind, that they will yield us not only a passing gratification of the lower kind, but rather a real satisfaction of the nobler order, and even lay up in store for us a "treasure in the heavens," enlarging the blessedness which is beyond the grave. (1) Is our wisdom limited to a superficial cleverness? If so, let us "become fools that we may be wise" indeed. (2) Are we making the *best* use of the various faculties and facilities God has committed to our trust? There are those who turn them to a very small account indeed, to whom they are virtually worth nothing; and there are those who are compelling them to yield a rich harvest of good which the longest human life will be too short to gather in.—C.

Ver. 5.—*Our indebtedness to our Lord.* "How much owest thou unto my Lord?" Taking these words quite apart from the context to which they properly belong, we may let them suggest to us the very profitable question, how much we, as individual men, owe to him who is the Lord of all.

I. WE OWE HIM FAR MORE THAN WE CAN ESTIMATE. Who shall say how much we owe our God when we consider: 1. *The intrinsic value of his gifts to us.* How much are we indebted to him who gave us our being itself; who gave us our physical, mental, and spiritual capacities; who has been preserving us in existence; who has been supplying all our wants? 2. *The wisdom of his gifts*; their moderation, not too large and liberal for our good; the conditions under which he grants them—in such wise that all manner of virtues are developed in us by our necessary exertions to obtain them. 3. *The love which inspires them.* The value of a gift is always greatly enhanced by the good will which prompted its bestowal. God's gifts to us his children should be very much more highly valued by us because all that he gives to us is prompted by his Fatherly interest in us; all his kindnesses are loving-kindnesses. 4. *The costliness of one supreme Gift.* "He spared not his own Son, but delivered *him* up for us all." The costliness of that surpassing Gift is such as we have no standards to compute, no language to express.

II. EACH ONE OF US HAS HIS OWN SPECIAL INDEBTEDNESS. "How much owest *thou* unto my Lord?" 1. One man has been long spared in sin, and has been reclaimed at last; he owes peculiar gratitude for long patience and merciful interposition at the last. 2. Another has had his rebelliousness suddenly and mightily broken down; he is under peculiar obligation for God's redeeming and transforming grace. 3. A third has been led almost from the first by the constraining influences of the home and the Church; he owes very much for the earliness and the constancy and the gentleness of the Divine visitation. Which of these three owes most to the heavenly Father, to the Divine Saviour, to the renewing Spirit? Who shall say? But we can say this, that—

III. WE ALL OWE MORE THAN WE CAN HOPE TO PAY. We are all in the position of him who "owed ten thousand talents," and *had not to pay* (Matt. xviii.). When we consider the unmeasured and practically immeasurable amount of our indebtedness to God, and also consider the feebleness of our power to respond, we conclude that there is but one way of reconciliation, and that is a generous cancelling of our great debt. We can only cast ourselves on the abounding mercy of God in Jesus Christ our Lord, and accept his forgiving love in him. For his sake he will forgive us "all that debt," will treat us as those who are absolutely free and pure: then will uprising and overflowing gratitude fill our hearts, and the future of our lives will be a holy and happy sacrifice, the offering of our filial love.—C.

Ver. 10.—*The wisdom of fidelity.* Between the text and the verse that precedes it there is some interval of thought. There may have occurred a remark made by one of our Lord's apostles: or we may supply the words,—"as to the supreme importance and obligatoriness of fidelity, there is the strongest reason for being faithful at all times and in everything;" for "he that is faithful in that which is least," etc. This utterance of our Lord is seen to be profoundly true, if we consider—

I. THE LAW OF INWARD GROWTH. The Lord of our nature knew that it was "in man" to do any act more readily and easily the second time than the first, the third than the second, and so on continually; that every disposition, faculty, principle, grows by exercise. This is true in the physical, the mental, and also in the spiritual sphere. It applies to acts of submission, of obedience, of courage, of service. One who is faithful to-day will find it a simpler and easier thing to be faithful to-morrow. The boy who faithfully studies at school, scorning to cheat either his teacher or his fellows, will be the apprentice who faithfully masters his business or his profession; and *he* will be the merchant on whom every one may rely in large transactions in the market; and *he* will be the minister of state who will be trusted with the conduct of imperial affairs. Fidelity of habit will grow into strong spiritual principle, and will form a large and valuable part of a holy and Christ-like character. "He that is faithful in that which is least will," in the natural order of spiritual things, "be faithful also in much." Of course, the converse of this is equally true.

II. THE PRINCIPLE OF DIVINE REWARD. God blesses uprightness in the very act, for he makes the upright man something the better and the stronger for his act of faithfulness. That is much, but that is not all. He holds out to faithfulness the promise of a reward in the future. This promise is twofold: 1. It is one of *heavenly wealth*, or wealth of the highest order. The proprietor of the estate (ver. 1) would remove the unfaithful steward altogether; but he would treat faithfulness very differently—he would be prepared to give him something so much better that it might even be called "true riches" (ver. 11); nay, he might even go so far as to give him lands, vineyards, which he should not farm for another, but for himself, which he should call "his own" (ver. 12). The Divine Husbandman will reward fidelity in his service by granting to his diligent servants "the *true* riches;" not that about which there is so much of the fictitious, the disappointing, the burdensome, as there is about all earthly good, but that which really gladdens the heart, brightens the path, ennobles the life—that noble heritage which awaits the "faithful unto death" in the heavenly country. 2. It is *inalienable wealth*, that will not pass. Here a man points to his estate and says complacently, "This is mine." But it is only his in a secondary sense. He has the legal use of it, to the exclusion of every other while he lives. But it is alienable. Disaster may come and compel him to part with it; death *will* come and undo the bond which binds it to him. It is only his in a certain limited sense. Of nothing visible and material can we say strictly that it is "our own." But if we are faithful to the end, God will one day endow us with wealth with which we shall not be called to part; of which no revolution will rob us, of which death will not deprive us—the inalienable estate of heavenly honour and blessedness; that will be "our own" for ever.

III. THE GROUND FOR PRAISE AND PATIENCE. 1. Bless God that he is now righteously endowing and enlarging his faithful ones. 2. Live in the well-assured hope that the future will disclose a much larger sphere for spiritual integrity.—C.

Ver. 11.—*The true riches.* We must gain our idea of the sense in which the word "true" is to be taken by our knowledge of Christ's use of it. And we know that he used it as distinguishing, not the correct from the incorrect, or the existing from the imaginary, but the valuable from the comparatively unimportant, the substantial from the shadowy, the essential from the accidental, the abiding from the transitory. It is in this sense that he says of himself, "I am the *true* Light;" *i.e.* "I am not that which renders the smaller service of revealing outward objects and the outward path, but that which renders the supreme service of making clear Divine and heavenly truth, and the way that leads home to God himself." Thus he speaks also of himself as "the *true* Bread;" *i.e.* not the food which sustains for a few hours, but that inward and spiritual nourishment which satisfies the soul and makes it strong for ever. Similarly he declares that he is "the *true* Vine;" *i.e.* the Divine Author of the soul's refreshment, strength, and joy. We shall, therefore, find in "the true riches" those treasures which are truly valuable, which permanently endow their possessor, in opposition to those other treasures which are of inferior worth. We glance at—

I. THE INFERIOR CHARACTER OF EARTHLY TREASURE. No doubt these riches, which are not entitled to be called the "true riches," have a worth of their own which is far from contemptible. Indeed, they render us services which we cannot help calling valuable; they provide us with shelter, with food, with raiment, with instruction, and even (in the sense of ver. 9) with friendship. But they neither supply to us nor secure for us lasting satisfaction. 1. *They do not supply it* in themselves. The possession of wealth may give, at first, considerable pleasure to the owner of it; but it may be doubted whether there is not more pleasure found in the pursuit than in the possession of it. And it cannot be doubted that the mere fact of ownership soon ceases to give more than a languid satisfaction, often balanced, often indeed quite outweighed, by the burdensome anxiety of disposing of it. 2. *They do not ensure it.* They can command a large number of pleasant things; but these are not happiness, much less are they well-being. That life must have been short or that experience narrow which has not supplied many instances in which the riches of this world have been held by those whose homes have been wretched, and whose hearts have been aching with unrest or even bleeding with sorrow.

II. THE SUPREME VALUE OF SPIRITUAL GOOD. 1. *There are true riches in reverence.* To be living in the fear of God; to be worshipping the Holy One; to be walking daily, hourly, continually, with the Divine Father; to have the whole of our life hallowed by sacred intercourse with heaven;—this is to be enriched and ennobled indeed. 2. *There is real wealth in love.* Our best possession at home is not to be found in any furniture; it is in the love we receive, and in the love we have in our own hearts: "The kind heart is more than all our store." And to be receiving the constant loving favour of a Divine Friend, and to be returning his affection; to be also loving with a true and lasting love those for whom he died;—this is to be really rich. 3. *There are true riches in the peace, the joy, the hope, of the gospel of Christ.* The peace that passes understanding; the joy that does not pall, and which no man taketh from us—joy in God and in his sacred service; the hope that maketh not ashamed, that is full of immortality;—these are the true riches. To be without them is to be destitute indeed; to hold them is to be rich in the sight of God, in the estimate of heavenly wisdom.—C.

Ver. 13.—*The dividing-line.* Ingenuity is an excellent thing in its way; it counts for much in the conduct of life; it renders valuable aid in our "taking possession of the earth and subduing it;" it has its place and function in the spiritual sphere. A holy love will press it into its service and make it further its benign and noble aims. But there is a dividing-line, which is such that no ingenuity will enable us to stand on both sides of it. We must elect whether we will take our place on this side or on the other of it. That line is found in the service of Jesus Christ. To be his servant is to have withdrawn from the service of the world; to remain in the latter is to decline "to serve the Lord." We may be loyal enough to this present world, may be animated by its spirit, governed by its principles, numbered amongst its friends, and—

I. YET MAKE A LOUD PROFESSION OF PIETY; or

II. YET ENJOY A GOOD REPUTATION FOR RELIGION,—witness the Pharisees of our Lord's time and the false prophets of an earlier age; or—

III. STILL COUNT OURSELVES AMONG THE PEOPLE OF GOD; for many of those whom God "knoweth afar off" are persuaded of themselves that they are quite near and very dear to him. In nothing do men make greater mistakes than in the estimation that they form of their own moral and spiritual worth. But no man can live under the dominion of any one sin or with his heart yielded to the objects and interests of time, and—

IV. YET BE A TRUE SERVANT OF CHRIST. For to be the servant and follower of Christ is: 1. To have surrendered self to him, and the spirit of selfishness is the essential spirit of worldliness. 2. To have sworn undying enmity to all the false doctrines and pernicious habits which abound in "the world," and which both characterize and constitute it. 3. Not to be living for time, but to be building for eternity.—C.

Ver. 14.—*The explanation of false judgment.* "Herein is a marvellous thing," that the men who were reputed to be the best and wisest among the people of God went so far astray in their judgment and their behaviour that they treated with positive contempt the Good and the Wise One when he lived before their eyes and spoke in their hearing. It demands explanation.

I. AN APPARENTLY UNACCOUNTABLE FACT. Here we have: 1. Heavenly wisdom derided by those who were divinely instructed. The Pharisees had the Law of God in their hands. Moreover, they had it in their minds and memories; they were perfectly familiar with it; they knew it well to the last letter. They had the great advantage of the devotional Scriptures following the legal, and the didactic and the illuminating prophetic Scriptures added to both. Then, to crown all, came the enlightening truths of the great Teacher himself; yet they failed to appreciate and even to understand him. Nor did they simply turn from him without response; they took up the position of acute and active opposition—"they derided him;" they sought to bring his doctrine into popular contempt. 2. Divine goodness derided by those who were exceptionally devout. No man could impeach the devoutness of the Pharisees, that is to say, so far as manner and habit were concerned. Their outward behaviour was reverent in the extreme; their habit of life was regulated by rules that brought them into frequent formal connection with God and with his Word. Yet with all their exterior piety they saw the Holy One of God living his transcendently beautiful, his positively perfect life before them, and, instead of worshipping him as the Son of God, instead of honouring him as one of the worthiest of the sons of men, they actually judged him to be unholy and unworthy, and they endeavoured to bring him under the contempt of all good men! Such was their moral perversity, their spiritual contradictoriness.

II. THE TRUE EXPLANATION OF IT. That which accounts for this radical and criminal mistake of theirs was *spiritual unsoundness.* They were all wrong at heart; they loved the wrong thing, and a false affection led them, as it will lead all men, very far astray. Everything is explained in the parenthetical clause, "who were covetous." For covetousness is an *unholy selfishness.* It is a mean and a degrading carefulness about a man's own circumstances, a small and a withering desire for an enrichment at other men's expense; it is an affection which lowers and which enslaves the soul, ever dragging downwards and deathwards. And it is also a *guilty worldliness.* It is not that ambition to make the most and best of the present, which may be a very honourable aspiration; for "all things are ours [as Christian men], things present" as well as things to come (1 Cor. iii. 22); it is rather the moral weakness which allows itself to be lost and buried in the pursuits and pleasures of earth and time; it is the narrowing of the range of human attachment and endeavour to that which is sensuous and temporal, excluding the nobler longings after the spiritual and the eternal. This worldliness is not only a guilty thing, condemned of God; but it is a disastrous thing, working most serious evils to mankind. 1. It distorts the judgment. 2. It leads men into wrong and mischievous courses of action; it led the Pharisees to take such an attitude and to initiate such proceedings against Christ as culminated in his murder. 3. It ends in condemnation—such severe judgment as the Lord passed on these blind guides (see Matt. xxiii.). If we would be right at heart and in the sight of God, it is clear that "our righteousness *must* exceed the righteousness of the scribes and Pharisees." (1) Multiplied ceremonialism will not suffice. (2) Perfected proprieties will not avail. (3) Only a humble, trustful, loving heart will make us right. A true affection, the love of Christ, will lead us into truth and wisdom, will commend us to God, will land us in heaven.—C.

Ver. 15.—*Divine and human judgment.* This declaration of Christ was a judgment in a double sense. It was drawn down upon themselves by the Pharisees, who had been doing their worst to bring into derision the doctrine and the character of our Lord. This reply was not indeed a retort, but it was of the nature of a judgment. It declared the mind of Christ, and it declared it in strong disapproval of evil-doing and strong condemnation of an evil spirit. It brings before us three subjects of thought.

I. OUR DESIRE TO STAND WELL WITH OUR BRETHREN. "Ye . . . justify yourselves before men." The desire to be justified of man is almost universal. 1. It may be a right and worthy sentiment. When the approval of man is regarded in the light of a confirmation of God's acceptance of us or of the commendation of our own conscience, then is it right and honourable. 2. But it may be of very little value indeed; it is so when it is sought merely as a matter of gratification, irrespective of the consideration of its true moral worth. For the approval of man is often a very hollow and always a transient thing; change the company, and you change the verdict; wait until a later day, and you have a contrary decision. The hero of the past generation is the criminal of the present time. And it may be that the man or the action the multitude are praising is the one that God is most seriously condemning. Of what value, then, is "the honour that cometh from man"? (1) Care nothing for the opinion of the selfish and the vicious. (2) Care little for the judgment of those whose character you do not know. (3) Be desirous of living in the esteem of the good and wise.

II. God's searching glance. "God knoweth your hearts." Men do not see us as we are; we do not know ourselves with any thoroughness of knowledge; the power we have and use to impose on others reaches its climax when we impose on ourselves, and persuade ourselves that those things are true of us which are essentially false. Only God "knows us *altogether*;" for it is he alone that "looketh upon the heart," that is "a Discerner of the thoughts and intents of the heart." His glance penetrates to the innermost chambers of our soul. He sees: 1. *The motives* by which we are actuated in our deeds; seeing often that apparently good deeds are inspired by low or even bad motives, and that deeds which society condemns are relieved by unselfish promptings. 2. *The feeling* that accompanies our expression; whether it is slight or whether it is deep; often perceiving that it is more or that it is less than we imagine it to be. 3. *The purpose of our heart* toward himself; determining whether, in the presence of much profession, there is genuine devotedness; whether, in the absence of profession and even of assurance, there is not true godliness in the soul.

III. The Divine reversal. "That which is highly esteemed," etc. Of those things concerning which these strong words are true, there are: 1. *Assumed and also unpractical piety.* The *hypocrite* is hateful in the sight of Absolute Purity; we know what Christ thought of him. Less guilty and yet guilty is the *mere ceremonialist*—he who has no more piety than is found in a multitude of sacred ceremonies, who has not learned to regulate his life or to regard the claims of others. To frequent the sanctuary on one day, and the next to take a mean advantage of some weak brother, is odious in the sight of the common Father. 2. *Self-seeking philanthropy*—the show of doing good to others which is nothing more than a profitable pretence, a course of conduct which has a benevolent aspect but which is secretly aiming at its own enrichment. 3. *Irreverent activity.* Men often yield great admiration to those whose lives are full of successful labour, who build up large fortunes or rise to great eminence and power by much energy and unremitting toil. But if those men are living godless lives, are excluding from the sphere of their thought and effort that Divine One, "with whom they have [everything] to do," and whose creative, preserving, and providing love has everything to do with their capacity, must we not say that the lives of these men are so seriously defective as to be even "abomination in the sight of God"?—C.

Vers. 19—26.—*The sin and doom of selfish worldliness.* This parable, taken (as I think it should be), not in connection with the immediately preceding verses (16—18), but with those that come before these (with vers. 1—15), is a very striking confirmation of the doctrine delivered by Christ concerning selfishness and worldliness. He brings its sinfulness and its doom into bold relief.

I. Where the rich man was wrong. 1. Not in being rich. He is not brought forward as the type of those whose very possession of wealth—because ill-gotten—is itself a crime and a sin. He may be supposed to have entered on his large estate quite honourably. 2. Not in being vicious. There is no trace of drunkenness or debauchery here. 3. Not in being scandalously cruel. It is not a monster that is here depicted; not one that took a savage and shameful pleasure in witnessing the sufferings of others. He was so far from this that he consented to the beggar being placed at his gate, and (it may be taken) that he allowed his servants to give the suppliant broken pieces from his table; he was not at all unwilling that the poor wretch outside should have for his dire necessity what he himself would never miss. This is where he was wrong. 4. He was *living an essentially selfish and worldly life.* God gave him his powers and his possessions in order that with them he might glorify his Maker and serve his brethren. But he was expending them wholly upon himself, or rather upon his present personal enjoyment. If he parted with a few crumbs which he could not feel the loss of, that was an exception so pitifully small as to serve no other purpose than that of "proving the rule." It went for nothing at all. His spirit was radically and utterly selfish; his principles were essentially worldly. It was nothing to him that outside his gates was a world of poverty, of which poor Lazarus was only one painful illustration; that sad fact did not disturb his appetite or make his wines lose anything of their relish. It was nothing to him that there were treasures of a better kind than those of house and lands, of gold and silver; that there was an inheritance to be gained in the unseen world; enough for him that his palace was his own, that his income was secure, that his pleasures there was no one to interrupt. Selfishness and worldliness characterized his spirit; they darkened and degraded his life, and they sealed his doom.

II. THE SEVERITY OF HIS DOOM. "In hell he lift up his eyes, being in torments;" "There is a great gulf fixed." Jesus Christ was not now unveiling the future world for curious eyes; he was simply using current language and familiar imagery to intimate to us that the man who has lived a selfish and worldly life will meet with severe condemnation and grievous penalty in the next world; a penalty in regard to which he has no right to expect either mitigation or release.

1. Are our lives governed *by the spirit of active benevolence?* To throw the crumbs to Lazarus is far from "fulfilling the law of Christ" (Gal. vi. 2). We must go a very long way beyond that infinitesimal kindness. We must have a heart to pity the poor and needy; a soul to sympathize with them and share their burdens (Matt. viii. 17); a generous hand to help them (ch. x. 33—37). The sorrow and the sin of the world must be upon our heart as a serious and heavy weight, and we must be ready to make an earnest effort to soothe the one and to subdue the other. 2. Have we regard to the *day of trial and the future of retribution* (see Matt. xxv. 41—46)?—C.

Vers. 19, 20.—*Poverty at the gate of wealth.* Here is a picture which we recognize in England in this nineteenth century quite as readily as it would be recognized in Judæa in the days of our Lord; it is that of poverty and wealth in very close association. It is not only a picture to look upon but a problem to solve, and one of much urgency as well as great difficulty.

I. POVERTY AND WEALTH IN CLOSE JUXTAPOSITION. As the rich man of the parable could not enter his house without seeing Lazarus lying in rags and sores at his gate, so are we unable to pass our days without being impressed with the fact that "the poor [even the very poor] we have with us," and indeed all around us. *Lazarus lies at our gate.* Not only have we the *professional beggar,* who has adopted "begging" as his means of livelihood, but we have the whole army of *the unfortunate,* who have been incapacitated by some means, and who cannot "work that they may eat;" and we have also another large and equally pitiable multitude of *the ill-paid,* who cannot earn enough by the honest industry in which they are employed to sustain themselves and their families. And so it comes to pass that in England to-day, side by side with competence, with wealth, with inestimable affluence, is poverty walking in rags, lying in loneliness, shivering with cold and hunger, working without reward that is worthy of the name. It is a sad sight in a Christian land; and it is not sad alone, it is alarming; for such extremes are full of evil and of peril.

II. THE PAINFUL ASPECT OF THIS FEATURE OF OUR MODERN LIFE. For who can doubt: 1. *The dangers attending great wealth?* It leads to luxury, and luxury favours sloth, indulgence, a false standard of the worth and purpose of life, a proud heart, and a haughty bearing. In circumstances where there is no necessity for energetic and patient labour, and where there is every opportunity of enjoyment, many evil weeds grow fast, and there the best flowers that grow in the garden of the Lord too often languish. Or who can doubt: 2. *The perils of extreme poverty?* These lead down by a straight and steep path to servility, to craftiness and cunning, to falsehood, to dishonesty, to envy and hatred. And who can fail to see: 3. *The evil influence on the State* of these two extremes? Here there can be no true brotherhood, no proper association and co-operation; here is separation from one another, a division as great as that which is interposed by the high mountain range or the broad sea; nay, greater than that! Many English people see more and know more of the inhabitants of Switzerland than they see and know of the denizens of the streets of another part of their own parish. It is the uninteresting and objectionable poor at their gate who are the "strangers."

III. One mitigating feature. This juxtaposition of poverty and wealth provides an opportunity for the exercise of sincere benevolence and of the highest Christian wisdom. To the Christian heart there is a plaintive plea which cannot be unheard or disregarded, even though Lazarus be kept out of sight and hearing by judicious arrangements. And to the honest patriot there is an inviting and urgent problem to which, far more than to the questions of fortifications and armaments, he will give earnest heed, viz. how to bring about an approachment, an intermingling, of all classes and conditions of men, a better distribution of the great resources of the land.

IV. The true hope of adjustment. Whither shall we look for a better distribution of the riches of the land? 1. *Almsgiving* can only touch the fringe of the difficulty. 2. *Economic changes* may have a valuable part to play in the matter; but we are not yet agreed as to the best course to take. 3. *Beneficent legislation* will certainly bring its large contribution; it can do two things: it can (1) educate the whole nation, and so provide every citizen with necessary weapons for the battle of life; and it can (2) do much to remove temptation from the path of the weak. But it is: 4. *Spiritual renewal* which must prove the main source of social reconstruction. Change the character, and you will change the condition of men. And the one force which will effect this is the redeeming and regenerating truth of God, made known by the holy lives and in the loving words of the disciples of Jesus Christ.—C.

Vers. 27—31.—*A dangerous delusion.* The rich man found himself undergoing the penalty of a selfish and worldly life, and, bethinking himself of his five brethren, he desired for them the advantage which he himself had not possessed; he prayed that a visitant from the unseen world might appear to them and warn them of the danger in which they stood. He thought this extraordinary privilege would accomplish for them what the ordinary influences around them had not wrought. He was assured that in this notion he was mistaken; if they were not hearing "Moses and the prophets, neither would they be persuaded though one rose from the dead."

I. The one hope for erring and sinful men—that they may *be persuaded.* They are living in sin; for selfishness and worldliness are such in the sight of God that they may be said to be sin itself; they are the soul turning from the living God to find its centre, its sphere, its satisfaction, in its own poor self, in the material and transitory good of this present world. And living in sin, men are living under God's high displeasure, under his solemn and awful condemnation, in peril of final banishment and penalty in the future. The one hope for them is that they will *be persuaded:* 1. *To consider.* To consider whence they came, whose they are, unto whom they owe their powers and their possessions, what is the true end and aim of human life, their accountableness to the God whom they have neglected and displeased, the nearness of death, the greatness of eternity. 2. *To repent.* That is, not to be convulsed with a strong and passing agony of soul, nor to use the current and approved language of contrition, but to change their minds, their views, their feelings; to have in their hearts a deep sense of shame and of regret that they should have so sadly misspent their powers and lost their opportunities. 3. *To resolve.* To come to a deliberate and fixed resolution to live henceforth unto God their Saviour.

II. The refuge of the disobedient. There are many who, when they thus recognize their duty, are "not disobedient to the heavenly vision;" they say, "Lord, what wilt thou have me to do?" and proceed without delay to do his holy will. But there are others who weakly and wrongly postpone the hour of decision and of return. They think that the time will come for them to enter the kingdom of God, but it has not yet arrived. There has not happened to them any great visitation. God has not appeared in any striking and overwhelming form. There will come an hour when it will be made manifest to them that they must no longer delay; when they will be mightily constrained to yield themselves to the service of the Supreme; *then* they will freely and gladly respond; meantime they will pursue the old path of selfishness and worldly pleasure.

III. The vanity and the folly of this resort. 1. *The vanity of it.* Jesus Christ taught that men, if they were unmoved by the sacred truths they learned in Deuteronomy and Isaiah, would not be stirred to newness of life even by an apparition from the unseen world; that it was not by the extraordinary and the startling, but by the *divinely true*, that souls were to be saved. And this doctrine is in conformity with the known facts of our human experience. Men that know their Lord's will but delay to do it will find some excuse for disobedience when the unusual or even when the supernatural is before them. The disobedient heart goes on in sinful procrastination, with a vague and feeble hope that this hour will come; but it does not arrive. He has a vision of sudden death, but he rises from the sick-bed to pursue the old path; he loses some companion and is powerfully admonished of his own mortality, but he returns from his friend's grave the same man that he was before; he goes to hear the wonderful preacher and listens with admiration not unmixed with fear or even trembling, but he awakes on the morrow with a closed mind, with an unbroken heart. Some great trouble overtakes and overthrows him, but his soul is hardened, and the "sorrow of the world worketh death" and not life in his case. His hope is a vain one. 2. *The folly of it.* Why should he wait for the extraordinary, the supernatural? Has he not at hand everything he needs to convince him and to induce him to take the step of spiritual decision? Why want some one from heaven to bring down the word of truth or the Saviour himself (Rom. x. 6)? All that we want we have. (1) Our conscience is urging us to a life of holy service. (2) Our reason tells us that our present and eternal welfare is bound up with the forgiveness and the favour of the living God, in whose power we stand and who holds all our future in his sovereign hand. (3) Our Divine Father is summoning us to his side, to his hearth, to his table, and is waiting to welcome us. (4) Our gracious Saviour is inviting us to an immediate and to an absolute trust in himself. (5) The Holy Spirit of God is pleading and striving with us. There is no reason, there is no excuse, for a single day's delay. Every one to whom it is right to listen, everything to which it is wise to yield attention, says, "Come." It is only the evil voices around us and from below that say, "Wait." Delay means the doom of Dives; immediate obedience leads along the paths of heavenly wisdom and holy service to the home of the blessed.—C.

Vers. 1—13.—*Money as a means of grace.* The previous chapter was spoken against the *pride* of the Pharisaic party, who were too exclusive to welcome publicans and sinners to the same feast of privilege as themselves. The parable now before us was spoken against their *covetousness.* It will be found that, as the graces are to be found and grow together, so do the vices of mankind. The idolatry of wealth goes hand-in-hand with pride. In warning his disciples, however, against the vice, our Lord inculcates positive truth, and brings out in his parables the important fact that money may either be a means of grace to men, or a temptation and a snare. The first parable, about the unjust steward, shows us one who was wise in time in the use of money; the second parable, about the rich man and Lazarus, shows us one who became wise when it was too late and his doom was sealed. The story need be no moral difficulty to us. The all-important point is the deprivation of his stewardship. It was taken from him on the ground of injustice of some kind. In view of his exodus from the stewardship, he prudently makes his lord's debtors his debtors too, by largely reducing their liabilities. Having thus made friends with them all, he awaits his dismissal with confidence, and expects befriendment when out of his situation. It is his *prudence*, not his motives, that our Lord commends. Now, to our Lord's spiritual eye, this was a beautiful representation of what a soul may do in prospect of dismissal from his earthly stewardship at death. He may take the money he happens to possess, and, feeling that it is not his own absolutely, but God's, and that he is only a steward of it, he can use it liberally, making the troubles of his brethren lighter, so that, having laid them under obligations to him, he can calculate with certainty upon their cordial sympathy in the world beyond the grave. A prudent outlay may make hosts of friends among the immortals beyond; in a word, money may be utilized as a very important means of grace.

I. Mammon is a bad master. (Ver. 13.) We start with this thought as a kind of background to the more comforting teaching which our Lord here emphasizes. The soul that is enslaved by mammon becomes miserable. Is not this implied in the term "miser," which designates the slave of money? The poor slave is kept grinding away, amassing more and more, and yet never getting any benefit from all the lust of gold. Nothing seems more foolish and insane than the race for riches; nothing more ruinous than the snares into which the runners fall. When life's end comes and the accumulated hoard has to be left behind, the condition of the soul is pitiful indeed.

II. ON THE OTHER HAND, MONEY MAY BE MADE A VERY USEFUL SERVANT. (Vers. 1—9.) For nothing is gained by denying that money is a great power. How much it can accomplish! Every department of enterprise regards money as the "one thing needful." So powerful is it, that people by the use of it may become thoroughly *hated*, as many selfish speculators and covetous people are every day. On the other hand, it may be so wisely laid out as to increase our friends to troops. A judicious use of money can gather friends around us by the thousand. It may serve us by increasing our list of friends.

III. MONEY CAN BE USED BY US TO SERVE GOD. (Vers. 10—12.) This is the gist of Christ's teaching in the parable before us; and we never use money aright until we have got this idea driven home of serving God by it. And to emphasize this, let us notice: 1. *Money is God's, and we are never more than stewards of it.* This truth underlies the whole parable. The very rich man who has the steward is God. We are all his stewards, faithful or unfaithful, as the case may be, in our use of *his* money. It is never ours apart from God; it is ours only as his stewards. Other things are held far more surely—for example, education, thoughts, culture. They enter our being and become ours, we have reason to believe, for evermore. But money is only ours for a time—a loan from God to be put out to a proper use. 2. *We are faithful in our stewardship when we give ungrudingly to those who are in real need.* God gives us "enough *and to spare*" for the purpose of laying the needy under obligation. In this way we transmute our money into gratitude. The gratitude of the assisted is better than the money, for it abides and can be enjoyed when money cannot. 3. *God guarantees the gratitude and the reward.* Some of the recipients may turn out to be ungrateful, but "he that giveth unto the poor lendeth unto the Lord," and "Inasmuch as ye have done it unto one of the least of these my brethren, ye have done it unto me." We are, therefore, sure of the highest recognition when for the Lord's sake we help our fellows.

IV. THE TRULY GENEROUS AND LIBERAL SOUL HAS A WELCOME AWAITING HIM IN THE ETERNAL TABERNACLES. (Ver. 9.) The expression, "eternal tabernacles," to adopt the Revised Version, seems to indicate everlasting *progress* to be realized in the next life. We shall be moving onwards even there to higher and higher attainment. Those we have befriended here will receive us into their eternal tents. There will be recognition and fellowship and its accompanying progress. What a judicious outlay to have all this awaiting us in the world to come! What a means of grace money may thus become! and what a help to glory! Let the so-called unjust steward, then, admonish us to make the most of our capital on earth, that we may have the best heavenly return from it when we have left the money behind us for ever.—R. M. E.

Vers. 14—31.—*The misuse of money.* The possibility of making "friends of the mammon of unrighteousness" has been clearly set before us by our Lord in the preceding parable. The "eternal tents" may afford us warmest welcome if we have conscientiously used our money. But the Pharisees who needed the warning against covetousness only derided him for his pains. It is supposed that it was his poverty which they thought took away his right to speak as he did of riches. He is consequently compelled to turn upon them a severer rebuke, and he does so in the sentences preceding, as well as in the substance of, the next parable. The intermediate sentences need not long detain us. Christ charges the Pharisees with *self-justification.* Now, this can only take place "before men." It is an appeal to a mere human tribunal—to those who can only judge by the appearance, but cannot search the heart. God, he tells them plainly, will not endorse this justification. He will reverse the sentence of self-complacency. He follows up this by stating the *permanence of the Law.* The reputation of the Pharisees may wither and decay, but not one tittle of the Law shall fail. And in present circumstances he declares that the Divine kingdom is being stormed by anxious men who have learned to humble themselves in penitence and pass into exaltation through pardon. They ought to see to it that they are not induced by lust to play fast and loose with the unchanging Law, and to imagine that they can divorce their wives on the usual pretexts, and be guiltless. But now we must proceed to the striking parable of the rich man and Lazarus. Upon the details of the story we do not tarry. It is an exquisitely powerful picture. The artist is here at his best. The rich man in his "purple and fine linen, faring sumptuously every day;" the poor man "laid at his gate, full of sores," and thankful for the crumbs that fall from the rich man's table and for the attention of the dogs; then two deaths, when lo! the positions are reversed, and the poor man finds himself in the bosom of Abraham and with his good things all about him, while the rich man finds himself in utter poverty, in need of everything and sure of nothing. The picture closes, too, all hope for such a selfish soul as the rich man proved himself to be. The following lessons are here taught us.

I. EVERY ONE WITH MEANS HAS AMPLE OPPORTUNITY IN THIS LIFE OF BEING GENEROUS. (Ver. 20.) The friends of the poor man laid him, or, as the word (ἐβέβλητο) may mean, "threw him down" at the rich man's gate.[1] There could be no doubt about the rich man's opportunity; it was pressed upon his notice. And amid all the artificial separations which civilization makes between rich and poor, there is always some friendly hand to force opportunity upon us. "The poor we have with us always." They appear, do what we may, at the feast of life, and we cannot exclude them from our considerations. It requires an effort to be utterly ungenerous. Now, we ought to bless God that he has not left us with any excuse for hard-heartedness. He brings the world's needs to our very gates. He emphasizes opportunity. He gives us outflow for our generosities. He will not leave us in our hard-heartedness, but calls us evermore to nobler things.

II. SELF-INDULGENCE MAKES PEOPLE ABSOLUTELY PITILESS. (Ver. 21.) Mosheim, in a suggestive discourse from this parable, reminds us at the outset of the words of Peter about "fleshly lusts warring against the soul."[2] It is wonderful how hard-hearted luxurious living can make people. The rich man in the parable can find in his heart to pass out and in and never once to relieve his poor brother. The latter may have got crumbs from the rich man's table, but if he did, it was more likely by the servants' charity than by the master's orders. From the self-indulgent worldling he got no consideration. He is ignored, for the selfish soul has become pitiless. When self is supreme, it can shut out all consideration of others from one's thoughts. When they obtrude themselves or are obtruded upon our attention, we say, alas! that they have no claim upon us, forgetting that they are our brothers. Against such hard-heartedness we should all be upon our guard.

III. DEATH, IN DEPRIVING THE SELFISH SOUL OF HIS GOOD THINGS, LEAVES HIM NECESSARILY IN TORMENT. (Vers. 22, 23.) Good living is a most dangerous habit when it constitutes any man's *all*. A soul, to be confined to this tariff, is in danger of dying *into* utter want. The round of sensual indulgence goes on day after day, the appetites are gorged, and man sinks down into the animal pure and simple. Now, if the world beyond makes no provision for such gross indulgences; if it has no venison and champagne; if the appetites are left without a larder and the famine of the senses has come;—what kind of life must the poor soul have? It needs no furnace of actual fire to secure his torment. The burning desire, within which nothing can quench, leaves him of necessity in torment. If God has made no provision for the intemperate, for the gourmand, for the dissolute, in their environment beyond the grave, must not their lusts, denied satisfaction, be perpetual torment? The torment of unsatisfied desire, the hunger of a self-centred spirit, must be terrible!

IV. UNBELIEF IS INEXCUSABLE, AND MAY BE INVINCIBLE. (Vers. 27—31.) The selfish worldling had evidently been living without regard to a future life. In his torment he realizes that his five brethren are living the same heedless life. Lest, therefore, they should come and *increase his torment*, he asks that Lazarus be sent on a special mission to warn them about their doom. Now, it is plain that, with Moses and the prophets in their hands, they were without excuse. What, then, did Moses and the prophets teach? They do *not* teach with great distinctness the doctrine of a future life. They undoubtedly *imply* that doctrine. But the question is—Did the rich man or his brethren need that doctrine to guard them against inhumanity of life? Must I tremble before prospective torment ere I am convinced that I ought to be

[1] Cf. Bruce's 'Parabolic Teaching of Christ,' p. 388.
[2] 'Heilige Reden,' erster theil, s. 65, etc.

generous and considerate?[1] Nay, do I not know by the law of conscience that such conduct as is inhuman must incur the curse of God? Even the pagans are inexcusable when they live inhuman lives. Besides, we must not, with the rich man, imagine that a prescribed miracle may overbear all unbelief. Unbelief may be invincible. No miracle may be strong enough to defeat self-will. May we all be kept from such a hardened state!

V. ABRAHAM, AS HE CHERISHES LAZARUS IN THE OTHER LIFE, SHOWS US HOW A RICH MAN MAY PERPETUATE HIS KINDLY OFFICES AND INFLUENCE. (Vers. 23—25.) It has been very properly observed that in Abraham we have a rich man in blessedness, as a set-off to the other rich man in torment. Abraham was very probably the richer of the two while in life, but he had used his wealth for the good of his fellows. He had cherished the poor and needy. And so it is to good-hearted, faithful Abraham that the consolation of Lazarus is committed. Here the habits of helpfulness which the patriarch had cultivated upon earth find exercise in the better world. What a prospect is thus opened up to the large-hearted! Heaven will be full of opportunity for ministration. Those whose lot has been a hard one in this world will be taken to the bosom of the patriarchs of God—those who have become "seniors" in his house of many mansions —and receive from them the compensation which God has in store for all who have learned to love him.—R. M. E.

EXPOSITION.

CHAPTER XVII.

Vers. 1—37.—*The Master's teaching on the subject of the injury worked on the souls of others by our sins. The disciples pray for an increase of faith that they may be kept from such sins. The Lord's reply. His little parable on humility. The healing of the ten lepers. The ingratitude of all save one. The question of the Pharisees as to the coming of the kingdom. The Lord's answer, and his teaching respecting the awful suddenness of the advent of the Son of man.*

Vers. 1, 2.—Then said he unto the disciples, It is impossible but that offences will come: but woe unto him, through whom they come! It were better for him that a millstone were hanged about his neck, and he cast into the sea, than that he should offend one of these little ones. The thread of connection here is not very obvious, and many expositors are content with regarding this seventeenth chapter as simply containing certain lessons of teaching placed here by St. Luke without regard to anything which preceded or succeeded them in the narrative, these expositors regarding the contents of this chapter as well authenticated sayings of the Master, which were repeated to Luke or Paul without any precise note of time or place, and which appeared to them too important for them to omit in these memoirs of the Divine life. Notwithstanding this deliberate opinion, endorsed by Godet and others, there does seem a clear connection here with the narrative immediately preceding. The Divine Master, while mourning over the sorrowful certainty of offences being committed in the present confused and disordered state of things, yet pronounces a bitter woe on the soul of the man through whose agency the offences were wrought. The "little ones" whom these offences would injure are clearly in this instance not children, although, of course, the words would include the very young, for whom Jesus ever showed the tenderest love; but the reference is clearly to disciples whose faith was only as yet weak and wavering—to men and women who would be easily influenced either for good or evil. The offences, then, especially alluded to were no doubt the worldliness and selfishness of professors of godliness. The sight of these, professedly serving God and all the while serving mammon more earnestly, would bring the very name of God's service into evil odour with some; while with others such conduct would serve as an example to be imitated. The selfish rich man of the great parable just spoken, professedly a religious man, one who evidently prided himself on his descent from Abraham the friend of God, and yet lived as a heartless, selfish sinner, who was eventually condemned for inhumanity, was probably in the Lord's mind when he spoke thus. What fatal injury to the cause of true religion would be caused by one such life as *that! It were better for him that a millstone were hanged about his neck, and he cast into the sea.* This was a punishment not unknown among the ancients. The ancient Latin Version, and Marcion in his

[1] Cf. Bruce, *ut supra.*

recension of St. Luke, read here, "It were better for him that he had never been born, or that a millstone," etc. The awful sequel to a life which apparently had given the offence to which the Lord referred, endorses this terrible alternative. Yes; better indeed for him had that evil life been cut short even by such a death of horror as the Master pictures here, when he speaks of the living being cast into the sea bound to a millstone.

Ver. 3.—**Take heed to yourselves: If thy brother trespass against thee, rebuke him; and if he repent, forgive him.** "But do you take heed," the Lord went on to say, "my disciples; you too are in danger of committing deadly sin yourselves, and of doing my cause irreparable injury. Soft living in selfish luxury, about which I have been speaking lately, is not the only wrong you can commit; there is sore danger that men placed as you are will judge others harshly, even cruelly, and so offend in another way 'the little ones' pressing into the kingdom: this is your especial snare." Things Jesus had noticed, perhaps congratulatory, self-sufficient comments he had heard them make on the occasion of the lately spoken parable of Dives, very likely had suggested this grave warning. So here he tells them, the future teachers of his Church, how they must act; while ever the bold, untiring, fearless rebukers of all vice, of every phase of selfishness, they must be never tired of exercising forgiveness the moment the offender is sorry. The repentant sinner must never be repelled by them.

Ver. 5.—**And the apostles said unto the Lord, Increase our faith.** The disciples, moved by the severe and cutting rebuke of their Master—a rebuke they probably felt their *harsh*, self-congratulatory state of mind had well merited—come to him and ask him to give them such an increased measure of faith as would enable them to play better the difficult and responsible part he had assigned them. They evidently felt their weakness deeply, but a stronger faith would supply them with new strength; they would thus be guided to form a wiser, gentler judgment of others, a more severe opinion too of themselves.

Ver. 6.—**And the Lord said, If ye had faith as a grain of mustard seed, ye might say unto this sycamine tree, Be thou plucked up by the root, and be thou planted in the sea; and it should obey you.** The Lord signifies that a very slight *real* faith, which he compares to the mustard seed, that smallest of grains, would be of power sufficient to accomplish what seemed to them impossible. In other words, he says, "If you have any real faith at all, you will be able to win the victory over yourselves necessary for a perpetual loving judgment of others." The sycamine tree here mentioned in his comparison is not the sycamore; he was probably standing close by the tree in question as he spoke. The sycamine is the black mulberry, *Morus nigra*, still called *sycamenea* in Greece.

Vers. 7, 8.—**But which of you, having a servant ploughing or feeding cattle, will say unto him by-and-by, when he is come from the field, Go and sit down to meat? and will not rather say unto him, Make ready wherewith I may sup, and gird thyself, and serve me, till I have eaten and drunken; and afterward thou shalt eat and drink?** And here we have the Lord's answer to his disciples' request to increase their faith. They were asking for a boon he would not, nay, could not, grant them yet. A small measure of *real* faith was sufficient to teach them that God would give them strength enough to keep themselves from committing this offence against love and charity of which he warned them so solemnly; but they prayed for more. "They were asking for faith, not only in a measure sufficient for obedience, but for a faith which would exclude all uncertainty and doubt. They were looking for the crown of labour *before* their work was done, for the wreath of the conqueror *before* they had fought the battle.... In other words, the 'increase of faith' for which the apostles prayed was only to come through obedience to their Master's will" (Dean Plumptre). The little parable was to teach them that they were not to look to accomplishing great things by a strong faith given to them in a moment of time, but they were to labour on patiently and bravely, and *afterwards*, as in the parable-story, *they too should eat and drink*. It was to show them that in the end they should receive that higher faith they prayed for, which was to be the reward for patient, gallant toil. *And gird thyself, and serve me.* It is scarcely wise, as we have before remarked, to press each separate detail of the Lord's parables. Zeller, quoted by Stier, "makes, however, an application of this to the 'inner world of the heart,' in which there is no going straightway to sit down at table when a man comes from his external calling and sphere of labour, but we must gird ourselves to serve the Lord, and so prepare ourselves for the time when he will receive us to his supper." This is interesting, but it is doubtful if the Lord intended these special applications. The general sense of the parable is clear. It teaches two things to all who would be, then or in the ages to come, his disciples—*patience* and *humility*. It reminds men, too, that his service is an arduous one, and that for those really engaged in it it not only brings hard toil in the fields during the day, but also further duties often in the evening-tide. There is no rest for the faithful and true servant of Jesus, and this restless work must be *patiently* gone through, perhaps for long years.

Vers. 9, 10.—**Doth he thank that servant because he did the things that were commanded him? I trow not. So likewise ye, when ye shall have done all those things which are commanded you, say, We are unprofitable servants: we have done that which was our duty to do.** And for the loyal, patient, unwearied worker there must be no saying, "What shall we have therefore?" (Matt. xix. 27). No spirit of self-complacency and of self-satisfaction must be allowed to brood over the faithful servant's thoughts. In much of the Lord's teaching at this period of his life the position of man as regards God seems to have been dwelt on. God is all; man is nothing. In God's great love is man's real treasure; man is simply a steward of some of God's possessions for a time; man is a servant whose duty it is to work ceaselessly for his Master, God. There are hints of great rewards reserved for the faithful steward in heaven, promises that a time should come when the unwearied servant should sit down and eat and drink in his Master's house; but these high guerdons were not *earned*, but were simply *free, gracious gifts* from the Divine Sovereign to his creatures who should try to do his will. This patient, unwearied toil; this deep sense of indebtedness to God who loves man with so intense, so strange a love; this feeling that we can never do enough for him, that when we have taxed all our energies to the utmost in his service, we have done little or nothing, and yet that all the while he is smiling on with his smile of indescribable love;—this is what will increase the disciples' faith, and only this. And in this way did the Lord reply to the disciples' prayer, "Increase our faith."

Ver. 11.—**And it came to pass, as he went to Jerusalem.** Just a note of time and place inserted by St. Luke to remind the reader that all these incidents took place, this important teaching and the momentous revelations concerning man's present and future were spoken, during those last few months preceding the Crucifixion, and generally in that long, slow progress from the north of Palestine through Galilee and Samaria to the holy city.

Vers. 12, 13.—**And as he entered into a certain village, there met him ten men that were lepers, which stood afar off: and they lifted up their voices, and said, Jesus, Master, have mercy on us.** These met him somewhere outside the village, separated, by the fact of their unhappy malady, leprosy, from their fellows, in accordance with the old Mosaic Law of Lev. xiii. 46, "He is unclean: he shall dwell alone; without the camp shall his habitation be." These had no doubt heard of the many lepers who had been healed by the Galilæan Teacher who was then drawing nigh the village. They did not venture to approach him, but they attracted his attention with their hoarse, sad cry. The legal distance which these unfortunates were compelled to keep from passers-by was a hundred paces. He does not seem to have touched them, or talked with them, but with an impressive majesty bids them go and return thanks for their cure, which his will had already accomplished. They evidently believed implicitly in his healing power, for without further question they went on their way as he had commanded, and as they went the poor sufferers felt a new and, to them, a quite strange thrill of health course through their veins; they felt their prayer was granted, and that the fell disease had left them. They were not sent to the capital city; any priest in any town was qualified to pronounce on the completeness of a cure in this malady (Lev. xiv. 2—32).

Ver. 16.—**And he was a Samaritan.** Apparently nine of these lepers were Jews, and only one a Samaritan. This man would not have been allowed to associate with Jews but for the miserable disease with which he was afflicted, and which obliterated all distinction of race and caste. It is the same now at Jerusalem; in the leper-houses, termed "Abodes of the Unfortunate," Jews and Mohammedans will live together. Under no other circumstances will these hostile peoples do this.

Ver. 17.—**Where are the nine?** It has been suggested that the priests, in their hostility to Jesus, hindered the return of the nine. The one who was a Samaritan would naturally pay little heed to a remonstrance from such a quarter. From the terms of the narrative it is, however, more likely that the strange Samaritan, as soon as he felt he was really cured, moved by intense, adoring gratitude, at once turned back to offer his humble, heartfelt thanks to his Deliverer. The others, now they had got what they so earnestly required, forgot to be grateful, and hurried off to the priests to procure their certificate of health, that they might plunge at once again into the varied distractions of everyday life—into business, pleasure, and the like. The Master appears especially moved by this display. He seems to see in the thanklessness of the nine, contrasted with the conduct of the one, the ingratitude of men as a whole, "as a prophetic type of what will also ever take place" (Stier).

Ver. 19.—**Thy faith hath made thee whole.**

This was something more than the first noble gift, which he, in common with his nine fellow-sufferers, had received. A new power was his from that day forth. Closely united to his Master, we may think of the poor unknown Samaritan for ever among the friends of Jesus here and in the world to come. There are degrees in grace here. The nine had faith enough to believe implicitly in the Master's power, and in consequence they received his glorious gift of health and strength; but they cared to go no further. The one, on the other hand, struck with the majesty and the love of Jesus, determined to learn more of his Benefactor. From henceforth we may consider the Samaritan was one of "his own." SS. Luke and Paul gladly recorded this "memory," and no doubt not once or twice in the eventful story of their future lives used the incident as a text for their teaching when they spoke to the stranger Gentiles in far cities. Being a hated Samaritan, they would say, argued no hardness of heart, nor was it any bar to the bestowal of Jesus' most splendid gifts, first of life here, and then of life glorious and full in the world to come.

Ver. 20.—**And when he was demanded of the Pharisees, when the kingdom of God should come.** The following discourse of the Lord in reply to the Pharisee question, "When cometh the kingdom?" was delivered, clearly, in the closing days of the ministry, probably just before the Passover Feast, and in the neighbourhood of Jerusalem. The query was certainly not put in a friendly spirit. The questioners had evidently caught the drift of much of our Lord's late teaching, and had seen how plainly he was alluding to himself as Messiah. This seems to have been the starting-point of their bitter, impatient inquiry. We must remember that the great rabbinic schools in which these Pharisees had received their training connected the coming of Messiah with a grand revival of Jewish power. If in reality this Galilæan Rabbi, with his strange powers, his new doctrines, his scathing words of reproach which he was ever presuming to address to the leaders in Israel,—if in reality he were Messiah, when was that golden age, which the long looked-for Hope of Israel was to introduce, to commence? But the words, we can well conceive, were spoken with the bitterest irony. With what scorn those proud, rich men from Jerusalem looked on the friendless Teacher of Galilee, we know. We seem to hear the muttering which accompanied the question: "*Thou* our King Messiah!" **The kingdom of God cometh not with observation.** This answer of our Lord's may be paraphrased: "The kingdom of God cometh not in conjunction with such observation and watching for external glorious things as now exist among you here. Lo, it will burst upon you suddenly, unawares." The English word "observation" answers to the signification of the Greek as meaning a singularly anxious watching.

Ver. 21.—**Neither shall they say, Lo here! or, lo there! for, behold, the kingdom of God is within you.** That kingdom will be marked out on no map, for, lo, it is even now in your midst. It may be asked—How "in your midst"? Scarcely not as Godet and Olshausen, following Chrysostom, think, *in your hearts.* The kingdom of God could not be said to be in the hearts of those Pharisees to whom the Master was especially directing his words of reply here. It should be rather understood *in the midst of your ranks;* so Meyer and Farrar and others interpret it.

Ver. 22.—**And he said unto the disciples.** The Master now turns to the disciples, and, basing his words still upon the question of the Pharisees, he proceeds to deliver a weighty discourse upon the coming of *the kingdom* which will be manifest indeed, and externally, as well as internally, exceeding glorious, and *for which* this kingdom, now at its first beginning, will be for long ages merely a concealed preparation. Some of the imagery and figures used in this discourse reappear in the great prophecy in Matt. xxiv. (a shorter report of which St. Luke gives, ch. xxi. 8—36). Here, however, the teaching has no reference to the siege of Jerusalem and the destruction of the Jewish polity, but only to "the times of the end." **The days will come, when ye shall desire to see one of the days of the Son of man, and ye shall not see it.** In the first place, our Lord addressed these words to the disciples, who, in the long weary years of toil and bitter opposition which lay before them, would often long to be back again among the days of the old Galilæan life, when they could take their doubts and fears to their Master, when they could listen without stint to his teaching, to the words which belonged to the higher wisdom. Oh, could they have him only for one day in their midst again! But they have a broader and more far-reaching reference; they speak also to all his servants in the long Christian ages, who will be often weary and dispirited at the seemingly hopeless nature of the conflict they are waging. Then will these indeed long with an intense longing for their Lord, who for so many centuries keeps silence. These will often sigh for just one day of that presence so little valued and thought of when on earth.

Ver. 23.—**And they shall say to you, See here; or, See there: go not after them, nor** follow them. Again addressed to the disciples in the first instance, but with a far more extended reference. In the early days of Christianity such false reports were exceedingly frequent; false Messiahs, too, from time to time sprang up; unhealthy visions of an immediate return disturbed the peace and broke into the quiet, steady work of the Church. Nor have these disturbing visions been unknown in later ages of Christianity. Dean Alford has a curious comment here. He sees in the words of this verse a warning to all so-called expositors and followers of expositors of prophecy who cry, "See here! or, See there!" every time that war breaks out or revolutions occur.

Ver. 24.—**For as the lightning, that lighteneth out of the one part under heaven, shineth unto the other part under heaven; so shall also the Son of man be in his day.** "Yes," went on the Master, "let not delusive expectations interrupt you or turn you aside out of the narrow way of patient faith, for my coming will, like the lightning, be sudden, and will gleam forth on every side. There will be no possibility of mistake *then*."

Ver. 25.—**But first must he suffer many things, and be rejected of this generation.** But, and here again he repeats "as a solemn refrain to all his teaching," the warning to his own of the fearful end fast coming on him. If he is to come again with glory, he must first go away with shame, persecuted, forsaken, by the generation then living. *The suffering Messiah must precede the glorified Messiah.* After this rejection and suffering would begin the period alluded to above (ver. 22) as the time when men should long to have him only for one day in their midst. During this period Messiah should continue invisible to mortal eye. How long this state was to continue, one century or—— (eighteen have already passed), Jesus himself, in his humiliation, knew not; but he announced (vers. 26—30) that a gloomy state of things on earth would be brought to a close by his reappearance. Ah! "when the Son of man cometh, shall he find faith on the earth?"

Vers. 26—28.—**As it was in the days of Noe (Noah) . . . as it was in the days of Lot.** The prominent sin of the antediluvian, he reminds them, was *sensuality* in its varied forms. The torch of religious feeling will have waned in that unknown and possibly distant future when Messiah shall reappear, and will be burning with a pale, faint light. The bulk of mankind will be given up to a sensuality which the higher culture then generally reached will have been utterly powerless to check or even to modify. Men, just as in the days when the ark was building and Noah was preaching, as in the days when the dark cloud was gathering over the doomed cities of the plain and Abraham was praying, will be entirely given up to their pursuits, their pleasures, and their sins. They will argue that the sun rose yesterday and on many yesterdays; of course it will rise to-morrow. Perfect security will have taken possession of the whole race, just as, on a smaller scale, was the case in the days of Noah and of Lot, when the floods came and the fire, and did their stern, pitiless work; so will that day of the second coming of Messiah, with its bloody and fiery dawn, assuredly come on man when he is utterly unprepared.

Ver. 30.—**Even thus shall it be in the day when the Son of man is revealed.** "Is revealed," that is to say, he has been present all along, through those long ages of waiting; only an impenetrable veil has hid him from mortal eyes. In that day will the veil be lifted, "and they shall look upon me whom they have pierced" (Zech. xii. 10).

Vers. 31, 32.—**In that day, he which shall be upon the house-top, and his stuff in the house, let him not come down to take it away: and he that is in the field, let him likewise not return back. Remember Lot's wife.** The Lord, with this striking imagery, describes, not the attitude which men who would be saved must assume when he appears with power and great glory—there will be no time then to shape any new way of life—but it pictures the attitude they must always maintain, if they would be his servants, towards the things of this world. His servants must be ready to abandon all earthly blessings at a moment's notice; none but those who have been sitting loosely to these will be able, when the sudden cry comes, at once to toss away all, and so to meet the long-tarrying Bridegroom. The reminder of Lot's wife—a very familiar story to Jews—warned all would-be disciples of the danger of the double service, God and the world, and how likely the one who attempted it would be to perish miserably.

Ver. 33.—**Whosoever shall seek to save his life shall lose it; and whosoever shall lose his life shall preserve it.** Very deep must have been the impression which this saying made upon the early Church. So literally did many interpret it, that the wiser and more thoughtful men in the congregations during the days of persecution had often to prevent persons of both sexes recklessly throwing away their lives in the conflict with the Roman authorities. Very many in the first three centuries positively *courted* martyrdom.

Vers. 34, 35.—**I tell you, in that night there shall be two men in one bed; the one shall be taken, and the other shall be left. Two women shall be grinding together; the one**

shall be taken, the other left. How taken? Not, as some scholars have supposed, *taken only to perish*, but taken away by the Lord in the way described by St. Paul in 1 Thess. iv. 17, where he paints how the faithful servant who is living when the Lord returns in glory, will be caught up in the clouds, to meet the Lord in the air. The *other* will be left. Thus, as it has been strikingly observed, "the beings who have been most closely connected here below shall, in the twinkling of an eye, be parted for ever."

Ver. 36 is wanting in nearly all the oldest authorities. It was subsequently inserted in this place by copyists from Matt. xxiv. 40—a passage in which much of the imagery here used was repeated by the Master. In one important feature this discourse differs from that delivered at Jerusalem a little later, and reported at length by St. Matthew in his twenty-fourth chapter. There is no reference here (in St. Luke) to the siege of Jerusalem; the whole teaching is purely teleological, and deals exclusively with what will take place at the close of this age.

Ver. 37.—**And they answered and said unto him, Where, Lord?** The disciples were still unable to grasp the full meaning of their Master's words when he spoke of his second advent being visible in all parts of the world, comparing it to a flash of lightning which gleams at the same instant in every point of the horizon. "Where, Lord, will all this take place which thou hast been telling us about?" **And he said unto them, Wheresoever the body is, thither will the eagles be gathered together.** The imagery is taken from Job xxxix. 30, "Where the slain are, there is she" (the eagle); the bird intended being most probably the great vulture, well known in Syria. It is seen, for instance, travellers tell us, in hundreds on the Plain of Gennesaret; it is a hideous-looking bird, equal to the eagle in size and strength, and acts as a scavenger to purify the earth from the putrid carcases with which it would otherwise be encumbered. "Do you ask where all this will take place? As the curtain of the future rolls up before my inward eye, I see the vultures of Divine vengeance flying in flocks athwart the whole area of the earth; the sky is darkened with their numbers; far as my eye can reach, I still see them. Alas! for the habitable earth, my Father's goodly world . . . it is rank everywhere with corruption . . . wheresoever the carcase is, there the vultures will gather together" (Dr. Morrison). The Lord's answer to the question—"Where?" was that his words applied to the whole earth. The terrible and awful scenes he had pictured would take place everywhere. The carcase, as Godet phrases it, is "humanity, entirely secular and destitute of the life of God. . . . The eagles (vultures) represent punishment alighting on such a society." There is another interpretation of these words, which, although many great expositors favour it, must be rejected as improbable, being so alien to the context of the whole passage." The dead body (the carcase), according to these interpreters, is the body of Christ, and the eagles are his saints, who flock to his presence, and who feed upon him, especially in the act of Holy Communion.

HOMILETICS.

Vers. 1—10.—*The Addition Besought.* We are not informed of the circumstances which called forth the discourse condensed in the first ten verses of the chapter. An occasion was, by some incident, provided for a solemn warning against the sin of an unforgiving and uncharitable spirit. And this warning apparently intensified a conviction which had been simmering in the minds of the disciples, and led to the prayer, "Lord, Increase [or, 'add to us'] faith." Have we not a part in this cry? Are there not some of us who feel that, although we live in the light of Christ's Word and kingdom, we yet need one great addition—faith?—

> "The childlike faith that asks not sight,
> Waits not for wonder or for sign."

I. The prayer supposes a want. Trace this want from two or three positions. 1. Reflect how sorely we *are wanting in a lively sense of the great truths of our holy faith.* These truths are not mere opinions; they are facts. The seat of the doctrine is the fact; it is with the facts that faith has primarily to do. Are we receiving the facts with our whole mind and strength? That God is; that Jesus Christ is; that the Holy Spirit of God is witnessing with our spirits and helping our infirmities;—what of these fundamental verities? Realize what a thorough grasp of these facts would involve; what manner of persons they ought to be to whom they are matters of experience and consciousness. And what are we? Alas! is it not too certain that, between the truths in which we declare our belief, and the affections and attitudes of our minds, there is a sad disproportion; that whilst we say, "Lord, I believe," we have need of the addition, "Help our unbelief; add to us faith"? 2. Reflect again, how *constantly we are reminded that the words of Christ are "too deep, too high," for us.* Even when we follow him as our Master, how dim are our apprehensions of his truth! Perhaps this was the immediate reason of the apostles' prayer. They had been listening to wonderful teaching—*e.g.* the cycle of parables in the fourteenth and fifteenth chapters—and after hearing all, how poor was the vision of the realities with which the sayings were charged! And the demand made on them in respect of forgiveness, how could they meet such a demand in a world like this? "O Lord, thy thoughts are very deep, thy commandment is exceeding broad; add faith!" Can we not sympathize? Do we not often feel that Christ's doctrine is pitched on a note far above the level of our mind? We think that it will not do to interpret it too literally, that we must take only broad and general views. The teaching as to conduct seems too fine, too pure and other-worldly for the state of things about us. How can we realize it? "Lord, add to us faith." 3. Reflect, once more—when we look around, *what is one of the chief wants of the time?* Is it not faith? How much of the instruction given in Christian churches is halting and confused!—the sceptic too evidently looking over the shoulder! Religion is a thing talked about rather than lived in. And when we scrutinize the countenances of the "anonymous many-sided" force which we call society, what furrows appear in it! what lines betokening the absence of trust—man in man, having its root in the absence of trust; man in the living God! Is not this signified in the conflict of interests—labour and capital, class against class. To bridge the yawning social chasms, oh for a new spirit of faith! We need a chasm-bridging Church—a Church presenting, with a new force, the ideal of Christian brotherhood. "Lord, add to those who call on thy Name the faith by which the just live, through which 'they work victories, obtain promises, stop the mouths of lions'!" It is because of the lack of an heroic trust in the living God and his government that so few sycamine trees are plucked up by the root, so few mountains of sin and pride are cast into the sea. "Lord, bid us stretch forth our palsied hand, that we may take the fulness of thy grace! Add to us *faith!*"

II. So much for the want which the prayer supposes. Consider THE SCOPE AND IMPORT OF THE PRAYER ITSELF. First, it suggests the *way of the addition;* secondly, it reminds us of the *conditions on which the increase sought is realized.* 1. *The way of the addition.* "The apostles *said unto the Lord.*" It is the only example of a common appeal, the only instance of the apostles, as distinct from the disciples, having a special concerted supplication. Sometimes there was a holy restraint on them, and they durst not ask him. But this is a matter on which they could speak; it came out of the sense of their relation to him that they should go, with their great weakness, direct to his presence. Sometimes, when the hard saying was uttered, they reasoned one with another. But this is not a matter for conference. Only the hand of the Lord opened wide can supply the needed addition. For so it is. In pressing with the little we have to the Lord himself, we get the addition, we have the faith. Any faith, any trust whatsoever in the eternal love and righteousness, is a gift of God, a hold which God has on you, and which, if you only go whither it would lead, will bear you to a confidence more complete and unreserved. The one thing is, do not stop, mourning over what you have not; use what you have; it is enough to lead you to the Lord. Little-faith, at least thou canst cry. Cry the more, the more that the noisy world within or without bids thee hold thy peace. Cry the more, the less thou dost seem to have. "To them that have no might, he increaseth strength." "This poor man cried, and the Lord heard him." 2. Further, connecting the apostles' prayer with the Lord's reply, we see *the condition on which the increase sought is realized.* The reply is given in vers. 8—10. There is a twofold type, with a twofold promise. (1) The mustard seed, smallest of all seeds, which yet grows into the tallest of trees. Let there be faith, even of the dimensions of this seed, any measure whatsoever, then be sure of a Divine power co-operating, which is able to do exceeding abundantly above all that can be asked. As the seed is the promise of the tree, so is this your small faith the promise of a greater and ever greater. "Not by might, nor by power, but by my Spirit, saith the Lord of hosts." (2) Nay, says the Lord, pointing to some mulberry tree at hand, "does that seem strong? Strength which may be compared to that of tearing the tree up by the roots and casting it into the sea is, through Divine co-operation in that grain-like faith. It can tear up by the roots and cast into the sea the selfishness against which the commandment of love has struck." But now follows the condition. What I take the words from ver. 7 to mean is, "If you would have that faith, if you would have more faith, you must cease from all self-trust, you must renounce all self-complacency, you must be as nothing before God. The highest possible excellence is only the fulfilment of an obligation. You are only unprofitable servants. Your life is a bright life only when, instead of thinking of what you are to get from God, or of thanks from God for service, you take the servant's place, and are only and wholly God's. Do not aim at accomplishing great things. Let your one point be an unwearied continuance. Work now, and rest afterwards when all is done. The less there is of self and self-feeling, the more you are busied with him as his servants and sons, the purer, larger, and more victorious will be your faith. All true faith has the certainty of addition; and this addition will be in the measure in which the faith leaves the heart alone with God, worshipping and obeying his holy will.

"So in the darkness I may learn
To tremble and adore,
To sound my own vile nothingness,
And thus to love thee more.

"To love thee, and yet not to think
That I can love so much,
To have thee with me, Lord, all day,
Yet not to feel thy touch."

Vers. 11—19.—*The ten lepers.* Our minds have been so occupied by the fulness of teaching contained in the three last chapters, that we have almost lost sight of the progress of our Lord to the capital. Now the evangelist recalls our attention. He presents the little party, followed no doubt by many who were attracted from one motive or from another, as "passing through the midst of," or rather "between Samaria and Galilee"—Samaria on the right, Galilee on the left, and before them the river Jordan. It is in the immediate neighbourhood of a certain village, no name given, that the company are met by the fellowship of misery. A sad spectacle indeed, but one not unfrequent in the sunny isles of Southern seas, and in Eastern cities and thoroughfares. "Sauntering down the Jaffa road," says Dr. Thomson, "on my approach to the holy city, in a kind of dreamy maze, with, as I remember, scarcely one distinct idea in my head, I was startled out of my reverie by the sudden apparition of a crowd of beggars, without eyes, nose, hair. They held up to me their handless arms, unearthly sounds gurgled through throats without palates; in a word, I was horrified." It is a group of these miserables which clamours to Jesus as he nears the village walls. Those with him had heard the wild "Tamé, tamé! Unclean, unclean!" when suddenly the cry was exchanged for "Jesus, Master, have mercy on us!" These ten, each a homeless man; some with the recollection, perhaps, of happy homes, of other days, of the solaces of human love,—all drawn together by virtue of that gregarious instinct which acts on even the wretched. Class distinctions, even the estrangement of opposite nationalities, are forgotten in the one uniting circumstance—a common woe. No man would have allowed the dust of the Jew to have the same place of sepulture as the dust of the Samaritan; but these men, dead while they live, may herd as they please. Oh, what a sight to that heart in whose consciousness there survived the feeling of the morning stars and the triumph of the sons of God over the creation on which God had pronounced his "Very good"! What resistless eloquence in the cry, "Jesus, Master, have mercy"! He hears, and he answers in his own way; for in the Gospels there is a striking variety in the dealings of the Lord with those who call on him. Each person is a specialty to him. His way with these ten is not to respond as he did to the leper who knelt to him, beseeching, "If thou wilt, thou canst." To them he gives no direct answer; he bids them at once go and show themselves to the priests. This was the trial of their faith. The priests could only pronounce a person cured; for the ten to obey was equivalent to a trust that the power of the cure lay with Jesus the Master. They go; and shortly the limbs no longer drag, the sensations of health, as of new fresh currents coursing through the frame, tell them that they are cleansed. And now for the point of the incident. One, and only one, turns back, and he a Samaritan; and with a loud voice he gives God the glory, and, falling down before his Benefactor, renders thanks and praise. "Were there not the ten cleansed? Where are the nine? There are not found that returned to give glory to God, save this stranger." It is the old story of the thankless heart. Note some of the lights and shadows of the picture of ingratitude.

I. ALL HAD BEEN EARNEST UNDER THE PRESSURE OF THE GREAT WANT AND IN THE PRESENCE OF THE DELIVERER. There was faith enough for prayer, not for praise. Is this uncommon? We have heard that, overtaken by unexpected calamity—fire, shipwreck, etc.—knees which for long years refused to bow, have bowed, and lips that uttered the adorable Name only in blasphemy have uttered the most fervent pleadings for mercy. The record of the great plague in London is a most graphic description of a new earnestness which nearly the whole population manifested, so that there were not clergy enough, services enough, to meet the demand for prayer. Have we not the tokens of this same state of feeling in ourselves? Oh, there is no difficulty in a cry when the life hangs in doubt, when the shadow of death creeps up the wall of the home and lies across the bed of the dearly beloved. The heart needs no book then to teach to pray; it will cling to any plank; somehow, anyhow, the voice must rise like a fountain, "Jesus, Master, have mercy!"

II. WHERE ARE THE NINE WHO WERE EARNEST?

"Even he who reads the heart—
Knows what he gave and what we lost,
Sin's forfeit, and redemption's cost—
By a short pang of wonder crost,
Seems at the sight to start."

They are cleansed. The need is relieved. They are so far on their way. Perhaps there had been some discussion between the one and the nine, and they may have argued, "Let us get to our homes. Grateful to him? Certainly; but he will never miss us." Have we not all illustrated the reasoning? How did the writing of Hezekiah when he was sick condemn him when he was well! "I will go softly all my days" was part of the writing which contained the reflections and purposes of the recovery. How did that harmonize with his pride and ostentation to the messengers of Baladan? Alas! how quickly is the love which special moments originate overborne by the return of the old things, or the influence of new scenes and circumstances?

"Not showers across an April sky
Drift when the storm is o'er,
Faster than those false drops and few
Fleet from the heart, a worthless dew."

Most of all is this true when the record borne is of blessings bestowed, when the prayer which brought to the feet of Jesus has been answered even in a manner which can be traced. What healings are received! and yet there is no turning back of the soul to glorify the Healer! What plenteousness of redemption! and yet there is no loud voice to confess the Redeemer! The proportion is the nine thankless to the one thankful. And is not ingratitude among the most common of vices?—the Aaron's rod which swallows up and comprises in itself all the baser vices? Archdeacon Farrar quotes the lines of Wordsworth—

"I've heard of hearts unkind
Kind deeds with coldness still returning:
Alas! the gratitude of men
Hath left me oftener mourning."

And he adds, "If Wordsworth found gratitude a common virtue, his experience must have been exceptional." "Give thanks unto the Lord at the remembrance of his holiness. Give unto the Lord the glory due unto his Name. Bring an offering, and come into his courts."

Vers. 20—37.—*The kingdom and the day of the Son of man.* This passage is not to be isolated as if it were a definition complete in itself of Christ's view of the kingdom of God. Some, doing this, have found in it a justification of the teaching that God's kingdom has no external character, that the coming of the Lord is only a revelation of truth in and to the heart of man. This is to do violence to the language of Jesus. In what he says afterwards to his own, in the solemn discourse reported two chapters hence, he refers to the coming of the Son of man as a fulfilment which would have its outward signs and effects, and for which his people are to wait. On the occasion before us he sets his Word in the sharpest possible antagonism to the carnal and unworthy notions which prevailed among the Pharisees who had demanded a statement from him as to how the kingdom should come. *E.g.* the Pharisees conceived of this kingdom as a victorious world-power. "Not so," is the assertion (ver. 20); "God's kingdom does not come with observation, does not lend itself to such outwardness as your vision contemplates." The Pharisees separated the citizenship in the Divine kingdom from character. The right to partake of its glories was a political right. It measured the extravagance of their social caste. It was not a chastening and purifying expectation. It was a dream of conquest and outward abundance which kept their minds on the stretch, which made them dupes of those who claimed to be Messiahs or forerunners of Messiahs. "The kingdom of God," says Jesus, "is not heralded by loud professions, by cries of, 'Lo here! or, lo there!' Unobserved, often unthought of, are its marches and movements, its surprises and its conquests" (ver. 21). As the concluding touch of the answer, Jesus warns against a restless asking "when the kingdom shall come," as if it were a prospect wholly future. He reminds us (ver. 21) that the kingdom is here and now, that it is verily and indeed among us. And the caution is as timely for us to-day as it was for the Pharisee then. For we are all apt to associate God's kingdom with some distant prospect or some condition removed from the world in which we live. And the doctrine of the Lord's advent is too often mixed up with schemes of prophecy, with calculations of catastrophes and the like, which men profess to expound or to forecast, crying, "Lo here! or, lo there!" Not, therefore, without meaning for more than the old Hebrew separatists is the counsel, "Look into the region of character for the reality of the kingdom. Where the King is, there is the court. If God has possessed your souls, his kingdom is among, is in you." Observe the solemn discourse to the disciples suggested by the demand which he has met. The words which follow from ver. 22 may be regarded either as an epitome of longer addresses, or as an address in itself complete. Look on it as an instruction preliminary, and preparatory, to the fuller opening up of the time of the end. The shadows are getting longer and longer; Jerusalem is not far ahead; the night is at hand in which, under the form of his first appearing, the Son of man cannot work. The look forward in the verses before us is to (1) a day of distress; (2) a day calling for patient faith; (3) a day of retribution and judgment.

I. A DAY OF DISTRESS. When (ver. 22) the mind would cast a regretful retrospect on the time when the Lord was with them—their Sun and Shield. Ah! would that he, the Bridegroom of our souls,

"Our Shepherd, Husband, Friend,
Our Prophet, Priest, and King,"

were going before us as in the days of old! But no; the shadow on the dial of time cannot be put back. The Church must face perplexities and follow its path through them. It hears voices crying, "Lo here! and lo there!" and the voices are so delusive that even the elect are often bewildered. The Master's word is, "Onwards!" He bids us look up where Stephen beheld him—standing, bending forward in sympathy and help. In the struggle, through the din, although it seems as if he were not, he is with his Church until the end of the age.

II. A DAY CALLING FOR PATIENT FAITH. There are incertitudes and excitements which sometimes almost suspend the action of faith. There are complications in the Church and the world which induce a feverishness of tone. What the Lord enjoins (ver. 25) is a calm, although wakeful, vigilance. He reminds his followers that the way to the crown is by the cross, that the offence of the cross must be exhausted, and then the end shall come. Thus, whilst the sentence is (vers. 26—30), "The coming may be at any moment, it will be, as was prefigured in the days of Noah and Lot, when men are least expecting it," the balancing thought is added, that a testimony must be given to all the nations. And the right kind of waiting is that which seeks to fill up what remains of his sufferings, so that, when he shall appear, his people may be found "not sleeping in sin, but diligent in his service, and rejoicing in his praises." It is in this connection that the reference is made (ver. 29) to the tradition concerning the wife of righteous Lot. "She looked back, and became a pillar of salt." The world-clinging heart was stiffened into a very column of worldliness. Remember, there are to be no regrets, no glances behind. A heart single, and free for the Lord, is the condition of the disciple who shall escape all these things that shall come to pass, and stand before the Son of man. "Whosoever shall seek to save his life shall lose it; and whosoever shall lose his life shall preserve it" (ver. 33).

III. A DAY OF JUDGMENT. The revelation of Christ is a judgment—in the fuller meaning of the word, a making manifest, a bringing to light of the hidden bents of mind and separation of the true from the false. Whenever Christ is presented, the judgment is set and the books are opened. The end is simply the full apocalypse of the judgment which is now proceeding. The lightning (ver. 24) "that lighteneth out of the one part of heaven, shining to the other," is the manifestation of the electricity with which the atmosphere is charged. What of this day of judgment? It is (vers. 27, 28) the condemnation of the world as to its worldliness in both its more sensual and its more cultured aspects—the *sensuality* typified in the days of Noah; the *culture*, with coarseness, typified in the wealthy citizen of Sodom. It is (vers. 34, 35) the disjunction of the closest of life's fellowships—the two in the bed, the two at the mill, the two in the field. The issues that, unobserved by many, are being adjusted and completed will be set forth in their reality. What men would not believe men will be brought to know. "The Lord cometh; he cometh to judge the earth." "Where?" ask these simple men, affrighted—"where, Lord?" and the enigmatical response (ver. 37) is given. Wherever there is corruption, wrong, death, there is the scene of the judgment of God. Jerusalem was the carcase more immediately in view, and the eagle, sign of the Roman empire, that was raised over its battlements was the sign of other eagles that were already gathering. But may we not ask whether the Jerusalem that is in bondage, the Christendom that is, is not ripening for judgment? "Receiving the kingdom which cannot be moved, let us have grace whereby we may serve God acceptably, with reverence and godly fear: for our God is a consuming fire."

HOMILIES BY VARIOUS AUTHORS.

Vers. 1, 2.—*Spiritual resistance.* Our Lord here delivers very weighty truth of a practical kind to the whole body of his adherents—to "the disciples." It is truth which remains as appropriate and as necessary as it was when it was uttered.

I. OUR NEED OF THE POWER OF SPIRITUAL RESISTANCE. "It is impossible but that offences will come." Knowing the human world as Christ knew it, he perceived that his disciples would, through many generations, be subjected to continual and severe trial of their faith. With such error, such selfishness, such despotism, such heartlessness, such iniquity in the world, it was inevitable that temptations should abound. The path of Christian life must lie through a country beset with moral evil; the journey home must be attended by the most serious perils. 1. *The aim of the enemy.* This would be, as it is still, to lead the disciples of Christ into (1) doubt, disbelief, denial, apostasy; (2) indecision and irreligion; (3) half-heartedness in worship, in sacred service, in domestic and individual devotion; (4) worldliness of tone and spirit; (5) unworthy and (ultimately) injurious and even fatal methods of presenting the truth and advocating the cause of Christ; (6) laxity of speech and of behaviour, leading down to positive and destructive sin. 2. *The weapons of his attack.* These are (1) evil suggestion; (2) bad example; (3) specious argumentation; (4) commandment and constraint. 3. *Our resources of resistance.* These are (1) a simple sagacity; such a knowledge of the evil that is in men as will ensure vigilance, a wise carefulness, a hesitation to commit ourselves to every plausible spokesman, to every inviting and well-sounding doctrine (1 John iv. 1). (2) A spirit of fidelity; a steadfastness of purpose and earnestness of spirit that is born of pure devotedness to a Divine Saviour, and that is sustained by intimacy of fellowship with him. (3) Strength in God—that strength which comes from God's own indwelling in the soul and direct action upon it (Isa. xl. 29—31).

II. Our Lord's regard for his disciples of humbler rank. "Woe unto him" through whom it results that the stumbling-block is in the way and the weak disciple falls! "It were better for him" that the worst disaster should befall him than that he should contract such guilt as that and be open to such condemnation. Nothing could more strongly mark the deep interest our Lord takes in his humbler disciples than the severity of this his indignation against those who wrong them. The intensity of his wrath is the measure of the depth and tenderness of his love. Among his followers are those who occupy high places—in ecclesiastical position, in social honour, in mental equipments, in constitutional strength. But there are also those who take the lower place; not the children only—the "little ones" in years and size—but the inexperienced, the unsophisticated and unsuspecting, the mentally weak, the spiritually feeble; those who are much at the mercy of the strong; those who, for some cause and in some one respect, are unendowed and unequipped with the ordinary means of defence. These "little ones" are often: 1. The object of disregard. Many pass them by as unworthy of consideration; they will not repay attention; they will not contribute anything considerable to the cause in hand. 2. The mark at which iniquity aims. For it is one that can be easily hit; it is a victim ready for the blow. 3. But it is for us to remember that they are always the object of our Lord's peculiar interest and affection. He cares for them the more that men care for them so little. He remembers them in "their low estate;" and as a mother lets her heart go most freely to her weakest child, so does he bestow upon these members of his Church all the fulness and all the tenderness of his Divine love. He indicates to us here how he feels toward those that do them harm; and, conversely, it is safe for us to infer that he is peculiarly pleased with those who, entering into his own spirit, love and guard and guide these disciples of lowlier rank.

III. Christ's estimate of sin and suffering. "It were better," etc. We have sometimes to choose between sinning and suffering; *e.g.* the martyr in time of persecution; the son or servant commanded to do that which to him would be sin because "not of faith." This word of our Lord reminds us that any physical suffering, any bodily evil, any temporal misfortune, of whatever magnitude it be, is much to be preferred to any serious sin. Be sunk in the sea, be utterly extinguished, let the worse come to the worst, but *do not* descend to anything which is mean, which is unholy or impure, which would stain your own conscience or injure and perhaps slay a brother's or a sister's character, which would grieve the Father and Saviour of us all.—C.

Vers. 3, 4.—*Our duty when wronged.* The opening words of this passage, "Take heed to yourselves," point to our Lord's sense of the great difficulty we are likely to experience in learning the forthcoming truth, or to the great stress he lays upon its illustration in our lives—it might well be either or both of these. For it *is* a difficult lesson to learn well; and our Master *does* make much, as other passages show, of this particular grace.

I. Our openness to injury. 1. We come into the world with a strong sense of what is due to us. We all feel that there is due to us a certain measure of *respect* as human beings, as those made in the image of God; also that we can claim *just and equitable treatment.* Men may not withhold or remove from us that which we consider to belong to us. If they do we are aggrieved; we have a sense, more or less deep, of having been wronged—our sense of injury rising and falling with the sensitiveness of our nature and the character of the offence. There is neither virtue nor vice, honour nor shame, in this. It is an instinct of our nature which we have in common with our kind. 2. There are many possibilities of offence. In our present condition we touch one another at so many points that there is great likelihood of offence being given and taken. At home; in all the complications of our business life; in all our social relations; in the Church of Christ and the worship of God; in the field of philanthropy:—in all these domains we "have to do" with one another; and it is improbable in a very high degree, it is almost impossible, that we should always comport ourselves as our neighbours would expect; it is inevitable that we should occasionally differ as to what is due from one to another.

II. OUR DANGER UNDER A SENSE OF INJURY. 1. The *mistake* we are likely to fall into when we have a sense of injury is that of instantly concluding that we have been wronged; we are apt to hurry to the conclusion that some one has slighted or injured us. But before we give way even to a strong feeling, we should make quite sure that things are as they seem to be. There are many possibilities of mistake in this world of error and misunderstanding. 2. The *sin* into which we are tempted to fall is that of giving way to unbecoming anger and unchristian retaliation—a *feeling* of bitter resentment, vindictive, passionate, such as does not become the children of God; and *action* which is intended to result in suffering on the part of the wrong-doer; we proceed to "avenge ourselves."

III. OUR DUTY WHEN WRONGED. 1. *Direct communication*, and, where it is necessary, *friendly remonstrance.* Matthew tells us that Christ enjoined upon us that, under a sense of injury, we should "go and tell our brother his fault between ourselves and him alone." This is surely most wise. Instead of *dwelling upon* it and magnifying it in our own mind; instead of *talking about* it and causing it to be spread abroad and discoloured and misrepresented,—the one right thing to do is to go at once to our offending neighbour and tell him our grievance. It is very likely he will explain everything, and there will be no need of any overlooking on our part; or, if wrong has been done, it is very likely he will appreciate our fairness and friendliness in coming straight to him, and will make the apology that is due on his part. Then must come: 2. *Free and full forgiveness.* "If he repent, forgive him." If he should refuse to repent, we must pity him and pray for him, that his eyes may be opened and his action amended, and himself raised by doing the right and honourable thing. But if he repent, then it is our high and Christian duty *to forgive.* And how shall we forgive? Even as God, for Christ's sake, forgives us (Eph. iv. 32). (1) *Immediately.* (2) *Frankly and heartily;* reinstating the one who has wronged us in the place he occupied before in our confidence, affection, kindness. (3) *Uncalculatingly.* "Seven times in a day." However often our child, our servant, our neighbour, may offend, if there be sincere penitence on his part, and therefore an honest effort to amend, we do well to forgive. The more of this grace we have in our heart and life, the closer is our resemblance and the fuller is our obedience to our forgiving Saviour.—C.

Vers. 5, 6.—*Effective faith.* It is the part of a wise teacher to endeavour both to elevate and to humble his disciples. He will not discharge his whole duty nor realize his full opportunity unless he imparts elevating aspirations and unless he promotes a deep humility of heart; he will thank God and congratulate himself when he knows that his hearers are happily sensible of progress, and also when he learns that they are profoundly dissatisfied with their attainments. Both these results ensued from the teaching of our Lord.

I. THE DISCIPLES' DISSATISFACTION WITH THEMSELVES. Evidently the apostles of our Lord felt that there was something lacking in their souls which they would gladly possess. The doctrine of the great Teacher, perhaps, was not so clear to them as they could have wished; or perhaps they felt themselves a painfully long distance behind their Leader in their spirit and bearing; or it may be that they found themselves unable to do such works as they judged they ought to be able to do, in and through the Name of the great Healer. But whencesoever their source of dissatisfaction, they agreed that they were in spiritual want.

II. THEIR CONCLUSION AS TO THE REMEDY THEY NEEDED. They agreed that what was wanted was an increase of faith. And they were perfectly right in their judgment. 1. They wanted to believe in Christ in a way *not then open to them.* They became "greater in the kingdom of heaven" afterwards, more enlightened, more spiritual, more devoted, more useful, because afterwards they had a deep and a firm faith in Jesus Christ as their almighty Saviour, as their Divine Lord. But they did not know him yet as such; for as such he had only begun to reveal himself to them. 2. But they needed a fuller faith in him *as they did then know him.* A more complete and implicit confidence in him (1) would have led them to eject from their minds all their own old prejudices and prepossessions, and so have made way for the reception of his truth in its fulness and in its power; (2) would have evoked a profounder reverence and a more fervent affection, and thus have led to a nearer likeness to him in spirit and in character; (3) would have given them power over the forces of evil outside them, and made them equal to the emergencies to which they were unequal (see Matt. xvii. 19, 20). They did well, therefore, to make of their Lord the request they made, "Increase our faith."

III. The truth contained in our Lord's reply. "If ye had faith as a grain of mustard seed," etc. This truth is surely *not* that the possession of a faith *as slight* as the mustard seed is small will suffice, *but* that the faith which *is full* as is the mustard seed *of life and power of appropriation* will avail for all occasions. For it is not true that a slight and feeble faith does suffice. It failed the apostles on one memorable day (ch. ix. 40). It has been failing ever since. Only a faith which is a living and a growing power, like the mustard seed in the soil, will triumph over the difficulties to be met and mastered. The fact is that: 1. A formal faith is worth nothing at all; indeed, less than nothing, for it deludes and misleads. 2. A feeble faith will accomplish little. It sinks in the hour of trial (Matt. xiv. 30); it shrinks from open avowal, and makes feeble fight in the hour of battle (John iii. 1; vii. 50; xix. 38); it enters upon, but abandons, the goodly enterprise (Acts xiii. 13). 3. A living, appropriating faith is the only effective power. A faith that, like the mustard seed in the soil, puts forth the power of life, and appropriates to itself the riches that are around it in order that, further on, it may bear fruit—this is a power that will be felt. It will accomplish great and even wonderful things; it will surprise the unbelieving as much as if it actually did the very thing which the Master speaks of in his illustrative language. (1) It will uproot great evils in God's Name and strength. (2) It will upraise noble structures of good, when inspired at the same source.

1. Is there anything seriously lacking in our spirit, character, life, work? 2. May it not be traced to the absence or to the feebleness of our faith? If we believed more truly in Jesus Christ, if we realized more thoroughly what we accept, should we not be more to God and do more for him? 3. Shall we not come to our Saviour, unhesitatingly, earnestly, perseveringly, with this prayer of the apostles?—C.

Vers. 7—10.—*The spirit of Christian service.* The hardest nut may have the sweetest kernel; the least inviting and most difficult parable may have the most strengthening and stimulating truth beneath the surface. So with this passage. We may be even repelled from treating it because it seems to represent our Father in a light in which we do not like to look at him. It *seems* as if we were required to regard him as a hard taskmaster, indifferent to the past labour and present weariness of his servants, accepting their service without sign or token of recognition. We don't recognize the portrait in this picture. But when we look longer and see more, we understand that Jesus Christ *did not* for a moment *intend to convey this impression* of his Father and ours. 1. It is inconsistent with the revelation of God which Christ gave us both in his doctrine and in his own Person and life. For in both of these God is revealed to us as a Father who gives rather than receives. Jesus Christ himself was "amongst us as he that serveth;" he "came not to be ministered unto but to minister, and to give his life;" it is not from him that we can receive the impression that God is one that exacts everything and makes no response. 2. Christ's method of teaching does not require us to interpret the parable in this sense. He argued not only from comparison, but from contrast; not only from the less to the more worthy, but also from the unworthy to the excellent. He said, "If an *unjust* judge for a *bad* reason will do right, how certainly will the *just* Judge for a *high* one!" He said, "If an ungracious neighbour, prompted by a selfish consideration, will listen and comply, how much more surely will the gracious God, from beneficent considerations!" So here. The slave, when he returns from his day's laborious duties, prepares, unthanked, for his master's comfort before he thinks of his own necessities; and he does this unquestioningly, uncomplainingly. How much more ready, more eager, should *we* be to serve our God!—*we* who are not slaves, but children; to serve *him*, who is no unresponsive and inconsiderate taskmaster, but who is Considerateness itself, who is Responsiveness itself, who is Encouragement itself. We should be ready and eager to serve him to the uttermost, and when we have done everything we can do, be prepared to say, "It is nothing of all that we should do and would do for thee." Now, there are certain *occasions to which this more particularly applies*; and here we have a touch of *resemblance* in the parable. As the master there requires of his slave something over and above his day's work in the field, so does our Lord sometimes ask of us *more than we thought he would* when he first said to us, "Follow me," and we said, "Lord, I will." This may be in the way—

I. OF ACTIVE SERVICE; *e.g.* when parents have clothed and fed, taught and trained their own children, they may be directed, in God's providence, to take charge of the children of others; or when the minister, superintendent, missioner, teacher, finds that the duty he has undertaken involves a great deal more of costly work than he had counted upon—more time, trouble, patience, self-mastery, self-sacrifice.

II. OF SACRIFICE; *e.g.* when the young man leaves home or college for work in the foreign field, he finds that the privations he has to endure, the scenes he has to witness, the discouragements he has to bear, the parting with his children he has to go through, are a great deal more than he realized when he started on his way.

III. OF SUBMISSION. When life seems to have been lived through, its strength spent and its work done, the weary human spirit craves rest, the rest of the heavenly home; but God may allot many months or even years of patient waiting before the summons is sent to "come up higher." And in whatever way, or to whatever degree, the heavenly Father may ask of his children the service which they did not look for, such should be and may be their spirit of (1) *perfect trustfulness*, and of (2) *fervent love*, that they will gladly and faithfully respond; doing with alacrity and bearing with cheerfulness all his holy will, and quite disposed at the end to say, "All is not half enough to give unto the 'Lamb that was slain,' who is worthy to receive the *riches* of our hearts and of our lives."—C.

Vers. 11—19.—*The commonness of ingratitude, etc.* Under the guidance of this narrative, we think of—

I. THE COMMONNESS OF INGRATITUDE. Only one of these ten men had a sufficient sense of indebtedness to return to Christ to offer thanks. The ingratitude of the remaining nine touched, smote, wounded our Lord, and he used the reproachful words of the text (ver. 17). This ingratitude was not a remarkably exceptional illustration of our nature; it is one of those things in respect of which "he that increaseth knowledge increaseth sorrow." For that which youth refuses to believe, experience obliges us to acknowledge, viz. that to accept a great boon from the hand of love, and to show no proper sense of gratitude, is not a rare but a common thing. It is likely enough that we may go much out of our way to do a man a kindness, and that when we look for his response we shall be disappointed. What then? Shall we be diverted from the path of beneficence by this unlovely fact? Shall we say, "Since it is very likely that my services will not be appreciated, they shall not be rendered"? Certainly not. For: 1. There *is* gratitude to be gained and to be enjoyed. This proportion is not representative. It is not the case that nine men out of ten are insensible to kindnesses shown them. It is as likely as not, perhaps more likely than not, that if we do help our brother in his hour of need, if we do sustain him in sorrow, succour him in distress, stand by him in temptation, lead him into the kingdom of God, we shall win his gratitude, and we *may* secure the profound, prayerful, lifelong affection of a human heart. And what better reward, short of the favour and friendship of God, can we gain than that? 2. If we fail to obtain this, we shall stand by the side of our Divine Master; we shall share his experience; we shall have "fellowship with the sufferings of Christ." He knew well what it was to serve and be unappreciated, to serve and be disparaged. To be where he stood, to

"Tread the path our Master trod,
To bear the cross he bore,"

—this is an honour not to be declined. 3. If man our brother does not bless us, Christ our Saviour *will*. The most heroic deed of love may go, has gone, unrewarded of man. But the smallest act of kindness rendered to the humblest child will *not* go unrewarded of him. "Whosoever shall give to drink unto one of these little ones a cup of cold water only . . . shall *in no wise* lose his reward."

II. THE UNCOUNTED DEBT DUE TO JESUS CHRIST. These nine men having received the greatest good one man could receive from another—deliverance from a living death—failed to recognize their obligation, did not stop to consider it. They were not the last to be guilty in this respect. 1. How much more do many owe to Christ *than they think they do!* They say, "We do not choose to range ourselves under him and call him 'Master;' we can construct our own character, can build up rectitude and purity and benevolence of spirit apart from his truths or his will; we can do without Christ." But suppose we subtract from the elevating and purifying influences which have made these men what they are all those elements which are due to Christ, how much is left? How *little* is left? The influences that come from him are in the air these men are breathing, in the laws under which they are living, in the literature they are reading, in the lives they are witnessing; they touch and tell upon them at every point, they act silently and subtly but mightily upon them; they owe to Jesus Christ the best they are and have; they ought to come into direct, living, personal relations with the Lord himself. 2. How much more do some men owe to Christ *than they stay to consider!* These nine men would not have disputed their obligation had they been challenged, but they were so anxious to get home to their friends and back to their business that they did not stay to consider it. Have we *stayed to consider* what we owe to him who, though he has not indeed cured us of leprosy, has at infinite cost to himself prepared for us a way of recovery from that which is immeasurably worse —from sin and death? to him who, "though he was rich, for our sakes became poor, that we through his poverty might be rich"?

III. THE PERIL OF EARLY PRIVILEGE. It is significant enough that the tenth leper who did return to give glory to God was a Samaritan—was "this stranger." Taking this fact with that concerning the Roman soldier whose faith surprised our Lord, and that of the Syro-Phœnician woman whose importunity prevailed over every obstacle, we may conclude that the Hebrew mind was so familiarized with "signs and wonders," that those outside the sacred circle were far more impressed by what they witnessed than the people of God themselves. It is well to be the children of privilege; but there is one grave peril connected with it. We may become so familiar with the greatest of all facts as to become insensible to their greatness. The Swiss peasant who lives on the Alpine slopes sees no grandeur in those snow-clad summits on which his eyes are always resting; the sailor who lives by the sea hears no music in "old ocean's roar." We may become so familiar even with the story of the cross that our minds are unaffected by its moral grandeur, by its surpassing grace. It behoves us to take earnest heed that we fall not into this fatal snare; lest many should come "from the north, and the south, and the east, and the west, and sit down in the kingdom of God," and we, the children of the kingdom, be excluded. We must do our utmost to *realize* the great truths which have so long been uttered in our hearing.—C.

Vers. 20, 21.—*Radical mistakes respecting the kingdom of God.* Pharisaism took its hostile attitude toward Christianity because it entirely failed to understand it. It made two radical mistakes which completely misled it.

I. THE MISTAKES WHICH PHARISAISM MADE. 1. As to the *character of the coming kingdom.* It thought it was to be outward, earthly, political, temporal; it was looking and longing for the time when another David, another Judas Maccabæus, should come, should liberate the Holy Land from the grasp of the pagan power, and make Jerusalem the metropolis, the centre and glory of the earth. 2. As to the *evidences and signs of its coming.* It looked for a grand display of power, for overwhelming evidences that would strike every eye and startle and convince every mind that One was at hand who should assume the sovereignty awaiting him. And so it came to pass that when Jesus was born at Bethlehem, a Babe cradled in a manger; when he grew up to be a Carpenter at Nazareth; when he gathered no army, and struck no blow for national deliverance; when there was no ostentation about his method; when he lived to bless and teach individual men and women, and wrought his work quietly and unpretendingly;—Pharisaism decided that he was not the Coming One, and that his reign was not to prove the kingdom of God. Pharisaism entirely mistook God's purpose, and fatally misinterpreted his procedure.

II. THE MISTAKES INTO WHICH WE ARE LIABLE TO FALL. Not, of course, the same but similar, and equally disastrous. 1. When we look for blessedness in outward circumstances instead of in inward peace. We say, "If I could but win that prize, gain that post, secure that friendship, earn that income, how bright would be my lot, how glad my heart, how radiant my life!" But we are wrong. Gladness of heart and excellency of life are not to be found in sunny circumstances, but in a pure heart, a heart that is at rest, a heart at home with God. "Out of the heart are the issues of life;" the fountain of lasting joy rises from our own breast; the kingdom of God is *within* us. 2. When we look for blessedness in the time that is beyond. "Man never *is*, but always *to be* blessed." There is even an unchristian longing for the heavenly future. When "to abide in the flesh" is more needful for those for whose welfare we are largely responsible, then the "kingdom of God" for us is not in the distance; it is in the present sphere of duty; it is in present peace, present joy, present service, in the blessedness which Christ gives to his servants

"Before they reach the heavenly fields,
Or walk the golden streets,"

in those "heavenly places" of holy service and happy fellowship in which he "has made them to sit" (Eph. ii. 6). 3. When we wait for heavenly influences to fall upon us instead of availing ourselves of those we have. Not only is there no need for any soul to wait for some remarkable and overwhelming influences before entering the kingdom, not only is it *wholly unnecessary*, but it is *positively wrong* to do so. It is in those quiet influences which are now working within your heart that God comes to you. He will never be nearer to a human soul than when his Spirit fills it with a holy longing, and makes it eager to know what it must do to enter into life. Wait not for anything that is coming: act on the promptings that are within you, and your feet shall then surely stand within the kingdom of God.—C.

Vers. 22—25.—*The brief day of opportunity.* The thought of our Master in this passage (as I understand it) is this: "I have been asked when the kingdom of God will come: my reply is that it has come already; that you have not to look about in this and that direction; here, in the midst of you, impersonated in him that speaks, *is* the kingdom. It is present in the Present One. But," he says to his disciples, "he is present in a very strict sense. The time will soon be here when you will greatly long for his fellowship, and you will not be able to possess it. Do not believe those who will tell you that the Son of man is still on earth; it will not be true. His life below will be of the very briefest; it will be but as a lightning-flash which passes through the darkened heavens in a moment, and is gone again; so brief will be his stay, so soon will he be gone. But before he goes he must suffer many things; much must be done, for much must be endured, before his short day is done."

I. The brief day of our Lord's opportunity. When we think of the long centuries that preceded, and of those that have already succeeded, the day of Christ, we may well regard his short visit to our world as a mere flash of light for transitoriness. What were those few months of his short stay among men compared with all those dark ages, and to all those that have been illumined by the light which his truth has shed upon them! But, transient as it was, it sufficed. It does not take long to utter or to illustrate the most Divine and the most vital truths; it did not take long to undergo the most mysterious and the most availing sorrows—it took but a few agonizing hours to die the death of atonement. Into that short day of opportunity our Divine Redeemer compressed: 1. The utterance of all needful truth—all the truth we need for our guidance into the kingdom of God, and for our passage through life and death into the kingdom of glory. 2. The illustration of every human grace; the living of a human life in all its perfect loveliness and grandeur. 3. The endurance of sorrow such as constituted him for ever the Man of sorrows, and the High Priest of human nature, touched with the feeling of our infirmities (Heb. iv. 15). 4. The dying of that death which is the all-sufficient sacrifice for sin. A few months of time sufficed to complete his work and make him the Divine Teacher, Leader, Friend, Saviour, of the whole race of man for all time to come.

II. Our brief day. 1. Measured by hours, our day is very brief. Human life is short at the longest. We are "but of yesterday," and to-morrow we shall not be.

The rocks and even the trees look down on many generations. And in all the bustle and battle, in all the pursuits and pleasures of our life, the little time we have hastens away and is gone far sooner than we thought it would go. It is not only our poetry that sings, but our experience that testifies of the swiftness of our course beneath the sun. 2. Yet it holds manifold and precious opportunities of regaining our position as the children and heirs of God; of doing "many things" that shall tell even in future years for truth and God; of "suffering many things" after Christ our Lord, and in holy and noble fellowship with him (Phil. iii. 10). 3. Its transiency is an urgent reason for (1) immediate decision, and (2) constant and earnest action in the cause of righteousness. Whilst we have the light that shines, let us walk and let us work in the light.—C.

Vers. 26—30.—*The unlearnt lesson.* Man differs from the brute creation in that he learns and profits by experience—he advances. He passes through stage after stage toward the perfection of his life upon the earth. He is the hunter at one period, then the shepherd, then the agriculturist. From the lowest barbarism he reaches, in time, the most refined civilization. But he is very slow indeed to learn, if he does learn at all, moral and spiritual truths. The excellency of thrift, of temperance, of purity, of patience,—how long a time it is taking man to acquire these virtues! Our text opens to us the truth of the danger of spiritual trifling, and indicates that what men were long ages ago, that they still are in this respect.

I. SPIRITUAL TRIFLING. The men of the time of Noah were living in a state of utter worldliness and impiety. They were not without remonstrance and rebuke; Noah was himself "a preacher of righteousness" unto them. But they hearkened not, nor heeded; they made light of his admonitions and his warnings. They found some pretext under which they could easily hide the truth he reminded them of, and they went on their way of materialism and enjoyment. The same with the people of Sodom, and the character and instruction of Lot. And so with us. 1. Men are living in sinful selfishness and worldliness—many in crime, many more in vice; but a very large multitude in practical godlessness. God is not in all, he is not in many if in any of their thoughts. His will is not *the* object of their inquiry, is not *the* rule of their life. 2. The religious teacher comes and admonishes; he says, "Man cannot live by bread alone;" the claims of the Divine Father, of the holy Saviour, are the supreme claims, etc. 3. But still the same course is pursued; the better thoughts that are momentarily stirred in the heart are silenced; sacred truths are extinguished; the truth of God is treated lightly; the world and the things that are in the world are uppermost and are victorious.

II. THE PALPABLE FOLLY OF SUCH TRIFLING AS THIS. 1. It is attended with immediate and certain injury. For it is impossible for a human soul to reject the truth or to quench the Spirit of God, and not be seriously the worse for such an act. 2. There is the grave peril of a great disaster. The generation is eating and drinking and marrying, and behold! the Flood sweeps them away. The cities are trading and feasting, and lo! the fires of heaven come down and consume them. They who trifle with the most sacred things are sure to find that, suddenly, in such an hour as they think not, the end arrives. The business plans are all broken off; the brilliant career is concluded; the flow of pleasures is arrested. Death suddenly appears, and deals his fatal blow. These sacred opportunities which have been so little prized, so much disparaged, recede with terrible rapidity and disappear. Opportunity that waited by the side, and waited all in vain, melts and vanishes in a moment. The soul awakes from its long lethargy to see that its powers have been wasted and that its chance is gone!

III. THE ELUSIVENESS OF THIS SOLEMN LESSON. Men have always known this, and they have always acted as if they were ignorant of it. "As it was . . . so shall it be." So is it to-day. By spiritual trifling men fritter away the golden chance that Divine love puts into their hands. Be wise in time. Realize what you are doing, what injury you are working, what risk you are running.—C.

Vers. 34—36.—*Accidents.* "The one shall be taken, and the other left." And who or what is it that decides which one shall be taken and which left? Events are often occurring which convey to us the impression of—

I. THE LARGE AMOUNT OF ACCIDENT which enters into the fabric of human life. Take, for example, a bad railway accident. How accidental it seems that one man should just miss that train and be saved, and that another should just catch it and be killed; that one should take a seat in the carriage which is crushed, and another in the carriage which is left whole; that one should be sitting exactly where the bent and twisted timber pierced him, and another exactly where no injury was dealt, etc.! It is the same with the battle-field, with the thunderstorm, with the falling house. One is taken, and another left; and the taking of the one and the leaving of the other seems to be pure accident—not the result of reason or forethought, but entirely fortuitous.

II. OUR CORRECTED THOUGHT CONCERNING IT. 1. Of accident in the sense of *chance* we know there is nothing. Everything is "under law;" and even where there is no law apparent, we are assured, by the exercise of our reason, that there must be the operation of law, though it is out of our sight. In this world of God's, pure chance has not an inch of ground to work upon. 2. There is usually much more play of reason and habit in "accidental events" than seems at first sight. Things result as they do because habit is stronger than judgment, or because foolish men disregard the counsel of the wise; because thoughtful men take the precautions which result in their safety, and because thoughtless men take the action which issues in their suffering or death. 3. The providence of God covers the entire field of human life. May we venture to believe that the hand of God is in the events and issues of life? I think we may. (1) It is clearly within the range of the activities of an Infinite Being to whom nothing is small as nothing is great. (2) His Fatherhood would lead him to follow the course of every one of his children with parental interest, and to interpose his hand wherever he saw it was wise to do so. (3) Scripture warrants the conclusion: "Precious in the sight of the Lord is the death of his saints;" "The way of man is not in himself; it is not in man that walketh to direct his steps;" "Not a sparrow falleth to the ground without your Father: ye are of more value than many sparrows."

III. THE LARGE MEASURE OF UNCERTAINTY THAT REMAINS AND MUST REMAIN. Human science has introduced many safeguards, but it has also introduced new perils. The "chapter of accidents" is as long as it ever was in the contemporary history of mankind. God is supreme, but he lets many things happen we should antecedently have supposed he would step in to prevent; he lets good men take the consequence of their mistakes; he permits the very holy and the very useful to be overtaken by sad misfortunes and even by fatal calamities. We cannot guarantee the future; we cannot ensure prosperity, health, friends, reputation, long life. To one that seems to be heir to all these good things they will fall; to another who seems equally likely to inherit them they will be denied: one is taken, the other left. Therefore let us turn to—

IV. THE ONE GOOD THING ON WHICH WE CAN ABSOLUTELY COUNT. There is "a good part which shall not be taken away." This is a Christian character; its foundations are laid in repentance and faith; it is built up of reverent study, of worship, of the obedience of love. Its glory is in resemblance to Jesus Christ himself. This is within every man's reach, and it *cannot* be taken; it *must* be left. He who secures that is safe for ever. No accident can rob him of his heritage. His treasure and himself are immovable; for "he that doeth the will of God abideth for ever."—C.

Vers. 1—19.—*Graces stimulated and strengthened.* The preceding chapter urges most powerfully, by precept and parable, consideration for others. Money is to be used for this end. But consideration may be shown in many other ways. And want of consideration may be one of those "occasions of stumbling" (so in Revised Version) to the Lord's little ones which shall be visited with such overwhelming retribution. Our Lord consequently begins by teaching—

I. THE GREAT DANGER OF CAUSING A LITTLE ONE TO STUMBLE. (Vers. 1, 2.) In this way he urges his disciples to watchfulness. He plainly implies that defenceless individuals who fall through stumbling-blocks placed in their path shall have in God a most terrible Avenger. Better the most fearful physical death than the fate of those who cause them to stumble. Of Judas it was expressly stated it would have been better if he had never been born; and the same might be said of every one who, like him, throws stumbling-blocks in his brother's way. The ruin of the innocent, through exposing them to temptation, will be visited by God's most terrible indignation.

II. THE DISCIPLES OF CHRIST MUST GUARD AGAINST AN UNRELENTING AND UNFORGIVING TEMPER. (Vers. 3, 4.) The disciples are to take heed to themselves. *They* are not to be avengers. They have not the solidity of judgment or of character to exercise vengeance. It is to be left to God. If, therefore, a brother trespass against us, we are to pursue such a path as will result in forgiveness and reconciliation. We are to rebuke him courageously; then, if he repents, if he shows signs of sorrow and confesses his fault, even though it should be repeated seven times a day, we are to forgive him. Now, this forgiving spirit is Divine. It is God-like. It is the spirit God has manifested in Christ, and which we should cultivate most diligently.

III. OUR LORD'S EXHORTATIONS LED THE DISCIPLES TO SEEK AN INCREASE OF FAITH. (Vers. 5—10.) When we have discovered how small our forgiving spirit is, we then begin to see how small other graces are, and to cry, "Lord, Increase our faith." It is most instructive to notice how our Lord responds to the disciples' desire. And: 1. *He shows them how very small their faith is.* His statement implies that it was less than a grain of mustard seed, for, if they had even so little a measure of genuine faith, they could remove any difficulty out of their path. Even a sycamine tree might be plucked up by the roots, or any difficulty which such an obstacle would represent, and be cast by faith into the sea. The first lesson we have got to learn is how small our faith is, and then it will soon increase. 2. *He impresses on them the cultivation of a sense of their own unprofitableness to God.* He likens them to a farm-servant who, when he has finished in the field, comes home and is then put to wait at table on his lord. His work is never done. He turns from one occupation to another; and only laments at the close that he could not do more and better. Now, this sense of unprofitableness really arises out of the magnificence of the Christian ideal. The Christian system sets before us such incomparable excellency, that we are always coming short of it. All Christian progress is just conditioned upon this sense of unprofitableness. Our faith will grow exceedingly when this sense of unprofitableness has been secured and is maintained. Of course, this teaching of our Lord is quite consistent with the reward promised in his grace, of "Well done, good and faithful servant." The servant looks at his labours in the light of strict justice, and acknowledges his shortcoming. The Master looks at them in the light of grace and love, and rewards them with overflowing bounty. Even when receiving the reward at last, it will be with surprise, and with the consciousness that we have been but unprofitable servants.

IV. THE DISCIPLES ARE INSTRUCTED AT THE SAME TIME REGARDING HUMAN INGRATITUDE. (Vers. 11—19.) It so happened that ten lepers cross the Saviour's path, and their cry for mercy meets with immediate response. But their cure is given on their way to the priests, who could only give them a certificate of cure. The sense of cure came upon the ten, we may believe, at the same time. But only one, and he a Samaritan, returned to express his gratitude. The other nine, all Jews, passed on to the priest with a joyful sense of cure, but little sense of gratitude. It was such ingratitude as called for the animadversion of Jesus, while the Samaritan's gratitude led our Lord to say his faith hath made him whole. It seems clear that he became attached to Jesus in a way the others did not. The expression of his gratitude led to an assurance of faith. Now, this was a wholesome lesson for the disciples, as it is also for us. How many blessings have we all got from the hands of Christ, for which we have returned no thanks at all! And, if we have been ungrateful to our Lord, should we not put up with a good deal of ingratitude? It is a sense of personal ingratitude which will stimulate the grace within us, and make us less surprised when we are the objects of ingratitude on the part of others we have befriended. In this plain and practical fashion our Lord stimulated and strengthened the graces of his disciples, and indicates how our graces may be stimulated likewise.—R. M. E.

Vers. 20—37.—*The advent of the kingdom and the King.* Jesus was on journey to Jerusalem when the ingratitude of the nine lepers, just noticed, took place, and this gave rise to speculation as to the near approach of his kingdom. His enemies, the Pharisees, put the sarcastic question when the kingdom of God should come, as much as to say, "We have heard of it long; we should like to see it."[1] This leads our Lord to unfold the nature of his kingdom's advent and of his own.

I. HIS KINGDOM COMES IN THE HEARTS OF MEN. (Vers. 20, 21.) The characteristic of worldly kingdoms has always been *ostentation*. They try to impress the senses by noisy advents, brag, advertisement, the blare of bugle and roll of drum. And some think that there is nothing worth talking about which can come in any milder way. The Jews expected a kingdom of God to supersede the Roman, and that its advent would be seen in the defeat and expulsion of the conquerors of Canaan. But, no; the kingdom was coming in men's hearts; it was there it had its sphere and home. 1. *How superficial is the sovereignty which is not founded in the heart!* This is the world's experience daily. The outward sovereignty is a name and based on fear. 2. *How noble is the sovereignty which is based upon people's hearts!* It is here Jesus reigns. We love him. We would die for him. Thus his kingdom progresses wherever a heart is touched by Christ's love. His triumph is over the selfishness of mankind. He conquers them by self-sacrificing love.[2]

II. THE KING HIMSELF IS TO COME AS SUDDENLY AS THE LIGHTNING-FLASH. (Vers. 22—24.) He is not to give warning of his approach. There will be no need to go here or there under the impression that he has come quietly and privately, to prepare for his public manifestation; but suddenly like the lightning-flash, and publicly like its heaven-enlightening beam, is he to come for judgment. Hence the awful suddenness of his advent is distinctly implied. He will give no premonitory warnings, but overwhelmingly sudden and awful will be his approach. No wonder in such circumstances that many shall desire to see one of the days of the Son of man, one of those seasons of quiet philanthropy such as the Saviour was now leading among men. The Pharisees were mistaking altogether the significance of his present mission.

III. THE RESULTS OF THE PRESENT MISAPPREHENSIONS. (Vers. 25—30.) 1. The *first* sad result will be the rejection and martyrdom of Jesus (ver. 25). Misapprehending the significance of his meek and lowly philanthropic life, his generation united in rejecting him, and secured his crucifixion on the tree. They would not have the King when actually among them in flesh and blood. 2. Men will act like the *antediluvians* and *Sodomites* up to the very time of our Lord's advent. A sense of *carnal security* characterized these sinners. They thought in Noah's day that no harm would overtake them. There was no sign of the Deluge except Noah's precautions against it, and they would not act upon such signs. In Sodom it was the same. The inhabitants thought no change would come over their selfish, sensual dream. But the Deluge came, and the fire and brimstone descended, notwithstanding. So will it be with the advent of Christ—it will come as a sudden, unexpected judgment upon many. And this carnal security is a present danger with many. They fancy they are safe, that nothing will interfere with their security; but the Saviour makes his advent suddenly, and they are overwhelmed.

IV. THE REALITIES OF THE ADVENT. (Vers. 31—37.) Now, the truth is clearly brought out that some shall be saved and others lost at the advent. 1. Let us look at *the lost*. They are brought under our notice here in several ways. Thus *Lot's wife is taken as a type of the lost*. Now, we know that she was lost through looking longingly back to her worldly things. God, by his angels, had set the family's faces towards the mountains and himself. Were they prepared to take him and his favour as their portion, and give up all their property in Sodom? If they looked longingly behind them, it would show that the world was still more to them than God. The poor wife could not resist the temptation, and so she was changed into a pillar of salt. She is, then, the type of those who are almost saved, but worldliness gets the better of them, and they are lost. Again, the lost ones are represented as *food for eagles* (ver. 37). This brings out the *corruption* characterizing them. They have become moral carrion, which only the eagles can consume. There is, doubtless, a reference to the Roman invasion under Titus, and to the destruction of corrupt Jerusalem. The Roman armies were God's scavengers to destroy a corrupt people. This was one way in which Christ made an advent to judgment. Lastly, we have the lost described as those who are *continually seeking to save themselves* (ver. 33). Those whose one aim in life is self-

[1] Robertson's 'Human Race and other Sermons,' p. 63.
[2] Cf. Liddon's 'Church Troubles,' serm. i.

preservation, the saving of themselves at every turn, who think of self as the supreme concern, are only *losing themselves.* The curious paradox is that those who save themselves at every turn lose themselves; while those who do not count their lives dear, but Christ's concern as supreme, find themselves safe at last. Let us see to it, therefore, that we are neither worldly minded, nor corrupt, nor given up to selfishness, else we are among the lost. 2. But let us look at the *saved ones.* These are those who have kept Christ before them as their Lord and Master, whose interests should be supreme (ver. 33). They value him more than life, and so he saves them. The nature of salvation is thus plainly unfolded. The saved ones are those with whom Christ is all in all. They prefer him to everything else. The instinct of self-preservation has in them given place to an instinct to preserve the honour and promote the kingdom of the Master. And those who have trusted him and honoured him so thoroughly shall find that he will not disappoint them. Let us wait for his appearing, then, and *love* it; and when it flashes across the world, we shall be allowed to escape the judgments that come upon the earth, and to stand before the Son of man.—R. M. E.

EXPOSITION.

CHAPTER XVIII.

Vers. 1—14.—*The Lord speaks the two parables on prayer—the importunate widow, and the Pharisee and publican.*

Ver. 1.—**And he spake a parable unto them to this end, that men ought always to pray, and not to faint.** The formula ἔλεγε δὲ καί, literally, "and he spake also," calls attention to the fact that the parable-teaching immediately to follow was a continuation of what had preceded. Indeed, the connection between the first of the two parables, which urges restless continued prayer, and the picture which the Lord had just drawn of men's state of utter forgetfulness of God, is obvious. "The Son of man has been rejected; he has gone from view; the masses are plunged in gross worldliness; men of God are become as rare as, in the days of Abraham, they were in Sodom. What, then, is the position of the Church? That of a widow whose only weapon is incessant prayer. It is only by means of this intense concentration that faith will be preserved. But such is precisely the disposition which Jesus fears may not be found even in the Church at his return" (Godet).

Ver. 2.—**There was in a city a judge, which feared not God, neither regarded man.** Probably enough the whole scene was a sketch from life; under such a rule as that of Herod Antipas there were, doubtless, judges of the character here portrayed.

Ver. 3.—**And there was a widow in that city; and she came unto him, saying, Avenge me of mine adversary.** The petitioner was a woman and a widow, the latter being in the East a synonym for helplessness. With no one to defend her or plead her cause, this widow was ever a prey to the covetous. Not once nor twice in the noble generous words of the chivalrous Hebrew prophets we find this readiness on the part of those in power to neglect, if not to oppress these helpless widow-women, sternly commented upon. So in Isaiah we read (i. 23), "They judge not the fatherless, neither doth the cause of the widow come unto them." While Jesus (Matt. xxiii. 14) includes this cowardly sin among the evil deeds of the rulers of the Israel of his day: "Ye devour widows' houses, and for a pretence make long prayer." A more desperate situation, as regards any hope of obtaining the object of her earnest prayer, could not well be pictured—a careless, corrupt judge of the lawless Herod period for the tribunal in Israel, and a poor helpless widow for the suppliant. The forlorn woman of the parable represents the Church or people of God in dire straits, overborne by an unbelieving world and seemingly forgotten even of their God. The story is a reminder that there is hope even in that extreme situation sketched in the parable, if the petitioner only continues persistent in her prayer. The argument which lies on the surface of the parable-teaching is obvious: if such a judge will in the end listen to the prayer of a suppliant for whom he cares nothing, will not God surely listen to the repeated prayer of a suppliant whom he loves with a deep, enduring love? Such is the argument of the story. Importunity, it seems to say, must inevitably triumph. But underlying this there is much deep teaching, of which, perhaps, the most important item is that it insists upon the urgent necessity for us all to continue in prayer, never fainting in this exercise though no answer seems to come. "The whole life of the faithful," as Origen once grandly said, "should be one great connected prayer." That is the real moral of the story; but there are a number of minor bits of Divine teaching contained in this curious parable setting, as we shall see. ***Avenge me of mine adversary.*** We must not suppose that mere vengeance in the vulgar sense is what the widow prayed for; *that* would be of no use to her; all she wanted was that the judge should deliver her from the oppression which her adversary exercised over her, no doubt in keeping from her the heritage to which she was lawfully entitled. Of course, the granting her prayer would involve loss and possibly punishment to her fraudulent oppressor.

Ver. 7.—**And shall not God avenge his own elect, which cry day and night unto him?** The Master tells us that God permits suffering among his servants, long after they have begun to pray for deliverance. But we are counselled here to cry day and night unto him, and, though there be no sign of reply, our prayers shall be treasured up before him, and in his own good time they will be answered. **Though he bear long with them.** With whom does God bear long? With the wrong-doers, whose works and words oppress and make life heavy and grievous to the servants of God; with *these* who have no claim to consideration will God bear long. And this announcement gives us some clue to the meaning of the delay we often experience before we get an answer to many of our prayers. The prayer is heard, but God, in the exercise of mercy and forbearance, has dealings with the oppressors. It were easy for the Almighty to grant an immediate answer, but only at the cost often of visiting some of the oppressors with immediate punishment, and this is not his way of working. God bears long before his judgments swift and terrible are sent forth. This has ever been his way of working with individuals as with nations. Was it not thus, for instance, that he acted towards Egypt and her Pharaohs during the long period of the bitter Hebrew bondage? We who would be God's servants must be content to wait God's time, and, while waiting, patiently go on pleading, sure that in the end "God will avenge his own elect, which cry day and night unto him."

Ver. 8.—**I tell you that he will avenge them speedily.** "Non *bientôt*, mais *bien vite*" (Godet). It means that God will act in accordance with his servant's prayer, not soon, but suddenly; sure and sudden at the crisis the action of Divine providence comes at the last "as a thief in the night." **Nevertheless when the Son of man cometh, shall he find faith on the earth?** These difficult words seem to point at least to a fear lest, the second coming being long delayed, true faith would have died out of the hearts even of the godly. Such a *fear* might be Jesus'; for we know, from his own lips, that to him, while on earth and wearing the body of humiliation, the day and hour of the second advent was not known. Was not our Lord speaking with the same sad onlook in his parable of the virgins, when he said, "they *all* slumbered and slept," wise virgins as well as foolish (Matt. xxv. 5)? "It is often the case that God's action as a Deliverer is delayed until his people have ceased to hope for deliverance. So it was with Israel in Egypt; so was it with her again in Babylon. 'Grief was calm and hope was dead' among the exiles when the word came that they were to return to their own land; and then the news seemed too good to be true. They were 'like them that dream' when they heard the good tidings. This method of Divine action—long delay followed by a sudden crisis—so frankly recognized by Christ, is one to which we find it hard to reconcile ourselves. These parables help us so far, but they do not settle everything. They contain no philosophy of Divine delay, but simply a proclamation of the fact, and an assurance that, in spite of delay, all will go well at the last with those who trust in God" (Professor Bruce).

Ver. 9.—**And he spake this parable.** With this parable, "the Pharisee and the publican," St. Luke concludes his memories of the last journeyings toward Jerusalem. The incidents which directly follow took place close to Jerusalem; and here St. Luke's narrative rejoins that of SS. Matthew and Mark. No note of time or place assists us in defining exactly the period when the Master spoke this teaching; some time, however, in these last journeyings, that is, in the closing months of the public ministry, the parable in question was certainly spoken.

Ver. 10.—**Two men went up into the temple to pray; the one a Pharisee, and the other a publican.** This parable constitutes an important chapter in Jesus' apology or defence—if we may dare use the word—for loving the sinful, for consorting with publicans and sinners. It tells men, in very simple language, how they are saved; not by works of righteousness which they have done, but of grace; in other words, by God's free mercy. Jewish religious society in the time of our Lord, as represented by the great Pharisee sect, totally misunderstood this Divine truth. They claimed salvation as a right on two grounds: (1) because they belonged to the chosen race; (2) because they rigidly and minutely obeyed the precepts of a singular code of laws, many of them devised by themselves and their fathers. Upon these two grounds they claimed salvation, that is, eternal blissful life. Not content with this claim of their own, they condemned, with a sweeping, harsh condemnation, all other peoples, and even those of their own race who neglected rigidly to observe the ordinances and ritual of a law framed in great measure in the schools of their own rabbis. Two extreme instances are here chosen—a rigid, exclusive, self-satisfied member of the religious society of Israel; and a Jewish officer of the hated Roman government, who knew little or nothing of the Law, but yet who longed after a higher life, and craved for an inward peace which he evidently was far from possessing. These two, the Pharisee and the publican, both went up to God's holy house, the temple, with a view of drawing near to the eternal King.

Ver. 11.—**The Pharisee stood and prayed thus with himself, God, I thank thee that I am not as other men are.** How closely drawn from the life is this picture of a Pharisee will be seen by a comparison of the prayer here with the prayer of a rabbi contained in the Talmud. When Rabbi Nechounia Ben Hakana left his school, he used to say, "I thank thee, O Eternal, my God, for having given me part with those who attend this school instead of running through the shops. I rise early like them, but it is to study the Law, not for futile ends. I take trouble as they do, but I shall be rewarded, and they will not. We run alike, but I for the future life, while they will only arrive at the pit of destruction" (from the treatise 'Berachôth').

Ver. 12.—**I fast twice in the week.** There was no such precept in the Law of Moses. There only a single fast-day in the year was enjoined, *the Day of Atonement* (Lev. xvi. 29). By the time of Zechariah the prophet (viii. 19) the one fast-day had grown into four. But this fasting twice every week was a burthensome observance imposed in the later oral Law. Thursday and Monday were the appointed fasting-days, because tradition related how, on those days, Moses ascended and descended from Sinai. Compare the Talmud (treatise 'Bava Khama,' fol. 82. 1). **I give tithes of all that I possess.** Here, again, the Mosaic ordinance only enjoined tithes of corn, wine, oil, and cattle. The later rabbinic schools directed that everything should be tithed, down to the mint and anise and cummin. And so this poor deluded Pharisee dreamed he had earned his eternal salvation, *forgetting* that the tithes he so prided himself on paying were merely tithes of goods of which he was steward for a little time, tithes, too, given back to their real Owner—God. Could this be counted *a claim* upon God? He boasted, too, that he was no extortioner: did he forget how often he had coveted? He was no adulterer: what of those wicked thoughts which so often found a home in his heart? He rejoiced that he was not like the publican and others of that same class: did he think of the sore temptations to which these and the like were exposed, and from which he was free? He gloried in his miserable tithes and offerings: did he remember how really mean and selfish he was? did he think of his luxury and abundance, and of the want and misery of thousands round him? did his poor pitiful generosity constitute *a claim* to salvation? All this and more is shrined in the exquisite story of Jesus, who shows men that salvation—if it be given to men at all—must be given entirely as a free gift of God.

Ver. 13.—**And the publican, standing afar off, would not lift up so much as his eyes unto heaven, but smote upon his breast, saying, God be merciful to me a sinner!** Utterly sad and heart-broken, the publican neither recounts nor thinks of good kind deeds done, or special sins committed; no thoughts came into that poor heart, such as, "I have done some fair deeds; I am not altogether vile and sinful." He felt that with him evil so far overbalanced good that he could make no plea for himself, and yet he, too, longed for salvation, so he threw himself wholly upon God's mercy and love in his sad prayer, "God be merciful to me *the* sinner!" for so the words should be rendered. Different to the Pharisee, who thought himself better than his neighbours, this man, in his sad humility, evidently thought other men better than himself, but still he so trusted in God that he felt even for him, the sinner, there might be mercy.

Ver. 14.—**I tell you, this man went down to his house justified rather than the other: for every one that exalteth himself shall be abased; and he that humbleth himself shall be exalted.** And the publican was right; there was mercy even for him, all sin-stained though he was. The words with which the Lord closes his teaching are full of comfort. *That* prayer he tells us was heard and granted. The "I tell you" of Jesus here means, as Stier well puts it, "*I tell you*, for I know, I have seen, I have heard all this in many such a case, and in many such prayers." With this example of prayer favourably heard, there is surely no sin-burthened soul on earth who may not take courage in seeking God's face. One great object of this parable, we may believe, was to suggest some such thoughts, to embolden sorrowful, heart-broken sinners simply to go to God, trusting in his great pitying love. It should not be forgotten that the publican's prayer was heard *in the temple;* a silent approval seems given to his having thus sought out the appointed consecrated place of prayer.

Vers. 15—30.—*Jesus and the children. The young ruler refuses to give up his riches. The Lord speaks of the reward of them that leave all for his sake.*

Ver. 15.—**And they brought unto him also**

The poor, indeed, with all their trials, stand fairer for the kingdom than do their envied richer brothers and sisters.

Ver. 25.—**For it is easier for a camel to go through a needle's eye, than for a rich man to enter into the kingdom of God.** This simile, taken in its plain and obvious sense, appears to many an exaggerated one, and various explanations have been suggested to soften it down. The best is found in Lord Nugent's 'Lands Classical and Sacred,' who mentions that in some modern Syrian towns the narrow gate for foot-passengers at the side of the larger gate by which waggons, camels, and other beasts of burden enter the city, is known as the "needle's eye." It is, however, very uncertain whether this term for the little gate was known in ancient times. But the simile was evidently a common one among the Jews. The Talmud, for instance, gives us the parallel phrase of an elephant passing through a needle's eye. The Koran repeats the very words of the Gospel. It is the object of the proverb to express human impossibility.

"I would ride the camel,
Yea leap him flying, through the needle's eye
As easily as such a pampered soul
Could pass the narrow gate."
(Southey.)

It seems strange that the three evangelists, SS. Matthew, Mark, and Luke, who tell this story of the young questioner and the Master's conversation with him, do not mention his name. And yet he must have been a conspicuous personage in the society of the time. First of all, his riches were evidently remarkable. One account tells us that he was "very rich." Two of the Gospels mention his "great possessions." St. Luke tells us that he was "a ruler." He was, then, certainly a very wealthy Jew holding a high official position, not improbably a member of the Sanhedrin council. Why is he nameless in the three Gospels? Dean Plumptre has a most interesting theory that the young wealthy ruler was *Lazarus of Bethany*. He bases his hypothesis upon the following data: He begins by stating that "there is one other case in the first two Gospels which presents similar phenomena. In the narrative of the supper at Bethany, St. Matthew and St. Mark record the passionate affection which expressed itself in pouring the precious ointment of spikenard upon our Lord's head as the act of 'a woman' (Matt. xxvi. 7; Mark xiv. 3), leaving her unnamed. In John xii. 3 we find that the woman was Mary, the sister of Lazarus. The train of thought thus suggested points to the supposition that here also there may have been reasons for suppressing in the records a name which was familiar to the narrator. What if the young ruler were Lazarus himself? The points of agreement are sufficiently numerous to warrant the conjecture. The household of Lazarus, as the spikenard ointment shows, were of the wealthier class. The friends who came to comfort the bereaved sisters were themselves, in St. John's language, 'of the Jews,' *i.e.* of the chief rulers (John xi. 19). The young ruler was obviously a Pharisee, and the language of Martha (John xi. 24) shows that she, too, believed in eternal life and the resurrection of the dead. The answer to the young ruler, 'One thing thou lackest' (as given by St. Mark and St. Luke), is almost identical with that to Martha, 'One thing is needful' (ch. x. 42). In such a case, of course, nothing can be attained beyond conjectural inference; but the present writer must avow his belief that the coincidences in this case are such as to carry the evidence to a very high point of probability."

Ver. 26.—**And they that heard it said, Who then can be saved?** This hard saying appeared to the disciples to be terribly comprehensive in its scope; the longing to be rich was confined to no one class or order, it was the universal passion. Were *they* guiltless here? Were *they* not looking for riches and glory in the Messianic kingdom of the immediate future? And of all peoples the Jews in every age have been credited with the blindest devotion to this idol, wealth. In St. Mark (x. 24) we find certainly an explanatory statement: "How hard is it for them that *trust* in riches to enter into the kingdom of God!" But this explanatory and softened statement is not found in the older authorities; these read instead, in Mark x. 24, simply the words, "How hard is it to enter the kingdom of God!" Hard alike, the Master meant, for rich and poor, though harder for the former.

Ver. 27.—**And he said, The things which are impossible with men are possible with God.** Yes, impossible, the Divine Teacher repeated, from a man's point of view; impossible from the platform of legal obedience on which the young ruler (ver. 21) had taken his stand, or the Pharisee in his prayer (vers. 11, 12); but it was not impossible with God. *He* might give this salvation as a perfectly free gift, utterly undeserved, perfectly unmerited, as he did to the *prodigal son* when he returned, or to the *publican* when he beat his breast in almost voiceless mourning, or still more conspicuously, not many days later, to the *penitent thief* dying on the cross.

Ver. 28.—**Then Peter said, Lo, we have left all, and followed thee.** Again the question of Peter, evidently acting as spokesman of the twelve, is repeated by the first three evangelists. Strangely faithful in their accounts of their own dealings with their adored Master, they never veil or hide any human weakness or error of their own which led to an important bit of teaching from their Lord. Now, in this place, they, in the person of Peter, gave utterance to a very worldly, but a very natural, thought. The ruler had failed when the test was applied to him; he was a conspicuous example of failure in the rich to enter the kingdom. But *they* had not failed when the test had been applied to them; they had given all up for his sake: what would be their reward?

Vers. 29, 30.—**And he said unto them, Verily I say unto you, There is no man that hath left house, or parents, or brethren, or wife, or children, for the kingdom of God's sake, who shall not receive manifold more in this present time, and in the world to come life everlasting.** Evidently, from the reports of the three evangelists, the reply of Jesus was a lengthy one, and contained much deep teaching. St. Luke only gives us, however, one section, so to speak, of the great discourse which followed upon Peter's question. Here and in St. Mark Peter and the twelve receive a quiet rebuke in this general promise. The Master seems to say, "My promises are not especially to you, my first followers, but to all who, not for any selfish hope of recompense or reward, but for the kingdom of God's sake, give up what they hold dearest; there will be real, true happiness for them even in this world, and in the world to come unspeakable joy will be their portion; theirs will be the life that knows no ending." St. Mark adds, with rare truth, that the happiness which his faithful are to enjoy in this world will be accompanied *with persecutions*. It is the same beautiful thought which the Master had put out before, only the gem now is set in different words. "Blessed are they which are persecuted for righteousness' sake: for theirs is the kingdom of heaven" (Matt. v. 10; see, too, vers. 11, 12). St. Matthew deals especially with another division of the Lord's discourse. Here Jesus speaks of the future of the twelve; and, looking forward to the generally noble and self-devoted lives he saw these would live, he tells them of the great destiny surely reserved for them if they remained faithful to the end. But even here, in his words, "the first shall be last" (Matt. xix. 30), and still more pointedly in the parable of the labourers which followed (Matt. xx. 1—16), he warned these devoted but often mistaken men of the danger of self-complacency. It was only because he foresaw that in these really great ones this spirit would in the end be overcome (at least in eleven of them) that he made the grand and mysterious promise of Matt. xix. 28.

The narrative here, in the three synoptical Gospels, is not continuous; at this point there is a break. There is little doubt but that the sickness and death of Lazarus of Bethany, and the summons of the sisters to Jesus, took place about this period. The three synoptical evangelists are silent here for reasons we have discussed elsewhere.

Between vers. 30 and 31 there probably should be inserted the hasty journey to Bethany. The Master was not far when the news of his friend's death reached him. Immediately after the miracle there appears to have been a meeting of the Sanhedrin, when it was decided to put Jesus to death, though not during the ensuing Passover, with such precautions as were possible. The terrible decision became known. Jesus then retired to Ephraim, an obscure village about twenty miles from the city. Here a very short time was spent in absolute retirement and seclusion. But the Passover Feast was nigh at hand. In company with some of the crowded pilgrim caravans, and secure under their protection till his last few days of work were accomplished, Jesus journeys to Jerusalem At this point the three synoptical Gospels take up the story again. The eleventh chapter of St. John fills up this gap in the connected story.

Vers. 31—42.—*Jesus again tells them of his Passion. The healing of the blind at Jericho.*

Ver. 31.—**Then he took unto him the twelve, and said unto them.** St. Mark (x. 32) prefaces this announcement with the words, "And they were in the way going up to Jerusalem; and Jesus went before them: and they were amazed; and as they followed, they were afraid." There was something unusual, evidently, in the manner and behaviour of the Master; silently, wrapped up in his own lofty meditations, he strode on in front of the company of his followers. A feeling of awe and fear stole over them as they watched the silent Master with the shadow of the coming cross falling, perhaps, across his countenance. Much had happened lately: the teaching growing more and more solemn as the end drew near; the raising of Lazarus; the intense enmity of the great men of the nation; the fixed determination to put the Master to death; his short retirement; then the announcement that he was going up to face his enemies at the great feast in Jerusalem; and now alone and silent he walked at their head. What was coming? thought the twelve and their friends. He read their thoughts, and, calling them round him, told them what was about to happen. **Behold, we go up to Jerusalem, and all things that are written by the prophets concerning the Son of man shall be accomplished.**

Vers. 32, 33.—**For he shall be delivered unto the Gentiles, and shall be mocked, and spitefully entreated, and spitted on: and they shall scourge him, and put him to death: and the third day he shall rise again.** The outlines of the Passion he had sketched for the disciples before on two occasions, but never so clearly as now. He even tells them the manner of his end, and how his own countrymen would give him up to the Romans, and how these Gentiles, amidst every conceivable circumstance of horror, would do him to death. And the Master closed his dread revelation by predicting his speedy resurrection.

Ver. 34.—**And they understood none of these things: and this saying was hid from them, neither knew they the things which were spoken.** But they listened all dazed and confused; they could not take it in, neither the shame of the death of their loved Leader, nor the glory of the Resurrection which was to follow immediately after. They could not persuade themselves that the hopes of an earthly Messianic glory in which they were to share must positively be given up. "We must learn to *love* Divine truths before we can understand them," said Pascal. "Toward everything which is contrary to natural desire," wrote Riggenbach (in Godet), "there is produced in the heart a blindness, which nothing but a miracle can heal."

Ver. 35.—**And it came to pass, that as he was come nigh unto Jericho.** Jericho was once called "the City of Palms," afterwards "the City of Perfumes." It was about eighteen miles from Jerusalem. In the Herodian times it became a popular resort, owing to the affection the great Herod entertained for it. Its palm-groves and balsam-gardens were a present from Antony to Cleopatra. Herod the Great bought them from her, and made it one of his royal cities, and adorned it with many stately buildings, and eventually died there. It is now a miserable village. **A certain blind man sat by the wayside begging.** An apparent discrepancy exists in the three accounts given of this act of our Lord. St. Luke speaks of one blind man who was healed as our Lord was *entering* the town. St. Matthew and St. Mark mention that the miracle took place as our Lord was leaving the place, and St. Matthew mentions that two blind men received their sight at the bidding of Jesus. Several solutions of this little difficulty have been proposed. Perhaps the most probable is that the sufferers were sitting near the town gates as the Lord entered. They, hearing who was passing by, eagerly called to him for help. Surrounded by the crowd, he probably did not hear the cry, or possibly wished to test the earnestness of their faith by allowing them to wait. They follow him through the place, and in the open space outside the city they attract his attention, and he heals them. Or, in the words of Dr. Morrison, "the case seems to have begun as he entered into the city, but it culminated in all likelihood as he departed." A later explanation, apparently preferred by Godet and Farrar, is that, as Josephus and Eusebius distinguish between the old and the new Jericho—the old town on the ancient site, and the new Herodian town which had sprung up at a little distance from it—the blind man might, according to some traditions, have been healed as Jesus was leaving old Jericho; according to others, as he was entering the new town. The fact of SS. Mark and Luke only mentioning one blind man is easily explained. There was one evidently (as we shall suggest further on), a well-known character in Christian story—Bartimæus. Two of the evangelists recorded his cure, as being of special interest to the Church, leaving the second among the numberless unrecorded miracles of healing of Jesus. ***A certain blind man.*** St. Mark names him Bartimæus. It may be inferred that, as St. Mark specially names him, this man was well known in early Christian story. We know that after the cure he joined the company as one of the followers of Jesus.

Ver. 37.—**And they told him, that Jesus of Nazareth passeth by.** The Lord's name was by this time a household word in Palestine, and among the sick and afflicted a most precious and welcome sound.

Ver. 38.—**Jesus, thou Son of David.** This form of address distinctly shows that the idea that the Rabbi of Nazareth, the great Wonder-worker, the wise kind Teacher, was in some way or other the long looked-for Deliverer, was now taking possession of the people's mind. "Son of David" was distinctly a Messianic salutation.

Ver. 39.—**And they which went before rebuked him.** It must be remembered that our Lord was surrounded by a great host of Passover pilgrims, by many of whom he was reverenced as "some great One," perhaps the King Messiah. Such a low wailing cry on the part of a blind beggar, asking to be brought into the presence of him they wondered at and admired and hoped so much from, seemed a great presumption: hence these rebukes.

Vers. 40, 41.—**And Jesus stood, and commanded him to be brought unto him.** St. Mark here adds, "And they call the blind man, saying unto him, Be of good comfort, rise; he calleth thee." These kindly sympathizing words of the disciples to the beggar, doing their loving Master's behest, were one of Peter's own memories of the scene under the walls of Jericho. **And when he was come near, he asked him, saying, What wilt thou that I shall do unto thee?** Many besides the governor Pilate, who a few days later put the query to him, "**Art thou a King, then?**" during this period must have often asked silently the same question. We shall soon see the whole multitude carried away with enthusiasm, giving him a royal welcome as he entered the city. Here, with a majesty truly royal, as Godet well remarks, Jesus seems to open up to the beggar the treasures of Divine power in "What wilt thou that I shall do unto thee?" and to give him, as it were, *carte blanche*. **And he said, Lord, that I may receive my sight.** There is a curious variation in the terms of this request in that ancient Syriac Version known as "the Curetonian," in the account of St. Matthew, "That our eyes might be opened, and we shall see thee."

Ver. 42.—**And Jesus said unto him, Receive thy sight.** "Magnifique aumône du Christ" (Pressensé). **Thy faith hath saved thee.** The American Longfellow has united the cry for mercy of the blind, the kindly sympathizing words of the disciples (reported by St. Mark), and the gift of Jesus Christ, in his exquisite poem of 'Blind Bartimæus.'

"Those mighty voices three—
Ἰησοῦ, ἐλέησόν με!
Θάρσει, ἔγειρε· φωνεῖ σε!
Ἡ πίστις σου σέσωκέ σε!"

HOMILETICS.

Vers. 1—8.—*The importunate widow.* The importance which Christ attaches to prayer is evidenced by the frequency with which he recurs to it in his teaching, and the variety of his illustration of its duty and blessedness. The sermon on the mount enforces it as one of the cardinal virtues of the perfect disciple. In the eleventh chapter of this Gospel both the manner after which we are to pray, and the assurance on which faith should rest, are presented. Again, towards the close of the ministry we are introduced to two parables bearing on it, each with the lesson which the Master would teach clearly defined. The former of these two has this as its object (ver. 1), "that men ought always," *i.e.* unremittingly, "to pray, and not to faint;" *i.e.* not to be scared by hindrances, or induced to desist by the sickness which comes through hope deferred. The structure of the parable is very simple. There is a judge who neither fears God nor regards man. A poor widow, who has been wronged, claims his interposition. He pays no regard to her suit. But she importunes him; day by day she presents herself, until, though he has no regard to the justice of her case, he listens to her pleading in order that he may be relieved of her solicitations. If man, unjust and selfish, thus yields to unceasing prayer, how much more, argues Jesus, will he, who is the Absolutely Just and the Infinitely Loving, yield to the cry, day and night, of his own people! Notice three features in the delineation.

I. God in contrast with the human avenger. The latter consults his own ease. He acts in mere selfishness. The Eternal Righteousness is ever consistent with itself. "To this man will I look, even to him that is humble and contrite in spirit."

II. God's people in contrast with the widow. They resemble her in one thing—in the sense of need, of helplessness. But the widow stands in no special relation to the judge. God's people are his own elect. They are part of the blood-bought, ransomed family. "As many as are led by the Spirit of God, they are the sons of God;" and "the secret of the Lord is with them that fear him." Each of them is in the most intimate relation to the Eternal. "I am poor and needy, yet the Lord thinketh on me."

III. The long-suffering of God in contrast with the long-suffering of man. The long-suffering of man is in consequence of the indisposition to act; if in the end it is dispelled, if the action after a lengthened interval follows, it is only that repose may be purchased by the effort, and that the mind may be free to carry out its unloving projects. God bears long with his elect, not because he is unwilling to bless, but that he may draw them closer to himself, that he may prepare them for fuller measures of blessing, that he may chasten their wills into completer union with his will, and so ultimately bestow the higher gifts of his Fatherhood. When they cry, there is much that needs to be corrected; they desire only what they regard as the best or what will relieve them from some pressure. There is still a distance between their will and his; he delays the answer that they may be brought in true self-emptiness to his heart, and that, their faith being purified, they may be enriched out of his exceeding abundance. So the Lord bore long with Job; in him patience had its perfect work; he learned to "abhor himself, and repent in dust and ashes;" he was "attuned also to finer issues" by the charity which led him to pray for his friends. And the Lord turned his captivity when his prayer was thus disciplined and enlarged, and he received "twice as much as he had before." So, too, the woman of Canaan cried, and "the Lord answered her not a word" (Matt. xv.). Then came she "and *worshipped* him." She bowed her whole soul before him, and she received the reward of the "great faith." "Therefore," says the Lord, "*faint not.*" "Pray without ceasing." The heavens above are not brass. There is a flexibility in the ordering of the universe which admits of the answer, direct and real, to prayer. "More things are wrought by prayer than the world dreams of." "O thou that hearest prayer, unto thee shall all flesh come." The Lord anticipates a decadence in the belief as to the efficacy of prayer, for he adds a "nevertheless" (ver. 8). Is this loss of faith true of the Church and of Christians in this day?

Vers. 9—14.—*The Pharisee and the publican.* The lesson as to prayer is continued. The parable which follows exhibits the spirit and conditions of effectual prayer. Mark the two features of the audience specially addressed. He speaks to certain (1) who trusted in themselves as being righteous; (2) who, as the outcome of this trust, despised others. He spoke in the previous parable of "God's own elect." Now, the Pharisees accounted themselves the elect of God. They were puffed up by this confidence. They regarded themselves as the righteous, who kept the Law, both oral and written. And, indeed, they were most scrupulous as to every requirement; nay, they were willing to burden themselves with minute and vexatious observances. And the sin which beset them was the pride shadowed forth in one of the two who went up to pray. As the illustration of the elect, the Lord chooses a tax-gatherer, one of a hated class, for whom, in Pharisee-thought, there was no place in the kingdom of heaven. The instruction is suitable to every time. Pharisee separation and pride are features to be recognized in the Church of this day, as they were prominent in the Jewish Church of our Lord's day. Ever to be studied is the antithesis—*respectability* in the Pharisee, non-*respectability* in the publican. See the two. The one, with his broad phylactery, his supercilious bearing, his Pharisaism reflected in every feature of his sallow countenance, as with measured step he proceeds to the temple. In its inner court he stands erect; he arranges his prayer-robe, he looks around, the face darkened by a scowl as he observes the publican in a distant corner of the sacred building. And then he lifts his eye. No prayer trembles in any tone; no pleading escapes through any word; he "speaks with himself" rather than with God. It is a soliloquy, a self-gratified recital of his own piety. If he says, "God, I thank thee" (vers. 11, 12), it is not for any grace that he has received, it is not in acknowledging that only through a higher mercy and strength he is what he is; nay, with something of familiarity in the address, he bids the Almighty join him in admiration of his virtues, on account of which he is lifted above other men. Only by certain averages of his own striking does he measure his excellence, the climax being reached, when there comes the contemptuous "even as this publican." Oh, what a superior person, to be sure! With what satisfaction must highest Heaven regard one who fasted twice in the week, and gave tithes of all he possessed! The other, with hurried gait, as one intent only on pouring out his heart before God, takes his place far off. He has no wish to disturb the complacency of his fellow-worshipper. He claims nothing; self-assertion in every form is absent from his heart. The only presence with him is the Holy One of Israel. Beneath the vision of his holiness all that is of the earth must keep silence. He will not even lift up his eyes. He has not much to record; human righteousness even is but a filthy rag when held up to the light of that Perfect Holiness. And as for him, oh, there can be only the one prayer, "God be merciful to me a sinner!" (ver. 13). He is overpowered with the conviction of sin. His only refuge is the mercy of the Eternal. "I tell you" (ver. 14), concludes Christ, "this man is manifested to be one of God's elect. He, not the other, returns to his house the one accepted and justified." The parable is most suggestive.

I. IT IS THE EXPOSURE OF SPIRITUAL PRIDE IN ITS ROOT AND FRUIT. Its root, the measurement of self by "other men." God is not in the thought. The song of the seraphim, "Holy, holy, holy, Lord God of hosts," sounds faintly in the ear. The mind is not occupied with him and his holiness. It looks around rather than above. The standard is a social one. There is "a zeal for the Law, but not according to knowledge." Having settled the constituents of righteousness, and having in conduct realized these constituents, it looks from the legal vantage-ground on others. And, seeing the many below the elected level, it whispers within itself, "I thank thee that I am not as they." The *I* struts abroad with a distinct sense of superiority. This pride is the parasite of religiosity. And religiosity is the whole religion of many. Religiosity means the performance, punctilious and sincere, of acts and offices, functions and services. It may comprehend a wide area of the existence. It may fill up much of time and much of thought, and he who abounds in it is held to be a religious man. But it is a morality untouched by the emotion of the broken and contrite spirit. There is no distinctively evangelical motive force. On an earlier occasion, the contrast between the routine religiosity and the warm religion of the heart was presented at the dinner-table where Simon the Pharisee presided, and the woman washed the Lord's feet with her tears. Of her he said, "She hath loved much." Here the Pharisee is in opposition to the publican, who had the inner spirit of poverty. Now, one who has the religiosity, not the religion, is apt to rest on the duties which he discharges, on the zeal which he manifests. He trusts in himself as being righteous, and, wherever there is this trust, there creeps around it a feeling of superiority. "I am not as other men are." It engenders the separatist's haughty spirit. It brings in the sentiment of a caste. The "I" belongs to the religious world, "others" are without. Let us beware lest we rest satisfied with a righteousness like that of the Pharisee, lest we substitute the outward for the inward—what we do for what we are. Let us beware of that which always develops with this tendency—the habit of comparison of self with others on levels lower than our own, instead of realizing "the vision splendid" of that righteousness which demands the entire self. It is this trust, this self-elevation, this pride of righteousness, which vitiates the sacrifice of many who go up to the temple to pray.

II. It is the COMMENDATION OF HUMILITY, IN ITS ESSENTIAL NATURE AND BLESSEDNESS. What is humility? It is not so much a self-consciousness as a God-consciousness; not so much a mean thinking of ourselves as a thrilling, penetrating consciousness of him who is perfect holiness and truth. There is a self-abhorrence, but that follows the seeing of God with the opened inner eye. The Pharisee had no conviction of sin, because he had no real discernment of the Eternal. His god was the property of his caste, one on whom he had a claim because of his belonging to the caste and doing what was required by it. The publican felt God at his heart; and the sight awoke the longing to be holy as God is, and the longing to be holy called out the sense of wrongness. Oh, how he had offended! how selfish and grasping and wicked he had been! All else fades into indistinctness; in that temple there are to him but the two presences, God and his soul, and the soul cries, "God be merciful!" It is the first cry of the soul which God has appropriated. There is no real prayer until that cry. A genuine earnest pleading is evoked. The beginning of all prayer, Christ reminds us, is the taking of the sinner's place, and the simple appeal to mercy. And as it is the first, so it is the cry ever pulsing through prayer. It is never wanting from the justified. The pardon has been received. The blood cleanses from all sin; but not the less, all the more, is the knowledge of sin and the need of the ever-renewed application of mercy. This is humility—sinful self cast on Divine mercy, and, forgiven much, loving much. There is no measurement with other men, for God is the all in all. And this is blessed. The Pharisee returns—his pride more deeply written into his nature, its blight and curse; no spring in the heart, no visitation of any day-spring from on high. Remaining in his pride, he was truly abased. The publican returns—a burden rolled off from his heart, a new elasticity in his step, a new light in his countenance. "The winter is past, . . . the flowers appear on the earth." He is at peace with God, justified, sanctified, righteous in the communion of the Righteous One. "I, yet not I, for he lives in me." In his humility he was exalted.

Vers. 18—25.—*The ruler who refused the crown.* It is a certain ruler, a young man, who accosts our Lord. And the question which he asks represents one of the deepest cravings of the human breast. Is it only in the Gospels that we find this question? It is written into all the religions, into the best of all the philosophies, the poetries, the guesses at truth, which have commanded the thought of the ages. It is as old as human nature, as manifold in its complexion as the human experience, as abiding in its persistence as the human need. It is our question—one compared with which the hundred things which claim our attention are only as strivings after wind. Let us listen. The eternal life: what is it? and how is it realized?

I. What did the young man mean when he came running and kneeling and asked, "What shall I do to inherit eternal life?" The answer may indicate the essential features of the desire that has haunted the breast. Clearly he meant three things: 1. *A real, personal existence*—one implying distinct consciousness and activity. He is too prosaic, too selfishly in earnest, to mean less than this. 2. *An existence removed from the imperfections of the present time.* His notions of immortality may have been crude; but he certainly desired a life which, as contrasted with the changeful and limited, is an eternal life. 3. *A life in relation to a moral or spiritual system.* He has possessions. Sirens are ever luring him to the fateful shores of pleasure. Against them "the categorical imperative" of conscience is ever dominant. It says, "Root thy conduct in the everlastingly true. The eternal life is not mere endlessness. It is endless goodness, truth. And to be in harmony with this is to live eternally." Now, such being the contents of his thought, the burden which he brings to the Master is—how it comes that, although the harmony of his conduct with this system is complete, he is still unsatisfied; nay, that the more he seems to approach the ideal the more conscious he is that it is far ahead of him. "Explain it to me" is the passionate entreaty; and who does not love him for this sublime passion? "What is the missing quantity? What is the *plus* yet to be possessed that I may have eternal life?"

II. Turning to the answer of Christ, and connecting it with words elsewhere, what is Christ's exposition of the eternal life? The question is, "What shall I do?" And to this the specific reply is, "Be free. Your life does not consist in the abundance of your possessions. Can you part with them, that you may the more unreservedly obey the vision which has dawned on you?" (ver. 22). Thus the truth probed him. He might not have been called actually to sell his estate, any more than Abraham was called to offer up Isaac. But the trial of his will was made; and, in the trial, he was found wanting (ver. 23). Do we blame him?—we whom the truth is proving every day, only to find that we are caught up by all kinds of vanities! He turned away; and, alas! what of us? But the demand of the Lord reminds us of the requirement essential to the eternal life. Life, we are told by scientists, consists in an adaptation of organism to surrounding. When the adaptation is complete, and the surrounding nourishes the organism, there is health. When it is impaired, there is sickness; when it is broken, there is death. Human life has both a spiritual and a material environment. As the ruler rightly supposed, the eternal life implies correspondence to the spiritual environment. Where there is no such correspondence, where, in Scripture phrase, the life is "without God," there is death. Where the correspondence has been formed, and the inner life is nourished by the system which surrounds it, there is spiritual, eternal life. But are not the phrases, "systems," "environments," too vague and abstract? Do we not need something more concrete, something nearer us, than such abstractions? *This* is more concrete, *this* is nearer us, "Take up the cross; come, follow me" (ver. 22). A perfect Man has walked this earth—One in whom the correspondence with the heavenly environment was complete, who lived in and with a Father in heaven, and whose meat was to do his will. His existence, in its details, we cannot copy; but his life, in its principles, inspirations, in all that gave it its beauty and glory, we can realize, under varying conditions. To be joined to him; to live in his light; to be the manner of person that he was; to be affianced to him as the Lord and Friend and Brother of our perfect choice; and have his flesh as meat indeed, and his blood as drink indeed;—this is the way to the eternal life. But what is this life whose way is thus defined? It must be kept always in view that *eternal* is not merely another name for *endless*. Endless time would not be eternity. The eternal is the timeless. Everlasting existence may be involved; but this is because the life is what it is—Divine, and therefore imperishable. Christ has supplied many unfoldings of this Divine life (see John iii. 1—13; vi. 32—53; xvii. 3). May the guidance of the Holy Spirit illumine this teaching! and may we all realize the secret of St. John: "He that hath the Son hath the life!"

III. THIS RULER INTERESTS US. The narrative concerning him suggests reflections which may be dwelt on with profit. 1. *The difficulty, the hindrance, to salvation that is interposed by riches.* (Vers. 24, 25.) Great possessions, Christ declares, increase the risk of losing the true spiritual health, are apt to stand in the way of the eternal life. It is not the riches themselves that are evil; it is, as one of the evangelists explains, the trust in them, the sensation of them, that is the evil. And may there not be a trust in riches, even when they are not actually possessed? We may have very little, and yet have such a craving for more as proves that the ungotten wealth stands for our best. More than this, with little there may be as much of earthliness and love of the world as when there is much. It is a wretched slavery which one often sees, and the feeling of which one often detects in one's own breast. Persons are miserably ruled over by the sense of wealth. Neither do they get the good, nor does the world get the full good, of what they have. On the other hand, the poor cannot rise to the real dignity of their being because they set possessions on the height which they regard as the *summum bonum*. Social life is honeycombed by that trust in riches. "How hard it is," says Christ, "for those that have riches to enter into the kingdom of God!" (ver. 24). 2. *A crown is refused.* Who the ruler was we cannot tell. On a sudden he appears, on a sudden he disappears. Is he wrecked, like a ship with full sail, at the harbour-bar? It is noticeable that Jesus "loved him;" in this distinction he is bracketed, in the Gospels, with Martha and Mary and Lazarus. For a moment the crown hangs over his head. Did he finally reject it? But he waves it aside. Oh, not the last who has missed the flood-tide—the blessing offered to the man, and the man turning from it! Young men, all, reflect!

Vers. 35—43.—*Bartimæus.* Here are two noises suggestive of the human life with which we are all familiar. There is the tramp, tramp, tramp, of the swaying multitude, the din of the many minds, many experiences, many mouths, all moving in obedience to a common impulse. Men and women, when they become mere units of a crowd, forget for the time their personal histories. They are swept on by the current, sharing and adding to its excitement. There is nothing more unaccountable sometimes than the impulses which are communicated from person to person, and pass by infection to the multitude. Different days have their different idols. Those who are shouting themselves hoarse with their hosannahs at Jericho will shout themselves hoarse with the cry, "Away with him! Crucify him!" at Jerusalem. Oh, fickle popularity! The Lord knew what the applause of the crowd was worth. The children crying in the temple were far more to him than the loud voice and the tremendous enthusiasm of the thousands who had swelled the triumph of the entry into the city of David. But through that tumult, in the midst of that noise, there is another—that which always reaches the ears of the Lord of Sabaoth. Only one voice, at most two voices, shrill and clamorous—the voice of misery and want and prayer! Had he not heard that same voice in highest heaven? Had it not pierced through the praises of angel and archangel, of cherubim and seraphim—the cry of a sinful and weary world? A little one only in the system of the universe, but the least in need has a special way of access to the Eternal Love. Far off the great Shepherd hears the bleat of the sheep that has strayed into the wilderness. He who heard the sigh of the world from the excellent glory will not turn from the piteous pleading of the poor and needy. God's tenderness individualizes. "*This* poor man cried, and the Lord heard him, and saved him out of all his troubles."

I. REGARD THIS POOR MAN. Perhaps we shall realize that he is our near kinsman. 1. *He has been sitting by the wayside begging.* And what are we all but beggars at the world's wayside? Even the mind most richly endowed, the heart most wealthy in love and imagination, needs "the life more and fuller." Is there no begging from heaven? no consciousness of a fountain of living waters? This Bartimæus, taking his place day by day on the thoroughfare and asking an alms, is only too faithful a picture of me, wanting, desiring, and, alas! too often trying to satisfy my soul with some dole of happiness or excitement thrown to me—a beggar all the while, blind. 2. *What is this?* An unusual bustle and din. What does it mean? We can imagine the question addressed, with only a languid interest, to some person at hand—a languor which vanishes when the answer is given, "It is Jesus of Nazareth who is passing by." Ah! the newness of cry, sign of newness of life! What and how he had heard of this Jesus we know not; but he had heard enough to open the gates of the soul. The one argument is need, the one reasoning, "I am here; he is there. Son of David, have mercy on me!" It is the great hour of a human life when speech is begun between the soul and heaven. Such speech arrests the love of God in the way. "We enter heaven by prayer." 3. *Those around bid the one who cries hold his peace.* So speak the many to the one in earnest. Notice how often in the Gospels the disciples are represented as keeping back from Christ instead of helping to him (see ver. 15). They did not know the heart of God. And men do not know it still. There is often a "send away" in the minds of even the well-disposed. Earnestness meets discouragements where it leasts expects them. Cry on, thou who hast felt the breath of the passing Saviour. If those about thee are unsympathetic, throw thyself the more on thy Lord; the more they protest, cry thou the more, "Son of God, they will not take me up. Father and mother even forsake me. Thou, thou only art my hope. Make no tarrying, O my God."

II. Think of the Saviour, in whom the living God is revealed. 1. There is *the Christ-commandment.* "Bring him hither to me." It is the commandment to an often misunderstanding and misinterpreting Church. Christ has much to bear at the hand of the world; he has much also to bear at the hand of his Church. How frequently those who are his repel rather than attract, send away rather than bring! "Bring"—there is no gainsaying this charge. Instantly the tone of the multitude changes. Now it is, "Rise, be of good comfort; he calleth thee." And what alacrity in the Bartimæus-obedience! The old tattered garment connected with the past time of, it may have been, a sinful life is thrown away. There is no stopping to inquire how the blind can reach that blessed presence. He has called. In the call there is the pledge of a sufficient grace. O mirror of Divine condescension! O word, preparing for work, of power! "The blind, the poor, bring to me!" 2. There is *the Christ-question.* "What wilt thou that I shall do unto thee?" The question is put when the presence is reached. The presence is the help to the answer. Now, the great underlying want is expressed, "Lord, that I may receive my sight." Is it not the prayer of the human heart when the quickening presence of God is realized? It is to prepare for the revelation that the will is gently besieged. He cannot force; he can only draw. Stooping to thee, the person thou art, and as thou art, the word of grace and truth is, "What wilt thou?" 3. And then *the Christ-action.* "He touched the eyes," says St. Matthew. "Receive thy sight: thy faith hath saved thee," says St. Luke. His faith had been a trust in the dark. He could not make the light, but he could call for it. And he had called, he had pressed to Christ, awfully in earnest, unboundedly confident. The faith saved through what it did. It brought him to the Lord; and that is salvation. The first use of the new sight was to behold the Deliverer. The first face that wrote its image in the heart was the face of God in Christ. Saved, whole, because that face was formed in the heart of hearts, never more to fade from it. "I was blind; now I see." "Go thy way," says the Lord. "Nay, dearest Master, where thou goest I will go. Where thou dwellest I will dwell. Thy way is mine. Mine the new song which thou hast given. Thou hast touched my eyes—

"'And in that light of life I'll walk
Till travelling days are done.'"

HOMILIES BY VARIOUS AUTHORS.

Vers. 1—7.—*Continuance in prayer: Divine delay.* We have first to consider what is—

I. The argument in the text. It is one from the less to the greater, or rather from the unworthy to the worthy. If a bad man will, for a poor reason, accede to the request of one for whom he cares nothing, how much more certainly will the Righteous One himself, for a good reason, espouse the cause of those who are so dear to him! The reasons for confidence in God's faithfulness and interposition are therefore threefold. 1. If an unprincipled judge amongst men will finally do justice, assuredly the righteous Judge of all the earth will do so. His character is something which cannot fail; we may build on that as on the most solid rock. 2. If justice is granted by us for so poor a reason as that of fearing vexatious annoyance, surely God will listen and will respond to reverent and believing prayer. He is far more certain to be won by that in us which pleases him than is an unjust judge by that in his appellant which annoys him. And our approach to him in prayer, our reverent attitude, our faith in his goodness, our trust in his Word,—all this is very pleasing unto our Father. 3. If a man will yield a demand made by one to whom he does not feel himself related, and in whom he is absolutely uninterested, how confident we may be that God will interpose on behalf of those who, as his own sons and daughters, are dear to his parental heart, and who, collectively, constitute "his own elect"—those who are most tenderly and intimately related to him in Jesus Christ his Son!

II. The serious fact of the Divine delay. "Though he bear long with them" (ver. 7), or, "and he delays [to interpose] in their cause" (Dr. Bruce). It is certain that, *from our point of view*, God does delay to vindicate his people; his answer does not come as soon as we expect it; it is held back so long that we are ready "to faint" (lose heart). Thus was it many times in the history of Israel; thus has it been frequently in the history of the Church of Christ. How many times have suffering bands of noble martyrs looked up piteously and despondently to heaven as they cried, "How long, O Lord, holy and true, dost thou not judge and avenge our blood?" Thus has it been in multitudes of individual instances; men have been oppressed, or they have been embarrassed, or they have been disappointed, or they have been otherwise afflicted; they have appealed to God for his delivering grace; and they have looked long in vain for the Divine response. They say, "O my God, I cry, . . . but thou hearest not" (Ps. xxii. 2).

III. The explanation that will be found. The time will come when we shall understand why God did delay to answer us. But we may be quite sure that when it comes it will be seen: 1. That it was not in him—not in his absence from us, nor his indifference to us, nor his unreadiness to help us. 2. That it was in us—in our unreadiness to receive his interposition, or in the misuse we should make of it, or in the greater and truer good to be gained by our patience than by our relief; and thus in the ultimate gain to our own well-being by his withholding.

IV. The blessed fact that it is only a delay. "I tell you that he will avenge them speedily." 1. It is probable that when God does manifest his power he will work speedy and overwhelming destruction to the guilty; he will avenge "speedily," *i.e.* quickly, instantaneously. "How are they brought into desolation, as in a moment! they are utterly consumed with terrors. As a dream when one awaketh; so, O Lord, when thou awakest, thou shalt despise their image" (Ps. lxxiii. 19, 20). 2. It is certain that in his own time and way God will defend his people, that he will relieve his children, that he will redeem and bless his "own elect." His faithfulness to his Word; his love for them that love him; his intimacy of relation to those who are "in Jesus Christ;"—this is a sure and absolute pledge that the appeal to him cannot be and will not be in vain. Men ought continuously, perseveringly, to pray, and never to lose heart. The day of Divine appearing is entered in the books of God.—C.

Ver. 8.—*Our unbelief.* "Nevertheless when the Son of man cometh, shall he find faith on the earth?" These words have no special reference, if they have any at all, to the condition of the world at the "second coming" of Christ. In order to understand and appreciate them, we must consider—

I. What is the force and range of this expression, "the coming of the Son of man." And it will be found on investigation that it signifies any special manifestation of God's power or any special appearance of Christ either in Person or in providence. This may be: 1. *In mercy;* including the Incarnation, when the Son of man came "not to destroy but to save" the world; the Resurrection, when he came in power and triumph from the other world; the Day of Pentecost, when he came in marvellous outpouring of Divine influence upon the world. 2. *In judgment;* including the destruction of Jerusalem; the day of death to each human being; the day of judgment itself, when "before him shall be gathered all nations."

II. What is the application of it in the text. A widow appeals for redress against "her adversary" (the defendant) to an unprincipled judge. He puts her off until her importunity makes him listen and respond in order to save himself from annoyance. Arguing *à fortiori*, our Lord contends that God, the righteous Judge, will most certainly grant to his own people (children) the requests they make of him (see previous homily). But, continues the great Teacher, who had such a perfect insight into our nature, when he *does* that, and "comes" in judgment to his foes and in mercy to his friends, will he find his friends expecting him? will they be looking for his appearing? will their attitude be one of holy expectation, of instant recognition, and of devout thankfulness? or will they not, after all their asking, be positively surprised and even incredulous at his manifestation? He *will* come most assuredly, but when he comes, will he find faith on the earth?

III. What illustrations we have of the truth of it. 1. We have two striking *scriptural* illustrations. (1) Christ's own coming, after his resurrection, to his disciples. Instead of looking for him and welcoming him, according to his word (ver. 33), they were astounded and incredulous (ch. xxiv. 11, 22, 23, 37). He did not "find faith" in them. (2) His coming in providential deliverance to Peter. When the Church had been praying without ceasing for him, they should have been hoping for a Divine visitation in response to their prayer. Nevertheless, when it came, were they not found unbelieving and astonished (Acts xii. 5, 15)? Are we much better than they? 2. Christ's coming *in judgment.* Such narrow and false interpretations as the Jews were apt to put upon sudden and sad calamities (ch. xiii. 1—4) we must scrupulously avoid. But when we see a man who has defied all laws, human and Divine, brought down into shame and ruin, or when we see a guilty empire which was founded on violence, sustained by force, and nourished in corruption, stricken down by defeat and reduced to dishonour and disaster, shall we be surprised as if a strange thing had happened? or shall we not rather feel that this is precisely what we had every reason to expect from the righteousness of the Divine Ruler? 3. Christ's coming *in grace and mercy.* When the Christian family, in answer to earnest and continued prayer, is just saved from serious embarrassment and perhaps from disgrace; when the Christian Church, after much pleading for God's Spirit, receives marked and manifest tokens of the presence and power of God in the midst of it; when the Christian teacher or preacher, as the issue of much devout and faithful work, finds many souls to be seeking the life which is of God;—is the attitude of that family, that Church, that teacher, one of calm expectation and devout acquiescence? or is it not rather one of surprise, if not even of incredulity? When we have been imploring the Son of man to come, and he comes at our appeal, does he find us awaiting and expecting him? Surely, with fuller and deeper faith on our part, there would be a more frequent coming on the part of our gracious Lord in life-giving power and blessing.—C.

Vers. 9—14.—*The Pharisee and the publican.* The scene indicated by our Lord's opening sentences is easily realized. We readily picture to our minds the place and the two persons in whom we are interested—the haughty Pharisee and the humble-minded publican. We readily imagine their demeanour as they enter, their posture as they pray, their reception as they pass through the courts going and returning. But we ask how and why was it that the Pharisee was rejected and the publican accepted. And in reply we say: 1. In some respects the two men stood on the same ground. Both were free from the taint of idolatry and were worshipping God; both appreciated the privilege of prayer; both came to the same building, and, using the same invocation, each uttered the uppermost thought in his mind. 2. In some aspects the Pharisee seemed to have the advantage. (1) He had the respect of the public, the good and God-fearing public, of the respectable people of his day; (2) he had lived the worthiest life in all social and political relations; (3) he was much the more "religious" of the two, in the sense that his habit of life was devout and charitable, while that of the publican had been godless and avaricious. 3. The terms of their respective prayers are not decisive of their acceptableness in the sight of God. (1) A truly humble man might speak to God in the strain, though not in the spirit, of the Pharisee. It is quite right to thank God for being preserved from presumptuous sins and being kept in the path of rectitude and devotion (see Ps. xli. 12, 13). (2) A thoroughly formal worshipper might present the petition of the publican. How often, since then, have these or very similar words been used by "penitents" who have been impenitent, by those who have taken the language of humility on their lip while they "have regarded iniquity in their heart"! A modern writer (T. T. Lynch) represents these two men as going up again to the temple; but this time the Pharisee, adopting the publican's form of words in hope of acceptance, is again rejected; while the publican, giving thanks to God for his reconciliation and renewal, is again accepted—

"For sometimes tears and sometimes thanks,
But only *truth* can please."

How, then, do we explain the fact that "this man went down to his house justified rather than the other"?

I. THE PHARISEE HAD FORMED A RADICALLY FALSE ESTIMATE of his own character, and the publican a true one of his. The Pharisee thought he was everything God wished him to be, and was miserably wrong in his estimate; he was reckoning that God cared chiefly if not exclusively for the outside in religion, that his favour was secured by ceremonies, by proprieties, by punctualities, by utterances of prescribed forms. He failed to understand that this was only the shell and not the kernel, and that the shell of correct behaviour is nothing without the kernel of a reverent and loving spirit. The publican, on the other hand, believed that he was very far from right with God; that he had been living a guilty life, and was condemned of God for so doing; and his thought was true.

II. THE PHARISEE'S FALSE ESTIMATE LED HIM INTO SELF-FLATTERY; the publican's true estimate into frank, penitential acknowledgment. Under the cover of gratitude, the one man paid himself handsome compliments, and held on high his great meritoriousness, thus confirming in his own mind the delusion that he was a favourite of Heaven; the other, moved by a deep sense of personal unworthiness, made honest confession of sin, and sought the mercy he knew he needed.

III. GOD HATES THE PROUD, AND HONOURS THE HUMBLE-HEARTED. Old and New Testaments may be said to be full of this truth. God has said and has repeated, he has most plainly and emphatically declared, that pride is odious and unpardonable in his sight; but that humility shall live before him (ver. 14; see also Ps. xxxii. 5; cxxxviii. 6; Prov. xxviii. 13; Isa. lvii. 15; Matt. v. 3; 1 Pet. v. 6; 1 John i. 8, 9). Here is: 1. *A message of solemn warning.* It concerns those who are the spiritual descendants of the Pharisee; who are satisfied with their spiritual condition but have no right to be so; who are building the hope of their hearts on things which are external, but in whom the love of God does not dwell. And here is: 2. *A message of gracious encouragement.* It concerns those who are burdened with a sense of sin and need not remain so. The way of mercy is open to every penitent soul. Jesus Christ is the "Propitiation for the sins of the whole world," and the grace of God in him far more than suffices for every guilty heart. In him we have forgiveness of sins; in him we have peace and hope and joy, even eternal life.—C.

Vers. 15, 16.—*Christ and the children: a sermon to children.* This familiar and attractive scene is well conceived and described in the lines commencing, "Over the hills of Jordan." It contains valuable lessons for the young.

I. THE KINDLINESS OF JESUS CHRIST. Some kind men are not kindly. They will do a great deal for you, will give much to you, will run serious risks or even make serious sacrifices on your behalf; but they are not gracious, genial, winning. They are not *approachable;* you are not drawn to them; you are not inclined to address them and make friends with them; they rather repel than invite you. Such was *not* Jesus Christ. He was not only kind at heart, but kindly in manner and in bearing. The children of his day went freely and gladly to him. That "he was never seen to smile" is a wholly unauthorized and, we may be quite sure, an entirely false statement. Did he not take those infants into his arms with a smile upon his face? Did he not frequently, ay, *constantly,* smile as he looked upon innocency, upon hopefulness, upon childhood? Think of Jesus Christ as not only the kind but the kindly One, as not only the good but the gracious One, as not only the wise but the winning One. Think of him as that One to whom, if he were with us now as he was with men of old, you would be drawn with an irresistible attraction, and to whom you could, without any effort, unburden your heart. And believe that just what he was on earth he is in heaven.

II. JESUS CHRIST STILL RECEIVES US TO THE SHELTER OF HIS LOVING POWER. He took them up into his arms. The arms of the parent are the place of shelter to the child; to them in all time of danger or of distress he naturally and eagerly resorts. It is the place of strength, of defence, of succour. But youth needs more than human sympathy and help; it needs a refuge in Divine tenderness and power. It does so always; but more particularly when parental care is lost, because the parents themselves have "passed into the skies." Very seriously is this need felt when parental care is *left behind,* when youth or young manhood goes forth from the shelter of the home. Then how priceless is the shelter of the loving power of the Divine Friend! In that unknown "world" which lies beyond the home-life are perils that cannot be anticipated, and that are all unknown. Take care to secure the invaluable refuge of the Divine arm; for only in the protection of the all-wise Leader and almighty Friend will safety be found.

III. JESUS CHRIST STILL LAYS HIS HAND UPON US. Mark tells us (x. 16) that he "put his hands upon them, and blessed them." You still sing, "I wish that his hands had been laid on my head." It is a right and becoming thought. But the laying of the hand of flesh on those children's heads may not have wrought any great spiritual change in them; they may have grown up to reject him. Of far more consequence is it that Christ should now lay the hand of his Divine power and grace upon your heart; that he should so act upon you by his Divine Spirit that your mind should be illumined, and that you understand what is the good and the wise thing to do; that your heart should be touched so that you will live to love him who is worthiest of all that is best. "His touch has still its ancient power." Yes; and more than the healing touch which gave sight to the blind and wholeness to the poor leper is that benignant power which opens the closed mind and cleanses the unholy heart.

IV. JESUS LOOKS AND WAITS FOR YOUR SUBMISSION. He says that it is *you* who, of all people, can most readily enter his holy kingdom. He must have your free and full consent. When he made the world, and sent the sun on its course, and gave to the sea its bounds, "he spake, and it was done; he commanded, and it stood fast." He *compels* all things in nature to do his bidding; but he *asks,* he *invites* your trust, your worship, your love. He cannot bless you as he would unless you consent to receive him as your own personal Lord and Saviour and Friend. But he assures you that this is open to you as it is not to others; the young can readily give their attention, their docility, their love, their obedience. Fewer and slighter hindrances are in your way than are in the path of those who have travelled further. Of such as you are now "is the kingdom of God." This is the golden chance of your life.—C.

Ver. 17.—*The child of man and the kingdom of God.* Jesus Christ not only opened the gate of his kingdom to the little child as he opened his arms to the little children whom the mothers of Judah brought to him; he also took the little child as a type of the true disciple. He taught us that if we wish to enter his kingdom, our spirit must be the child-spirit. "Whosoever shall not receive the kingdom of God *as,*" etc. And what is this spirit? It is that of—

I. DOCILITY, or readiness to accept what is told us. The ideal child is teachable; it will learn because it is ready to receive; it has not found out the way of distrust and of rejection; it takes in the light, the truth, which is offered and it grows thereby. Men of mature years and powers, who have had all the advantages of Christian privileges, often stand without the kingdom because they will not receive the truth that is offered them; their mind is preoccupied with theories, systems, imaginations, of their own. They seem to know much; they believe they know much, for they are familiar with some things of which many (perhaps most) are ignorant; they could easily puzzle their neighbours by asking questions which these could not answer; they have a number of facts and laws, and a much larger number of names at their command; they "seem to be wise" (1 Cor. iii. 18). But their knowledge is very small in comparison with all that has to be acquired; it is partly (largely) local, temporary, evanescent (1 Cor. xiii. 8); it is nothing to the wisdom of God. It becomes them, as it becomes us all, to feel toward God as our little children feel towards us—to cherish a spirit of docility. How much more he has to tell us than we have to teach them! How much greater is our ignorance in his sight than theirs is in ours! He who will not accept the doctrine of the Divine Fatherhood; he who will not yield himself to a Divine Saviour; he who will not pursue the path of holy service, hoping to find at the end of it a heavenly home,—because this does not square with some favourite theories, or because it transcends the range of some intellectual faculties, cannot enter the kingdom of truth, and therefore shuts himself out of the kingdom of God. We shall fail to stand on the first rung of the ladder that reaches heavenly wisdom unless we realize that we are all of us but very little children in the presence of our Father, and unless with docile spirit we come to his feet and say, "Lord, we are very ignorant; wilt thou teach us?"

"Lead us, O Father, in the path of truth;
Unhelped by thee, in error's maze we grope."

II. SIMPLICITY. The little child (of our thought and our affection) is simple, transparent, sincere; he says just what is in his mind, does not pretend he is naughty when he believes himself to be good—is *real*. This God demands of us—"truth in the inward parts," sincerity of spirit. It does not further our cause with him to affect a piety that is not genuine; to simulate a penitence of which our heart knows nothing; to use the language of humility while pride is reigning within. He would rather we tell him just what we feel, just what we are, than adopt the most appropriate confessions or petitions. We must be like the children of our home; we must mean what we say when we draw nigh to him.

III. TRUSTFULNESS. Christianity is a religion which centres in a Person, in one Divine Being. "He that believeth in me," "that abideth in me,"—that is the prevailing note. Trust in Jesus Christ as the Teacher, Saviour, Sovereign of the human soul, is the way of life. He who has that stands within "the kingdom of God." Where shall we learn *to trust?* Is it not of the little child? As the child flees for refuge to its parent's arms, confides itself and all it has or hopes for to its parent's wisdom and love, so the human soul is invited to commit itself and all its everlasting interests to the Almighty Saviour, to say with implicit, childlike confidence and self-surrender—

"Jesus, Refuge of my soul,
Let me to thy bosom fly."

C.

Vers. 18—22.—*The golden chance: a sermon to the young.* Many features combine to make this incident one of peculiar interest.

I. THE PRINCIPAL ACTOR IN THE SCENE A YOUNG MAN. Matthew tells us this quite incidentally (xix. 22), but it adds great interest to the occurrence. For our hearts are drawn towards youth. Youth is innocent, ingenuous, frank, trustful, hopeful, loving. There is, moreover, some mystery about it. We know what the old man has been; we know what the man of middle life will be; but of youth we cannot tell; it may accomplish great things; it is covered with the delicate buds, with the beautiful flowers of promise.

II. A YOUNG MAN OF WEALTH AND INFLUENCE. This might not make him more interesting to Christ; but it does to us. The rich young heir may be of no more intrinsic worth than the beggar by the wayside; but because he is the heir of fortune, we care about him, we watch his career; we are specially glad if he takes a wise course, and are specially grieved if he goes astray.

III. A YOUNG MAN WITH SOME OF THE NOBLER QUALITIES OF YOUTH. 1. We note *his reverence.* Youth should be reverent. Ignorance and inexperience should pay to knowledge and wisdom the regard which is their due. We like this young man because he saw in that homeless Teacher a wisdom superior to his own, and came and prostrated himself before him in becoming homage. 2. We note *his ardour.* He came running (Mark x. 17) to meet and to learn of Christ. Youth should be, as in the person of this inquirer it was—eager, ardent, enthusiastic, sanguine of good things. 3. We note *his religiousness.* "Heaven lies about us in our infancy," etc. Youth is the time when heavenly visions are most and best seen; when Divine claims, spiritual realities, are strongest and clearest to the soul; then "life eternal" has the deepest meaning. So was it with him. To him life held something larger and better than all his lands and houses; other and higher voices than those of debtors and stewards reached his ear; he had a vision of a holy service in which he might be engaged; of a Divine life he might be living; and running in his eagerness, and kneeling in his reverence, he looked up into the face of Christ and said, "Good Master, what good thing shall I do, that I may have eternal life?"

IV. A YOUNG MAN IN THE PRESENCE OF CHRIST, exciting his special interest. A young man, with his life before him and a soul not yet stained by the evil which is in the world, standing in the very presence of him who knew what human life might include and what the human soul was worth, who could tell him how to enlarge the one and how to ennoble the other, and who (Mark x. 21) took a tender and loving interest in this earnest spirit,—what could we have more profoundly interesting than this?

V. JESUS CHRIST REVEALING TO HIM THE TRUE STATE OF HIS HEART. Our Lord's treatment of inquirers differed much; it was, no doubt, determined by the state of their heart, *as he alone knew it.* He replied to this young man as he did, because he wished him to know where he actually stood; he wished to show him that, in order to be prepared to lay hold on eternal life, it was not only necessary to have such sincerity as he had, and such earnestness as he had, but such earnestness as would make him ready to yield everything to the Lord of his life; *and that this he had not.* So, after leading him up to the point, he said, "Sell all that thou hast," etc. And then the inquirer knew that he lacked one thing—one essential thing; he wanted that thoroughness of purpose toward God which made self-surrender possible to him. It was a glorious, golden chance, then used or then lost when this interview was held. It must have been *the crisis of his career,* on which everything hung for all the future. Similar in its nature, though not alike in its circumstances, is the opportunity offered to each one of us. 1. All the life of Christian privilege is the golden chance of our existence. "Now is the accepted time," the period when everything is open to us, when a noble and immortal future stretches out before us and is within our power. 2. Youth is the golden chance of life. It is in the days that are now passing, when the heart is warm, and the mind is open, and the conscience tender, and the life unburdened and unembarrassed, that Christ should be approached and his lasting friendship gained. 3. The day of Divine visitation is the golden chance of youth—that day when the truth and the grace of Jesus Christ are most powerfully felt, and a voice from heaven is heard saying of the path of life, "This is the way: walk ye in it."—C.

Ver. 24.—*Wealth and piety.* Wherein lies *the* difficulty of a rich man entering the kingdom? This young ruler shrank from parting with his property; but Jesus Christ does not ordinarily ask men of wealth to "sell all that they have, and give to the poor." His difficulty, therefore, is not the common one. 1. It is not that the rich man is not as welcome to the friendship of Christ as the poor man. He does not make distinctions in his invitation, or in his desire that men should come to him. In him in whom is neither male nor female, bond nor free, there is neither rich nor poor. The poor as much as the rich, and also *the rich as much as the poor,* are the objects of his love and of his seeking. The Lord of our nature regards us, and concerns himself for us, not on account of our circumstances, but because he knows the value of our souls. 2. Not because the rich man cannot illustrate the distinctive graces of Christianity.

The sale and distribution of property in apostolic times was an expedient which was adopted for the occasion; but it was not insisted upon as necessary even then (Acts v. 4), and it was very soon abandoned. Paul, writing to Timothy, wrote on the supposition that the Christian Church included many wealthy men (1 Tim. vi.). Every age and every country has witnessed the lives of wealthy Christian men, who have illustrated every grace that the great Teacher has commended. It is clear that a rich man *may be* as humble, as generous, as temperate, as pure, as devout, as any poor man can be; and he sometimes *is* so. The explanation of our Lord's language is found in the fact that *riches are apt to put a serious obstacle* in the way of entrance into the kingdom. If we would find our way into that holy and blessed kingdom, it is necessary that we should have a sense of our personal emptiness and need. We come to Christ to be filled with his fulness, to be enriched by his grace and love. He is a Physician, and it is they who feel that they are sick that are likely to apply for his healing power. He is the Divine Source of all wealth and enrichment (Rev. iii. 18), and they must know themselves to be poor who come to buy of him gold that they may become rich. Hence the difficulty. It is for this reason that—

I. A MAN WHOSE MIND IS FULL OF KNOWLEDGE finds it hard to receive distinctive Christian truth. He is rich, as compared with his fellows, in the acquisition of knowledge. He is proud of this possession of his, and is bent on making the most of it. Jesus Christ comes to him, and says that he must lay aside his own views and notions, and sit at his feet and receive the truth he brings to him from God. Then the "rich" man has to sacrifice his favourite theories, has to make nothing of his learning, that he may admit to his mind the wisdom that is from above; and he finds it very "hard" to do this.

II. A MAN WHO IS CLOTHED WITH HONOUR finds it hard to take a very humble view of himself. For honour is an order of wealth, and one that is highly prized. But the natural and common effect of it is to lead those who are the objects of it to form a flattering view of themselves; it is hard to get them to believe that in God's sight they may be as sinful as those held in very much less regard by their fellow-men. But the ground on which human souls must come to Christ is that of humility. "Blessed are the poor in spirit: for *theirs* is the kingdom of heaven."

III. A MAN WHOSE CHAMBERS ARE FULL OF TREASURE is tempted to seek his satisfaction in the lower good. We have to make our choice, as Divine truth is presented to us, whether we will live for the service of Christ or for our own personal enjoyment and aggrandizement. To the poor, to the afflicted, to the suffering, to those who know they have not long to live, the temptation to live for this present world is not so strong; on their ear the overtures of the gospel of grace fall as that very thing they need for their comfort and their peace; they have little to surrender, they have much to gain. But to those to whom every avenue of enjoyment is open; to those who may look hopefully, perhaps confidently, for place, for power, for society, for pleasure, for honour,—the inducement is very strong and urgent to cast in their lot with those "whose portion is in this life." Many voices very close to their ear, very clear and convincing, call for their strength to be given to the material rather than the spiritual, to the temporal rather than the eternal, to the human rather than the Divine; and it is "hard" for them to resist and to overcome. 1. Let poverty find its ample consolation in the accessibility of the riches that always satisfy and never flee. 2. Let those who know neither poverty nor riches thank God for the happy mean in which his providence has placed them—not subjecting them to the temptations of either. 3. Let wealth beware lest it make a sad, a supreme, mistake; lest, in the great spiritual strife, it—

"Clutch the tinsel gilding, and let go the crown of life."

C.

Vers. 28, 29 (comp. Mark. x. 29, 30).—*Christ's estimate of a Christian life.* It is certain that no literalist could ever understand Jesus Christ. Men of this order of mind utterly failed to understand him in his own time (see particularly John vi. 41—46), and they are equally at fault to-day. It is clearly impossible to give a literal interpretation to these words of the Lord; the facts of the case do not permit it. But going to the heart of this Divine utterance, we understand that any one who for Christ's sake suffers the loss of kindred and of worldly goods, shall have that which, in the sight of

God and in the light of his truth, *is worth* a hundred times more than any human or earthly blessings can be. We shall better see the truthfulness of this declaration if we approach the main thought from a little distance, and consider that *human life is something the value of which depends not on the quantity but on the kind of it.* A small quantity of human life outweighs in value a large amount of animal life. A very small portion of the higher human life transcends in value a large extent of lower human life. "Better fifty years of Europe than a cycle of Cathay." Bailey has well written—

"Life's more than breath and the quick round of blood;
It is a great spirit and a busy heart.
We live in deeds, not years; in thoughts, not breaths;
In feelings, not in figures on a dial.
We should count time by heart-throbs. He most lives
Who thinks most, feels the noblest, acts the best."

And there is wisdom as well as strength in the lines—

"One crowded hour of glorious life
Is worth an age without a name."

Lifting up this truth to the spiritual level of the teaching of Jesus Christ, we find that in such a life as that which is *of* him and *in* him—for the attainment of which we may have to make very great sacrifices—

I. There is an elevated and transporting joy experienced in the very endurance of persecution; and this alone goes far towards fulfilling the Saviour's word. This statement is simply historical. The apostles returned from the council, condemned and severely scourged, "rejoicing that they were counted worthy to suffer shame for his Name." Paul and Silas sang the praises of God in the darkness and foulness of a Philippian dungeon. And under every sky since then, men and women, old and young and in the midst of life, have gone to the dungeon and to the stake and to the open grave in which they were to be buried alive, not with tears in their eyes and lamentations on their tongues, but with songs of praise upon their lips, and with keen, exultant triumph in their hearts. To-day there is far more of real and lasting joy to be found under the roof of the missionary compound than in the palatial buildings of European capitals, profounder and more lasting satisfaction in the self-sacrificing labours of the evangelist than in the lounging idleness of the sons and daughters of fashion and of pleasure.

II. In true discipleship there are sources of joy which altogether outweigh any losses that may be entailed by fidelity. Some people know just enough of "religion" to find it a weariness, a burden, an anxiety. This is neither piety nor policy; it does not secure God's favour, and it gives no satisfaction to them. But the true and thorough servant of Jesus Christ, heartily surrendering himself to his Divine Redeemer, and devotedly engaging in his service, has "manifold more" of blessedness than he loses by anything with which he parts. He has (1) the favour, the forgiving and abiding love of God his Father; his lifelong, his unfailing friendship; (2) happy, holy fellowship with Jesus Christ, and, through him, with the true and pure and good amongst men; (3) a share in that holy service, outside of which is no rectitude for man, in which is rightness and wisdom, and therefore peace and joy; (4) the luxury, the blessedness of usefulness, of doing good and communicating, of being a source of strength and healing to the poor and needy; (5) "And in the world to come *eternal life:*" not the lingering and lasting shadows into which Greek and Roman shrank from descending; not the uninviting *sheôl* of the Hebrews; but everlasting day, eternal life—life in its fulness, its freedom, its blessedness, its glory, life never ceasing but enlarging and unfolding evermore. What commanding, convincing, constraining reasons are here for choosing the Master's service! What is it that he asks us to surrender for his sake? Anything in the way of profit, or pleasure, or companionship? Perhaps something in these ways. But what we gain by accepting him as Saviour and Friend is a thousand times more precious than all that we can be called upon to renounce. Even here and now God gives to us *far* more than he takes from us; and, beside this, in the world to come is "eternal life." We may well do as Peter said he and his associates had done—leave all to follow Christ.—C.

Vers. 31—34.—*God's concealing kindness, etc.* The clear prevision which the Lord Jesus Christ had of the future which was before him may suggest to us the thought—

I. God's kindness in concealment. We often try to forecast the future, and sometimes wish that we could do so less imperfectly than we can. But our very inability to do this is to us a valuable shield that saves us from great unhappiness. For who of us would care to proceed at all if he knew all the sorrowful experiences through which his path would lie? We sometimes feel a humane satisfaction that the sheep and cattle that browse so contentedly to-day in the field have not their short enjoyment marred by any expectation of the slaughter-house they are to enter to-morrow. And we may well be thankful that so thick a veil hangs over our future, that we cannot possibly tell what are the troubles that will befall us, or where our life will be darkened with its deeper shadows. Even when, as with Paul, we know that "bonds and afflictions abide us," still, like him, we do "*not* know the things that will befall us" then. And whilst, on the one hand, we very commonly have enough of premonition to make desirable preparation for coming evil, on the other hand our life is so ordered that we go happily and hopefully on our way, untroubled by the evils which are in front of us but which are mercifully hidden from our view.

II. Our Lord's leadership in the experience of apprehension. Our happy inability to anticipate the future is not the whole of the truth, though it is a large part of it. It remains true that there is a considerable amount of apprehension in the structure of our life. There are times when we clearly foresee some trial ahead of us. We may not know precisely the time of its arrival, nor the elements of which it will be composed. But we can tell that "our hour is coming." Before us, at no great distance, is suffering, is separation, is loss, is loneliness, is heart-ache. The road we are travelling along will soon descend, and we shall go down into the darkly shaded valley. Of that we have no doubt; and our spirit trembles, our heart is full of foreboding and, perchance, misgiving. How shall we pass through that dark valley? How bravely or how weakly, how worthily or how unbecomingly, shall we undergo that experience when it comes? There are many sources of encouragement to which we might resort. But this passage speaks to us of one of the best of them. Christ has gone this way before us—this way of keen and anxious apprehension. He knew that the most trying experiences were only a little way in front of him. He knew that the last extremity of human hatred and of human cruelty would be visited upon him. The Jews would condemn him with all their malignity, and the Gentiles would maltreat him with all their disdainful and powerful heartlessness. The sad and shameful future immediately before him stood clear to his sight, clearer far than any coming sorrow can shape itself to us. Therefore we may feel that: 1. We are treading in the footsteps of our Lord, and it is enough for the disciple to be as his Master. 2. We may be confident of his tenderest and fullest sympathy. He has suffered just what we are suffering now. 3. He will help us in our time of need. As he himself sought of man the succour he did not find, and was glad to receive from heaven the comfort he did not ask (Mark xiv. 34, 37; and ch. xxii. 43), we may be well assured that he will not refuse us all the aid we need and ask of him when the trial-hour of our experience shall have come.

III. The difficulty of discipleship—to learn unwelcome truth. There was no inherent incomprehensibleness in the words Christ here employed; yet "they understood none of these things." Why did they not comprehend such intelligible language? Because the truth conveyed was so exceedingly unwelcome. It cut across all their cherished hopes respecting the Messiah; it dashed their natural expectations to the ground; and it went sorely against all that their affection prompted them to believe and cherish. "It could not, must not, did not mean *that*," they said in their hearts. It is not the strangeness nor the profundity of truth which is too much for us; it is its *remoteness from that on which we have set our heart.* We do not understand that which clashes with our prejudices, or our passions, or our affections. The apostles of Christ would have saved themselves from many hours of awful sorrow and abject hopelessness and painful incredulity, if their feelings had allowed them to understand the truth which their Master put so plainly and so repeatedly before them (Matt. xvi. 21; xvii. 22; xx. 17). Can it be that Jesus Christ is saying something to us which we ought to understand, but do not because it is unwelcome to our hearts, or because it is at variance with all our old and strong habits of thought? Is it possible that he is calling us to repentance, to self-surrender, to a full confession of our faith, to a nobler life, to some field of active work, and we do not understand what he is saying to us? Where his own apostles so greatly failed, may not we be found at fault? Shall we leave it to future darkness and a great surprise and a mortifying discovery of error to set us straight? Or shall we not rather recognize in time our liability to mistake; seek to have an open mind to receive all his holy will concerning us; ask God to help us to remove the bandages of prejudice and of earthly attachments from the eyes of our understanding; seek by docility and devoutness of spirit to be such disciples of the Master that, when he speaks even unwelcome truth to us, we shall understand him and obey?—C.

Ver. 37.—*Present but passing opportunity.* Pathetic stories are told of those who, in circumstances of the greatest danger or distress, have suddenly found themselves almost within reach of blessed deliverance, but who just failed to realize their hope. It is the captive knight past whose dungeon a friendly host is filing, and the sound of the clarion drowns his pleading cries; or it is the shipwrecked sailor on the lonely island whose laboriously constructed signal the ship that is homeward bound does not descry, and who sees his one chance of rescue vanishing away. Those who have never known a supreme misfortune, together with a possibility, which was only a possibility, of deliverance, cannot realize the thrilling and all but intolerable suspense of such moments of present but passing opportunity as Bartimæus now knew. He was blind, helpless, shut out from all the sights and nearly all the enjoyments of human life; his lot was of the darkest and the saddest; and there was passing by One who could turn darkness into day, dreariness and gloom into blessedness and beauty, if only he could win his ear and make his plea. This glorious Healer was within a few paces of him, would soon be actually in front of him, would all too soon be gone beyond his call. "Jesus of Nazareth was *passing by!*" We see here—

I. The soreness of our spiritual need. We are blind, helpless, suffering the worst privations, under the dominion of sin. We recognize not our Father, our brethren, our true selves, our true opportunities, our chief perils, our real interests; and our blindness is not only immeasurably reducing the value of our present life, but is leading us to that which is darker still and sadder far.

II. The near presence of Jesus Christ. A Divine Deliverer is at hand. Quite near to us, within reach of our voice, within touch of our hand, is One who can open our eyes and make us see clearly all that we need to know. At our very door is One who is not only ready at our entreaty, but even prepared already and eager to supply all our need. Here is One who offers to: 1. Enlighten our mind. 2. Restore the relationship to God our Father we have lost by our sin. 3. Constitute himself our almighty and unchanging Friend and Guide through all our life. 4. Conduct us and receive us to a heavenly home.

III. The passing of present opportunity. This priceless chance is ours to-day; but how long will it remain within our reach? Jesus of Nazareth is near, but he is passing. 1. We know nothing of Christian privilege beyond the grave, and our life is hastening on; it may close at any hour, and it is hurrying away on the swift wings of duty and of pleasure. 2. The favoured period of youth is still more transient. Christ is very near us in the golden days of youth, when the spiritual nature is so open and so responsive; but how fast these days are fleeing! how soon will they be gone! 3. The hour of special grace and of rare privilege is but an hour—that time when Heaven puts forth its most constraining influences, and we see and feel that the gates into the kingdom of God are opened wide for our entrance. We cannot afford to delay when Jesus of Nazareth is near us. When eternal life is within our grasp, we must compel every other interest to take the second place; and this, not only because it is of such transcendent value, but because we may never have so golden an opportunity again. There is "a tide" in the history of every man which leads on to something more than "fortune;" it leads *unto life*—the life that is Divine and everlasting. On no account whatever must *that* be "omitted." Foolish beyond all reckoning, as well as guilty before God, is the soul that lets Jesus of Nazareth pass by without seeking his feet and finding his favour.—C.

Ver. 41.—*What we want of Christ.* Our hearts are drawn towards blind Bartimæus; we compassionate him for his long-continued blindness; we enter into his feeling of keen hopefulness when he hears of the passing of Jesus Christ; we like the importunity of the man, his sturdy refusal to be put down by popular clamour; we like also his manly directness in reply to the question asked him, "Lord, that I may receive my sight!" We owe him some gratitude in that it was his necessity which provided our Lord with one more opportunity of illustrating his power and his pity, and of carrying on the great redemptive work he came to accomplish. For these miracles he wrought were a part, and a valuable part, of that work of his. If apprised of less value than they once were, they are very far indeed from being valueless. And amongst other things they illustrate Christ's *personal* dealing with men. As he did not heal in troops and companies but addressed himself to each individual man or woman that was sick or suffering, blind or lame, so does he now make his appeal to each individual heart, and say to this man and to that man, "What wilt *thou* that I shall do unto thee?" And what *do* we want of him, as he thus approaches us?

I. Those who want nothing in particular. They meet with their neighbours to worship him and to hear about him, but they have no sense of need in their hearts; their souls are not suffering and smarting under a painful sense of sin; their hearts are not athirst for the living God and Saviour. They wish for "bread enough," but it is not the bread of life for which they hunger; they would like much to be wealthy, but they are not careful to be "rich toward God."

II. Those who want nothing of Christ now. The time will come when they will be glad of a Saviour and Friend—some future hour of sorrow, or difficulty, or loneliness, and certainly the hour of death; they would like to keep open the line of communication, but at present they do not feel that they want anything of the great Healer of hearts. But let us look rather at—

III. What we all do really want of him. If our Divine Father is not to be disappointed in us, if our lives on earth are not to be miserable failures, then may we all urge, with this blind man, "Lord, that we may receive our sight!" For it is essential to the life of our life that we should be enlightened upon: 1. The transcendent value of the human spirit, and thus understand of how much more value we ourselves are than any of our earthly surroundings, or than the body which is our temporary residence. 2. The intimate and tender relation in which we stand to God. That God is the one Being with whom we have to do, from whom we cannot withhold our love and service without doing him and ourselves the greatest wrong, who is "earnestly remembering" and patiently seeking us in our distance and estrangement. 3. The supreme and abiding blessedness of the service of Christ; that this is the soul's only true rest and portion, its peace and its inheritance. We want that these great saving truths should stand out before the eyes of our soul as *the* solid and living facts, in comparison with which all other things are of small account; we want to recognize in them *the* great verities which alone will satisfy and save us. If we would that Christ should do this for us, we must remember that what he is saying to us is this: (1) "Learn of me;" (2) "Believe in me;" "Have faith in me;" (3) "Abide in me;" (4) "Follow me."—C.

Vers. 1—14.—*Lessons in prayer.* Our Lord, in the two parables composing the present passage, gives the disciples encouragement to pray. The one brings out the need of perseverance and importunity in prayer; the other brings out the spirit of self-abasement which should be cultivated in prayer. They are thus linked together as twin lessons in the art of prayer.

I. Let us notice the needful importunity of God's elect as illustrated by the importunate widow. (Vers. 1—8.) The story is about an earthly judge of unscrupulous character, to whom a widow in her weakness, but with a deep sense of injury, appeals for redress. The weak woman is able by her importunity to extort from the heartless judge the redress which he would give on no other conditions. He even becomes facetious and humorous over it, and declares that he will avenge her, lest "by her continual coming she *strike* me." Having related this story, our Lord makes certain deductions from it. And: 1. *He declares that at his coming there will be little faith in his advent.* (Ver. 8.) Now, this unbelief about his advent can be accounted for on several grounds. (1) The procession of nature is so uniform. All things seem to continue as they were from the creation. Nature is on so large and grand a scale that we do not appreciate the real progress, and imagine that we are in the midst of a standstill. Uniformity, however, is *not* standstill. (2) Hope deferred will make many hearts sick. And so what has been so long talked of and yet has never appeared will be thought at last as never to appear. And (3) stoicism will lead many just to take things as they are, and entertain no concern about any change. It is astonishing how easy-going people tolerate manifest wrongs rather than take the trouble either to pray about them or to work for their removal. But: 2. *Our Lord acknowledges the wrong to which his elect ones have been exposed.* Their cry is for justice, for redress, like the widow. Now, our Lord admits that his people have not got justice from the world. The world has not been worthy of them. The world has made them time after time martyrs. It is a great assurance that the Lord acknowledges his servants' wrongs. 3. *He intimates at the same time that, like the widow, they will need importunity.* The one weapon must be wielded and wielded incessantly. He keeps us waiting doubtless for our good. If we got all the moment we asked it, how should we ever learn patience? But: 4. *He promises a sudden redress.* The idea seems to be not "speedily" but "suddenly" he will avenge them. It will be a sharp and decisive deliverance when it comes. We thus see that all life's discipline is planned to stimulate prayer. And when we have least taste for it, we should, like Luther, pray on. This is the importunity the Lord loves and will answer.

II. Let us notice the spirit of self-abasement which should characterize our prayer as illustrated in the parable of the Pharisee and the publican. (Vers. 9—14.) And in this second story we have a Pharisee first presented whose prayer is an outburst of self-confidence. He thanks God that he is so much better than his neighbours. For in these he recognizes extortioners, unjust men, and adulterers. A self-righteous spirit is censorious; its prayer is a criticism; even a publican's modesty in standing afar off, and his contrition in smiting on his breast, are set down to his disparagement. Then the Pharisee can congratulate himself on fasting twice a week, and on giving tithes of all he possesses. But he was not a bit the better for all this so-called prayer, this bit of blatant self-praise. On the other hand, the publican, though he remained afar off and hardly ventured to look up, but smote on his breast and cried, "God be merciful to me a sinner!" went down to his house a happier and better man. For the important point is not their *consciousness*, but God's attitude towards their respective spirits. To the one spirit God responds by justification and a sense of acceptance. The other is sent empty away. Hence the principles Jesus deduces are twofold. 1. *Self-exaltation always precedes abasement.* The proud will sooner or later get his fall. The Pharisaic spirit is always humiliated in the end. The man who is filled with self-satisfaction is only demonstrating his own self-ignorance and distance from God and his great ideal. 2. *Self-abasement always leads to exaltation.* It is when we feel "as a beast" before God, like Asaph in the seventy-third psalm, that we are on the way to spiritual rapture. For God has provided for the abased sinner the *pardon* he needs, and, besides the pardon, *sanctification and everlasting progress.* Let us, then, pray in the penitential key continually, and let us pray determined not to be denied; and heights of spiritual exaltation and rapture will be seen rising from our very feet, and inviting us to sit down on them with Jesus.—R. M. E.

Vers. 15—30.—*The children of the kingdom.* During the progress of the King towards Jerusalem, his personal influence and benediction were greatly valued. It would seem that mothers brought their children to him to be blessed, and ended by producing the very little ones. The disciples thought the line should be drawn somewhere, and so ventured to forbid the anxious mothers, only, however, to receive the significant rebuke from him, "Suffer little children to come unto me, and forbid them not: for of such is the kingdom of God." We are thus introduced to the important principle that—

I. Childlikeness is the qualification for God's kingdom. (Vers. 15—17.) Now, that is only another way of stating that God's government is paternal, and that his subjects are sons. It is, in fact, "a mighty family" of which he is himself the Head.

It is when we recognize in him our Father, and are prepared to accept as little children all he sends, and to do all he commands, that we truly belong to his kingdom. Hence the two characteristics specially brought out are (1) *trust*, and (2) *obedience*. It is thus we are to test ourselves. Do we *trust* God our Father as little children trust their fathers according to the flesh? and do we *obey* our heavenly Father as little ones obey their earthly parents? Then are we in the kingdom.

II. CHRIST EXPECTS THE RICHEST RULER TO TRUST AND TO OBEY HIM LIKE A LITTLE CHILD. (Vers. 18—27.) We have here an interesting case of anxiety, and how Christ dealt with it. And here we have to notice that: 1. *Neither his wealth nor his position satisfied the young ruler.* Something more was needed. The heart cannot content itself with either rank or gold. Hence his anxiety to lay hold on eternal life, which he felt was something more than he had yet obtained. 2. He fancied he could *entitle himself to it by a stroke of public service.* Hence his inquiry, "Good Master, what shall I *do* to inherit eternal life?" His notion was that he could claim it as a right, if he could only find out the additional duty he felt able to discharge. 3. *Jesus destroys with a single stroke his overestimate of human nature.* The flattery of human nature coincides with self-esteem. The young ruler believed in his own goodness and capabilities, and he complimented Jesus as "good Master," because he believed in the existence of any number of good men—himself, of course, included. Now, Jesus will not accept a false compliment. Human nature is *not* good; and it is not as a mere man that he is going to receive such flattery. Hence he tells the ruler that there is no mere man good; that God alone is good. There is here no repudiation of goodness as belonging to himself, but simply a repudiation of goodness as an attribute of unaided humanity. 4. Jesus insists on *examination of past conduct in the light of the Divine Law.* He asks the young ruler if he has kept the second table of the Decalogue, and been dutiful to his fellow-men. Looked at from without, the self-sufficient mind imagines it is a simple thing to keep the Law. But when for "law" we substitute "love," the self-examination does not so assure us. Meanwhile the young ruler is strong in the belief that he has kept the whole Law. 5. *Jesus now demands, as a test of his trust in him, the surrender of his riches to the poor, and the subsequent following of him.* The demand was for faith. When we consider that Jesus was apparently but a poor artisan, then, unless the young ruler would absolutely and implicitly trust him, he would never think of obeying his demand. The result proved that he was not yet ready to trust Jesus. He trusted his money more! Hence his sorrow as he leaves the Lord. And herein lies the money-danger. It bids for the trust of the soul. Moneyed men find it hard to trust any one more than money. They think it only natural that they should feel independent. But if money leads men away from Jesus, it is a curse, and not a blessing. When tempted to be covetous, let us remember that money has its special dangers, and makes it harder and even impossible for some to enter into God's kingdom. 6. *Jesus, while stating the difficulty which rich men find in entering God's kingdom, shows that God manifests his great power in saving some of them.* Money is such a barrier that we might well despair of the salvation of any rich men. Poor men have a chance. They have so little that they dare not trust in it, but in God only. But the rich man is tempted to trust in the uncertain riches, and leave God out of the account. But for this very reason God magnifies his grace in saving some rich men—in saving some in spite of all their temptation to trust in their abundance. A rich yet real believer is a splendid illustration of the grace of God. He sees through his riches and forbids them to come between his soul and his Saviour.

III. CHRIST INDICATES THE RECOMPENSE AWAITING ALL THOSE WHO HAVE SACRIFICED THEIR ALL FOR HIM. (Vers. 28—30.) Peter, as spokesman for the others, asks Christ what they shall have, seeing they have sacrificed their worldly positions to follow him. They thought that they should have some recompense. Nor were they mistaken; for Christ shows that they shall have: 1. *A recompense in kind in this world.* Often when a home is left for the sake of Jesus, a happier home is found in the midst of the Lord's work. When rich prospects are renounced for the Saviour's sake, unexpected recompense comes round in the shape of riches. When relatives are resigned that Christ's cause may be promoted, new relations spring up around the devoted soul and bring compensation. And the spirit of loving appreciation which appropriates all things makes ample amends for all our self-denial for our Saviour (1 Cor. iii. 21—23).

2. *A recompense in the world to come in the shape of eternal life.* So that self-denial, self-renunciation, becomes the path to the life eternal. The opportunity of living in God and for God awaits all sincere souls in the other life, and satisfies them. Let us consequently rejoice in hope of the glory, and have grace to fear no evil.—R. M. E.

Vers. 31—43.—*Blindness, mental and physical.* Having spoken to the disciples about recompense, he balances his consolation by giving them fair warning of his own approaching humiliation and death. But they were so infatuated about the honours that they were totally blind to the humiliation. Christ's words were no better than idle tales to them. It suggests—

I. THE ONE-SIDED WAY IN WHICH PEOPLE MAY READ THE BIBLE. (Ver. 31.) What was about to happen to Jesus was prophesied ages before. The Old Testament presented a suffering as well as an exalted Messiah. But the Jews totally overlooked the humiliating aspect. And in the very same way people go still to God's Word, and find there only what they want to find. It needs great trials oftentimes to expound some passages of the Divine Word to us. We are partial students; we do not enter into the wide meaning of the Word as God would have us!

II. GREAT TRIALS ARE NEEDED TO OPEN OUR EYES TO THE OVERLOOKED REALITIES. (Vers. 32—34.) It is plain that they did not take in Christ's meaning until he was actually taken from them and crucified. In the terrible suffering which seemed to extinguish all their fond hopes, the overwhelmed men got the spiritual vision, and were enabled to see a suffering as well as an exalted Messiah revealed in the Divine Word. And do we not often, when crushed and broken by trial, come to appropriate passages of God's Word which formerly were blank to us? We ought to bless God for the opened eye, even though the process of opening it be painful.

III. THE RESURRECTION OF CHRIST MADE AMENDS FOR ALL THE PREVIOUS SUFFERING. (Ver. 33.) For resurrection was exaltation; it was glory which could only be reached through the tomb. No possibility was there of Jesus being raised if he had never died. It is an experience cheaply purchased, perhaps, through death and the grave.

IV. LET US CONTRAST WITH THIS THE CURE OF BLIND BARTIMÆUS. (Vers. 35—43.) From blind disciples—mentally blind—Luke proceeds to speak of the blind beggar and his physical cure. Jesus was proceeding to Jerusalem to enter it as King. It was a royal progress. Here was one of the splendid accompaniments of it. 1. *The condition of the poor blind beggar.* He was blind, and, as he could not keep himself by work, he had to beg. He was thus perfectly helpless and dependent. And he knew his deficiencies. There was no unconsciousness of them or indifference to them. 2. *The knowledge he possessed of Jesus.* He had heard of Christ's miracles, how he had cured several blind men previously. He knew he was the Son of David, and regarded him as true Messiah. Hence his knowledge of Christ was sufficient to lead him to throw himself upon his mercy as soon as he had the chance. 3. *The visit of Jesus to his neighbourhood.* Jesus was passing on, and the crowd surged mightily around him. The noise fell upon the blind man's acute ear, and led him to ask what it all meant. Then, as soon as he learned that Jesus was passing by, he began to cry, "Jesus, thou Son of David, have mercy on me!" Noble example! Should not all who feel their need of mercy cry as Bartimæus did? 4. *Discouragement only intensifies his eagerness for blessing.* The crowd rebuked him, but Bartimæus persevered. The more discouragement, the more importunity. So let it be with us in our seasons of discouragement. 5. *The call of Jesus.* The importunate one is summoned to the Saviour's presence. Those who once discouraged him now urge him forward. 6. *The inquiry of Jesus.* Bartimæus is asked what mercy he desires; and his whole soul goes forth in the words, "Lord, that I may receive my sight!" It is surely well when we clearly know our need and desire its supply. 7. *The cure conferred and its consequences.* Bartimæus is thrown upon his faith; according to this is his cure. But his faith was strong enough for the occasion. He consequently sees plainly, and his fresh sight is used to guide him after Jesus. So is it with us if we receive from Jesus our spiritual healing. Then we see the Saviour plainly, and we learn and are proud to follow him. The people, too, in seeing us follow Christ, will learn to glorify the God of grace who has enabled us to do so.—R. M. E.

EXPOSITION.

CHAPTER XIX.

Vers. 1—10.—*Jesus lodges in the house of Zacchæus, "the chief among the publicans" at Jericho.* This episode, which took place at Jericho just before the Lord's entry into Jerusalem the last time, is peculiar to this Gospel. That the source was Hebrew (Aramaic) is clear from the wording of the narration. Some brief Hebrew (Aramaic) memoir was given to St. Luke, whence he derived his information of this most interesting and instructive incident of the last journey of the Master.

Vers. 1, 2.—And Jesus entered and passed through Jericho. And, behold, there was a man named Zacchæus, which was the chief among the publicans, and he was rich. Jericho, under the Herods, had become again an important centre of trade. It lay on the road from Peræa to Judæa and Egypt, and had, of course, an important custom-house. The balm which came especially from the Gilead district was sent through there into all parts of the world. Zacchæus was at the head of this customs department at Jericho. The exact position of such an official in those days is not known. He probably farmed the customs revenue under some great Roman capitalist of the equestrian order. In such an appointment it was easy to commit even involuntary injustices. The temptations to such an official to enrich himself at the expense of others, besides, were sadly numerous. *Named Zacchæus. Zakkai* signifies "pure" (see Ezra ii. 9; Neh. vii. 14). It is curious that we find in the Talmud a man named Zakkai, the father of the famous rabbi Jochanan, living at Jericho.

Ver. 3.—He was little of stature. Such a curious detail comes, of course, from some memoir written just at the time.

Ver. 4.—Into a sycomore tree. *Ficus sycomorus*, the fig-mulberry, is here meant. It grew in the Jordan valley to a considerable height; the low, spreading branches were easy to climb. "We can picture the scene to our mind's eye. The eager, wistful, supplicating face looking down from the fresh green foliage—it was early spring—and meeting the gaze of Jesus as he passed" (Dean Plumptre).

Ver. 5.—Zacchæus, make haste, and come down; for to-day I must abide at thy house. Jericho was one of the cities of the priests, and yet our Lord, setting public opinion at defiance, passed over their houses, and announced his intention of lodging for the night with one whose life's occupation was so hateful to the Jewish religious world. The Master recognized in the intense eagerness of Zacchæus to get a sight of him, and possibly a word from him, that it was in the chief publican's house where lay his Father's business for him in Jericho.

Ver. 7.—They all murmured. This very inclusive statement, "they all," shows the general intensely Jewish spirit of the age, narrow and sectarian. The people could not imagine goodness, or earnestness, or generosity in one who served the hateful Roman power. Probably in priestly Jericho this stern exclusive spirit was especially dominant.

Ver. 8.—And Zacchæus stood, and said unto the Lord; Behold, Lord, the half of my goods I give to the poor; and if I have taken anything from any man by false accusation, I restore him fourfold. Zacchæus's memorable speech was addressed not as an *apologia* to the murmuring, jealous crowd, either in the room or the courtyard of the house, but to his Divine Guest, who, he felt, understood him, whose great heart, he knew, sympathized with him in that life of his, so tempted and yet so full of quiet, noble acts; for the chief publican's words do not refer to a *future* purpose, but they speak of a *past* rule of life which he had set for himself to follow, and probably had followed for a long period. So Godet, who paraphrases thus: "He whom thou hast thought good to choose as thy host is not, as is alleged, a being unworthy of thy choice. Lo, publican though I am, it is no ill-gotten gain with which I entertain thee." In a profession like his, it was easy to commit involuntary injustice. There may, too, have been, probably was, many a hard if not an unjust act worked by the chief of the taxgatherers and his subordinates in their difficult employment.

Ver. 9.—And Jesus said unto him, This day is salvation come to this house. This solemn announcement on the part of the Redeemer was something more than a mere comforting assurance to a man who, in spite of difficulties and temptations, had striven manfully to lead a brave and generous life, helping, it is clear, the very multitude who were so ready to revile him. It is an assurance to the world that men might work in *any* profession or calling, and at the same time live a life pleasing to God. It repeats with intense emphasis—and this is the great lesson of this striking scene—that it is never the work or the position in life which ennobles the man in the sight of

God, but only the way in which the work *is done*, and the position *used*, which are of price in his pure eyes. The hated publican at the receipt of custom—the servant of Rome, might so live as to win the smile of God, as well as the priest in the sanctuary, or the rabbi in his theological school. He also is a son of Abraham. That is to say, a spiritual son—a son in the highest and most real sense. Zacchæus was a faithful follower of Abraham, in his life and in his faith.

Ver. 10.—**For the Son of man is come to seek and to save that which was lost.** A quiet rebuke to the Pharisees and priests and their followers, who would limit the redeemed. Surely the "publicans" and the great tempted mass of mankind needed him more than the happy privileged class. It was for the sake of *these* poor wandering sheep that he left his home of grandeur and peace. But there was a vein of sad irony running through these words of the Master. Between the lines we seem to read some such thoughts as these: "You know, O priests and Pharisees, *you* do not want me. You think you are safe already. But these poor despised ones, *they* want, they welcome me, like this Zacchæus." This, too, was a lesson for all time. This scene probably took place the evening of the Lord's arrival at Zacchæus's house at Jericho, after the evening meal, when the room and court of the house were filled with guests and curious spectators. Dean Plumptre has an interesting suggestion that Zacchæus the publican was one and the same with the publican of ch. xviii. 10—14, who in the temple "smote upon his breast, saying, God be merciful to me a sinner!" "Is it too bold a conjecture that he who saw Nathanael under the fig tree (John i. 48) had seen Zacchæus in the temple, and that the figure in the parable of ch. xviii. 14 was in fact a portrait?"

Vers. 11—27.—*The parable of the pounds.*

Ver. 11.—**And as they heard these things, he added and spake a parable.** The words which introduce this parable-story indicate its close connection with the events which had just taken place. "He added, and spake (προσθεὶς εἶπε)." **Because he was nigh to Jerusalem, and because they thought that the kingdom of God should immediately appear.** Thus were briefly stated the reasons which determined the Master to speak the following parable. First, "he was nigh to Jerusalem," only at most a few hours' journey from the holy city—his last solemn, awful visit, when the mysterious act of stupendous love would be accomplished. So he determined to give a veiled parabolic picture of himself and of his chosen people. Second, "they thought that the kingdom of God should immediately appear." In his parable he proposed to moderate the wild romantic enthusiasm of his immediate followers and of the Passover crowds by painting for them a quiet picture of the future of work and waiting which lay before them. The parable contains three sets of lessons. (1) The varieties of reward apportioned to different degrees of zeal and industry in the Master's service. (2) The eternity of loss and shame which will be the portion of the slothful and unfaithful servant (3) The terrible doom of his enemies.

Ver. 12.—**He said therefore, A certain nobleman went into a far country to receive for himself a kingdom, and to return.** There was a singular fitness in the Master's choice of a framework for his parable, which at first sight would seem strange and unreal. Two nobles, Herod and Archelaus, in that age had literally gone from Jericho, where the Speaker of the parable-story then was, to a far country across the sea—to Rome, to receive a kingdom from Cæsar (Josephus, 'Ant.,' xiv. 14; xvii. 9). And one of these two nobles, Archelaus, had rebuilt the stately royal palace of Jericho, under the very shadow of which the Speaker and the crowds were perhaps standing.

Ver. 13.—**And he called his ten servants, and delivered them ten pounds, and said unto them, Occupy till I come.** No doubt when our Lord spoke these parables he considerably enlarged the details, made many parts of the framework clearer than the short reports which we possess can possibly do. The meaning of the great noble's action here is that he wished to test his servants—to try their various capabilities and dispositions, intending, when he should return from his long journey, having received his kingdom, to appoint them to high offices in the administration, to such positions, in fact, as their action in regard to the small deposit now entrusted to them should show themselves capable of filling. The Greek verb rendered "occupy" (πραγματεύσασθε) occurs here only in the New Testament: a compound form of it is rendered (ver. 15) by "gained by trading."

Ver. 14.—**But his citizens hated him.** Again history supplies the framework. This was what the Jews had done in the case of Archelaus. They had sent a hostile deputation to complain of their future king before the emperor's court at Rome. In the parable, in these "citizens who hated him" a thinly veiled picture is given of those Jews who utterly rejected the mission of Jesus, and by whose designs the Crucifixion was brought about.

Ver. 16.—**Thy pound.** At first the smallness of the sum given to each of the servants is striking. Was it not a sum unworthy of a noble about to receive a kingdom?

The Attic pound was in value somewhat less than £4 sterling. In the parable of the talents (Matt. xxv. 14—30), where although very different lessons are inculcated, yet the imagery is somewhat similar, the amounts, however, are vastly larger, varying from five talents, which would represent about £1000. Here the very smallness of the sum entrusted to the servants has its deep meaning. The "nobly born" one who is about to receive a kingdom, represents our Lord, who *here* is in a state of the deepest poverty and humiliation. The little sum in one sense represents the work he was able *then* to entrust to his own. Again, the paltriness of the sum given them seems to suggest what a future lay before them. No sharing in what they hoped for—the glories of a Messianic kingdom on earth. No rest in repose under the shadow of the mighty throne of King Messiah. The "very little" (ver. 17) told them—if they would only listen—that their future as his servants would be a life of comparatively obscure inglorious activity, without rank or power, landless, homeless, well-nigh friendless. But the sequel of the parable told more than this. It proclaimed that their Master was able to estimate the moral worth of those who had been faithful and true in a "very little;" ay, more, was in a position to reward the faithful servant. And the recompense, a city for a pound, just hints at the magnificent possibilities of the heaven-life, just suggests the splendour of its rewards.

Ver. 17.—**Well, thou good servant.** It is noticeable that, in the bestowal of the "five cities" upon the servant who had with his one pound gained five, no expression of praise like this "good servant" is used by the King on his return. Now, what does this omission teach us? Christ, we know, was very careful and very sparing in his use of moral epithets. "Why callest thou me good?" was his stern address to the young ruler who used the expression, not because he was convinced of its applicability, but because he was desirous of paying a flattering compliment to the wise Rabbi from whom he desired information. We may safely conclude that, from the second servant in the story, the one who had earned but five pounds, he withheld the noble appellation "good" because he felt he had not deserved it. He had done *well*, it is true, and was splendidly recompensed, but he might have done *more*. He had won a high and responsible place in the kingdom; he was appointed the ruler over five cities; but he had not earned the noble title ἀγαθος, "good." Very accurately, indeed, it seems, will places and names and power be awarded in the heaven-life, exactly in proportion to merits and deserts.

Vers. 20, 21.—**And another came, saying, Lord, behold, here is thy pound, which I have kept laid up in a napkin: for I feared thee, because thou art an austere man: thou takest up that thou layedst not down, and reapest that thou didst not sow.** This is the third class into which the servants who knew their Lord's will are roughly divided. We have, first, the devoted earnest toiler, whose whole soul was in his Master's work—great, indeed, was his reward. And, second, we have the servant who acquitted himself fairly respectably, but not nobly, not a hero in the struggle of life; he, too, is recompensed magnificently, far above his most ardent hopes, but still his reward is infinitely below that which the first brave toiler received at his Lord's hands. The third falls altogether into a different catalogue. He is a believer who has not found the state of grace offered by Jesus so brilliant as he hoped; a legal Christian, who has not tasted grace, and knows nothing of the gospel but its severe morality. It seems to him that the Lord gives very little to exact so much. "Surely," such a one argues, "the Lord should be satisfied with us if we abstain from doing ill, from squandering our talent." The Master's answer is singularly to the point: "The more thou knowest that I am austere, the more thou shouldest have tried to satisfy me!" The Christian who lacks the experience of grace ought to be the most anxious of workers. The punishment here is very different from that awarded to the enemies (ver. 27). We hear nothing of darkness and gnashing of teeth; it is simply *deprivation*. Still, even this modified penalty seems to tell of an eternity of regret and loss. Instead of the ten cities, or even the five, there is not even the poor pound left to the hapless condemned one, unworthy even to retain that little heritage.

Ver. 23.—**Wherefore then gavest not thou my money into the bank, that at my coming I might have required mine own with usury?** Many in "the bank" have seen mirrored those Christian societies and religious organizations to which every believer may entrust the resources which he is uncertain how best to use himself. Without particularizing, however, it seems better to understand the Lord here simply intending to teach, by his image of the bank, that no man in this world is doomed to inactivity or uselessness, but that there will be opportunity afforded to every one who is willing to use his talent in a humble and obscure, if not in a heroic and conspicuous, way.

Ver. 27.—**But those mine enemies, which would not that I should reign over them, bring hither, and slay them before me.** An obvious reference to the Lord's dealings with the chosen people, and an unmistakable reference to the awful ruin and disaster which was so soon to overwhelm the city and temple and the whole nationality. But behind this temporal reference there looms in the background the vast shadow of a terrible eternal doom reserved for the enemies of the Redeemer. Godet has a beautiful and suggestive note on the signification of the ten and five cities, the reward of the faithful toiler here. "They," the "cities," "represent mortal beings in a lower state of development, but whom the glorified faithful are commissioned to raise to their Divine destination."

Vers. 28—48.—*Jesus enters Jerusalem as King Messiah* (vers. 29—44). *His work in the temple* (vers. 45—48). St. Luke here passes over in silence the events which happened after the episode at the house of Zacchæus at Jericho and the speaking the great parable of "the pounds." This parable may have been spoken in the house of Zacchæus before leaving Jericho, but it seems better to place it somewhere in the course of the walk from Jericho to Bethany, a distance of some twelve miles.

St. John fills up the gap left in the narrative of St. Luke.

The main body of pilgrims to the feast, with whom Jesus and his company were travelling, left him on the Jericho road at Bethany: they going on to their caravanserai in the holy city, he remaining for two nights with his friends at Bethany—the next evening Jesus was entertained at Bethany in the house of Simon the leper (Matt. xxvi. 6—13; Mark xiv. 3—9)—the feast at which Lazarus the risen sat a guest and Martha served, and to which Mary brought her precious ointment and her contrition (John xi. 1—9).

Jesus must have arrived at Bethany before sunset on Friday, Nisan 7, and therefore before the sabbath began.

The sabbath was spent in quiet. The supper probably took place directly after the end of the sabbath. The next morning (Palm Sunday) the Lord started for Jerusalem, and entered the holy city in the triumphant way as King Messiah related by St. Luke in our Gospel.

Ver. 29.—**And it came to pass, when he was come nigh to Bethphage and Bethany.** Bethphage is never mentioned in the Old Testament, but in the Talmud we find it specified in some interesting ceremonial directions. It was evidently an outlying suburb of Jerusalem. Bethphage, which lay between the city and Bethany, was by the rabbis legally counted as part of Jerusalem. Bethany signifies "House of Dates," no doubt so called from its palm trees. Bethphage, "House of Green Figs," from its fig-orchards. The modern Bethany is known as *El-Azarieh* or *Lazarieh*, the name attaching to its connection with the history of Lazarus.

Ver. 30.—**Ye shall find a colt tied, whereon yet never man sat: loose him, and bring him hither.** The account of this transaction is less circumstantial in St. Luke than in the other evangelists. The reference to the prophecy of Zech. ix. 9 is here left out. This prophecy is, however, necessary for the full understanding of the mystic act of riding upon an ass's colt. St. Luke, compiling especially for Gentile readers, would feel that such a reference to the old Hebrew story would scarcely interest a foreigner, and would serve to distract such a one's interest in the progress of the great recital. For us, however, the meaning of the scene, read in the light of the Zechariah (ix. 9) words and of Hebrew story generally, is as follows: The disciples and multitude wished their Master to claim a kingdom. At this moment in his eventful history, aware that death awaited him in the course of the next few days, he chose to gratify them; so he claimed his kingdom, but a kingdom utterly unlike what *they* longed for. He came to his royal, sacred city in the strange guise foreshadowed by Zechariah, as a Prince of Peace, not with chariot and horse, but meekly riding on an ass's colt, claiming, too, a dominion from sea to sea, from the river to the ends of the earth (Zech. ix. 10). *Whereon yet never man sat.* For this reason specially adapted for a sacred use (see Numb. xix. 2; Deut. xxi. 3; 1 Sam. vi. 7).

Ver. 31.—**And if any man ask you, Why do ye loose him? thus shall ye say unto him, Because the Lord hath need of him.** Had he not right here? surely the cattle on a thousand hills were his! St. Matthew not only mentions the colt, but also the ass. This little detail is unnoticed by St. Luke. Probably the colt, though not broken in, would go the more quietly accompanied by its mother. But the reason of St. Matthew's special mention of the ass as well as of the colt was the reference to Gen. xlix. 11, in which Justin Martyr, in a curious chapter of the 'Dialogue with Trypho,' finds a direct reference to the ass and the foal (see Justin Martyr, 'Dialogue with Trypho,' c. liii.).

Ver. 35.—**They cast their garments upon the colt.** "An extemporized housing in default of the purple trappings. Doubtless the fittest of the proffered robes would be selected by the disciples" (Morrison).

Ver. 36.—**And as he went, they spread their clothes in the way.** A common act of homage to a king or royal personage. So in the case of Jehu, the officers of the army offered him this tribute (2 Kings ix. 13). So Agamemnon walked on costly carpets and tapestry when he entered his palace at Mycenæ. Clytemnestra, in the 'Agamemnon' of Æschylus, says—

"But, my loved lord,
Leave now that car; nor on the bare ground set
That royal foot, beneath whose mighty tread
Troy trembled. Haste, ye virgins, to whose care
This pleasing office is entrusted, spread
The streets with tapestry; let the ground be covered
With richest purple, leading to the palace,
That honour with just state may grace his entry."

(905—911.)

Ver. 37.—**At the descent of the mount of Olives, the whole multitude of the disciples began to rejoice and praise God with a loud voice for all the mighty works that they had seen.** At this point on the Bethany road the city of Jerusalem comes into view. Here a crowd of pilgrims to the Passover Feast, many of whom were well acquainted with Jesus, came out to meet and welcome him with their branches of palm. These joined his friends who accompanied him from Bethany. This enthusiasm was excited among the Passover pilgrims in great measure owing to the report which by this time had got abroad of the raising of Lazarus (see John xii. 17, 18). Many had already gone out from the city to Bethany to see Jesus and Lazarus. Of the Messianic shouts of welcome which sounded in the crowd, St. Luke does not mention the "Hosanna!" of St. Matthew, no doubt because this peculiar Hebrew cry would not have conveyed any meaning to the Gentile readers to whom his story was especially addressed. The two incidents which follow—the crying out of the stones, and the weeping of the Master over his beautiful doomed city (vers. 39-44)—occur only in St. Luke. His source of information here was evidently quite different to the other two synoptists or St. John.

Vers. 39, 40.—**And some of the Pharisees from among the multitude said unto him, Master, rebuke thy disciples. And he answered and said unto them, I tell you that, if these should hold their peace, the stones would immediately cry out.** These Pharisees were probably some of that great and influential sect who had all along listened with respect and attention to the Master, looking upon him as a most able and powerful Rabbi, but refusing to entertain any of the growing Messianic conceptions respecting his person. Godet graphically paints the scene in his suggestion that the words, "Rebuke thy disciples," were accompanied with an irritated and anxious look towards the frowning citadel of Antonia, where the Roman garrison of Jerusalem lay. It was there in full view of Jesus and the crowds. The anxious look seemed to say that the Romans were on the watch for any signs of disaffection on the part of the hated and suspected Jews. The answer of Jesus, continues the same writer, has a terrible majesty. "If I could silence all these," looking round on the impassioned faces of the multitude as they waved their palm branches in homage to their King, "the very stones on the ground would cry aloud." This striking imagery was a memory of our Lord of the prophecy of Habakkuk: "The stone shall cry out of the wall, and the beam out of the timber shall answer it" (ii. 11).

Ver. 41.—**He beheld the city.** It was a very different view to what the traveller of the present day would see from the same spot. Though Jerusalem, when Jesus Christ was teaching on earth, was subject to the stranger Herodian, and the Herodian to the great Italian power, yet the beauty and glory of the city were remarkable. Still glittered in the midst of the great city that "mass of gold and snow" known as the temple. The far-extending suburbs were covered with the gardens and palaces of the wealthy Jews. But the mighty memories which hung so thickly round the sacred city and the glorious house of God after all constituted its chief charm. What might not that city have been! what splendid and far-reaching work might it not have done! and now the cup of its iniquities was just brimming over; only a few more short years, and a silence the most awful would brood over the shapeless ruins of what was *once* Jerusalem and her house on Zion, the joy of the whole earth. **And wept over it.** No merely silent tears of mute sorrow, but ἔκλαυσεν, he wept aloud. All the insults and the sufferings of the Passion were powerless to elicit from the Man of sorrows that expression of intense grief which the thought of the ruin of the loved city called forth.

Ver. 42.—**If thou hadst known, even thou, at least in this thy day.** The emphatic repetition of the "thou," and the broken form of the sentence, tell of the intense feeling of the Divine Speaker. "In this thy day." There was still time, still one day left, before his terrible trial-time began, which filled up the measure of Jerusalem and her people's iniquity. *Still one day* in which, had they only known "the things which belonged to their peace," they might have won a forgiveness for all the past centuries of sin.

Vers. 45, 46.—**And he went into the temple.** The recital of St. Luke here is more general and less precise than that of the other two synoptists. The Lord on that "Palm Sunday" evening simply went into the temple, "and when he had looked round about upon all things" it was then evening, and he returned to his lodging at Bethany with the twelve (Mark xi. 11). The expulsion of the money-changers, mentioned in the next verse (46), took place on the following day. St. Matthew adds another interesting detail respecting the excitement caused by the presence of Jesus in the city. "When he was come into Jerusalem, all the city was moved, saying, Who is this?" (Matt. xxi. 10). **And he went into the temple, and began to cast out them that sold therein, and them that bought; saying unto them, It is written, My house is the house of prayer: but ye have made it a den of thieves.** This visit of the Lord to the temple, in which he spoke and acted as King Messiah, was a fulfilment of Mal. iii. 1, 2. In the outer court of the temple stalls had been erected in which money-changers were located (*geld-wechsel comptoir — change de monnaies*), in order that pilgrims from foreign lands might be able to exchange their foreign coins for the purchase of sacrificial victims. These also seem to have been sold in the precincts. All this made the courts of the Lord's house a scene of noise and tumult, and, from the Master's stern words, a scene often of cheating and overreaching. The words of Jesus were taken from Isa. lvi. 7 and Jer. vii. 11.

Ver. 47.—**And he taught daily in the temple.** This and the following verses give, after the manner of St. Luke, both in his Gospel and in the Acts, a general picture of the Lord's life in these last days of his public ministry in Jerusalem; and of the effect of his last teaching (1) upon the priests and scribes, etc., and (2) upon the mass of the people. The Greek word rendered "very attentive to hear (him)" is an expressive one, and describes the intense attention with which the people generally listened to the last solemn public utterances of the Master. It means literally, "they hung upon his lips."

HOMILETICS.

Vers. 1—10.—*Zacchæus.* Very pleasant was the city of Jericho when our Lord passed through it; and very pleasant is the Scripture which records the visit of Jesus to it. It has a fragrance like that of the roses and palms in which the gardens of Jericho were luxurious; its verses remind us of the cells of the many honeycombs for which it was famous. Each verse is full of sweet and holy thought. A child can understand it; an angel will desire to look into it. One of the two incidents which have made Jericho memorable in connection with the life of the Saviour of men has been already considered. That which is told in the verses before us points to a different series of circumstances, a different and perhaps fuller illustration of the more Catholic aspect of Christ's mission. Consider three points.

I. The incident illustrates A PURPOSE TRIUMPHANT OVER HINDRANCES. These hindrances connect with social position, with wealth, with personal disqualifications. 1. *He was a tax-gatherer.* His place was usually filled by Roman knights, who farmed the taxes that they might replenish their empty coffers. It was a calling which aroused the hostility of the Jews. And to be a social Ishmael is hurtful to all that is generous and noble in the breast. He was "chief among the publicans"—a great man to whom many deferred; with the temptation, therefore, to imagine that the crowd was a vulgarity to be shunned, and so to isolate himself from the enthusiasms of the townsfolk. 2. *He was rich.* Almost insensibly a kind of pride grows in the person who is wealthy. He is conscious of his means. And the comfort with which they surround him tends to dull the edge of more spiritual feeling, to withdraw the interest from truths which imply the sense of need and poverty. He might have said to himself, "This Jesus of Nazareth, what is he to me? I have all that heart can desire: why should I make an ado about this travelling Prophet?" 3. *He was short of stature.* A little man: what hope was there that he would obtain a glimpse of the passing Nazarene? Why should he expose himself to the risk of being laughed at, especially when the chances were against his obtaining even a glimpse of the Stranger? Against all such hindrances the purpose to see Jesus is supreme. He must; the necessity of his soul makes him quick in invention. He forces his way through the crowd, climbs the small sycamore tree, and there he waits. He knows, confusedly enough, but by a kind of intuition, that the Poorest of all who on foot treads the street is his Lord; that with him is the wealth wanting which a man has no real inheritance. When the fountains of the inner deep are broken up, when any one is in earnest about the kingdom of God and his righteousness, the mere accidents of position and circumstance are forgotten. The Princess Alice of England, on her dying-bed, acknowledged her debt to a Scotsman in humble life for the help he had given in bringing her soul back to its rest in Christ. Zacchæus, chief among the publicans, heeds not appearances, thinks not of dignity, runs before the multitude, perches himself on the branch of the fig tree that he might see him whom his soul loved.

II. The incident illustrates THE MEETING BETWEEN A SUPREME PURPOSE IN MAN AND THE PURPOSE OF THE LOVE OF GOD. It may be said that the publican's motive was mere curiosity. Supposing that it was, it brought about the sight of the Lord. Curiosity impelled Augustine to the church of Ambrose in Milan, and there Christ found him. It is a gain to get people, even from an inferior desire, within the reach of the gospel of grace: who knows whether the one who came to scoff may not remain to pray? But was there not a cause deeper than mere curiosity at work in Zacchæus? He may not have had the same kind of plea as blind Bartimæus, but he had his own plea; and what Christ asks from each of us is that, as we are, in the specialties of our need and condition, we come to him. Faith carries an "I must" in its bosom. It always presses: "To-day I must see thee who thou art." That day the two "I musts," the one in the sinner, the other in the Saviour's heart, meet and touch. "Zacchæus, to-day I must abide at thy house" (ver. 5). What a journey that "*I must*" of Jericho represents! Has it not come from the heaven of heavens, out from the bosom of the great God himself? The fig leaves and branches cannot hide from Christ. The eyes of the two are seeking each other. He looks up; the one for whom he is in search receives the gaze. That one knows that he is looked into; he is understood; he is named. And the fellowship is formed from which neither things present nor things to come can separate.

III. The incident illustrates THE PURPOSE OF A MIND RENEWED IN ITS SPIRIT. What is the response to the Lord's "make haste"? "He made haste, and came down, and received him joyfully" (ver. 6). The whole heart opens to this new Master. There is no further asking who he is. That has been answered by the heart itself; and the welcome to his home, to all, immediately follows. If Christ will take one such as he,

> "Love so amazing, so Divine,
> Demands the soul, the life, the all."

There is more than this. We need not discuss whether the noble speech recorded in ver. 8 is the vindication of the publican as against the calumnies of those around him, indicating that he had not been the unjust extortioner whom they took him to be; that he had been in the habit of giving half of his goods to the poor. The latter part of the verse at least is the expression of a solemn purpose formed in Christ's presence. It indicates a change of character. "Is his *pocket* converted?" was a question put, when the conversion of one who had been greedy and selfish was announced. Hitherto this Zacchæus had lived to make money; now he will live to use it. Hitherto he had lived for himself; now he will live for God. Henceforth he will aim, not only at being just, but at making others the better and happier for him. When Christ is received joyfully, the narrow becomes the broad, the hard becomes the generous; the levels of the life are altered: "Old things pass away, and all things become new."

IV. Reflecting on the incident, two points are to be noted—its revelation of Christ, and its enforcement of the solemn word "opportunity." 1. *Christ the Brother and Saviour.* (1) It is interesting to observe that, on the same day, poor and rich were visibly embraced within the love of God. That love stretches from pole to pole in human experience and condition. Christ's sympathies are not with class as against class; for he is the Son of man. When the beggar comes he is so polite: "What wilt thou?" As to Zacchæus, he turns to the Jews (ver. 9). Everywhere he recognizes a something of God—a jewel to be snatched from among the ruins. "He is not afraid of consorting with the rich lest people should say he cares too much for money, any more than he is of consorting with the poor lest they should say he cares too little for respectability. He will dine with the Pharisee, if invited; and he will dine with a publican, even when uninvited, if the man's heart be indeed a guest-chamber." The most brotherly of hearts is the heart of God. (2) The Brother and the Saviour. See the sentence in which the conjunction is realized (ver. 10). It was spoken with immediate reference to Zacchæus. He was lost, for he had lived alone; and whoso lives alone, away from the light of God, out of sympathy with his brethren, an outside person, is really one lost. And is not Christ among us to bring the outsiders in, to awaken up dead worldly souls, and restore them to communion with the Father in heaven and the Father's children on earth? Christ is the Saviour because he is the Brother, and he is the Brother because he is the Son. Look at the Saviour in his work of love. The royalty of his grace shines marvellously forth. Note the *self*-invitation: "I love him because he first loved me." Note also the joy of salvation—not a passing glimpse —"I *must abide*." There is a new rule, a new companionship, a new mirth. 2. *The word "opportunity" is enforced.* That word contains the lesson most obviously taught in every part of the story. Jesus is passing; to-day and to-day only. There is no time to trifle. "Make haste, and come down."

Vers. 11—27.—*The parable of the pounds.* This parable closely resembles that reported in Matt. xxv. 14—30. The two are undoubtedly different, but they have much in common. We cannot rightly understand each without balancing it by the other. Certainly we realize the full effect of their application when, to borrow an expressive figure, we look on them "as twin parables, resembling one of those trees whose main trunk separates just above the earth into two equal towering stems." Thus connecting them, let us extract a portion of the instruction conveyed, our topics these: (1) *The endowments bestowed;* (2) *the trading recommended;* and (3) *the dealing of the Master with his servants presented.*

I. Observe the two principles which run in parallel lines as THE PRINCIPLES OF GOD'S DISTRIBUTION OF ENDOWMENTS. 1. *The parable of the talents* suggests an inequality in the gifts or faculties with which God enriches men: one gets five talents, another two, and another one. And this description is entirely consistent with fact. It is true as to even the commonest things; it is true as to higher qualities of intellect and will. There is no dead level. There are hills and plains; there are gardens and deserts in man's world as well as in the physical universe. God takes fact into account. He distributes according to ability; he imposes responsibility according to ability. He does not demand that the one with two talents make the ten—only the four. Let the vessel, according to its possibilities, be full; the smaller vessel is not required to hold the amount of the larger. One farm may not be as extensive as another, but it is still a farm. Cultivate to the measure of the farm; make full use of the capital such as it is. "What but this, O man, does the Lord thy God require of thee?" 2. But *observe the teaching in the parable of the pounds.* If talents are unequally bestowed, remember every one has his pound. The pound was of very small value as compared with the talent—£3 or a little more as compared with £160. The ten servants get each one pound—the same sum in every case. We have varying capacity, but we have all some capacity—"a little knowledge, a little love, a little experience, a little money, a little favour with men, a little conscience, a little pity, a little time, a little opportunity." We have one mina, one pound. Work, my brother, with thy pound, rather with the pound that the Lord has given thee. It may be increased tenfold, and the gain is (ver. 17) a city for every added pound—a blessing in possession, and rule, wholly unmerited by, yet graciously corresponding to, the servant's faithfulness.

II. WHAT MEANS THE OCCUPYING OR TRADING WHICH THE LORD ENJOINS ON ALL TO WHOM HE GIVES HIS GOODS? Let it be remembered that, in the olden time, the relation between master and servant was different from that in our time. It is not usual to leave sums of money to the servant to be put out by him in his master's behalf when he takes a journey into the far country. But it was a common practice to make such arrangements as allowed the slave to transact business, either on condition of paying a yearly sum to his master, or on the footing of a man with so much of another's wealth committed to his charge to be invested for the other's benefit. To this custom our Lord refers. "Occupy [or, 'trade'] till I come." The two persons opposed are the trader and the idler; and the striking feature is that the idler is denounced as "the slothful and wicked servant." All start with some advantages; they are not persons just hired; they have been in his service, they know his character, and they know what he wants. The one who does not trade is lying when he excuses himself; his slothfulness (ver. 22) is sheer wickedness. The point of the exhortation can very readily be apprehended. God wants his interest, as the merchant wants his. How is this interest to be gained? The purpose and destination of life must be kept steadily in view—

"Not enjoyment, and not sorrow,
Is our destined end and way;
But to act that each to-morrow
Find us farther than to-day."

Recollect that the self in each of us connects with two factors—God who made us; and our brother, whose good is to be as sacred to us as our own. We cannot be making increase unless we are true to him whose we are, and to every one who is near us; unless both God and man are benefited, and benefited the more the greater our means and ability are. Consider how we can best lay out our influence, whatever that may be; how we can best use our time; how we can get the best percentage for whatever capacity, whatever force, we possess. As it is essential to a prosperous business that there be a good administration, reflect how we are administering the affairs with which, in one sphere or another, we are entrusted—in a word, on what plan, with what aim, and by what methods, our life is being fulfilled. Give two men five pounds each; in the hands of the one they may remain five pounds neither more nor less, or they will gradually melt away; the other will spend the sum wisely, will so invest it that it will increase to him tenfold. We have read the story of the successful merchant of Bristol—the beginning of whose merchant life was the horseshoe that he picked up one day on his way to school, and carried for three miles and sold to the blacksmith for a penny. That penny was the foundation of a business pronounced, after his death, the largest in the West of England, turning nearer millions than thousands in the course of the year. All was the result of the judicious use of that which he had. In our Christian life and service this is the lesson which we most need to learn. Is there not comfort in the thought that, whilst the talents increase only twice, the pounds increase ten times? The more ordinary gifts which we all have, when faithfully applied, are capable of indefinite increase. We cannot keep unless we add; and it is God's law that to him who, thus adding, has, much is given. In spiritual, as in every other kind of commerce, much always tends to the making of more. The trader and the idler! Notice, neither the talent nor the pound is absolutely lost. It is not a spendthrift who is held up to contempt. It is the awfully careful man. It is the one who hoards. "There is that scattereth, and yet increaseth; and there is that withholdeth, . . . and it tendeth to poverty." Here is the one who withholds. And a distinction is delicately hinted at. The pound is carefully wrapped in the napkin; the man intends to do something with it when the convenient season comes; in the mean time it is safe in the napkin. But the talent is not in a napkin; it is hidden in the earth—"a precious thing," as it has been said, "made worthless because abandoned to be useless. And within how many a man's earthiness is there a talent hidden and wasted?" Take that thought home—the Master's antipathy to the idler. Who of us, in these harvest-days of God, is standing all the day idle?

III. Consider THE DEALING OF THE LORD WITH HIS SERVANTS. That is very striking and solemn as it is set before us in both the parables, especially the one as to the talents. In that of the pounds we are told only that the unused, napkin-hidden, pound is taken from the unprofitable servant and given to the one who has ten pounds. "Lord," his hearers exclaim, "he hath ten pounds" (ver. 25). The thriftiest, the most diligent, will get the addition. Why not? He has proved himself the ablest, the one who has given the most abundant guarantee that it will not be wasted. But in that of the talents the judgment is, "Let the unfaithful be bound hand and foot, and cast into the outer darkness." The wasted life, the life that has buried its force in mere earthiness, is that for which the outer darkness is reserved. The soul consigns itself to an unspeakable loneliness that, by indolence and engrossment with what is perishing, loses the grace of God. Abiding alone is the second death—the outer darkness. Most noteworthy are the scathing sentences to the poor trembling idler! How he stammers out his lame and impotent excuses (vers. 20, 21)! The very words are sent back. The mouth is the witness against the man. He might have known, should have known, if he had done right would have known, that his excuse was a falsehood. Hard thoughts of the Lord are certain if the Lord's work is shirked. The man would not be foolish if he were not wicked. O man, woman, with thy pound kept, but not traded with, who shall abide the day of his coming? who shall stand when he appeareth? Very different are the sentences on the nine who have been faithful, who have seen in their pound the Lord's pound, and traded with it for him. Humbly, joyfully, the first and the second meet the Master's eye (vers. 16, 18). What is the award? It is so gracious (ver. 17): "Thou hast been faithful *in a very little.*" To faithful service, rule is given. The one who can best serve is the one who can best rule.

"Strive, man, to win that glory;
Toil, man, to gain that light;
Send hope before to grasp it,
Till hope be lost in sight."

Vers. 28—44.—*From Jericho to Jerusalem.* The last glimpse which we obtain of Moses presents him wending his way up the slope of Mount Nebo, thence to give one fond gaze towards the land he might not enter, and, having so done, then to lay himself down and die. Imagination has often attempted to portray the working of the great lawgiver's mind, the emotion of his heart, the thoughts which must have crowded on him as he took that last solitary journey to the sepulchre which no man must know, in which the Lord alone was to bury him. Jesus Christ, by whom came grace and truth, is now facing the hill of sacrifice. He has begun the ascent to Mount Calvary, not alone and yet alone; the people crowd behind, but of the people there is none with him in the region of consciousness and desire. Only the Father knows the Son. Let us not attempt to draw aside the veil. Words to be pondered, but not commented on, are these (ver. 28): "When he had thus spoken, he went before, ascending up to Jerusalem." Coming near the capital, Jesus and his apostles made for Bethany. It was Friday evening. He must spend the last sabbath on earth in the quiet of the rural village. We can suppose what that sabbath was—not so much to him, for now he is moving in a sphere beyond our vision, but to those with whom he passed the hallowed hours. When the sun sets and the sabbath is over, a family feast is made in the house of Simon, once a leper. Lazarus, the man raised from the dead, one of the party, Martha for the time resuming her old ways, and Mary filling her heart with his love, until, swayed by an irresistible impulse, she pours on him the contents of an alabaster box of ointment—the preparation against the approaching burial. It was on the Sunday morning that the Lord set out for Jerusalem, at first in the ordinary guise of a pilgrim. People were hovering around the home, waiting for him, and at every step of the journey the number increased. Then occurred the transaction mentioned in vers. 29—35. From a place not now to be identified, but not far from Bethany, called Bethphage, or "the house of figs," the Saviour "in lowly pomp rides on to die." Verily, the King comes, "meek and lowly." His state, his pageant, at best is humble. And yet its simplicity is its royalty; its want of the poor tinsel and trapping of earthly greatness is the sign of the kingdom which is in the world, yet not of it. "Behold the Man!" "Behold your King!" The procession sweeps onward, along the southern shoulders of Olivet, until the road, having gained the summit of the hill, turns northward and begins the descent. And there the stream that had poured out from Jerusalem when the news was borne that the Prophet was on his way to the city met the stream pouring towards Jerusalem, and the disciples, inspired by an enthusiasm which was caught up and prolonged by the multitude, rent the air with songs (ver. 38) of joy and praise to God, and rock and cave and peak sent it back in gladsome echoes. Truly, a soul-stirring entry! The whole city is moved as Jesus of Nazareth rides through its gate, and passes towards Mount Zion and the holy and beautiful house which glitters on its heights. Before we think of him there, pause over two characteristic signs of the King given in his journey on that day.

I. THE KING'S WORD OF POWER. (Ver. 31.) "Say, The Lord hath need of him." We do not believe that there was any secret agreement between Christ and the owner of the colt. But he was a man prepared for the announcement; he was at least in the outer circle of believers. He understood who was meant by "the Lord," and the Lord's need was the one irresistible argument. So should it be. That the Lord needs, that there is a use for us and ours, should be enough. First, the King's word has its bond over us personally. Man, woman, it is for thee that Jesus calls. He needs thy heart, for he redeemed it; thy life, for it is his; thyself, for "he is thy Lord, and worship thou him." Shall not the response "straightway" be, "Now to be thine, for ever thine"? And then the possessions. Art thou ready to give him what thou hast, however dear it may be? Ah! the life is a new life when Christ's voice, as the voice of the life's true Master, is heard, and the answer is returned, "Here am I; for thou didst call me."

II. THE KING'S SORROW. (Ver. 41.) "He beheld the city, and wept over it." It has been noticed that "at the grave of Lazarus he had dropped silent tears, but here he wept aloud. All the shame of his mockery, all the anguish of his torture, was powerless to extort from him a single groan, or to wet his eyelids with one trickling tear, but here all the pity that was in him overmastered his human spirit, and he not only wept, but broke into a passion of lamentation in which the choked voice seemed to struggle for its utterance." It was the agony of the Saviour over the lost. There had been the time of the visitation, and Jerusalem had not known it. Now was the day, the hour, the last offer, the last opportunity; and it was to be rejected. The city was hardened in ignorance. It was blinded by its own deceived heart, and all that remained was ruin. And thus he weeps still; for still men hear their own passions and inclinations, not the voice of the prophets whom he rises early and sends.

"Ye hearts that love the Lord,
If at this sight ye burn,
See that in thought, in deed, in word,
Ye hate what made him mourn."

Ver. 45—ch. xx. 18.—*Passion Week.* The last of the old Hebrew prophets, Malachi (iii. and iv.), had announced that the Lord, the Sought One, would come "suddenly" into his temple, and manifest himself there in a threefold character—that of Judge, that of the Purifier and Refiner, and that of the swift Witness of the kingdom of heaven. It is in this threefold character that Christ is presented during the week in which he suffered. *The Judge.* St. Mark, with his usual delicacy of touch, informs us that, after the procession which swept through the gates of the city halted at the foot of Mount Moriah, Jesus advanced to the temple, walked through its courts, and looked round about on all things (Mark xi. 11). Every part of the building, every arrangement, every feature, was comprehended in that gaze. It was the act of the Judge. The survey completed, the *Purifier and Refiner* disposes his crucible. At the beginning of the ministry he cleansed the house of his Father, which had been rendered a den of merchandise; at the end of the ministry he repeats the cleansing (vers. 45, 46). Jerusalem was crowded; outside the city wall there was a vast city of pilgrims' booths. For the sale of victims for sacrifice, and no doubt for the vending of many wares besides, the temple precincts were for the time a huge holy fair. One could scarcely distinguish that its real purpose was an asylum for weary hearts, a refuge for sin-stricken consciences, a place for quiet meditation and prayer. Where, amid the hubbub of buyer and seller, could the pious Israelite "dwell in the courts of Jehovah, beholding his beauty and inquiring in his temple"? It is this that kindles the wrath of the Son of God, and incites to the action portrayed by the synoptic evangelists. "Who shall stand when he appears who is like a refiner's fire, and like fuller's soap?" This purging of the holy house of that which made it like a cave of brigands was the work of that first day, which has been called Palm Sunday. The night which followed was spent in Bethany, perhaps on the slope of Olivet. On the second day we find the Lord again in the temple, and now in the third of Malachi's characters—as the *swift Witness* against the enemies of God. This was the aspect of his countenance on the days which remained until the night came on which, in the form of his human presence, the Lord could no more work. "He taught daily in the temple" (ver. 47). The events of the Monday would seem to be these: In the keen-aired early morning, Jesus, on his way to the temple, is hungry. He sees (Matt. xxi. 19; Mark xi. 12—14) a fig tree, evidently a conspicuous one, which, rich in leaves, gave the promise of fruit. There is nothing but leaves, a mere *simulacrum*, the semblance without the reality of goodness. As a lesson to all the ages, a swift witness against all part-acting, he pronounces over it the curse of the Eternal Truth, and leaves it to wither and rot. The temple gained, again the dense crowd gathers around the Prophet of Nazareth. The phrase is most expressive: "The people were very attentive to hear him" (ver. 48). The tide had not yet turned. He was still engirt by the hosannahs of the multitude; when, lo! cries are heard, "Make way for the chief priest!" and, followed by a retinue of priests and scribes, the head of the temple-worship confronts the Teacher. Poor, purblind souls! they do not look for his authority to the truth with which he is filled, to the works which he does. To bigots like them the certificates which the truth supplies are unintelligible; their only point is a formally expressed delegation of power (ch. xx. 2). Had not Jesus met similar cavils at the Feast of Tabernacles two years before? Had he not argued (John v. 32—47) that it is impossible for minds brimful of prejudice, loving and courting the honour of men, to understand him, to know whose he is, whence he comes, and by what right he speaks? But now he will not thus argue. They are there to browbeat and overawe him; they shall themselves be silenced by a thrust impaling them on the horns of a dilemma from which they will escape only in confusion and chagrin. Question is replied to by the question of ch. xx. 3, 4. They cannot answer. Then, rejoins the Truth, "Neither tell I you by what authority I do these things" (ver. 8). And there follows a series of parables bearing on and bringing out the obstinacy which had just been exemplified: the two sons; the wicked husbandmen; and the marriage of the king's son. Only the second of these is quoted by St. Luke (xx. 9—16). The parable is in harmony with well-known prophetic symbols; *e.g.* Isa. v. 1—7. The vineyard is the kingdom of God, which had been planted in Israel; the husbandmen are the priests and scribes to whom had been committed the care of the vineyard; the servants sent—first one, then another, and then a third—to demand the fruit, represent the prophets, ending with John the Baptist; and the climax of the wickedness of the husbandmen is the rejection and death of the beloved Son. "What will the owner do with such men?" Christ demands. He pauses for the reply; and, not perceiving that it is pronouncing its own judgment, his audience answers, "He will miserably destroy them, and give the vineyard to others." Ah! priest and Pharisee, out of your own mouth are you condemned. "The kingdom of heaven shall be taken from you, and given to a nation bringing forth the fruits thereof." And from startled consciences comes back the shuddering, "God forbid!" He has not done with them. The eye, flashing its holy fire, fastens on the crouching multitude, and, resuming the discourse, he sends straight home the words of Ps. cxviii. 22, 23. Solemn, memorable words! Pause and ponder them. The spurning of the Incarnate Love and truth by those amongst whom he came often seems to us a miserable infatuation, a double-dyed sin against the Holy Ghost. Are we sure that Christ, coming as the swift Witness, would be welcomed even in the house of his friends to-day? The late General Gordon said, "*No;* he would be a Stranger, rejected, if not despised, by the society which is professedly Christian." One thing, at all events, is strange; and that is that men and women should live in such marvellous light as that into which we are called, and remain the men and women they are, unmoved by, unresponsive to, the voice of God, willing to live apart from him whose service is their perfect freedom. May we not summon ourselves before the great white throne of truth, and ask whether God is receiving from us the fruit of his own vineyard; whether we are consciously and really living to him; whether our attitude towards the Son of his love is that of a whole-hearted and loyal acceptance; or only like that which has been strikingly compared to "some fever-reduced patient, lifting himself up for an instant from the bed on which he is lying, and putting out a hand, and then falling back again, the vacillating, fevered, paralyzed will recoiling from the resolution, the conscience having power to say, 'Thou oughtest,' but with no power to enforce the execution of its decrees, and the heart turning away from the salvation that it would have found in the love of God to the loss that it finds in the love of self and earth." That vacillation, that impotence, is the strange, sad thing. Reflect intensely, prayerfully, on the house which the builders rejected. Which of the two ways is it, will it be: this House taken as the Head of the corner, the reconciling centre of all the days—pride, wilfulness falling on it, and through the fall broken? or, the house rejected, and the Corner-stone falling on the disobedient soul, grinding its very strength to powder? Love rejected—the wrath of the Lamb: who can measure that force?

HOMILIES BY VARIOUS AUTHORS.

Vers. 1—9.—*Zacchæus; the triumph of earnestness.* The incident here recorded provides a very good opportunity for the imagination. We can picture the scene before us quite vividly; it is a subject for the sacred artist. But let us look at *the triumph of earnestness* as illustrated in the story of Zacchæus.

I. It triumphed over THE PERIL WHICH ATTENDS WEALTH. This man was rich (ver. 2). Riches are unfavourable to religious earnestness; we have Christ's own word for it (ch. xviii. 24; see homily). They present a very strong inducement to their owner to forsake the fountain of living waters, and to quench his thirst in the lower streams. Far too often they lead to luxury, to indulgence, to spiritual indifference. But Zacchæus did not suffer this calamity to befall him, this fatal injury to be wrought upon him. His spiritual solicitudes won the victory over his temporal circumstances.

II. It triumphed over THE DEMORALIZING CALLING IN WHICH HE WAS ENGAGED. Our daily vocation must necessarily have a very great influence over us for good or evil; and if it be one that tends to lower and degrade a man, he is placed in the greatest possible peril. Much wisdom of mind, much resoluteness of soul, and much devoutness of spirit must be required to withstand the adverse powers. But though Zacchæus was engaged in a pursuit that invited avarice and oppression, still he did not lose his religious earnestness.

III. It triumphed over AN EVIL REPUTATION. Few things are more degrading than a bad name. Men quickly become what they are supposed to be and what they are called. Let all his neighbours consider and call a man a rogue, and it will be strange indeed if he maintains his integrity. Yet, although Zacchæus was denominated and dismissed as "a publican," spoken of by a term which was full of the strongest reproach, he did not descend to that level.

IV. It triumphed over THE OBSTACLES WHICH STOOD BETWEEN HIM AND CHRIST. He could not venture to solicit an interview with this holy Prophet; that he knew was completely barred by his vocation. He found it difficult to secure even a view of him as he passed along; his smallness of stature was against him. But such was his determination that he disregarded all considerations of dignity and decorum, and ran any risk of popular derision and affront, and climbed up, as if he had been a boy, into a tree to command a view of Jesus of Nazareth. So he prevailed.

V. IT WON WHOLLY UNEXPECTED GOOD. 1. The honour of entertaining this great Prophet at his own house; thus securing a standing to which he had long been a stranger. 2. The advantage of a protracted interview, an extended privilege, in which he could not only secure a few sentences from the great Teacher, but could unburden his heart to him and learn his holy will.

VI. IT LED TO NEWNESS OF LIFE. (Vers. 8, 9.) Zacchæus from that day forth was a new man. His character was thenceforth determined: whatever selfishness or wrongness there had been, it should be renounced, and, where possible, reparation should be made. Character and life were to be cleansed and renewed; and Christ took him up into his favour and friendship. He was to be perfectly restored to the position he had lost. By his pursuit and practice he had become an alien, disinherited, no longer admitted to the services of the sanctuary. But now he was to be, in the fullest and deepest sense of the word, "a son of Abraham," a far truer son of his than many who prided themselves on their descent from the "father of the faithful."

Thus *earnestness* of spirit completely prevailed. 1. *Only earnestness* will prevail. *Indifference* will go down to the death from which it is already not far removed. *Half-heartedness* will go only a very little way towards the goal; it will have to take some trouble and to suffer some pains, but it will not win the prize. Even *impulsiveness*, which bears a considerable resemblance to earnestness, but is not the same thing, will fail before the way is trodden and the end secured. Only earnestness wins. 2. *It always must.* Whatever comes in the way; whatever inward or outward obstacles present themselves; whatever personal or social hindrances intervene; however victory be delayed; notwithstanding that the case may again and again seem hopeless;—still in the end earnestness will succeed. Jesus Christ will manifest himself; he will found in the home; his presence and his grace will fill the soul with joy; he will declare sonship and heirship to his devoted and determined follower.—C.

Ver. 9.—*Forfeiture and recovery.* Our Lord's words refer in the first instance to—

I. THE LOSS AND RECOVERY BY ZACCHÆUS of his place in the commonwealth of Israel. 1. He had forfeited this. It was by no means inalienable. Only they were the true children of Abraham who did the deeds, who lived the life, who were possessed with the spirit, of Abraham. So our Lord taught himself (see John viii. 39). This was Paul's doctrine also (Rom. ii. 28, 29; ix. 7; Gal. iii. 7). The true child of Abraham was he who walked by faith, who was the servant and the friend of God (Isa. xli. 8). But Zacchæus had lost this true, this real and effectual sonship. For he had been living the life of sense, and not of faith; he had departed from the service of God, and engaged in the practice of extortion and corruption. He had ceased to be the friend of God, and made friendship with an evil world. 2. But now he was in the path of restoration. He was penitent; he was a seeker after heavenly wisdom in Jesus Christ; and this meant renewal of heart and life; it meant rising into a new and elevated region, breathing the pure air of devotion, of service, of righteousness; it meant the recovery of the forfeited birthright. Salvation had come to himself and his household; once more he was "a son of Abraham." We are thus led to look at—

II. THE SAD POSSIBILITIES OF FORFEITURE open to all the children of men. God made us to be heirs of all that is good and blessed—of liberty, of truth, of honour and of love, of himself and of his kingdom. But sin comes in and spoils our heritage; under its evil ban we lose our good estate; our inheritance is forfeited; instead of being the "sons of God" and the "children of wisdom," we become rather the "children of wrath." We may forfeit: 1. *Our liberty.* We may become, how many do become, enslaved by some evil habit which holds them fast in its strong coils—some bodily or mental habit! 2. *Our hold upon the truth.* We may lose our faith in, and our appreciation of, the leading and vital doctrines which bring us into close and conscious fellowship with God. 3. *Our very manhood.* For there are many who suffer themselves to sink so low in the moral scale that they forfeit all claim to be accounted men; their lives are simply brutal. 4. Our rightful place *in the estimate of our fellow-men.* We may lose all the esteem, the confidence, and (consequently) the affection of our neighbours. 5. *The friendship of Jesus Christ.* Too often those who once walked with him and worked for him stand aside, and "walk no more" by his side; they leave his service, they lose his loving favour, they cannot be any longer counted among his friends. And with all this there must be the sad and grievous forfeiture of: 6. *The hope of eternal life.* For when fidelity is lost, hope is lost also.

III. THE BLESSED OPENING FOR RESTORATION provided by the Saviour of souls. There is no "house," however fallen, to which "salvation" may not come; no human being, however sunk in sin and wrong, who may not be restored in the mercy of God by the power of Jesus Christ the Saviour. It is when *he* is admitted to the home and to the heart that recovery is attained. In him, for all earnest seekers, is escape from bondage and from error and unbelief; in his service is found the gradual but effectual return of the trust and the love of man; he offers the renewal of his friendship, and opens again the closed door of hope to the penitent and the believing spirit. The slave of sin becomes the son of God; the companion of the evil-doer becomes the friend and co-worker of Christ; the candidate for condemnation becomes the heir of heaven.—C.

Ver. 10.—*The great purpose of Christ.* Mankind had lost its way utterly, its way from the home of God, from the fields of truth, from the path of holiness, from the fountains of joy; was wandering, blind and miserable, in forbidden ways; was stumbling on the dark mountains of error and sin. And the Son of man came to seek this erring and lost race, to lead it back again, to restore it to its heritage in wisdom, in righteousness, in God. This great and most beneficent purpose is enough of itself to explain such action as he took on this occasion; it covers the propriety of the conduct which seemed at the time so inexplicable to the good people of his day. For on what more fitting errand could the Saviour be engaged than on that of saving another human soul from its sin and its shame, and lifting it up into the light and liberty of the truth? But there are three reasons which we gain from the words or the actions of our Lord which perfectly justified him (and would justify us) in seeking out and saving a lost human soul.

I. An appeal to our finer and nobler instincts. If you have a hundred sheep, and of these all but one are safely sheltered from the cold and protected from every peril, but that one is shut out, is away shivering in the blast, is exposed to the attack of the wild beast, is nearing the deadly precipice,—your heart prompts you to leave those that are safe, and to go and seek and rescue the one that is lost. Christ's heart prompts him to find that human soul which is lost in the mazes of error, or caught in the meshes of vice, or starving on the barren plains of unbelief. The most generous instincts of our nature will help us to understand his action when he went to the house of the publican, or suffered the daughter of shame to come in penitence to his feet.

II. An appeal to our higher interests. We should put forth that labour in the field of sacred usefulness which is most remunerative. But which answers best—attention to the pretentious Pharisee, or to the shamefaced publican? To forgive fifty shillings to him who will first dispute the claim and then think nothing of your readiness to forego it will not be so satisfactory as to forgive five hundred pounds to him who is constrained to acknowledge the indebtedness, and is filled with gratitude to you for cancelling it. To endeavour to convince the scribe and the Pharisee of sin would have proved vain and fruitless work; but to lead some guilty ones to penitence and purity was to earn unbounded gratitude, and to unloose streams of devoted love that should refresh the parched and thirsty soil.

III. An appeal to our sense of duty. The physician has several patients; some of them are not very ill, and these have the idea that they know what ails them and what remedies will do them good; but there are two or three that are dangerously, perhaps desperately ill, who do not know what they should do for recovery, and who will gladly take his advice and adopt his measures. To whom should he go but to those who need him most and will receive him best?

1. *Let us enter more into the pitifulness of spiritual degradation.* Sin is to be condemned, and strong indignation is often a duty and even a grace. But it is also very *pitiful.* Whether we find it in publican or harlot, in the covetous man or in the degraded woman, it is a thing to grieve over, even as Christ our Lord did, with a generous compassion; to affect our hearts with a pure and even deep distress. And if we should feel thus as we contemplate the condition of *one* lost human being, what should our emotion be in view of the multitudes who are sunk in superstition, in wrong-doing, in utter hopelessness and helplessness! When we "see these multitudes," should we not, like the Master, be "moved with compassion for them, because they as sheep without a shepherd"? May we not well exclaim—

"My God, I feel the mournful scene,
And my heart bleeds for dying men,
While fain my pity would reclaim
And snatch the firebrands from the flame"!

2. *Let us avail ourselves of every means for seeking and saving the lost:* whether it be individual effort, or action in combination with others, or liberal contribution to the missionary institution, let every opportunity be taken to follow in the path of love once trodden by "those sacred feet."—C.

Ver. 10.—*Saving the lost.* It has been questioned whether there can be mentioned one word which is more pathetic than any other. It might be well maintained that this word would be found in our text. What truly and profoundly pathetic pictures are called up before us by the sound of the word, "lost"! It speaks to us of the *vessel* far out of its track and drifting toward the rocks where it will find its ruin; it speaks of the *traveller* lost among the mountains, moving toward the precipice over which he is bound to fall and perish; it speaks of the *firm* whose affairs have been growing serious and have now become desperate, before which there is no other prospect than the closed door and a place in the gazette; and it speaks of the sad story, old as sin but young as yesterday, of one that has been deceived and led astray, over whose character and over whose future the darkest shadows rest. But our text reminds us of—

I. THE LOST WORLD WHICH CHRIST CAME TO SAVE. 1. There was a day in the history of heaven when it was announced that a new world was lost; that a race created in its Divine Maker's image was lost, had departed from the truth and wisdom of God, had left its home in his love, and had wandered away in guilt and wrong. 2. Only God himself could comprehend what *that* meant; what evil, what sorrow, what error, what darkness of soul, what wretchedness of life, what degradation of character, what deathfulness. 3. But the Son of God determined to restore it; ordered everything in his holy providence that would prepare for his own personal intervention; in due time manifested himself in the flesh, spake, wrought, lived, suffered, died, arose, reascended; left behind him the great work of redemption in all its fulness and fitness—the gospel of the grace of God.

II. THE LOST SOUL WHICH HE IS EVER SEEKING AND SAVING. 1. *The sense in which each sinful human soul is lost.* (1) It has lost *its way*; it is a traveller going in the wrong direction, away from his home toward the perilous precipice. (2) It has lost *its treasure*, its heritage; for it has lost its peace, its harmony, its accordance with all those beings to whom it is most nearly and vitally related; it has lost its hopes. (3) It has lost *its worth*, its likeness to the Holy One; it has been brought down to folly, to that which is unbeautiful and unworthy. 2. *The fact that Christ is seeking it.* (1) *He is tenderly interested in every human soul.* At all stages in its history. When it is in the far country he is regarding it with infinite compassion and Divine yearning; when the first thought of returning is kindled in the heart and the beginnings of penitence are seen; when there is earnestness which makes toward, but does not amount to, actual repentance (see Mark x. 21); when the soul is seeking its Saviour. (2) *He is endeavouring to win it.* He is coming to it by various approaches, laying a loving hand upon it at many points, addressing it in many tones, returning again and again to it in patient solicitude. "Behold, he stands at the door, and knocks." (3) *Our only possible response.* Not, indeed, that we *cannot* reject and refuse him; *we can*; it is open to us to do that. But, then, *how can we?* If we would not be shamefully and guiltily ungrateful, if we would not make his dying and ever-living love to be of no avail to us, if we have any regard for our own present and immortal blessedness, if we would win the prize and enjoy the heritage of eternal life, the only possible response we can make to the seeking Saviour is to open wide the door of our hearts and bid him enter and take full possession of our grateful and loving spirit.—C.

Vers. 12—27.—*Probation and award.* Jesus Christ here invites us to do two things.

I. TO TREAT THIS LIFE AS A TIME OF SACRED OPPORTUNITY. The "nobleman" of the parable gave to his servants a certain sum, of which they were to make good use during his absence. His charge was this: "Occupy till I come." 1. The time of the nobleman's absence stands for our mortal life. Whether it be long or short, our present life is a period during which we have to be preparing for another of far greater consequence. It is a probationary period, that on which the larger and more serious future depends. This is in harmony with our experience; for one part of our life is a preparation for another, and the nature of the succeeding period depends upon the character of that which precedes it—childhood for youth, youth for young manhood, etc. 2. The "pound" of the parable stands for God-given opportunity—for the constitutional capacity with which we are endowed; for the favouring circumstances and facilities by which we are surrounded; for the Christian privileges with which we are blessed. 3. The smallness of our endowment affords no escape from responsibility. Only "one pound." It seems a very small sum for a nobleman to give in charge; but clearly it was large enough for a righteous requirement. No plea could be found in the littleness of the sum; it is not even urged. No man is entitled to say that his human spirit is worth nothing to God, his life worth nothing to the cause of righteousness; only God knows how valuable one human spirit, one earthly life, is. 4. No slavish timidity will excuse the most faint-hearted (vers. 21, 22). Our God is not a Being from whose service we have to turn because we shrink from his severity (Ps. ciii. 8—14; Isa. xl. 29; lvii. 16; 2 Cor. viii. 12).

II. To LOOK FORWARD TO A DAY OF ACCOUNT AND OF AWARD. 1. There will be a day of judgment. The nobleman will return and call his servants before him (ver. 15). This may stand for some one great day, or we may still better look upon it as the day, when our earthly life terminates, and when we shall, as individual souls, stand before the Judge. 2. God will require of us the use we have made of our opportunity; what we have gained; what we have done in the direction (1) of self-culture, ministering to the growth of our spiritual faculties; (2) of the service of our kind, enlightening and aiding and blessing them; (3) of magnifying the Name of our Divine Lord. 3. He will express his Divine judgment concerning us—his warm approval of those who have been most faithful (ver. 17); his acceptance of those who have not been unfaithful (ver. 19); his displeasure with the unworthy (ver. 22). We are to look for the clearly and fully expressed decision of Jesus Christ upon the character of our life-work, upon the comparative excellency or faultiness of our Christian life. 4. He will determine the measure of our award by the degree of our fidelity (see vers. 17, 19). The more faithful and devoted the life on earth, the larger the recompense, the brighter the crown, the broader the sphere, in the heavenly kingdom. The doctrine of Matt. xx. 14, 15 does not contradict this; it simply teaches that those to whom God gives a smaller share of bounty and of grace are not to complain because there are those to whom he grants a larger one. God is righteous, and he not only will not forget our work and labour of love (Heb. vi. 10), but he will not allow those of his servants who have devoted their powers to his cause with the greatest energy, constancy, and self-sacrifice to miss the most generous and gracious recognition at his loving hand.—C.

Vers. 12—24.—*Life a sacred opportunity.* We may bring out the main thought of our Master in this parable if we consider the four points of—

I. GOD'S SOVEREIGNTY OF OUR LIFE. He is the Divine Lord of our life. It came from him; it is continued by him; it is enriched perpetually and liberally from his bountiful stores; and it is subject to his sway. He has a sovereign right to determine what it shall be—what shall be its aim and its issue. He is the "nobleman;" we are "his servants." If we do think of objecting to his claim (ver. 14), we shall only be disappointed and defeated in our rebelliousness of heart. He cannot be dethroned; against his right to rule there can be no appeal. Submission is our true wisdom, as it is our first and last obligation.

II. THE SACRED CHARGE HE LAYS UPON US. He gives to each of us money (silver)—a talent (Matt. xxv.), a "pound" (text), and he says to each of us, "Occupy till I come." 1. The time of the nobleman's absence represents our mortal life, or (more correctly) the period between our first sense of responsibility and the last hour of consciousness. 2. The pound (talent) represents the opportunity of service which he places within our reach. This opportunity is compounded of (1) our natural capacity—bodily, mental, spiritual; and of (2) all the favourable circumstances by which we are attended as we pass through our life—education, home influence, capital, facilities for entering a sphere of activity, etc. And this sacred opportunity looks out in three directions: (1) the cultivation of our own nature; (2) the service of mankind; (3) the worship of God, and work in his broad field. The Lord of our life is saying to us, "Occupy till I come;" *i.e.* put out this pound, employ this sacred opportunity now within your reach, turn it to good account, use your capacities and your circumstances for high and noble ends—for your own spiritual enlargement, for the good of your brethren, for the glory of Christ.

III. THE REWARD OF FAITHFULNESS. (Vers. 16—19.) Here are two principles on which we may depend as guiding the Divine hand when the day of account arrives. 1. Those who have done well will receive God's gracious commendation and reward. To them he will express his good pleasure, and to them he will give an award. 2. They who have been more faithful will receive the more gracious approval and the larger sphere. He who turns his one pound into ten has a warmer welcome and a more liberal reward; to him are those most gladdening words addressed, and to him are entrusted not five but ten cities over which to rule (ver. 17). "Then shall every man have praise of God." But then shall those who have striven hard and toiled long and suffered much in the cause of Jesus Christ have a full measure of benediction; and to such will be apportioned a crown that will be bright indeed, a sphere that will be broad indeed.

IV. THE PENALTY OF NEGLIGENCE. (Vers. 20—24.) The slothful servant may make excuses, but they will be brushed aside; he himself will be severely condemned; he will be divested of what he has left him; he will be sent into saddest exile (Matt. xxv. 30). It is not the atheist, or the criminal, or the perpetrator of vicious deeds; it is not the outward and flagrant transgressor, who is here condemned and sentenced; it is the man who *made nothing of his life;* it is the man who had no sense of sacred responsibility; it is he who withheld his powers from the service of God;—it is he who is pronounced to be so guilty. To let our lives go by without making them a service and a blessing, to let our powers and our opportunities rust in mere disuse, is to be accumulating a debt which we shall not be able to discharge, and which will make us to appear bankrupt at the great account.—C.

Ver. 26.—*The law of spiritual increase.* Here we have one of those paradoxes of Jesus Christ into the heart of which many have failed to find their way. Why, it is asked, should one who *has* have more? will he not have too much? Why should he who *has but little* lose the little he has? will he not be still worse off than ever? Where is the wisdom, where the righteousness of this course? This criticism arises from a pure misunderstanding of Christ's meaning. We shall see what he meant if we consider—

I. THE VIEW CHRIST TOOK OF POSSESSION. When may a man be said *to have* anything? When he has legal documents to prove that it belongs to him? Or when it is securely locked up in a box or buried in the earth? Not at all. It is when *he is using it*, when he is turning it to account, when he is making it answer the purpose for which it exists. If a man lets an object rust in disuse, remain unemployed, he has it not, virtually and practically. It is not his at all; it does him no good, renders him no service, is to him as if it were not; he has it not, in truth. This accords perfectly with Christ's usage in Matt. xxv. There the men who put out their talents *had* them; the man who hid his latent *had it not.* He who does not make use of that which is at his command only "seemeth to have" (or thinketh he has) it (ch. viii. 18). It is use that really constitutes possession. This is not a mere fancy or conceit; it is the language of truth, it is the verdict of experience. The miser does not really possess his gold; it answers to him none of the ends which make it the valuable thing it is. He might as well own as many counters. He seems to have (thinks he has) money, but in truth he *has* it not. It is thus with men of great intellectual capacity which they do not employ; their faculties, unused, are of no value to themselves or to others; they might as well be non-existent. According to the wise and true usage of the great Teacher, we have the things we use; those we use not we have not. Now we can understand—

II. THE DIVINE LAW OF INCREASE AND DECLINE. For this is not a mere action done on one particular occasion; there is nothing exceptional or arbitrary about it. It is a Divine method invariably adopted; a Divine principle running through the whole economy; a Divine law with illustrations on every hand. It affects us at every turn of our life, in every part of our nature. It applies to us considered: 1. *Physically.* The muscle that is used is developed; that which is neglected shrinks, and in time becomes wholly powerless. To him that has is given; from him that hath not is taken away. 2. *Mentally.* The boy who cultivates his intellectual capacities becomes mentally strong; every acquisition of knowledge is an increase of power; the more he knows the better he can learn: to him that has is given. But the boy who does not study, but wastes his youth in idleness, not only does not acquire knowledge; he loses the faculty of acquisition: from him that has not is taken away that (capacity) which he has. 3. *Spiritually.* (1) *Spiritual perception.* The little child can readily understand the elements of the Christian faith, and, apprehending them, go on to master "the deep things of God." But the aged man who has learnt nothing of Divine truth through a long life of godlessness, is quite unteachable; he is dull of apprehension: from him has been taken away, etc.; his faculties have become shrivelled. (2) *Christian work.* Every one has a certain capacity for usefulness; and he is bound to put it out at once; if he waits until his capacity has grown into a power, he will find that not only will he not gain the skill he is waiting for, but he will lose the capacity he now has. But if, on the other hand, he uses what he has, the exercise of his humblest talent will bring increase, and he will soon acquire the strength and facility he is eager to possess. What, therefore, we wish to be able to do—teach, preach, pray, etc.—we must set about doing; every intelligent, devout effort to do good means not only a little good done, but a little power gained. What we do poorly to-day we shall do fairly well to-morrow; be ourselves to-day, we shall surpass ourselves to-morrow. Aptitude comes with effort and exercise: to him that has is given. (3) *Spiritual sensibility.* The little child is open to impression, and, if he yields to the truth he knows, that truth will always be effective; but if he rejects it his heart becomes hardened, and he becomes increasingly unresponsive: from him that *has not*, etc. Thus God's holy Law engirts us on every side; we cannot step outside it. It is determining our character and our destiny. We must act upon it, must turn it to good account. We must see to it that we really have what we seem to have, that we are using the talent, the opportunity, that is at our command. Then to us will be given—here, on the earth, in the shape of increased faculty and multiplied usefulness; there, in the heavens, in the way of a far broader sphere of celestial service.—C.

Vers. 28—38.—*Christ's royalty.* Something like a royal procession is here described. On the foal of an ass, on which it comported as well with Oriental ideas of *honour* as with Christian ideas of *peace* that he should ride, the "King came, meek," but not without attention and acclaim, into Jerusalem. A large company of the curious, the devout, and even the enthusiastic, welcomed him as "the King that came in the Name of the Lord." At last, thought his disciples, his hour is come; at last their Master was entering on his heritage, was assuming his kingdom; at last their long-delayed hopes were to be fulfilled. Gladly they accepted and sustained the greetings of the multitude, and fondly, we may be sure, they hoped that a triumphant issue was at hand. But it had no such ending as they looked for. Jesus went into the temple, healed the sick, received the adoration of the children, whose voices (as we can well believe) were the last to sink into silence, and went quietly back to Bethany. What, then, did it mean? What was the service and significance of the scene?

I. A VALUABLE REMINDER OF HIS POWER OF SELF-RESTRAINT. He had been moving among men as "one that serveth," as one that "ministered." He had moved as a very humble traveller along the path of human life. But how easy it would have been for him to call forth the honour of the people, and to live amid the excitements of popularity, and to reach the high places of power! But this he resolutely declined to do, choosing deliberately the lowlier but the nobler path of humble, holy service.

II. A STRIKING INDICATION OF HIS ACCEPTANCE WITH THE PEOPLE. No one can say that Christ's teaching was not profound; it was deep as the very fountains of truth. No philosophy went further; he went down into the deep places of the human soul. Yet, while the philosophers made their appeal to the cultured, Christ addressed himself to the multitude, to the common human heart. And "all the people were very attentive to hear him." So here, while the men who prided themselves on their knowledge looked on with angry disdain (ver. 29), the people and the children were enthusiastic in his favour—they recognized in the Prophet of Nazareth the true Teacher that had come from God. Better be numbered among the simple-hearted who can appreciate the Divine than among the wise and learned who misread the providence of God, and stand sullen and silent while everything is inviting to joy and praise. Better be the ignorant cottager whose heart is full of reverence, or the little child who has the songs of Zion on his lips and the love of Jesus in his heart, than the learned critic who never bends the knee or bows the heart in homage to the true and the eternal.

III. A HINT OF CHRIST'S TRUE ROYALTY. The Messiah of the Jews was to be a King. To that conclusion prophecy pointed with unfailing finger, and on that event Jewish faith rested with gathering hope. The Son of David was to occupy his father's throne, the daughters of Jerusalem were to rejoice because "her King was coming."

Claiming the Messiahship, Jesus was bound to claim this sovereignty, but how do this without encouraging the current fallacy as to his temporal and visible royalty? Is not this simple scene the answer? Christ then and thus said, "I am the King you are awaiting." But its extreme simplicity and its transiency showed that he did not intend to wear the trappings and be surrounded with the common grandeurs of earthly royalty; it showed that he came not for pomps and pageantries and outward triumphs, but to seek a sovereignty of another kind in another realm altogether. That very simple and passing regal state was only an emblem of the spiritual sovereignty which was immeasurably higher and more to be desired. Sweet to his ear may have been the acclaim of the populace and the hosannas of the children; but how much sweeter is the voice of man or woman or of little child who goes in glad submission to his feet to offer loyal service to the Divine Redeemer, to place heart and life beneath his gracious and benignant sway!

IV. A PROPHECY OF FAR FUTURE GLORY. Never on this earth will that scene be re-enacted; but there is an hour coming when, in another realm, it will be amplified and perpetuated. Christ will be acknowledged King by all the hosts celestial and terrestrial. The transient gladness of the sacred city will be nothing to the everlasting joy of the new Jerusalem; the passing enthusiasm of that happy demonstration to the abiding blessedness of the life in the heavenly land. Yet may we take that one hour of Jerusalem's acceptance of her King as a prelude and a prophecy of the adoration which the redeemed of every kindred and tribe shall pay him when they cast their crowns at his feet.

"Oh that with yonder sacred throng
We at his feet may fall," etc.!

PRACTICAL LESSONS. We gather: 1. That Jesus Christ is now claiming the real, spiritual sovereignty of ourselves. He is calling upon us not to strew his path with palm branches, but to offer him the first place in our heart; to yield him our perfect trust, our unfailing and unfading love, our cheerful and constant obedience. 2. That the rest of soul which follows such surrender of ourselves is incomparably better than the passing exultation of a triumphal entry. 3. That by loyal and devoted service in his cause we shall gain a place in the acclaiming company that will praise the King in his celestial glory.—C.

Ver. 28.—*Eagerness in the upward path.* "He went before, ascending up to Jerusalem." "To go to Corinth" once meant to give way to dissipation. What did it mean to "go to Jerusalem"? To the Jews generally it meant to go to some sacred service, to visit the temple of Jehovah, to enter the sacred precincts where sacrifice was offered to God. To Jesus Christ, now, it meant to go on to martyrdom and to death. But still to go thither was to "go up," was to "ascend," and in his progress to that sacred city he did not lag behind, nor even walk abreast; he "went before," he showed great eagerness in that upward and most honourable path. Such was his eagerness of soul that the disciples were astonished and even awed as they beheld it (Mark x. 32); they were profoundly impressed with the ardour and intensity of his spirit: "As they followed they were afraid." We may share the Saviour's spirit of holy ardour and elevation as we tread—

I. THE PATH OF HOLY PRIVILEGE. When may we be said to be on the upward road so far as our activities are concerned? When we are presiding? or when we are ruling? or when we are winning? or when we are rejoicing? It may be so. But assuredly we are then on the way that slopes upward and heavenward when we are in the path of sacred privilege, when we are "on our way to God"—to his nearer presence, to the worship of the Holy and the True One, to communion with the righteous Lord of all, to fellowship with Christ, to gathering at his table of love, to work in his vineyard. Then are we in the high places—"in the heavenly places;" then are we engaged in an exercise of human power which is most worthy of our highest faculties and reflects dignity on our human nature; then are we "ascending" in spirit; and we do well to feel that it is not a time for slackness of speed, for exhaustion of spirit, for signs of weariness. We should show a sacred ardour, a holy eagerness, like unto him who "went before" as he ascended to Jerusalem

II. The way of witness-bearing. To go to Jerusalem was, to our Lord, to go where he should "bear witness to the truth" (John xviii. 37); should bear witness by *words*, of which many would be utterly misunderstood, and many treated with high disdain; should bear witness by *suffering*, by calm, brave, patient endurance of wrong. And to do this was to go up, to ascend; as it is to-day, and will always be. Where shall we find the martyr-witnesses among mankind? Not as we look down, but as we look up—up to the very loftiest altitudes that human foot has ever trodden. Kings and statesmen walk not along such lofty, such truly celestial paths as do they who speak amid derision or suffer without flinching to attest the living truth of God. When we go forward toward self-sacrifice for Christ's sake we "ascend up" to the high places of the kingdom of God. It may well be with no faltering or lingering step, but with a free and forward movement, like him who now "went before," that we move to those sacred and noble levels.

III. The mount of translation. Jesus went up to Jerusalem, to Calvary, to that wondrous redeeming death which is the world's great sacrifice. We may well say that he ascended to that. That was the culminating point of his career; that not only concluded, but crowned his course. And after receiving all the light which he has shed upon it, we need not be ever speaking of death as a dark valley down which we must descend; we may rather regard it as a mount of translation up which we move. In all things physical, indeed, we descend to die; our powers become lower, our life grows less. But we walk by faith in Christ Jesus. And by faith we regard ourselves as going up to the gateway which admits to the celestial glories. In view of that which immediately afterwards awaits us, we need not lag behind; we may press forward, like our Master, as we draw toward the close, and may eagerly pass on the way which ends in death and victory.—C.

Vers. 39, 40.—*Suppression and expression.* It is not difficult to find the meaning of our Lord in this hyperbolical utterance of his. "Why should I silence my disciples?" he says. "Of what use would it be to suppress such strong feelings as theirs? Feeling will always find its vent. If suppressed in one form, it will express itself in another; if driven underground in one spot, it will only come up in another; if these human beings whose hearts are so filled with exultation were silenced, the very stones would cry out." It is useless, and worse than useless, to try to extinguish enthusiasm by a hard repressive commandment. The folly of suppression and the wisdom of allowing and inviting, indeed of providing, the means of suitable expression will apply to many things.

I. Youthful curiosity. Curiosity is an irrepressible thing; it will be satisfied. Age cannot extinguish it, try how it may. It may have occasion to check it, but its true wisdom is to guide it—to take the necessary trouble to satisfy it in the best possible way. Curiosity is not a plant of the evil one; it is rooted in the soul by the heavenly Father; it is a main source of knowledge; it ought to be wisely but amply nourished. If we endeavour to suppress it we shall find that it will *not be* suppressed, but will find other ways of satisfaction than those we disallow.

II. The love of liberty. A desire for freedom and independence is a strong sentiment of the human soul. Where intelligence exists there it will arise and assert itself. It will not be put down; it cannot be put out. Authority may "rebuke" it, as the Pharisees wanted Christ to act on this occasion; but the Lord of our nature knows that it will be heard and must be respected. Neither domestic, nor social, nor national, nor ecclesiastical despotism can survive beyond a certain time. The aspirations of the human soul for freedom will not be denied. If not permitted a wise and rightful form of action, they will take improper and harmful ones.

III. The religious sentiment in man. Philosophy has tried to silence the voice of faith; it has undertaken to rebuke the disciples; and it has temporarily and superficially succeeded. But it has found that so deep and so strong is the religious sentiment in man that when religion is driven down below the surface it comes out again in superstition in some form or other. The sense of the Supreme, a yearning of the human heart for the living God, is not to be erased from the soul, is not to be removed from the life of man.

IV. Definite religious convictions. These also are not to be suppressed. Men have taken very various views of the doctrines of the Christian faith; and, as we know too well, opponents have not only "rebuked," but tried arrogantly and forcibly to silence, those who have differed from them. But they have not succeeded. Religious conviction is an inextinguishable force; slain in the persons of its champions, it rises again and reappears, often in tenfold power.

V. RELIGIOUS ENTHUSIASM. To this the words of our Lord primarily and most properly apply. Religious fervour may frequently be disposed to take a form which we do not think the best, or even the suitable and becoming. But we must take care how we deal with it. It is not a thing to be suppressed; it is to be encouraged and enlightened and guided. It is, or it has within it, a true, living power; this power is of God, and is for good. Abruptly and harshly rebuked and silenced, it will only assert itself in other and probably still more questionable forms. Treated with Christian sympathy and encouragement (see ch. x. 49, 50), informed and enlightened by superior intelligence, directed into wise channels, it may do a noble work for the Master and mankind. 1. Let not a young enthusiasm be mindful only of its own exuberance; let it be regardful of the judgment and feeling of experience. 2. Let experience be tolerant of eager-hearted enthusiasm, and be prepared to count it amongst its friends.—C.

Ver. 41.—*The tears of Christ.* We are touched by the tears of a little child; for they are the sign of a genuine, if a simple, sorrow. Much more are we affected by the tears of a strong and brave man. When a man of vigorous intelligence, accustomed to command himself, gives way to tears, then we feel that we are in the presence of a very deep and sad emotion. Such were the tears of Christ. Twice, at least, he wept; and on this occasion we understand that he gave free vent to an overpowering distress. The tears of Christ speak of two things more especially.

I. HIS TENDER SYMPATHY WITH HUMAN SORROW. The grief which now overwhelmed the Saviour was (as we shall see) very largely due to his sense of its past and its approaching guilt. But it was also due, in part, to his foreknowledge of the sufferings its inhabitants must endure. An intense sympathy with human woe was and is a very large element in the character and life of Jesus Christ. 1. It was his compassion for our race that brought him from above—that we by his poverty might become rich. 2. It was this which, more than anything else, accounts for the miracles he wrought. He could not see the blind, and the lame, and the fever-stricken, and the leprous without tendering them the restoring grace it was in his power to bestow. He could not see mourning parents and weeping sisters without healing the heart-wounds he was able to cure. 3. It was this which drew to himself the confidence and affection of loving hearts. It was no wonder that pitiful women and tender-hearted children, and men whose hearts were unhardened by the world, were drawn in trust and love to the responsive Son of man, whose step was always stopped by a human cry, to whose compassion no stricken man or woman ever appealed in vain. 4. It is this feature of his character which makes him so dear to us now as our Divine Friend. For in this world, where sorrow treads so fast on the heels of joy, and where human comforters so often fail us, of what priceless value is it to have in that Everlasting One, who is the Ever-present One, a Friend who is "touched" with our griefs, and who still carries our sorrows by the power of his sympathy! (1) Let us thank God that we *have* such a Friend in him; and (2) let us resolve before God that such a friend will we seek and strive *to be*.

II. HIS PROFOUND REGRET FOR THOSE WHO ARE IN THE WRONG. With what eyes do we look upon human sin when we see it at its worst? How are we affected by the sight of a drunkard, of a thief, of a foul-mouthed and fallen woman? Are we filled with contempt? Many bad things are indeed contemptible; but there is a view to be taken which is worthier and more Christ-like than that; a view which is more humane and more Divine—a feeling of profound pitifulness and sorrowful regret. It was this which filled the heart of Christ when he looked upon Jerusalem, and that called forth his tearful lamentation. Much was there about that city that might well move his righteous anger, that did call down his strong, unsparing indignation (Matt. xxiii.)—its spiritual arrogance, its religious egotism, its fearful pretentiousness, its deep-seated hypocrisy, its heartless cruelty, its whitewash of ceremony *without* with all its corruptness and selfishness *within*. But Jesus forebore to denounce; he stopped to weep. He was most powerfully affected by the thought that Jerusalem might have been so much to God and man, and was—what she was. Jesus Christ was not so much angered as he was saddened by the presence and the sight of sin. He might have withered it up in his wrath, but he rather wept over it in his pity. This is the Christian spirit to be cherished and to be manifested by ourselves. We must contemn the contemptible; but we rise to higher ground when we pity the erring because they are in error, when we mourn over the fallen because they are down so low, when we grieve for those who are afar off because they are astray from God and blessedness. But we must not only *weep* for those who are in the wrong because they are in the wrong. We must *do* our utmost to set them right. "How often" did Christ seek to gather those sons and daughters of Jerusalem under the wings of his love! How often and how earnestly should we seek to reclaim and to restore!—C.

Vers. 41, 42.—*Judæa and England.* Did Jesus Christ grieve over Jerusalem as a patriot over his own country? Was there an element of patriotic sorrow in that touching and tearful lament? Did he love that land any the more because, as concerning the flesh, he was the Son of David, was born at Bethlehem, and regarded the Jews as his fellow-citizens? The idea is open to one objection. To be a patriot seems to put a man under limitation. To love our own country more than others is to love others less than our own. We shrink from associating with him anything that even looks like partiality or partisanship. On the other hand, we must take care that we do not lose the human in our desire to preserve the Divine. Might not the same consideration be urged against our Lord cherishing a peculiar regard and affection for his mother, his sisters, his brothers, his personal friends? But who can doubt that there was especial love in his heart for these? There was then, probably, something of patriotic grief in those tears of Christ, an additional pang in his heart, as he thought that it was Jerusalem itself, the city round which so many associations gathered, whose guilt and doom stood in clear, sad vision before him. However that may be, he felt deep compassion as he looked forward to—

I. THE FUTURE OF THE HOLY LAND. We speak of the land or country, though it was the city of Jerusalem over which he wept. But in the sense in which "Paris is France" Jerusalem was Judæa, was Israel itself. It was the strength, the light, the glory, of the land; it was the centre to which all the inhabitants looked and journeyed; it was the source of the people's habits and beliefs. The capital taken, everything was well-nigh gone, the fate of the country was settled. Concerning this people, this nation, Jesus Christ felt, as he beheld the city: 1. That it had been *enriched with peculiar privilege.* (1) Commencing with a signal and glorious deliverance from bondage; (2) continued with the granting of a Law and a system admirably fitted to save them from surrounding superstitions and impurities; (3) multiplied by the coming of psalmist and of prophet with inspiring song and elevating speech and life, uplifting their imagination and cleansing their conscience; (4) enhanced by the strong and severe, but yet kind and merciful, discipline through which they were made to pass; (5) culminating in the presence, the teaching, the life, of him, in whom One wiser than Solomon, mightier than David, devouter than Samuel, nobler than Elijah and John, "was there." 2. That it was *charged with a high and sacred mission.* It was designed by God to be the depository and guardian of his Divine truth, to hold fast and to hold high those great verities which are the strength, the life, and the glory of our manhood. Just what part it was to have played, and what exact service it would have rendered our race had it been loyal and true, may be questioned by us. But it would undoubtedly have played a very great part, and been, as a nation, the great factor in the restitution of mankind. 3. That it had now *missed its chance,* and was *hastening to its doom.* (1) The Hebrew faith had become a hollow formality, a mere ritual, from which true reverence, love, charity, earnestness, were all absent; and (2) the nation was in the very act of rejecting and was about to slay its Messiah, thus going down into the darkest crime and then going on to the saddest disaster. We glance at—

II. THE FUTURE OF OUR OWN COUNTRY. There is no little parallelism between Judæa and England. 1. God has enriched our land with *peculiar privileges.* We have (1) a large share of religious liberty; (2) a good measure of spiritual enlightenment, not indeed without some dark shadows of ignorance and superstition; (3) numerous and strong organizations covering the land, whose function is to teach, to guide, to guard, to rescue, and redeem. May *we* not say, "He hath not dealt so with any nation; as for his statutes and commandments, they have not known them" as we have known them? 2. God has given us a high and a *great mission* to perform. Responsibility goes with privilege; it is, indeed, the obverse side of the same thing. We have not only to present to his view "a holy nation" within our own borders, to raise our own community to the height of Christian knowledge, of social purity, of national well-being in all its forms; but also to diffuse the light of Divine truth far and wide, and to make our influence tell for peace, righteousness, and truth in every quarter of the globe. 3. We have to consider whether we are *declining* that *mission* or are *fulfilling it.* That is a question which cannot be determined by public professions; nor by the number or character of our sanctuaries; nor by the number or constitution of our Churches. It can only be determined by the actual spiritual and moral condition of our people, of the multitudes and millions of our citizens; and by the earnestness and devotedness of Christian men and women in the field of sacred work. By these criteria we stand or fall.—C.

Ver. 44.—*The time of visitation.* "This thy day;" "The time of thy visitation." What is it that makes man, everywhere and under all conditions, so deeply interesting? He is found on savage shores in nakedness and barbarism, in idolatrous lands living in saddest superstition, in the slums and purlieus of great cities as debased and vicious as the brutes of the field, yet still most interesting. It is because God made man for himself, and, far as he has wandered from his side, it is still open to him to return. It is because man was created to move along the loftiest levels, and, low as he has fallen, *it is in him to rise.* Bring to bear the right influences upon him, and from the very lowest depths of debasement and dishonour he may attain to noble heights of excellency and power. Again and again in the history of mankind and of individual men has this been proved to be true. Illustrative and reassuring instances can be adduced in which whole tribes, or even nations, and in which particular men and women, have been visited with "the truth and grace of Jesus Christ," and have been lifted up to knowledge, to virtue, to piety, to spiritual beauty, to preparedness for the heavenly sphere. But the serious aspect of this truth is that which is here suggested, viz. that God's dealings with us *may reach a climax which is ignorantly and fatally neglected.* We know how true this was of the Hebrew people. God's dealings with them (see previous homily) were long-continued, varied, gracious; they culminated in the coming of the King's Son. Then Divine Wisdom uttered its voice in their hearing; then Divine Power wrought its marvels of mercy before their very eyes; then Divine Purity lived its life of loveliness; and Divine Love manifested itself in a hundred forms of kindness and of pity in the very midst of them. But "this their day," this "time of their visitation," they did not know. Israel missed its golden chance, and went down, as a nation, to rise no more. But looking at God's redemptive dealing with ourselves, as individual spirits, we see—

I. How OFTEN GOD VISITS US in his redeeming love. In childhood, by a mother's tenderness; in youth, by a father's wisdom; in young manhood (womanhood), by many voices of the home and of the Church, uniting to say, "Thy God hath commanded thy strength;" in prime, by some chastening providence, laying his hand upon us and constraining us to listen and to understand.

II. How HIS DEALINGS WITH US CULMINATE in some day of grace. There comes a time in the history of souls—it may come in any period of life—when "the powers of the world to come" are most strongly felt, when God's nearness is most vividly realized, when the claims of Christ most forcibly touch and move the soul, when the kingdom of God is very near, and its gates are seen to stand wide open. It is "this thy day," it is the "time of visitation" to such a human heart.

III. How WISE, THEN, IS IMMEDIATE ACTION! How wise and well for us to *know* the time of our visitation, to recognize our great and priceless opportunity, to flee to the seeking Saviour "swift as the morning light," lest the golden chance be gone, the gates of opportunity be closed!—C.

Ver. 46.—*The house of prayer.* The strong indignation of our Lord shown on this occasion is a plain indication of the importance he attached to right thought concerning the sanctuary, and to the right use of it. He brought into prominence the act of prayer as that which should, above all things, characterize the house of God. We enter into his thought if we consider—

I. THE SENSE IN WHICH SACRIFICE WAS PRAYER. The temple existed primarily and pre-eminently for sacrifice. There, and there alone, might sacrifices be offered to the Lord. It was the one place in all the land where the sin offerings and the burnt offerings could be presented. Was it not, then, essentially, the *place of sacrifice?* Truly; but sacrifice, when rightly viewed, was a *form of prayer.* In it and by it the offerer drew near, consciously, to the loving God; in it he made confession of sin to God; in it he made acknowledgment of his continual indebtedness to God; in it he supplicated the mercy and the grace of God. But *this is* prayer; it is prayer in the form of offering rather than in words. Less than this—this conscious approach, this confession, thanksgiving, and supplication—is not prayer at all. Inasmuch, then, as the temple was the place of sacrifice, it was the place of prayer.

II. THE FACT THAT THERE WAS ROOM IN THE TEMPLE FOR PRAYER AS WE ORDINARILY UNDERSTAND IT. We gather from our Lord's own words that the temple was the place commonly chosen by the people for the offering of prayer (ch. xviii. 10). It was toward the temple that the exiled Jews looked when they knelt down to pray in distant lands; and it was in the temple that they stood to pray when that sacred building was within reach. It was, no doubt, regarded as of all places in the world the very fittest in which to realize the presence of Jehovah, and to spread forth the soul's desires and aspirations before him. There were many places for prayer, but that was *the* place of prayer.

III. THE PLACE OF PRAYER IN THE CHRISTIAN SANCTUARY. By what, above all things else, should the Christian sanctuary be characterized? 1. It should be the place of *common assembly.* Where all classes of the people meet together, the rich and the poor, and feel that the Lord is the Maker of them all (Prov. xxii. 2); where the learned and the unlearned worship and bow down together, and "kneel before the Lord their Maker" (Ps. xcv. 6); it is the place where human spirits meet, and where earthly circumstances are of no account whatever—where wealth does not weigh, and rank creates no distinction. 2. It should be the place of *spiritual enlightenment.* (1) Where the Word of God is read, and should be read (as it may be) impressively and effectually; for there is nothing in literature which is more fitted to attract and interest a miscellaneous assembly; (2) where the will of God is faithfully delivered, and the gospel of Christ expounded and enforced; (3) where the cause of the Master and of mankind is fully and earnestly pleaded. But most especially is it: 3. The place of *prayer.* Here, either in sacred psalmody, or through some prepared formula, or led by the extemporaneous thought and aspiration of the minister, the worshippers draw nigh to God in every way in which he is approached by man—in adoration, in communion, in thanksgiving, in confession, in supplication, in consecration. No worshipper in the house of the Lord can reach a higher level of spiritual attainment than when he pours out his heart in prayer to God in these various utterances; and no minister in the house of the Lord can render to the people gathered together a truer or higher service than when he helps them thus to approach the Father of spirits, and thus to come into direct communion with him. Then is the house of God put to its noblest and worthiest use when it is made by those who meet within its walls "the house of prayer."—C.

Ver. 46.—*Desecration.* Our Lord was touched and troubled with a holy indignation as he saw the temple of Jehovah turned into a place of traffic; that which was intended for the approach of the human spirit to God made to serve the purpose of hard bargaining, and even, as we judge from the language of the text, of dishonest dealings. It was a shocking, an intolerable desecration, and, exerting the authority which always resided in him and which he occasionally put into exercise, he drove these hucksters from the sacred place which they were desecrating by their presence and their practices. What places are we now tempted to desecrate?

I. THE SANCTUARY. When, instead of making it a place of worship, of drawing near to God, of speaking to him or for him, of learning something more of his holy will, we make it a place for distinguishing ourselves, or for advertising our respectability, or for gaining enjoyment which is wholly unspiritual.

II. THE HOME. When that which should be the abode of peace, of love, of purity, of fellowship, of tenderness, of gracious ministry, of quiet growth and joy, is turned into a scene of bitterness, of recrimination, of estrangement, of deterioration, of unhappiness.

III. THE PLACE OF BUSINESS. That might be a sphere where valuable virtues and most acceptable graces are manifested and are strengthened—truth, equity, courtesy, honour, courage, sagacity; too often it is nothing better than a sphere in which deceit, low cunning, dishonesty, a mean and miserable selfishness, are sown and reaped bountifully.

IV. THE HUMAN BODY. In our treatment of this bodily frame, so skilfully and so wonderfully made, so nicely adjusted to receive and convey impressions from and to the outside world of man and nature, we may and we should act as if we were dealing with a very sacred thing. By cleanliness, by moderation, by purity; by entertaining through the ear and the eye God's own truth and wisdom; by employing the tongue to speak his love and to sing his praise; by letting the graces of Christian character write themselves, as they will, in lineaments of beauty upon our countenance; by letting our bodies be, as they may be, the very temples of the Holy Ghost (1 Cor. vi. 19),—we may make them worthy and sacred in the sight of God. But when we regard them as mere instruments of gratification, and make them the ministers of sinful and even shameful pleasure, how great is such desecration before God!

V. HUMAN LIFE. It is here that the Holy One most often sees with Divine regret a pitiful desecration. He gave us our life that it might be spent, through all its stages, in sacred service, in spiritual growth, in elevating joy, in excellent preparation for the larger and fuller life beyond. How grievously is it desecrated when it is turned into a time for mere pecuniary acquisition, or for mere fleshly enjoyment, or for mere emptiness and aimlessness of existence! 1. What a pitiful waste is this! and how it will one day be deplored as absolutely irreparable! 2. How perilous to form such evil habits of the soul, every day becoming more fixed! how wise to hear the Master's voice summoning us to noble service, "Why stand ye all the day idle? go, work in my vineyard"!—C.

Ver. 48.—*Christ's popularity.* That Jesus Christ, as a Teacher, had no small share of popularity is beyond all question. "The people were astonished at his doctrine; for his word was with power;" "He taught them as one that had authority." His hearers wanted to know "whence hath this Man this wisdom?" The officers of the Sanhedrin declared that "Never man spake like this Man." His enemies' purpose was defeated: "They could not find what they might do: for all the people were very attentive to hear him." Large companies of men and women flocked to hear him; he had not to seek an audience; he had to seek shelter from their curiosity and intrusion. "Whence had this Man" this popularity? What was the source and the secret of it? There were—

I. THREE THINGS IN SPITE OF WHICH HE WAS POPULAR WITH THE PEOPLE. 1. *The depth of his doctrine.* Many gain a ready audience with the people by carefully restricting themselves to those truths which their hearers can easily understand: superficialities are generally acceptable. Not so with the great Teacher. He struck far below the surface, and was frequently announcing and enforcing truths which the majority of his hearers must have found "hard to be understood." Many of his utterances were "hard sayings" (John vi. 60). 2. *The height of his purpose.* Christ would have "got on" with the multitude much further and faster if he had but brought down his teaching to the level of their national aspirations. But when they were thinking of something as shallow and as transitory as a political revolution, he was laying broad and deep the foundations of a spiritual, universal, everlasting kingdom of God. His lofty purpose was high as the heavens above their hopes. His and their aims were altogether diverse and inconsistent with one another. 3. *The strength and straightness of his charge.* "Do you suppose these men were extraordinary sinners? I tell you, Nay; but except ye repent," etc.; "Except ye be converted, and become as little children, ye cannot *enter* the kingdom;" "Except your righteousness exceed the righteousness of the scribes," etc. (ch. xiii. 2, 3; Matt. xviii. 3; v. 20).

II. Two things which contributed to, without accounting for, his popularity. 1. The *illustrativeness* of his style. He called to his aid all visible nature, all homely occupations, the familiarities of social and domestic life.

"He talked of grass and wind and rain,
And fig trees and fair weather,
And made it his delight to bring
Heaven and the earth together.
He spoke of lilies, vines, and corn,
The sparrow and the raven;
And words so natural, yet so wise,
Were on men's hearts engraven."

2. The *fearless front* he showed to those who were the worst enemies of the people. He denounced in unsparing terms the selfishness and rapacity as well as the pretentiousness and actual impiety of those who were fastening the bonds of a merciless and oppressive legality on the necks of their victims; and the people looked on with approval and with enjoyment. Men always listen with delight when oppression is unsparingly denounced. They always like to see the mask torn off the face of falsehood. But it is not here that *the* secret of the popularity of Jesus is to be found.

III. Four things which made Christ's teaching acceptable to those who heard him, and may well make his doctrine acceptable to us to-day. 1. He spoke of those things the *truth of which* the people *most wanted to know*. They did not want to know a number of legal niceties and small social and domestic proprieties of which the scribes spoke to them. They wanted to know what God thought of them, and how he felt toward them, and what was the way by which they could gain and claim his favour; what was the meaning and the purpose and the possibility of human life; what followed death; and what was the true hope for the after-time. On such themes Jesus spoke to men, and we need not wonder that "all the people listened attentively" as he spake. 2. *He spoke as one that knew.* He spoke "with authority, and not as the scribes;" "His word was *with power*." He did not indulge in hair-splitting argumentations, nor in vague and dreamy imaginings, nor in doubtful and unreliable guesses. He spake as one that knew; as one who could speak about God, because he came forth from him, and dwelt with him; about prayer, because he was in constant communion with Heaven; about righteousness, because he himself was pure in heart; about love, because his whole life was one act of self-denial. Out of the depths of a living soul he gave the known facts of experience, the certain truths of God. 3. His teaching was that *of helpfulness and hopefulness.* He saw men "as sheep without a shepherd, tired out and lying down," wandering, smitten, dying. He grieved over the multitudes that were being misled, and he longed to do them good, to lead them back; he knew that he could help, that he could restore them. So he announced himself as that One who came "to preach good tidings to the poor, to heal the broken-hearted, to preach deliverance to the captive;" he offered himself as One to whom all the heavy-laden might repair, and in whom they would find rest unto their souls. He stretched forth an uplifting hand to those who were thought by every one else to have fallen beyond recovery. He breathed hope and life into despairing and dying ears. 4. His doctrine was *sustained by his character and his life.* Men listened to him, not only because he "spake as never man spake," but because he lived as never man lived before—in such perfect purity, in such constant devotion, in such self-forgetting love, with such gracious and tender sympathy in his heart and upon his countenance. They listened to him with such wrapt attention because they loved him for his goodness and for his love. (1) Such popularity as springs from such sources as these we may desire and seek to obtain. (2) For these same reasons we should be as attentive to hear the Master as were "the common people who heard him gladly" when he lived amongst us.—C.

Vers. 1—10.—*A son of Abraham found in Zacchæus the publican.* The healing of blind Bartimæus was not the only saving act done by Jesus at Jericho. A notable publican, called Zacchæus, becomes the object of our Lord's compassion and the subject of his grace. He was at the head of the custom-house, as we should now call it, and in his important post he had become rich. Having heard of Jesus and seen the advancin[g] crowd, his curiosity prompted him to have a look at him if possible; but, being little of stature, he could not from the ground obtain the view he wished. Accordingly he ran before, climbed up into a sycamore tree, one of whose branches it has been supposed may have extended across the road, and, perched upon this, he awaited the advent of Jesus. How astonished he must have been to find Jesus pausing below his perch, looking up, naming him, and telling him, "Zacchæus, make haste, and come down; for to-day I must abide at thy house"! Thus invited, he came down with all haste, and received Christ joyfully. Doubtless the Pharisees will murmur at Christ becoming the publican's guest; but what does it matter when Zacchæus is gathered into the kingdom of God, makes his declaration about future conduct, and receives the Lord's assurance of being Abraham's son? Let us notice the points of interest as they present themselves in this case.

I. Zacchæus needed a Saviour. For success is not sufficient for any man. He needs besides, salvation from sin, that is, from selfishness, and often from success itself. It is well when even curiosity leads a man to the Saviour, and to a sense of his great need. Zacchæus's case is instructive for us all. His need of a Saviour ought to emphasize our need.

II. His hindrances in seeking the Saviour. And of these we shall only mention three. 1. *His riches.* These are often a great hindrance to souls. They compete with Christ as a ground of trust. Men are tempted to trust in uncertain riches instead of in the living God. Zacchæus had, however, got over this hindrance, and, rich man though he was, he was not ashamed to climb the sycamore to get a sight of Jesus. 2. *His business.* For the tax-farming had been denounced and excommunicated by the Jewish authorities, so that Zacchæus, because of his business, did not enjoy the means of grace in the measure and amount he might otherwise have done. Jesus had, however, overcome this hindrance by his own manly and merciful policy, and insisted on associating with publicans and sinners to save them. Every one should ask himself the question, however, if his business is a hindrance or a help to his salvation. Can we ask Christ to meet us in it and save us in it? or can we only expect him to save us *from* it? 3. *His physical state.* His stature hindered him for a time from seeing Jesus, as the physical state of others often hinders them. But when one is thoroughly in earnest, he can overcome all hindrances as Zacchæus did by climbing the sycamore. Hindrances may be changed by energetic action into helps and spiritual gains.

III. Salvation means heartfelt sympathy with a personal Saviour. For salvation comes to us clothed in loving personality, and the advent of Jesus to our souls, as in the case of Zacchæus, is the advent of salvation. What we are asked in the gospel to do is to trust a Person, and to accept of safety in his blessed society. There is no abstract and confusing process to be passed through, but a concrete and real fellowship to be entered on and enjoyed.

IV. The saved soul proves his salvation by liberality and restitution. As soon as Zacchæus enters into sympathy with Christ, he makes a public profession. Here is his resolve deliberately made to Christ, "Behold, Lord, the half of my goods I give to the poor; and if I have wrongfully exacted aught of any man, I restore fourfold" (Revised Version). His riches are now to be made a means of grace, enabling him, in the first place, liberally to make restitution to all wronged ones; and secondly, to dedicate largely to the poor. Contact with Christ has opened his heart and made him open-handed. Murmuring Pharisees might restrict their ostentatious almsgiving to a tenth, but converted Zacchæus will dedicate a half to the wants of the poor! A rich man may thus make his wealth the basis of princely generosity, and reap a reward in the gratitude of God's poor people.

V. Jesus gives Zacchæus a blessed assurance of sonship. For Zacchæus, if originally a Jew, had forfeited through his tax-gathering his position in the Jewish Church. No longer would the Jewish authorities regard him as a son of Abraham or heir of the promises. But Jesus interposes and reinstates him in his position of privilege. He declares before the guests that Zacchæus has been saved by his visit to his house, and that this salvation-visit is because the publican is also a son of Abraham. In this beautiful way the selecting love of God in Christ is set before the people and the assurance of Abrahamic sonship conveyed to the new convert. It is thus the Lord comforts those who trust in him.

VI. CHRIST THUS DEMONSTRATES HIS MISSION TO SEEK AND SAVE THE LOST. Not by the parables of the fifteenth chapter merely does he demonstrate the merciful character of his mission, but also by such a missionary act as the salvation of Zacchæus. As "the Son of man" he is interested in the welfare of his race, and finds in the lost the sphere of his gracious operation. It is thus he comforts the lost ones, by enabling them to see that they are the proper objects of his compassion.—R. M. E.

Vers. 11—27.—*The law of capital in Christ's kingdom.* Zacchæus's conversion and all the stir on leaving Jericho led many in the crowd to imagine that Christ was immediately to assume a visible kingdom. To remove misapprehension, therefore, he proceeds to tell them a parable which would at once rouse them to the necessity of working instead of indulging in lackadaisical waiting. Comparing himself to a nobleman who is going into a far country to receive a kingdom and to return, he compares his disciples to servants left to make the best of what is entrusted to them. The worldly minded as distinct from the servants are called his citizens, whose spirit is manifested in the message transmitted to him, "We will not have this man to reign over us." Then the return of the crowned king is to be celebrated by the distribution of rewards and punishments as the case may be. Out of this significant parable we may learn the following lessons.

I. IT IS IN HEAVEN, AND NOT ON EARTH, OUR LORD IS TO RECEIVE HIS KINGDOM. This is the great mistake many have made about Christ's kingdom and reign. They localize head-quarters on earth instead of in heaven. It is not by a democratic vote, by a *plébiscite,* our Lord is to receive his kingdom, but by donation from the Father. When he went away by death, resurrection, and ascension, therefore, it was to receive a kingdom that he might return crowned. Hence we are to regard him as now reigning over his mediatorial kingdom. He is on the throne. His government is administered from the heavenly places.

II. IT IS PERILOUS TO REFUSE TO ACKNOWLEDGE HIS PRESENT REIGN. The citizens that hate the absent King will be slain before him when he returns for judgment. Hostility, enmity, to Christ, if continued, must lead to utter discomfiture at last. Rebellion of spirit is, therefore, to be diligently uprooted if we would have any share in Christ's kingdom. It is at our peril if we refuse his loving and righteous reign.

III. CHRIST'S SERVANTS LIVE UNDER A LAW OF CAPITAL IN HIS KINGDOM. In this parable we have "pounds," and not "talents," referred to. The question is, therefore, of some equal endowment which all receive in common, not of unequal endowment distributed in sovereign wisdom. In the parable of the talents, given in another Gospel, we have equal diligence exhibited in the use of unequal endowments; and the reward is righteously equalized in the completed kingdom. Here, on the other hand, we have an unequal use of equal endowments, with the unequal reward attached in proportion to the diligence. We discern in the arrangement, therefore, that law of increase which has been denominated the law of capital. But first we have to settle the signification of the pounds. We shall not be far astray if, with Godet, we regard them as indicating those donations of Divine *grace* which are offered to the Lord's servants, we may suppose, in equal measure. These endowments are put to use in some cases, utterly neglected in others. It will be found at last that the law of capital has obtained in the Lord's arrangements. One man, by judicious use of what the Lord has given, finds his grace growing tenfold, so that by the time the Lord returns he is ready to undertake the government of ten cities. Another man, by diligence, but not so persevering as the former, finds his graces growing fivefold, so that in the final arrangement he is equal to the oversight of five cities. A third is represented as making no use whatever of his endowment, under the impression that the Lord is a grasping speculator, who wants to make the most he can out of men. He ventures to return his trust just as it was. He finds, however, that his selfish idleness is visited with utter ruin. He has the misused endowment recalled and made over to the better trader. "To him that hath shall be given." Accumulated capital tends to increase in proper hands, and it is right it should do so. It follows, then, from this law of capital as thus applied: 1. *That we should use diligently every means to increase our Christian graces.* Sanctification should be our life-work, and all action, meditation, prayer, should be utilized for the one great object of becoming the best servants of our

Master our circumstances admit of. 2. *We shall find ourselves thereby becoming rulers of men.* It is wonderful the influence exercised by consecrated lives. It is easy understanding how we may become kings and priests unto God the Father. As consecrated by his grace, we begin immediately to influence others for good and to reign. 3. *The influence on earth will have its counterpart in the reign enjoyed by us in heaven.* For heaven will be the home of order. It will be no happy, musical mob. It will be a great society, with recognized kings of men, under the gracious authority, of course, of him who is "King of kings, and Lord of lords." Influence, character, all that is gracious, is destined to be continued and to abide. Those who have done men most good, and made the most of their opportunities here, shall be rewarded with corresponding influence in the well-ordered commonwealth above. 4. *Wrong views of Christ's character may also be perpetuated, with their corresponding judgments.* The pitiful servant who thought his Master austere, hard, grasping, was only attributing his own hard character to his superior. He failed to understand him. So is it with some souls. They insist on misunderstanding God, and the result is that their misunderstanding continues and is its own punishment. How important, therefore, that we should have correct views of God our Saviour! It will save us from misuse of his gifts and graces, and from the doom awaiting all faithless souls.—R. M. E.

Vers. 28—48.—*The advent of the humble King.* To illustrate still more thoroughly the character of his kingdom as one not of ostentation and worldly glory, but of humility, our Lord directed two of his disciples to procure for him a colt, the untrained foal of an ass, that he might ride into Jerusalem thereon. The marvellous way in which the ass was lent to him indicated preternatural knowledge. Upon this colt, then, he sat, and passed amid the hosannas of the people into the sacred city. But his advent was in tears, and his terminus was not a palace, but the temple. The whole character of the procession and its termination tended to upset all vulgar Messianic hopes and lead thinking minds to reflection. Let us look at the different stages of the royal progress and such lessons as they suggest.

I. The humble character of the procession. (Vers. 28—40.) For it was on an *ass*, not on any royal mule, he rode; to fulfil the prophecy of Zechariah, "Rejoice greatly, O daughter of Zion; shout, O daughter of Jerusalem; behold, thy King cometh unto thee: he is just, and having salvation; lowly, and riding upon an ass, and upon a colt the foal of an ass" (Zech. ix. 9). The very fact of his selecting such a lowly and despised animal indicated his humility. At the same time, his perfect command of the untrained colt revealed his sovereignty in animated nature—that, like an unfallen Adam, he was lord of the lower creatures. It was akin to his being with the wild beasts and unscathed in the wilderness. But secondly, the *extemporized character of the procession was humiliating.* A great king gets the parade organized, and knows what will for the most part compose his escort. But this King of kings rests his escort upon the extemporized enthusiasm of the crowd, and values at its proper figure the measure of enthusiasm that is evoked. He knew that the same people who then shouted, "Hosanna; Blessed be the King that cometh in the name of the Lord: peace in heaven, and glory in the highest!" would a few days after cry out, "Crucify him!" And so he was humiliated rather than honoured by the shallow enthusiasm of the motley crowd. Thirdly, *the unseemly interruptions of the Pharisees rendered it humiliating.* So irritated were they that they urged him to rebuke the disciples for crying out as they were doing. But the Lord only declared that, if the disciples were silent, the very stones would get tongues to sound his praise. This Pharisaic jar, this unseemly interruption, must have been humiliating to the Lord. To bear it as he did demonstrated the humility and meekness of his spirit. Truly he was "meek and lowly in heart."

II. The tears of the advancing King are notable. (Vers. 41—44.) For instead of a city welcoming him, instead of this city of the great King recognizing the day of her visitation, and opening her arms for her Deliverer, there was apathy and scorn for his methods and aims. No wonder, therefore, that he had to speak about the siege of Titus, which he saw plainly must come. Pursuing their poor worldly policy, they must be encompassed ultimately by the Roman eagles. And so he wept those tears of deepest sorrow over the impenitence of Jerusalem. How different from the processions of earthly monarchs or great captains! The very last thing looked for on such occasions would be tears. The sympathy of this Saviour for Jerusalem sinners was deep indeed when it led him to such a weeping-time as the processionists witnessed.

III. HIS SECOND PURIFICATION OF THE TEMPLE WAS THE CULMINATION OF THE PROCESSION. (Vers. 45, 46.) The tempter wanted him to begin his Messianic work by a harmless descent from the temple-pinnacle; he began his work by entering into the temple and casting out the traffickers. And now he has to finish his work by repeating the purification. Usually the processions of kings end at palace gates and in palace halls; but the procession of Christ ends at the temple and in its court. He must convert it from a den of thieves to a place of prayer. The meaning of his kingdom could not be better represented. It was really the sphere of religion and of worship that he made his own; in the regulation thereof he was supreme, and exercised his influence.

IV. HE TAUGHT DAILY IN THE TEMPLE UNTIL THE END. (Vers. 47, 48.) He was surrounded by his enemies. They were on the *qui vive* to secure him and put him away. But now that his hour of self-sacrifice is near, he feels himself immortal till his work is done. It is the interests of others that occupy him. He must teach to the last. And so from Bethany he comes in morning by morning to instruct the interested crowds. What solemn lessons they must have been, those closing ones of Jesus! And they attracted great attention, and their popularity restrained his enemies, although it must have intensified their determination to put him out of the way. Thus we have seen how this humble King entered Jerusalem to work reformation there, and, if possible, save the people by enlightening and teaching them. If his mission failed with most, it succeeded with some, and inaugurated the new kingdom, which is "righteousness and peace and joy in the Holy Ghost."—R. M. E.

EXPOSITION.

CHAPTER XX.

Vers. 1—8.—*Question of the priests and scribes as to the nature of the authority under which Jesus was acting.*

Vers. 1, 2.—**And it came to pass, that on one of those days, as he taught the people in the temple, and preached the gospel.** We are now in the midst of the so-called Passion week. Probably the events related in this chapter took place on the Tuesday. The first day of the week, Palm Sunday, was the day of the public entry into the city. The purification of the temple took place on the Monday, on which day also the barren fig tree was cursed. We are now considering the events of the Tuesday. The Greek word εὐαγγελιζομένου is especially a Pauline word; we find it rarely used save in his writings, and of course in those of St. Luke. St. Paul uses it twenty times, and St. Luke twenty-five. **The chief priests and the scribes came upon him with the elders, and spake unto him, saying, Tell us, by what authority doest thou these things?** This appears to have been a formal deputation from the supreme council of the Sanhedrin. The three classes here specified represented probably the three great sections of the Sanhedrin—(1) priests, (2) scribes and rabbis, (3) Levites. These came upon him evidently with hostile intent, and surrounded him as **he was walking in the temple.** The jealous anger of the rulers of the Jews had been lately specially excited by the triumphant entry on Palm Sunday, and by the stir and commotion which the presence of Jesus had occasioned in the holy city. And in the last two or three days Jesus had evidently claimed especial power in the temple. He had publicly driven out the money-changers and vendors of sacrificial victims who plied their calling in the sacred courts. He had, in addition, forbade the carrying vessels across the temple (Mark xi. 16), and had allowed the children in the temple, probably those attached to its choir, to shout "Hosanna!" to him as the Messiah. From the point of view of the Sanhedrin, such a question might well have been looked for. His interlocutors made quite sure that Jesus, in reply, would claim having received a Divine commission. Had he made openly such a formal claim in reply to their question, then he would have been cited before the supreme court to give an account of himself and his commission. Then, as they thought, would have been their opportunity to convict him out of his own mouth of blasphemy.

Vers. 3—6.—**And he answered and said unto them, I will also ask you one thing, and answer me: The baptism of John, was it from heaven, or of men? And they reasoned with themselves, saying, If we shall say,**

From heaven; he will say, Why then believed ye him not? But and if we say, Of men; all the people will stone us: for they be persuaded that John was a prophet. The reply of Jesus was one of strange wisdom. He—Jesus—as was well known, had been introduced to the people by this very John. If the Sanhedrin acknowledged John the Baptist as a divinely accredited messenger, then surely they could not question the claims of one borne special witness to by him, brought forward and introduced to public notice by him! If, on the other hand, the Sanhedrin refused to acknowledge the authority of John as a Heaven-sent messenger, which would have been the course they would have preferred, then the popularity and influence of the Sanhedrin would have been sorely imperilled, for the people generally held firmly that John the Baptist was really a prophet of the Lord. They even feared—as we read, "All the people will stone us"—personal violence on the part of the people whose favour they so zealously courted.

Ver. 7.—**And they answered, that they could not tell whence it was.** The reply of Jesus, which so perplexed the Sanhedrin, really inflicted a grave blow to their prestige, thus compelling the grave doctors of the Law, who claimed the right of deciding all momentous questions, to decline to pronounce a judgment on so grave a question as "the position of the Baptist," that mighty preacher who had so stirred and roused Israel and who had with his life paid the forfeit of his boldness in rebuking crime in high places, thereby no doubt enormously enlarging his already vast popularity with the people.

Ver. 8.—**And Jesus said unto them, Neither tell I you by what authority I do these things.** Jesus, on hearing their plea of ignorance, now contemptuously declines to answer the Sanhedrists' question in the direct way they desired, but at once proceeds to speak a parable which unmistakably contains the reply.

Vers. 9—19.—*Parable of the wicked husbandmen in the vineyard, and the simile of the corner-stone.*

Ver. 9.—**A certain man planted a vineyard, and let it forth to husbandmen.** Under a very thin parabolic veil, Jesus foretells the awful tragedy of the next few days. He adopts a well-known imagery, and seems to say, "Listen to Isaiah's well-known story of the vineyard, the vineyard of the Lord of hosts, which is the house of Israel. I will expand it a little, that I may show you how it stands with you as regards this matter of 'authority,' that we may see whether you have as much respect for the ascertained will of God as ye pretend, so that ye should be sure to submit to me if only ye were satisfied that I was an accredited Messenger of God" (Professor Bruce). **For a long time.** Representing the nearly two thousand years of Jewish history.

Vers. 10—12.—**He sent a servant to the husbandmen, that they should give him of the fruit of the vineyard.** After the pains and care bestowed upon the vineyard, that is, after the many mighty works done in Israel's behalf, the Lord of hosts looked for *fruits* of gratitude and fidelity in some proportion to the mighty favours which it had received from him. The people were intended to be the example to, and the educators of, the world, and, instead of carrying out these high functions, they lived the poor selfish life so sadly depicted in the long story contained in the historical and prophetical books. "He looked that it [his vineyard] should bring forth grapes, and it brought forth wild grapes" (Isa. v. 2). **But the husbandmen beat him, and sent him away empty. And again he sent another servant: and they beat him also, and entreated him shamefully, and sent him away empty. And again he sent a third: and they wounded him also, and cast him out.** These represent the prophets, those faithful servants of the Lord, whose toils and trials and fate are painted in the Epistle to the Hebrews (xi.) in such glowing and eloquent language. *And again he sent.* In vers. 11 and 12, προσέθετο πέμψαι, literally, "he added to send another"—a Hebraism. This shows St. Luke here based his account on a Hebrew (Aramaic) original. Professor Bruce well puts the thoughts which possessed the wicked husbandmen thus: "When the servants came for fruit, they were simply surprised. 'Fruit! did you say? We have occupied the position of vine-dressers, and have duly drawn our wages: what more do you want?' Such was the actual fact in regard to the spiritual heads of Israel. They were men who never thought of fruit, but only of the honour and privilege of being entrusted with the keeping of the vineyard. They were triflers, men utterly devoid of earnestness, and the practical purpose of the property committed to their charge they habitually forgot. Generally speaking, they had utterly lost sight of the end of Israel's calling." Their anger flamed forth when accredited messengers of the Lord visited them and reminded them of their forgotten duties; they vented their furious wrath by persecuting some and killing others of these faithful men.

Ver. 13.—**Then said the lord of the vineyard, What shall I do? I will send my beloved son.** The guilt of the husbandmen who acted as vine-dressers here reached its highest measure. The words represented here by Jesus as spoken by God, possess the deepest doctrinal value. They, under the thin veil of the parable-story, answer the question of the Sanhedrin (ver. 2), "By what authority doest thou these things?" The deliberative words, "What shall I do?" recall the Divine dialogue alluded to in Gen. i. 26. St. Luke here represents the Father as calling the Son, "*my Beloved.*" St. Mark adds that he was *an only Son.* Such sayings as this, and the remarkable prayer of Matt. xi. 25—27, are a clear indication of the Christology of the synoptists. Their estimate of the Person of the blessed Son in no wise differed from that given us by St. John at much greater length and with fuller details.

Ver. 14.—**But when the husbandmen saw him, they reasoned among themselves, saying, This is the heir: come, let us kill him, that the inheritance may be ours.** The husbandmen are represented as knowing the son and heir. Nor can we resist the conclusion that some at least of those grave learned men who sat in the Sanhedrin as priests or scribes well knew who the Speaker of the awful words claimed to be, and, in resisting him and seeking his destruction, were deliberately sinning against the voice of their own hearts.

Vers. 15, 16.—**So they cast him out of the vineyard, and killed him.** The parable-story *of itself* was an improbable one. The conduct of the husbandmen, the long patience of the owner of the vineyard, his last act in sending his beloved and only son,—all this makes up a history without a parallel in human experience. Yet this is an exact sketch of what did actually take place in the eventful story of Israel! **What therefore shall the lord of the vineyard do unto them? He shall come and destroy these husbandmen, and shall give the vineyard to others.** Again a hint of a solemn deliberation in heaven, a prophetic picture of the future of the Jewish race fulfilled with terrible exactness. **And when they heard it, they said, God forbid!** Well understood they the Speaker's meaning here. He foreshadowed, in no veiled language, the utter ruin of the Jewish polity. When they heard this, forgetting to be scornful, they exclaimed, in deprecation of the ominous and terrible prediction, Μὴ γένοιτο! which we render accurately, though not literally, "God forbid!"

Vers. 17, 18.—**And he beheld them, and said, What is this then that is written, The stone which the builders rejected, the same is become the head of the corner? Whosoever shall fall upon that stone shall be broken; but on whomsoever it shall fall, it will grind him to powder.** In spite of the deprecating expression, the severity of the tone of Jesus increases in his next words, when, looking at them with grave anger (ἐμβλέψας), he proceeds to speak of himself under the figure of the rejected stone. Quoting a well-known psalm (cxviii. 22), and using the imagery of Isa. viii. 14, 15 and Dan. ii. 44, he describes his fortunes under the image of a corner-stone—that stone which forms the junction between the two most prominent walls of a building, and which is always laid with peculiar care and attention. In ch. ii. 34 of our Gospel Simeon refers to the same well-known prophetic saying. The husbandmen who had just been described as vine-dressers are now described as builders, and the murdered son is reproduced under the image of a corner-stone tossed aside as useless. In the first part of the picture, the earthly humiliation of Messiah is portrayed when the stone is laid in the earth. In the second, the stone falling from the top of the building represents the crushing of all earthly opposition by Messiah in his glory. Woe to the builders, then, who had scornfully rejected him!

Ver. 19.—**And the chief priests and the scribes the same hour sought to lay hands on him; and they feared the people: for they perceived that he had spoken this parable against them.** Again the Sanhedrin take counsel. They long to arrest him on some capital charge; but they dared not, for the people, joined by the Passover pilgrims, had exalted him to the rank of a hero. Not a few evidently looked on him at that period as King Messiah. But the feeling of the great council was intensely bitter. They felt *their* power and influence was slipping away from them. These last parables were scarcely veiled attacks on them. In the last spoken words he had calmly announced that he was to die, and *their* hands were to carry out the bloody work. And then, in the simile of the corner-stone, he, in no ambiguous terms, told them that in killing him they will not be done with him, for that in the end they will be utterly crushed by his power.

Vers. 20—26.—*The question of the tribute money.*

Ver. 20.—**And they watched him, and sent forth spies, which should feign themselves just men, that they might take hold of his words, that so they might deliver him unto the power and authority of the governor.** In their intense hatred, conscious that the populace were on the whole in sympathy with Jesus, the Sanhedrin, to carry out their design on his life, determined to avail themselves of the hated Roman military police. Their hope henceforward is to substantiate a charge of treason against him. This was, in those troublous times, when insurrection against the detested Gentile rule was ever being plotted, a comparatively easy matter. The incident of the tribute money, which immediately follows, was part of this new departure in the Sanhedrin policy respecting the murder they so longed to see carried out.

Vers. 21, 22.—**And they asked him, saying, Master, we know that thou sayest and teachest rightly, neither acceptest thou the person of any, but teachest the way of God truly: Is it lawful for us to give tribute unto Cæsar, or no?** SS. Matthew and Mark both tell us that in this plot the Herodians were united with the Pharisees (and Sanhedrin). The great Nazareth Reformer was equally hateful to both these hostile parties; hence their union in this matter. It was a well and skilfully laid question. This "tribute" was a capitation tax—a denarius a head assessed on the whole population, the publicans who farmed it being answerable for it to the Roman treasury. As a direct personal tax it was most unpopular, and was looked on by scrupulous legalists and the more zealous Jews as involving a greater humiliation than the ordinary import or export customs dues. It occasioned at times popular tumults, as in the case of Judas of Galilee (Acts v. 37). If Jesus answered the question in the affirmative: "Yes, it is lawful for the Jews to give this tribute to Cæsar," then the Pharisees would use this decision of his as a means of undermining his credit with the zealous populace. "See, after all," they would say, "this pretended Messiah of yours is but a poor-hearted traitor. *Think of King Messiah paying tribute to a Gentile.*" If, on the other hand, the Master had said such payment of tribute was unlawful, then the Herodians, who were watching him, hoping for some such expression of opinion, would at once have denounced him to their Roman friends as One who taught the people—only too ready to listen to such teaching—lessons of sedition. In the latter case Pilate and the officials of Rome would have taken good care that the Galilæan Master had troubled the Sanhedrin no more.

Ver. 24.—**Show me a penny;** literally, *a denarius*, a coin of the value of 7½*d.*, but really representing a larger sum in our money. It seems probable, from the language of Mark xii. 15, 16, that his interrogators had to borrow the Roman coin in question from some of the neighbouring money-changers. These Jews would scarcely carry any but Jewish coins in their girdles. That the Roman denarius, however, was evidently a coin in common circulation in those days, we gather from the parable of the labourers in the vineyard. **Whose image and superscription hath it? They answered and said, Cæsar's.** "On one side would be the once beautiful but now depraved features of Tiberius; the title 'Pontifex Maximus' was probably inscribed on the obverse" (Farrar).

Ver. 25.—**And he said unto them, Render therefore unto Cæsar the things which be Cæsar's, and unto God the things which be God's.** As regarded the immediate issues the Lord's answer was in the affirmative: "Yes, it is lawful under the present circumstances to pay this tribute." The Roman money current in the land, bearing the image and title of the Cæsar, bore perpetual witness to the fact that the rule of Rome was established and acknowledged by the Jewish people and their rulers. It was a well-known and acknowledged saying, that "he whose coin is current is king of the land." So the great Jewish rabbi Maimonides, centuries after, wrote, "Ubicunque numisma regis alicujus obtinet, illic incolæ regem istum pro Domino agnoscunt." The tribute imposed by the recognized sovereign ought certainly to be paid as a just debt; nor would this payment at all interfere with the people's discharging their duties God-ward. The tithes, tribute to the temple, the offerings enjoined by the Law they revered,—these ancient witnesses to the Divine sovereignty in Israel might and ought still to be rendered, as well as the higher obligations to the invisible King, such as faith, love, and obedience. Tribute to the Cæsar, then, the acknowledged sovereign, in no way interfered with tribute to God. What belonged to Cæsar should be given to him, and what belonged to God ought to be rendered likewise to him. Godet, in a long and able note, adds that Jesus would teach the turbulent Jewish people that the way to regain their theocratic independence was not to violate the duty of submission to Cæsar by a revolutionary shaking off of his yoke, but to return to the faithful fulfilment of all duties toward God. "To render to God what is God's was the way for the people of God to obtain a new David instead of Cæsar as their Lord. To the Pharisees and Zealots, 'Render unto Cæsar;' to the Herodians, 'Render unto God.'" Well caught the great Christian teachers their Master's thought here in all their teaching respecting an institution such as slavery, in their injunctions concerning rigid and unswerving loyalty to established authority. So St. Paul: "Be subject to the powers . . . not only from fear of punishment, but also for conscience' sake" (Rom. xiii. 1 and 1 Timothy).

Vers. 27—40.—*The scornful question of the Sadducees bearing on the doctrine of the resurrection, and the Lord's reply.*

Vers. 27, 28.—**Then came to him certain of the Sadducees, which deny that there is**

any resurrection; and they asked him, saying, Master, Moses wrote unto us, If any man's brother die, having a wife, and he die without children, that his brother should take his wife, and raise up seed unto his brother. This is the only occasion related in the Gospels where our Lord comes in direct conflict with the Sadducees. They were a small but very wealthy and powerful sect. The high priests at this period and their families seem to have belonged generally to this party. They acknowledged as Divine the books of Moses, but refused to see in them any proof of the resurrection, or indeed of life after death. To the prophets and the other books they only attached subordinate importance. Supercilious worldliness, and a quiet indifference to all spiritual things, characterized them at this period. They come, comparatively speaking, little in contact with Jesus during his earthly ministry. While the Pharisee hated the Galilæan Master, the Sadducee professed to look on him rather with contempt. The question here seems to have been put with supercilious scorn. SS. Matthew and Mark preface the Lord's answer with a few words of grave rebuke, exposing the questioners' utter ignorance of the deep things involved in their query.

Vers. 29—33.—**There were therefore seven brethren: and the first took a wife, and died without children. And the second took her to wife, and he died childless. And the third took her; and in like manner the seven also: and they left no children, and died. Last of all the woman died also. Therefore in the resurrection whose wife of them is she? for seven had her to wife.** The question here put to the Master was a well-known materialistic objection to the resurrection, and had on several occasions been asked by these shallow Epicureans—as the Talmud calls them—to the great rabbis of the schools of the Pharisees. Their usual answer was that the woman in question would be the wife of the first husband.

Vers. 34—36.—**And Jesus answering said unto them, The children of this world marry, and are given in marriage: but they which shall be accounted worthy to obtain that world, and the resurrection from the dead, neither marry, nor are given in marriage: neither can they die any more.** How different are the few rare pictures which our Master draws of the heaven-life to those painted by the great founders and teachers of other world-wide religions! In his world beyond the grave, while he tells us of a continuing existence, of varied and ever-increasing activity, in contradistinction to the Nirvâna of Buddha, in these pictures of Jesus the sensual paradise of Mohammed, for instance, finds no place. Marriage is, according to our Lord's teaching, but a temporary expedient to preserve the human race, to which death would soon put an end. But in the world to come there will be no death and no marriage. We may assume from his words here that the difference between the sexes will have ceased to exist. **They are equal unto the angels.** Equal with the angels in being immortal; no death; no marriage. Jesus in this place asserts that angels have a body, but are exempt from any difference of sex. The angels are here introduced because our Lord was speaking with Sadducees, who (Acts xxiii. 8) denied the existence of these glorious beings. He wished to set the seal of his teaching on the deeply interesting question of the existence of angels.

Vers. 37, 38.—**Now that the dead are raised, even Moses showed at the bush.** You Sadducees, in your own arbitrary fashion, set aside the authority of the prophets and all sacred books save the Pentateuch; well, I will argue with you on your own, comparatively speaking, narrow ground—the books of Moses. Even he, Moses, is singularly clear and definite in his teaching on this point of the resurrection, though you pretend he is not. You are acquainted with the well-known section in Exodus termed 'the Bush:' what read you there?" **When he calleth the Lord the God of Abraham, and the God of Isaac, and the God of Jacob. For he is not a God of the dead, but of the living;** more accurately rendered, *not a God of dead beings, but of living beings.* The meaning of the Lord's argument is, "God would never have called himself the God of Abraham, of Isaac, and of Jacob, if these patriarchs, after their short lives, had become mere crumbling dust. God cannot be the God of a being who does not exist." So Josephus—who, however, no doubt drew his argument from these words of Christ, for this strong and conclusive argument from the Pentateuch for the immortality of man does not appear to have occurred to rabbis before the time of our Lord—so Josephus writes: "They who die for God's sake live unto God as Abraham, Isaac, and Jacob, and all the patriarchs." The expression, "at the bush," should be rendered "in the Bush," that is, in that division of Exodus so named. So the Jews termed 2 Sam. i. and following verses "the Bow;" Ezek. i. and following section, "the Chariot."

Vers. 39, 40.—**Then certain of the scribes answering, said, Master, thou hast well said. And after that they durst not ask him any question at all.** "This prompt and sublime answer filled with admiration the scribes, who had so often sought this decisive word in Moses without finding it; they cannot restrain themselves from testifying their joyful surprise. Aware from this time forth that every snare laid for him will be the occasion for a glorious manifestation of his wisdom, they give up this method of attack" (Godet).

Vers. 41—44.—*The question respecting Christ's being David's Son.*

Ver. 41.—**And he said unto them, How say they that Christ is David's Son?** St. Matthew gives us more details of what went before the following saying of Jesus in which he asserts the Divinity of Messiah. Jesus asked the Pharisees, "What think ye of Christ? whose Son is he? They say unto him, *The Son* of David. He saith unto them, How then doth David in spirit call him Lord, saying, The Lord said unto my Lord," etc.? (Matt. xxii. 42—44). This is one of the most remarkable sayings of our Lord reported by the synoptists; in it he distinctly claims for himself Divinity, *participation in omnipotence.* Unmistakably, lately, under the thinnest veil of parable, Jesus had told the people that he was Messiah. For instance, his *words* in the parable of the "wicked husbandmen;" in the parable of "the pounds;" in his late *acts* in the temple—driving out the sellers and buyers, allowing the children in the temple to welcome him with Messianic salutation, receiving as Messiah the welcome of the Passover pilgrims and others on Palm Sunday as he entered Jerusalem. In his later *parables*, too, he had with startling clearness predicted his approaching violent death. Now, Jesus was aware that the capital charge which would be brought against him would be blasphemy, that he had called himself, not only the Messiah, but Divine, the Son of God (John v. 18; x. 33; Matt. xxvi. 65). He was desirous, then, before the end came, to show from an acknowledged Messianic psalm that if he was Messiah—and unquestionably a large proportion of the people received him as such—he was also Divine. The words of the psalm (cx.) indisputably show this, viz. that the coming Messiah was Divine. This, he pointed out to them, was the old faith, the doctrine taught in their own inspired Scriptures. *But this was not the doctrine of the Jews in the time of our Lord. They, like the Ebionites in early Christian days, expected for their Messiah a mere "beloved Man."* It is most noticeable that the Messianic claim of Jesus, although not, of course, conceded by the scribes, was never protested against by them. *That* would have been glaringly unpopular. So many of the people, we know, were persuaded of the truth of these pretensions; Jesus had evidently the greatest difficulty to stay the people's enthusiasm in his favour. What the scribes persistently repelled, and in the end condemned him for, was *his assertion of Divinity.* In this passage he shows from their own Scriptures that whoever was Messiah *must be Divine.* He spoke over and over again as Messiah; he acted with the power and in the authority of Messiah; he allowed himself on several public occasions to be saluted as such: who would venture, then, to question that he was fully conscious of his Divinity? This conclusion is drawn, not from St. John, but exclusively from the recitals of the three synoptists.

Ver. 42.—**And David himself saith in the Book of Psalms, The Lord said unto my Lord, Sit thou on my right hand.** The Hebrew runs thus: "Jehovah said to my Lord (*Adonai*)." The Eternal is represented as speaking to David's Lord, who is also David's Son (this appears clearer in St. Matthew's account, xxii. 41—46). The Eternal addresses this Person as One raised to sit by him, that is, as *a Participator in his all-power*, and yet this one is also David's Son! The scribes are asked to explain this mystery; alone this can be done by referring to the golden chain of Hebrew Messianic prophecy; *no scribe in the days of our Lord would do this.* Such passages as Isa. ix. 6, 7; Micah v. 2; and Mal. iii. 1, give a complete and exhaustive answer to the question of Jesus.

Ver. 44.—**David therefore calleth him Lord, how is he then his Son?** That Jesus was the acknowledged descendant of David during his earthly ministry, is indisputable; we need but refer to the cries of the populace on Palm Sunday, the words of the woman of Canaan, of blind Bartimæus, and others. History bears its witness to the same fact. The Emperor Domitian, it is well known, summoned the kinsmen of Jesus, the sons of Jude, his so-called brother, to Rome as "the sons of David."

Vers. 45—47.—*St. Luke's brief summary of the Lord's denunciation of the scribes and others.*

Vers. 45, 46.—**Then in the audience of all the people he said unto his disciples, Beware of the scribes.** Here, in St. Matthew, follows the great denunciation of the Sanhedrist authorities with the other rabbis, Pharisees, and public teachers and leaders of the people. It fills the whole of the twenty-third chapter of the First Gospel. The details would be scarcely interesting to St. Luke's Gentile readers, so he thus briefly summarizes them. **Which desire to walk in long robes.** "With special conspicuousness of fringes (Numb. xv. 38—40). 'The supreme tribunal,' said R. Nachman, 'will duly punish *hypocrites who wrap their talliths round them* to appear, what they are not, true Pharisees'" (Farrar).

Ver. 47.—Which devour widows' houses. Josephus specially alludes to the influence which certain of the Pharisees had acquired over women as directors of the conscience. **For a show**; rather, *in pretence*. "Their hypocrisy was so notorious that even the Talmud records the warning given by Alexander Jannæus to his wife on his death-bed against *painted* Pharisees. And in their seven classes of Pharisees, the Talmudic writers place '*Shechemites*,' Pharisees from self-interest; '*Stumblers*,' so mock-humble that they will not raise their feet from the ground; '*Bleeders*,' so mock-modest that, because they will not raise their eyes, they run against walls, etc. Thus the Jewish writers themselves depict the Pharisees as the Tartuffes of antiquity" (Farrar). **Shall receive greater damnation**; rather, *judgment*. The translators of our beautiful English version are most unhappy in their usual rendering of κρίμα.

HOMILETICS.

Ver. 19—ch. xxi. 38.—*The last working day.* It is Tuesday, the last of the Lord's working days; for Wednesday and the early part of Thursday were spent apparently in the quiet of his Bethany home. A busy, trying day, crowded with events in which we see the Son of God enduring against himself the contradiction of sinners. Let us gather up a part of its teaching. When, in the early morning, Christ entered the outer courts of the temple, he encountered a deputation of persons secretly commissioned by the Pharisees to entrap him into admissions which might be used against him (vers. 19, 20). The deputation consisted (Matt. xxii. 16) of some of the more prominent scholars of the rabbis, and some politicians who were attached to the Herodian dynasty. For so it often is—a common hatred will unite those whose positions, mental or moral, are antagonistic. This has been frequently exemplified in religious and religio-political movements. The emissaries of priest and politician, thus leagued together, submit their question with ceremonious politeness (vers. 21, 22). He to whom they speak knows what is in man (ver. 23). And, demanding the penny, with the coin held before them he returns the famous sentence on which so much has been spoken and written, which has been rendered the catchword of heated ecclesiastical controversy (ver. 24), "Whose image and superscription hath this penny?" It is the image and superscription of the proud Tiberius. "Then," is the reply, "if you use his coin, give back to him what is his due, and to God, whose is the image and superscription on the human soul, give back what is God's" (ver. 25). The confusion of the spies is complete. "They marvelled at his answer, and held their peace" (ver. 26). As the day passes, another deputation appears on the scene. This time the Sadducees (ver. 27) measure the sword of their wit against the Witness for God. The Sadducee mind, cold, cynical, cavilling, pronouncing all earnestness fanaticism, with no definite views as to a life beyond the present, but willing enough to toy over the subject —faith and the things of faith being only a matter to be talked about—has its representative in all ages. And it has some trafficking with Christ. It has its problems, its questions, its discussions. Behold an illustration of their kind in the problem submitted as to the seven brothers (vers. 28—33). A more foolish issue than that raised it is scarcely possible to conceive, and it might have been treated with contemptuous silence. But truth may be taught even though the occasion of the teaching is unworthy. And, by the incident related, a weighty, suggestive instruction is elicited, one which gives, as by a lightning flash, not only a glimpse into the invisible, but a discernment of the spirit of the old Mosaic economy. First of all, disabusing the thought of his hearers of their carnal conceptions of the resurrection-life (vers. 34—36), he reminds them (ver. 37) of the character which, by their own admission, belonged to God; of the great covenant word which Moses uttered when he called the Eternal "the God of Abraham, Isaac, and Jacob." Could they conceive him (ver. 38) the God of mere empty names? Does not the word imply that Abraham, Isaac, and Jacob are not mere dust and ashes, but still living persons, heart to heart with him? It is not wonderful that the quickness and keenness of the reply, and the light which it shed on human destiny, impressed all who were present; so that the multitude hearing were astonished at his doctrine, and from the admiring crowd (Matt. xxii. 23) came the approbation, echoed (ver. 39) by certain of the scribes, "Master, thou hast well said." But not yet does the temptation cease. A jurist, or student of the Law, accustomed to hair-splitting distinctions and controversies over mere pin-points, exclaims, "Master, which is the great commandment in the Law?" (Matt. xxii. 35). In the school to which he belonged, the precepts of the moral and ceremonial law were reckoned to be more than six hundred, although the great Rabbi Hillel reminded his pupils that, after all, the word, "Do justly, love mercy, and walk humbly with God," is the essence of the Law, the rest being only commentary. "Which commandment," asks this lawyer, "is the greatest, Master? What sayest thou?" Let us thank the tempting jurist whose question evoked the golden wisdom of the emphatic enforcement of the two sentences to which all obedience returns and from which all worthy conduct departs—the first commandment bidding us love God with all the heart, and the second, which is like to it, bidding us love our neighbour as ourselves (Matt. xxii. 37—40). Pharisee, Sadducee, and scribe have all been defeated in their trial of Jesus. It is his turn to try them. He will not let them go until he has shown them the slowness of their minds, and left with them a question to be afterwards inwardly digested. He puts the query, "What think ye of Christ?" (Matt. xxii. 42). And when they answer, "He is the Son of David," he reminds them (vers. 41—44) of the language of the psalmist, implying that there is another than the merely filial relation: "If David call him Lord, how is he then his Son?" Who can abide the thrusts of Jesus? No more questions are asked. No; and pointing to his discomfited tormentors, he preaches the terrible denunciation epitomized in vers. 45—47, given at fuller length in the eight crushing woes of Matt. xxiii. It is a scene that beggars description—the grandest moment in the ministry of Christ, the Prophet and King. The evangelist, guided, perhaps, by the sense of fitness to that scene, represents the tone of the speech as changing, at the close of the commination, from indignation hot and strong to the moaning, saddened cry of a heart breaking with grief—the cry, already considered, over impenitent, hard-hearted Jerusalem. So the Lord moves towards the gate of the temple. It is on his way thither that he observes (ch. xxi. 1—4) the action of the poor widow, who cast into one of the chests which were placed in the temple courts her poor little all. How calm was the soul which, even in the heat of that day of temptation, could pause, observe, and speak of a deed apparently so insignificant! It is observable that the last word of Christ in the temple should be one concerning the love and the love-offering, which are better than formal sacrifices. Ever to be remembered, too, is the sentence, "He looked up, and *saw* the gifts cast into the treasury." The gifts that men and women furtively cast, thinking that none will observe the meanness, or the ostentatiously cast money expecting that all will applaud the munificence, he sees. He is always looking to the treasury; he estimates the real value of the offering. What is the principle of the commendation? "One coin," says an old Father, "out of a little is better than a treasure out of much; for it is not considered how much is given, but how much remains behind." "He went out and departed from the temple." It is the "Ichabod," the departing of the glory. Thirty-five years later the holy and beautiful house was left desolate; the prediction (ver. 6) as to the great costly stones was fulfilled. The ploughshare of a fearful retribution was driven through Israel's palace, as through Israel itself. The quitting of the temple by the Son of God was the beginning of the end. Thenceforth it was the whited sepulchre, beautiful in appearance, but within full of the dead bones of religion and all spiritual uncleanness. Lo! the house is left to these Pharisees desolate. As the closing feature of that great Tuesday, we behold Christ and his apostles seated on the slope of Olivet. The golden radiance of the setting sun is flung over the glorious city. The pinnacles of the temple, the palaces, and massive buildings and endless houses of the Jews are, one by one, bathed in the georgeous reflection. There, in the vale below, are Gethsemane and the Kedron, and around are the well-known features of the landscape so dear to the Israelite. It is with this prospect full in his view that Jesus gives the instruction as to the end of the age in those mysterious intimations in which the downfall of the city of the great King is so blended with other and greater catastrophes that it is difficult to distinguish what relates specially to the one and what relates specially to the others. Oh, how urgent the exhortation to vigilance! How real and solemn for all the injunction "to pray always, that we may be accounted worthy to escape all these things that shall come to pass, and to stand before the Son of man" (ver. 36)!

HOMILIES BY VARIOUS AUTHORS.

Vers. 1—8.—*The great Teacher's silence.* The refusal of Jesus Christ to answer the question proposed to him demands explanation and suggests remark.

I. THE DIFFICULTY WE FIND IN HIS SILENCE. Had not the Sanhedrin a right to ask this of him? It was a legally constituted body, and one of its functions was to guide the people of the land by determining who was to be received as a true Teacher from God. John had recognized their right to formally interrogate him (John i. 19—27). As Jesus was claiming and exercising authority (ch. xix. 45), it seems natural and right that this council of the nation should send a deputation to ask the question in the text; and, if that be so, it seems only right that our Lord should give them a formal and explicit answer. Why did he not?

II. ITS EXPLANATION. There was: 1. *A formal justification.* The Sanhedrin had not yet declared its mind on the great Prophet who had been before the public, and in regard to whom an official decision might well be demanded. Jesus Christ, as a Jew, had a right to ask this question concerning one whose ministry commenced before his own, and had already been concluded. If they were unwilling or unable to pronounce a judgment, they ruled themselves unfit or incompetent to do what they undertook to do. As the event proved, they declined to say, and their refusal justified Jesus in withdrawing his own case from a tribunal which confessed its own incompetence. But there was also: 2. *A moral ground* on which our Lord might base his action. The Sanhedrin was not solicitous to guide the people in the ways of truth and righteousness; they wanted to *entrap their enemy* (see ch. xix. 47). Their aim was not holy, but unholy; not patriotic, but malevolent. They were not seeking the public good, but their own personal advantage; they desired to crush a rival, and so to maintain their own position of authority. Such an object as this deserved no regard; it was one not to be respected, but to be defeated; and our Lord, with Divine wisdom, adopted a course which cut the ground completely from beneath their feet.

III. ITS SIGNIFICANCE TO OURSELVES. Jesus Christ will not always answer our questions. Whether or not he will do so depends on the spirit in which he is approached by us. 1. *Mere curiosity* has nothing to expect of him (see ch. xiii. 23, 24; Acts i. 6, 7). 2. *Unmeaning and unspiritual utterance* makes no way with him (see ch. xiv. 15). The formalities and proprieties of religious language fall on his ear, but they do not touch his heart or move his hand. 3. *Malevolent activity* can look for nothing but defeat from his wisdom and his power (see text and following verses of this chapter). 4. *Presumption* will be turned away unrewarded. To see the Father as he is in himself is an impossible and impracticable desire; our wisdom is to understand him as he is revealed in his Son (John xiv. 8, 9). We may not ask of Christ those things which are beyond the range of our powers. 5. *Impatience* must be postponed, and must wait the fitter time (John xvi. 12). Christ will sometimes, perhaps often, be silent when we would that he should speak to us. But there is—

IV. ONE CONDITION UNDER WHICH HE WILL SPEAK TO US. *Practical, spiritual earnestness* will draw down his blessing, will command his gracious and life-giving word. If we earnestly and perseveringly seek our own spiritual well-being or that of others, we shall not fail to hear him say, "According to your faith be it unto you."—C.

Ver. 16.—*Deprecation and doom.* We may regard—

I. THE FORCE OF THESE WORDS AS ORIGINALLY APPLIED. The people who listened to this parable: 1. *Deprecated a guilt in which they were to be partakers.* "God forbid," said they, "that we should do such shameful things as these, that we should be in any way involved in such crimes as these! Whosesoever hands may be dyed with the blood of the Husbandman's Son, ours shall be stainless." Yet were they moving on to the last and worst enormity, and already were they doing their best to bring about the guilty consummation. 2. *Deprecated a doom to which they were descending.* "God forbid," said they, "that we should be subjected to the Divine wrath, and that we should lose that place of privilege we have so long enjoyed! May Heaven avert from us the calamity of having to yield to another nation or kingdom the post of honour, the place of privilege, which our fathers handed down to us!" But they were then pursuing the course which led inevitably to this very doom. If they only walked on in the path along which they were then hurrying, they were bound to reach that "miserable" end.

II. ITS APPLICATION TO OUR OWN HEARTS AND LIVES. 1. We may be supposing ourselves incapable of wrong-doing the seeds of which are already sown in our heart. Hazael proved to have "dog" enough in him to do the worst things he shuddered at when he spoke (2 Kings viii. 13). David discovered that he was capable of a selfishness which he was condemning to death in another (2 Sam. xii. 5—7). These Jews shrank from an action which was described to them, as a thing too base for them to commit; and yet they were in the very act of committing it. We little know what possibilities of evil are within us; we cannot estimate aright our own capacity for wrong-doing. Probably every man has in his heart something of which sin may lay hold in some dark hour, and by which he may conceivably be led down to guilt and shame. The declension and fall of those who once stood among the worthiest and the most honoured speaks to us in earnest tones of the possible wandering of our own souls from God and goodness. Even Paul realized this stern possibility, and acted upon it (1 Cor. ix. 27). The histories of the erring and ruined souls of men who once seemed beyond the reach of wrong and crime, but who became entangled in their meshes and were slain by them, call upon us to be (1) watchful with a constant vigilance, and (2) prayerful with an unflagging earnestness, lest we too fall under the power of temptation (Matt. xxvi. 41). 2. We may be supposing ourselves safe from a doom which lies straight in front of us. How many a youth imagines himself secure from a degradation and a darkness toward which he has, in the sight of God, already set his foot! How many a man considers himself safe from a low and dishonourable level, when he is already on the slope that leads down to it! What if we could see the goal to which the path we tread is tending! "God forbid," we say, "that this should be our destiny!" and all the while our face is turned in that direction. There is "an earnest need for prayer" that God would show us what is the way in which we are walking; that, if we are in the wrong road, he would "apprehend" us even as he apprehended his chosen messenger (Phil. iii. 12), and turn our feet into the way of his testimonies (Ps. cxxxix. 23, 24).—C.

Ver. 17.—*The rejection and exaltation of Christ.* We look at—

I. THE REJECTION OF JESUS CHRIST. *Its strangeness.* 1. From an *evidential* point of view. How came the builders to reject that valuable Stone? How was it that all the *miracles* of Jesus, so wonderful, so beneficent, so simple, and so credible as they were; that the *life* of Jesus, so holy and so beautiful, so gracious and so winning as it was; that the *truth* spoken by Jesus, so profound, so original, so lofty, so satisfying to the deepest wants of man as it was;—how came it to pass that all this left him the "despised and rejected of men"? 2. From a *providential* point of view. How do we account for it that there should have been such a long and complicated preparation for the coming of the Messiah of the Jews, and of the Redeemer of mankind, and that he should fail to be recognized when he came? Does not all that Divine arrangement of Law and ritual and prophecy, of privilege and discipline, seem to have been attended with failure? Of what use was all that elaborate preparation, when the people of God rejected the Son of God? when he to whom everything pointed, and of whom everything foretold, was not welcomed and honoured, but denounced as a deceiver and slain as a criminal?

II. CONSIDERATIONS WHICH ACCOUNT FOR IT; or which, if they do not account for it, lessen our surprise concerning it. 1. As to the *evidential* difficulty. We need not wonder that the very strongest evidence failed to convince those who were unconvinced. What evidence *can* prevail against bigotry (or prejudice) and selfishness combined? Our knowledge and experience of mankind must have abundantly proved that either of these can repel the clearest and weightiest proofs; much more can both of them. And surely prejudice and self-interest never found a firmer seat than they found in the minds of the "chief priests and the scribes" who led the opposition to our Lord. 2. As to the *providential* difficulty. We must take into our consideration (1) the fact that God's dealings with our race include such apparent failures as this, and oblige us to wait the issue before we judge; (2) the fact that the long preparation of Israel was by no means wholly an *apparent* failure. There is evidence of much fulfilment of prophecy; there is the valuable contribution of all that is contained in Old Testament Scripture, which is a rich and precious heritage to the human race; and there is, above all, the formation of a pure and reverent people, distinguished from and raised above all surrounding nations in the supreme element of moral character, which supplied the human material for the first great missionary epoch. Moreover, the very rejection of Jesus Christ has proved to be the beginning and foundation of ultimate success, and of a success far deeper and larger than any contemporary and national triumph would have been. It has led up to—

III. HIS EXALTATION. 1. *Notwithstanding his humiliation.* That Stone was rejected indeed; that Teacher was silenced, that Prophet slain, that cause covered with infamy; those hopes, cherished by a few disciples, were laid in the tomb and covered from sight; yet, notwithstanding all that apparent defeat and discomfiture, that "Stone has become the Head of the corner," that Teacher the great Teacher of Divine wisdom, that Prophet the acknowledged Saviour of mankind, that cause the kingdom of God upon earth. 2. *As the reward of his humiliation.* "*Wherefore* also God hath highly exalted him" (Phil. ii. 6—11; Heb. ii. 9, 10). 3. *As the result of his humiliation.* "I, if I be lifted up, will draw all men unto me." The cross has been the great loadstone which has been attracting the world. It is to a crucified Saviour, once slain for our sins, dying in mercy toward our race, that we are drawn in faith and love. It is he "who loved us, and gave himself for us" unto such shame and sorrow and death—it is he whom we rejoice to make the Friend of our heart and the Sovereign of our life.

1. Learn the *place of privilege.* It is well for us that we stand where we do stand—at a point in time where we can recognize the Corner-stone. The mountain is best seen afar off, the city or the sea is best seen from above, the character of the generation is best understood after some interval of time. We know Jesus Christ better than we should have done had we lived when he was the Stone rejected of the builders. We could not be better placed than we are by the providence of God for understanding him and rejoicing in his worth. 2. Know the *day of opportunity.* Recognizing the true character of that once-slighted "Stone," knowing Jesus Christ as we know him now, it is for us to accept him without delay as our personal Redeemer, and to commend him, with all devotedness, to the estimation and trust of all beholders.—C.

Ver. 18.—*Contact and conflict with Christ.* There is one thing which, as a stone or rock, Christ is willing and waiting to be to us; there is that also which, in spite of his own desire concerning us, we may compel him to be to us.

I. THE ROCK ON WHICH WE MAY BUILD. 1. Christ desires to be as the Corner-stone or Foundation-stone on which the whole structure of our character and of our destiny is resting. 2. If we exercise a living faith in him, we shall find him to be all this to us. (1) Building on him, our confidence in the forgiving love of God will be well grounded and our peace of mind will be secure; (2) building on him, our character will be strong and saintly, our life will be useful and noble; (3) resting on him, our souls will be sustained in hours of trial; (4) abiding in him, we shall have peace at the last.

II. THE ROCK AGAINST WHICH WE ARE BRUISED OR EVEN BROKEN. We cannot come, in any sense or degree, into *conflict* with Christ without being injured by the act. 1. To turn from him is to deprive ourselves of the best; it is to rob ourselves of the highest motives to rectitude and spiritual worth, of the deepest springs of goodness and of beauty, of the heavenliest influences that can breathe upon the soul, of the purest and most elevating joys that can fill the heart, of the noblest activities that can occupy and crown our life. 2. To reject him, whether by deliberate and determined refusal or by a foolish and guilty procrastination, is to do conscious wrong to ourselves; it is to injure our conscience, to weaken our will, to suffer constant spiritual deterioration, to be moving along that downward slope which ends in darkness of mind and in self-despair. 3. To disobey the commandments of Christ is to come into collision with those laws of God which are also laws of our spiritual nature, any and every infraction of which is attended with inward and serious injury; *e.g.* to hate our brother without a cause, to look with lustful eye, to love our own life rather than the cause of God and righteousness,—this is to suffer harm and damage to the spirit. 4. To work against Christ and his gospel is to be constructing that which will be destroyed, is to be delving and building on the sand with the tide coming in which will wash everything away. In no way can we take up an attitude of resistance to Jesus Christ without "wronging our own soul;" it may be by a cruel renunciation of all that is best, or it may be by incurring the judgment which must fall and does fall upon folly and sin.

III. THE ROCK WHICH MAY CRUSH US IN ITS FALL. "On whomsoever it shall fall," etc. The snow-drift and the glacier are magnificent objects on which to gaze; but how terrible is the descending, destructive avalanche! It is simply inevitable that the brightest light should cast the deepest shade; that fullest privilege and most abounding opportunity should, in the case of the guilty, end in deepest condemnation and severest penalty (John iii. 19; Heb. vi. 4—8; Phil. iii. 18, 19). "When God arises to judgment," when the rock of Divine dissatisfaction falls, when the "wrath of the Lamb" is revealed, then must there be made known what God intends by "everlasting destruction from his presence." All that is meant by that we do not know: we may well resolve that, by timely penitence and loving faith, we will never learn by the teaching of our own experience.—C.

Vers. 19—26.—*The sacred and the secular.* There are three preliminary truths which may be gathered before considering the proper subject of the text. 1. *The worthlessness of heartless praise.* What value do we suppose Jesus Christ attached to the eulogium here pronounced (ver. 2)? How worthless to him now are the epithets which are uttered or the praises which are sung by lips that are not sincere! 2. *The evil end of a false attitude* toward Christ. The attitude of hostility which his enemies had definitely taken up led them to resort (1) to shameful deceit (ver. 20), and (2) to a malign conspiracy against the one Teacher who could and would have led them into the kingdom of God. 3. *The final discomfiture of guilt.* (Ver. 26.) It is silenced and ashamed. Respecting the principal subject before us, we should consider—

I. TWO NOTIONS THAT FIND NO COUNTENANCE IN OUR LORD'S REPLY. 1. When Jesus answered, "Render unto Cæsar," etc., he did *not* mean to say that the spheres of the secular and the sacred lie so apart that we cannot serve God while we are serving the state. Let none say, "Politics are politics, and religion is religion." That is a thoroughly unchristian sentiment. If we ought to "eat and drink," if we ought to do everything to the glory of God, it is certain that we ought to vote at elections, to speak at meetings, to exercise our political privileges, and to discharge our civil duties, be they humble or high, to the glory of God. A man may be, and should be, serving Christ as truly and as acceptably in the magistrates' court, or in the lobby of the House of Commons, as he can be in the school or the sanctuary. 2. Nor did Christ mean to say that these spheres are so apart that a man cannot be serving the state while he is engaged in the direct service of God; for, indeed, there is no way by which we render so true and great a service to the whole body politic as when we are engaged in planting Divine truth in the minds and hearts of men; then are we sowing the seeds of peace, of industry, of sobriety, of every national virtue, of a real and lasting prosperity. 3. Nor yet that there are no occasions whatever when we may act in opposition to the state. Our Lord encouraged his apostles in their refusal to obey an unrighteous mandate (Acts v. 28, 29).

II. THE LEADING TRUTH WHICH CHRIST'S WORDS CONTAIN, viz. that our obligation to God does not conflict with our ordinary allegiance to the civil power. If the latter should enjoin apostasy, or blasphemy, or positive immorality, then disobedience would become a duty, and might rise into heroism, as it has often done. But ordinarily, we can serve God and be loyal citizens at the same time, and this none the less that the rulers whom we serve are Mohammedans or pagans. To be orderly and law-abiding under the rule of an infidel is as far as possible from being unchristian. On the contrary, it is decidedly Christian (see 1 Tim. ii. 2; Rom. iii. 1—7). Indeed, service rendered to "the froward" has a virtue not possessed by service to "the good and gentle;" and faithful citizenship in "a strange land" may be a more valuable and acceptable service than in a Christian country. Our duty, in the light of Christ's teaching, is not that of discovering conscientious objections to the support of the civil government; it is rather that of rendering a hearty obedience to the Divine will, and also of conforming in all loyalty to the requirements of human law.—C.

Vers. 27—38.—*Foundations of Christian hope.* On what foundation do we build our hope for the future? Not now on any philosophical deductions; these may have a certain measure of strength to some minds, but they are not firm enough to carry such a weight as the hope of immortality. We build on the Word that cannot be broken—on the promise of Jesus Christ. Our future depends upon the will of our Divine Creator, on the purpose of our God, and only he who came from God can tell us what that purpose is. Here, as elsewhere, we have—

I. THE FIRM GROUND OF CHRISTIAN PROMISE. Our Lord tells us, from his own knowledge, that there is a future for the sons of men. And he indicates some features of this future. 1. Our life will be one *of perfect purity.* There is to be nothing of the grosser element that enters into our social relations here (ver. 35). Great founders of great faiths have promised to their disciples a paradise of enjoyment of a lower kind. Christ leads us to hope for a life from which everything that is sensual will be removed. Love will remain, but it will be spiritual, angelic, absolutely pure. 2. It will be a life *without end,* and therefore *without decay.* "Neither can they die any more" (ver. 36). How blessed the life that knows no fear of interruption, of dissolution, of sudden cessation, and, more particularly, that is free from the haunting consciousness of passing on to a time when faculty must fade, or the sadder sense of decline already commenced or even hastening to its end! What will it be to live a life that becomes ever brighter and fuller as the periods of celestial service pass away! 3. It will be a life *of highest honour and elevation.* "They are equal unto the angels; and are the children of God, being the children of the resurrection" (ver. 36). "*Now* are we the sons of God," and when the future life is disclosed our sonship will mean yet more to us—it will be life on a loftier plane, in a deeper and fuller sense; we shall be nearer to God, and more like him in our faculty and in our spirit and our character.

II. THE ADDITIONAL SUPPORT OF CHRIST'S INFERENCE. To be "the God of Abraham," he argued, meant to be the God of a living soul; he whose God was the living God was a living man in the fullest sense. For God to be *our* God includes everything we need. The living God is the God of living men; the loving God of loving men; the blessed God of happy men; the holy God of holy men. All the highest good for which we long in our noblest hours is guaranteed to us in that "the everlasting God," the righteous and the faithful and the loving One, is *our God.* 1. The heritage of the future is not promised unconditionally; there are "those accounted worthy to obtain" it; therefore there are those who are not worthy, and who will miss it. 2. The condition that is implied is that of a living personal connection with God himself. Those who can truly claim him as "their God" may confidently look forward to an eternal home in his presence and in his service. To us, to whom he has revealed himself in his Son, this means a living union with Jesus Christ our Saviour. To know *him,* to live unto him, to abide in him,—this is life eternal.—C.

Vers. 40—44.—*The lowliness and the greatness of Jesus Christ.* This is the subject of these verses; but they are suggestive of minor truths. We have—

I. A PROOF OF UTTER FALSITY. (Ver. 40.) How came these men to be afraid to ask questions of Christ? Others did not shrink from him, or fear to ask things of him. The children were not afraid of him; nor were "the strangers"—those not of Israel; nor were the women who waited on him and learned of him; nor the simple-hearted and genuine inquirers. It was only the men who sought his overthrow, because they dreaded his exposure; it was only those who shrank from his heart-searching gaze and his truth-telling words, that dared not approach him and ask questions of him. No man however ignorant, no child however young, need shrink from the Lord of love, from asking of him what he needs; it is only the false who are afraid.

II. THE TIME FOR AGGRESSIVE ACTION. The successful general may act long on the defensive, but he waits and looks for the moment of attack. Jesus bore long with the questionings of his enemies, but the time had come for him to ask something *of them.* We may well *bear* long *with* the enemies of Christ, but the hour comes when we must *bear down upon* them with convincing and humbling power.

III. THE OCCASIONAL DUTY OF PUTTING MEN INTO A DIFFICULTY. On this occasion our Lord placed his hearers in a difficulty from which he did not offer to extricate them. His prophetic function was to enlighten, to liberate, to relieve. But here was an occasion when he best served men by placing them in a difficulty from which they found no escape. Such service may be rare for a Christian teacher, but it does occur. There are times when we cannot render a man a better service than that of humbling him, of showing him that there are mysteries in presence of which he is a little child.

IV. THE WISDOM OF FURTHER INQUIRY. These Pharisees imagined that they knew everything about the Scriptures that could be known. They were learned, but they were unwise; they had a large verbal and literal acquaintance with their sacred books, but they had missed their deepest meaning. They had not inquired humbly, intelligently, reverently enough. How much more is there in our New Testament than we have yet found! What depth of wisdom in the words of Christ! What enlightenment in the letters of his apostles! Though we may not have missed our way so grievously as the scribes had done, yet may there be very much of Divine truth we have not yet discovered, which patient and devout inquiry will disclose.

V. THE LOWLINESS AND THE GREATNESS OF JESUS CHRIST. He is the Son of David, and he is also his Lord. We understand that better than the most advanced and enlightened of his disciples could at that point. "As concerning the flesh" he was "born of a woman, made under Law;" yet is he "exalted to be a Prince and a Saviour;" Son of man and Son of God. Only thus could he be what he came to be: 1. Our Mediator between God and man. 2. Our Divine Saviour, in whom we put our trust and find mercy unto eternal life; our Divine Friend, of whose perfect sympathy we can be assured; our rightful Lord, to whom we can bring the offering of our hearts and lives.—C.

Vers. 45—47.—*Character and precept, etc.* These verses suggest five truths of practical importance.

I. THAT CHARACTER IS OF MORE CONSEQUENCE THAN PRECEPT. "Beware of the scribes;" they "sit in Moses' seat, and teach things that you should do" (Matt. xxiii. 2); but their conduct is such that they are to be avoided rather than sought after. Beware of the bad man, though he be a good teacher; the influence of his life will be stronger than the effect of his doctrine; the one will do more harm than the other will do good. In a religious teacher, character is the principal thing; if that be unsound, proceed no further; seek some one else, one that you can respect, one that will raise you by the purity of his heart and the beauty of his behaviour.

II. THAT UNGODLY MEN FALL INTO A FOOLISHNESS THE DEPTH OF WHICH THEY DO NOT SUSPECT. How childish and even contemptible it is for men to find gratification in such display on their own part and in such obsequiousness on the part of others as is here described (ver. 46)! To sink to such vanity is wholly unworthy of a man who fears God, and who professes to find his hope and his heritage in him and in his service. They who thus let themselves down do not know how poor and small is the spirit they cherish and the behaviour in which they indulge; they do not suspect that, in the estimate of wisdom, it is at the very bottom of the scale of manliness.

III. THAT FAMILIARITY WITH DIVINE TRUTH IS CONSISTENT WITH THE COMMISSION OF THE WORST OFFENCES. The scribes themselves, familiar with every letter of the Law, could descend to heartless misappropriation in conjunction with a despicable hypocrisy (ver. 47). Guilt and condemnation could go no further than this. It is a solemnizing thought that we may have the clearest view of the goodness and the righteousness of God, and yet may be very far on the road to perdition. Paul felt the solemnity of this thought (1 Cor. ix. 27). It is well that the children of privilege and the preachers of righteousness should take this truth to heart and test their own integrity.

IV. THAT THE AFFECTATION OF PIETY IS A SERIOUS AGGRAVATION OF GUILT. The "making long prayers" entailed a "greater condemnation." Infinitely offensive to the Pure and Holy One must be the use of his Name and the affectation of devotedness to his service as a mere means of selfish acquisition. The fraud which wears the garb of piety is the ugliest guilt that shows its face to heaven. If men will be transgressors, let them, for their own sake, forbear to weight their wrong-doing with a simulated piety. The converse of this thought may well be added; for it is truth on the positive side, viz.—

V. THAT DEVOUT BENEVOLENCE IS GOODNESS AT ITS BEST. To serve our fellow-men because we love Christ, their Lord and ours, and because we believe that he would have us succour them in their need, is to do the right thing under the purest and worthiest prompting; it is goodness at its best.—C.

Vers. 1—19.—*Christ's collision with the Sanhedrin.* We have studied Christ's triumphal entry into Jerusalem and his cleansing of the temple. And now we have to notice the interruptions to which he was subjected as he improved his last days of ministration in the temple-court. He had exercised authority in God's house, he was also teaching with authority the people; hence the Jewish rulers came, demanding from him the sign of his authority to do so. As with many still, there is great demand for signs, certificates, orders. In these circumstances Jesus throws them back on John the Baptist, and asks if they had made out *his* authority. This so "cornered" them that they decline giving an opinion, and Jesus consequently is warranted in declining to tell them by what authority he takes the course he does. Now, here it is to be noticed—

I. The ministry of Jesus was bound up historically with the claims of John. It was to the Baptist he went for baptism. It was when being baptized by John that he received the gifts of the opened heaven, descending dove, and assurance of Sonship. It was from John he received the first start in securing disciples, when the Baptist pointed to him and said, "Behold the Lamb of God, which taketh away the sin of the world!" How natural, therefore, that Jesus should take the chief priests back to John! It was no able manœuvre on the Master's part, but *simple historic defence.* "John recognized my authority and mission; he set his seal upon them: should this not satisfy you?" And surely this course taken by our Lord has deep significance. If ever one in this world might have stood in his own individual right and said, "My work and teaching are surely self-evidently Divine," he was the Man; but no, he takes his questions along the historic line, and shows how he stands on prophetic ground, as successor of the last of the prophets. It was the recognition of the prophetical succession rather than any independent assumption.

II. Fear of man will incapacitate men for the simplest act of judgment. What Jesus asks these rulers to decide is whether John the Baptist, in introducing baptism, was taking a Heaven-inspired course or not. "The baptism of John, was it from heaven, or of men?" Instead of facing the question like men, they fenced with it. They saw clearly that in either case their answer would put them in a difficulty. If they said that John's baptism was from heaven, Jesus would immediately say, "Why then believed ye him not?" but if they declared it was a mere human innovation, they would come into such collision with the people as to run the risk of being stoned. In fear of man they decline judgment. Now it is instructive here to notice that such temporizers never can be martyrs. They have no notion of *dying* for their conviction about John. Why should they be stoned? They prefer being silent on the whole subject. As long as we fear man more than God, as long as we value man's esteem more than truth, we are unfit for judgment. We only become *impartial* when we are ready to take truth with all its consequences upon us.

III. The incompetent do not deserve to be treated as judges. These rulers have demonstrated their utter incompetency to undertake any decision upon a prophet's claims. They are consequently treated by Jesus as undeserving of the position of judges. It were well if this rule were faithfully observed. Men are treated often as if they had the judicial spirit, capacity, and temper, when they are simply *man-fearing partisans.* It is lost time putting such people in the judgment-seat. Better far to spend the time in teaching the common people, as the Master did, than in trying to convince the partisans who interrupt good work and do none themselves.

IV. By a parable of judgment he reveals to these partisans their danger. The vineyard indicates the theocratic people, the husbandmen the men who exercised government among them, and the naturally expected fruit was the loyalty and spiritual service which prophets called for but seldom secured for their Master in heaven. Instead of rendering the fruits, the rulers of the Jewish people subjected the line of prophets to increasing indignities. Last of all, the only Son is sent; but, instead of reverencing him and yielding to Divine demands, they cast him out of the Jewish Church and kill him. How clearly does Jesus thus claim Sonship to God, and indicate his approaching and dreadful doom! The result of this murder of God's Son is to be the transference of the theocracy from the Jews to other husbandmen. The chief priests and scribes are to be supplanted by apostles; and Judaism to give place to Christianity. Seeing that the parable was spoken against them, they cry, "God forbid!" but Jesus clinches his argument by apt quotation from their own Scriptures. He asks, "Is not the stone rejected of the builders to become the head of the corner? And will not all who collide with it be either broken or ground to powder?" In this way he claims to be the test of men, and his rejection to be fatal and final.—R. M. E.

Vers. 20—40.—*Christ supreme in debate.* We have seen in the last section how our Lord told a parable whose bearing was unmistakably against the Jewish rulers. They are determined, in consequence, to so entrap him in discussion as, if possible, to bring him within the grasp of the Roman governor. But in entering the doubtful field of debate with a base purpose such as this, it was, as the sequel shows, only to be vanquished. Jesus proves more than a match for the two batches of artful men who try to entrap him. Let us look at the victories separately, and then at Jesus remaining Master of the field.

I. His victory over the revolutionary party. (Vers. 21—26.) This party was composed mainly of Pharisees. They corresponded to the modern revolutionary party in settled or conquered states. They were constantly fomenting sedition, plotting against the Roman power, the sworn enemies of Cæsar. They come, then, with their difficulty about tribute. But notice: 1. *Their real tribute to Christ's character in their pretended flattery.* (Ver. 21.) They own to his face that he was too brave to make distinctions among men or to accept their persons. In other words, their testimony clearly is that, like God his Father, Jesus was "no respecter of persons." No one is fit to be a teacher of truth who panders to men's tastes or respects their persons. Only the impartial mood and mind can deal with truth truthfully. In the hollow flattery of the Pharisees we find rich testimony to the excellency of Jesus. 2. Notice their *scruple about paying tribute.* (Ver. 22.) The law of the nation might possibly be made to teach the duty of being tributary to none. It was this they wished to elicit from him, and so hand him over to the governor as seditious. They wished a pretext for revolution, and if he furnished them with one and perished for it, so much the better, they imagined. The baseness of the plot is evident. Their hearts are hostile to Cæsar, but they are ready to become "informers" against him for the sake of getting rid of him. 3. Notice *how simply he secured a victory.* Showing them at once that he knew their designs, he asks them to show him a penny. In his poverty he hardly possessed at this time a spare penny to point his teaching. Having got the penny, he asks about the image on the currency, and receiving for answer that it was Cæsar's, he simply instructs them to give both Cæsar and God their due. Cæsar has his domain as the currency shows. He regulates the outward relations of men, their barter and their citizenship, and by his laws he makes them keep the peace. But beyond this civil sphere, there is the moral and the religious, where God alone is King. Let God get his rights as well as Cæsar, and all shall be well. These words of Christ sounded the death-knell of the Jewish theocracy. They point out two mutually independent spheres. They call upon men to be at once loyal citizens and real saints. We may do our duty by the state, while at the same time we are conscious citizens of heaven, and serve our unseen Master in all things.[1]

II. His victory over the Sadducees. (Vers. 27—38.) The Pharisees having been confounded by his subtle power, he is next beset by the rival party, the party of sceptical and worldly tendencies. They have given over another world as a no-man's land, the region of undoubted difficulty and puzzle. Especially do they think it impossible to settle the complicated relations into which men and women enter here in any hereafter. Accordingly they state a case where, by direction of the Mosaic Law, a poor woman became successively the wife of seven brothers. In the other life, ask they, whose wife shall she be? Christ's answer is again triumphant through its simplicity. In the immortal life to which resurrection leads there shall be no marrying or giving in marriage. All shall be like the angels. No distinction in sex shall continue. All are to be "sons of God, being sons of the resurrection" (Revised Version). The

[1] Cf. Bersier's 'Sermons,' tome iv. p. 239, etc.

complicated earthly relations shall give place to the simplicity of *sonship*. God's family shall embrace all others. His Fatherhood shall absorb all the descending affections which on earth illustrate feebly his surpassing love, and our sonship to him will embrace all the ascending affection which his descending love demands. The simplicity of a holy family, in which God is Father and all are brethren, and the angels are our high-born elder brethren, will take the place of those complex relationships which sometimes sweeten and sometimes sadden human love. But, in addition, our Lord renders Sadduceeism ridiculous by showing from the Scriptures these sceptics revered that the patriarchs had not ceased to be, but were still living in the bosom of God. For God, in claiming from the burning bush to be the God of Abraham, Isaac, and Jacob, revealed the reality of life beyond death. It was a demonstration of the resurrection. The patriarchs must have been living worshippers when God was still their God, and this life unto him demands for its perfection the resurrection. The plenitude of life is guaranteed in the continued and worshipful life beyond the grave. In this simple and perfect fashion Jesus silences the Sadducees.

III. He remains complete Master of the field. (Vers. 39, 40.) They are beaten in the field of debate. Jesus is Victor. There is no question now which they can ask him. All is over on the plane of intellectual and moral argument. Not even a Parthian arrow can be shot against him. But treachery and brute force remain, and they can have him betrayed and crucified whom they cannot refute. Resort to weapons like these is always proof of weakness. Victory has always been really with the persecuted party. Persecution on the part of any cause or organization demonstrates its inherent weakness. Hence we hail the Christ in the temple as the supreme Master and Conqueror of men. The very men who put unholy hands upon him must have felt that they were doing the coward's part after ignominious defeat. The weapons of our warfare should always be spiritual; with carnal weapons we only confess defeat and court everlasting shame.—R. M. E.

Ver. 40—ch. xxi. 4.—*Vindications and judgments.* We saw on the last occasion how Christ had vanquished all who had tried with him the fortunes of debate. And now we find him putting a pertinent question to them about himself, and effectually puzzling them. Not, of course, that he had this in view in presenting it. His purpose was always a clear and pure one; it was, as Godet suggests, to vindicate beforehand those claims to Divine Sonship on the ground of which they are so shortly to condemn him to death.

I. Consider Christ as David's Son and Lord (Vers. 41—44.) It is clear from the Gospels and from the Targums that the Messiah wanted by the Jews was not necessarily to be Divine. It was a temporal prince, a military Messiah, they longed for; and no Divinity was needful to play the *rôle* of "conquering hero" which they desired. A merely human Messiah would have suited them admirably. When they got one, therefore, who claimed to be Divine, they condemned him for blasphemy, and never stopped until they had made away with him by crucifixion.[1] Our Lord's question in the temple was to arouse them to a sense of Messiah's proper claims. This suggests: 1. *How prone we are to be satisfied with mere human saviours.* The Jews wanted a Messiah to collect armies, to deliver them from Roman bondage, and to give them all good situations in the new kingdom. They wanted nothing that a clever leader could not do for them. And there are plenty of people whose only desired salvation is from hunger and thirst and discomfort of a physical kind. They have no real longing after deliverance from sin and covetousness and discontent. Their one thought is to find somebody who can help them on a bit. 2. *David's royal line produced a Prince who was also David's Lord.* Now, it is plain from the psalm (cx.) which Jesus quotes that David realized in the Messiah his present Lord. He ruled over David, and was recognized by David as his Lord. When we add to this the fact that David was the greatest monarch of his time, we see that the only interpretation of this Lordship is the Divinity of Messiah. This Messiah is made by the Most High to sit at his right hand until his enemies are made his footstool. The whole picture involves and implies Christ's Divinity. Now, if these scribes and Pharisees had acted honestly, they would have said, "Here is a point which escaped us; this Lordship over David is a claim which

[1] Cf. Treffry, on 'The Eternal Sonship,' 4th edit., pp. 77—99.

the sonship does not cover; there must be more in the Messiahship than we suspect; we must reconsider our attitude towards Jesus, and do him justice." But instead of this, they deliberately ignored the difficulty, and went on with their persecution of the Divine Messiah. Now, this is surely to show us that we need a Divine Saviour, for the salvation must be from the power and guilt of sin. We need a Saviour who will be our Lord; to whom we not only owe allegiance, but give it cheerfully. It is a Divine Lord of the ages, the King of kings, the Lord of lords, the infinite Majesty, whom we need to give us the emancipation which can alone profit our souls.

II. CONSIDER CHRIST'S CONDEMNATION OF THE SCRIBES. (Vers. 45—47.) Seeing how they reject the scriptural evidence of his claims, Jesus proceeds to warn his disciples against them. He knows them thoroughly. And: 1. He charges them with *skilfully manufacturing a religious reputation.* They wore peculiar garments; the man-milliners of the day had been brought into requisition. They welcomed recognition from the people in the markets; they took, as their right, the highest seats in the synagogue and the chief rooms at social feasts. They manufactured such a reputation as secured them abundant honour. 2. *They traded upon their reputation.* Widows got their advice and intercession, and paid them well for giving it. In fact, our Lord charges them with devouring widows' houses in their greed. Instead of the widows inspiring pity, they seemed eligible because defenceless victims. 3. *Their condemnation shall be proportionally great.* Professions which are traded upon will ultimately procure a deeper condemnation. How needful that the genuineness of our profession should be tested! If it is for God's dear sake, and not for the sake of worldly advantage, it will stand the test at last.

III. CONSIDER CHRIST'S ENCOMIUM UPON THE POOR WIDOW. (Ch. xxi. 1—4.) Sitting over against the treasury, our Lord saw both rich and poor depositing their gifts. Some of the rich gave largely out of their abundance, and Jesus noted doubtless the proportion. But one poor widow came along, and she deposited in the temple-chest a single farthing. It was little, but it was her all. Behind her sackcloth Jesus discerned the biggest heart in all the company. Now, we are taught by this circumstance: 1. That *all our gifts are deposited in sight of Christ.* As Divine Saviour he sits, so to speak, over against every treasury, and notes what the people deposit there. There is no such thing as secret giving so far as Jesus is concerned. We may give so that the right hand knows not what the left is giving, but Jesus knows all the same. 2. It is *the heart which determines the character of our liberality.* It is not the quantity of money, but the quality of the act, which is important. A farthing from a widow is more in the sight of God than thousands from a millionaire. Hence we ought to examine ourselves, and see clearly what our motives may be. 3. *Hence it is possible even for the poorest to be liberal.* It is this which we require to have driven home. When poor as well as rich give with large-heartedness, the Church's "golden age" shall come. It is to this that our Lord would lead us.—R. M. E.

EXPOSITION.

CHAPTER XXI.

Vers. 1—4.—*The widow's mite.* We find this little sketch only here and in St. Mark (xii. 41—44). The Master was sitting—resting, probably, after the effort of the great denunciation of the scribes and Pharisees—in the covered colonnade of that part of the temple which was open to the Jewish women. Here was the treasury, with its thirteen boxes in the wall, for the reception of the alms of the people. These boxes were called *shopheroth*, or trumpets, because they were shaped like trumpets, swelling out beneath, and tapering upward into a narrow mouth, or opening, into which the alms were dropped. Some of these "trumpets" were marked with special inscriptions, denoting the destination of the offerings.

Ver. 1.—**And he looked up, and saw the rich men casting their gifts into the treasury.** It is not improbable that a special stream of almsgivers were just then passing through the temple court, many being specially impressed by the solemn words they had just been listening to.

Ver. 2.—**And he saw also a certain poor widow casting in thither two mites.** The mite (λεπτόν) was the smallest current coin. Two of these little pieces were the smallest legal offering which could be dropped into the "trumpet." But this sum, as the Heart-reader, who knew all things, tells us (ver. 4), was *every particle of money she had in the world;* and it was this splendid generosity on the part of the poor solitary widow which won the Lord's praise, which has touched the hearts of so many generations since, which has stirred up in so many hearts an admiration of an act so strangely beautiful, but well-nigh inimitable.

Vers. 5—7.—*The temple—its impending ruin. The disciples' questions.*

Ver. 5.—**And as some spake of the temple.** After the Lord's remark upon the almsgiving of the rich men and the poor widow to the treasury of the temple, the Master left the sacred building for his lodging outside the city walls. As far as we know, his comment upon the widow's alms was his last word of public teaching. On their way home, while crossing the Mount of Olives, they apparently halted for a brief rest. It was then that some of his friends called attention to the glorious prospect of the temple, then lit up by the setting sun. It was, no doubt, then in all its perfect beauty, a vast glittering mass of white marble, touched here and there with gold and colour. Whosoever had not gazed on it, said the old rabbis, had not seen the perfection of beauty. It is possible that the bystander's remark was suggested by the memory of the last bit of Divine teaching they had listened to. "Lord, is not the house on Zion lovely? But if only such gifts as those you have just praised with such unstinting praise had been made, never had that glorious pile been raised in honour of the Eternal King." More probable, however, the sight of the great temple, then bathed in the golden glory of the fast-setting sun, recalled some of the Master's sayings of that eventful day, notably such as, "Your house is left unto you desolate," which occurred in the famous twice-spoken apostrophe, "O Jerusalem, Jerusalem, thou that killest the prophets!" (Matt. xxiii. 38; ch. xiii. 35). "What, Lord! will *that* house, so great, so perfect in its beauty, so loved, the joy of the whole earth,—will *that house* be left desolate and in shapeless ruins?" **With goodly stones.** The enormous size of the stones and blocks of marble with which the temple of Jerusalem was built excited the surprise of Titus when the city fell. Josephus mentions ('Bell. Jud.,' v. 5) that some of the levelled blocks of marble or stone were forty cubits long and ten high. **And gifts;** better rendered, *sacred offerings*, such as the "golden vine," with its vast clusters, the gift of Herod—which probably suggested the discourse, "I am the true Vine" (reported in John xv.)—such as crowns, shields, vessels of gold and silver, presented by princes and others who visited the holy house on Zion. The temple was rich in these votive offerings. The historian Tacitus, for instance, calls it "a temple of vast wealth" ('Hist.,' v. 8).

Ver. 6.—**There shall not be left one stone upon another.** There is a remarkable passage in 2 Esdr. x. 54, "In the place wherein the Highest beginneth to show *his* city, there can no man's building be able to stand." The Lord's words were fulfilled, in spite of the strong wish of Titus to spare the temple. Josephus, writing upon the utter demolition of the city and temple, says that, with the exception of Herod's three great towers and part of the western wall, the whole circuit of the city was so thoroughly levelled and dug up that no one visiting it would believe that it had ever been inhabited ('Bell. Jud.,' vii. 1. 1).

Ver. 7.—**And they asked him, saying, Master, but when shall these things be? and what sign will there be when these things shall come to pass?** St. Mark (xiii. 3) tells us that these questioners were Peter and James, John and Andrew. They said to their Master, "When shall these things be, and what sign shall precede them?" They asked their question with mingled feelings of awe and gladness: *of awe*, for the ruin of their loved temple, and all that would probably accompany the catastrophe, was a dread thought; *of gladness*, for they associated the fall of city and temple with the manifestation of their Lord in glory. In this glory they would assuredly share. But they wished to know more respecting the times and seasons of the dread event. Of late the disciples had begun dimly to see that no Messianic restoration such as they had been taught to expect was contemplated by their Master. They were recasting their hopes, and this solemn prediction they read in the light of the late sad and gloomy words which he had spoken of himself and his fortunes. Perhaps he would leave them for a season and then return, and, amid the crash of the ruined city and temple, set up his glorious kingdom. But they longed to know when this would be; hence the question of the four.

The Lord's answer treated, in its first and longer portion, exclusively of the destruction of Jerusalem and its temple—the fair city and the glorious house on which they were then gazing, glorified in the light of the sunset splendour; then, as he spoke, gradually the horizon widened, and the Master touched upon the fortunes of

the great world lying beyond the narrow pale of the doomed, chosen people. He closes his grand summary of the world's fortunes by a sketch of his own return in glory. The disciples' hearts must have sunk as they listened; for how many ages lay between *now* and *then!* Yet was the great prophecy full of comfort, and in later days was of inestimable practical value to the Jerusalem Christians. The discourse, which extends from ver. 8 to ver. 36, has been well divided by Godet into four divisions. (1) The apparent signs of the great catastrophe, which must not be mistaken for true signs (vers. 8*b*—19). (2) The true sign, and the destruction of Jerusalem, which will immediately follow it, with the time of the Gentiles, which will be connected with it (vers. 20—24). (3) The coming of the Lord, which will bring this period to an end (vers. 25—27). (4) The practical application (vers. 28—36).

Vers. 8—19.—*The apparent signs which would show themselves, but which must not be mistaken for the true signs immediately preceding the catastrophe.*

Ver. 8*b*.—**Many shall come in my name, saying, I am Christ.** Many of these pretenders appeared in the lifetime of the apostles. Josephus mentions several of these impostors ('Ant.,' xx. 8 §§ 6—10; 'Bell. Jud.,' ii. 13. § 5). Theudas, one of these pretenders, is referred to in Acts xxi. 38 (see, too, Josephus, 'Ant.,' xx. 5. § 1). Simon Magus announced that he was Messiah. His rival Dositheus, his disciple Menander, advanced similar pretences. Mr. Greswell (quoted by Dean Mansel, 'Speaker's Commentary,' on Matt. xxiv. 5) has called attention to the remarkable fact that, while many of these false Messiahs appeared in the interval between the Lord's ascension and the Jewish war, there is no evidence that any one arose claiming this title before the beginning of his ministry. It was necessary, he infers, that the true Christ should first appear and be rejected by the great body of the nation, before they were judicially given over to the delusions of the false Christs.

Vers. 9, 10.—**Wars and commotions . . . nation shall rise against nation, and kingdom against kingdom.** Josephus the Jewish, and Tacitus the Roman, historian—the former in his 'Jewish Wars,' and the latter in his 'Annals'—describe the period which immediately followed the Crucifixion as full of wars, crimes, violences, earthquakes. "It was a time," says Tacitus, "rich in disasters, horrible with battles, torn with seditions, savage even in peace itself."

Ver. 11.—**Great earthquakes.** These seem to have been very frequent during the period; we hear of them in Palestine, Italy, Greece, Asia Minor, Crete, Syria. **Famines and pestilences.** The Jewish and pagan historians of this time—Josephus, Suetonius, Tacitus, and others—enumerate several memorable instances of these scourges in this eventful time. **Fearful sights and great signs.** Among the former may be especially enumerated the foul and terrible scenes connected with the proceedings of the Zealots (see Josephus, 'Bell. Jud.,' iv. 3. § 7; v. 6. § 1, etc.). Among the great signs "would be the rumour of monstrous births; the cry, 'Woe! woe!' for seven and a half years of the peasant Jesus, son of Hanan; the voice and sound of departing guardian-angels; and the sudden opening of the vast brazen temple gate which required twenty men to move it" (Farrar).

Ver. 12.—**But before all these, they shall lay their hands on you, and persecute you.** The Master continues his prophetic picture. From speaking generally of wars, and disasters, and tumults, and awful natural phenomena, which would mark the sad age in which his hearers were living, he proceeded to tell them of things which would surely befall *them*. But even then, though terrible trials would be their lot, they were not to be dismayed, nor to dream that the great catastrophe he had been predicting was yet at hand. Some doubt exists as to the meaning of "before" (πρό) in this twelfth verse. It usually has been understood in a temporal sense, *i.e.* "Before all the wars, etc., I have been telling you of, you will be persecuted." A more definite sense is, however, produced by giving the word πρό (before) the signification of "before," equivalent to "more important"—"more important for you as signs will be the grave trials you will have to endure: even *these* signs must not dismay you, or cause you to give up your posts as teachers, for the end will not be heralded even by these personal signs." **Delivering you up to the synagogues, and into prisons, being brought before kings and rulers for my Name's sake.** What may be termed instances of many of these special persecutions are detailed in the Acts (see, for instance, Acts v. 40; and portions of vi., vii., viii., xii., xiv., xvi., xxi., and following).

Ver. 15.—**For I will give you a mouth and wisdom, which all your adversaries shall not be able to gainsay nor resist.** Instances of the splendid fulfilment of this promise are supplied in the "Acts" report of St. Stephen's speech (vii.), and St. Paul's defence spoken before the Roman governor Felix (xxv.) and before King Agrippa (xxvi.).

Ver. 16.—**And ye shall be betrayed both by parents, and brethren, and kinsfolk, and friends.** His disciples must be prepared to pay, as the price of their friendship with him, the sacrifice of all home and domestic life and peace. How often in the records of the early Christians are these terrible sufferings added to public persecution! Literally, his own would have very often to give up mother, father, friends, for his sake. **And some of you shall they cause to be put to death.** This was literally true in the case of several of those then listening to him.

Ver. 17.—**And ye shall be hated of all men for my Name's sake.** All the records of early Christianity unite in bearing witness to the universal hatred with which the new sect were regarded by pagans as well as Jews. The words of the Roman Jews reported in Acts xxviii. 22 well sum this up, "As concerning this sect, we know that everywhere it is spoken against" (see, too, Acts xxiv. 5 and 1 Pet. ii. 12). The Roman writers Tacitus, Pliny, and Suetonius, bear the same testimony.

Ver. 18.—**But there shall not an hair of your head perish.** Not, of course, to be understood literally; for comp. ver. 16. Bengel's comment accurately paraphrases it: "Not a hair of your head shall perish without the special providence of God, nor without reward, nor before the due time." The words, too, had a general fulfilment; for the Christian community of Palestine, warned by this very discourse of the Lord's, fled in time from the doomed city, and so escaped the extermination which overtook the Jewish people in the great war which ended in the fall of Jerusalem (A.D. 70).

Ver. 19.—**In your patience possess ye your souls.** Quiet, brave patience in all difficulty, perplexity, and danger, was the attitude pressed upon the believers of the first days by the inspired teachers. St. Paul constantly strikes this note.

Vers. 20—24.—*The true signs which his people are to be on the watch for.*

Ver. 20.—**And when ye shall see Jerusalem compassed with armies, then know that the desolation thereof is nigh.** This is to be the sign that the end has come for temple, city, and people. Wars and rumours of wars, physical portents, famine and pestilence succeeding each other with a terrible persistence, all these will, in the forthcoming years, terrify and perplex men's minds, presages of something which seems impending. But his people are to bear in mind that these were not the immediate signs of the awful ruin he was foretelling. But when the holy city was invested, when hostile armies were encamped about her—then this would surely come to pass, and some of these very bystanders would behold it—*then*, and not till then, let his people take alarm. Let them at once and at all cost flee from temple and city, for there would be no deliverance, God had left his house, given up the chosen people. "Jerusalem shall be trodden down of the Gentiles" (ver. 24). It is probable that these solemn words of the Master, becoming, as they did, at a comparatively early date, the property of the Church, saved the Christian congregations in Palestine from the fate which overtook the Jewish nation in the last great war. Clearly warned by Jesus that the gathering of the Roman armies in the neighbourhood of Jerusalem was the unmistakable sign of the end of the Jewish polity, the Christian congregations fled to Pella beyond Jordan. The Jews never ceased to the last trusting that deliverance from on high would be vouchsafed to the holy city and temple. The Christians were warned by the words of the Founder of their faith—words spoken nigh forty years before the siege—that the time of mercy was hopelessly past.

Ver. 24.—**And they shall fall by the edge of the sword, and shall be led away captive into all nations.** It is computed that 1,100,000 Jews perished in the terrible war when Jerusalem fell (A.D. 70). Renan writes of this awful slaughter, "that it would seem as though the whole (Jewish) race had determined upon a rendezvous for extermination." **Jerusalem shall be trodden down of the Gentiles.** After incredible slaughter and woes, Titus, the Emperor Vespasian's son, who commanded the Roman armies, ordered the city (of Jerusalem) to be razed so completely as to look like a spot which had never been inhabited (Josephus, 'Bell. Jud.,' v. 10. § 5). The storied city has been rebuilt on the old site—*but without the temple*—and since that fatal day, more than eighteen centuries ago, no Jew save on bare sufferance has dwelt in the old loved and sacred spot. In turn, Roman and Saracen, Norseman and Turk, have trodden Jerusalem down. Literally, indeed, have the sad words of Jesus been fulfilled. **Until the times of the Gentiles be fulfilled.** These few words carry on the prophecy past our own time (how far past?)—carry it on close to the days of the end. "The times of the Gentiles" signify the whole period or epoch which must elapse between the destruction of Jerusalem and the temple, and the beginning of the times of the end when the Lord will return. In other words, these "times of the Gentiles" denote the period during which they—the Gentiles—hold the Church of God in place of the Jews, deposed from that position of favour and honour. These words separate the prophecy of Jesus which belongs solely to the ruin of the city and temple from the eschatological portion of the same prophecy. *Hitherto* the Lord's words referred solely to the fall of Jerusalem and the ruin of the Jewish race. *Now* begins a short prophetic description of the end and of the coming of the Son of man in glory.

Vers. 25—27.—*The prophecy of the coming of the Son of man in glory. The signs which shall precede this advent.* **And there shall be signs in the sun, and in the moon, and in the stars; and upon the earth distress of nations, with perplexity; the sea and the waves roaring; men's hearts failing them for fear, and for looking after those things which are coming on the earth: for the powers of heaven shall be shaken. And then shall they see the Son of man coming in a cloud with power and great glory.** The Lord continues his solemn prophecy respecting things to come. Now, the question of the four disciples—to which this great discourse was the answer—was, When were they to look for that awful ruin of city and temple of which their loved Master spoke? *But they, it must be remembered, in their own minds closely connected the temple's fall with some glorious epiphany of their Master, in which they should share.* He answers generally their formal question as to the temple, describing to them the very signs they are to look for as heralding the temple's fall. He now proceeds to reply to their real query respecting the glorious epiphany. *The temple's ruin*, that belonged to the period in which they were living; but the glorious epiphany, *that* lay in a far distance. "See," he said, "city and temple will be destroyed; this catastrophe some of you will live to see. The ruin will be irreparable; a new epoch will set in, an epoch I call 'the times of the Gentiles.' These once despised peoples will have their turn, for I shall be their Light. Ages will pass before these 'times of the Gentiles' shall be fulfilled, but the end will come, and then, and not till then, will the Son of man come in glory. Listen; these shall be the signs which shall herald this glorious advent: *Signs in the sun, and in the moon, and in the stars.*" St. Matthew (xxiv. 29) supplies more details concerning these "signs." The sun would be darkened, and the moon would not give her light; the stars would fall from heaven. These words are evidently a memory of language used by the Hebrew prophets to express figuratively the downfall of kingdoms. So Isaiah (xiii. 10) speaks thus of the destruction of Babylon, and Ezekiel (xxxii. 7) of the fall of Egypt (see too Isa. xxxiv. 4). It is, however, probable that our Lord, while using language and figures familiar to Hebrew thought, foreshadowed a literal fulfilment of his words. So Godet, who picturesquely likens our globe just before the second advent to "a ship creaking in every timber at the moment of its going to pieces." He suggests that "our whole solar system shall then undergo unusual commotions. The moving forces (δυνάμεις), regular in their action till then, shall be, as it were, set free from their laws by an unknown power, and, at the end of this violent but short distress, the world shall see him appear" (see 2 Pet. iii. 10—12, where it is plainly foretold that tremendous physical disturbances shall precede the second coming of the Lord). *The Son of man coming in a cloud.* The same luminous cloud we read of so often in the Pentateuch: the flames of the desert-wanderings; the pillar of cloud and fire; the same bright cloud enveloped the Lord on the Mount of Transfiguration; it received him as he was taken up (Acts i. 9). Nothing is said in this place as to any millennial reign of Christ on earth. The description is that of a transitory appearance destined to effect the work upon quick and dead—an appearance defined more particularly by St. Paul in 1 Cor. xv. 23 and 1 Thess. iv. 16, 17.

Vers. 28—36.—*Practical teaching arising out of the foregoing prophecy respecting the fall of Jerusalem and the "last things."*

Ver. 28.—**And when these things begin to come to pass, then look up, and lift up your heads; for your redemption draweth nigh.** There is no doubt that the first reference in this verse is to the earlier part of the prophecy—the fate of the city and the ruin of the Jewish power. "Your redemption" would then signify "your deliverance" from the constant and bitter hostility of the Jewish authority. After A.D. 70 and the fall of Jerusalem, the growth of Christianity was far more rapid than it had been during the first thirty or forty years of its existence. It had no longer to cope with the skilfully ordered, relentless opposition of its deadly Jewish foe. Yet between the lines a yet deeper meaning is discernible. In all times the earnest Christian is on the watch for the signs of the advent of his Lord, and the restless watch serves to keep hope alive, for the watcher knows that that advent will be the sure herald of his redemption from all the weariness and painfulness of this life.

Ver. 29.—**And he spake to them a parable.** "It is certain," went on the Lord to say, "that summer follows the season when the fig tree and other trees put forth their green shoots. It is no less certain that these things—the fall of Jerusalem, and later the end of the world—will follow closely on the signs I have just told you about."

Ver. 32.—**Verily I say unto you, This generation shall not pass away, till all be** fulfilled. In the interpretation of this verse, a verse which has occasioned much perplexity to students, any non-natural sense for "generation" (γενεά), such as being an equivalent for *the Christian Church* (Origen and Chrysostom) or *the human race* (Jerome) must be at once set aside. Γενεά (generation) denotes roughly a period of thirty to forty years. Thus the words of the Lord here simply asserted that within thirty or forty years all he had been particularly detailing would be fulfilled. Now, the burden of his prophecy had been the destruction of the city and temple, and the signs they were to look for as immediately preceding this great catastrophe. This was the plain and simple answer to their question of ver. 7, which asked "when these things should come to pass." The words he had added relative to the coming of the Son of man did not belong to the formal answer, but were spoken in passing. This mighty advent the Lord alluded to as probably a very remote event—an event certainly to be postponed, to use his own words, "until the times of the Gentiles be fulfilled." Not so the great catastrophe involving the ruin of Jerusalem and the temple, the prophecy concerning which occupied so much of the Lord's reply. *That* lay in the immediate future; *that* would happen in the lifetime of some of those standing by. Before forty years had elapsed the city and temple, now lying before them in all its strength and beauty, would have disappeared.

Ver. 33.—**Heaven and earth shall pass away: but my words shall not pass away.** A general conclusion to the whole prophecy. "No word of mine," said the Master, "will ever pass away unfulfilled. Some of you will even live to see the terrible fulfilment of the first part of these utterances. All that mighty pile of buildings called Jerusalem will pass away, but my words which told of their coming ruin will remain. All this vast creation, earth, and stars will disappear in their turn, but these sayings of mine, which predict their future passing away into nothingness, will outlive both earth and heaven."

Ver. 34.—**And take heed to yourselves.** The Master ended his discourse with an earnest practical reminder to his disciples to live ever with the sure expectation of his return to judgment. As for those who heard him then, conscious of the oncoming doom of the city, temple, and people, with the solemn procession of signs heralding the impending ruin ever before their eyes, no passions or cares of earth surely would hinder *them* from living the brave, pure life worthy of his servants. As for coming generations—for the warning voice of Jesus here is equally addressed to them—they too must watch for another and far more tremendous ruin falling upon their homes than ever fell upon Jerusalem. The attitude of his people in every age must be that of the "watcher" *till he come.*

Ver. 37.—**And in the daytime he was teaching in the temple; and at night he went out, and abode in the mount that is called the Mount of Olives.** This brief picture of the last days of public work is retrospective. This was how our Lord spent "Palm Sunday" and the Monday and Tuesday of the last week. The prophetic discourse reported in this twenty-first chapter was, most probably, spoken on the afternoon of Tuesday. After Tuesday evening he never entered the temple as a public Teacher again. Wednesday and Thursday were spent in retirement. Thursday evening he returned to the city to eat the last Passover with his own.

HOMILIES BY VARIOUS AUTHORS.

Vers. 1—4.—*Worth in the estimate of wisdom.* What is the real worth of a human action? Surely, to us who are acting every wakeful hour of life, a very serious question. How shall we decide that an action of ours is worthy or unworthy, and what is the standard by which we shall estimate the comparative excellence of worthy deeds? Our text gives us one principle by which to judge. There are, however, two others which are essentially Christian, that should be placed in the foreground. Acts are worthy—

I. As THEY ARE USEFUL; as they tend to promote well-being. And here we should note that their usefulness is greater: 1. As they affect character rather than circumstance. 2. As they are free from drawback; for the usefulness of many a course of action is the difference between the intentional good and the incidental evil that is wrought. 3. As they are permanently influential and therefore reproductive. Many a deed, being done, is *done with;* it has no appreciable results; but many another is as seed in the soil—there is a fruitful harvest to be reaped from it in the after-time.

II. ACCORDING TO THE SPIRIT IN WHICH THEY ARE DONE. If useful things are done in the spirit of rivalry, or for the purpose of display, or in the hope of social or material remuneration, their worth in God's sight is nothing or next to nothing. If they are done to honour and to please Jesus Christ, or prompted by pure benevolence, or in the spirit of filial obedience, they have a real worth and are the objects of Divine approval. But the teaching of our text is that actions are worthy—

III. MEASURED BY THEIR UNSELFISHNESS. If at heart they are selfish, then in the judgment of God they are without virtue; in proportion to their generosity, and that is to say, to their costliness, they are beautiful, and even noble. 1. *The gift of money.* The widow's mite was more in the sight of God than the rich men's gold; and it was so because they gave of their abundance a sum the loss of which they would not feel—a sum that entailed no reduction of their comfort and constituted no sacrifice at all; but she gave all that she had—a sum she would miss much, a truly generous sacrifice. How often we applaud the donation of some hundreds of pounds, when the ten shillings contributed by some struggling worker has a higher place in the heavenly ledger! 2. *The gift of time.* The man whose easy circumstances allow him to give much time to religion or philanthropy may be less worthy and may be making a really smaller contribution than he who, pressed hard by pecuniary obligations and having a heavy burden of family responsibility to carry, yet squeezes a few hours from toilful days to lend a helping hand to the cause of Christ and of man. The *horæ subscecivæ* are of more account than many leisure days. 3. *Active service* in the field of Christian labour. Some men are so constituted that they can render service in the pulpit, on the platform, in the class-room, *almost without cost;* they can speak without previous preparation and without subsequent exhaustion. But others can only serve at much cost to themselves; their strength is taxed to be ready for the hour of opportunity, they expend themselves freely in the act of utterance or in the outpouring of sympathy, and they know what the miseries of prostration mean. A slight service, as reckoned by the time-table or the census, on the part of these latter may be more than equal to very prominent and much-appreciated work rendered by the former. 4. *The sacrifice of life.* It might seem that those who gave their life for their Lord or for their kind were all offering a gift of the same value. But not so. Life has very different values at different stages. It is comparatively little for the man who has spent his days and his powers to surrender the short and uninteresting remainder; it is much for the young man who has all the pleasures and prizes of life within his reach to part with the bright, inviting future in order to serve his fellows; the deed is nobler, for the sacrifice is greater. (1) Let us take care that we do not judge by the appearance only, or we shall be unjust. (2) Let us be sure that every true act of worthy service is appreciated and will be owned of Christ.—C.

Vers. 5, 6.—*The destructible and the indestructible.* We have our Lord's own authority for comparing the temple with a human being (John ii. 19). He, however, compared it with his body; we may without any impropriety make the comparison with a human spirit—with the man himself. We look at it in regard to its destructibleness.

I. THE BUILDING ITSELF, AND OUR BEING ITSELF. The temple was the pride and the delight of every Jew. Among other things that gratified him, he rejoiced in its strength; he felt that it was secure. Generations of men would come and go, but that building would remain. Built of the most durable materials, it would defy the action of the elements; placed in the strong city and guarded with such ramparts, the enemy would assail it in vain. Where it then stood, there after many centuries it would be found. But the Jew was wrong; already those elements were at work which would bring on the fatal conflict, and that generation was not to pass (ver. 33) until that glorious fabric should be cast down and "not one stone left upon another." A very slight thing in comparison with such a great and imposing structure seems a human being How easily destroyed! "crushed before the moth;" "destroyed between the morning and the evening." Yet is there within the compass of the smallest and feeblest man that which is more lasting than the temple, that which will survive the strongest structure that art or nature ever reared. Not that the human soul is absolutely indestructible: "*He* can create and he [can] destroy it." But it is created and intended for immortality. And if only it be on the side of truth and in the service of God—*in* Christ Jesus, it is *destined* for immortality; it will survive the strongest temples and the most impregnable castles; no wrath of man, no lapse and wear of time, no shock of material forces, can destroy it; it is indestructible.

II. ITS STRENGTH AND BEAUTY, AND OUR OWN. The temple was "adorned with goodly stones and gifts." But strong as these massive stones were, and carefully as those gifts were guarded, the day came, and came in the experience of that very generation, when not one stone was left upon another, and nothing of the exquisite offerings was preserved; everything perished in the fire or was ploughed up by the ruthless share. Now, there is one thing which no fire can consume and no violence shatter—*a spiritually strong and spiritually beautiful character;* a holy and lovely character rooted in Christ and sustained by his indwelling Spirit. Buildings massive and solid, fortunes large and brilliant, kingdoms fortified by great armies and costly navies,—these may be broken to pieces and perish. But the character of a Christian man, who is simply loyal to his Master, cannot be broken. Character that is not rooted in faith and that is not sustained by devotion may fall and be broken, and great and sad is the fall of it. But (1) let a man build on the foundation which is laid for it, even Jesus Christ; (2) let him abide in Christ by a living faith; (3) let him seek the continual sustenance of the Spirit of God;—and no opposing or wasting forces will touch him to harm him. The strength and beauty of his character will remain, will become stronger and fairer with the passing years, will be the object of commendation when the eye of the great Judge shall rest upon them at last.—C.

Ver. 13.—*Afterwards.* "No chastening for the present seemeth to be joyous, but grievous: nevertheless *afterward* it yieldeth the peaceable fruit of righteousness." Concerning any course we take the question *how it affects us now* is not so important as is the question *to what it leads*, or, in the words of the text, "to what it turns." And while that which is very pleasant often "turns to" much that is painful and bitter, or even shameful (see Rev. x. 10), on the other hand, that which is very trying and even saddening at the time often "turns to" an issue that is full of honour and of joy. The context suggests that—

I. PERSECUTION TURNS TO TESTIMONY—to a most valuable proof of sincerity and faithfulness. When a man endures the blows and buffetings of the cruel hand of the persecutor, "we know the proof of him;" we write him down a true, loyal, noble servant of Christ. To how many men, not of the earliest age only but of all ages, has this steadfastness in the hour of trial been accepted by us as a "testimony" of the very greatest worth, so that their names are treasured by us as those of men that have done highest honour to their race! And their martyr-sufferings have turned to a testimony in the heavenly country; they have gained for them there the commendation of their Lord and the greeting of their glorified brethren. When, from "wandering in deserts, and in mountains, and in dens and caves of the earth," the persecuted Christians of Madagascar came forth to be welcomed by those who were then living under a kindly rule, they were greeted as such faithful and heroic men deserved to be; their persecution had turned into a testimony. In a similar way we may say that—

II. TOIL TURNS INTO ACHIEVEMENT. The toil of the desk, of the field, of the shop, of the factory, may be hard and wearisome; our back may bend beneath our burden; our mind may be strained to its utmost capacity of continuance; but let us take courage and work on at our task; further on is the precious goal of achievement; after a while we shall look with unspeakable satisfaction on the work that has been done, the result that has been reached.

III. PRIVATION TURNS INTO ENRICHMENT. Sad and serious indeed are the privations, the losses, which are suffered when men are suddenly reduced in their temporal possessions, or when they are bereaved of near relatives or most intimate friends. Yet is there something more than compensation when the loss of the one leads, as it has often led, to the enrichment of the soul, by its finding refuge in God and in his service; or when the loss of the other has brought to the soul the fulness of the sympathy and friendship of Jesus Christ; privation has turned to enrichment.

IV. SERVICE TURNS INTO RULE. The soldier in the ranks becomes an officer of the army; the apprentice becomes the master; by long and faithful service in any one of the fields of human activity we prepare to rule. Thus is it in the spiritual realm. Obedience to Divine law turns into a perfect self-command, which is another name for liberty. And a lifelong service of Jesus Christ will turn to an occupancy of that heavenly sphere for which our fidelity shall have fitted us; the "faithful and wise servant" his Lord will "make ruler over all his goods" (Matt. xxiv. 45—47). Faithful service here "turns to" happy and helpful rule hereafter.

V. PATIENT WAITING TURNS TO BLISSFUL PARTICIPATION. Some souls have much waiting for the hour of deliverance, for "the redemption of our body;" it is a weary and a trying time. To "learn to wait" is the hardest of all lessons. But though the night seem very long, the morning will come in time; and if the steadfast soul wait patiently the holy will of God, the long endurance shall turn to a full and joyous participation in the glory that is to be revealed—the "glorious liberty of the children of God."—C.

Vers. 14—19.—*Inevitable trial and unfailing resources.* Here we have one more illustration of the faithfulness of Jesus Christ toward his apostles. So far was he from encouraging in them the thought that their path would be one of easy conquest and delightful possession, that he was frequently warning them of a contrary experience. It was not his fault if they failed to anticipate hardship and suffering in the near future; he told them plainly that his service meant the cross, with all its pain and shame. In reference to the apostles of our Lord, we have here—

I. THE SEVERITY OF THE TRIALS THAT WERE BEFORE THEM. Jesus Christ had already indicated the fact that fidelity to his cause would entail severe loss and trial; here he goes into detail. He says that it will include: 1. *General execration.* They would be "hated of all men." This is a trial of no small severity; to move among men as if we were unworthy of their fellowship; to be condemned, to be despised, to be shunned by all men; to be the object of universal reprobation;—this is a blow which, if it "breaks no bones," cuts into the spirit and wounds the heart with a deep injury. Fidelity to their Master and to their mission would entail this. 2. *Desertion and treachery* on the part of their own friends and kindred. (Ver. 16.) Very few sorrows can be more piercing, more intolerable, than desertion by our own family, than betrayal by our dearest friends; it is the last and worst calamity when "our own familiar friend lifts up *his* heel against us." Those who abandoned the old faith, or rather the Pharisaic version of it, and who followed Christ had to be prepared for this domestic and social sorrow. 3. *Death.* (Ver. 16.)

II. THE UNFAILING RESOURCES ON WHICH THEY COULD DEPEND. 1. Everything they suffered would be endured for the sake of Jesus Christ; all would be "for my Name's sake" (ver. 17). We know how the thought that they were experiencing wrong and undergoing shame for Christ's sake could not only alleviate, not only dissipate sorrow, but even turn it into joy (see Acts v. 41; Phil. i. 29). To suffer for Christ's sake could give a thrill of sacred joy such as no pleasures could possibly afford. 2. They would have the shield of the Master's power (ver. 18). Not a hair of their head should perish until he allowed it. That mighty Friend who had kept them in perfect safety, though enemies were many and fierce, would be as near to them as ever. His presence would attend them, and no shaft should touch them which he did not wish to hurt them. 3. They should have the advantage of his animating Spirit (vers. 14, 15). Whenever wisdom or utterance should be needed, the Spirit of Christ would put thoughts into their mind and words into their lips. His animating power should be upon them, should dwell within them. 4. They should triumph in the end; not, indeed, by martial victories, but by unyielding loyalty. "In patience" (in persistency in the right course) "they would possess their souls." *Losing* their life in noble martyrdom, they would *save* it (ch. ix. 24); loving their life, they would lose it; but "hating their life in this world, they would keep it unto life eternal" (John xii. 25). The bright promise of an unfading crown might cheer them on their way, and help them to pursue without flagging the path of devoted loyalty.

APPLICATION. 1. *Similar trials await the faithful now.* The dislike, the aversion, the opposition, of some, if not the active and strong hatred of all; the opposition, perhaps quiet enough, and yet keen and injurious enough, of our own friends or relatives; loss, struggle, suffering, if not fatal consequences of enmity. Downright loyalty to Jesus Christ, tenacity and intensity of conviction, usually carry persecution and trial with them. 2. *We have the same resources* the apostles had. (1) The constant, sustaining, inspiring sense that we are enduring all for Christ our Saviour—for him who suffered all things for us. (2) His protecting care. (3) His indwelling, upholding Spirit. (4) The strong assurance that he will cause us to triumph, that he will help us to be faithful unto death, and will then give us the crown of life; that by "patient continuance in well-doing" (patience, perseverance) we shall have "eternal life" (shall possess our souls).—C.

Ver. 28.—*The second redemption.* "Lift up your heads; for your redemption draweth nigh." Jesus Christ led his disciples to think that beyond the redemption which he was working out for them, and subsequent to it in time, was another great deliverance which should prove of unspeakable value to them. This is true now of our discipleship; we look for and we sorely need a second redemption.

I. ITS CHARACTER. It is not, like the first, distinctively and purely spiritual. *That was;* men were yearning for a political revolution and redemption. But the kingdom of heaven was not to be "of this world;" it was to be wholly inward and spiritual; it was to be our redemption from sin and restoration to the favour and the likeness of our Divine Father. But the second redemption is not distinctively and primarily that of the soul; it is to be "the redemption of our body" (Rom. viii. 23). It will have a gracious and beneficent effect, a redeeming and elevating influence, upon the soul; but in the first instance it is a redemption from a troublous and trying condition; it is being taken away, by the appearance of Christ, in the providence of God, from a state in which happy service is almost impossible; it is a removal from storm to calm, from hostile to friendly forces, from turbulence to serenity; from hard conflict, or tense anxiety, or painful suffering, to "the rest which remaineth for the people of God." It is a blessed and merciful change from unfavourable to favourable conditions.

II. OUR HUMAN NEED OF IT. We are not *of* this world, we who have been redeemed by Jesus Christ and renewed by the Spirit of God. And we may be nobly, even grandly, victorious over it, being "always caused to triumph" by that Divine Spirit that dwells within us, and "strengthens us with all might." Yet are we actually, and by universal experience, seriously affected by it, and we suffer many things as we pass through it. We may suffer, as the early Christians did (to whom these words were addressed), from persecution, and thereby be made "most miserable" (1 Cor. xv. 19). Our life may be made worthless, or worse than worthless, to us by the cruelties of our fellow-men. Or we may suffer so much from privation of privilege, or from the struggles of daily life, or from grief and disappointment, or from a steadily advancing decrepitude, that we may earnestly long for this second redemption, the redemption of our body. We may be in sore need of its approach, of its presence.

III. ITS KINDLY SHADOW. It will then be much to us, perhaps everything, that our redemption *draweth nigh.* 1. It is *something* that at any moment we may be within a step of the heavenly sphere; for anything we know, Christ may be about to say concerning us, "This day ye shall be with me in Paradise." 2. It is *more* that we may be confident that a life of holy activity will rapidly pass away and bring us to the day of rest and of reward. 3. It is very much indeed that the duration of the blessed future will prove to be such that any number of years of earthly trouble will be nothing in comparison. 4. It is also a truth full of hope and healing that every day spent in faithful service or patient waiting brings us that distance nearer to the blessedness that lies beyond.

"We nightly pitch our moving tent
A day's march nearer home."

Beneath the varied and heavy burdens of time we are fain to bow our heads; but we shall lift them up with strength and eager-hearted expectation as we realize that every step forward is a step onward to the heavenly horizon.—C.

Ver. 33.—*The immortality of Christian truth.* These striking words suggest to us—

I. CHRIST'S CONSCIOUS CONNECTION WITH THE ETERNAL FATHER. Had there not been in him a profound and abiding consciousness that, in a sense far transcending our own experience, God dwelt in him and he in God, these words would have been wholly indefensible; they would have been in the last degree immodest. Proceeding from any other than the Son of God himself, they would have simply repelled us, and would have cast grave discredit on every other utterance from the same lips. It was because he was Divine, and felt the authority which his Divinity conveyed, that he could and did use such words as these without any trace of assumption; without violating that "meekness and lowliness of heart" which he claimed to possess—the possession of which neither friend nor enemy has attempted to dispute.

II. THE PERMANENCE OF TRUTH COMPARED WITH THE TRANSITORINESS OF MATTER. It is only in a limited and figurative sense that we can speak of material things as eternal. The hour will come when they will perish; indeed, they are perishing as we speak. The immovable rocks, the everlasting hills, are being disintegrated by sun and rain; the fixed earth rises and falls; the "changeless rivers" are cutting new courses for their waters. Only truth abides; it is only the words in which the thought of the Eternal is expressed that do not pass away. Fashions do not touch it with their finger; revolutions do not overthrow it; dispensations leave it in its integrity. We look particularly at—

III. THE IMMORTALITY OF THE THOUGHTS OF CHRIST. 1. We have found him a true Prophet. Events have happened according to his word. 2. We are finding him to be the Divine Teacher of truth to-day. He has that to say to us which, in our better moods and worthier moments, we hunger and thirst to hear. In his deathless words there are still treasured for us salvation from our sin, comfort in our sorrow, sanctity in our joy, strength in our struggle, companionship in our loneliness, and peace and hope in our decline and death. Unto whom shall we go if we sit at his feet no longer? 3. We shall find him the Source of truth in the after-life. Death will not make his words less true, even of it makes some of them less applicable than they are here and now. His thoughts will never lose their hold upon our heart, never cease to affect and shape our course. The truths which Jesus spake eighteen centuries ago will beautify our life and bless our spirit in the furthest epochs and the highest spheres of the heavenly world. (1) If we would render the truest service to ourselves, we shall do our utmost to fill our minds with the thoughts of Christ; for these will prepare us for any and every condition, here or hereafter, in which we can possibly be placed. (2) If we would serve our race most effectively, we shall consider in how many ways we can impress his thoughts upon the minds of men and weave them into the institutions of the world. And we shall find, at any rate, these three: (*a*) The testimony of a Christian life. (*b*) The utterance, in public or in private, of Christian doctrine. (*c*) The support of Christian institutions.—C.

Ver. 34.—*Christian and unchristian carefulness.* Take care not to be overtaken and overweighted by care is the simple and intelligible paradox of the text; in other words, have a wise care lest you have much care that is unwise. There is a carefulness that is eminently godly and worthy, the absence of which is not only faulty and dangerous, but even guilty and fatal; but there is another carefulness which is an excess, a wrong, an injury in the last degree.

I. A WISE ORDINATION OF GOD. Surely it is in pure kindness to us that God has ordained that if we will not work neither shall we eat; that possession and enjoyment involve thoughtfulness and activity on our part. To be provided with everything we could wish for without the necessity for habitual consideration as well as regular exertion is found to be hurtful, if not positively disastrous to the spirit. The necessity for care, in the sense of a thoughtful provision for this life, involves two great blessings. 1. The formation of many homely but valuable virtues—the cultivation of the intellect, forethought, diligence, sobriety of thought and conduct, regularity of daily habits, the practice of courtesy, and the avoidance of offence, etc. 2. The practice of piety; there is perhaps no better field in which we can be serving God than in that of our daily duties as citizens of this world. Whether it be the counting-house, the desk, the factory, the shop, the home, the school,—in each and in all of these there is a constant opportunity for remembering and doing the will of God; there will true and genuine godliness find a field for its exercise and its growth.

II. OCCASION FOR FILIAL TRUST. Care, in the sense of anxiety, about our temporal affairs is an evil to be met and mastered by Christian thought. Christ has said to us,

"Take no thought [be not anxious] for your life" (Matt. vi. 25); Paul writes, "Be careful [anxious] for nothing," etc. (Phil. iv. 6); Peter says, "Casting all your care upon him; for he careth for you" (1 Pet. v. 7). Clearly our Christian duty is to do our best with head and hand, by thoughtfulness and diligence, to ask for God's direction and blessing, and then to put our trust in him, resting humbly but confidently on his Word of promise. This is a promise where there is much occasion for filial trustfulness. When the way is dark we must not yield to an unspiritual anxiety, but rise to a holy, childlike faith in our heavenly Father.

III. A SPHERE FOR DETERMINED LIMITATION. The great and the growing temptation is to fill our lives and hearts with the affairs of time. No more needful or seasonable counsel could be given us than this of our Lord, "Take heed to yourselves, lest your hearts be *overcharged* with . . . the cares of this life." Undue and unwise carefulness about these mundane interests does two evil things: *it wears out that which is good*—good health, good spirits, good temper; and *it shuts out that which is best*—for it excludes the worship and the direct service of God; it leaves no time for devout meditation, for profitable and instructive reading, for religious exercises, for Christian work. It shuts men up to the lesser and lower activities; it dwarfs their life, it starves their soul; they "lose their life itself for the sake of the means of living." Two things are requisite, requiring a very firm and vigorous hand. 1. To resist the temptation to enlarge our worldly activities when such enlargement means spiritual shrinkage, as it very often does. 2. To insist upon it that the cares of life *shall not* exclude daily communion with God and the culture of the soul. If we do not exhibit this wise care against the unwise carefulness, we shall (1) displease our Divine Lord by our disobedience; (2) sacrifice ourselves to our circumstances; (3) be unready for the advancing future; "that day will come upon us unawares," and we shall not be "worthy to stand before the Son of man" (see next homily).—C.

Ver. 36.—*Standing before Christ.* "Watch . . . and pray that ye may be accounted worthy . . . to stand before the Son of man." What is involved in this worthiness? It must include our being—

I. PREPARED TO GIVE ACCOUNT TO HIM. We know that we shall have to do that (Rom. xiv. 10; 2 Cor. v. 10); and we must expect, when we do stand before the Judge, to account to Jesus Christ for (1) the relation which we have voluntarily sustained to himself—how we have received his invitation, and with what fulness we have accepted him as the Redeemer, the Friend, the Lord of our heart and life; (2) the way in which we have served him since we called ourselves by his Name—*i.e.* how closely we have followed him, how obedient we have been to his commandments, how earnest and faithful we have showed ourselves in his cause; in fact, how true and loyal we have proved to be as his servants here.

II. CONFORMED TO HIS LIKENESS. Will not our Lord expect to find those who professed to be his disciples, who had access to so many and such great privileges, stand before him *such as he lived and died to make them?* We know what that is. "He gave himself for us, to redeem us from all iniquity;" he has "called us to holiness;" he came and wrought his work in order that he might make us to be in our spirit and character the children of God, bearing our heavenly Father's image. He will therefore look to those who stand before him as his redeemed ones for: 1. *Purity of heart;* the abhorrence of all that is evil, and love for that which is good and true and pure. 2. *A loving spirit;* a spirit of unselfishness, of devotedness, of generosity, of tender solicitude for the well-being of others. 3. *Reverence and consecration of heart to God.*

III. READY FOR THE HEAVENLY SPHERE. To "stand before" the king meant to be ready to fulfil his royal behest, prepared to do at once and to do effectively whatever he might require. To stand before our Divine Sovereign means to be ready to do his bidding, to execute his commandments as he shall employ us in his heavenly service. We naturally and rightly hope that he will entrust us with the most honourable errands, will appoint us to elevated posts, will charge us with noble occupations that will demand enlarged ability and that will contribute great things to his cause and kingdom. We may be sure that the devoted and faithful discharge of our duties here will prove the best preparation for celestial activity and usefulness. He that is faithful in a few things now will be made ruler over many things hereafter. He who puts out his talents here will be found worthy to stand before the King, and to be employed by him in broad and blessed spheres of service there. If we would be "accounted worthy" to do this, we must "watch and pray." 1. We must spend much time with God—in the study of his will and in supplication for the quickening influences of his Spirit. 2. We must often examine our own hearts, observing our progress or retrogression, ready for the act of penitence, or of praise, or of reconsecration as we find ourselves declining. We must also observe the forces that are around us, and distinguish carefully between the hostile and the friendly, between those which make for folly and for sin and those which lead up to wisdom and to righteousness.—C.

Vers. 5—38.—*Preliminaries of the second advent.* It would seem that, as an interlude amid his diligent teaching in Jerusalem, Jesus and the disciples, on their way back to Bethany, had paused on the Mount of Olives and contemplated the temple. The building was a superb one, and so well put together that the disciples and people generally believed it would last till doomsday. Hence, amid their admiration for the gorgeous pile, came their question about the end of the world, which would, they believed, synchronize with that of the temple. Now, our Lord, while prophesying its destruction, warns them not to be mistaken about times and signs.

I. OUR LORD WARNS THE DISCIPLES AGAINST FALSE ALARMS. (Vers. 7—9.) He indicates that many false Messiahs will arise, declaring their Messiahship and the speedy approach of the end. They are to be for the most part of the military type, for this was the kind of Messiah Israel wanted. The result will of necessity be "wars and tumults." But the disciples ought not to be alarmed at these mere preliminaries. The end would *not* be "immediately" (Revised Version). It is well known that between our Lord's time and the destruction of Jerusalem quite a number of military and mushroom Messiahs arose, "making confusion worse confounded." They were only the outcome of the people's false hopes, and of no prophetic import.

II. THE DISCIPLES, AS THEIR LORD'S WITNESSES, WOULD EXPERIENCE BOTH PERSECUTIONS AND INSPIRATIONS. (Vers. 10—19.) And here the Lord states that persecution of his people would precede national and natural troubles. War, earthquake, and pestilence would be the providential judgment upon unrighteous persecution. But the persecuted witnesses should receive the inspiration needful to speak resistlessly. They might be betrayed and martyred, but no real injury would overtake them. "There shall not an hair of your head perish." In this remarkable deliverance of our Lord about persecution he implies that his people are really imperishable. The world might do its best to annihilate them by fire and sword; their bones might be scattered, no marble tells whither; but the Lord who loves and prizes his people's dust will reorganize the scattered remains, and demonstrate how absolutely imperishable his people are. Hence he urges patience. "In your patience," he declares, "ye shall win your souls." So that it was a most wonderful preparation of these marked men for martyrdom and all preceding tribulation. Were we more dependent on Divine inspirations, we should be more calm and influential before a hostile world.

III. THE DESTRUCTION OF JERUSALEM IS DISTINCTLY FORETOLD AS AN INSTANCE OF DESERVED VENGEANCE. (Vers. 20—24.) And here the Lord gives his people directions to escape from the doomed city as soon as they should see the armies gathering round it. The siege was drawn upon it by no misconduct of theirs, but by the misconduct of their enemies: why, therefore, should the Christians lay down their lives for a false policy and cause? Their duty was, if possible, to escape. He also hints at the horrors of the siege, and how mothers with their infant children would suffer terribly. The issue of the investment would be the slaughter of multitudes and the exile of the rest. The Jews became wanderers and exiles from that moment.

"Tribes of the wandering foot and weary breast,
How shall ye flee away and be at rest!
The wild dove hath her nest, the fox his cave,
Mankind their country—Israel but the grave!"

IV. REDEMPTION MAY BE DISCERNED AS DRAWING NIGH. (Vers. 25—33.) Our Lord indicates that distress of nations, perplexity, and faint-heartedness through fear will precede his second coming. But his people need be no sharers in this fear. So far from this, as soon as the judgment-signs begin they are to lift up their heads, assured that redemption is drawing nigh. The outlook may be wintry for the world, but it is summer for the saints of God. And here we may notice: 1. *The parable of the spring trees.* (Vers. 29, 30.) Our Lord reminds the disciples that every spring, in the buds and shoots of the various trees there is the promise of the summer. The progress is gradual, yet noticeable. In the same way his people are to look for the signs of coming summer, and to manifest a hopeful spirit in beautiful contrast to the despairing spirit of the world. 2. *The imperishable character of the Christian stock.* (Vers. 31—33.) All the world's opposition and persecution will not annihilate the Christian stock. As the martyrs fall before their persecutors, it is only to summon fresh witnesses for the Master from the ranks of their enemies. The Christian stock abides. There need be no fear. Let this be left to the unbelieving world.

V. THE LORD'S PEOPLE OUGHT CONSEQUENTLY TO BE WATCHING AND PRAYING FOR THE ADVENT. (Vers. 34—38.) And in the conclusion of this discourse our Lord clearly indicates: 1. *That it is possible to escape the judgments which are coming on the earth before the advent.* For there is no merit in allowing one's self to be involved in judgments which others by their unbelief have invited. It is our duty to escape, if possible, the catastrophe. 2. *It can only be by a watchful and prayerful spirit.* Self-indulgence, everything that would dull our sense of the impending advent, must be avoided. It is to come as a thief and a snare upon those that dwell on the face of the whole earth. Hence the imperative necessity of watching. And it is prayer which will help us in our watching. We must wrestle with the coming King, that he may count us worthy to escape the world's judgments and to stand before him. 3. *How great a privilege it will be to be permitted to stand in the presence of the Son of man!* No such privilege is afforded even by the greatest of earthly kings. It becomes us, therefore, to be in downright earnest about this privilege, and by persevering prayer to secure it.

VI. OUR LORD GAVE THE DISCIPLES THE EXAMPLE OF THE WATCHFUL PRAYER REQUIRED. (Vers. 37, 38.) For it would seem that, in the closing days, the people came so early to the temple to be taught, that he could not go as far as Bethany to spend the night. He went out, therefore, at nightfall to the Mount of Olives, and spent the night-watches more in prayer than in sleep. He was showing what persevering prayer in the crises of history must be. Let our Lord's Gethsemane habits call each of us to privacy and patient prayer such as will alone secure the proper public spirit.—R. M. E

EXPOSITION.

CHAPTER XXII.

Ver. 1—ch. xxiii. 56.—THE LAST PASSOVER.

Vers. 1, 2.—*Short explanatory introduction.*

Ver. 1.—**Now the Feast of Unleavened Bread drew nigh, which is called the Passover.** These words show that many of the readers for whom this Gospel was intended were foreigners, who were unacquainted with Jewish terms such as the "Passover." *Passover* (τὸ πάσχα, פסח) means, literally, "a passing." The feast so named commemorated the manner in which the chosen people were spared in Egypt when the destroying angel of the Lord passed over all Israelitish houses, which had been sprinkled with the blood of the lamb, *without* slaying the firstborn. Dr. Farrar suggests that the Greek word πάσχα is a transliteration, with a sort of alliterative allusion to the Greek πάσχω, "I suffer." This greatest and most important of the Jewish feasts, which ever brought a great host of pilgrims to Jerusalem, was kept in the first month of the Jewish year (Nisan), from the 15th of the month, the day of full moon, to the 21st. Roughly, this corresponded to the end of our March.

Ver. 2.—**And the chief priests and scribes sought how they might kill him; for they feared the people.** The determination, long maturing, had, during the last few days of public teaching, been come to on the part of the Sanhedrin. They had determined to put the dangerous public Teacher to death. The bitter hatred on the part of the Jewish rulers had been gradually growing in intensity during the two years and a half of the public ministry of Jesus of Nazareth. The raising of Lazarus seems to have finally decided the governing body with as little delay as possible to compass the Reformer's death. The temporary withdrawal of the Lord after the great miracle deferred their purpose for a season; after, however, a retirement for a few weeks, Jesus appeared again, shortly before the Passover, and taught publicly in the temple, at a season when Jerusalem was crowded with pilgrims arriving for the great feast. Never had his teaching excited such interest, never had it stirred up such burning opposition as at this juncture. This decided the Jewish rulers to carry out their design on the life of the Galilæan Teacher with as little delay as possible. The only thing that perplexed them was *how* this could safely be accomplished, owing to the favour in which he was held by the people, especially by the crowds of pilgrims from the provinces then in Jerusalem.

Vers. 3—6.—*Judas Iscariot betrays his Master.* **Then entered Satan into Judas surnamed Iscariot, being of the number of the twelve. And he went his way, and communed with the chief priests and captains, how he might betray him unto them. And they were glad.** This was their chance. In the very heart of the Galilæan Teacher's own company a traitor showed himself, one who knew well the plans of his Master. With his help the Sanhedrin and the priestly party would be enabled to effect the arrest privately. They then must trust to Roman jealousy to help them to carry out their evil design. The expression, "Then entered Satan into Judas," is a strong one, and definitely shows that, in the opinion of these inspired compilers of the Gospels, there was *a person* who bore rule over the powers of evil. The character and history of the faithless friend of Jesus is mournfully interesting. For one to whom such splendid chances were offered to fall so low, is an awful mystery. It is clear that the betrayal was no sudden impulse. He set up self as the one object of all his thoughts, and followed Jesus because he believed that, in following him, he could best serve his own interests. His ambition was cruelly disappointed by his Master's gradual unfolding his views respecting his kingdom, *which was not to be of this world.* He was still further shocked by the undisguised announcement on the part of his Master, whose greatness and power Judas recognized from the first, that he would be rejected by the nation, and even put to death. It has been suggested, as an explanation of the betrayal, that at the last he seems to have fancied that he could force the manifestation of Christ's power by placing him in the hands of his enemies; but the acceptance of a reward, miserable though it was, seems to point to vulgar greed, and to the idea of making friends with the dominant party in the state now that his Master evidently looked forward to a violent death, as the real motives of the betrayal. The question has been asked whether Christ, in his choice of Judas as one of the twelve, read the inmost depths and issues of his character. Canon Westcott, in a profound note on John xiii. 18, writes "that the records of the gospel lead us to believe that the Lord had perfect human knowledge realized in a human way, and therefore limited in some sense, and separable in consciousness from his perfect Divine omniscience. He knew the thoughts of men absolutely in their manifold possibilities, and yet as man, not in their actual future manifestation." These mysteries "underlie all religious life, and, indeed, all finite life—for finite being includes the possibility of sin and the possibility of fellowship between the Creator and the creature. . . . Thus we may be content to have this concrete mystery as an example—the most terrible example—of the issues of the two fundamental mysteries of human existence."

Vers. 7—13.—*The disciples Peter and John are directed to prepare for the last Passover.*

Ver. 7.—**Then came the day of unleavened bread.** This was the Thursday, Nisan 13. On this afternoon all leaven was carefully and scrupulously put away; hence the name.

Ver. 8.—**Go and prepare us the Passover, that we may eat.** The three synoptists unite in describing this solemn meal, for which Peter and John were sent to prepare, as the ordinary Paschal Supper. But, on comparing the record of the same Supper given by St. John, we are irresistibly led to a different conclusion; for we read that on the following day those who led Jesus into the Prætorium went not in themselves, "lest they should be defiled; *but that they might eat the Passover*" (John xviii. 28); and again it is said of the same day, that "it was the preparation of the Passover" (John xix. 14). So the time of the Supper is described by St. John (xiii. 1) as "before the Feast of the Passover." It appears that our Lord was crucified on the 14th of Nisan, *on the very day of the sacrifice of the Paschal Lamb*, a few hours before the time of the Paschal Supper, and that his own Last Supper was eaten the night before, that is, twenty-four hours before the general time of eating the Passover Supper. The most venerable of the Fathers preserved this as a sacred tradition. So Justin Martyr: "On the day of the Passover ye took him, and on the day of the Passover ye crucified him"

('Dial. cum Trypho,' ch. iii.). To the same effect write Irenæus ('Adv. Hær.,' iv. 23) and Tertullian ('Adv. Judæos,' ch. 8). Clement of Alexandria is most definite: "The Lord did not eat his last Passover on the legal day of the Passover, but on the previous day, the 13th, and suffered on the day following, being himself the Passover" (Fragment from 'Chron. Paschal.,' p. 14, edit. Dindorf). Hippolytus of Portus bears similar testimony. The question—as to whether the famous Last Supper was the actual Passover Supper, or the anticipatory Paschal Feast, which we believe it to have been—is important; for thus the language of St. Paul (1 Cor. v. 7), "Christ our Passover is sacrificed for us," is justified. "The apostle regarded not the Last Supper, but the death of Christ, as the antitype of the Paschal sacrifice, and the correspondence of type and antitype would be incomplete unless the sacrifice of the Redeemer took place at the time on which alone that of the Paschal lamb could legally be offered" (Dean Mansel).

Ver. 9.—**And they said unto him, Where wilt thou that we prepare?** It is probable that the disciples, in asking this question, concluded that the Passover was to be eaten by them and their Master at the same time with the rest of the Jews on the following day; but our Lord gave directions for its being eaten the same evening.

Ver. 10.—**And he said unto them, Behold, when ye are entered into the city, there shall a man meet you.** The name of the man who should meet them was omitted—purposely, think Theophylact and others, lest the place of meeting should be prematurely known to Judas. **Bearing a pitcher of water.** This would be an unusual sight in an Oriental city, where the water is drawn by women. It is probable that the "man" whom the Master foretold John and Peter would meet, was the master of the house, who, according to the Jewish custom on the 13th of Nisan, *before the stars appeared in the heavens*, had himself to go to the public fountain to draw the water with which the unleavened bread for the Passover Feast was kneaded.

Ver. 12.—**And he shall show you a large upper room furnished: there make ready.** The house which possessed so large an upper chamber must have been one of considerable size, and evidently belonged to a man of some wealth and position, possibly to Nicodemus or Joseph of Arimathæa. That it perhaps belonged to St. Mark's family has also been suggested. It had evidently been prepared beforehand for the purpose of the feast, in obedience to a previous direction of Jesus. "Furnished" (ἐστρωμένον) applies specially to carpets spread over the couches for the reception of guests. "In this large upper chamber thus prepared," said the Lord, "make the necessary arrangements for the Paschal Supper; procuring and preparing the lamb, the unleavened bread, the herbs, and other customary dishes." It seems probable that this "large upper room," evidently belonging to a disciple, or at least to one friendly to Jesus, was the same room which, in the happier hours *after* the Resurrection, witnessed the appearance of the Risen to the eleven, and, later, the descent of the Holy Ghost at Pentecost.

Vers. 14—38.—*The Last Supper.*

Ver. 14.—**And when the hour was come, he sat down, and the twelve apostles with him.** The preparation had been made in the "large upper room," and the Lord and the twelve sat down, or rather reclined on the couches covered with carpets, the tables before them laid with the dishes peculiar to the solemn Passover Supper, each dish telling its part of the old loved story of the great deliverance. There was the lamb the Paschal victim, and the bitter herbs, the unleavened bread and the reddish sweet conserve of fruits—commemorating, it is said, by its colour the hard labours of brick-making, one of the chief burdens of the Egyptian bondage—into which the Master dipped the sop, and gave it to the traitor-apostle (John xiii. 26). The Lord reclined, probably, at the middle table; St. John next to him; St. Peter most likely on the other side; and the others reclining in an order corresponding more or less closely with the threefold division of the twelve into groups of four. The Supper itself had its special forms and ceremonies, which the Lord transformed as they proceeded in such a way as to change it into the sacred Supper of the New Testament.

Ver. 15.—**And he said unto them, With desire I have desired to eat this Passover with you before I suffer.** This peculiar expression, "with desire," etc., is evidently a reproduction by St. Luke of the Lord's very words repeated to him originally in Aramaic (Hebrew). They seem to be a touching apology or explanation from him to his own, for thus anticipating the regular Passover Supper by twenty-four hours. He had been longing with an intense longing to keep this last Passover with them: *First* as the *dear human Friend* who would make this his solemn last farewell. (Do not *we*, when we feel the end is coming, long for a last communion with our dearest ones?) And, *secondly*, as the *Divine Master* who would gather up into a final discourse his most important, deepest teaching. We find this teaching especially reported by St. John in his Gospel (xiii.—xvii.). And *thirdly*, as the *Founder of a great religion*, he purposed, on this momentous occasion, transforming the most solemn festal gathering of the ancient Jewish people, which commemorated their greatest deliverance, into a feast which should—as age succeeded age—commemorate a far greater deliverance, not of the old chosen race only, but of every race under heaven. These were three of the reasons why he had desired so earnestly to eat this Passover with them. "To-morrow, at the usual hour, when the people eat their Passover, it will be too late for us." This he expresses in his own sad words, "*before I suffer.*"

Vers. 16—18.—**For I say unto you, I will not any more eat thereof, until it be fulfilled in the kingdom of God.** There was yet one other reason for the Master's special desire once more to eat the solemn Passover with his chosen disciples. He would, by some significant action and word, show that the great Jewish feast, for so many centuries the central act of the ritual observances under the Mosaic Law, from henceforth would be superseded by a new and a yet more solemn religious rite. The Jewish Passover was to give place to the Christian sacrament. He, their Master, would with them share in the Passover meal that evening for the last time. The next time that he would partake would be still with them, but it would be in the kingdom of God, that is to say, in the Church of God, which was to be founded after his resurrection. The kingdom of God commenced with the resurrection of Jesus. The constant celebration of the Holy Eucharist commenced from that time; it is more than probable that our Lord partook of it, after his resurrection, with his own (see ch. xxiv. 30; Acts x. 41). **I will not any more eat thereof, until . . . I will not drink of the fruit of the vine, until, etc.** These statements, which speak of a final partaking (eating and drinking), are closely parallel to the command contained in vers. 19, 20. The first statement seems solemnly to close the celebration of the Passover Feast; the second, to institute with equal solemnity a new feast in its place—

"*With desire I have desired to eat this passover with you before I suffer*" (ver. 15); for—

The Passover Feast is solemnly put an end to.	*The Holy Eucharist is solemnly instituted.*
"I will not any more *eat* thereof, until it be fulfilled in the kingdom of God" (ver. 16).	"He took *bread*, . . . and brake it, and gave unto them: . . . This do in remembrance of me" (ver. 19).
"I will not *drink* of the fruit of the vine, until the kingdom of God shall come" (ver. 18).	"Likewise also the *cup* after Supper" (ver. 20).

It was in the course of the great ritual Supper on some of the occasions when the cup was passed round, and the unleavened bread formally broken or dipped in one of the Passover dishes, that the Lord found his opportunity solemnly to announce the formal abrogation of the old Paschal Supper and the institution of the new communion feast. The above *literal* interpretation of the Lord's mystic words, "until that day when I drink it new with you in my Father's kingdom" (Matt. xxvi. 29), or, as St. Luke reports them, "I will not drink of the fruit of the vine, until the kingdom of God shall come"—which literal interpretation in the main is that preferred by Dean Mansel (Commentary on Matt. xxvi. 29); see, too, St. Chrysostom in Matt. Hom. lxxii., who adopts the same literal interpretation—does not exclude a yet deeper and more spiritual meaning which lies beneath the surface, and which speaks of another and spiritual banquet in the heavenly realm, which not only the Redeemer, but also his redeemed, will partake of. Heaven-life under the form of a banquet was imagery well known and often painted by the Jewish masters in the old rabbinic schools before and contemporary with the earthly life of Christ. The New Testament writers in several places have adopted the similar imagery, notably in Matt. viii. 11; ch. xxii. 30; Rev. xix. 9. How widespread and well loved was this Jewish representation of the heaven-life under the form of a banquet is clear from the three above-quoted references taken from SS. Matthew, Paul (Luke), and John.

Vers. 19, 20.—**And he took bread, and gave thanks, and brake it, and gave unto them, saying, This is my body which is given for you: this do in remembrance of me. Likewise also the cup after supper, saying, This cup is the new testament in my blood, which is shed for you.** Around these words, and the parallel passages in SS. Matthew and Mark, for more than a thousand years fierce theological disputes have raged. Men have gone gladly to prison and to death rather than renounce what they believed to be the true interpretation. Now, a brief exegetical commentary is not the place to enter into these sad controversies. It will be sufficient here to indicate some of the lines of thought which the prayerful earnest reader might wisely follow out so as to attain certain just ideas respecting the blessed rite here instituted—ideas which may suffice for a practical religious life. Now, we possess a Divine commentary on this sacrament instituted by our Lord. It is noticeable that St. John, whose Gospel was the latest or well-nigh the latest of the canonical writings of the New Testament, when at great length he relates the story of the last Passover evening and its teaching, does not allude to the institution of that famous service, which, when he wrote his Gospel, had become part of the settled experience of Church life. He *presupposes* it; for it had passed then into the ordinary life of the Church. In another and earlier portion of his Gospel, however, St. John (vi. 32—58) gives us a record of the Lord's discourse in the synagogue of Capernaum, in which Jesus, while speaking plainly to those who heard him at the time, gave by anticipation a commentary on the sacrament which he afterwards instituted. The truth which was taught in this discourse is presented in a specific act and in a concrete form in the Holy Communion. In the fifty-third verse of that sixth chapter we read, "Verily, verily, I say unto you, Except ye eat the flesh of the Son of man, and drink his blood, ye have no life in you." How is this now to be done? We reply that our Lord has clothed these ideas and brought them near to us in this sacrament; while, by his teaching in the sixth chapter of St. John, he guards this sacrament from being regarded on the one hand as an end in itself, or on the other as a mere symbol. Certain truths, great *landmarks* laid down in this discourse, have to be borne in mind. (1) The separation of the flesh of the Son of man into flesh and blood (John vi. 53) presupposes a violent death submitted to for the sake of others (John vi. 51). (2) Both these elements, the flesh and the blood, are to be appropriated individually by the believer (John vi. 56). (3) How appropriated? St. Bernard well answers the question which he asks: "What is it to eat his flesh and to drink his blood, but to *share in his sufferings and to imitate the life he lived when with us in the flesh?*" (St. Bernard, on Ps. iii. 3). "If ye suffer with him, ye shall also reign with him." The Holy Eucharist is from one point of view a great truth dramatized, instituted for the purpose of bringing before men in a vivid manner the great truths above alluded to. *But it is something more.* It brings to the believer, to the faithful communicant, to the one who in humble adoring faith carries out to the best of his ability his Master's dying charge—it brings a blessing too great for us to measure by earthly language, too deep for us to fathom with human inquiry. For the partaking of this Holy Communion is, first, the Christian's solemn public confession of his faith in Christ crucified; his solemn private declaration that it is his deliberate wish to suffer with his Lord and for his Lord's sake; that it is, too, his firm purpose to imitate the earthly life lived by his Lord. The partaking of this Holy Communion, too, is the Christian's most solemn prayer for strength thus to suffer and to live. It is, too, his fervent expression of belief that this strength will be surely given to him. Further, the partaking of this Holy Communion is, above all, the Christian's most solemn prayer for living union with Christ—"that Christ may dwell in his heart by faith." It is, too, his fervent expression of belief that "then we dwell in Christ, and Christ in us; we are one with Christ, and Christ with us." This confession, declaration, and prayer he constantly renews in obedience to the dying command of his Master. It is difficult to understand how any belief in a physical change in the elements of bread and wine, such as is involved in the theory of transubstantiation held in the Roman Church, or of consubstantiation in the Lutheran community, can be supposed to enhance the reverence of the communicant, or to augment the blessing promised. The words of the Lord, "This is my body . . . my blood," cannot surely be pressed, seeing that the same Divine Speaker was in his discourses in the habit of using imagery which could not literally be pressed, such as "I am the Bread of life," "I am the Door of the sheep," "I am the true Vine," etc. Nothing that can be conceived is more solemn than the simple rite, more awful in its grandeur, more Divine and far-reaching in its promises to the faithful believer. Human imaginings add nothing to this Divine mystery, which is connected at once with the Incarnation and the Atonement. They only serve to envelop it in a shroud of earth-born mist and cloud, and thus to dim if not to veil its Divine glory.

Vers. 21—23.—*The Lord's sorrowful allusion to Judas the traitor.*

Ver. 21.—**But, behold, the hand of him that betrayeth me is with me on the table.** This is the second mention of the traitor in St. Luke's account of the Last Supper. From St. John's recital, we gather that Jesus returned several times in the course of that solemn evening to this sad topic. That one of his own little inner circle, so closely associated with him, should so basely betray him, was evidently a very bitter drop in the Lord's cup of suffering. In his dread experience of human sorrow it was needful that the Christ should fulfil in his own experience what even the noblest of the children of men—David, for instance—had felt of the falseness of friends. What suffering can be inflicted on a generous heart comparable to it? Surely he of whom it was written, "Whose sorrows are like unto my sorrows?" must make trial of *this* bitterness. Chrysostom thinks that the Master, in some of these repeated allusions during the "Supper," tried to win Judas over to a better mind.

Ver. 22.—**Woe unto that man by whom he is betrayed!** We seem to hear a wailing in this woe, although the denunciation was so firmly pronounced. St. Matthew, in his account, here adds some more words spoken by the Master, "It had been good for that man if he had not been born." Dean Plumptre, on this saying of Christ, very suggestively remarks, "Awful as the words were, they have their bright as well as their dark side. According to the estimate which men commonly form, the words are true of all except those who depart this life in the faith and fear of God. In his applying them to the case of the traitor in its exceptional enormity, there is suggested the thought that for others whose guilt was not like his, existence even in the penal suffering which their sins have brought upon them may be better than never to have been at all."

Ver. 23.—**And they began to inquire among themselves, which of them it was that should do this thing.** That all the disciples, on hearing this statement of their Master, should at once question their own hearts with the "Is it I?" (of St. Matthew's Gospel), shows with what cunning skill the arch-traitor must have concealed not merely his plans but his very sentiments. No suspicion on their parts ever seems to have fallen on Judas, their companion for so long a time. The direct colloquy of the Lord with the traitor, reported at length in the other Gospels on the occasion of dipping the sop into one of the Paschal dishes, was most probably carried on in a whisper (see John xiii. 26—29, where mention is specially made of the disciples' ignorance of the dread meaning of their Master's words to Judas).

Vers. 24—30.—*The jealousy among the disciples.*

Ver. 24.—**And there was also a strife among them, which of them should be accounted the greatest.** The Lord's words in these verses are peculiar to St. Luke. The strife among the disciples which suggested the Lord's corrective sayings was evidently no mere dispute as to precedence in their places at the supper, but some question as to their respective positions in the coming kingdom of which their Master had said so much in the course of his later instructions. It is closely connected with the "feet-washing" related at length by St. John (xiii. 4—17). This has been well described as a parable in action, exhibited to illustrate forcibly the novel and sublime truth which he was teaching them, the world-teachers of the future, that in self-sacrifice consisted the secret of true greatness. In the kingdom of heaven this would be found to be conspicuously the case.

Ver. 25.—**Are called benefactors** (εὐεργέται). Those who were listening knew well how utterly false these high-sounding human titles often were. Εὐεργέτης (*Euergetes*), Benefactor, was the well-known title appropriated by Ptolemy Euergetes and other hated royal tyrants well known to the Jewish people.

Ver. 28.—**Ye are they which have continued with me in my temptations.** But after the gentle rebuke of their jealous ambition, which rebuke was veiled in the great instruction, their Master, with the tenderest grace, referred to their unswerving loyalty to him. Their faithfulness stood out at that hour in strong contrast with the conduct of Judas. It is always thus with their Master and ours. Every good deed, every noble thought, each bit of generosity and self-forgetfulness on our part, is at once recognized and rewarded a hundredfold *now* as *then*.

Ver. 29.—**And I appoint unto you a kingdom, as my Father hath appointed unto me.** This promise refers to earth and this life. *They* and their successors in his Church would bear sway over men's hearts. His kingdom would be administered by them. With strangely literal accuracy has this promise been fulfilled. From the hour when the despised Master, already doomed to a shameful death, uttered this seemingly improbable prediction, his kingdom over men's hearts has been extending. *Then* at most the kingdom numbered a few hundreds; *now* it can only be reckoned by millions. For centuries the story of the civilized world has been the story of this kingdom.

Ver. 30.—**That ye may eat and drink at my table in my kingdom, and sit on thrones judging the twelve tribes of Israel.** While the words just considered (ver. 29) referred to a success and a reward, the scene of which was to be this world, the Master now continues his promises of reward to his chosen faithful followers—a reward which will be their blessed portion in eternal life, which will follow this. *First*, the endless bliss to be shared with him is pictured under the old favourite Jewish image of the heavenly banquet; and *second*, in that heavenly realm a special place of honour and a distinct work is promised to these his chosen faithful servants.

Vers. 31—38.—*The Lord foretells Simon Peter's fall. He tells the disciples of the hard times coming on them.*

Ver. 31.—**And the Lord said, Simon, Simon, behold, Satan hath desired to have**

you, that he may sift you as wheat. The majority of the more ancient authorities omit the words, "and the Lord said." These words were possibly inserted at an early date to obviate the abruptness of this sudden change in the subject-matter of the Lord's discourse. The more accurate translation would be, "Satan obtained you by asking that he," etc. Bengel comments with "*not content with Judas.*" This saying of Jesus is a very mysterious one; it reveals to us something of what is going on in the unseen world. A similar request was made by the same bitter, powerful foe in the case of Job (i. 12). Are we to understand that these are examples of what is constantly going on in that world so close to us, but from which no whisper ever reaches our mortal ears? Such grave thoughts lend especial intensity to those words in the prayer of prayers, where we ask "our Father which is in heaven" *to deliver us from evil*, or *the evil one*, as so many of our best scholars prefer to translate *ἀπὸ τοῦ πονήρου*. Satan asks that he may test and try the apostles. Judas he had already tempted, and he had won him. Possibly this signal victory emboldened him to proffer this request. We may imagine the evil one arguing thus before the Eternal: "These chosen ones who are appointed to work in the future so tremendous a work in thy Name, are utterly unworthy. Let me just try to lure them away with my lures. Lo, they will surely fall. See, *one* has already."

Ver. 32.—**But I have prayed for thee, that thy faith fail not.** The prayer of Satan *apparently* was not refused. Jesus, however, says, that *for one* of that loved company, who he knew from his peculiar temperament was in especial peril, *he had prayed*. The prayer was answered thus: the temptation came to all the apostles; all fell; Peter, though, more disastrously by far than his brethren, but the result of the fall was not hopeless despair as in the case of Judas, but bitter remorse and a brave manly repentance. "It is said by Roman divines (*e.g.* Maldonatus, à Lapide, and Mai, here) that this prayer and precept of our Lord extends to all bishops of Rome as St. Peter's successors, and that in speaking to St. Peter our Lord spoke to them. Would they be willing to complete the parallel, and say that the bishops of Rome specially need prayer, because they deny Christ? Let them not take a part of it and leave the rest" (Bishop Wordsworth). **When thou art converted.** "Converted" must not be understood here in its technical sense; it should rather be translated, "And thou, when thou hast turned (*i.e.* to God) **strengthen thy brethren.**"

Ver. 33.—**And he said unto him, Lord, I am ready to go with thee, both into prison, and to death.** This kind of confident enthusiasm is usually a sign of weakness. Jesus, *the Heart-reader*, knew too well what such a wild protestation was worth, and went on at once to predict his friend's and servant's awful fall, *that very night*.

Vers. 35, 36.—**And he said unto them, When I sent you without purse, and scrip, and shoes, lacked ye anything? And they said, Nothing. Then said he unto them, But now, he that hath a purse, let him take it, and likewise his scrip; and he that hath no sword, let him sell his garment, and buy one.** The Lord speaks one more word to his own before leaving the upper room. More occupied with the future trials of his disciples than with his own tragic destiny, which he knew was about to be fulfilled, he reminds his friends of the comparatively quiet and serene existence they had been spending during the last two years and a half with him. In that period, generally speaking, they had been welcomed and kindly entertained by the people, sometimes, they would remember, even with enthusiasm. But they must prepare now for a different life—cold looks, opposition, even bitter persecution, would be their lot for the future. They must order themselves now to meet these things. No ordinary prudent forethought must be omitted by them. He had more than hinted that this future lay before them in his words, "Behold, I send you forth as lambs in the midst of wolves;" now he plainly tells them what kind of life awaited them in the immediate future. Of course, the advice as to the sword was not meant to be taken literally. It was one of those metaphors the Lord used so often in his teaching. For a similar metaphor still more elaborately developed, see Eph. vi. 17, and following verses.

Ver. 37.—**For I say unto you, that this that is written must yet be accomplished in me, And he was reckoned among the transgressors.** Here he shows them what he meant. They, as disciples of One treated as a malefactor, had surely nothing to expect but hatred and persecution. Stier remarks that this is the first time that the Lord himself directs us to the fifty-third chapter of Isaiah, that most pre-eminent and complete text of the Passion. **For the things concerning me have an end.** The tragic end of his earthly ministry is close at hand. The prophetic description of the suffering Servant of the Lord will soon be found to have been terribly accurate.

Ver. 38.—**And they said, Lord, behold, here are two swords. And he said unto them, It is enough.** As so often, the disciples took their Master's words with curious literalness, and, as a reply, produced two swords, as if these two poor weapons *could* help them in the coming times of sore need. If they were to stand firm in the long trial-season which lay before them, they must surely provide themselves with very different weapons to these; their arms in the campaign of the future must be forged in no earthly workshop. But our Lord sadly declined then to enter into further explanation. His meaning would be all clear to them soon, so he closed the dialogue with the words, "It is enough." This verse was curiously perverted in the famous Bull of Pope Boniface VIII., "Unam sanctam," to prove his possession of both secular and spiritual power: "Dicentibus apostolis, *ecce gladii duo*, in Ecclesiâ scilicet, quum apostoli loquerentur, non respondit Dominus *nimis esse*, sed *satis*. . . . Uterque ergo in potestate est Ecclesiæ, spiritualis scilicet gladius et materialis."

Vers. 39—46.—*The agony in the garden.* This eventful scene is recounted in detail by all the three synoptists. St. Matthew's account is the most complete. St. Mark adds one saying of the Lord's containing a deep theological truth, "Abba, Father, all things are possible unto thee." These remarkable words, occurring as they do in the midst of the most solemn scene of prayer in the Redeemer's earth-life, tell of the vast *possibilities* of prayer. What may not be accomplished by earnest supplication to the throne of grace?

St. Luke's account is the shortest, but it contains the story of the angelic mission of help, and the additional detail of the "bloody sweat."

St. John alone of the four omits the scene; but, as in other most important recitals where he refrains from repeating the story of things thoroughly known in his Master's Church at the period when he committed his Gospel to writing, he takes care, however, often to record some hitherto unrecorded piece of the Lord's teaching, which is calculated to throw new light upon the momentous twice and thrice told incident, the story of which he does not deem it necessary to repeat. So in ch. ii. he throws a flood of light upon Christian baptism. Ch. vi. is a Divine commentary on the Holy Eucharist. While in ch. xii. 23—28 he gives us, in his Master's words, a new insight into that awful sorrow which was the source of the agony in Gethsemane.

Canon Westcott suggests that the succession of the main events recorded by the four evangelists was as follows:—

Approx. time.	
1 a.m.	The agony.
	The betrayal.
	The conveyance to the high priest's house, probably adjoining "the Booths of Hanan."
2 a.m.	The preliminary examination before Annas in the presence of Caiaphas.
About 3 a.m.	The examination before Caiaphas and the Sanhedrin at an irregular meeting at "the Booths."
About 5 a.m.	The formal sentence of the Sanhedrin in their own proper place of meeting—Gazith or Beth Midrash (ch. xxii. 66; Matt. xxvii. 1, πρωΐας γενομένης; comp. Mark xv. 1; ch. xxii. 66, ὡς ἐγένετο ἡμέρα).
	The first examination before Pilate at the palace.
5.30 a.m.	The examination before Herod.
	The scourging and first mockery by the soldiers at the palace.
6.30 a.m.	The sentence of Pilate (John xix. 14, ὥρα ἦν ὡς ἕκτη).
7 a.m.	The second mockery of the condemned "King" by the soldiers.
9 a.m.	The Crucifixion, and rejection of the stupefying draught (Mark xv. 25, ἦν ὥρα τρίτη).
12 noon	The last charge.
12—3 p.m.	The darkness (Matt. xxvii. 45; Mark xv. 33; ch. xxiii. 44, ἦν ὡσεὶ ὥρα ἕκτη . . . ἕως ὥρας ἐννάτης).
3 p.m.	The end.

Ver. 39.—**And he came out, and went, as he was wont, to the Mount of Olives.** In the other evangelists we find the place on the Mount of Olives described as Gethsemane. The word *Gethsemane* signifies "oil-press." It was a garden; one of the many charming gardens which Josephus tells us old Jerusalem abounded with. It perhaps belonged to a friend of Christ, or else was with others of these gardens, or "paradises," thrown open at the great festival seasons to the faithful pilgrims who on these occasions crowded the holy city and its suburbs. There is at the present day just beyond the brook Kedron, between the paths that go up to the summit of the mount, about three quarters of a mile from the Jerusalem wall, an enclosed garden

called Gethsemane. It belongs to the Latin community in Jerusalem. In it are eight very ancient olive trees. When Henry Maundrell visited the spot, in 1697, these eight aged trees were believed to be the same that stood there in the blessed Saviour's time. Bové the botanist, in Ritter's 'Geography of Palestine,' vol. iv., quoted by Dean Mansel, says these venerable olive trees are two thousand years old. Josephus, however, relates that in the great siege the soldiers of Titus cut down all the trees in the Jerusalem suburbs. Even if this be assumed, these soldiers, from some feeling of awe stirred up by the tradition which hung, of course, round this hallowed spot, might have spared this little sacred grove; or they might at the time have been still young saplings, of no use for the purpose of the siege operations. "In spite of all the doubts that can be raised against their antiquity, the eight aged olive trees, if only by their manifest difference from all others on the mountain, have always struck even the most indifferent observers. They will remain, so long as their already protracted life is spared, the most venerable of their race on the surface of the earth. Their gnarled trunks and scanty foliage will always be regarded as the most affecting of the sacred memorials in or about Jerusalem—the most nearly approaching to the everlasting hills themselves in the force with which they carry us back to the events of the gospel history" (Dean Stanley, 'Sinai and Palestine,' p. 455).

Ver. 40.—**Pray that ye enter not into temptation.** The temptation in question was the grave sin of moral cowardice into which *so* soon the disciples fell. Had they prayed instead of yielding to the overpowering sense of weariness and sleeping, they would never have forsaken their Master in his hour of trial and danger.

Ver. 42.—**Saying, Father, if thou be willing, remove this cup from me: nevertheless not my will, but thine, be done.** The three synoptists give this prayer in slightly varying terms; "but the figure of *the cup* is common to all the three; it was indelibly impressed on tradition. This cup, which Jesus entreats God to cause to pass from before (παρά) his lips, is the symbol of that terrible punishment, the dreadful and mournful picture of which is traced before him at this moment by a skilful painter with extraordinary vividness. The painter is the same who in the wilderness, using a like illusion, passed before his view the magical scene of the glories belonging to the Messianic kingdom" (Godet). *If thou be willing.* He looked on in this supreme hour, just before "the Passion" really began, to the Crucifixion and all the horrors which preceded it and accompanied it—to the treason of Judas; the denial of Peter; the desertion of the apostles; the cruel, relentless enmity of the priests and rulers; the heartless abandonment of the people; the insults; the scourging; and then the shameful and agonizing lingering death which was to close the Passion: and, more dreadful than all, the reason why he was here in Gethsemane; why he was to drink this dreadful cup of suffering; the memory of all the sin of man! To drink this cup of a suffering, measureless, inconceivable, the Redeemer for a moment shrank back, and asked the Father if the cross was the only means of gaining the glorious end in view—the saving the souls of unnumbered millions. Could not God in his unlimited power find another way of reconciliation? And yet beneath this awful agony, the intensity of which we are utterly incapable of grasping—beneath it there lay the intensest desire that his Father's wish and will should be done. That wish and will were in reality his own. The prayer was made *and answered.* It was not the Father's will that the cup should pass away, and the Son's will was entirely the same; *it was answered* by the gift of strength—strength from heaven being given to enable the Son to drink the cup of agony to its dregs. How this strength was given St. Luke relates in the next verse.

Ver. 43.—**And there appeared an angel unto him from heaven, strengthening him.** The Lord's words reported by St. Matthew were no mere figure of rhetoric. "My soul is exceeding sorrowful, even unto death." The anguish and horror were so great that he himself, according to his humanity, must have before the time become the victim of death had he not been specially strengthened from above. This is the deep significance and necessity of the angel's appearance. So Stier and Godet, the latter of whom writes, "As when in the wilderness under the pressure of famine he felt himself dying, the presence of this heavenly being sends a vivifying breath over him,—a Divine refreshing pervades him, body and soul, and it is thus he receives strength to continue to the last the struggle."

Ver. 44.—**And his sweat was as it were great drops of blood falling down to the ground.** Some (for instance, Theophylact) understand this "as it were" to signify that the expression, "drops of blood," was simply parabolic; but it is far better to understand the words in their literal sense, as our Church does when it prays, "By thine agony and bloody sweat." Athanasius even goes so far as to pronounce a ban upon those who deny this sweat of blood. Commentators give instances of this blood-sweat under abnormal pathological circumstances. Some, though by no means all, of the oldest authorities omit these last two verses (43, 44). Their omission in many of these ancient manuscripts was probably due to mistaken reverence. The two oldest and most authoritative translations, the Itala (Latin) and Peshito (Syriac), contain them, however, as do the most important Fathers of the second century, Justin and Irenæus. We have, then, apart from the evidence of manuscripts, the testimony of the earliest Christianity in Italy and Syria, Asia Minor and Gaul, to the genuineness of these two famous verses. They are printed in the ordinary text of the Revised English Version, with a side-note alluding to their absence in some of the ancient authorities.

Vers. 45, 46.—**He found them sleeping for sorrow, and said unto them, Why sleep ye? rise and pray, lest ye enter into temptation.** The events of the past evening; the long excitement stirred up by listening to such words as their Master had been speaking to them during the sad hours of the Last Supper; the sure consciousness of coming sorrow; then the walk through the silent city;—all predisposed them to sleep. Commentators are never weary with pressing these excuses for the slumber of the eleven at that awful moment. But all these things, though they may well have predisposed them to slumber, are not sufficient to account for that strange heavy sleep which seems to have paralyzed the eleven in Gethsemane. In spite of their Master's solemn injunction to watch and pray, he finds them, several times during that dreadful watch of his in the garden, asleep, in spite of his asking them for sympathy and prayer, in spite of his evident longing for their sympathy—each time he cast his eyes on them, he sees them, not watching, but sleeping! Many a time in their work-filled lives those fishermen he loved so well, John and Peter and Andrew, had toiled all night with their nets; but on this night of sorrow, when their pleading voices were listened for, possibly their hand-press waited for, their silent sympathy certainly longed for, they slept, seemingly forgetful of all save their own ease and comfort. Surely on this night of temptation they were influenced by some invisible power, who lulled them to sleep during those precious moments when they should have been agonizing with their Master in prayer, and so arming themselves against the supreme moment of temptation just coming upon them. But swayed by the power of evil of whom the Lord had been warning them, but in vain, they let the moments slip by, and the hour of temptation came on them unawares. We know how grievously they all fell.

"'Forsake the Christ thou sawest transfigured! him
Who trod the sea and brought the dead to life?
What should wring this from thee?'—ye laugh and ask.
What wrung it? Even a torchlight and a noise,
The sudden Roman faces, violent hands,
And fear of what the Jews might do! Just that;
And it is written, 'I forsook and fled:'
There was my trial, and it ended thus."
(Browning, 'A Death in the Desert.')

Vers. 47—53.—*The arrest of the Redeemer.* All the four evangelists tell the story of the last hours, in the main the same, though the language is often quite different, and fresh and important details appear in each memoir.

The general effect on the thoughtful reader is that the Crucifixion and the events leading up to it were very far from being the result of the counsels of the Jewish leaders, the outcome of their relentless enmity. The death and all the attendant circumstances took place in their solemn order, then, when the public teaching of the Redeemer was finished, *because* it had been determined by some higher and grander power than was possessed by Jerusalem Sanhedrin or Roman Senate.

So St. Matthew, in his account, twice (xxvi. 54, 56) gives the ground for the arrest, "That the Scriptures might be fulfilled." And the Scriptures were but the echoes of that other and grander power.

Ver. 47.—**And while he yet spake, behold a multitude.** Different to his disciples, their Master, who had prayed and received as an answer to his prayer the angel's visit, was now, when the hour of mortal danger struck, in possession of the profoundest calm. Nothing disturbed his serenity any more. With calm majesty he advanced to meet the traitor as he guided his Master's deadly enemies into the garden. From this hour Jesus welcomes the cross, from which for a brief moment he had seemed to shrink. The company who was thus guided to Gethsemane to effect the arrest in the dead of the night was composed of Roman legionaries detailed for this duty from a cohort on guard in the Antonia Fort by the temple, and of Levitical guards belonging to the temple—an armed force of police, part of the temple watch at the disposal of the priests. **He that was called Judas, one of the twelve.**

Each of the evangelists mention the presence of the traitor. It was evidently a strange and startling detail for the writers of these memoirs that one of the chosen twelve should have been the betrayer! **And drew near unto Jesus to kiss him.** This was the sign agreed upon between Judas and his employers. They knew that it would be night, and that Gethsemane was shaded with olives, and that therefore some conspicuous sign would be necessary to indicate to the guards which of the company of twelve was the Master whom they were to seize. But the signal was superfluous, for, as St. John tells us, Jesus of his own accord advanced before the others, telling those who came for him who he was. Because of this kiss the early Christian Church discontinued the customary brotherly kiss on Good Friday.

Ver. 50.—**And one of them smote the servant of the high priest, and cut off his right ear.** The name of the disciple who smote the servant of the high priest is given by St. John: it was Peter. He gives, too, the servant's name, Malchus. John wrote many years later, when Jerusalem had long ceased to exist; Peter, too, had passed away. Before this incident, St. John relates how the Roman and Jewish guards "went backward, and fell to the ground." *What* overawed the party of armed men is uncertain—whether some supernatural or merely a natural cause; possibly something of majesty in the Lord's appearance impelled these men to retire and reverently to salute him they were ordered to seize. St. John mentions this to show that it was of his own free will that he rendered himself up.

Ver. 51.—**Suffer ye thus far.** The exact meaning of these words has been much debated. They probably were addressed to the company of armed men, and contained a plea for the mistaken zeal of his disciple Peter. "Excuse this resistance." **And he touched his ear, and healed him.** This miraculous cure of the wound inflicted by the zealous disciple is related by the physician Luke.

Ver. 53.—**When I was daily with you in the temple, ye stretched forth no hands against me: but this is your hour, and the power of darkness.** These words of the Lord may signify, "It was from a cowardly fear of the people whom you felt were my friends that you did not dare to arrest me in the full light of day." But it is better to take the last clause as possessing a deeper meaning: "I have often been in your power before, when, without concealment, I taught publicly in that sacred house where you are the appointed guardians; you never dared to lay hands on me *then*. But this, I know, is *your* hour, the moment God has given up to you to effect this sad triumph, and this (*i.e.* the power by which you work) is the power of darkness (*i.e.* the power of the spirit of darkness)."

Vers. 54—62.—*The denial of Peter.*

Ver. 54.—**Then took they him, and led him, and brought him into the high priest's house. And Peter followed afar off.** There has been some discussion here on the question of harmonizing the separate accounts. There is, however, no real difficulty if the following historical details be borne in mind. The actual high priest at this juncture was Caiaphas, son-in-law to Annas, who was the legal high priest, but had been deposed by the Roman power some time before. Annas, however, although prevented by the Roman government from bearing the high priestly insignia, was apparently looked upon by the people as the rightful possessor of the dignity, and evidently exercised the chief authority in the Jewish councils. It seems that he and his son-in-law Caiaphas, the Roman nominee, occupied together the high priest's palace. There were three trials of our Lord by the Jews: (1) Before Annas (John xviii. 12—18). (2) Before Caiaphas and what has been termed a committee of the Sanhedrin (John xviii. 24; Matt. xxvi. 59—68; Mark xiv. 55—65). (3) Formally before the whole Sanhedrin at dawn (ch. xxii. 66—71; Matt. xxvii. 1; Mark xv. 1). The thrice-repeated denial of Peter took place: (1) On his first going in (he was admitted through the influence of John, who was known to the officials) to the court-yard of the high priest's palace, in answer to the female servant who kept the door (John xviii. 17). (2) As he sat by the fire warming himself, in answer to another maid (Matt. xxvi. 69) and to other bystanders (John xviii. 25; ch. xxii. 58), including the kinsman of Malchus (John xviii. 26). (3) About an hour later (ch. xxii. 59), after he had left the fire to avoid the questioners, and had gone out into the porch or gateway leading into the court-yard, in answer to one of the maids who had spoken before (Mark xiv. 69; Matt. xvi. 71), and to other bystanders (ch. xxii. 59; Matt. xxvi. 73; Mark xiv. 70).

Ver. 55.—**And when they had kindled a fire in the midst of the hall, and were set down together, Peter sat down among them.** We know that the arrest in Gethsemane was followed by the flight of the eleven apostles. John and Peter, however, once out of reach of the armed band, seem in some way to have recovered from their first panic, and to have followed their Master and his guards into the city. Arrived at the high priest's house, John, who was known to the high priest, had no difficulty in procuring admission for himself and his companion. Peter's motive in pressing into what he knew for him was a locality full of peril, is given by St. Matthew (xxvi. 58), "to see the end." There was no doubt there was in the heart of the impulsive, loving man, sorrowful anxiety and deep sorrow for his dear Master's fate. But, alas! with the feverish sad expectation to see what he felt would be the end, there was no earnest prayer for guidance and help. The fire is mentioned because, generally speaking, the nights in the Holy Land about the Passover season are warm. The cold on this night appears to be spoken of as something unusual. *Peter sat down among them.* "St. John (it must be supposed) had passed on into the audience-chamber, so that St. Peter was alone. St. John, who remained closest to the Lord, was unmolested; St. Peter, who mingled with the indifferent crowd, fell" (Westcott).

Ver. 56.—**But a certain maid beheld him as he sat by the fire, and earnestly looked upon him, and said, This man was also with him.** Comparing the several accounts of the evangelists together, we see how naturally the incidents followed each other. As he entered, the portress first thought she recognized him as one of the followers of the well-known Teacher just arrested on a capital charge. Then as, weary and chilled, he drew near the fire, the firelight shone on his face, a face known to many who had listened during the last few days to his Master as he taught, with his disciples grouped round him in the temple-courts before crowds of listeners. Thoroughly alarmed, he drew aside from the friendly warmth of the fire into the outer shade of the gateway; yet he could not tear himself away from the neighbourhood of the spot where his dear Master was being interrogated by his deadly foes; and even there, while lurking in the shadow, he was recognized again, and then, just as he was in the act of fiercely denying, with oaths and curses, his friendship for and connection with Jesus, came the Master by, after the second examination before Caiaphas and certain members of the Sanhedrin, being conducted by the guard to another and more formal court. And as the Master passed, he turned and looked upon his poor cowardly disciple.

Ver. 59.—**For he is a Galilæan.** The strong provincial dialect of the fisherman of the Lake of Galilee at once told these Jerusalem Jews, accustomed to the peculiar pronunciation of the Galilee pilgrims at the Passover Feast, that the man whom they suspected certainly came from the same province as Jesus the Accused.

Ver. 61.—**And the Lord turned, and looked upon Peter.** As he was passing from the interrogation before Caiaphas to be examined before the Sanhedrin assembled in solemn council, he heard his servant's well-known voice raised and accompanied with oaths and curses, assuring the by-standers he had no connection with and knew nothing of Jesus of Nazareth. Then, as he passed, the Master turned and looked on his old friend, that disciple who so lately had declared that even if all others deserted the Lord, he never would! The glance of Jesus was full of the tenderest pity; it was not angry, only sorrowful; but it recalled Peter to his better, nobler self. SS. Matthew and Mark (Peter's own Gospel) record how, when he heard the cock crow, which St. Luke tells us happened as our Lord turned to look on the recreant disciple, he remembered all, and burst into bitter weeping. We meet him again on the Resurrection morning in company with St. John (John xx. 3), whence, it would seem, that in his bitter sorrow he had turned to his old friend, who had probably heard his denial. St. John, who briefly in his narrative touches upon the "denial," omits to mention the repentance, but, according to his custom, specially illustrates it in the scene by the lake (John xxi. 15, and following verses).

Vers. 63—65.—*After the second examination, the officials of the Sanhedrin mock and ill treat Jesus as one doomed to death.*

Ver. 63.—**And the men that held Jesus mocked him, and smote him.** The position of the Redeemer when the cruelties took place, described in this and the two following verses, was as follows: After the arrest in Gethsemane, the guards, Jewish and Roman, escorted the Prisoner to the palace of the high priest in Jerusalem. There both Annas and Caiaphas apparently lodged. In the first instance, Jesus was brought before Annas, who was evidently the leading personage of the Sanhedrin of that day. Details of the preliminary examination are given apparently by John xviii. 13, 19—24. In this first and informal trial Caiaphas was evidently present, and took part (ver. 19). At the close of this unofficial but important proceeding, Annas sent him to Caiaphas. The true reading in John xviii. 24 is ἀπέστειλεν οὖν, "Annas therefore sent him." That is, at the close of the first *unofficial* examination, which took place in Annas's apartments in the palace of the high priest, Annas sent him to be examined *officially* before Caiaphas, the reigning high priest, and a committee of the Sanhedrin. This, the second trial of Jesus, is related at some length by St. Matthew (xxvi. 59—66) and St. Mark (xiv. 55 64). The priests on that occasion sought false witnesses, but their witness did not, we know, agree. Jesus kept silence until Caiaphas arose, and with awful solemnity adjured him to say whether he was the Christ, the Son of God. So adjured, Jesus answered definitely in the affirmative. Then Caiaphas rent his robe, and appealed to the assembly, who answered the appeal by a unanimous cry, "He is guilty of death." After this hearing before Caiapnas and a committee of the Sanhedrin, the condemned One was conducted before the full assembly of the Sanhedrin. While being led across the court, he heard Peter's third denial. It was during the interval which elapsed before the great council assembled, that the mocking related in these verses (63—65) took place.

Ver. 64.—**And when they had blindfolded him, they struck him on the face, and asked him, saying, Prophesy, who is it that smote thee?** The Jews, in this terrible scene (see, too, for further details of the outrages, Matt. xxvi. 67; Mark xiv. 65), were unconsciously working out a literal fulfilment of Isaiah's picture of the righteous Sufferer (Isa. l. 6; liii. 3—7).

Vers. 66—71.—*The third trial before the Sanhedrin.*

Ver. 66.—**And as soon as it was day.** The Sanhedrin as a council could only meet by day; all the preliminaries had been settled and the course of procedure fully arranged when the legal time for the meeting of the state council arrived. **The elders of the people and the chief priests and the scribes came together, and led him into their council.** These were the three constitutional parts of the Sanhedrin. The name of the famous Sanhedrin, curiously enough, is a Greek, not a Hebrew or Aramaic word, being derived from συνέδριον, an assembly. We first come on the word, says Dr. Farrar, when this state council summoned before them Hyrcanus II., son of Alexander Jannæus. In the time of our Lord, the Roman government had taken from them the power of carrying out capital sentences; hence their bringing Jesus before Pilate. There is a remarkable tradition that the council left their proper place of assembly, Gazith, and sat in another chamber (forty years before the destruction of the temple). Now, it was forbidden to condemn to death except in Gazith (see 'Avoda Zara,' pp. 61, etc.). Dr. Westcott quotes from Dérenbourg ('Essai sur l'Histoire et la Géographie de Palestine'), who suggests the probability of the night sitting of Annas and Caiaphas and the members of the Sanhedrin favourable to their policy (the second trial) being held at "the Booths of the Sons of Hanan" (Annas). These booths, or shops, were under two cedars on the Mount of Olives (Jerusalem Talmud, 'Taanith,' iv. 8). There were four of these booths, which were for the sale of objects legally pure. In one of these pigeons were sold for the sacrifices of all Israel. Dérenbourg conjectures that these booths on the Mount of Olives were part of the famous Booths of the Sons of Hanan (Annas) to which the Sanhedrin retired when it left the chamber Gazith.

Ver. 67.—**Art thou the Christ? tell us. And he said unto them, If I tell you, ye will not believe.** In his answer Jesus evidently refers to something which had preceded this interrogation on the part of the Sanhedrin. He referred, no doubt, to that night examination before Caiaphas and certain chosen members of the council—the meeting passed over by St. Luke, but recounted by SS. Matthew and Mark. In this earlier trial, which we (see above) term the second, a similar question had been put to Jesus, but, as Lange and Stier point out, *now* the political significance of the charge, the claim to Messianic royalty, is brought into prominence. They were desirous to formulate an accusation which they could bring before the Roman tribunal of Pilate. The words, "*Son of God*," which the fury of jealous anger had wrung from Caiaphas (Matt. xxvi. 63), is here left out of sight, and is only brought forward again by the fierce Jewish wrath excited by the Lord's quiet words telling of his "session at the right hand" (vers. 69, 70). *If I tell you, ye will not believe.* If you, who have seen my life, have heard my words, and seen my works, believe not, to what end is it to say it again now?

Ver. 68.—**And if I also ask you, ye will not answer me.** The Lord here especially refers to those public questions of his put to members of the Sanhedrin and others in the last days of his public ministry, such as we find in Matt. xxii. 45, to which the rulers had attempted to give no answer.

Ver. 69.—**Hereafter shall the Son of man sit on the right hand of the power of God.** Jesus decided to put an end to this weary and useless trial, and supplied his judges with the evidence they were seeking to extort from him. The Master's words would recall to the teachers of Israel, sitting as his judges, the words of their loved prophet Daniel (vii. 13, 14). These solemn words of his were, and they perfectly understood them as such, a claim on the part of the Prisoner who stood before them—*a direct claim to Divine glory.*

Ver. 70.—**Then said they all, Art thou then the Son of God?** Now bringing forward the loftier title formerly suppressed (in ver. 67). "And *art* thou, then, dost *thou*, poor Man, vain in thy imagining, dost thou assert thyself to be the Son of God?" So Stier. **And he said unto them, Ye say that I am.** This form of reply is not used in Greek, but is frequent in rabbinic. By such an answer the one interrogated accepts *as his own* *affirmation* the question put to him in its entirety. We have, then, here, in the clearest possible language: (1) A plain assertion by our Lord of his Divinity. (2) The reply of the Sanhedrists, showing that *they* for their part distinctly understood it as such, but to make it quite clear they asked him if that *was* his meaning, *i.e.* the assertion of his Divinity. (3) We have the Lord's quiet answer, "Yes, that was his meaning." The next verse (71) shows that they were satisfied with the evidence which they proceeded without delay to lay before the Roman governor, Pilate.

HOMILETICS.

Vers. 1—30.—*Wednesday and Thursday of Passion Week.* Look at *that* picture—the Son of God awaiting the hour; spending the last day before the arrest and the trial in the deep seclusion of the Bethany home. Over that day the veil of an impenetrable secrecy hangs. One thing only is certain—it was a time in which the shrinking spirit, whilst feeling even unto death the shadow of the exceeding heaviness, nevertheless drank of the brook by the way, the comforting "I am not alone, for the Father is with me." Look at *this* picture—the priests and scribes, defied and denounced in the temple and in the presence of the people, have resolved that, by fair means or by foul, they must get rid of this "Swift Witness" against them. These men, united by a common hatred, consult (ver. 2) how they may kill him. We can imagine the conferences in the dimly lighted chamber—the partial light only casting deeper shadows, and bringing into fuller relief the lines of fierce resentment on the faces of the councillors. There is no debate as to the object; the only and the long debate is simply as to the means of accomplishing the object. Their deliberations are unexpectedly aided. The evangelist informs us of the satisfaction which lightens their countenances as they conclude the bargain with Judas of Karioth, and receive from him the assurance that he will find "the opportunity to betray him to them" (ver. 6) without the risk of exciting a tumult. Thus, whilst heaven is calm, hell is agitated at its depths; whilst love is directing its prayer and looking up, pride and envy are laying their plots and meditating the darkest crime which blots the page of history. "Mark the perfect, and behold the upright; for the end of that man is peace." "But the wicked are like the troubled sea, when it cannot rest, whose waters cast up mire and dirt." The early hours of Thursday swiftly pass. The next day is the great Passover day; and the disciples have begun to press the inquiry, "Where shall we keep it?" In the forenoon (ver. 8) Jesus gives Peter and John his instructions. A place is in the Lord's view. That the one to whose house the apostles are directed was a believer may be inferred (1) from the word which the three synoptists represent the Lord as using, "The Master saith" (ver. 11); and (2) from the confidential character of the message. The two are commanded to go in advance of the party, and have all in readiness for a celebration of the Paschal meal, which probably anticipated by one day the usual celebration of the Lord's Passover. Christ and the remaining ten apostles follow in the evening. Nothing is told us of that journey, whether, *e.g.*, it was private, or whether, as usual, Jesus was accompanied by a multitude of people. It is the last time on which the feet of the Christ who had been known after the flesh shall press the grassy slope of the hill he loved. But he had spoken to his own of another day, that foretold in prophecy, when "his feet shall stand on the Mount of Olives, which is before Jerusalem on the east . . . the day when the light shall not be clear nor dark, but one day known to the Lord. And living waters shall go out from Jerusalem; half of them toward the former sea, and half of them toward the hinder sea; . . . and the Lord shall be King over all the earth" (Zech. xiv. 4—9). All that is reported is this: "When the hour was come, he sat down, and the twelve apostles with him" (ver. 14). The details of that memorable evening are full of interest; and, regarding them, the narratives of the evangelists are singularly explicit. "The four streams that go forth to water the earth in that tale meet in a common channel; the four winds of the Spirit are in it, united and one." The scene is (vers. 11, 12) "a large upper room"—the guest-chamber of the house. (For distinction, emphasize "the *guest-chamber*.") 1. *Its object.* To receive and entertain the Friend, the one to be honoured. Is not Christ the Guest (Rev. iii. 20)? 2. *Its characteristics.* The *best room.* Is he not entitled to the best? A *large room.* The whole breadth of the life's aims, the whole strength of the heart's love, is due to him. An *upper room*. Poor and sorry is the life that has no upper room; blessed is the life whose upper room is reserved for him. A *furnished room*, all in readiness for his presence—a heart and will furnished for every good work. 3. *Its consecration*. How realized? On *our* side, by an *unreserved* surrender: "The Master saith;" and by the ready-making of faith and love, as symbolized in Peter and John. On *his* side, by the coming as the Lamb of God with the gospel of forgiveness, and as the Bread of life to have communion with us and we with him. When Jesus enters the room there is a strife for precedence, for the places nearest him. St. Luke places the strife (ver. 24) along with the questioning among themselves who would be false to Christ; but his language, "there was also," is inexact, and it seems consistent with the fitness of things that the contention should occur when seats were being taken. The Master, observing it, administers the rebuke recorded in vers. 26, 27; and, having so done, he proceeds to comply with the ceremonial of the feast. It was wont to begin with the passing of a cup of wine, blessed and hallowed. The word recorded in vers. 15, 16 is spoken before the dispensation of the cup; the word in vers. 17, 18 accompanies the dispensation; both words intimating the declinature to partake of the shadowy rite when the substance is so soon to be realized. "Suffer it to be so *now*," said Jesus to John at the baptism. The *now* is exhausted. "I will not any more" is the sentence of the supper-table. As they divide the cup, he rises. He is minded to give them the lesson never to be forgotten, as his sharpest rebuke of all their contentions for priority—the lesson so graphically related in John xiii. 1—17. Resuming his place at the table, lo! a troubled look flits across the countenance. A little later in the evening he can no longer refrain. There is one seated near him over whom the heart yearns, though it recoils from his baseness (ver. 21). The hand of the betrayer is with him. "*One of you.*" Startled, deeply moved, the question passes from one and another, "Lord, is it I?" Simon whispers to John, "Ask who it is;" and John, leaning forward, his head close to Jesus, puts the question. He gets the sign by which the one will be identified—a morsel to be dipped in the dish that is before the Lord will be given to him. It is given to Judas, hitherto silent, something of the better self still struggling within. But, after the sop, the Satanic spirit gains in boldness. He has the effrontery to ask, "Is it I?" What is the answer? "Thou hast said . . . That thou doest do quickly." O Judas, there is no need to linger; thou art detected. "The Son of man goeth, as it is written: but woe unutterable to thee!" It is difficult to determine the precise stage in the keeping of the feast at which the sacrament of the Lord's Supper was instituted. Matthew makes the departure of the traitor precede the appointment of the ordinance. Luke seems to place the institution of the Supper at an earlier period than the departure. But the fact of the institution is beyond doubt (vers. 19—21). The Christian Church, in all ages, has obeyed the command of her beloved Lord, spoken in the guest-chamber when keeping the Passover with his disciples: "This do in remembrance of me." The central point of the interest attaching to the Thursday evening is this consecration of the bread and the cup as the abiding pledges of redeeming love. It is sad to think that over the gracious words of Christ in the consecration so many controversies should have been waged. Why cannot men recognize the language of figure and symbol? Those who insist that in the sentence, "Take, eat; this is my body," there is implied the transubstantiation of the cake of bread held in the hand, claim for that sentence a narrow literalism which they themselves do not observe when they read, "I am the true Vine," or "I am the Door." Let us receive, with all possible oblation of praise, the earthly creatures as, in sacramental use, the hallowed representations to the eye and pledges to the soul of the never-failing nourishment of the body that was broken and the blood that was shed for us. Let all who would feed on Jesus in their heart with thanksgiving reflect on the words of the Thursday evening which mirror his consciousness, and let them examine themselves in the light of this consciousness. "With desire I have desired" (ver. 15). O my Lord, if thy desire was thus vehement; if, because of it, thou didst overlook all that lay in the immediate future; if thou didst so long to share thy feast with men, why the want of desire in me? why the backwardness and slowness of my soul to receive thee in the mysteries of thy love? Lord, lead me in thy truth, and teach me. "Until the kingdom of God shall come" (ver. 18). O my Lord, how vivid to thee was the future consummation of thy sacrifice! As, in perspective, the distant is often near, the intervening spaces being lost to sight, so was it with thee. Thou didst behold thy kingdom in glory as at hand, and thy soul stretched forward whither thy prayer afterwards pointed,—"Father, that which thou hast given me, I will that where I am they also may be with me." Why beats my pulse so slow and feeble in response to the hope of thy kingdom? Why is my Lord's Supper so much of a mere commemoration, so little of a prophetic joy, of a prayer, as already in the vision of the kingdom? "Come, Lord Jesus, come quickly."

"Thou strong and loving Son of man,
  Redeemer from the bonds of sin,
'Tis thou the living spark dost fan
  That sets my heart on fire within.
Thou openest heaven once more to men—
  The soul's true home, thy kingdom, Lord;
And I can trust and hope again,
  And feel myself akin to God."

Vers. 31—34.—*The special word to Simon.* Its solemnity is indicated by the twice-repeated "*Simon.*" Observe, when the warning is given, this is the name used; afterwards (ver. 34), in reply to the disciple's protestation, "I am ready to go both to prison and to death," the name is changed, "I tell thee, *Peter.*" How gentle, how pathetic, the irony! Of the Peter, the rock, it is to be said, "The cock shall not crow until thou shalt thrice deny that thou knowest me." Note three points in the word of Christ.

I. The temptation. To him the personality of the tempter is always real. Real, in respect of his own temptations: "Get thee hence, Satan;" "The prince of this world cometh." Now we are reminded that it is real in respect of the temptations of men. Beware of foolish speaking and jesting in connection with the actual existence of the Satan. "Behold!" says Jesus. All is vividly present to him; he would have the agency of the adversary vividly present to his follower. The expression employed is very striking (see the Revised Version, "Satan asked to have you"). The phrase recalls the scene in Job ii. But this is memorable—the tempter recognizes the proprietary of the Lord. Of Judas it is said, "Satan entered into him." Of Simon it is said, "He asked to have you." This is one over whom he has no right. He belongs to the Son of God—a man given him by the Father. And he makes request that the disciple be sifted. In the margin of the Revised Version it is put as an alternative reading: "He obtained you by asking." All is so suggestive. The Christian Father speaks of the Christian's *fasting-days.* Such days are often part of the experience of God's people. The sieve, as if with God's permission, is applied. The tempter obtained the Lord himself by asking, and the sieve was applied to him. It was similarly applied to his apostle; it is similarly applied, in one form or another, to those who are his. God will have his wheat winnowed. Remember, there is the sieve: "Watch and pray."

II. The intercession. It is spoken of (ver. 32) as *past*, and as a transaction accomplished in the invisible world. And who knows what transactions are there realized? How blessed is the assurance that

"Where high the heavenly temple stands,
The house of God, not made with hands,
A great High Priest our nature wears,
The Guardian of mankind appears"!

"I *made intercession* for thee." Ah! in the day when all secrets are declared, with what marvellous light will this word be illumined! Ye Simons of all ages, thyself, O my soul, what a reflection it is that between the one tempted and the outer darkness there is the intercession of the ever-living and ever-mighty One, who is able to "save to the uttermost"! What is the intercession? Not that the sieve be withdrawn, that the sifting fail? It is needful. Simon would not have been the Peter he became without the sieve and without the discipline. The tempter and the trial are used as discipline. He who would not pray that his own be taken out of the world, will not pray that the Satan-request be refused. No; but he intercedes that the "faith fail not" (ver. 32). The great feature of Simon was his confidence in Christ. Why should he have been selected as the Rock-man, who was so often rash, and who so weakly denied his Master? Through all there was still the faith. He had quicker insight into the secrets of his Master's power and presence than any of his fellows; he had a higher and fuller perception of and trust in him. Were this to fail, all would fail. And the fruit of the intercession was evidenced in the springing back of his faith—nay, in its rising to a still higher measure of knowledge on the ruins of the old self-confidence; there was created the new heart that by-and-by was ready to go to prison and death.

III. The exhortation. Simon will turn again. When the Lord turns, in the day of the trial, and looks on the apostate disciple, there is born a godly sorrow which works repentance not to be repented of. Out of this repentance there comes the earnest, "Lord, thou knowest all things; thou knowest that I love thee." And the charge is, "Do thou, when once thou hast turned again, stablish thy brethren" (ver. 32, Revised Version). The most helpful man is he who has himself been tempted, who has passed, not without scars, through the fight of faith. It is the sympathy of the soul that has come through great tribulation that has the delicate touch, the magnetic force, the faculty of establishing the brethren. All discovery of the Lord is to be utilized in the way of strengthening, cheering, building up human souls in the kingdom of God. What we receive we hold in trust for others, and, in giving as we receive, what we have gained becomes doubly ours.

"Heaven does with us as we with torches do,
Not light them for themselves."

Experience of God and his love is the best teacher. What we learn, even through falls and failures, turns most to the profit of poor human nature. Simon, after the sifting, through the turning again, was the confirmer of the brethren.

Vers. 39—46.—*Gethsemane.* It is now dark. On the way to the Mount of Olives, the customary retreat of Jesus (ver. 39), at the point where the upward slope begins, there is a shady place, belonging, perhaps, to one of those who believed in him, whither "Jesus had often resorted" (John xviii. 2). The site of the garden of Gethsemane may, with sufficient accuracy, be identified. It may not have been the exact spot, overshadowed by the eight venerable trees, which immemorial tradition has distinguished as the scene of the lonely vigil, but it must have been close to that spot. It was a place where there were many olives, and, as the name suggests, an oil-press; a place of perfect quiet and seclusion, where, beyond the voices of rude men, there was the peace of heaven. To this place he who had uttered the high-priestly prayer brought the high-priestly sacrifice; and there he began the walk through the valley of the shadow of death. The tale of the sore amazement and exceeding heaviness is told, with more fulness of detail, by the Evangelists Matthew and Mark (see homiletics *in loc.*). Here, without enlarging on the meaning and scope of the features of the narrative, note—

I. The agony. (Ver. 44.) It has always been felt that in this there is immeasurably more than a mere revolt from imminent pain and death. The anguish is marked by an intensity for which this revolt cannot account. A brave man, however sensitive, can face, with unflinching fortitude, a high enterprise, even though its fatal consequence is evident. "The sweat becoming as it were great drops of blood," speaks of a conflict in the soul for which the impending physical dissolution cannot account. Some references supply us with suggestions. 1. The announcement made at the Supper-table (John xiv. 30), of the coming of the prince of the world, speaks to us of a temptation, intensified by the circumstances of the hour, in the line of the wilderness-temptation, to grasp the power of the Messiah otherwise than through the suffering of the cross (see, in this connection, Matt. xxvi. 53). 2. The sorrow which cast its shade over his countenance when the betrayal was mentioned (John xiii. 21); the horror with which he regarded the perfidy (ver. 22; Matt. xxvi. 24); the utterance by which he awoke the disciples, marking out the betrayal as the bitterness of the hour at hand (Matt. xxvi. 45); the appeal to Judas (ver. 48);—these things indicate the *amazement* and pain caused by the action of the son of perdition. 3. The word of the Son to the Father as to the cup so full of woe that he humbly besought its removal, reminds us of a region beyond all that our thought can trace, in which the Christ of God was treading the wine-press alone. Better, in view of this, a holy reticence than a zeal which is eager with explanations. If we must speak of the special fearfulness and trembling of Gethsemane, let us simply say that there, in all its crushing weight, was realized the bearing of the sin of the world.

II. THE PRAYER. 1. *Observe its characteristics.* (1) *Humility.* "He kneeled down." More strongly still St. Mark says (xiv. 35), "He fell on the ground." It was the attitude of deepest reverence, of entire prostration. In the high-priestly prayer, "he lifted up his eyes to heaven;" but now, in human weakness and dependence, he is prostrate before his Father. Sign of the "godly fear" (Heb. v. 7) for which he was heard. (2) *Importunate repetition.* Thrice he prayed, "saying the same words" (Matt. xxvi. 44). It is not the eloquence, but the sincerity of desire in the prayer which God regards. (3) *Increasing earnestness.* "Being in an agony, he prayed more earnestly." The greater the pressure on the soul, the more fervent became the cry. The sorrow of the disciples sent them to sleep; his sent him to the Father. "Love overmasters agony," not agony love. Let the disciple learn of the Master. 2. *Observe its subject-matter.* (Ver. 42.) "Remove this cup from me;" or (as in Matt. xxvi. 30), "Let this cup pass from me." It was the pleading of the sensitive human soul. And we may be assured that to plead for the removal of a cup of pain, for relief from burdens which seem greater than we can bear, is in the way of the child's privilege; only there must be the spirit of entire dependence. "If thou be willing." There is to be no "if" where God's promise is absolute. We do not need to say, "If thou be willing, make thy grace sufficient." His pledge as to this is distinct and unequivocal: "My grace *is* sufficient." From this, on this resting, we pray. But when we desire that concerning which we have no definite assurance of the Father's mind, then all is to be subordinated to him. This is to abide in the Son as he is revealed in Gethsemane. "If we ask any thing according to God's will, he heareth us." The godly McCheyne spoke of getting into tune for prayer. We get into tune when we learn Christ's "If it be possible;" "If thou be willing."

"Renew my will from day to day;
Blend it with thine," etc.

3. *Observe its answer.* The answer is manifest: (1) In the *righting "Nevertheless."* (Ver. 42.) In the prayer the soul realized "God my Rock." From what might have been self-seeking, it was delivered.

"Do thou thy holy will:
I will lie still; I will not stir,
Lest I should break the charm."

"In the day when I cried, thou answeredst me, and strengthenedst me with strength in my soul." (2) In the *comforting angel.* (Ver. 43.) The holy one, sign of the sympathy in heaven above. For to the one who prays in an agony the heavens are not brass. There are ministries of love. God's angels are all ministering spirits. In visible form the angel may not appear; but we know that he is with us in the comfort and peace. Have we not the Comforter himself?—

"A gracious, willing Guest,
While he can find one humble heart
Wherein to rest."

And thus, though the cup does not pass, the will of the Son is strengthened into perfect harmony with the will of the Father. He rises up from prayer, ready, "strong in the Lord, and in the power of his might."

III. Observe, finally, THE REMONSTRANCE. Very touching the *word to Peter* (Matt. xxvi. 40). The one hour never again to come, the one hour of watching, lost in sleep! And now (ver. 46). May not the pathetic question ring in the ears of the Christian? Why do *we* sleep—we whom the Son of man has associated with himself in his prayers and pains? We asleep, and he toiling! We asleep, and the world lying in darkness! Ah! in the solemn light of Gethsemane, what is the utmost Christian activity but a slumber? and how many who claim to be Christ's are fast asleep, not for sorrow, but in self-indulgence and sin! Oh that the gentle, reproachful "why?" may be as an alarum-clock to conscience, a continual incitement to will and heart! The spirit may be willing, but the flesh is ever weak. "Rise and pray, lest ye enter into temptation!"

Ver. 47—ch. xxiii. 46.—*Thursday night to Friday evening.* It is time to be going. The footfall of the coming host has already been heard, and the gleam of the lanterns and the flashing of the swords have been detected at no great distance. Guiltily, under shadow of night, the conspirators have approached. "While Jesus is yet speaking" (ver. 47), the traitor is bending forward to give the salute of friendship. Note the question, so full of gentle dignity, "Companion, wherefore art thou come? Betrayest thou the Son of man with a kiss?" Note what follows down to the flight of the apostles, when to them it seems that the end has come. "We trusted that it had been he who should have redeemed Israel;" and now? Betrayed into the hands of sinners, he is "led as a lamb to the slaughter, and as a sheep dumb before her shearers." Priest, Pharisee, scribe, he who scourged you with the whip of his holy indignation is now the Prisoner on whose bleeding body the furrows of your scourge may be made long. No legion of angels will interpose. The Son of God only waits to die. There are: (1) *a precognition by Annas;* (2) *an arraignment before Caiaphas and the Sanhedrin;* and, finally (3), *the deliverance to the judicature of the governor.* Briefly trace the narrative.

I. THE PRECOGNITION BY ANNAS. Annas, or Hanan, to whom first the fettered Jesus is borne, occupied at the time a peculiar position. His son-in-law, Joseph Caiaphas, was the actual high priest. But Annas, having been deposed by the Roman governor, was still regarded as the priest *jure divino*, and his influence seems to have been immense. Five of his sons and his son-in-law were raised to the pontifical throne. It was under the last of his five sons that James, the brother of our Lord, was put to death. He was an unscrupulous intriguer. A Sadducee, who had been mixed up in foul plots and conspiracies, the head of "a viper brood," as a Jewish chronicler says, which amassed wealth by unlawful gains. Farrar has called attention to the fact that, when the capture of Jesus is determined, the Pharisees disappear from the scene; his implacable enemies are the chief priests and scribes. Before this Annas Jesus stands (John xviii. 13—23). Some questions are put as to his disciples and doctrine. And these, as has well been remarked, Jesus answers "with dignified repulsion"—a repulsion so sharp that the first blow inflicted on that sacred face was bestowed by one of the menials of the court. "Answerest thou the high priest so?" How complete the self-restraint expressed in the only action which followed—the reply, "If I have spoken evil, bear witness of the evil; but if not, why strikest thou me?"

II. THE ARRAIGNMENT BEFORE CAIAPHAS AND THE SANHEDRIN. All that Annas could do was to order his Prisoner to be still more tightly bound, and to send him to the portion of the temple court which was occupied by the priest, his son-in-law, Caiaphas. The morning had not yet dawned, and until dawn no meeting of council could be convened. It was during this interval that the predicted denial of the Lord by Peter occurred (vers. 54—62). The clock marks the hour of six, when Caiaphas and his assessors confront the Nazarene. Their object is to establish a charge of blasphemy, and suborned witnesses are cited. They are clumsy perjurers, who contradict one another and contradict themselves. And the evidence breaks down. Then the tactics are changed. The high priest, directly addressing the Prisoner, demands a "yea" or "nay" to the interrogation, "Art thou the Christ?" Jesus has been silent, but now (vers. 60—71), calmly and solemnly, he answers, "Thou hast said;" and adds that, by-and-by, they should see "the Son of man sitting on the right hand of the power of God." It is enough. "Blasphemy!" is the shout, and he is condemned as worthy of death. And there ensues a scene of brutal ferocity. The wretches in attendance spit on the face, buffet, strike him with the palms of their hands, and rend the air with ribald cries. For the world shows its baseness when a man is down; then the many rush forward to have their fling and kick.

III. JESUS IS DELIVERED TO THE JUDICATURE OF THE GOVERNOR. What priests and elders could do has been done. The procurator alone could inflict the sentence of death. Their next movement must be to coerce him into the carrying out of their plan. And they know that in Pontius Pilate, stained with violences the report of which to his imperial master would cost him his government, if not his life, they have the ruler whom they can rule. Two appearances (ch. xxiii.) of our Lord before the governor are recorded, and between them stands the episode with which the name of Herod is associated. There is nothing more sad than the record of the expedients, the shufflings to and fro, the efforts to save One whom Pilate felt to be guiltless, whilst yet he dared not give effect to his convictions. A record most sad, but most instructive. Is it not a portrait, many of whose features suggest cowardly concessions, timidities, struggles between conscience and policy in which conscience is worsted, with which, in one form or another, too many of us are familiar? A character-sketch, like that of Pilate in the trial, gauges the directions and the possibilities of the human nature which is common to us all. In the afternoon of Friday the Saviour of sinners was crucified. An incident on the way to Calvary is related by the evangelist, which is touching in itself, and which reminds us of the attitude of mind, the kind of feeling towards him, the Crucified, which he denies and accepts. We are told that he was "followed by a great company of women, who bewailed and lamented him" (vers. 27—31). Observe his saying, most tenderly prefaced by the phrase, "Daughters of Jerusalem." Virtually, he declines tears and cries, which express only sorrow over his fate. He wishes those who bewail to estimate the significance of the spectacle, to realize what it foreboded for them and theirs; to weep not *for* him, but *with* him in his sadness concerning Jerusalem, in his baffled longing to gather its children together, in his thwarted purpose to save and bless. The events of that day were the prophecy of a doom not to be long delayed: in his thought and emotion as to this doom, and in this alone, he sought their sympathy. And so, remember, Christ desires not a luxury of sentiment, which ends in lamentations on account of his suffering. He desires partnership in his suffering. His cross is to be our cross. We are to hold ourselves identified with him in it. The apostle's words are the interpretation of the genuine Christian sentiment: "I was crucified with Christ: nevertheless I live; yet not I, but Christ liveth in me: and the life which I now live in the flesh I live by the faith of the Son of God, who loved me, and gave himself for me;" "God forbid that I should glory, save in the cross of our Lord Jesus Christ, through which the world has been crucified to me, and I to the world."

HOMILIES BY VARIOUS AUTHORS.

Ver. 2.—*Piety, pedantry, and formalism.* Of all those who in any and every way were responsible for the death of Jesus Christ, the largest share of guilt lies at the door of the religious leaders of the time. The Roman soldiers were only the *immediate instruments* of it; the Jewish populace were only the *blind agents* of it; but these scribes and chief priests were the *guilty instigators of it:* they brought it about. It was they who first conceived the idea; it was they who suggested and urged it; it was they who ceased not to agitate and direct until the dark deed was done. How came they to go so far astray? How came it to pass that while "all the people came early in the morning to him in the temple for to hear him" (ch. xxi. 38), thus bearing witness to the sincerity of their discipleship and their desire to know the truth he taught, *they*, the leaders of the land—scribes who were familiar with every letter of the Law, priests who were daily occupied in the services of the sanctuary, learned doctors, and pious ministrants—were actively and earnestly compassing his death? The fact is that—

I. Religious pedantry may be very learned, and yet wholly wrong. These men knew their Scriptures with a fulness and nicety of detail that surpasses the knowledge we have of our sacred writings; and they had also a perfect familiarity with the teachings of traditional lore. They despised the ignorance of the common people in these respects (see John vii. 47). Yet they were not wise with the wisdom of God; they entirely failed to understand the Divine will and the way to eternal life. The religion they taught and lived was utterly heartless; it was a service without any soul in it, a mechanism without any life in it; it was an elaborate error, a great and sad misconception of the mind of God; it was a surrender of freedom that did man no good and gave God no pleasure; it was a toilsome and torturing imposition that neither satisfied the intellect, nor cleansed the heart, nor elevated the life. And it so perverted the judgment that, when the Truth himself came to reveal the Father, these learned but unwise leaders, instead of being eager to hear him like the people (ch. xxi. 38), were "seeking how they might kill him."

II. RELIGIOUS FORMALISM WILL GO TO GREAT LENGTHS OF WRONG-DOING. If the scribes were men of pedantry, the chief priests represented the evil and error of religious formalism; and the latter were in no way behind the former in either spiritual blindness or malevolence. They, too, failed to recognize their Messiah, and were actively engaged in compassing his murder. In every age and land religious formalism has been blind and cruel; it has failed to recognize the reformer when he has come to speak in God's name; and it has been forward to accuse and to slay him. Such has been its spirit and its course, that the home of love and mercy has been converted into the hotbed of hatred and of cruelty. It is another illustration of the truth that the corruption of the best becomes the worst of all; the piety that runs into ordinances, utterances, abstinences, formalities, will in time degenerate into utter error and shameful wrong. This is a truth which applies to many more Churches than one; it is, indeed, more or less applicable to all religious circles. There lies a deep-seated tendency in our nature which accounts for the facts in our Lord's time and in every age since then. Let us, therefore, learn that—

III. TRUE PIETY IS FOUND IN RECTITUDE OF HEART AND LIFE. Not in holding and professing certain correct formulæ; not in going through certain ceremonies or observing a number of rules and regulations. These have their place in the kingdom of God, but they do not by any means assure us of our place in it. It is rightness of heart toward God our Father and our Saviour, and consequent integrity of life, which make us to "stand before God" as his loyal subjects now, and will make us "worthy to stand before the Son of man" when he shall call us to his nearer presence.—C.

Vers. 3—6.—*The deepest wound, etc.* When everything has been allowed for Judas that the most ingenious and the most charitable have begged us to consider, we must judge him to be a man whose conduct is to be solemnly and seriously condemned. It is Divine Love itself that decides this question (see ver. 22; Matt. xxvi. 24; John xvii. 12). The text suggests to us—

I. THAT OUR DEEPEST WOUNDS ARE THOSE WE RECEIVE AT THE HAND OF OUR NEAREST FRIENDS. How much force is there in the parenthesis, "*being of the number of the twelve*"! What deep pathos is in those sad words of the Lord, "Verily I say unto you, that *one of you* shall betray me" (Matt. xxvi. 21)! This was a "sword that entered into his soul," a keen distress, one of the very bitterest of all the sorrows of the Son of man. That one whom he had admitted to his intimate fellowship, of whom he had made a friend, who had partaken of his confidence and shared his strong affection,—that *he* should be the one to betray him to his foes! There is no trouble possible to us so great as that which lies open to us on the side of our purest and strongest affections. It is not our avowed enemy, nor the man to whom we are indifferent, but it is our dearest friend, who has it in his power to lacerate our soul with the sharpest thrust, and to spoil our life by throwing over it the darkest shadow (see Ps. xli. 9). 1. Be slow to admit to the inner sanctuary of the heart; for he who has entrance there holds your happiness in his own right hand. 2. Realize the responsibility of intimate friendship; it is not only a privilege, but an obligation; it gives you power to gladden and to bless, but also opportunity to mar and to destroy.

II. THAT MONEY PLAYS A LARGE PART, FOR GOOD OR EVIL, IN HUMAN LIFE. They "covenanted to give him money." It seems hardly credible that any man who had lived in the society of Jesus Christ, and had witnessed his kindness and his purity, should take money for betraying him. Other motives—those of resentment or ambition—are far less shocking and revolting than this mercenary one. To betray his Master, his Friend, for thirty pieces of silver, fills us with wonder and excites the deepest reprobation. But for what has not money been responsible in human history? How large a part it plays in the great drama! What untold good it is instrumental in effecting! What admirable virtues it is the means of illustrating! To what deeds of folly and even of infamy the desire to obtain it has conducted! It is clear that men who have been trained to hate immoral and criminal behaviour with an intense hatred have been induced to part with every principle they have honoured, and to do the worst deeds they have denounced, in order to obtain money, when they have *found themselves pressed* for its possession. Probably no man who has not felt it knows the deadly force of the temptation. Who shall say that he is safe from this powerful snare? It is probable that to obtain money more evil deeds have been done than under any other inducement whatever. Therefore let every man beware lest he subjects himself to this strong and fell temptation. Let neither an overweening ambition nor extravagance of habit lead where the possession of more money becomes an imperative demand. Moderation in desire and economy in habit save men from a temptation in which, it may be, their souls would be entangled and their very life taken away.

III. THAT EARNESTNESS IS SURE TO SEEK ITS OPPORTUNITY UNTIL IT FINDS IT. He "*sought opportunity* to betray him." By whatever motives inspired, Judas was intent on compassing the act he had undertaken. And he did not wait idly until an opportunity offered itself. He *sought it.* If evil is thus in earnest, how much more so should righteousness and mercy be! *These* should surely be about their holy and loving work "with both hands earnestly." Opportunity to raise, to help, to redeem, to restore,—this is not to be passively waited for, but to be actively sought out. There is a very marked difference between readiness to work when we are invited and even urged to do so, and that noble zeal which will not be contented without finding material for activity. It is the difference between a goodness that you do not blame and a goodness that you admire; between a life that will not stand condemned and a life that will be crowned with victory and honour. If there are those who, in the interest of error and of evil, will set about diligently to promote these ends, shall we not put forth our utmost energy on behalf of truth and heavenly wisdom? If men can be found who will "seek opportunity" to *betray*, shall not we with deeper devotedness "seek opportunity" to *honour* our Lord?—C.

Vers. 15, 16.—*The Passion, from two standpoints.* I. AS IT LOOKED TO OUR LORD WHEN HE WAS APPROACHING IT. It was to him a terrible trial, which he was eager to reach and pass through. "With desire he desired" the time to arrive when he should suffer and should complete his work. He did not wish to escape it; he was not looking about for an alternative; he knew that he could not save himself if he would save the world; and he longed for the trial-time to come and to be passed. Here was the heroic, and here was also the human. Here was the determination to endure, and, at the same time, the natural, human anxiety to know the worst and to exchange an almost intolerable suspense for the suffering that awaited him. 1. Having chosen the path of self-sacrifice, and having entered upon and pursued it, it behoved him to continue and to complete his appointed work. He could not turn back without suffering defeat; he accepted the dark future that was before him as a sacred duty. From it there must be no turning aside to other ends; and *there was none.* He never wavered in his purpose from beginning to end. "This shall not be unto thee," from Peter, appears to have been a strong shock of temptation to him (Matt. xvi. 21—23). But nothing induced him to turn aside by a single step from the path of sacrificial service. 2. Yet we have here a glimpse of the extreme severity of the trial he underwent. He knew that his "suffering" would immediately follow this Passover, and he "earnestly desired" that Passover to come, that the sufferings might follow. With perfect reverence we may say that he could not realize what they would include, for they had never before been experienced; they stood absolutely by themselves, and could not be known until they were actually felt. And this element of suspense and uncertainty must have added a great weight of trouble to the sorrows of our Lord. "How bitter that cup no heart can conceive;" not even *his* heart did conceive until it was in his hands. (1) Like our Lord, we should go on without faltering to the darkest future which we feel it becomes us to face. (2) As with him, the uncertainty of the actual elements of our grief may oppress our spirit and fill us with eager desire for its coming (see also ch. xii. 50). (3) We shall find, as he found, all needful Divine help when the hour does actually arrive.

II. AS HE WOULD HAVE US REGARD IT NOW. That is, as a completed work of redeeming love. That last Passover has been "fulfilled in the kingdom of God." All that the Passover prophesied has been fulfilled. The "Lamb of God" has been slain—that Lamb "which taketh away the sin of the world." Everything in the way of sacred endurance, of Divine preparation, is now completed, and the way into the kingdom is open. Those sufferings to which Jesus was so eagerly looking forward, to which he had now come, with nothing between them and him but that Passover Feast, had to be endured (see ch. xxiv. 26); and now *they have been* endured. Everything predicted in sacred rite or solemn utterance has been "fulfilled," and we wait for nothing more. We sit down to no predictive Passover Feast, because "Christ, our Passover, *is* slain for us." What we have to do is gratefully and eagerly to avail ourselves of the "finished" work of our redeeming Lord; to let that suffering, that death, that sacrifice, (1) evoke our humility; (2) call forth our faith; (3) kindle our love and command our obedience; (4) inspire us with sacred and abiding joy, inasmuch as his "sorrow unto death" is the source of our eternal life.—C.

Vers. 19, 20.—*The Lord's Supper.* A very simple rite as first observed was the Lord's Supper. But for certain passages in the Acts of the Apostles and in the Epistles, we should not have known that Jesus Christ intended to create a permanent institution. But though the simpler the ceremony is the more scriptural it is, yet are the ideas associated with it and suggested by it many and important. They are these—

I. The near presence of our Lord. Not in the elements but presiding over the company. It is a table at which he entertains his friends; and can he, the Divine Host, himself be absent?

"Around a table, not a tomb,
He willed our gathering-place should be;
When going to prepare our home,
The Saviour said, 'Remember me.'"

And at that table, meeting and communing with his friends, we may feel sure and can realize forcibly that our living Lord is, in spirit and in truth, "in the midst of us."

II. Christ our Strength and our Joy. The chosen elements are bread and wine, the sources of strength and of gladness. He, our Lord, is the one constant Source of our spiritual nourishment and strength, of the joy with which our hearts are for ever glad.

III. Christ our Propitiation. The *broken* bread, the *outpoured* wine—of what do these speak to our hearts? Of the "marred visage," of the weariness, of the poverty and privation, of the toilfulness and loneliness of that troubled life, of the griefs and pains of that burdened and broken heart, of the shame and the darkness and the death of the last closing scene. We stand with bowed head and reverent spirit at that cross and see—

"Sorrow and love flow mingled down."

And our hearts are full as we ask—

"Did e'er such love and sorrow meet;
Or thorns compose so rich a crown?"

And we realize that that sorrow was borne, that death died, *for us.* "This is my body, 'given for you;' my blood, 'shed for you.'" It is the Propitiation for *our* sins.

IV. Our individual appropriation of our Lord's great work. Each one eats of that bread and drinks of that cup. As he does so, in and by that act he declares his own personal need of a Divine Saviour; he affirms his conviction that the sacrifice was offered for him; he renews his faith in the Divine Redeemer; he recognizes the claim of him that loved him unto death; he rededicates himself to Jesus Christ and to his service; he rejoices, in spirit, in his reconciled Father, in his Divine Lord and Friend.

V. Happy and holy communion with one another. Gathered round one table, in the felt presence of our common Lord, *all* invited to drink of the same cup (Matt. xxvi. 27), we are drawn to one another in the bonds of Christian love. We realize our oneness in him as a strong bond which triumphs over all the separating influences of the world. Faith, joy, love, are kindled and "burn within us;" and we are strengthened and sanctified, built up, enabled to "abide in him."—C.

Vers. 21, 22.—*Jesus and Judas; our Lord and ourselves.* The ordinance of the

Lord's Supper was closely connected, not only in time but in apostolic thought, with the act of the betrayal (see 1 Cor. xi. 23)—the institution of the greatest privilege with the commission of the darkest crime. Our Lord's demeanour on this occasion is well worthy of our most reverent thought.

I. Jesus and Judas. 1. *His length of sufferance.* After knowing that Judas was seeking to betray him (ver. 6), Jesus might well have expelled him from his society. He might have done so, acting *judicially*, as being no longer worthy to be classed among his apostles. He might have done so, acting *prudentially*, as one (1) whom it was not wise to admit to his counsels and his plans; and as one (2) whose association with the eleven would be a source of evil. He might very appropriately have declined to acknowledge him as an officer and a friend. But Jesus did not press his right. On the contrary, he let him continue as one of the twelve, he let him come under the same roof with himself, he permitted him to share the Paschal feast: the hand of him that was betraying him was "with him on the table." To such a length as that his long-suffering went. 2. *His dignity in rebuke.* He did not break forth into passionate invective; he did not use words of natural and permissible vehemence; he quietly said, "Woe unto that man," etc.! Matthew tells us that he added, "It had been good for that man if he had not been born." What a transcendent calmness and serenity of spirit we have here! What a contrast between two children of men! One man preparing to betray his Teacher, his Friend, his Master; the other compassionating his betrayer for the depth of his fall and the sadness of his doom. Jesus went on to his sacrificial death and to his throne; Judas went out into the night (John xiii. 30)—into the dark night of guilt, of shame, of despair, of death.

II. Our Lord and ourselves. 1. The wrong against our Lord it is still open to us to commit. We cannot betray him *as* Judas did; yet may we do that which answers to, and is almost if not quite as deplorable as that sad and shameful act. Let us consider that: 1. We know more about Jesus than Judas then did; for we have all the light of his resurrection and of the teaching of his apostles. 2. He has granted to us mercies as many and as great in intrinsic value as those he bestowed on Judas. 3. Owing him as much as Judas did, we may do even greater injury to his cause than the traitor did. The act of Iscariot ultimately issued in the all-sufficient sacrifice; this did not extenuate or lessen his guiltiness by a simple grain; but it nullified the *mischief* of the crime. We may do incalculable and irreparable mischief to the cause of our Master by our unfaithfulness, our infidelity, our disobedience, our criminal negligence. 4. By such disloyalty we may wound and grieve his Spirit almost as severely as his betrayer did. Wherefore let us: (1) *Be humble-minded.* "Let him that thinketh he standeth," etc. If we could find the man who has smitten Christ and his cause the severest blow that was ever struck, it is probable that we might easily find an hour in that man's history when he would have shrunk with holy horror from such a guilty act. (2) *Be prayerful;* ever looking heavenward with the supplication, "Hold thou me up," etc. (3) *Be diligent* in the field of earnest Christian work. It is the idler in the vineyard whom the tempter will assail. It is the faithful workman who is in a position to say, after his Lord and Leader, "The prince of this world cometh, and hath nothing in me" (John xiv. 30).—C.

Vers. 24—27.—*Greatness after Christ.* Three things claim our attention.

I. Apostolic failure. When the apostles of our Lord came to look back on this most memorable evening, how pained and how ashamed they must have felt as they recollected this unseemly contest (ver. 24)! At the very hour when their Lord was manifesting his love and his forethought for his Church in two most striking and touching ways—at the very hour when his heart was torn with distracting sorrow by the desertion and treachery of one of his chosen band, and when he might well have been looking for some consolation in the attachment and the obedience of the others, they must needs show their unlikeness to himself and their unworthiness of their position by an untimely dispute about their own importance! In connection with that condescending service of their Lord's, how small such a controversy seems! And in connection with such a trial as that through which he was passing, how unbecoming and ill-timed was any anxiety about their own affairs! It was in their power to render to Jesus Christ a most helpful sympathy, and, instead of doing that, they grieved him by the exhibition of a contentious and an ambitious spirit. It was a sad failure on their part. How often do his disciples fail him now! How often do they let the opportunity of loving and effective service pass unused! When the hour strikes for faithfulness, or for courage, or for self-sacrifice, or for humility, or for energetic action, is there not found unfaithfulness, or timidity, or selfish time-serving, or pride, or a culpable inactivity, that loses everything and leaves behind nothing but failure and regret?

II. WORLDLY VANITY. (Ver. 25.) What a poor thing indeed is mere official dignity, or even arbitrary power, or servile flattery! *Official dignity* without moral worth is a miserably hollow thing. *Arbitrary power*, exercised in caprice and apart from a pure desire to do good and to enrich, is an evil thing; it is injurious to the possessor and it is burdensome to the objects of it. *Servile flattery* is a false thing. It is simply contemptible on the part of those who pay it; it is morally ruinous to those who accept it. Let the "Gentiles" act thus if they must; but "*ye* shall not be so." Ye who care to be true, to be loving, to be humble—ye shall not sit on *that* seat of honour, ye shall not run into that serious temptation, ye shall not pursue such a worthless prize. Other and better things are within your reach; for you there is—

III. CHRISTIAN GREATNESS. (Vers. 26, 27.) 1. Jesus Christ, the greatest One, was the Servant of all. He *came* to serve; it was his holy, heavenly errand; he came to seek and to save the lost. He *lived* to serve. That act of menial service in which he had just been engaged (John xiii. 1—5) was only a picture and illustration of the whole spirit and substance of his life; to bear the burden of others was the law of his life (Gal. vi. 2). He lived to heal, to help, to comfort, to enlighten, to redeem; his life from end to end was a loving ministry, a gracious and generous service (Mark x. 45). He *suffered* to serve. He *died* to serve. He had a perfect right to say, "I am among you as he that serveth." 2. We are nearest to our Lord as we live to serve; we rise towards the spiritual stature of Jesus Christ as we are filled with this his spirit and as we live this his life. There *is* a path for ambition to tread in the kingdom of Christ; but it is not the path that leads to high office and official dignity and popular applause: these things may come unsought, and be used for good. But the one road along which true Christian greatness travels is the way of self-forgetting service. To be touched and moved by the sorrows and the sins of our fellow-men; to be stirred to helpful, earnest, sacrificial effort on their behalf; to pity the poor and needy; to seek and to save the lost; to breathe the air and to do the work of an unpretentious but effective kindness, to have the right to say, "I am among you as he that serveth;"—*that* is greatness after Christ himself.—C.

Vers. 28—30.—*Fidelity and its reward.* The lesson of the text is the bountiful reward of faithfulness to Jesus Christ; but taking these words of his in connection with the position in which he well knew himself to be, they speak to us of—

I. THE MAJESTIC CONFIDENCE OF OUR LORD. "I appoint [bequeath] unto you a kingdom . . . that ye may sit on thrones." And who is this thus calmly disposing of kingdoms and thrones?—a reigning emperor, a brilliant conqueror? Only a poor, homeless, soldierless Prophet! One who knew that he was about to be taken, tried, convicted, scourged, crucified! Yet he meant it all. What majestic confidence in God, in the power of his gospel, in his own integrity! With what reverent homage shall we bow before him who could make such royal offers when the shadow of the cross already rested on his path! And what nobler sight is there to be seen among men than that of one (missionary, minister, teacher, reformer, etc.) calmly going on his way when every one and when everything is against him, confident in the triumph of the cause for which he pleads! Taking these words of Christ in connection with the preceding verses, we see—

II. THE QUICKNESS WITH WHICH HE PASSED FROM CORRECTION TO COMMENDATION. Seeing that his apostles were not only silenced, but humbled by the rebuke he had administered to them (vers. 24—26), and wishing to reassure and revive them, our Lord turned to the fidelity they had shown toward himself, and spoke words of praise and of promise. "You are wrong altogether in your spirit and behaviour in this matter; I blame you for this. But be not cast down; I do not forget your constancy toward me in all my times of trial, and I will reward you." Such was, such is, the gracious, considerate, generous Master.

"His anger is so slow to rise,
So ready to abate."

It is the flying shadow which the wind-driven cloud casts upon the field, chased by the hastening sunshine. "O slow to strike and swift to spare!" might well have been written of him. Can it be said or sung of us, in our relations with one another? But the main truth here is—

III. THE REWARD OF FIDELITY IN THE MASTER'S SERVICE. Our Lord wished to assure his disciples that he was by no means unmindful or unappreciative of their faithfulness; and he found the best proof of this in their constancy toward himself in his times of trouble. Through all poverty, all persecution, all desertion, all apparent failure, they had been true and loyal—they had shared his sorrows, had kept step with him through the dark shadows; they had ministered to his bodily necessities (John iv. 8), and (so far as they could) had sympathized with him in his spiritual conflicts. "Ye are they who have *continued with me* in my trials." And what a reward he was prepared to give them (vers. 29, 30)! Not understanding these words literally, we take it that their Lord held out before them: 1. *Fulness of joy.* "Eat and drink at my table." 2. *Signal honour.* "Sit on thrones." 3. *Large and abiding power* and influence. "I appoint unto you a kingdom." This promise has been already fulfilled, though in a different form from that which they then expected—in the exalted privilege of being the first to publish the gospel of his grace to mankind; in the glorious work of writing those memorials and letters which show no sign of age and are esteemed the one *absolutely invaluable* literature of the world; in the celestial joy, dignity, influence, which they have long inherited. (1) What are the best proofs of loyalty *we* can give? These are (*a*) showing tender sympathy and untiring helpfulness towards his people (see Matt. xxv. 40); (*b*) having continual regard to his will in all the duties and details of our life (see John xiv. 15, 21, 23); (*c*) being practically concerned for the progress of his kingdom. (2) What is the reward he will grant *us*? A goodly measure *of joy*,—of sacred joy in worship, fellowship, work, life; *of honour*,—the esteem which purity and love rarely, if ever, fail to win; *of quiet power*,—the holy and blessed influence which spiritual beauty and earnest testimony exert on heart and life, which they transmit from generation to generation. This reward *here*; and hereafter joy, honour, power, such as we must wait to see and must resolve to experience.—C.

Vers. 31, 32 (first part).—*The worth of man.* These verses afford incidental but valuable evidence of the surpassing worth of the human spirit, and should help us to feel of how much greater account are we ourselves than anything that merely belongs to us. This is brought out by—

I. THE DESIGNS THAT ARE LAID AGAINST US. It was evidently in a very solemn and earnest strain that Jesus said, "Satan desired to have you [plural], that he may sift," etc. The evil one longed with eagerness, and strove with strength, to pass the apostles of Christ through the sieve of temptation, that he might compass their overthrow. And Peter, at a later hour, tells us that that is his attitude and habit in regard to all Christian disciples (1 Pet. v. 8). We may take it that: 1. All the unholy intelligences of the spiritual realm are bent on securing our overthrow. 2. In this malign intention they are supported by human agents. And this, not only because evil naturally propagates evil, and because the wicked feel stronger and more secure as they are more numerous, but because they recognize the value of one human spirit and the advantage secured by gaining it to their side. Hence there is a deliberate and determined design often made upon the individual man by the forces of evil. This is a fact by no means to be overlooked. As we go on our heavenward way there may be an ambush laid for us at any point; at any time strong spiritual foes may do their utmost to contrive our fall. The possibilities of evil and of ruin are manifold. We may fall by error and unbelief, by pride, by selfishness, by worldliness and vanity, by intemperance or impurity, by departure in spirit from the fear and love of God. There is room, there is reason, for vigilance on the part of him who believes himself well on the way toward or even nearing the gates of the celestial city.

II. THE SOLICITUDE OF OUR SAVIOUR ON OUR BEHALF. "I have prayed for thee." The strain of our Lord's address, "Simon, Simon," and the fact of his interceding on Peter's behalf, speak of a tender solicitude on his part for his disciple. Jesus knew well all Peter's infirmities; but he also knew how ardently he could love, how devotedly he could serve, *how much he could be.* Hence the intensity of his desire that he would not be overcome. And for this reason we may be sure that our Lord is regarding us all with a Divine interest. He knows the worth of any and every human spirit—how much it can know and can enjoy; whom and what it can love; what graces it can illustrate, and what truth adorn; what influence it can instil; what good, and even great, work it can accomplish for God and man. He knows also what sorrow it may bring upon itself, what shame, what ruin; and also what irreparable injury it may do. We need not hesitate, but should accustom ourselves to think that Jesus Christ is regarding us with a very tender interest; is following the choices we are making and the course we are pursuing with holy and loving solicitude; is grieved when he sees us wander from the way of wisdom, rejoices in us and over us when he sees us take the upward path.

III. THE REALITY OF OUR HUMAN RESPONSIBILITY. Jesus Christ prayed that Peter's faith might not fail. And it did not—we should naturally expect. But in part *it did.* It did not utterly break down as that of Judas did, but it failed to keep him loyal in a very trying hour. It did not save him from the act of denial and from the sorrow which succeeded the sin. It did not in any way relieve the apostle of his individual responsibility. He continued to "bear his own burden," as every man must. Not the very highest privilege, not even the intercession of the Lord himself, will relieve us of that. It must rest with us, in the last resort, whether we will strive and win, or whether we will yield and be lost.—C.

Ver. 32 (latter part).—*The privilege of spiritual maturity.* "When thou art converted, strengthen thy brethren." This forward-looking injunction of Christ reminds us of—

I. OUR NEED OF STRENGTHENING POWER. Such are the manifold and effective forces opposed to us, invisible as well as visible and human (see Eph. vi. 12); so strong and so subtle are the temptations that beset us on every side; that we urgently need, not only the presence of resisting principles within us, but the aid of friendly and helpful auxiliaries around us. We want, indeed, the help which is from above; *that* is the first thing to seek. And, having besought that, we do well to avail ourselves of all the strength we can gain from other sources. For the battle is severe, and we are often hard pressed by our vigilant and relentless foes.

II. THE HELP WE CAN FIND IN MAN. God is, as stated, *the* Source of spiritual strength. He renews our strength by the direct communications of his Divine Spirit. But man helps us also. "*A man* shall be as an hiding-place . . . as rivers of water . . . as the shadow of a great rock." Paul went through the region of Galatia, "strengthening the disciples" (Acts xviii. 23). Peter was to "strengthen his brethren." We can and we should do much to strengthen one another, to build one another up on our holy faith. We can do this: 1. By the force of a beautiful and attractive example. 2. By the utterance of invigorating truth. 3. By the inspiration of a cheerful, hopeful, loving spirit.

III. THE INCOMPETENCE OF INEXPERIENCE. Peter was not in a position to afford spiritual strength then. He was too inexperienced. He had not yet learned what the fierceness of the fire of temptation meant. He did not then understand where his true strength lay. He had not yet graduated in the school of experience. It is they, and only they, who know what spiritual struggle means who can impart to others the help they need. We must have passed through the waters before we can undertake to teach others how to swim the strong stream of trial and temptation.

IV. THE UNFITNESS OF UNFAITHFULNESS. Peter was about to fall. A few hours would find him in the power of the adversary. Before another day dawned he would have to reproach himself as a disloyal disciple. He was about to rest under the shadow of great guilt, and he would have to wait until he came forth from that shadow. Not until he "was converted," not until the spirit of overweening self-confidence had given place to that of humble trust in God, not until the knowledge of Christ "after the flesh" had passed, had risen into a knowledge of him that was truly spiritual and real, —not till then would he be fitted to "strengthen his brethren." His case was strikingly parallel with that of David (see Ps. li. 11—13). We have similar experiences now. When the Christian disciple loses ground spiritually and morally, it becomes him to "return unto the Lord" himself, and "*then* to teach transgressors" the way of God; it becomes him to undergo a change of spirit, to be "renewed in the spirit of his mind," and then to speak the helpful and sustaining truth of Christ. Unfaithfulness to our Lord, departure and distance from him,—this has no teaching function; its first duty is penitential; then it may think of useful work. But we should understand that all true usefulness rests on the foundation of spiritual integrity; it can find no other footing.

V. THE PRIVILEGE OF CHRISTIAN MATURITY. Peter was to look forward to a not distant future, when, having learnt truth by what he suffered, he should strengthen his brethren in all that was true and wise and good. This he did, and in this he found a noble heritage. To this we may look forward as the reward of spiritual struggle, as the goal of earthly good. What better portion can we ask for than to be the source of spiritual strength to our brethren and sisters as they bear the burdens and fight the battles of their life?—C.

Vers. 33, 34 (with 55—62).—*The apostle's fall.* From this most memorable incident, recorded with noticeable candour by all the evangelists, many lessons spring.

I. HOW IGNORANT OF HIMSELF EVEN A GOOD MAN MAY PROVE! (Ver. 33.) Peter believed himself to be capable of daring and enduring the very last extremity in the cause of his Master. He would have utterly ridiculed the idea that the sneer of a servant-girl could draw from him a denial of his Lord. The event showed how entirely he mistook himself. We ought to know ourselves well; but, in fact, we do not. We suppose ourselves to be strong and steadfast, when we are feeble and unreliable; or to be humble-minded, when we are proud of heart; or to be generous, when we are essentially self-seeking; or to be devout, when we are really unspiritual; to be near to God, when we are afar off (Rev. iii. 17; 1 Cor. x. 12; Ps. xix. 12, 13; cxxxix. 23, 24).

II. HOW PERFECT THE KNOWLEDGE OUR MASTER HAS OF OUR HEART AND LIFE! (Ver. 34.) Jesus knew how weak his disciple was, and he foresaw his speedy failure. He knows us altogether. He knows *our heart;* how sincere is our purpose, how frequent are our efforts, how many our disappointments, how faulty is our nature, how wounded and weak is our spirit. He knows also *our life.* He sees it as it lies before his all-beholding eye; he "knows the way we take," the path we are about to pursue. It is to One who has a thorough and complete knowledge of us that we belong, and it is to him we draw nigh in our best hours.

III. FROM WHAT A HEIGHT A GOOD MAN MAY FALL! This erring one is no other than the Apostle Peter, the very man who had made the great confession, and upon whom or upon whose testimony Christ would build his Church (Matt. xvi. 13—19). It is he who had been admitted to such close fellowship with Christ, and been allowed the high privilege of rendering him constant personal service. There is no office, however high it may be in the Christian Church, which will ensure to its occupant spiritual integrity. And even he who has been "raised up to heavenly places," and has known even the raptures of an exalted spiritual experience, may fall under the power of temptation. It is not the lofty but the lowly that stand on safe ground in the kingdom of God.

IV. HOW STEEP IS THE DESCENT OF SIN! From a presumptuous and blind self-confidence Peter fell to a half-hearted following (ver. 54); from that he fell to untruthfulness and denial of his Lord (ver. 57); from that to a more deliberate and repeated denial (vers. 58, 59), accompanied even (as Matthew tells us) with profanity. Sin is a slope which seems slight at the summit, but it becomes steeper and yet steeper as we go on our downward way. And it too often happens that we reach a point where we cannot arrest ourselves, but are compelled against our own desire to continue. Shun the first step in the downward course!

V. HOW MERCIFUL IS CHRIST'S METHOD OF CONVICTION! (Ver. 61.) Not a blow that smote him to the ground; not even burning words of condemnation that should sound ever afterwards in his soul; but one reproachful glance—the look of wounded love. So merciful and so pitiful is our Lord when we are unfaithful or disloyal to him now. He

bears long with us; he seeks to win us back through added privilege and multiplied mercy; he deals very patiently and gently with us; only when other and milder methods fail does he mercifully afflict us, that in some way and by some means he may redeem us from folly and from ruin.

VI. WHITHER CHRIST SEEKS TO LEAD THE ERRING. (Ver. 62.) He seeks to lead us, as by his reproving glance he led his fallen disciple, to a pure and saving penitence. He would have our hearts filled with a worthy and a cleansing shame, with a purifying sorrow; that this may lead us into a condition of (1) abiding humility, of (2) living faith, of (3) thorough reconsecration to himself and to his cause.—C.

Vers. 35—38.—*Misunderstanding Christ.* There is no teacher who has been so well heard, and none that has been so much honoured and obeyed, as Jesus Christ. Yet there can have been few who have been so much misunderstood as he has been. We have our attention drawn by the text to—

I. CONTEMPORARY MISUNDERSTANDING. 1. *By the apostles themselves.* (1) On this occasion their Lord wished to intimate to them, in strong and forcible language, that to whatever perils and straits they had been exposed before, the time was now at hand when, he himself being taken from their side and the saddest foreshadowings being fulfilled, they would be subjected to far severer trials, and would be (in a sense) cast on their own defences. The apostles, mistaking his meaning, put a literal interpretation on his words, and produced a couple of swords, as perhaps meeting the emergency! (2) On a previous occasion (Matt. xvi. 5—8) the Lord warned them against "the leaven of the Pharisees;" and they supposed him to refer to their neglect in forgetting the bread! (3) They completely failed to apprehend his meaning when he foretold his own sufferings and death (ch. xviii. 31—34). 2. *By his disciples generally.* (1) They could not comprehend what he meant by "eating his flesh and drinking his blood (John vi. 60). (2) They completely misunderstood the end he had in view, the character of that "kingdom of heaven" of which he spoke so much. (3) They did not enter into the great redeeming purpose for which he came. 3. *By his enemies.* (1) In so small a matter as his saying recorded in John ii. 19; (2) in so great a matter as that recorded in John xviii. 37.

II. SUBSEQUENT MISUNDERSTANDING. In how many ways has the Church of Christ, since apostolic days, misunderstood its Lord! It has done so in regard to the meaning of particular words; and in regard to the great end he had in view (the nature of his kingdom); and in regard to the means and methods he would have his friends employ. How pitifully and how painfully has it misunderstood him when it has interpreted his reference to the sword of the text (ver. 36), and his use of the word "*compel*" (ch. xiv. 23) as justifying every conceivable cruelty in the furtherance of his cause!

III. MODERN MISUNDERSTANDING. Judging from what we know has been, we conclude that it is likely enough that we also misunderstand our Master. 1. We may fail to reach the true significance of his words; we may find out, further on, that they have another and a larger meaning than that we have been ascribing to them. 2. We may mistake his will as to the object we should work for, or as to the right and the wise methods we should adopt to secure our end. 3. We may be wrong in our judgment of what Christ is doing with ourselves and with our life; we may misread his Divine purpose concerning us. There are three principles which we shall do well to keep in mind in our endeavour to understand the Divine Teacher. The thought of Christ is (1) profound rather than superficial; (2) spiritual rather than sensuous; (3) comprehensive and far-seeing (reaching through time to immortality) rather than narrow and time-bounded.—C.

Vers. 39—45.—*Gethsemane.* As we enter "the place which is called Gethsemane," we pass into the "holy place," the nearest of all to "the holy of holies"—that is, to Calvary itself. Thither our Lord went on this most memorable evening; and "his disciples followed him"—the eleven who remained faithful to him. But even of these only three were counted worthy to attend him into the secret place of prayer and struggle, and to witness his agony. Such sorrow as he was then to know seeks the secret place and chooses only the very closest and dearest friendship for its ministry. Then fell upon our Divine Lord a sorrow and a temptation; an agitation and agony of soul for which our language has no name, our heart no room, our life no experience. We ask—What *was* that intolerable and overwhelming anguish, which the Saviour asked might pass from him, and which had so marvellous and so terribly significant an effect on his bodily nature (vers. 42—44)? Our completest answer leaves much to be said, much to be explained. 1. We barely touch the outer line of the whole circle of truth when we speak of the *apprehension of coming torture and death* as events in the natural, physical sphere. It is an irreverent and wholly unworthy conception that what many men—many who have not even been good men—have faced without flinching, our Lord and Master shrank from with an overmastering dread. 2. We come nearer to the centre of the truth when we think that the *whole shadow of the cross*, with its spiritual darkness and desolation, then began to rest upon him. Something of that shadow had been darkening his path before (Mark x. 38; ch. xii. 50; John xii. 27). And this shadow darkened and deepened as he drew near to the dread hour itself. At this point the cross immediately confronted him in all its awful severity, and he knew that this was the time when he must finally resolve to endure everything or to retrace his steps. This, then, was the critical hour; then was "the crisis of the world." Great and terrible was the temptation to decline the fearful future now at hand; it was a temptation he struggled against with a spiritual violence that showed itself in the drops of blood; it was a temptation he only overcame by tearful supplications to the Eternal Father for his prevailing succour (Heb. v. 7). 3. But we miss our true mark if we do not include the thought that he was then bearing *something of the burden of human sin*. Whatever was intended by "bearing our sins in his own body," by "making his soul an offering for sin," and by expressions similar to these, we believe that Jesus Christ was then in the very act of fulfilling these predictions when he thus strove and suffered in the garden. As we look upon him there we see "the Lamb of God taking away the sin of the world." The scene may teach us very varied lessons and affect us in many ways; but it is certainly well fitted to be—

I. AN ATTRACTION TO SOULS STILL DISTANT FROM THE SAVIOUR. It says, "Behold how he loved you!"

II. AN INVITATION TO PRAYER FOR FAITHFULNESS IN THE HOUR OF TRIAL. Both before and after, the Master exhorted his disciples to pray that "they entered not into temptation" (vers. 40, 46). He himself triumphed through the strong efficacy of prayer (ver. 41). Prayer, appropriate at all times, is urgently needed as we enter the shadow of temptation; but it is positively indispensable when the greater trials of our life assail us.

III. A SUMMONS TO STRENUOUS AND UNFALTERING PERSEVERANCE. Christian pilgrim, Christian workman, do you weary of your way or of your work? Does the one seem long and thorny, or the other tedious and unsuccessful? Do you think you must sleep as the disciples did, or that you must put down the cup as their Master did not? Do you talk about giving up the journey, about retiring from the field? Consider him who went quite through the work the Father gave him to do, who strove and suffered to the very last; consider him, the agonizing but undaunted, the suffering but resolving Saviour; consider him, lest ye be wearied and faint in your minds.

"Go, labour on, spend and be spent,
  Thy joy to do the Father's will;
It is the way the Master went,
  Should not the servant tread it still?"

Ver. 42 (latter part).—*Self-surrender*. "Not my will, but thine, be done." These words are suggestive as well as expressive. They suggest to us—

I. THE ESSENTIAL NATURE OF SIN. Where shall we find the root of sin? Its manifold fruits we see around us in all forms of irreligion, of vice, of violence. But in what shall we find its root? In *the preference of our own will to the will of God*. If we trace human wrong-doing and wrong-being to its ultimate point, we arrive at that conclusion. It is because men are not willing to be what God created them to be, not willing to do what he desires them to do; it is because they want to pursue those lines of thought and of action which he has forbidden, and to find their pleasure and their portion in things which he has disallowed,—that they err from the strait path and begin the course which ends in condemnation and in death. The essence of all sin is in this assertion of our will against the will of God. We fail to recognize the foundation truth that we are his; that by every sacred tie that can bind one being to another we are bound, and we belong to him from whom we came and in whom we live, and move, and have our being. We assume to be the masters of our own lives and fortunes, the directors of our own selves, of our own will; we say, "My will, not thine, be done." Thus are we radically wrong; and being radically wrong, the issues of our hearts are evil. From this fountain of error and of evil the streams of sin are flowing; to that we trace their origin.

II. THE HOUR AND ACT OF SPIRITUAL SURRENDER. When does the human spirit return to God, and by what act? That hour and that act, we reply, are not found at the time of any *intellectual apprehension* of the truth. A man may understand but little of Christian doctrine, and yet may be within the kingdom of heaven; or, on the other hand, he may know much, and yet remain outside that kingdom. Nor at the time of *keen sensibility;* for it is possible to be moved to deep and to fervent feeling, and yet to withhold the heart and life from the Supreme. Nor at the time of *association with the visible Church of Christ.* It is the hour at which and the act by which the soul *cordially surrenders itself* to God. When, in recognition of the paramount claims of God the Divine Father, the gracious Saviour of mankind, we yield ourselves to God, that for all the future he may lead and guide us, may employ us in his holy service; when we have it in our heart to say, "Henceforth thy will, not ours, be done;"—then do we return unto the Lord our God, and then does he count us among the number of his own.

III. THE HIGHEST ATTAINMENT OF CHRISTIAN ENDEAVOUR. When do we reach our highest point? Not when we have fought our fiercest battle, or have done our most fruitful work, or have gained our clearest and brightest vision of Divine truth; but when we have reached the point in which we can most *cheerfully* and most *habitually* say, after Christ our Lord, "Not my will, but thine, be done;" when under serious discouragement or even sad defeat, when after exhausting pain or before terrible suffering, when under heavy loss or in long-continued loneliness, or in prospect of early death, we are perfectly willing that God should do with us as his own wisdom and love direct.—C.

Vers. 47—52, 63.—*Christianity and violence.* The use of the sword by Peter, and the presence of "swords and staves" in the hands of the officers, suggest to us the connection between Jesus Christ (and his disciples) and the employment of violence; and this both by them and against them.

I. THE UNSEEMLINESS OF VIOLENCE USED AGAINST JESUS CHRIST AND HIS DISCIPLES. It is true that there was something worse than the weapons of violence in that garden; the traitor's kiss was very much worse. We may be sure that Jesus was conscious of a far keener wound from those false lips of Judas than he would have been from the hands of those armed men had they struck him with their strength. The subtle schemes and the soft but treacherous suggestions of false friends are deadlier in their issue, if not in their aim, than the hard blows of open adversaries. But: 1. How unseemly was open violence shown *to Jesus Christ!* To come with sword and stick against the Gentle One from heaven; against him who never used his omnipotence to harm a single adversary; against him who "would not break the bruised reed" among the children of men; against him who had been daily employing his power to relieve from pain, to raise from weakness, to remove privation, to restore from death! 2. How unseemly is such violence shown to *Christ's true disciples!* His true disciples, those who are loyal and obedient to their Lord, are men and women in whom a patient and loving spirit is prevailing; they are peace-makers among their brothers and sisters; they have "put away bitterness, wrath, anger, clamour, railing;" they walk in love: they seek to win by a gentle manifestation and by a gracious utterance of the truth. How entirely inappropriate and unseemly is violence shown to them! And it may be added, how *useless* is such violence employed against the cause they advocate! It has never happened yet that sword and stave have crushed the living truth. They have smitten its champions to the ground, but they have only brought out into the light the heroic courage and noble unselfishness which that truth inspires. "So that those things [those persecutions] have fallen out rather unto the furtherance of the gospel." Cruelty strikes at its enemy, and smites itself.

II. THE UNLAWFULNESS OF VIOLENCE EMPLOYED ON BEHALF OF CHRISTIANITY. How vain and how foolish the act of "smiting with the sword" (ver. 49)! It was an act of intemperate and ill-considered zeal; it was calculated to do much more harm than good. Its effects had to be undone by the calm interposition and the healing power of Christ (ver. 51). It was rebuked by the Master in decided terms (Matt. xxvi. 52). And from that hour to the end of apostolic history the use of physical violence disappears. Well would it have been for the cause and kingdom of our Lord if it had never been revived. The sword and the stave have no place in the Christian armoury. The weapons of its warfare are not carnal. Such instruments do not, they cannot, serve it; they gain a momentary victory at the sad and great expense of entirely misrepresenting the spirit and the method of Jesus Christ. Compulsion is utterly out of place in connection with the Church of Christ; it loses immeasurably more than it gains by that resource. Let the disciples of Christ be assured that (1) the utterance of Divine truth, especially the truth that relates to the redeeming love of the Saviour himself; (2) living a life of blamelessness and beauty, of integrity and kindness; (3) dependence on the aid of the Divine Spirit to make the spoken Word and the living influence effectual and mighty;—that these are the weapons which will conquer the enemies of Christ, and will place him upon the throne of the world.—C.

Ver. 53.—*The power of spiritual darkness.* As our Lord, declining to avail himself of the physical forces at his command, surrendered himself to the will of his assailants, he used an expression which was full of spiritual significance. "This is your hour," he said, "and the power of darkness." By this he intimated (1) that the hour of his enemies' triumph had arrived—the brief hour of their outward success and inward exultation, the dark hour of his humiliation and visible defeat; and (2) that this passing hour was simultaneous with the prevalence of the power of darkness. Wicked men were to triumph because the forces of guilty error were for the time prevailing. We look at—

I. THE POWER OF DARKNESS. 1. *Its spiritual nature.* It is a state of spiritual blindness. We may not, with a great Greek philosopher, resolve all evil into error; but we may say that sin is continually, is universally, springing from inward blindness. Men do not see the truth; they call good evil, and evil good; they have the most false imaginations concerning all objects, from the Divine Being himself to the lowliest human duty; and hence they go far astray. 2. *Its most glaring manifestations.* It lays its unholy hand on innocence, on Divine Love itself, and leads it away to trial and crucifixion. It conducts the devoted servant of Christ to the brutal judge, to the shameful scaffold, to the devouring flame. It arms a vast multitude of men and leads them forth to a vain and useless strife, shedding human blood and wasting human labour, as if Christ would be pleased or could be served by such means as these. It covers with the sacred name of religion a system that holds millions of human beings in a degrading bondage. It sanctions all the sinful institutions the world has seen and suffered from. 3. *Its most deplorable effects.* These are not found in the deeds and the sufferings of men, but rather in their souls; the worst issue of spiritual misconception is in the utter darkness of spirit in which it ends. "If the light that is in us be darkness, how great must that darkness be!" It means: (1) *False thoughts.* Here were men who should have known better thinking the worst things of Jesus Christ—judging him to be a criminal, to be a traitor, to be a blasphemer; and there are men amongst us who, under the power of error, think altogether wrong thoughts of God and of the Saviour—thoughts which do him wrong, which misrepresent him to the mind, which repel rather than attract the soul. (2) *Bad feelings.* Here were men indulging in feelings of positive and perfect hatred against Jesus Christ; and there are men, misled by the power of darkness, hating instead of loving the Father of spirits, repelled from instead of being drawn towards good and true souls whom they have grievously misunderstood. (3) *Wrong purposes of heart.* Under this malignant influence men are purposing to injure their fellow-men. Instead of resolving to rescue, to raise, to ennoble them, they determine to put them down or to hold them down, to lay a hard hand upon them and keep them harmless because helpless. It is in the blinding, misleading, deteriorating effects upon the soul itself that the very worst results of darkness are to be seen.

II. OUR HOPE CONCERNING IT. The "power of darkness" was coincident with "the hour" of the enemies of our Lord. And that was *but an hour*; it was limited to the brief period of the Passion. Then came Christ's glorious hour—the hour of his resurrection; the hour of his ascent to the right hand of Power. The prevalence of this evil power of darkness is limited in time; it will not last for ever. Innocence, purity, truth, love, righteousness, may be led away to trial and death, as they were then in the Person of Jesus Christ; but the hour of their resurrection and their triumph will arrive. Let *faithful labour* do its noble part, and let calm and Christian *patience* bring its priceless contribution, and another hour will strike than that of the foes of Christ, and another power than that of moral darkness will take the sceptre and rule the world.—C.

Ver. 54.—*Distant discipleship.* "Peter followed afar off." 1. In this we find something that was *commendable.* The impulsive and energetic Peter did not exhaust his zeal in that unfortunate sword-stroke of his; nor was it quenched by the rebuke of his Master. Though it was far from an ideal discipleship to "follow afar off," it *was* discipleship still. We do not read that the others did as much as that; they probably sought their own safety by complete retirement. Peter could not do that; his attachment to Christ did not allow him to disconnect himself any further than was involved in a *distant* following. But: 2. In this we find something that was incomplete. The disciple desired to be near enough to his Master to know what the end would be, but he wished to be far enough off to be secure from molestation. He took counsel of his fears, and was so far from the scene that he was showing no sympathy with his Friend, and was running no risk from his enemies. It is not at all unlikely that this timidity, from which he succeeded in partially and momentarily shaking himself, was the beginning and the explanation of his subsequent failure.

I. GENUINE DISCIPLESHIP. This is found in *following Christ.* 1. Owning his claim as Lord and Leader of the soul; owning it by a willing and entire submission of our will to his will, a consecration of our life to his service, a perfect readiness of heart to say, "Lord, I will follow thee." 2. Endeavouring to walk even as he walked—in *reverence*, in *righteousness*, in *love.* 3. Striving to live this Christian life not only *after* him, but *unto* him.

II. DISTANT DISCIPLESHIP. We follow "afar off" when we are: 1. *Lacking in devotion.* He who is only found irregularly and infrequently with God, in the attitude of praise and prayer, and in the act of studying his holy will, must be at a great distance from that "beloved Son" who spent so much time with his Father, and found so much strength in his conscious presence and loving sympathy. 2. *Wanting in purity.* He whose spirit is much entangled with the cares, absorbed in the pursuits and prizes, hungering and thirsting for the pleasures of this world, and certainly he whose soul is to any considerable degree affected and tainted by the lower temptations of the flesh,—is a long way behind the holy Saviour; is far off from him who was "holy, harmless, undefiled, separate from sin," from him "in whose mouth *no* guile was found." 3. *Failing in generous and practical kindness.* He who is only sparingly offering his resources, spiritual or material, to the cause of human comfort and elevation, who is drawing the line of his service at the point of self-sacrifice, and declines to go across it,—is surely a very distant follower of that gracious and generous Friend of man who suffered the very last and the very worst that he might redeem us from sin and restore us to truth, to holiness, to God. This distant discipleship is, in every aspect, to be deplored. (1) It is *unfaithfulness to ourselves.* A departure from the position we took when we first "yielded ourselves unto God, as those alive from the dead." (2) It is *perilous to our own souls. That* way failure lies; and failure here means utter and disastrous defeat; it means suffering and shame; it may even mean death. (3) It is *disappointing to our Divine Lord.* He looks for a close following on our part; he wants us to be at his side, to be serving him with all our strength, to be like him in spirit and in character and in life. And when he sees us "afar off," he is grieved with us instead of rejoicing in us. (1) Let those who have been abiding in him, and therefore following him closely, be watchful and prayerful that they do not "drift away" and lag behind; (2) and let those who have to reproach themselves as distant disciples draw near to their Lord in renewed penitence and devotedness of spirit.—C.

Ver. 61.—*The look of our Lord.* "And the Lord turned, and looked upon Peter." What was there then, and what is there now, in the glance of Jesus Christ?

I. HIS LOOK OF PENETRATION. We read of one of the earliest disciples being convinced by our Lord's discernment of him under the thick foliage of the fig tree; he was then told to look for greater things than that (John i. 50). And surely one of those greater things was found in that penetration which saw through the thicker covering of the human flesh and of human speech and demeanour to the very thought of the mind, to the very desire of the heart, to the inmost secrets of the soul. He knew what was *in man.* It was his knowledge of men that directed him in his varying treatment of them; it *is* his penetrating insight into men now that determines his dealing with us all.

II. HIS LOOK OF COMPASSION. What did the sick and the suffering, the fevered and the paralyzed and the leprous, the men and women who had left afflicted ones behind them at their homes—what depths of tender compassion did these sons and daughters of Israel see in the eyes of Jesus Christ? And what inexhaustible fulness of pity, what unbounded sympathy, may not the stricken and the sorrowing souls who are badly bruised and wounded on life's highway still find in "the face of Jesus Christ"!

III. HIS LOOK OF SAD REPROACH. Sometimes there was that in the glance of Jesus Christ from which the guilty shrank. When "he looked round about on them with anger," we may be sure that his baffled enemies quailed before his glance. And when "the Lord turned, and looked upon Peter," what keen sorrowful reproach was then apparent in the face of Jesus Christ! how that look gathered up all possible words and tones of solemn expostulation, of sad disappointment, of bitter sorrow! It was a look which wrought great things in the apostle's soul, the remembrance of which, we may be sure, he carried with him to the end. Christ has all too many occasions now to turn toward us that reproachful glance. 1. When we fail to keep the promises we made him at the time of our self-surrender. 2. When we fail to pay the vows we made him in some hour of discipline. 3. When we fall seriously short of the allegiance which all his disciples owe to him—in reverence, in obedience, in submission. Let us, who are professing to follow him, ask ourselves what we should see in his countenance if we stood face to face with him to-day. Would it be the benign look of Divine commendation? or would it be the pained look of sorrowful reproach? To those who are inquiring their way to life it is a source of blessed encouragement that they will see, if they regard their Lord—

IV. HIS LOOK OF TENDER INTEREST. When the rich young man came and made his earnest inquiry of the great Teacher, he was not yet in the kingdom, and was not yet fully prepared to enter it; but he was a sincere and earnest seeker after God, and "Jesus, beholding him, loved him" (Mark x. 21). With such tender regard, with such loving interest, does he look down on every true suppliant who looks up to him with the vital question on his lips, "Good Master, what shall I do that I may inherit eternal life?"—C.

Vers. 63, 64.—*The patience of Christ.* In these touching words, which we cannot read without a sentiment of shame as members of the human race, we have—

I. A PICTURE OF SUPREME ENDURANCE. How much our Lord was called upon to endure, we shall be best able to realize when we consider: 1. The greatness of which he was conscious (see ver. 70). He knew and felt that he had a right to the most reverent homage of the best and highest, and was thus treated by the worst and lowest. 2. The power which he knew he wielded: with what perfect ease could he have extricated himself from these cruel insults! 3. The character of the men who were maltreating him—the lowest amongst the low. 4. The nature of the indignities to which they subjected him; these went from bad to worse—from binding him to beating him, from beating him to spitting upon him, from this most shameful indignity to the yet more cruel sneer at his holy mission, "Prophesy unto us," etc. They vented upon him the very last extremes of human contumely and shame.

II. A PICTURE OF SUBLIME PATIENCE. He bore it all with perfect calmness. Here shone forth in its full lustre "the meekness of Jesus Christ." "When he was reviled, he reviled not again; when he suffered, he threatened not;" "As a sheep before her shearers," etc. And wherein shall we find the source and explanation of this sublime patience? 1. He was bent on bearing, to the full and to the end, his Father's will. 2. He was determined to complete the work he had undertaken, and of that work those sufferings were a part. He was then "wounded for our trangressions," then was he "bruised for our iniquities," and by *those* "stripes were we healed."

APPLICATION. 1. Like our Divine Master, *we are called upon to endure.* In doing those things we believe to be right of which others do not feel the obligation, also in abstaining from those things we feel to be wrong, which other people allow, we come into conflict, we excite displeasure, we incur odium, we suffer censure, opposition, ridicule; we "bear his reproach." Thorough loyalty to our Lord and to our own convictions means exposure to the assaults and indignities of the world. 2. We have *the highest incentives to endure.* (1) As with our Master, it is *the Father's will* that we should suffer. (2) As with Christ, it is an important part of the testimony we are to bear and the work we are to do in this world. (3) Only thus can we completely follow our great Leader; he who does not go with Christ into the valley of humiliation does not follow him all the way he trod. (4) So doing, we are building up a strong Christian character, and are thus preparing for fuller and higher service. (5) Then are we especially pleasing our Master, and "great is our reward in heaven" (Matt. v. 10—12).—C.

Vers. 1—23.—*The last Passover of our Lord.* After the significant survey of Jerusalem's fate which is given in the previous chapter, Jesus seems to have remained quietly at Bethany, or in the Mount of Olives, until the time for the Passover. The season of solitude was brief, but all the more important in consequence. Every moment was utilized by our Lord that he might be ready for his great ordeal. But if he was making preparations, so were his enemies. Accordingly, we have an account here of the treason which led up to his sacrifice. We have, consequently, to consider—

I. THE TREASON OF JUDAS. (Vers. 1—6.) The Sanhedrin was in session, anxious to seize on Jesus and get him removed; for they feared that an attached populace would declare for him rather than for the old leaders. It was a vain fear. The people were fickle, and as ready to cry out for his crucifixion as they had been to cry "Hosanna!" Yet the fear of losing popularity goaded the Church leaders to desperation. Being beaten in debate by the Master-Mind who tabernacled among them, they can only expect by treachery to secure their purpose. They find their ready instrument in Judas. And here consider: 1. *The worldliness of Judas.* He had evidently joined the cause of Jesus in hope of a place in a world-kingdom. But our Lord's prophecies of his speedy suffering and death have blighted all these hopes. How can he best make his peace with the world, which is getting the upper hand, and before which Jesus is going down? Judas believes that he can best do this by betraying Jesus to his enemies, and, to make the transition the easier for himself, he consents to do the shameful work for thirty pieces of silver—the mean price of the life of a slave! It was not covetousness pure and simple which led Judas to such a bargain, but astute worldliness. He was making his peace with the world on the most liberal terms. 2. Notice *the Satanic inspiration under which Judas acted.* It is evident that Scripture represents the sphere of evil as under the domination of a great personality called Satan. He can enter into men and take possession of them. But we are not to suppose that he has the same intimate access to the human spirit which God the Holy Ghost enjoys. We have reason to believe that Satan moves men by presenting in all their attractiveness the worldly motives such as we have noticed. Further, the Satanic impulse is such as in no way to relieve the subject of it from responsibility. No one will be able to plead "not guilty" on the ground of Satanic temptation. 3. Notice *the mean prudence under which the traitor acted.* Had the band come in open day, when the entranced populace hung upon the lips of Jesus, there would have been a dangerous *émeute*, and life been lost. Accordingly, Judas seeks to betray Jesus "in the absence of the multitude." There is a meanness and cowardice about most of the diabolic wickedness which goes on in the world; a cowardice, moreover, which is generally overtaken by just and terrible retribution.

II. PREPARATIONS FOR THE LAST PASSOVER. (Vers. 7—13.) Jesus meanwhile directs the two disciples, Peter and John, to make ready the Passover. He so times the celebration as to have it over on the Thursday night of the Passover week, and without haste, to secure the further preparation which his spirit required. And here we have the facts set before us (1) that he owed accommodation to the consideration of a stranger; and (2) that his supernatural knowledge guided the disciples in their quest of a guest-chamber. There, then, in the guest-chamber of a stranger, without taking the lamb to the temple, but in the primitive fashion, the two faithful men made ready for their Master. It was a recurrence to the primitive ritual.

III. THE PASSOVER FEAST. (Vers. 14—18.) With the twelve accordingly he comes at the appointed hour, and sits down to the significant feast. He tells them with what desire he had contemplated this last Passover before he should suffer. He will not again eat of it till it is fulfilled in the kingdom of God. The order of celebration was first the passing round of the wine-cup; next, the bitter herbs, dipped, as salad would be, in a red sauce made of almonds, nuts, figs, and other fruits; next, another wine-cup, after which the father of the family explained the nature of the rite; then came the morsel of unleavened bread and the piece of the roast lamb, made palatable by the aforesaid sauce; the last act was the passing round of a third wine-cup (cf. Godet, *in loc.*). It must have been a touching and tender type in the eyes of him who was so soon to be offered. We should have listened to his explanations on that occasion with peculiar interest. His references must have been somewhat veiled in presence of the betrayer, yet sufficiently explicit to have broken ordinary hearts. It was a marvellous feast—the Paschal Lamb himself partaking of the Passover; the Antitype experiencing a special benefit through the study of the type! What a solemnity, moreover, is thrown over the whole scene through his indication that it is all shortly to be fulfilled!

IV. THE INSTITUTION OF THE LORD'S SUPPER. (Vers. 19, 20.) Upon the more formidable feast, which is to pass away on fulfilment, Jesus founds a simpler feast, to be celebrated till he comes again. It is to consist of bread and wine, two of the elements there at the table. The bread is to represent his body, which is to be broken for his people; and the wine his blood, which is for them to be shed. In this way a memorial more lasting than brass or marble is to be reared, and his gracious presence is to be experienced in the Christian Church. The new institution was a promise of the most gracious kind, regarding the season when he would be absent from them.

V. THE INTIMATION OF THE BETRAYAL. (Vers. 21—23.) Along with the solemn joy there is dashed profoundest sorrow at the intimation of betrayal by one of the apostolic band. A traitor is there, and they should know it. Good sign in that each man suspects himself! They all, except Judas, ask Christ if it is he. Last of all, it would seem, came the inquiry of the real traitor. But this unearthing of the false one does not shake him from his foul purpose. Christ could not do more for him than he here does, even though it does not save him. How salutary is self-suspicion! How dangerous self-confidence!—R. M. E.

Vers. 24—38.—*The proper Christian spirit.* Through our Lord's faithful dealing the disciples had been led to wholesome self-suspicion. They cried out at the possibility of a betrayal of the Master, "Lord, is it I?" But no sooner have their minds been relieved through the singling out of Judas than they swing round again to self-confidence and even base ambition. There, at the table of the Lord, in spite of the hallowed associations, they speculate who is to be greatest in the coming kingdom. Jesus has consequently to check this nascent ambition. He does so by ennobling—

I. THE SPIRIT OF SERVICE. (Vers. 24—27.) Now, the world's idea is that it is noble to exercise authority, to be able to order people about. In fact, the world has come to call men "benefactors" who have done nothing but command other people. What tributes are paid to princes, who have done nothing all their lives but issue orders and receive the homage and service of other people! A blear-eyed world is ready, as Christ here shows, to pronounce such princes the benefactors of their age and country. But he has come into the world to *ennoble the opposite idea*. Here at this very feast he has been as one that serveth. His whole life, moreover, has been a public service. Everywhere he has just considered how he could serve others. To minister, not be ministered unto, was his continual care. To make the service of others glorious in the eyes of discerning men was one great purpose of his earthly life. This reveals also the very spirit of the Divine life.[1] God is Lord of all because Servant of all. He sustains all, as he has created all; and his greatness is the greatness of ministration. It is only Oriental barbarism which supposes greatness to consist in indolent and luxuriant state. Here, then, is the field of genuine ambition. Let us try to be *first in the field of service;* let us do our best and most for the benefit of all about us; and then alone shall we become noble and Christ-like.

II. CHRIST INDICATES THE RESULTANT INFLUENCE. (Vers. 28—30.) To these disciples, who continue with Christ in his temptations, he appoints a kingdom. In this kingdom they are to have thrones, and to be judges of the twelve tribes of Israel. In this way our Lord indicates the influence which these men, who entertain his spirit of service, will acquire. And when we consider the history of Christianity, we see that even in the world of humanity these humble servants of God and mankind have become kings and judges. It is by their deliverances in the primitive age that men are judging themselves and being judged. The apostles are pre-eminently the *sovereigns of this new and better time.* And this posthumous influence on earth is only a faint reflection of their influence in heaven. Now, is not this to encourage every serviceable soul? Let each of us be only content to serve, to do whatever a brother needs, and by our service we acquire influence and kingship. The world is really ruled by obliging, serviceable, meek, and earnest men.

III. CHRIST NEXT POINTS OUT TO PETER HIS DANGER, RECOVERY, AND CONSEQUENT USEFULNESS. (Vers. 31—34.) For, strange to say, temptation is overruled as well as service to the creation of influence. There is in Peter's nature a good deal of pride and vain-glory to be winnowed out. There is wheat within him, but also chaff. Now, Satan had set his mind upon the fall of Peter; but Jesus has already prayed for him that his faith may not fail. Here was Peter's safeguard in the timely intercession of his Master.[2] How watchful the Lord was and is for souls! Oh, how our want of watchfulness stands rebuked! Yet Peter was permitted to fall under temptation; but he was won back again, converted the second time, so to speak, by the loving look of Jesus; and thus destined to become a strengthener of the brethren. So that our Lord's prayers for us may be that, through permitted humiliations and tears and penitence, we may pass on to power. It is only when self-confidence, as in Peter's case, has been purged out of us by humiliating discoveries of our personal weakness, that we are in a position to undertake the care and strengthening of brethren. Broken-hearted Simon becomes, after Pentecost, the reliable Rock-man, worthy of the new name, Peter.

IV. THE CONTRASTED POLICIES OF CONFIDENCE AND OF PRUDENCE. (Vers. 35—38.) In sending the disciples out on their first missions, Jesus relied on the hospitality of the people as a fitting support for his agents. Going to the people as philanthropists, working miracles, preaching the advent of Messiah, they would meet with such support as would be all-sufficient. This was the policy of confidence—the reliance on the people for entire support. But when the world turned against Christ, and realized how opposed he was to its worldliness, then the disciples would require to exercise all possible prudence. They would require to look out for themselves, and even to fight for their own hand. That is to say, there are times when we may trust the world, and times when we are warranted in distrusting it. When is it, we are inclined to ask, that the prudential temper must take the place of confidence? When the world is determined on injustice. Thus at this time the world is about to reckon Christ among the transgressors, and to do him manifest injustice. The *fit of unfairness* was upon it, and the disciples should then stand in self-defence. But other days would dawn again, when disciples will be warranted in pursuing a policy of public confidence, and thus giving the world the chance of compensation. Let us wisely consider the "signs of the times," and act accordingly. Christ will guide us to the policy which is best, if we prayerfully ask him.—R. M. E.

[1] Cf. Dr. Dykes's noble sermon on ver. 27: 'Sermons,' p. 291.

[2] Cf. Vinet's 'Nouvelles Études Evangeliques,' p. 238; also Woolsey's 'Religion of the Present and the Future,' p. 186; and Dykes's 'Sermons,' p. 263.

Vers. 39—53.—*Gethsemane.* After the Passover and the address given in John xiv., he led the disciples out through the vineyards, where most likely John xv. was delivered to them, and John xvi., until he reached his usual rendezvous in Gethsemane, part of the Mount of Olives. Here let us suppose the high-priestly prayer given in John xvii. took place, which being ended, he retired to an adjacent and secluded place for further prayer. Gethsemane was thus his preparation for suffering and death, as the Transfiguration had been for work. And here we have to notice—

I. HIS DREAD OF THE DENOUÉMENT WAS NOT A DREAD OF PHYSICAL PAIN AND DEATH. His cry for escape, if possible, was not prompted by physical fear. He always showed himself brave before danger of a mere physical kind. Socrates seems the braver man before he drank the hemlock, but this was because Socrates could not see the issues that were before him as Christ foresaw his fate. The cup he shrank from was not like that of Socrates. It was no literal cup, but the apprehension of isolation from his Father. Not the trial, nor the mockery, nor the physical pain, but the isolation from God, the sense of forsakenness, the constraint to cry, "My God, my God, why hast thou forsaken me?" which prompted the cry to escape. Now, the very elevation of his being rendered the dread of separation even for the shortest season from his Father intensely painful. Vulgar souls can take separation from others quietly, but the elect souls pass through deepest pains in consequence. That darkness which came on when Son was separated from Father because of the sin-bearing was what Jesus dreaded, and would gladly have escaped. Want of fellowship with the Father seemed to this holy Child Jesus something to be escaped if at all possible.

II. THE INTENSITY AND EFFICACY OF HIS PRAYER. Just as Jacob had to wrestle at Peniel to obtain the blessing, so had the Saviour in the garden. He was in an agony of earnestness, and was in consequence bathed in a bloody sweat. Time after time he prayed thus earnestly. And we are expressly told, "He was heard in that he feared" (Heb. v. 7). His prayer was efficacious. Now, let us consider what he prayed for. It was for deliverance from isolation from God—deliverance from death without a sense of the Divine fellowship. And when we consider the sequel, we find that he was heard, and his prayer answered. For (1) he enjoyed an *angelic visit* and was strengthened by it (ver. 43); (2) he was granted *light and fellowship with the Father before death* supervened; and (3) he was saved from death by *resurrection.* In these ways the Father undoubtedly heard and answered the cry of Christ in Gethsemane.

III. NOTICE THE DISCIPLES' SLEEP OF SORROW. For sorrow often induces sleep, while at other times it makes sleep impossible. In the present case the disciples ought to have been praying for Jesus, for themselves, seeking preparation for the trial he had forewarned them was at hand. Instead of doing so they slept. Here we have to notice: 1. *Opportunity for showing spiritual sympathy was missed.* Jesus, as we know, was most anxious they should watch with him. He needed and he sought their sympathy; but they, in thoughtlessness, denied it to him. It would be well if deepest consideration were exhibited for noble souls that are greatly tried. 2. *Opportunity for private preparation was missed.* They themselves needed spiritual help more than Christ. They could less afford than he to meet the crisis prayerlessly. Yet this was their condition when the trial fell upon them. 3. *Physical effort was their only resource when the crisis came.* They could lay on with the sword. It does not take much prayer to help men to fight. But other and better weapons were needed than Peter's sword, but they could only be taken out of the armoury by prayer.

IV. THE BETRAYAL. Judas and his band were upon them before the sleepy disciples had time to pray. He had planned the capture as only a coward can. He betrays Christ with the semblance of friendship, trying to give the Master the usual kiss. To this offer Jesus simply replies, "Judas, betrayest thou the Son of man with a kiss?" Force behind deceit is apparently overpowering the spirituality which had its home in that place of prayer.

V. THE DEFENCE OF THE DISCIPLES AND THE MIRACLE OF THE MASTER. The disciples, spiritually off guard, betake themselves to the carnal weapon, and Peter lays round him with the sword. He succeeds in cutting off the right ear of the high priest's servant. Here is fresh trouble created. If this servant has to go back thus wounded, a warrant will soon be out for the disciples, and the whole issue thrown into perplexity. Our Lord accordingly interposes, heals the sufferer's ear, and advises Peter to put up his sword. In this way Jesus rescues the disciples from the liability incurred through their own imprudence. It was a wonderful consideration manifested when his own troubles were rising to their height.

VI. THE REBUKE ADMINISTERED TO HIS ENEMIES. Why had they come out against him as against a thief? Had he not confronted them time after time in open day? They had not dared to lay hands upon him then. He thus convicted them of cowardice. It was "their hour, and the power of darkness." A deed of darkness dare not be done in open day. Thus was it that our Lord bravely met his adversaries. He was prepared, though the disciples were not.—R. M. E.

Vers. 54—71.—*Christ's trials in the high priest's palace.* The agony of Gethsemane is over, and our Lord has met his enemies in the calmness of real courage. He allows himself to be led to the palace of the high priest, and we have now to consider all the trials through which he passed there. The first of these is from Peter. Love to the Master keeps the disciple in the train of the procession, and even leads him to linger without until through John's good offices he gets into the hall. But, alas! instead of keeping near the Master, he lingers near the fire which was kindled in the hall to keep the cold at bay. And here let us notice—

I. PETER'S TEMPTATION. (Vers. 54—60.) It was identification with a lost cause. Here is Jesus down; no hope apparently lingers about him; he cannot now be saved. What use is there in further identifying himself with Jesus? Instead of responding boldly to the challenge and confessing Christ, he is tempted to deny him. And the denials are repeated, the last time with an oath. Peter's distant view of his Master and of his cause leads him to the fatal conclusion that it is safest to cut the connection and deny that he has ever known him. It is, alas! the temptation of men still. In the blazing light of society, when worldliness seems so strong and comfortable, it is convenient to ignore the Master and his cause. Peter's temptation is constantly repeated, and his fall has its counterpart continually in the cowardice of souls.

II. PETER'S RECOVERY AND REPENTANCE. (Vers. 61, 62.) The Master in warning him had given him a sign, that of the cock-crow. It acts as an alarum upon the dull ear of Peter. Along with this there comes the look ineffable of the loving Lord. The great heart is broken, and Peter passes out to weep bitterly. We have a great contrast between the sorrow of Peter and that of Judas. It is the sorrow of the world which worketh death in the one case; it is the sorrow which is godly and saving in the other. As Gerok, in an admirable discourse upon the subject, says, (1) *Peter's sorrow proceeds upon his sin*, Judas's upon the *consequences of his sin;* (2) Peter's sorrow turns him *from* the world, Judas's turns him *towards* the world; and (3) Peter's sorrow leads him *to life*, Judas's leads him *to death*.[1] Peter's repentance was thus the consequence of his Master's love, and the sign of his recovery. How sensible he must have been of the mighty wrong he had done the Master! Jesus knew when Peter slunk away out of the palace that he was safe in his bitter sorrow, and that he would come forth from it a better man. Our Lord's trial through Peter's faithlessness terminated when the disciple's heart was broken.

III. THE BUFFET-GAME. (Vers. 63—65.) The heavy hours till morning must be spent, and so the soldiers determine to get some amusement out of their notable Prisoner. They make Jesus, consequently, the centre in what is now known as the buffet-game. Blindfolding him, they proceed to strike him, and call upon him to tell who has inflicted the blows. They are terrible liberties they thus take with the Son of God. But they are unable to irritate this meek and lowly Man. Their blows are lost upon his magnificent meekness. They must have been struck at the majestic carriage of the Prisoner under their brutal horse-play. Yet the blows of the soldiers were less a trial, we may be sure, than the faithlessness of the disciple. But we are surely taught how essentially degrading it is to manufacture mirth out of the humiliation of others! The soldiers never were so *brutal* as when they treated Jesus in the style they did.

IV. HIS TRIAL BEFORE THE SANHEDRIN. (Vers. 66—71.) In the morning the Jewish authorities assembled, and their line of examination was as to the nature of his Messiahship. As we have seen, it was not a Divine, but a *military Messiah* the Jews

[1] Gerok's 'Evangelien-Predigten,' s. 276.

desired. To their question he replies first that they will not believe him if he answers them truthfully. They will only believe what they *like*. In other words, faith is largely a matter of the will as influenced by emotion. They were not prepared to accept truth and follow it to its consequences. After this preliminary, Jesus goes on to declare, "From henceforth shall the Son of man be seated at the right hand of the power of God" (Revised Version). That is to say, his Messiahship is to be a heavenly reign, not an earthly and temporal one. At once they saw in this a claim to Divine Sonship. Hence they challenge him upon the point, and get his manly reply that he is. On this ground they condemn him. It is plain, therefore, that this *Divine* Messiah was not what suited their fancy. It was not deliverance from such impalpable foes as sin and anxiety and suffering they desired, but from the Romans. They wanted a military leader—a pasha; and when God gave them his Son as their heavenly King, they condemned him to an ignominious death. It is thus that men despise their greatest blessings, and do their best to put them out of the way.—R. M. E.

EXPOSITION.

CHAPTER XXIII.

Vers. 1—4.—*The trial before Pilate: First examination.*

Ver. 1.—**And the whole multitude of them arose, and led him unto Pilate.** The Sanhedrin had now formally condemned Jesus to death. They were, however, precluded by the Roman regulations then in force from carrying out their judgment. A capital sentence in Judæa could only be inflicted as the result of a decision by the Roman court. The Sanhedrin supposed, and as we shall see rightly, that the judgment they had pronounced would speedily be confirmed by the Roman judge. The Sanhedrin condemnation to death was, however, from the Jewish standpoint, illegal. In capital cases judgment could not be legally pronounced on the day of trial. But in the case of Jesus, the Accused was condemned without the legal interval which should have been left between the trial and the sentence. The Prisoner was then at once hurried before the Roman tribunal, in order that the Jewish sentence might be confirmed and carried out with all the additional horrors which accompanied Gentile public executions in such cases of treason. Dérenbourg ('Histoire de la Palestine,' p. 201) attributes the undue illegal precipitancy of the whole proceeding to the overwhelming influence exercised in the supreme council by Annas and Caiaphas with their friends who were Sadducees, a party notorious for their cruelty as well as for their unbelief. Had the Pharisees borne sway in the Sanhedrin at that juncture, such an illegality could never have taken place. This apology possesses certain weight, as it is based upon known historical facts; yet when the general bearing of the Pharisee party towards our Lord during the greater part of his public ministry is remembered, it can scarcely be supposed that the action of the Sadducee majority in the Sanhedrin was repugnant to, or even opposed by, the Pharisee element in the great assembly. **Pilate.** Pontius Pilate, a Roman knight, owed his high position as Procurator of Judæa to his friendship with Sejanus, the powerful minister of the Emperor Tiberius. He probably belonged by birth or adoption to the gens of the Pontii. When Judæa became formally subject to the empire on the deposition of Archelaus, Pontius Pilate, of whose previous career nothing is known, through the interest of Sejanus, was appointed to govern it, with the title of procurator, or collector of the revenue, invested with judicial power. This was in A.D. 26, and he held the post for ten years, when he was deposed from his office in disgrace. His government of Judæa seems to have been singularly unhappy. His great patron Sejanus hated the Jews, and Pilate seems faithfully to have imitated his powerful friend. Constantly the Roman governor appears to have wounded the susceptibilities of the strange, unhappy people he was placed over. Fierce disputes, mutual insults arising out of apparently purposeless acts of arbitrary power on his side, characterized the period of his rule. His behaviour in the one great event of his life, when Jesus was brought before his tribunal, will illustrate his character. He was superstitious and yet cruel; afraid of the people he affected to despise; faithless to the spirit of the authority with which he was lawfully invested. In the great crisis of his history, from the miserably selfish motive of securing his own petty interests, we watch him deliberately giving up a Man, whom he knew to be innocent, and felt to be noble and pure, to torture, shame, and death.

Ver. 2.—**And they began to accuse him, saying, We found this fellow perverting the nation, and forbidding to give tribute to Cæsar, saying that he himself is Christ a King.** To understand this scene perfectly we must read St. John's account in his eighteenth chapter (ver. 28 and following). From the place of meeting of the Sanhedrin, Jesus was led to the palace of Pilate, the Prætorium. The Roman governor was evidently prepared for the case; for application must have been made to him the evening before for the guard which arrested Jesus in Gethsemane. St. John tells us that the delegates of the Sanhedrin entered not into the hall of judgment, "lest they should be defiled; but that they might eat the Passover." Pilate, who knew well from his past experience how fiercely these fanatics resented any slight offered to their religious feelings, wishing for his own purposes to conciliate them, went outside. These Jews, prior to eating the Passover, would not enter any dwelling from which all leaven had not been carefully removed; of course, this had not been the case in the palace of Pilate. The governor asks them, in St. John's account, what was their accusation against the Man. They replied that they had three charges: (1) he had perverted the nation; (2) he had forbidden that tribute should be given to Cæsar; (3) he had asserted that he was Christ a King.

Ver. 3.—And Pilate asked him, saying, Art thou the King of the Jews? Pilate then went again into his judgment-hall, where he had left Jesus, but before going back he could not resist addressing an ironical word to the accusing Jews: "Take ye him, and judge him according to your Law" (John xviii. 31), to which the Sanhedrists replied that they were not allowed to put any man to death, thus publicly confessing the state of comparative impotence to which they were now reduced, and also revealing their deadly purpose in the case of Jesus. Pilate, having gone into the judgment-hall again, proceeds to interrogate Jesus. The first two accusations he passes over, seeing clearly that they were baseless. The third, however, struck him. **Art** *thou*, poor, friendless, powerless Man, the King I have been hearing about? **And he answered him and said, Thou sayest it.** St. Luke gives only this bare summary of the examination, in which the prisoner Jesus simply replies "Yes," he was the King. St. John (xviii. 33—38) gives us a more full and detailed account. It is more than probable that John was present during the interrogatory. In the sublime answers of the Lord, his words explanatory of the nature of his kingdom, which "is not of this world," struck Pilate and decided him to give the reply we find in the next verse.

Ver. 4.—**Then said Pilate to the chief priests and to the people, I find no fault in this Man.** The Roman was interested in the poor Prisoner; perhaps he grudgingly admired him. He was so different to the members of that hated nation he had been brought into such familar contact with; utterly unselfish, noble with a strange nobility, which was quite unknown to officials and politicians of the school of Pilate; but as regards Rome and its views quite harmless. The Roman evidently was strongly opposed to harsh measures being dealt out to this dreamy, unpractical, generous Enthusiast, as he deemed him.

Vers. 5—12.—*Pilate sends Jesus to be tried by Herod.*

Ver. 5.—**And they were the more fierce, saying, He stirreth up the people, teaching throughout all Jewry, beginning from Galilee to this place.** On hearing the Roman governor's declaration that in his opinion the Prisoner was innocent, the Sanhedrists became more vehement, repeating with increased violence their accusation that Jesus had been for a long time past a persistent stirrer-up of sedition, not only here in the city, but in the northern districts of Galilee.

Vers. 6, 7.—**When Pilate heard of Galilee, he asked whether the Man were a Galilæan. And as soon as he knew that he belonged unto Herod's jurisdiction, he sent him to Herod, who himself also was at Jerusalem at that time.** Now, Pilate dreaded lest these Jews should make his clemency towards the Prisoner a ground of accusation against him at Rome. Pilate had enemies in the capital. His once powerful patron Sejanus had just fallen. His own past, too, he was well aware, would not bear examination; so, moved by his cowardly fears, he refrained from releasing Jesus in accordance with what his heart told him was just and right; and yet he could not bring himself to condemn One to whom he was drawn by an unknown feeling of reverence and respect. But hearing that Jesus was accused among other things of stirring up sedition in Galilee, he thought he would shift the responsibility of acquitting or condemning, on to the shoulders of Herod, in whose jurisdiction Galilee lay. Herod was in Jerusalem just then, because of the Passover Feast. His usual residence was Capernaum.

Ver. 8.—**And when Herod saw Jesus, he was exceeding glad: for he was desirous to see him of a long season, because he had heard many things of him; and he hoped to have seen some miracle done by him.** This was Herod Antipas, the slayer of John the Baptist. He was at that time living in open incest with that princess Herodias concerning whom the Baptist had administered the public rebuke which had led to his arrest and subsequent execution. Godet graphically sums up the situation: "Jesus was to Herod Antipas what a juggler is to a sated court—an object of curiosity. But Jesus did not lend himself to such a part; he had neither words nor miracles for a man so disposed, in whom, besides, he saw with horror the murderer of John the Baptist. Before this personage, a monstrous mixture of bloody levity and sombre superstition, he maintained a silence which even the accusation of the Sanhedrin (ver. 10) could not lead him to break. Herod, wounded and humiliated, took vengeance on this conduct by contempt."

Ver. 11.—**And Herod with his men of war set him at nought, and mocked him, and arrayed him in a gorgeous robe, and sent him again to Pilate.** He treated him, not as a criminal, but as a mischievous religious Enthusiast, worthy only of contempt and scorn. The "gorgeous robe," more accurately, "bright raiment," was a white festal mantle such as Jewish kings and Roman nobles wore on great occasions. It was probably an old robe of white tissue of some kind, embroidered with silver. Dean Plumptre suggests that we might venture to trace in this outrage a vindictive retaliation for the words which the Teacher had once spoken—with evident allusion to Herod's court—of those who were gorgeously apparelled (ch. vii. 25). It was this Herod of whom the Lord had spoken so recently with for him a rare bitterness, "Go ye, and tell that fox [literally, 'she-fox'] Herod" (ch. xiii. 32).

Ver. 12.—**And the same day Pilate and Herod were made friends together.** This union of two such bitter enemies in their enmity against Jesus evidently struck the early Church with sad wonderment. It is referred to in the first recorded hymn of the Church of Christ (Acts iv. 27). How often has the strange sad scene been reproduced in the world's story since! Worldly men apparently irreconcilable meet together in friendship when opportunity offers itself for wounding Christ!

Vers. 13—25.—*The Lord is tried again before Pilate, who wishes to release him, but, over-persuaded by the Jews, delivers him to be crucified.*

Vers. 13—16.—**And Pilate . . . said unto them . . . behold I . . . have found no fault in this Man . . . No, nor yet Herod: . . . lo, nothing worthy of death is done unto him;** more accurately rendered, *is done by him.* This was the Roman's deliberate judgment publicly delivered. The decision then announced, that he would scourge him (ver. 16), was singularly unjust and cruel. Pilate positively subjected a Man whom he had pronounced innocent to the horrible punishment of scourging, just to satisfy the clamour of the Sanhedrists, because he dreaded what they might accuse him of at Rome, where he knew he had enemies! He thought, wrongly as it turned out, that the sight of Jesus after he had undergone this dreadful and disgraceful punishment would satisfy, perhaps melt to pity, the hearts of these restless enemies of his.

Ver. 17.—**(For of necessity he must release one unto them at the feast.)** Probably, however, before the scourging was inflicted, the attempt to liberate Jesus in accordance with a custom belonging to that feast was made by Pilate. We know it failed, and a condemned robber called Barabbas was preferred by the people. The more ancient authorities omit this verse (17). It probably was introduced at an early period into many manuscripts of St. Luke as a marginal gloss, as an explanatory statement based on the words of Matt. xxvii. 15 or of Mark xv. 6. As a Hebrew custom, it is never mentioned save in this place. Such a release was a common incident of a Latin Lectisternium, or feast in honour of the gods. The Greeks had a similar custom at the Thesmophoria. It was probably introduced at Jerusalem by the Roman power.

Vers. 18, 19.—**And they cried out all at once, saying, Away with this Man! and release unto us Barabbas: (who for a certain sedition made in the city, and for murder, was cast into prison).** Barabbas, whose release the people demanded at the instigation of the influential men of the Sanhedrin, was a notable leader in one of the late insurrectionary movements so common at this time. St. John styles him a robber; this well describes the character of the man; a bandit chief who carried on his lawless career under the veil of patriotism, and was supported and protected in consequence by many of the people. The meaning of his name *Bar-Abbas* is "Son of a (famous) father," or possibly *Bar-Rabbas*, "Son of a (famous) rabbi." A curious reading is alluded to by Origen, which inserts before Barabbas the word "Jesus." It does not, however, appear in any of the older or more trustworthy authorities. Jesus was a common name at that period, and it is possible that "when Barabbas was led out, the Roman, with some scorn, asked the populace whom they preferred—Jesus Bar-Abbas or Jesus who is called Christ!" (Farrar). That this reading existed in very early times is indisputable, and Origen, who specially notices it, approves of its omission, not on critical, but on dogmatic grounds.

Ver. 23.—**And they were instant with loud voices, requiring that he might be crucified.** The Roman governor now found that all his devices to liberate Jesus with the consent and approval of the Jews were fruitless. After the clamour which resulted in the release of Barabbas had ceased, the terrible cry, "Crucify him!" was raised among that fickle crowd. Pilate was determined to carry out his threat of scourging the Innocent. *That* might satisfy them, perhaps excite their pity. Something whispered to him that he would be wise if he refrained from staining his life with the blood of that strange quiet Prisoner.

St. Luke omits here the "scourging;" the mock-homage of the soldiers; the scarlet robe and the crown of thorns; the last appeal to pity when Pilate produced the pale, bleeding Sufferer with the words, "Ecce Homo!" the last solemn interview of Pilate and Jesus, related by St. John; the sustained clamour of the people for the blood of the Sinless. "*Then he delivered Jesus to their will*" (ver. 25). (See Matt. xxvii., Mark. xv., and John xix., for these details, omitted in St. Luke.)

Of the omitted details, the most important piece in connection with the "last things" is the recital by St. John of the examination of Jesus by Pilate in the Prætorium. None of the Sanhedrists or strict Jews, we have noticed, were present at these interrogatories. They, we read, entered not into the judgment-hall of Pilate, lest they might be defiled, and so be precluded from eating the Passover Feast.

St. John, however, who appears to have been the most fearless of the "eleven," and who besides evidently had friends among the Sanhedrin officials, was clearly present at these examinations. He too, we are aware, had eaten his Passover the evening before, and therefore had no defilement to fear.

The first interrogatories have been already alluded to, in the course of which the question, "Art thou a King, then?" was put by Pilate, and the famous reflection by the Roman, "What is truth?" was made. Then followed the "sending to Herod;" the return of the Prisoner from Herod; the offer of release, which ended in the choice by the people of Barabbas. The scourging of the prisoner Jesus followed.

This was a horrible punishment. The condemned person was usually stripped and fastened to a pillar or stake, and then scourged with leather throngs tipped with leaden balls or sharp spikes.

The effects, described by Romans, and Christians in the 'Martyrdoms,' were terrible. Not only the muscles of the back, but the breast, the face, the eyes, were torn; the very entrails were laid bare, the anatomy was exposed, and the sufferer, convulsed with torture, was often thrown down a bloody heap at the feet of the judge. In our Lord's case this punishment, though not proceeding to the awful consequences described in some of the 'Martyrologies,' must have been very severe: this is evident from his sinking under the cross, and from the short time which elapsed before his death upon it. "Recent investigations at Jerusalem have disclosed what may have been the scene of the punishment. In a subterranean chamber, discovered by Captain Warren, on what Mr. Fergusson holds to be the site of Antonia—Pilate's Prætorium—stands a truncated column, no part of the construction, for the chamber is vaulted above the pillar, but just such a pillar as criminals would be tied to to be scourged" (Dr. Westcott).

After the cruel scourging came the mocking by the Roman soldiers. They threw across the torn and mangled shoulders one of those scarlet cloaks worn by the soldiers themselves—a coarse mockery of the royal mantle worn by a victorious general. They pressed down on his temples a crown or wreath, imitating what they had probably seen the emperor wear in the form of laurel wreath—Tiberius's wreath of laurel was seen upon his arms (Suetonius, 'Tiberius,' c. 17). The crown was made, as an old tradition represents it, of the *Zizyphus Christi*, the *nubk* of the Arabs, a plant which is found in all the warmer parts of Palestine and about Jerusalem. The thorns are numerous and sharp, and the flexible twigs well adapted for the purpose (Tristram, 'Natural History of the Bible,' p. 429). "The representations in the great pictures of the Italian painters probably come very near the truth" ('Speaker's Commentary').

In his right hand they placed a reed to simulate a sceptre, and before this sad, woebegone Figure "they bowed the knee, saying, Hail, King of the Jews!"

Hase ('Geschichte Jesu,' p. 573) is even moved to say, "There is some comfort in the fact that, even in the midst of the mockery, the truth made itself felt. Herod recognizes his innocence by a white robe; the Roman soldiery his royalty by the sceptre and the crown of thorns, and that has become the highest of all crowns, as was fitting, being the most meritorious."

It was *then* and *thus* that Pilate led Jesus out before the Sanhedrists and the people, as they shouted in their unreasoning fury, "Crucify him!" while the Roman, partly sadly, partly scornfully, partly pitifully, as he pointed to the silent Sufferer by his side, pronounced "Ecce Homo!"

But the enemies of Jesus were pitiless. They kept on crying, "Crucify him!" and when Pilate still demurred carrying out their bloody purpose, they added that "by their Law he ought to die, because he made himself the *Son of God*."

All through that morning's exciting scenes had Pilate seen that something strange and mysterious belonged to that solitary Man accused before him. His demeanour, his words, his very look, had impressed the Roman with a singular awe. Then came his wife's message, telling him of her dream, warning her husband to have nothing to do with *that just Man.* Everything seemed to whisper to him, "Do not let that strange, innocent Prisoner be done to death: he is not what he seems." And now the fact, openly published by the furious Jews, that the poor Accused claimed a Divine origin, deepened the awe. Who, then, had he been scourging?

Once more Pilate returns to his judgment-hall, and he says to Jesus, again standing before him, "Whence art thou?"

The result of this last interrogatory St. John (xix. 12) briefly summarizes in the words, "From thenceforth Pilate sought to release him."

The Sanhedrists, and their blind instruments, the fickle, wavering multitude, when they perceived the Roman governor's intention to release their Victim, changed their tactics. They forbore any longer to press the old charges of blasphemy and of indefinite wrong-doing, and they appealed only to Pilate's own dastardly fears. The Prisoner claimed to be a King. If the lieutenant of the emperor let such a traitor go free, why, that lieutenant emphatically was not Cæsar's friend!

Such a plea for the Sanhedrin to use before a Roman tribunal, to ask for death to be inflicted on a Jew because he had injured the majesty of Rome, was a deep degradation; but the Sanhedrin well knew the temper of the Roman judge with whom they had to deal, and they rightly calculated that his fears for himself, if properly aroused, would turn the scale and secure the condemnation of Jesus. They were right.

Ver. 24.—**And Pilate gave sentence that it should be as they required.** This sums up the result of the last charge of the Sanhedrin. Pilate's selfish fears for himself overpowered all sense of reverence, awe, and justice. There was no further discussion. Bar-Abbas was released, and Jesus was delivered up to the will of his enemies.

Vers. 26—32.—*On the way to Calvary. Simon the Cyrenian. The daughters of Jerusalem.*

Ver. 26.—**And as they led him away.** Plutarch tells us that every criminal condemned to crucifixion carried his own cross. There was borne in front of him, or else hung round his own neck, a white tablet, on which the crime for which he suffered was inscribed. Possibly this was what was afterwards affixed to the cross itself. **Simon, a Cyrenian.** Cyrene was an important city in North Africa, with a large colony of resident Jews. These Cyrenian Jews had a synagogue of their own in Jerusalem. It is probable that Simon was a Passover pilgrim. St. Mark tells us he was the father of "Alexander and Rufus;" evidently, from his mention of them, these were notable persons in the early Christian Church. Very likely their connection with the followers of Jesus dated from this incident on the road to Calvary. **Coming out of the country.** He was probably one of the pilgrims lodged in a village near Jerusalem, and met the sad procession as he was entering the city on his way to the temple. **On him they laid the cross.** Our Lord was weakened by the trouble and agitation of the past sleepless night, and was, of course, faint and utterly exhausted from the effects of the terrible scourging. The cross used for this mode of execution was (1) either the *Crux decussata* X, what is usually known as St. Andrew's cross; or (2) the *Crux commissa* T, St. Anthony's cross; or (3) the ordinary Roman cross +, *Crux immissa.* Our Lord suffered on the third description, the Roman cross. This consisted of two pieces, the one perpendicular (*staticulum*), the other horizontal (*antenna*). About the middle of the first was fastened a piece of wood (*sedile*), on which the condemned rested. This was necessary, else, during the long torture, the weight of the body would have torn the hands, and the body would have fallen. The cross was not very high, scarcely twice the height of an ordinary man. Strong nails were driven through the hands and feet. The victim usually lived about twelve hours, sometimes much longer. The agonies endured by the crucified have been thus summarized: "The fever which soon set in produced a burning thirst. The increasing inflammation of the wounds in the back, hands, and feet; the congestion of the blood in the head, lungs, and heart; the swelling of every vein, an indescribable oppression, racking pains in the head; the stiffness of the limbs, caused by the unnatural position of the body;—these all united to make the punishment, in the language of Cicero ('In Verr.,' v. 64), *crudelissimum teterrimumque supplicium*. From the beginning Jesus had foreseen that such would be the end of his life."

Ver. 27.—**And there followed him a great company of people, and of women, which also bewailed and lamented him.** The great company was made up of the usual concourse of curious lookers-on, of disciples, and others who had heard him in past days, and now came, with much horror, to see the end. *The women* specially noticed consisted mostly, no doubt, of holy women of his own company, such as the "Maries," together with some of those kindly Jerusalem ladies who were in the habit of soothing the last hours of those condemned ones—unhappily in those sad days so numerous—with narcotics and anodynes. These kindly offices were apparently not forbidden by the Roman authorities. This recital respecting the women is peculiar to St. Luke.

Ver. 28.—**But Jesus turning unto them said, Daughters of Jerusalem.** This address to them by the Lord indicates that the majority at least of this company of sympathizing women belonged to the holy city. **Weep not for me, but weep for yourselves, and for your children.** Again here, as on the cross, the utter unselfishness of the dying Master comes out. His thoughts in his darkest hour were never of himself. Here, apparently, for the first time since his last interrogation before Pilate does our Lord break silence. Stier beautifully calls this the first part of the *Passion sermon of Christ*. The second part consisted of the "seven words on the cross." "Weep," said our Lord here. It is noticeable that it is the only time in his public teaching that he is reported to have told his listeners to weep. "The same lips whose gracious breath had dried so many tears now cry on the way to the cross, 'Weep for yourselves, and for your children.'"

Ver. 29.—**Blessed are the barren.** A strange beatitude to be spoken to the women of Israel, who, through all their checkered history, so passionately longed that *this* barrenness might not be their portion!

Ver. 30.—**Then shall they begin to say to the mountains, Fall on us; and to the hills, Cover us.** The allusion, in the first place, was to the awful siege of Jerusalem and to the undreamed-of woes which would accompany it; and in the second place, to the centuries of misery and persecution to which the children of these "daughters of Jerusalem" would, as Jews, be subjected in all lands.

Ver. 31.—**For if they do these things in a green tree, what shall be done in the dry?** Bleek and others interpret this saying here thus: The *green wood* represents Jesus condemned to crucifixion as a traitor in spite of his unvarying loyalty to Rome and all lawful Gentile power. The *dry wood* pictures the Jews, who, ever disloyal to Rome and all Gentile authority, will bring on themselves with much stronger reason the terrible vengeance of the great conquering empire. Theophylact, however, better explains the saying in his paraphrase, "If they do these things in *me*, fruitful, always green, undying through the Divinity, what will they do to *you*, fruitless, and deprived of all life-giving righteousness?" So Farrar, who well summarizes, "If they act thus to me, the Innocent and the Holy, what shall be the fate of these, the guilty and false?"

Ver. 32.—**And there were also two other, malefactors, led with him to be put to death.** Many commentators suppose that these were companions of that Bar-Abbas the robber who had just been released. They were not ordinary thieves, but belonged to those companies of brigands, or revolted Jews, which in those troublous times were so numerous in Palestine.

Vers. 33—49.—*The Crucifixion.*

Ver. 33.—**And when they were come to the place, which is called Calvary;** literally, *unto the place which is called the skull.* The familiar name "Calvary" has its origin in the Vulgate translation, *Calvarium*, a skull. The name "Place of a skull," *Golgotha* (properly *Gulgoltha*, an Aramaic word גלגלתא, corresponding to the Hebrew *Gulgoleth*, גלגלת, which in Judg. ix. 53 and 2 Kings ix. 35 is translated "skull"), does not come from the fact that the skulls of condemned persons remained lying there, but it is so called from being a bare rounded mound like a skull in form. Dean Plumptre suggests that the spot in question was chosen by the Jewish rulers as a deliberate insult to one of their own order, Joseph of Arimathæa, whose garden, with its rock-sepulchre, lay hard by. A later legend derives the name from its being the burying-place of Adam, and that as the blood flowed from the sacred wounds on his skull, his soul was translated to Paradise. A tradition traceable to the fourth century has identified this spot with the building known as the Church of the Holy Sepulchre. St. Cyril of Jerusalem alludes to the spot repeatedly. In the time of Eusebius there was no doubt as to the site. The Bordeaux Pilgrim (A.D. 333) writes thus: "On the left side (of the original Church of the Holy Sepulchre) is the hillock (*monticulus*) Golgotha, where the Lord was crucified. Thence about a stone-throw distance is the crypt where his body was deposited." Recent research confirms this very ancient tradition, and scholars are generally now agreeing that the evidence in support of the *traditional site* is strong and seemingly conclusive. **And the malefactors, one on the right hand, and the other on the left.** St. John adds, "and Jesus in the midst," as holding the position of preeminence in that scene of uttermost shame. Even in suffering Christ appears as a King. Westcott thus comments on the next detail recorded by St. John (xix. 19), where the accurate rendering is, "And Pilate wrote a title *also*." This title (see further, ver. 38) was drawn up by Pilate, who caused it to be placed on the cross. The words, "wrote a title also," perhaps imply that the placing of the Lord in the midst was done by Pilate's direction.

Ver. 34.—**Then said Jesus, Father, forgive them; for they know not what they do.** These words are missing in some of the oldest authorities. They are found, however, in the majority of the most ancient manuscripts and in the most trustworthy of the old versions, and are undoubtedly genuine. These *first* of the seven words from the cross seem, from their position in the record, to have been spoken very early in the awful scene, probably while the nails were being driven into the hands and feet. Different from other holy dying men, *he* had no need to say, "Forgive *me*." Then, as always, thinking of others, he utters this prayer, uttering it, too, as Stier well observes, with the same consciousness which had been formerly expressed, "Father, I know that thou hearest *me* always." "His intercession has this for its ground, though in meekness it is not expressed: 'Father, I will that thou forgive them.'" In the same sublime consciousness *who he was*, he speaks shortly after to the penitent thief hanging by his side. These words of the crucified Jesus were heard by the poor sufferer close to him; they—with other things he had noticed in the One crucified in the midst—moved him to that piteous prayer which was answered at once so quickly and so royally. St. Bernard comments thus on this first word from the cross: "Judæi clamant, 'Crucifige!' Christus clamat, 'Ignosce!' Magna illorum iniquitas, sed major tua, O Domine, pietas!" **And they parted his raiment, and cast lots.** The rough soldiers were treating the Master as already dead, and were disposing of his raiment, of which they had stripped him before fastening him to the cross. He was hanging there naked, exposed to sun and wind. Part of this raiment was torn asunder, part they drew lots for to see who was to wear it. The garments of the crucified became the property of the soldiers who carried out the sentence. Every cross was guarded by a guard of four soldiers. The coat, for which they cast lots, was, St. John tells us, without seam. "Chrysostom," who may have written from personal knowledge, thinks that the detail is added to show "the poorness of the Lord's garments, and that in dress, as in all other things, he followed a simple fashion."

Ver. 35.—**And the people stood beholding.** A hush seems to have fallen over the scene. The crowd of by-standers were awed as they at first silently gazed on the dying form of the great Teacher. What memories must have surged up in the hearts of many of the gazers—memories of his parables, his mighty miracles, his words of love; memories of the raising of Lazarus, and of the day of palms! Such a silent awe-struck contemplation was dangerous, the rulers felt, so they hastened to commence their mockery—"to clear," as Stier remarks, "the stifling air, and deafen the voice which was stirring even in themselves." "Look now," they would cry, "at the end of the Man who said he could do, and pretended to do, such strange, unheard-of things!" They seem soon to have induced many to join in their mocking cries and gestures, and so to break the awful silence.

Ver. 36.—**And the soldiers also mocked him, coming to him, and offering him vinegar.** Three times in the Crucifixion scene we find a mention of this vinegar, or the sour wine of the country, the common drink of the soldiers and others, being offered to the Sufferer. (1) Matt. xxvii. 34. This was evidently a draught prepared with narcotics and stupefying drugs, no doubt by some of those compassionate women addressed by him on his way to the cross as "daughters of Jerusalem," a common work of mercy at that time, and one apparently permitted by the guards. This, St. Matthew tells us, "he tasted of," no doubt in courteous recognition of the kindly purpose of the act, but he refused to do more than taste of it. He would not dull the sense of pain, or cloud the clearness of his communion with his Father in that last awful hour. (2) The second, mentioned here by St. Luke, seems to imply that the soldiers mocked his agony of thirst—one of the tortures induced by crucifixion—by lifting up to his parched, fevered lips, vessels containing their sour wine, and then snatching them hastily away. (3) The third (John xix. 28—30) relates that here the Lord, utterly exhausted, asked for and received this last refreshment, which revived, for a very brief space, his fast failing powers, and gave him strength for his last utterances. The soldiers, perhaps acting under the orders of the compassionate centurion in command, perhaps touched with awe by the brave patience and strange dignity of the dying Lord, did him this last kindly office.

Ver. 38.—**And a superscription also was written over him in letters of Greek, and Latin, and Hebrew, THIS IS THE KING OF THE JEWS.** The older authorities omit "in letters of Greek, and Latin, and Hebrew," but the fact is indisputable, for we read the same statement in John xix. 20, where in the older authorities the order of the titles is, "in Hebrew, in Latin, and in Greek." Such multilingual inscriptions were common in the great provincial cities of the empire, where so many nationalities were wont to congregate. The four reports of the inscriptions slightly differ verbally, not substantially. Pilate probably (see note on ver. 33, on effect of accurate rendering of John xix. 19, "and Pilate wrote a title also") wrote a rough draft with his own hand, "Rex Judæorum hic est." One of the officials translated freely into Hebrew and Greek the Roman governor's Latin memorandum of what he desired to have written in black on the white gypsum-smeared board to be affixed to the upper arm of the cross.

ישו הנצרי מלך היהודים (John).
Ὁ βασιλεὺς τῶν Ἰουδαίων (Mark).
Rex Judæorum hic est (Luke).

Dr. Farrar suggests that the title over the cross was as above. St. Matthew's is an accurate combination of the three, and was not improbably, *as a combination of the three inscriptions*, the common form reproduced in the first oral Gospel.

Vers. 39, 40.—**And one of the malefactors which were hanged railed on him, saying, If thou be Christ, save thyself and us. But the other answering rebuked him, saying, Dost not thou fear God?** In the first two synoptists we read how, shortly after they were nailed to their crosses, both thieves "reviled" Jesus. The Greek word, however, used by SS. Matthew and Mark is ὠνείδιζον (reproached). The word used by St. Luke in this place of the impenitent one is ἐβλασφήμει, "began to use injurious and insulting language"—a much stronger term. Farrar suggests that at first, during the early hours of the Crucifixion, in the madness of anguish and despair, they both probably joined in the reproaches levelled by all classes alike at One who might seem to them to have thrown away a great opportunity They, no doubt, knew something, possibly much, of Jesus' career, and how he had deliberately prevented more than once the multitude from proclaiming him King. Watching him as he hung bravely patient on his cross, only breaking the dread silence with a low-muttered prayer for his murderers to his Father, one of these misguided men changed his opinion of his fellow-Sufferer, changed his opinion, too, of his own past career. There, dying with a prayer for others on his lips, was the Example of true heroism, of real patriotism. *If thou be Christ.* The more ancient authorities read, *Art thou not the Christ? But the other.* In the Apocryphal Gospel of Nicodemus the names of the two are given as Dysmas and Gysmas, and these names appear still in Calvaries and stations in Roman Catholic lands. **Seeing thou art in the same condemnation.** His words might be paraphrased, "How canst thou, a dying man, join these mere lookers-on at our execution and agony? we are undergoing it ourselves. Dost thou not fear *God?* In a few hours we shall be before *him.* We have at all events deserved our doom; but not this Sufferer whom you revile. What has he done?"

Ver. 42.—**And he said unto Jesus, Lord, remember me when thou comest into thy kingdom.** The majority of the older authorities omit "Lord." The translation should run thus: *And he said, Jesus, remember me when thou comest in thy kingdom—in,* not *into.* The penitent looked forward to the dying Jesus coming again in (arrayed in) his kingly dignity, surrounded with his power and glory. Very touching is this confidence of the dying in the Dying One who was hanging by his side, his last garment taken from him; very striking is this trust of the poor penitent, that the forsaken Lord will one day appear again as King in his glory. He, and he alone, on that dread day read aright the superscription which mocking Pilate had fixed above the cross, "*This is the King of the Jews.*" He read "with Divine clear-sightedness in this deepest night" (Krummacher). He asks for no special place in that kingdom whose advent he sees clearly approaching; he only asks the King not to forget him then. On this knowledge of the thief concerning the second advent of Christ, Meyer well writes, "The thief must have become acquainted with the predictions of Jesus concerning his coming, which may very easily have been the case at Jerusalem, and does not directly presuppose any instructions on the part of Jesus; although he may also have heard him himself, and still remembered what he heard. The extraordinary character of his painful position in the very face of death produced as a consequence an extraordinary action of firm faith in those predictions."

Ver. 43.—**And Jesus said unto him, Verily I say unto thee, To-day shalt thou be with me in paradise.** No strengthening angel could have been more welcome to the dying Redeemer than these words of intense penitence and strong faith. Very beautifully Stier suggests that the crucified King "cannot see these two criminals, cannot direct his glance to this last without adding to his own agony by movement upon the cross. But *that* he forgets, and turns with an impulse of joy as well as he can to the soul that speaks to him, thus making the nails more firm." With those solemn words, "Verily I say unto thee," with which he had so often in old days begun his sacred sayings, he replied to the sufferer by his side. One at least, St. John, of his disciples would have heard the well-known words from the well-known voice. What memories must they not have recalled to that disciple whom Jesus loved, as he stood hard by the cross with the Mother of sorrows! The Lord's answer was very striking. *Remember him*, who could call on him with such reverent faith at the moment of his deepest humiliation! Remember him! yes; but not in the far-off "coming," but on *that* very day, before the sun then scorching their tortured bodies set; he would not be remembered by him only, but would be in closest companionship with him, not, as he prayed, in some far-off time in the midst of the awful tumult of the bloody and fiery dawn of the judgment advent, but almost directly in the fair garden, the quiet home of the blessed, the object of all Jewish hopes. *There* would he be remembered, and *there*, in company with his Lord, would the tortured condemned find himself in a few short hours. Are we right in thinking that there was no fulfilment of the words till death had released the spirit from its thraldom? May there not even then have been an ineffable joy, such as made the flames of the fiery furnace to be as a "moist, whistling wind" (Song of the Three Children, ver. 27), such as martyrs have in a thousand cases known, acting almost as a physical anæsthetic acts? (Dean Plumptre).

"Non parem Paulo veniam requiro,
Gratiam Petri neque posco, sed quam
In crucis ligno dederis latroni
Sedulus oro."

This striking verse is engraved on the tomb of the great Copernicus, and alludes to this prayer and its answer. *Paradise.* This is the only instance we have of our Lord's using this well-known word. In the ordinary language used by the Jews, of the unseen world, it signifies the "Garden of Eden," or "Abraham's bosom;" it represented the locality where the souls of the righteous would find a home, after death separated soul and body. The New Testament writers, Luke and Paul and John, use it (Acts ii. 31; 1 Cor. xv. 5; 2 Cor. xii. 4; Rev. ii. 7). To Luke and Paul, probably, this was a memory of the word spoken on the cross, which they alone record in their Gospel. It may have been told Luke by the Mother of sorrows herself. John, who uses it in his Revelation, doubtless heard it himself as he stood at the foot of the cross. *Paradeisos* is derived from the Persian word *pardes*, which signifies a park or garden.

Ver. 44.—*The time of the Crucifixion.* **And it was about the sixth hour.** We have before given (see note on ch. xxii. 47) the approximate hours of the several acts of the last night and day. This verse gives us the time of the duration of the "darkness"—from the sixth to the ninth hour; that is in our reckoning, from 12 noon to 3 p.m. With this date the other two synoptists agree (comp. Matt. xxvii. 45; Mark xv. 33). Our Lord had then been on the cross three hours (see Mark xv. 25, where it is stated that he was crucified in the third hour, *i.e.* 9 a.m.). But while the three synoptists are in perfect harmony, we are met with a grave difficulty in St. John's account, for in ch. xix. 14 of his Gospel we read how the final condemnation of our Lord by Pilate took place about the sixth hour. At first sight, to attempt here to harmonize St. John with the three synoptists would seem a hopeless task, as St. John apparently gives the hour of the final condemnation by Pilate, which the three give as the hour when the darkness began, *i.e.* when the Sufferer had already hung on the cross for three hours. Various explanations have been suggested; among these the most satisfying and probable is the supposition that, while the three synoptists followed the usual Jewish mode of reckoning time, St. John, writing some half a century later in quite another country, *possibly twenty years after Jerusalem and the temple had been destroyed, and the Jewish polity had disappeared*, adopted another mode of reckoning the hours, thus following, probably, a practice of the province in which he was living, and for which he was especially writing. Dr. Westcott, in an additional note on John xix. 14, examines the four occasions on which St. John mentions a definite hour of the day; and comes to the conclusion that the fourth evangelist generally reckoned his hours from midnight. The Romans reckoned their civil days from midnight, and there are also traces of reckoning the hours from midnight in Asia Minor. "About the sixth hour" would then be about six a.m. Before touching upon the strange darkness which at the sixth hour seems to have hung over the land like a black pall, we note that somewhere in the first three hours, possibly *after* the words spoken to the dying penitent, must be placed the incident of the entrusting the virgin-mother to St. John (xix. 25, etc.). There is no doubt that on the surface of this, his third word from the cross, lay a loving desire to spare his mother the sight of his last awful suffering. Hence his command to John to watch over from henceforth the mother of his Lord. We may assume, then, that, in obedience to his Master's word, John led Mary away before the sixth hour. So Bengel, who comments here, "Great is the faith of Mary to be present at the cross; great was her submission to go away before his death." **And there was a darkness over all the earth until the ninth hour.** St. Matthew gives us additional particulars respecting this phenomenon. He says that besides this darkness there was also an earthquake, and that several graves were opened, and the dead during those hours of solemn gloom appeared to many in the holy city. Early Christian writers of high authority, such as Tertullian ('Apol.,' ch. 21) and Origen ('Contra Cels.,' ii. 33), appeal to this strange phenomenon as if attested by heathen writers. It was evidently no slight or imaginary portent, but one that was well known in the early Christian years. The narrative does not oblige us to think of anything more than an indescribable and oppressive darkness, which like a vast black pall hung over earth and sea. The effect on the scoffing multitude was quickly perceptible. We hear of no more cries of mocking and derision; only just at the end of the three dark hours is the silence broken by the mysterious and awful cry of the Sinless One related by SS. Matthew and Mark, "My God, my God, why hast thou forsaken me?" Godet's comment is remarkable: "The darkness, the rending of the veil of the temple, the earthquake, and the opening of several graves, are explained by the profound connection existing on the one side between Christ and humanity, on the other between humanity and nature. Christ is the Soul of humanity, as humanity is the soul of the external world." The darkness, he suggests, was perhaps connected with the earthquake with which it was accompanied, or it may have resulted from an atmospherical or cosmical cause. The phenomenon need not necessarily have extended over all the earth; it probably was confined to Palestine and the adjacent countries.

Ver. 45.—**And the veil of the temple was rent in the midst.** This was the inner veil, which hung between the holy place and the holy of holies. It was rich with costly embroidery, and very heavy. Before the willing surrender of life told of in the next verse (46), our Lord spoke twice more. These fifth and sixth words from the cross are preserved by St. John (xix. 28, 30). The first of these, "*I thirst*"—an expression of bodily exhaustion, of physical suffering—was predicted as part of the agony of the Servant of God (Ps. lxix. 21). The second, "*It is finished!*" tells that "the earthly life had been carried to its issue. That every essential point in the prophetic portraiture of Messiah had been realized. The last suffering for sin had been endured. The end of all had been gained. Nothing was left undone or unborne" (Westcott).

Ver. 46.—**And when Jesus had cried with a loud voice, he said.** This is better rendered, *and Jesus cried with a loud voice and said.* The cry with the loud voice is the solemn dismissal of his spirit when he commended it to his Father. The object of the receiving the refreshment of the vinegar—the sour wine (John xix. 30)—was that his natural forces, weakened by the long suffering, should be restored sufficiently for him to render audible the last two sayings—the "It is finished!" of St. John, and the commending his soul to his Father, of St. Luke. **Father, into thy hands I commend my spirit.** St. John (xix. 30) has related now already Jesus had uttered the triumphal cry, Τετέλεσται! "It is finished!" This was *his farewell to earth.* St. Luke records the words which seem almost immediately to have followed the "It is finished!" This commending his spirit to his Father has been accurately termed *his entrance-greeting to heaven.* This placing his spirit as a trust in the Father's hands is, as Stier phrases it, an expression of the profoundest and most blessed repose after toil. "It is finished!" has already told us that the struggling and combat were sealed and closed for ever. Doctrinally it is a saying of vast importance; for it emphatically asserts that the soul will exist apart from the body *in the hands of God.* This at least is its proper home. The saying has been echoed on many a saintly death-bed. Stephen, full of the Holy Ghost, in his great agony shows us the form of this blessed prayer *we* should properly use for ourselves at that supreme hour, when he asked the *Lord Jesus* to receive his spirit, and then fell asleep. Thus coming to the Son, we come through him to the Father. Huss, on his way to the stake, when his enemies were triumphantly giving over his soul to devils, said with no less theological accuracy than with sure, calm faith, "But I commit my spirit into thy hand, O Lord Jesus Christ, who hast redeemed it." **And having said thus, he gave up the ghost.** This setting his spirit free was his own voluntary act. He had already told his disciples of his own independent power to lay down and take up his life (John x. 17, 18). The great teachers of the early Church evidently lay stress on this (see Tertullian, 'Apol.,' ch. 21). Augustine's words are striking: "Quis ita dormit quando voluerit, sicut Jesus mortuus est quando voluit? Quis ita vestem ponit quando voluerit, sicut se carne exuit quando vult? Quis ita cum voluerit abit, quomodo ille cum voluit obiit?" and he ends with this practical conclusion: "Quanta speranda vel timenda potestas est judicantis, si apparuit tanta morientis?" "Under these circumstances," writes Dr. Westcott, "it may not be fitting to speculate on the physical cause of the Lord's death, but it has been argued that the symptoms agree with a rupture of the heart, such as might be produced by intense mental agony."

Ver. 47.—**Now when the centurion saw what was done, he glorified God, saying, Certainly this was a righteous Man.** This was the Roman officer who was in command of the detachment on guard at the three crosses. St. Paul—who, if he did not absolutely put together the Third Gospel and the Acts, had much to do with the compilation and arrangement of these writings—on his many journeys and frequent changes of residence in different parts of the empire, had many opportunities of judging the temper and spirit of the Roman army, and on several occasions speaks favourably of these officers (ch. vii. 2; xxiii. 47; Acts x. 1; xxii. 26; xxvii. 43). *Certainly this was a righteous Man.* The noble generosity, the brave patience, and the strange majesty of the Sufferer; the awful portents which for three hours had accompanied this scene—portents which the centurion and many of the bystanders could not help associating with the crucifixion of him men called "the King of the Jews;" then the death, in which appeared no terror;—all this drew forth the exclamation of the Roman. In St. Matthew, the words of the centurion which are reported are "the Son of God." Twice in those solemn hours had the centurion heard the Crucified pray to his Father. This may have suggested the words, "Son of God;" but this change in the later Gospel of St. Luke to "a righteous Man" seems to point to the sense in which the Roman used the lofty appellation.

Ver. 48.—**And all the people that came together to that sight, beholding the things which were done, smote their breasts, and returned.** We must remember that the condemnation of the Christ was no spontaneous deed of the multitude. Their miserable share in the act was suggested to them by their rulers. In the multitude very quickly revulsion of feeling sets in, and they often regret the past with a bitter, useless regret The wave of sorrow which seems to have swept across those wavering, unstable hearts, which induced them to smite their breasts in idle regret, was a dim and shadowy rehearsal of the mighty sorrow and true penitence which will one day, as their prophet told them, be the blessed lot of the once-loved people when "they shall look upon *me* whom they have pierced, and they shall mourn for him, as one mourneth for his only son" (Zech. xii. 10).

Ver. 49.—**Stood afar off.** Disciples open and secret, friends and acquaintances among the Jerusalem citizens and Galilæan pilgrims (with the exception of the little group of which Mary and John were the centre till the dying Lord bade them leave him), all alike lacked courage and devotion, all feared to stand by their Master and Friend at that awful season. *He trod the winepress alone* (see Isa. lxiii. 3). None possessed the heroic faith which through the sombre cloud of seeming failure could see the true glory of the Sun of Righteousness, which *so soon* was to arise and shine.

Vers. 50—56.—*The entombment.* The sequence of events which immediately followed the death of Christ appears to have been as follows.

Our Lord expired apparently soon after 3 p.m. The "even" alluded to by St. Matthew and St. Mark began at 3 p.m. and lasted till sunset, about 6 p.m., when the sabbath commenced. Some time, then, between 3 p.m. and 6 p.m. Joseph of Arimathæa went to Pilate to ask for the body of Jesus. The governor was surprised, not at the request, but at hearing that Jesus was dead already (Mark xv. 44), and, to assure himself of the fact, sent to inquire of the centurion on duty at the crosses. Somewhere about the same time, probably a little later in the "evening," but still before 6 p.m., the Jews, *i.e.* the Sanhedrin leaders, came to Pilate with a request that the death of the three crucified might be hastened by their legs being broken, in order that their bodies hanging on the crosses might not pollute the very sacred day which followed.

(It would be the sabbath, and the day of the Passover.)

This terrible, but perhaps merciful, end to the tortures of the cross seems not to have been uncommon in Jewish crucifixion inflicted by the Roman authority.

Crucifixion with this and all its attendant horrors was abolished by the first Christian emperor Constantine in the fourth century.

The two thieves apparently expired under this treatment. The soldiers, however, when they looked on the form hanging on the central cross, found the Crucified, as we know, dead already. To make sure of this, one of the executioners thrust his spear deeply into the side of the motionless body of Jesus, "and forthwith came there out blood and water" (John xix. 33, 34). Upon this, in accordance with the permission of the governor already obtained, the body of the Lord was delivered to Joseph of Arimathæa and his friends.

Vers. 50, 51.—And, behold, there was a man named Joseph, a counsellor; and he was a good man, and a just: (the same had not consented to the counsel and deed of them;) he was of Arimathæa. This Joseph was a member of the Sanhedrin, a personage of high distinction in Jerusalem, and evidently of great wealth. It is especially mentioned that his vote in the supreme council was not given when the death of Jesus was determined on. Nicodemus and his costly offering of spices for the entombment is only mentioned by St. John (xix. 39). Arimathæa, the place whence this Joseph came, is famous in Jewish history, being identical with Ramathaim Zophim, the "Ramah of the watchers," the native town of Samuel. Each evangelist speaks of Joseph in high terms, and each in his own way. "Luke styles him 'a counsellor, good and just;' he is the καλὸς κἀγαθός, the Greek ideal. Mark calls him 'an honourable counsellor,' the Roman ideal. Matthew writes of him as 'a rich man:' is not this the Jewish ideal?" (Godet). And St. John, we might add, chooses another title for this loved man, "being a disciple of Jesus:" this was St. John's ideal. In Joseph of Arimathæa and Nicodemus we have specimens of a class of earnest and devout Jews, perhaps not uncommon at that time—men who respected and admired our Lord as a Teacher, and half believed in him as the Messiah (the Christ), and yet from many mixed and various motives shrank from confessing him before men till after the cross had been endured. It was not only the Resurrection which so enormously increased the number and raised the character of the followers of Jesus. When he was gone, men reflected on the inimitable life, on the deep, heart-searching teaching, on the confirmatory works of power; and when the news of the Resurrection came, the little wavering, half-hearted band of followers and hearers became in a few months a great host, and in a few years they had spread over the then civilized world. There is a strange but interesting tradition which tells how this Joseph of Arimathæa came to Great Britain about A.D. 63, and settled in Glastonbury, and there erected a humble Christian oratory, the first in England. The miraculous thorn of Glastonbury, long supposed to bud and blossom every Christmas Day, was reported to have sprung from the staff which Joseph stuck in the ground as he stopped to rest himself on the hill-top.

Ver. 53.—And he took it down, and wrapped it in linen. The last sad rites of love seem all to have been performed by friendly hands. Joseph and Nicodemus, and those with them, reverently took down the pierced and bleeding body; then, after the usual ablution, the sacred head was covered with the napkin, the *soudarion* (St. John), and the holy body was wrapped tenderly and carefully in broad bands of the finest linen, covered with thick layers of the costly aromatic preparation of which Nicodemus had laid up such ample store (St. John). This was to preserve the loved remains of the Master from any corruption which might set in before they could proceed with the process of embalming, which was delayed necessarily until after the sabbath and Passover day were passed. St. John adds, "as the manner of the Jews is to bury," probably marking the Jewish custom of embalming and thus preserving the body, as contrasted with burning, which was the Roman usage. **And laid it in a sepulchre that was hewn in stone.** St. John tells us the sepulchre was in a garden. This seems not to have been an unusual practice with "the great" among the Jews. Josephus relates of Kings Uzziah and Manasseh that they were buried in their gardens ('Ant.,' ix. 10 and x. 3. 2). "He made his grave with the rich" (Isa. liii. 9). **Wherein never man before was laid.** St. John styles it "a new sepulchre." These details are given to show that the Lord's sacred body was not brought into contact with corruption.

Ver. 54.—And that day was the preparation, and the sabbath drew on. It was the preparation for the sabbath, but more especially for the great Passover Feast. St. John, for this reason, calls the coming sabbath "a high day." *Drew on;* literally *began to dawn;* although the sabbath began at sunset, the whole time of darkness was regarded as anticipatory of the dawn. The evening of Friday was sometimes even called "the daybreak."

Vers. 55, 56.—**And the women also, which came with him from Galilee, followed after, and beheld the sepulchre, and how his body was laid. And they returned, and prepared spices and ointments.** The real process of embalming, the women who were of the company of Jesus—the Maries, Salome, and others—proposed to undertake as soon as the sabbath was passed, that is, on the first day of the coming week—the Sunday. How little even his nearest and dearest friends dreamed of a resurrection of the body! It seems probable that they expected, at least some of them, a glorious reappearance of Jesus, *but when, but how,* they had evidently formed no definite conception. None, however, seemed to have thought of the bodily resurrection which took place on the first day of the week—on that Sunday morning. St. Matthew (xxvii. 62—66) relates how, after the entombment, the chief priests and Pharisees went to Pilate and asked that the sepulchre might, "until the third day," be made sure; and how the Roman governor bade them take such precautions as seemed good to them. These—his bitter opponents—were more clear-sighted than his friends. They had some dim fears of *something* which might still follow, while his disciples, in their hopeless sorrow, thought all was over. **And rested the sabbath day according to the commandment.** "It was the last sabbath of the old covenant. It was scrupulously respected" (Godet).

HOMILETICS.

Vers. 47—56.—*Friday night until Sunday morning. "It is finished!"* But there are witnesses to the solemnity of the moment and the significance of the word, whose testimony gives weight to the voice of conscience. The rumble and reel of the earthquake are felt. When "the loud voice" is uttered, the veil which separates the most holy from the holy place is torn in two; an ominous darkness covers the city; there is a crash as of rending rocks and opening tombs, and strange forms, as of those who were dead, flit before the vision. Three hours are marked by portents (vers. 44, 45), beneath whose impression even the officer in charge of the Roman soldiery exclaims (ver. 47), "Certainly this was a righteous Man. He must have been a Son of God." And when, besides, the multitude, hushed and solemnized, gazes on the countenance now calm and still in the repose of death, and the recollection of the life so pure and noble becomes vivid in the mind, the reaction from intense excitement sets in, and (ver. 48) smiting on their breasts in unavailing sorrow, they steal away from the scene of death. Only two groups remain—the soldiers, who must watch until the crucified are dead, and their bodies are removed; and "the acquaintance of Jesus, and the women who had followed him from Galilee, far off, in speechless amazement beholding these things" (ver. 49). All that remains is the burial. He whose cross was erected between the malefactors is dead. The priests and scribes had begged that the closing act of the death by crucifixion, that called the *crucifragium*—the smiting or breaking of the legs—might be hastened and the corpses removed, so that no offence to decency might be felt on the high day, "the double sabbath," at hand. Pilate had acceded to the request; and the forms of the two malefactors had been smitten. Not the form of Jesus. No spark of life, it was said, remained. Only, to make assurance sure, a spear is thrust into the side; the spear, it may be, pierced the pericardium of the heart, or that had already been ruptured; anyhow, a mixture of blood and water flows out. St. John is emphatic as to this, no doubt to silence the suggestion that Jesus had only seemed to die, or that the seeming death had been only a swoon. No, says the evangelist (John xix. 35), "I saw it myself." It is the symbolic meaning of that effusion which we set before us when we sing—

> "Let the water and the blood,
> From thy riven side which flowed,
> Be of sin the double cure—
> Cleanse me from its guilt and power."

Is the Lord buried in the sepulchre reserved for those who had been doomed to capital punishment? No. Here there comes into view the beautiful and striking incident recorded in vers. 50—53. And, in connection with it, we light on a word which is used at he hour when we should least have expected to find it. One of the Sanhedrists—a man universally esteemed for piety and prudence—Joseph of Arimathæa—had not consented to the counsel and deed of his colleagues. Hitherto he had never dared to avow the attraction which he felt. Why should he now risk his reputation, it may be his life, by an acknowledgment which he had withheld in his earlier days? Every dictate of worldly wisdom bade him be wholly silent. What do we read in Mark xv. 43? It is the death of Christ that dispels the fear, that at last prompts to decision. He goes in *boldly* to Pilate, and craves the body of Jesus. And the demand of the senator is granted. And as he bears away the sacred frame, he is joined by another (John xix. 39), the Nicodemus of whom we read at the beginning of the ministry (John iii.), who brings with him a princely offering of myrrh and aloes. The reverent and loving hands thus joined together wrap the body (ver. 53) in linen, and hastily and partially embalm it, laying it in the tomb which Joseph had scooped out for himself as his own last resting-place. What happened between this time and the third, the appointed day? Let us ask, first, *What, as it concerns our Lord?* secondly, *What, as it concerns the disciples?* and, thirdly, *What, as it concerns the world which crucified him?*

I. What happened as it concerns our Lord? Two or three words give us some hints concerning our Lord after his death and before the Resurrection. First, his own assurance given to Mary on the resurrection-day (John xx. 17), "I am not yet ascended to my Father." The place and condition into which he passed, in dying, were intermediate between the life on earth and the life in glory. He was not then, as the Man Jesus, in the glory of the Father. And, as bearing on this, we further recall the promise to the dying malefactor (ver. 43). "Lord, remember me," he had said, "when thou comest into thy kingdom." "To-day," was the reply, "shalt thou be with me in Paradise." Paradise, then, received the soul of Christ. Thither he bore with him the one who, in penitence and faith, had cast himself on his mercy. And Paradise meant the region in the under-world of the dead set apart for the faithful as their rest until the resurrection—a blessedness real, though incomplete; a garden with the tree of life in it, but not the full enjoyment of the beatific vision. This is the meaning of the clause in the Apostles' Creed, "He descended into hell," *i.e.* into Hades, the state of the dead. It is true that this clause has not the antiquity which may be claimed for other clauses; but it expresses the belief of all times that our Lord submitted to the conditions of the holy dead—that he was truly and verily numbered among them. The soul was actually in Hades, or Sheôl. What part in the great redemptive work was fulfilled by this descent? Had he a ministry in this short but significant period? There is a passage in 1 Peter too obscure to allow of being pressed as an answer to this question, but suggestive of interesting lines of thought (1 Pet. iii. 18—20). To many it has seemed that the preaching to the spirits in prison mentioned there was the work of the Hades-state; that he proclaimed his gospel to those who were kept in ward—not the righteous only, but those who were disobedient, *e.g.* the antediluvian generations to which Noah had preached in vain. And the inference drawn from this view of the passage has appeared "to throw light on one of the darkest enigmas of Divine justice—the cases where the final doom seems infinitely out of proportion to the lapse which has incurred it." No argument can be built on a passage whose interpretation is doubtful; but the exposition hinted at falls in with convictions which have been cherished from the time of the apostles. We are, at all events, on solid Scripture ground when we suppose that, in the world of the dead, the triumph over him that had the power of death, *i.e.* the devil, was completed. The descent was the following of the enemy into his innermost citadel; it was the spoiling of the principalities and power of darkness; it was the opening of the way through death into life by him who has the keys of Hades. Is not Paradise all the sweeter that Christ has been there? Is not the inheritance all the surer that through death he went to the Father? Is not this the symbol of our faith and hope—that "the Lord has set his cross in the midst of Hades, which is the sign of victory that will remain to eternity"?

II. What happened as it concerns the disciples. But what of those who weep and lament whilst the world is rejoicing—the sorrow-stricken, orphaned company of disciples? The last to leave the place where the body of Jesus was laid, as the first to hasten to the tomb when the sabbath is past, are the holy women (vers. 55, 56). We see them on Friday evening watching the tomb, and observing how the lifeless form was attended to, and then hastening into the city, that they may make ready the spices and ointments for embalming before the sabbath began. Their love is stronger than their faith. The heart's yearning is sometimes more than the heart's believing. A very dreary sabbath that was to all the disciples. "They rested according to the commandment" (ver. 56). A commandment—rest, and nothing more. What conflicts of thought and affection! What desolation of spirit! Peter—what a strange sabbath it must have been to him! Only one thing for all. The sense of relation to the crucified Jesus can never be effaced; but it has no glow of hope, it has only the darkness of a memory, the gloom of a despair. "They rested on the sabbath; *but*" (the first word of the twenty-fourth chapter should be "but" rather than "now"); but the running of the spirit, the movement of the love, is only towards the garden and its sepulchre. Is it not the type of Church, of Christian, wanting the power of the Holy Ghost? Work for Christ, loyal but cheerless, without sight of his glory, or waiting for his advent—this is suggested by the preparation of the spices and ointments, and the sabbath-keeping but without the true spiritual sabbath, the joy of the Lord; ordinances observed, but with no inner alacrity, only because of the commandment. This is suggested by the unrestful resting on that seventh day. Not yet is there the anointing of the Holy Ghost, the power of the Resurrection.

III. WHAT HAPPENED AS IT CONCERNS THE WORLD WHICH CRUCIFIED HIM. Is it not strange that what was absent from faith as a hope was present to unbelief as a fear? Those who had crucified the Lord have their memory wonderfully quickened. They recall (Matt. xxvii. 62—64) some words which he uttered nearly three years before, about a temple which he would raise in three days, and their dread gives a force to these words. Sabbath though it be, the chief priests and Pharisees seek an audience of Pilate, and beg him to "make the sepulchre sure until the third day, lest his disciples come by night, and steal him away, and say to the people, He is risen from the dead: and so the last error be worse than the first." They are told to go their way and do as they choose; and hence the sealing of the great stone and the setting of the watch. Is not all now secure? Have they not for ever dispelled the illusions as to the Deceiver? So thought the Jewish authorities; so men think still. They are always crying out that the Christian religion is effete, that the Christian's Christ has been slain. "Are there any Christians still?" asked a notable sceptic some years ago. O purblind souls! What avail your watch and seal? He whom you call Deceiver is yet alive; and there are compunctions of heart, convictions of guilt and wrong-doing, and needs of spiritual restoration and inward rectitude, which will assert themselves against all your philosophies! Pentecost days are never far distant days when a mighty remorse rolls over the minds of men, and the cry which never can be silenced, because it is the cry of the human soul in its most solemn hours, and with reference to its deepest wants, bursts through lips which are quivering with a genuine earnestness, "What shall we do to be saved?" On that sabbath the world religious and irreligious holds its rest. It cannot altogether forget; but it holds its Paschal feasts, and complies with all the etiquette of these feasts, as if there were no Calvary, as if no Jesus had lived and died. And is not this the feature of all times? Do not men push their ambitious projects, scheme and toil, spend their strength, and hold their sabbaths without the living consciousness of the Christ who died for their sins? May not we ourselves say—

"I sin; and heaven and earth go round
As if no dreadful deed were done,
As if Christ's blood had never flowed
To hinder sin or to atone"?

There is no word more solemn than that (Heb. vi. 4—6) in which the sacred writer reminds us that if those who have tasted the Word of God and the powers of the world to come fall away, they pass from the fold of the Church into the ranks of Christ's enemies, seeing "they crucify to themselves the Son of God afresh, and put him to an open shame."

HOMILIES BY VARIOUS AUTHORS.

Vers. 1—3.—*The Divine kingdom.* Deeply interesting is this interview between the Nazarene and the Roman, the Jewish Prisoner and the Roman judge; the *one* then brought forth as a malefactor and now seated on the throne of the world, the *other* then exalted on the seat of power and now sunk to the depth of universal pity if not of universal scorn. "Art thou a King?" asks the latter, in the tone of lofty superiority. "I am," replies the former, in the tone of calm and profound assurance. What, then, was this kingdom of which he spoke? What was that kingdom of God, that kingdom of heaven, that "kingdom of the truth" (John xviii. 37) which he foretold, which he came to this world and which he laid down his life to establish? It was *the sovereignty of God over all human souls.* God's claim—which is not founded on *prescription,* nor upon *force,* but upon *righteousness*—is his claim on the reverence, the affection, the obedience, of those whom he has created, preserved, enriched, who owe to him all that he demands of them. With us, who have revolted from his rule, this means nothing less than the restoration of our loyalty, and thus our return to his likeness and to his favour as well as to his sway. We look at—

I. The originality of the conception. We plume ourselves upon the originality of our ideas, upon our "creations." But when did the mind of man launch on the sea of human thought such a conception as this kingdom of God? Men had entertained the idea of founding by force a widely extended empire which should command the outward homage and tribute of hundreds of thousands of men, and should last for many generations. But who ever designed a creation like this glorious "kingdom of heaven"—a world-wide sway embracing all living souls whatsoever, exercised by an unseen King, in which the service of the lip, and even that of the life, would be of no account at all without the homage of the heart and the willing subjection of the spirit, characterized by universal righteousness, and crowned by abounding peace and lasting joy?

II. The immensity of the work to be accomplished. For what would be involved in the establishment of such a kingdom as this? Not only the formation and maintenance of a new religion that should hold up its head and keep its course amid surrounding faiths, but the utter intolerance and complete subversion of every other creed and *cultus;* the emptying of all the temples and all the synagogues in every land; the dissolution of all the venerable religious institutions which were rooted in the prejudice, fixed in the affections, wrought into the habits and the lives of men; it meant the establishment in the convictions and in the conscience of mankind of a faith which came into direct collision with all its intellectual pride, with all its social selfishness, with all its powerful passions.

III. Its sublimity as a purpose and a hope. Not merely to ameliorate the circumstances and conditions of a country, or of the world at large. That would have been a noble purpose; but that would have been slight and small in comparison with the aim of Jesus Christ. His view was to put away *the source* of all poverty and sorrow and death; to "put away sin by the sacrifice of himself;" to found in the hearts and therefore in the lives of men a kingdom of holiness, and therefore of true and lasting blessedness; to restore to God his rightful heritage in the love of his children, and, at the same time, to restore to men everywhere their high and glorious portion in the favour and friendship, in the likeness and glory, of God. Was ever scheme, was ever hope like this—so divinely new, so magnificently great, so unapproachably sublime? 1. The *way into* this kingdom is by a humble, living faith. 2. The way *on* to its higher places is the service of sacrificial love. The path which takes us to the cross is the way to the throne.—C.

Vers. 4—12.—*The majesty of meekness, etc.* Beautiful in the last degree, as a moral spectacle, is the sight of the meek but mighty Saviour in the presence of the scornful human sovereign. But there are many lessons which we may gather on our way to that striking scene.

I. How pitiful human authority may prove to be! Poor Pilate, occupying his high seat of authority and power, is "driven with the wind and tossed," as if he were a leaf upon the ground. He "finds no fault in Jesus" (ver. 4), but he dares not acquit him; he is afraid of the men he is there to govern. He casts about for a way of escape; he at lasts hits upon the poor expedient of shifting the difficulty to other shoulders. He presents to us a very pitiable object as a man who sits in the chair of office, and dares not do his duty there. Authority divested of a manly courage and shaking with fear of consequences is a deplorable thing.

II. How FEEBLE IS MERE PASSIONATE VEHEMENCE! The people, led by the priests, were "the more fierce" (ver. 5), insisting that Pilate should not release the Prisoner of whose innocence he was convinced. We see them, with hatred flashing from their eyes, indulging in frantic gestures of deprecation and incitement, loudly clamouring for the condemnation of the Holy One. Their urgency did, indeed, prevail for the moment, as vehemence frequently does. But into what a dire and terrible mistake it led them! to what a crime were they hastening! what awful issues were to spring from their success! How truly were they sowing the wind of which they would reap the whirlwind! Earnestness is always admirable; enthusiasm is often a great power for good; but passionate vehemence is nothing better than a noisy feebleness. It is not the presence of real power; it is the absence of intelligence and self-control. It leads men to actions which have a momentary success, but which end in a lasting failure and in sad disgrace.

III. How UNFRUITFUL IS IDLE CURIOSITY. (Vers. 8, 9.) Herod congratulated himself too soon. He reckoned on having a keen curiosity fully gratified; he thought he had this Prophet in his power, and could command an exhibition of his peculiar faculty, whatever that might prove to be. But he did not want to arrive at truth, or to be better able to do his duty or serve his generation; and Jesus Christ declined to minister to his royal fancy. He was silent and passive, though urged to speech and action. Christ will speak to our hearts, and will work for our benefit and blessing when we approach him in a reverent and earnest spirit; but to a worldly and irreverent curiosity he has nothing to say. It must retire ungratified, and come again in another mood.

IV. How INCONSTANT IS UNSPIRITUAL FRIENDSHIP! Herod had very little to thank Pilate for, on this occasion; he appears to have mistaken a cowardly attempt to evade duty for a mark of personal respect or a desire to effect a reconciliation (ver. 12). A friendship that had to be renewed, and that was patched up in so slight a way and on such mistaken ground, would not last long and was worth very little. Friendship that is not built on thorough knowledge and on mutual esteem is exceedingly fragile and of small account. It is only common attachment to the same great principles and to the one Divine Lord that binds together in indissoluble bonds. Sameness of occupation, similarity of taste, exposure to a common peril, or the possession of a common hope,—this is not the rock on which friendship will stand long; it rests on character, and on the character that is formed by close, personal intimacy with the one true Friend of man.

V. How WRONG AND EVEN WICKED IS UNENLIGHTENED SCORN! (Ver. 11.) Quite unimaginable is the uproarious laughter and the keen, low enjoyment with which the actors went through this wretched ribaldry, this (to us) most painful mockery. How little did they think that he whom they were so mercilessly insulting *was* the King he claimed to be, and was immeasurably higher than the highest of them all! Wrong and wicked is human scorn. Often since then has it mocked at truth and wisdom, and poured its poor ridicule on the head of holiness and true nobility! It is not only the "stranger" who may prove to be the "angel unawares entertained;" it is also the man whom we do not understand, whom we may think entirely in the wrong, whom we are tempted to despise. Many are the mockers who will be fain, one day, to receive a gracious pardon from the object of their derision.

VI. How MAJESTIC IS SPIRITUAL MEEKNESS! (Ver. 11.) We know well how our Lord bore this cruel trial. "A silent Man before his foes" was he. Able at any moment to bring them into utmost humiliation, to turn the mocking glance of triumph into the countenance blanched with unspeakable fear, and the brutal laugh of mockery into a cry for mercy, he stood without a blow, without a word on his own behalf, enduring as one that saw the invisible and the eternal. There is nothing more majestic than a calm endurance of wrong. To accept without return the strong buffeting of cruelty, to take without reply the more keen and piercing utterance of falsehood, because stillness or silence will advance the cause of truth and the kingdom of God,—

this is to be very "near the throne" on which it is our highest ambition to be placed; it is to be carrying out, most acceptably, the commandment of the meek, majestic Saviour as he says to us, "Follow me!"—C.

Ver. 16.—*Guilty compromise.* Twice (see ver. 22) Pilate made this offer to the Jews. He would chastise Jesus and release him; he would thus gratify them by putting the Object of their hatred to pain and humiliation, and he would satisfy his own conscience by saving an innocent man from the last extremity. It was a poor and a guilty compromise he proposed as a solution. If Jesus were as guilty as they claimed that he was, he deserved to die, and Pilate was in duty bound to condemn him to death; if he were innocent, he certainly ought not to have been subjected to the exposure and agony of scourging. It was a cowardly and ignoble endeavour to save himself at the expense either of public or of individual justice. Compromises are of very different character. There are compromises which are—

I. JUST, AND THEREFORE HONOURABLE. Two men in business have claims one against the other, and one cannot convince the other by argument; the proposal is made to adjust their respective claims by a compromise, each man consenting to forego something, the concession of the one being taken as a fair equivalent to that of the other: this is honourable to both. It very probably results in each man getting what is his due, and it saves both from the misery and expense of litigation, and preserves good will and even friendship.

II. WISE, AND THEREFORE COMMENDABLE. A society—it may be of a distinctly religious character—is divided by its members holding opposite opinions. Some advocate one course, the others urge a different one. The idea is suggested that a third course be adopted, which includes some features of the two; there is no serious principle involved, it is only a matter of procedure, a question of expediency. Then it will probably be found to be the wisdom of that society to accept the proposed compromise. Every one present has the double advantage of *securing something* which he approves, and (what is really better, if it could but be realized) that of *yielding something* to the wishes or the convictions of other people.

III. GUILTY, AND THEREFORE CONDEMNABLE. Such was that of the text. Such have been innumerable others since then. All are guilty that are effected: 1. At the *expense of truth.* The teacher of Divine truth may bring his doctrine down to the level of his hearers' understanding; he may make known the great verities of the faith "in many portions" (πολυμερῶς); but he may not, in order to "please men," distort or withhold the living truth of God. If he does that he shows himself unworthy of his office, and he exposes himself to the severe condemnation of his Divine Master. 2. At the *expense of justice.* However anxious we may be to preserve outward harmony, we may not, for the sake of peace, do any one man a wrong; may not asperse his character, injure his prospects, wound his spirit. Rather than do that, we must face the storm, and guide our bark as best we can. 3. At the *expense of self-respect.* If Pilate had been less hardened than he probably was, less accustomed to the infliction of human pain and shame, he would have gone back to the interior of his house ashamed of himself, as he thought of the lacerating scene that immediately followed that mockery of a trial. If we cannot yield without inflicting on our own soul a real spiritual injury, without doing (or leaving undone) an action the remembrance of which will not only shame but weaken us, then we must not compromise the matter in dispute. We must tell our tale, whatever it may be; we must make our motion, whomsoever it may offend; we must walk straight on in the road of rectitude, in the path of humanity.—C.

Ver. 24.—*The character of Pilate.* It is true that Pilate's opinion concerning Jesus of Nazareth was very different indeed from that of his accusers; but he little imagined that it would be to that poor suffering Prisoner that he would owe such immortality as he is to enjoy. Yet so it is; it is only because we are disciples of Jesus Christ that we care to ask who and what was Pilate. He is nothing but the gold upon the altar. In considering the elements of his character, we note—

I. THAT HE WAS POSSESSED OF ENERGY AND ENTERPRISE. He would hardly have reached the station he occupied, or held it as long as he did, if he had not had these two qualities in his character.

II. THAT HE WAS NOT DEVOID OF SPIRITUAL DISCERNMENT. It is clear that he was much impressed by all that he saw of Jesus. The calmness, patience, and nobility of our Lord called forth from Pilate a sincere respect. There was genuine admiration in his heart as he led forth the Divine Sufferer and exclaimed, "Behold the Man!" He was affected, and even awed, by the moral greatness he was witnessing. He may also have been moved to pity.

III. THAT HIS WORLDLINESS HAD WORN OUT HIS FAITH. He had probably had his visions, in earlier days, of the sacredness and supremacy of truth; he had indulged his idea of what was morally good and sound, more to be desired than riches, more to be pursued than honour or authority. But a life of worldliness had done for him what it will do for any of its votaries—it had eaten away his early faith; it had caused his fairest views and noblest purposes to melt and to disappear; it had left his spirit "naked to his enemies," without any assured belief in any one or in anything. "To bear witness to the truth." "What *is* truth?" asks the poor sceptic, whose soul was empty of all sustaining trust, of all ennobling hope.

IV. THAT HE HAD COME TO SUBORDINATE RIGHTEOUSNESS TO POLICY. That Prisoner on his hands was innocent: of that he was well assured. He would not condemn him to a cruel death unless he was obliged to do so. But he must not push his preference for righteousness too far. He must not seriously endanger his own position; he must not put a handle into the power of his enemies. No; rather than that, this pure and holy One must be scourged, must even die the death. As the trial proceeds, it appears that he is exciting a very strong hostility to himself. Let the poor Man go, then, to his doom; one more act of injustice, however regrettable in itself, will not make much difference. "And Pilate gave sentence that it should be as they required."

APPLICATION. 1. Outward circumstances prove very little. It is the judge whom we pity now; it is the bound and buffeted, the maltreated and maligned Prisoner whom we now honour and emulate. 2. Real strength is in righteousness and in love. Unrighteousness and selfishness, in the person of Pilate, resorted to shifts and expedients, and vacillated again and again between obligation and self-interest. Flawless integrity and abounding love for man, in the person of Jesus Christ, wavered not for an instant, but pursued its holy and gracious purpose through pain and shame. Policy prevails for a very little while; it goes back to its palace, but its end is exile and suicide. Poverty and love go through the deep darkness of earth to the unshadowed glory of the skies.—C.

Ver. 26.—*Compulsion and invitation; the human and the Divine methods.* Here we have an illustration of—

I. HUMAN VIOLENCE. "They laid hold upon" one Simon, and "him they compelled" (Matt. xxvii. 32) to bear his cross. What right had these Roman soldiers to impress this stranger into their service? What claim had they upon him? By what law of rectitude did they arrest him as he was entering the city, and insist on his bearing a burden, and going whither he would not? What justified them in laying hands upon him and violently enforcing this service? None whatever; nothing whatsoever. It was only another instance of the unscrupulousness of human power. Thus has it been everywhere and always. Let men but feel that they have the mastery, that theirs is the more powerful mind, the firmer will, the stronger hand, and they will ask no leave, consult no law, be restrained by no consideration of conscience. The history of man, where not under special Divine direction, has been the history of the assertion of strength over weakness; that has been the course of national, of tribal, of family, of individual life. The strong man, well armed, has "laid hold upon" the weak man, and laid some burden upon him to carry. He has virtually said, "I can command your labour, serve me; if you refuse to do so, you shall pay some penalty of my own choosing." Human violence (1) is essentially unrighteous, for it is based on no claim that can be properly so called; (2) has been found to be shamelessly unmerciful; (3) has been gradually, though slowly, subjected to the great rule of Christ (Matt. vii. 12); (4) is destined in time to make way for the rule of righteousness.

II. DIVINE PERSUASIVENESS. God does not compel us to serve him. He may, indeed, so wisely overrule all things as to make the life deliberately withheld from him or the action directed against him (*e.g.* the act of betrayal by Judas) contribute to the final issue; but he does not force the individual soul to serve him. Jesus Christ does not compel us to his service. It is true that his invitations have the authority of a command; but his commands have the sweetness of invitations. 1. He *invites us to approach* him and seek his favour. "Come unto me all ye that labour" is not a severe command; it is a most gracious invitation. "Whosoever believeth on me hath everlasting life" is not a peremptory injunction; it is a welcome and generous announcement. And while it is indeed true that Christ says, imperatively "Follow me!" it is also true that he does not force any one into his company; he makes his appeal to our conscience and conviction; he will not have any in his service who do not freely and whole-heartedly consent to come. 2. *He graciously influences us*, that we may see and follow the true light. Paul, indeed, does speak of Christ as "apprehending," or laying hold of, him (Phil. iii. 12). But this referred to the very exceptional manifestation of his Divine power, and the language is strongly figurative. The Spirit of God does illumine our understanding and affect our heart; but he does not compel us to decide without the consent of our own will. In the last resort we have to "choose life" or death. 3. He summons us to a *full discipleship by following him* as one that bore a cross (ch. ix. 23; Matt. xvi. 24). He lets us know that we shall not meet with his full approval if we do not bear the cross after him, if we do not follow him in the path of sacrificial love. But there is truest kindness, both of substance and manner, in this his urgent challenge. 4. He *promises us inward rest* here, and a *large reward* hereafter, if we do hear his voice and do thus follow him. Between human compulsion and Divine invitation or Divine constraint, there is exceeding breadth: the one is an intolerable tyranny; the other *is* essential righteousness, and *introduces* to true liberty, to spiritual rest, to abiding joy.—C.

Vers. 27—31.—*Sympathy and solicitude.* Before reaching Calvary an interesting and instructive incident occurred. Among the tumultuous crowd that surged round the soldiers and their victims were many women. These were better away, we are disposed to think, from a scene so brutal and so harrowing as this. But we will believe that something better than curiosity, that gratitude, that affection, that womanly pity, drew them, spite of their natural shrinking, to this last sad ending. By whatever motives impelled, they were certainly moved to strong compassion as they saw the Prophet of Nazareth, the great Healer and Teacher, led forth to die. Their loud laments did not fall on the ear of One too occupied with his own impending doom to hear and heed them. Our Lord made to these weeping women the reply which is here recorded, longer and fuller than we should have supposed the circumstances would allow. It suggests to us—

I. THAT HUMAN DISTRESS NEVER FAILS TO REACH AND TOUCH HIM. If there were any moments in his life when he might have been preoccupied, and might not have noticed the sounds of sorrow, it was this hour of his agony, this hour when the weight of the world's sin rested on his soul, when the great sacrifice was in the very act of being offered. Yet even then he heard and stopped to console the troubled. An appeal to Jesus Christ in circumstances of sorrow is never ill-timed.

II. THAT SUCH SYMPATHY WITH JESUS CHRIST IS ENTIRELY OUT OF PLACE. "Weep not for me." Some men speak and act as if it were appropriate to express sympathy with the Saviour on account of his sufferings. It is, indeed, impossible to read the story of his last hours, and *realize* what it all *meant*, without having our sympathetic feeling very keenly quickened; but Jesus Christ does not ask that we should express to him, or to one another, our sympathy with him as One that then suffered. These sufferings are past; they have placed him upon the throne of the world; they have made brighter than ever his celestial crown, deeper than ever his heavenly joy. So far as *we* are concerned, and so far as they speak of our sin, they may well humble us; in so far as *he* is concerned, we *rejoice with him* that he "was perfected through suffering."

III. THAT A HOLY SOLICITUDE FOR OURSELVES AND OURS IS OFTEN THE MOST APPROPRIATE SENTIMENT. "Weep for yourselves, and for your children." We know well what reason these Jewish women had, both as patriots and as mothers, to be concerned for the fate that threatened their country and their homes. Our Lord certainly would not condemn, would not disparage, an unselfish sympathy. He who wept at Bethany, and whose law of love was the law that covered and inspired a gracious burden-bearing

(Gal. vi. 2), could not possibly do that. Indeed, we seldom stand nearer to his side than when we "weep with them that weep." But there are many times when we are tempted to be troubled by our brother's smaller difficulty instead of being concerned about our own much greater one. Do not be blind to the bodily pains or the circumstantial struggles of your neighbour; but look eagerly and earnestly to the rent which is opening in your own reputation, to the gap that is increasingly visible in your own consistency, to the fact that you are palpably descending the slope which leads down to spiritual ruin.

IV. THAT THERE ARE SAD EXTREMITIES OF EVIL WHEN NOTHING IS LEFT BUT A HOPELESS CRY. (Ver. 30.)

V. THAT SIN AND PUNISHMENT BECOME DEEPER AND NEARER AS TIME GOES ON. The green tree is exposed to the consuming fire; but the green tree in time becomes the dry, and how much more certain and more fierce then will be the devouring flame! The nation goes from bad to worse, from the worse to the worst; from dark to darker guilt, from condemnation to calamity. So does a human soul, unguided by heavenly truth and unguarded by holy principle. At any and every time in danger, its peril becomes continually greater as its guilt becomes constantly deeper. Go not one step further in the course of sin, in the way of worldliness, into the "far country" of forgetfulness. Each step is an approach to a precipice. Return on thy way without a moment's lingering.—C.

Ver. 34.—*Magnanimity an attainment.* "*Then* said Jesus, Father, forgive them; for they know not what they do." When—at what particular point did he say that? It is commonly believed that he uttered this most gracious prayer just at the time of the actual crucifixion. Just when the nails were driven into those hands, the hands that had constantly been employed in some ministry of mercy; into those feet that had been continually carrying him on some errand of kindness; or just when the heavy cross, with its suffering Victim fastened upon it, had been driven into the ground with unpitying violence;—just *then*, at the moment of most excruciating pain and of intolerable shame, he opened his lips to pray for mercy on his executioners. We have here—

I. A RARE INSTANCE OF HUMAN MAGNANIMITY. 1. Conscious, not only of perfect innocence, but of the purest and even the loftiest aims, Jesus Christ found himself not only unrewarded and unappreciated, but misunderstood, ill treated, condemned on a totally false charge, sentenced to the most cruel and shameful death a man could die. What wonder if, under those conditions, all the kindliness of his nature had turned to sourness of spirit! 2. At this very moment he was the object of the most heartless cruelty man could inflict, and must have been suffering pain of body and of mind that was literally agonizing. 3. At such a time, and under such treatment, he forgets himself to remember the guilt of those who were so shamefully wronging him. 4. Instead of entertaining any feeling of resentment, he desired that they might be forgiven their wrong-doing. 5. He did not haughtily and contemptuously decline to condemn them; he did not hardly and reluctantly forgive them; he found for them a generous extenuation; he sincerely prayed his heavenly Father to forgive them. Human magnanimity could hardly go further than that.

II. A BEAUTIFUL EXAMPLE OF HIS OWN LOFTY DOCTRINE. When in his great sermon (Matt. v.—vii.) he said, "Love your enemies . . . pray for them which despitefully use and persecute you, that ye may be the children of your Father which is in heaven," he urged upon us to cherish and to illustrate the loftiest virtue on the highest grounds. This he now beautifully, perfectly exemplified. He was literally and truly praying for those who were using him despitefully. As the greatest generals and captains have proudly and honourably claimed that they "never bade men do that which they were not willing to do themselves," so this our glorious Leader, he who came to be the "Leader and Perfecter of the faith" (Heb. xii. 2: Alford), never desired of us any virtue or grace which he did not possess and did not himself adorn. He could and did say to his disciples, not only, "Go thither in the way of righteousness," but also, "Follow me in every path of purity and love." We may well love our enemies, and pray for those who despitefully use us, that we may be the children of our Father in heaven, and that we may be followers of our patient, magnanimous Master. And it is here, truly, that we have—

III. A CHALLENGE TO A GREAT ATTAINMENT. 1. To pray sincerely for those who do us wrong is one of the very highest points, if not actually the very loftiest, of human magnanimity. To dismiss all vindictive purpose, all resentful thought; to look at our enemy's procedure in a kindly light, and to take, as Christ did here, a generous view of it; to cherish a positive wish for his good; to put this wish into action, into prayer;—by these stages we reach the summit of nobility. 2. This is an attainment we should sedulously and devoutly pursue. There are those of noble nature, men and women whom God endows with a most "excellent spirit," to whom this may be plain and easy; to them it is not a steep ascent to be laboriously climbed, but a gentle slope along which they can walk without difficulty. But to most men it is an *attainment* and not an endowment. It is an attainment which can only be secured by earnest and continued cultivation. But we have for this great end the most effectual means: (1) the realization of the near presence of God, and the knowledge of his Divine approval; (2) the sense that when we succeed we win the greatest of all victories; (3) the efficacy of prayer—its *subjective* influence, and the aid which it brings us *from above;* (4) the inspiration of our Lord's example, and that of his most faithful followers (Acts vii. 60; 2 Tim. iv. 16).—C.

Ver. 34.—*Sin greater than it seems.* "They know not what they do." There is more in our actions, and therefore in our life, than there seems to be to ourselves (see "The largeness of our life," homily on ch. x. 16). There is more of good; more also of evil. These soldiers imagined that they were doing nothing more than executing a malefactor. They *were* murdering a Messiah; they were putting to death the Son of Man, the Saviour of mankind. They knew not what they did; they did not recognize the extreme seriousness, the actual awfulness, of the crime they were committing. Thus is it constantly. We suppose ourselves to be doing something of very little consequence; but he who knows the realities and the issues of all things sees in our action something far more serious than we see. We know not what we do when we err from the straight line of moral and spiritual rectitude. We do not know—

I. HOW WE HURT A HUMAN SPIRIT WHEN WE WOUND IT. Whether this be by something said or done, by a glance of the eye, by the withholding of the expected word or action, we often wound more deeply than we think. We suppose we have caused a momentary irritation. If we knew all, we should know that we have produced a soreness of feeling, a keenness of disappointment, or (it may be) a depth of distress, which it will take weeks or months to heal.

II. HOW WE WRONG OURSELVES WHEN WE SIN AGAINST OUR CONSCIENCE. It is, we assure ourselves, a very slight deviation from rectitude; it is a negligence for which we can easily make up a little further on. But, in truth, we have begun a slow, steady, spiritual descent, which will take us to the bottom. We know not what we do when we take the first step in moral laxity. We have started our soul on an evil course; we have done ourselves a wrong which we quite fail to measure.

III. HOW WE DAMAGE ANOTHER'S CHARACTER WHEN WE INJURE IT. We have only induced our neighbour to take a step which will open his eyes to that which he ought to know. So we say, and perhaps think. But, in fact, we have done much more than that. We have led him to do that which has injured his conscience, which has weakened his self-respect, which has enfeebled his character. He will be less strong, henceforth, in the evil hour of temptation; he will be more open to attack, less likely to resist and to conquer his adversary. When we lead into temptation and sin, we "know not what we do."

IV. HOW WE GRIEVE OUR SAVIOUR WHEN WE DISOBEY OR DISHONOUR HIM. We do not know how much he expects of his disciples, especially of those who have such opportunities as we have of knowing and doing his will—how much attachment, how strong an affection, how quick an obedience, how full and patient a submission, he has a right to look for, and does wait to receive. And we do not know the fulness and intensity of his feeling of disappointment and sorrow when we fail him. The disciples did not know what they did, how grievously they failed, when they slept in that hour through which they should have watched. What depth of touching, tenderest pathos we hear in these words of gentle remonstrance: "Could ye not watch with me one hour?"

V. How WE HINDER THE CAUSE OF CHRIST when we discredit it. We think, perhaps, that the evil impression we have conveyed by our inconsistency will soon be forgotten, lost entirely in the current of human affairs. But more harm is done than we know or think. Some souls are shocked, scandalized, injured; their faith is lessened, perhaps pierced; they will not count for Christ what they would have counted. Springs of anti-Christian influence are started; who shall say whither they will flow?

VI. How WE SIN AGAINST GOD WHEN WE WITHHOLD FROM HIM OURSELVES AND OUR SERVICE. We may imagine that we are only delaying till a more suitable or convenient time the duty we intend to discharge. But we are really disobeying a Divine command; we are refusing a Divine invitation; we are continuing in open rebellion, in unfilial estrangement. We are seriously sinning against our heavenly Father, our merciful Saviour, our rightful and righteous Sovereign. 1. Our ignorance of "what we do" is in part *a necessity of our finite nature;* for we cannot possibly look down into the depth of things; nor can we look on to the final issues. This is beyond the compass of our powers. 2. But it is in part also *the fault of our character.* We do not think, we do "not consider" (Isa. i. 3), we do not inquire. We do not use as we might our spiritual faculties. More patient, prayerful consideration of "what we do" would save us from many errors, many wrongs, and also from many painful memories and much self-reproach.—C.

Ver. 35.—*A sad spectacle and the supreme vision.* "And the people stood beholding." "Sitting down they watched him there" (Matt. xxvii. 36). Shall we envy those spectators the scene they then witnessed? Shall we wish that we had lived when, with our mortal eyes, we could have seen the Saviour crucified on our behalf? I think not. With this distance of time and space between us, we have a better, truer standpoint where we are. No doubt we lose much by that distance; but we gain at least as much as we lose. To those who "stood beholding," or who "sat and watched," there was—

I. AN EXCEEDINGLY SAD SPECTACLE. They saw: 1. A human being suffering the last extremity of pain and shame. Some among that company could look upon that scene with positive enjoyment, some with stolid indifference; but those of whom we think, the disciples, would witness it with intense, heart-piercing sympathy, with utmost agitation of spirit. His suffering must, in a large degree, have been theirs also—theirs in proportion to the love they bore him. 2. A Prophet who had failed to be appreciated, and was now a martyr nobly dying in attestation of the truth. 3. A sacred cause losing its Chief and Champion; a cause being wounded and almost certainly slain in the person of its Founder and Exponent. For who could hope that there would be found amongst his disciples any that would take the standard from his hands, and bear it on to victory? For Christ to die was for Christianity to perish. Such was the spectacle on which his disciples looked as they gathered about his cross. The scene was more vivid, more impressive, more powerfully affecting, as thus enacted before their eyes; but we see in reality more than they did. We have before us—

II. THE SUPREME VISION on which we can gaze on earth. We see: 1. *One who once suffered and died,* but whose agony is over; whose pain and sorrow are not now to him sources of evil, but, on the other hand, the ground and the occasion of purest joy and highest honour (see homily on vers. 27—31). Had we been present then, we must have shrunk from the spectacle before us as too painful for sensitiveness to endure. Now we can bear to dwell on his dying and his death, because the element of overwhelming and blinding sympathy is happily withdrawn. 2. *A grand spiritual victory.* We do not see in the crucified prophet One that was defeated; we see One that told us all that he came to tell, communicating to us all the knowledge we need in order to live our higher life on earth, and to prepare for the heavenly life beyond; that was not prevented from delivering any part of his Divine message; that completed all he came to do; that was amply entitled to say, as he did before he died, "*It is finished!*" 3. *A Divine Redeemer ensuring,* by his death, *the triumph* of his cause. Had he *not* died as he did, had he saved himself as he was taunted and challenged to do, had he not gone on to that bitter end and drunk that bitter cup even to the dregs, *then* he would have failed. But because he suffered unto death, he triumphed gloriously, and became "the Author of eternal salvation to all them that believe."

This is the supreme vision of human souls. We do well to gaze on nobility as we see it illustrated in human lives around us. We do well to look long and lovingly on human virtue as manifested in the lives and deaths of the glorious army of martyrs. But there is no vision so well worthy of our view; of our frequent, our constant, our protracted and intense beholding, as that of the merciful and mighty Saviour dying for our sins, dying in wondrous love that he might draw us to himself and restore us to our Father and our home. Before our eyes Christ crucified is conspicuously set forth (Gal. iii. 1); and if we would have forgiveness of sin, rest of soul, worthiness of spirit, nobility of life, hope in death, a blessed immortality, we must direct our eyes unto him who was once "lifted up" that he might be the Refuge, the Friend, the Lord, the Saviour of the world to the end of time. Better than the saddest spectacle man ever saw is that supreme vision which is the hope and the life of each looking and trusting human heart.—C.

Vers. 35—37.—*Self-saving and self-sacrifice.* We have two things here of which the latter is much the more worth looking at.

I. INHUMANITY AT ITS LOWEST. There are many degrees of inhumanity. 1. It is bad for men or women deliberately to shut themselves out of the society of the wrong and miserable, in order that, without distraction, they may minister to their own comfort or consult their own well-being. 2. It is worse to look on the wounded traveller as he lies within sight and reach of us, and to pass him coldly by "on the other side." 3. It is worse still to regard the overthrow of human greatness or prosperity with positive satisfaction of spirit, to find a guilty enjoyment in the humiliation of another. 4. It is worst of all to do as did these men at the cross—to mock at human misery, to taunt it in the hour of its agony, to add another pang to the keen sufferings that already lacerate the soul. Alas! what may not men become! what positively awful possibilities of evil are wrapt up in every human soul! that tiny hand, so soft and delicate, so beautiful, so harmless, what blow may it not possibly strike, some day, against all that is most sacred and most precious! It makes all the difference whether, under Christian principles, we are steadily climbing *up* toward that which is holy and Divine; or whether, under the dominion of evil forces, we are slowly sliding *down* toward all that is wrong and base. What an argument for ranging ourselves, while yet young, under the guidance of Jesus Christ, the Righteous and the Gracious One!

II. MAGNANIMITY AT ITS HIGHEST. 1. *The extremity of evil* to which our Lord was then submitting; the most excruciating bodily pain; the most terrible and almost intolerable mental distress; the apprehension of approaching death. 2. *The powerful temptation* presented to him to deliver himself from it all. By one volition of his will he could have descended from the cross, thus releasing himself and confounding his enemies. He had (1) the strongest possible *inducement* to do this from the instincts of the nature he had assumed; (2) the strongest possible *provocation* to do this in the bitter and cruel taunts of his enemies. 3. *His most magnanimous refusal* to exert his power in his own favour. He heard those derisive cries, but he heeded them not. He let those revilers think that he *was* unable to save himself; he knew that if he did save himself he could not save others (Matt. xxvii. 42). So he voluntarily continued to endure all that torture of body, to bear all that burden of shame and agony of spirit, to go on and down into the deepening shadow of death. Surely spiritual nobility could never strike a higher note than that, could never reach a loftier summit than that. How far can we follow our Lord along this upward path? There have been men who, at a certain point in their career, have clearly foreseen a dark and deathful ending, who have been entreated by their friends to go no further, to stand aside, to "save themselves" and think no more about the salvation of others (see Acts xxi. 12). And it is quite possible that, though we shall never be placed in a position just like that of our Master, we may have the choice offered us which was then offered him—we may have to choose between *saving ourselves and leaving others to their fate* on the one hand, or *sacrificing ourselves and saving our fellows* on the other hand. If that choice should be presented to us, what should we do? The answer depends very much on the measure of the *spirit of unselfishness* we are cherishing and practising continually. (1) Before us is a noble opportunity—that of teaching, enlightening, (instrumentally) redeeming men; but (2) we cannot use this opportunity to any extent without self-sacrifice. If we are determined to "save ourselves," we shall do but very little in the work of saving others. (3) We must choose between the two: either we must resolve to spare ourselves expenditure and endurance, and let the work of human elevation go on without our help; or we must resolve *not* to spare ourselves, not to save time or money, or trouble, or health, not to spare ourselves uncongenial acts or unpleasant endurances, that men may learn what they know not, may see that to which they are yet blind, that they may be led out of exile into the kingdom of God. If we are keeping our Master well in view, especially if we are beholding him on the cross refusing to save himself though challenged with utmost bitterness to do so, we also shall make the nobler choice.—C.

Vers. 39—43.—*True penitence.* These verses narrate what we may call a standard fact of the gospel of Christ—a fact to which appeal will always be made, as it has always been made, in reference to a late repentance. We have to consider—

I. THE BREVITY WITH WHICH A GREAT SPIRITUAL REVOLUTION MAY BE WROUGHT IN A HUMAN MIND. Twelve hours before, this man was a hardened criminal, habituated to a life of rapacious and murderous violence; his counterpart is to be found to-day in the cells of a penal establishment. And now, after a short companionship with Jesus, after hearing him speak and seeing him suffer, his heart is purged and cleansed of its iniquity, he is another man, he is a child of God, an heir of heaven. There are great capacities in these human souls of ours, which do not come often into exercise, but which are actually within us. Powerful speech, imminent peril, great emergencies, sudden inspiration from God,—these and other things will call them forth; there is a brilliant flash of remembrance, or of emotion, or of realization, or of conviction and resolution. And then that which is ordinarily wrought in many days or months is accomplished in an hour. The movements of our mind are not subject to any time-table calculations whatsoever. No man can define the limit of possibility here. Great revolutions can be and have been wrought almost momentarily. Not slowly toiling upward step by step, but more swiftly than the uprising of the strongest bird upon fleetest wing, may the human soul ascend from the darkness of death into the radiant sunshine of hope and life.

II. THE THOROUGHNESS OF THIS MAN'S CHANGE AS EVIDENCED BY HIS WORDS. 1. He recognizes the existence and the power and the providence of God (ver. 40). 2. He has a sense of the turpitude of his own conduct, a due sense of sin (ver. 41). 3. He recognizes the innocence and excellence of Jesus Christ (ver. 41). 4. He believes in his real royalty, though it is so hidden from sight, and though circumstances are so terribly against it (ver. 42). 5. He believes in the pitifulness as well as the power of this kingly Sufferer, and he makes his humble but not unhopeful appeal to his remembrance. 6. He does the one thing for Christ he can do as he is dying on the cross—he remonstrates with his companion in crime, and seeks to silence his cruel taunts. Here is penitence, faith, service, all springing up and in earnest exercise in this brief hour.

III. A SUDDEN TRANSITION FROM THE LOWEST TO THE HIGHEST ESTATE. (Ver. 43.) "What a day to that dying man! How strange a contrast between its opening and its close, its morning and its night! Its morning saw him a culprit condemned before the bar of earthly judgment; before evening shadowed the hill of Zion he stood accepted at the bar of heaven. The morning saw him led out through an earthly city's gates in company with One who was hooted at by the crowd that gathered round him; before night fell upon Jerusalem the gates of another city, even the heavenly, were lifted up, and he went through them in company with One around whom all the hosts of heaven were bowing down as he passed to take his place beside the Father on his everlasting throne" (Hanna). In view of this most interesting fact we gather two lessons. 1. *One of hopefulness.* It is never too late to repent; in other words, repentance, when real, is never ineffectual. None could be more undeniably impenitent until within a few hours of his death than this malefactor, and no man's penitence could be more decisively availing than his. It was real and thorough, and therefore it was accepted. It is a great thing for those who speak for Christ to be warranted, as they are, in going to the dying and despairing, and telling these departing ones, that true penitence, however late, avails with God; that his ear is not closed against the sigh of the contrite, even at the last hour of the day; that up to the last there is mercy to be had by them who truly seek it. But there is another lesson to be learnt. 2. *One of warning and of fear.* There is every reason to hope that true though late repentance is always accepted; but there is grave reason to fear that late repentance is seldom real and true. How often does experience prove that men in apparently dying hours have believed themselves to be penitent when they have only been apprehensive of coming doom! The dread of approaching judgment is far from being the same thing as repentance unto life. Not the last hour, when a selfish dread may be so easily mistaken for spiritual conviction, but the day of health and strength, when conviction can pass into action and honest shame into faithful service, is the time to turn from sin and to seek the face and the favour of the living God. Let none despair, but let none presume.—C.

Ver. 44.—*The shelter of the darkness.* The darkness which fell upon Jerusalem at midday and enshrouded the scene of the Crucifixion was a phenomenon for which it is impossible to account physically, and which it is not easy to explain morally. It is a matter for reverent conjecture, for thoughtful and devout inference, for sacred and solemn imagination. We are on sure ground when we say that it came from the Divine Father, and came on behalf of his beloved Son. We do not venture much when we suggest that it came in response to that Son's appeal in this dark "day of his flesh" (Heb. v. 7). We may do well to consider what was the probable impression it made on those who were concerned in that sad and sacred scene.

I. On the leaders of the people. Surely they were smitten with consternation. One would suppose that, as these men witnessed the wonderful works of Christ, *some doubts* as to the rightness of their antagonism to him must have darted into their minds, and that beneath their confident and defiant attitude of enmity there must have lain some secret misgivings as to the course they were taking. Probably they were not without their fears that something would happen at the last to disappoint them. But as the day wore on, and Jesus actually hung upon the cross, and his strength was certainly going, and the people quietly acquiesced if they did not possibly "assist," all seemed to be satisfactory, to be indeed triumphant. When, lo! a strange, unaccountable darkness, an impenetrable obscurity! The sun refuses to shine at midday. No man sees his fellow, or sees him only in the faintest light. The Crucified One is screened from view. The scoffs and shouts are silenced, and there is a terrible stillness and solemnity. What can that mean? God is speaking in his own chosen way, and is rebuking their guilty deed. There is a quaking at the proud Pharisee's heart, a trembling in the soul of the scribe; there are no more taunts from *their* bitter lips; an unspeakable terror invades even their closed hearts which no casuistry can bar. Is it, then, the blood of their Messiah that they have been shedding?

II. On the multitude. How must they have been subdued with awe, if not agitated with wild alarm! How overwhelming to their less cultured minds must so astounding an event have been! "Whither," we hear them say, "have our rulers led us? Surely there is something sacred and Divine in this Galilæan Prophet! Heaven is pronouncing in his favour. Have we crucified our King? Will his blood be upon us?" and the daughters of Jerusalem already begin to weep for themselves and for their children, as they think that some great calamity impends.

III. On the Roman soldier. Trained to face peril and to be calm even in the presence of overshadowing death, he probably remained quiet and firm, the least moved of all the throng. Nothing could be *done*, and he would lean on his spear, waiting the centurion's command when light should break; though exceedingly astonished and awe-struck, he would stand to his post with unmoved purpose and well-mastered fear.

IV. On the disciples. To them it must have come as a relief, if not a promise. Believing in their Lord, wondering with great amazement at his capture and crucifixion, they would feel that any miraculous interposition was not unlikely, was quite probable. It raised their hopes a few degrees above despair; possibly many degrees. If God interposed thus far, he might restore everything. At the least, this welcome darkness screened themselves, who were too near the cross for security, though too far from their Master for service; perhaps it quieted their fear while it comforted their conscience.

V. On the Saviour himself. To him we may be well assured that it was a most welcome succour. 1. It was a verdict from heaven attesting his innocency. It brought confusion to his enemies and confirmation to himself. It was "a sign from heaven" distinctly in his favour. The sun refused to shine on so guilty a crime as that then perpetrated; the darkness that wrapped them round was God's attestation of the darkness of the deed then being enacted. 2. It effectually shut the mouth of ribaldry and reproach. "It stopped each wagging head, it silenced each gibing tongue." We cannot tell how painful and how piercing to his sensitive spirit those cruel mockings were; nor can we, therefore, tell how much of a relief was the stillness that came with the darkness. 3. It screened him from shame. "Men would leave the Crucified exposed in shame and nakedness to die, but an unseen hand was stretched forth to draw the drapery of darkness round him and hide him from vulgar gaze." 4. It gave him a desired privacy for sorrow and for prayer. Sorrow and prayer always seek solitude; they desire to be alone with God. We do not like any others, except it be one that is most beloved, to witness the deeper griefs, or the sadder and sterner wrestlings of our soul. We seek the shade of some Gethsemane for such sacred experiences as these. What awful sorrow now rested upon Christ, now agitated his soul to its very depths, we may never understand. But we know that the burden he bore for us was at its very heaviest, that the sorrow he endured for us was at its extremest point just at this time, for it culminated in that terrible cry of desolation (Matt. xxvii. 45, 46) which we do not try to fathom, which silences all speech and subdues every spirit. Such sacred sorrow, accompanied, as it certainly was, with the most close communion and fervent prayer, was not for the curiosity of that heartless crowd. It needed the most perfect privacy. And so the Divine Father, in this supreme hour of his Son's great work and of the redemption of mankind, "made darkness, and it was night;" shut the Saviour round with the merciful folds of thick darkness, that he might be alone with that Father in whose sole presence the great sacrifice was to be completed.—C.

Ver. 45.—*The rent veil.* At the time when Jesus died it is exceedingly probable that there would be priests in the "holy place." It was now afternoon, it was drawing toward the time of evening sacrifice; they would be in attendance rendering the service of the sanctuary; they would certainly be aware of what was happening just outside Jerusalem, and would be powerfully affected by the fact. Suddenly, as if grasped and rent by unseen hands, that most sacred veil interposing between the antechamber and the reception-room of God himself, was torn in twain, "from the top to the bottom." The incident was undeniably miraculous. No Jew would have dreamed of daring to do an act that would have been so impious in a man. A Divine hand must have been there, and when they entered into the mysterious darkness and felt the earthquake, must not these priests have asked themselves whether the rending of the veil did not signify a new epoch in the kingdom of God? May not the conversion of a "great company of the priests" (Acts vi. 7) be partly accounted for by this striking and significant event? But what did it symbolize?

I. THAT GOD HAD ADOPTED A NEW METHOD OF ASSERTING HIS HOLINESS AND IMPRESSING IT ON THE MIND AND HEART OF THE WORLD. That veil was an essential part of a system of carefully graduated approach to God. It divided the "holy" from the "most holy" place, and beyond it none might pass but the high priest, and he only once a year. It was intended to teach the absolute holiness of God—that it was only as men were prepared, and as they were separated from sin that they could be admitted to his presence. It was not without effect on the Jewish mind; that nation had thus grasped the idea of the purity and perfection of God. But now his character was so revealed that all such symbolism was no longer needed. The death of Jesus Christ his Son, as the Sacrifice for the sin of the world, was an expression of Divine holiness incomparably superior to the symbolism of the temple and for ever superseding it. Henceforth, when men wanted to know what God felt about sin—how he hated it, what he thought it worth while to do and to suffer in order to expel it—they would look to that cross at Calvary, and there read his mind and know his will. Holy places were no longer needed.

II. THAT GOD HAD NOW PROVIDED ANOTHER AND BETTER WAY OF MERCY FOR MANKIND. Behind the veil was the innermost chamber; and of this chamber *the* furniture was the ark with the two tables of the Law, *and the mercy-seat above it;* we read of this compartment thus: "within the veil before the mercy-seat." *Mercy was thus resting on Law.* Mercy always must be founded on holiness; for without holiness there can be no mercy worthy of the name. And on the great Day of Atonement the high priest entered this "holy of holies," and sprinkled blood upon the mercy-seat for the cleansing of the sins of the nation. But the cross of Jesus Christ spoke of the Divine mercy as no temple furniture could do; there needed nothing to teach the supremacy of mercy above Law after the dying love of the Redeemer of mankind, and there needed no more sprinkling of blood upon a mercy-seat after *this* great Day of Atonement, when "by one sacrifice of himself for ever" the spotless Lamb of God presented "a Propitiation for the sins of the world." The temple rites then became obsolete; its services were past; there need be no more guarding of one sacred place from another; let the sacred curtain be taken down or rent in twain.

III. That the way to the Holy One himself is now open to all mankind. That veil was an instrument that not only secluded, but excluded; through it no eye might venture to glance, no intruding hand might reach, no presumptuous feet might step. To pass that limit was to incur the heaviest penalty; "the Holy Ghost this signifying, that the way into the holiest of all was not yet made manifest." But now "the good High Priest is come, supplying Aaron's place," and having offered up the one all-sufficient sacrifice, having obtained thereby "eternal redemption," that excluding veil is rent in twain, that barrier is broken down; there are no more limitations, no more distinctions; there is access for every child of man to the mercy-seat of God—to the Holy One himself, to seek his grace and find his favour. Are we drawing nigh? Are we entering in? Are we availing ourselves of this priceless privilege, this glorious provision for our spirit's need? In many words and ways God invites us to draw nigh to himself: he did so when his invisible hand rent in twain that separating veil. "Having therefore boldness to enter into the holiest by the blood of Jesus . . . let us draw near with a true heart in full assurance of faith."—C.

Ver. 46.—*How to die and to live.* Our text treats of the dying of our Lord. We may distinguish between death and dying. All men die, but all men have not a dying experience. Those who are killed instantaneously in war or by accident, those who are attacked by fatal apoplexy, those who die in their sleep, have no such experience. It is probable that we shall have *to face the fact* that we are passing away from life, that when a few more hours have come and gone we shall have entered the unseen world. It is therefore of no small value to us that our great Exemplar underwent not only death, but the conscious act of dying, and that in this respect also he "left us an example that we should follow his steps." We look at—

I. The dying of our Lord in the light of these words. The words he uttered just as his end drew near indicate: 1. *Deep serenity of spirit.* They show nothing of agitation or anxiety; they breathe a calm stillness of soul; they are fragrant of peace and tranquillity. They begin with that word, "Father," which all along had been a name of strength and peace; he was evidently resting in the assurance of parental love. And the words that follow are in a strain of entire spiritual composure. 2. *True and living faith.* Jesus was resigning his spirit to God's gracious charge, knowing that in his holy and mighty keeping it would be safe and blessed. Here was fullest confidence in God and in immortality. 3. *Holy resignation.* As a Son of man, Jesus felt still subject to the Divine Father of all; and as he came to do and bear his will, and had done and had borne it perfectly in every hour and act of life, so now in this last volition he yielded himself to God. Thus with a soul tranquil to its profoundest depths, realizing the unseen and eternal world, resigning his spirit to the Divine Father, he bowed his head in death.

II. Our own departure. Having found in the death of Jesus Christ that which is the ground of our pardon, our peace, our life before God; having lived in the love and in the service of a once crucified and now ever-living Saviour;—there is no reason to doubt that we shall die as he died, breathing the spirit he breathed, if we do not use the very language that was upon his lips. 1. Our departure will be *tranquil.* We shall not be terrified, alarmed, agitated; our spirit will look calmly forward to the moment of departure from this world and of entrance into another. We shall face the very near future with a smile. 2. For we shall be sustained by a *living faith.* (1) We shall feel that we are only going into the nearer presence of our own Father—of him before whom we have been living and in whom we have been rejoicing; only passing from one room to another in our Father's house. (2) We shall have faith in Jesus Christ himself. That death upon the cross constitutes him a Divine Saviour, in whom we hide; and we shall die in the calm assurance that we shall be "found in him," and accepted through him. We shall say, with deeper and fuller meaning than the psalmist could, "Into thine hand I commit my spirit: *thou hast redeemed me, O Lord God of truth*" (Ps. xxxi. 5). (3) *We shall yield ourselves to God in the spirit of consecration*, assured that in that new and unknown realm which we are entering we may spend our time and our powers, liberated and enlarged, in his holy and blessed service: and the spirit of consecration is the spirit of confidence and hope. And while these words are particularly appropriate to dying lips, and very probably suggested the last utterance of the first Christian martyr (Acts vii. 59), they need not be held in reserve for that occasion; they admirably express our true attitude in—

III. Our daily life. So David evidently felt (Ps. xxxi. 5), and so we may feel. In faith and in self-surrender we should be continually commending our spirit to our heavenly Father's charge: 1. When the day is done and we enter the nightly darkness and unconsciousness, during which we can take no charge of ourselves. 2. As we go forth each morning to duties, trials, temptations, opportunities, to which our own unaided strength is quite unequal. 3. If we feel that we are entering some dark cloud of adversity and trial in which we shall have peculiar need of Divine support. 4. When we are called to new spheres and weightier responsibilities, wherein other graces will be required than any that have yet been demanded of us. At all such times should we, in faith and consecration, commit the keeping of our souls to our heavenly Father, to be sheltered in his faithfulness, to be enriched by his love and his power.—C.

Ver. 48.—*Sacred impressions.* There was a considerable company of spectators at the Crucifixion. They were attracted not only by the spectacle of a triple execution, but, far more, by the fact that the Prophet whose fame had filled the land was to be led forth to die. It was not the riffraff of Jerusalem merely that "beheld the things that were done." The sense of impropriety in attendance at such sanguinary and harrowing scenes is quite modern. It did not prevail there and then. Probably the leading citizens were present—the well-to-do, the educated, the refined—male and female. All classes and all characters were there—the devout and the profane, the rough and the gentle, the selfish and the sympathetic. And of that large company of people there would be present men and women very variously affected toward Jesus Christ. We may say, without hesitation, that the eleven were there; though it is more than likely that, for a time at any rate, they stood afar off, we cannot doubt that they were there, waiting and wondering; hoping with a faint hope, fearing with a terrible and mastering dread. Many true and loyal disciples were there, among whom, truest among the true, were the women who had followed him and "ministered to him" (Matt. xxvii. 55). Besides these were the fickle, doubled-minded multitude, who cried, "Hosannah!" one day, and a few days later shouted, "Crucify him!" And beyond these in spiritual distance were his implacable and bitter enemies. What may we suppose to have been the effect of the Crucifixion on the minds of "the people that came together to that sight"?

I. Immediate effects probably produced. 1. There were *physical elements* sure to excite their wondering imagination. When an unnatural darkness brooded over the entire scene for three long dread hours, when the earth trembled, when the loud death-cry of the suffering Saviour pierced the air, there was a combination of strange marvels and unusual experiences which must have shaken their souls and filled them with a great awe. 2. And there were *moral elements* there fitted to touch their hearts. There was the presence of *death*—death, "the great reconciler," that quenches strong animosities, that awakens an unwonted pity, that subdues the hardened soul to a surprising softness. There was the death of a Man still young, of a Man who had rendered undeniably great services to many hearts in many homes. There was death met with heroic fortitude, undergone with a calmness, a magnanimity, a moral greatness, such as their eyes had never seen before. These two elements together powerfully affected the people that drew to that sight; and with whatsoever thought in their mind they "came together," it is certain that a very great majority of them went home astonished, if not ashamed and alarmed; they returned "smiting their breasts." But what were—

II. THE ULTIMATE EFFECTS PRODUCED? 1. Some effects were permanently good. Surely it was partly, if not largely, the remembrance of what they had seen and done and felt on this great day that led to the "pricking of heart" they experienced when Peter spoke so faithfully, and led them to Christian baptism (Acts ii. 22, 23, 37—41). Was not the "smiting of the breast" more than an antecedent in time to that being smitten in heart when they listened and responded? 2. Others, we may be sure, were *evanescent and unfruitful.* It would have been a very singular case if there were not many who felt much agitation that day, and the next, and, perhaps, the day after; but who soon allowed pressing cares or passing pleasures to drive convictions from the soul. They "smote their breasts, and returned;" but, instead of returning to God, they went back to the old routine and the old formalism and unspirituality. It is well to be affected by the facts of God's providence, whether these be simple and ordinary, or whether unusual and startling. It is well indeed to be affected by the view of a Saviour's death, however that death may be presented to our souls. But let no man rest contented with such emotion as was in the breast of the people who "came together to that sight." It is wholly undecisive; if it lead not to something better than itself, it will bring forth no fruit of life. It must pass, and should pass quickly, into an intelligent conviction of sin, into a real and living faith in him who was then the Crucified One, and so into newness of life in him and unto him.—C.

Vers. 1—25.—*Jesus vindicated by his enemies.* We pass now from the ecclesiastical to the secular sphere. The charge brought forward in the Sanhedrin is *blasphemy;* before Pilate and Herod the charge must be *sedition* and *treason.* Yet amid his unscrupulous enemies unimpeachable testimony is forthcoming of his innocence.

I. THE TESTIMONY ELICITED BY PILATE. (Vers. 1—7.) The accusation made against Christ was twofold: (1) forbidding to pay tribute; (2) assuming royalty. Now, the first part of the accusation was totally false. Jesus, when asked about the tribute, had expressly advised the people to "render unto Cæsar the things that are Cæsar's." There could be no conflict of interests between the emperor and Christ so far as tribute was concerned. Doubtless upon this first point Pilate received ample assurance that it was groundless. When, again, he inquired about Christ's *royalty,* he was told that his kingship was not earthly, but *spiritual.* Although Pilate could not grasp its exact meaning, he saw sufficient to assure him that it was on a different plane from that of Cæsar's. Hence Pilate declared his innocence before his accusers. Upon this the chief priests and scribes were reduced to the complaint that he was stirring up the people from Galilee to Judæa. Strange complaint, that Jesus was rousing up his fellows! He was troubling Israel very much as Elias had done. Men are in desperate need of an accusation when they resort to this one, which merely means that the accused one is in downright earnest![1] As soon as Pilate hears of Christ's earnestness in Galilee, he inquires if he belongs to Herod's jurisdiction, and is happy to hand him over for trial to the Idumean.

II. THE TESTIMONY BORNE BY HEROD. (Vers. 8—12.) We have next to notice how Herod has unconsciously to testify to Christ's innocence. The murderer of the Baptist thinks, now that Jesus is brought before him, that he has only to express a wish for a miracle, and it will be gratified. To his great surprise and humiliation he receives no answer to his numerous questions; nor do the fierce calumnies of the Jews elicit from the meek Messiah a single word in mitigation or defence. The treatment of Herod was that of *silent contempt.* The wicked king deserved no other fate. And his only revenge was to mock Christ and set him at naught. So they array him in a robe such as the high priests wore, white and brilliant, indicating at once what he pretended to be and how innocent he really was. Herod, in sending him back in this scornful fashion, conveyed to Pilate's mind clearly that he had no more fault to find with him than the Roman governor had.[2] This was the second testimony to the innocency of Jesus.

III. THE TESTIMONY IMPLIED BY THE DEMAND FOR BARABBAS. (Vers. 13—19.) In no clearer way could the chief priests have shown the utter groundlessness of their first charge than in demanding Barabbas in preference to Jesus. Here was a real rebel,

[1] Cf. Saurin's 'Sermons,' tome xi. p. 236.
[2] Cf. Godet, *in loc.;* also Gerok's 'Evangelien-Predigten,' s. 319.

who had committed murder in the insurrection, and he is made the idol of the Jewish populace. They show in this their *sympathy with sedition.* They show clearly to Pilate that Jesus must be thwarting in some way their seditious designs, else they would not clamour so eagerly for his blood. Instead of substantiating their accusation against Jesus, therefore, they really formulate an accusation of treason against themselves. They were guilty; he was innocent. They were the dangerous class; Jesus occupied a region altogether outside the interests of Cæsar.

IV. JESUS SACRIFICED TO POPULAR CLAMOUR. (Vers. 20—25.) There is no show of justice in condemning Christ. All accusation against him fails, and all which can be done is to *shout him down.* If Jesus be not crucified, Jerusalem will go into revolt. Will not an *émeute* be worse than the death of an individual? And so the worldly governor, charged by Rome to keep the peace in the province at all hazards, prefers to deliver the innocent to the will of the guilty than to brave their wrath. It is clamour that secures his condemnation. The judge, who should be the protector of the innocent, unites with the populace in doing him to death. Alas! that men should be so bent on peace as to be ready to sacrifice the innocent to secure it! And yet our Lord's character never shone with so bright a lustre as when he submitted to such wrongs as these. He was truly meek and lowly in heart when he bore so quietly the wrath of the Jews and the time-serving policies of Pilate and Herod. This friendship of Herod and of Pilate, resting on a common indifference to Jesus, is the emblem of those worldly truces which men make who wish to enjoy immunity from trouble; but they do not wear well.—R. M. E.

Vers. 26—46.—*The merciful Saviour on the cross.* Delivered unto the will of the Jews by the indecision of Pilate, Jesus accepts the cross, and proceeds under its crushing weight towards Calvary. But seeing him fainting under it, they press Simon the Cyrenian into service, and he has the everlasting honour of carrying the end of the beam after Jesus. Thus is it in all life's burdens—the weighty end of them is carried by the sympathetic Master, while the lighter end he allows his people to carry after him. And here we must notice—

I. HIS CONSIDERATION FOR JERUSALEM'S WEEPING DAUGHTERS. (Vers. 27—31.) The victim of Rome's cruelty, he has enlisted the sympathy of many weeping women. They see in his death the departure of their best earthly Friend. It is the moment of their deepest sorrow. But Jesus tells them to reserve their tears for themselves. This death of his will lead inevitably to the destruction of Jerusalem and to the dire calamities of the nation. These will be much more lamentable than any sorrows through which he is now to pass. Why, then, does he call upon them to weep? Manifestly that their timely repentance may ensure their escaping the troubles which are so surely coming upon the earth. But the *self-forgetful* attitude of Jesus is surely most instructive. He thinks not of himself, but of their hard case, even though on his journey to the cross. It is the most perfect consideration for others' welfare, and the most beautiful forgetfulness of one's own, that he here exhibits.

II. HE WAS NUMBERED WITH THE TRANSGRESSORS. (Vers. 32, 33.) There was something peculiarly contemptuous in the arrangement of Jesus between two notable criminals. They were robbers—perhaps had been associates of Barabbas. They had committed, most probably, murder in the insurrection, so that the cross was the rightful end of such careers. But to number Jesus, the innocent, with them, to make him one with the greatest criminals then available, was diabolical! And yet he does not protest. Nay, he is willing to be thus identified that he may save even one of his associates. And yet, is not this arrangement, which numbered him with the transgressors, simply the outward expression of the great fact which is the foundation of our salvation? If Jesus had not voluntarily taken up the position of substitute, and identified himself with sinners, we should never have been redeemed.

III. INTERCESSION FROM THE CROSS. (Ver. 34.) It was ignorance on the part of many which led to this great crime, but *culpable* ignorance. They should have known better. They needed forgiveness for it. They are the subjects of his intercession. He prays, "Father, forgive them; for they know not what they do." There never had been such a forgiving spirit manifested since the world began. No wonder that the dying scenes took on ever after a new halo, and that martyrs were able, in spite of suffering, to forgive their murderers and intercede for their salvation! It was the glory of patience which was manifested upon the cross.

IV. THE CHARGE OF SELF-NEGLECT. (Vers. 35—38.) As they walk round the cross in their selfishness, the Jews charge Jesus with self-neglect. He had saved others, but now he does not try to save himself. If he would only show that he can take care of "number one," they would believe on him. Assuredly we have here the self-revelation of the world. The world believes in the selfish, self-seeking leaders of men. A Napoleon or Cæsar, who is willing to sacrifice millions of men to gratify his ambition, is believed in—at all events for a time! But Jesus, who sacrifices himself, is derided. Yet in the end the kingship of the self-sacrificing Saviour is acknowledged. The true King of the Jews is he who could lay down his life for his subjects, and so redeem them.

V. THE FIRST RECOGNIZER OF CHRIST'S KINGSHIP. (Vers. 39—43.) One in the vast assemblage, however, sees below the surface, and recognizes the sovereignty of self-sacrifice. At first reviling Christ, he had come to see, beneath the meek exterior of the Saviour, the real regal spirit. Hence he changes sides, begins to rebuke the other malefactor who continues his unholy maledictions, and then quietly implores the Lord to remember him when he comes in his kingdom. The poor robber, who had perhaps fought under some false Messiah, and knew what Jewish hopes were, believes that this meek and suffering One upon the cross beside him will yet come to his kingdom. When that advent is to be he knows not. But even in the far-off time it will be well for him to be remembered by him. Thus he prays, and is answered. But "To-day shalt thou be with me in Paradise," is the blessed hope set before him. Paradise is part of his kingdom, and the dying robber will be with Jesus in its peaceful bowers that very day. What a hope to be opened up to the dying man! What comfort it gave him, and should give to us!

VI. THE CONSUMMATION. (Vers. 44—46.) After these preliminaries are settled, the dealing of Jesus with the Father himself comes on. It was meet that a veil of darkness should surround the suffering Son and the righteous Father. The Priest and the Victim, who offered himself without spot to God, should in deep darkness pass through the act of unexampled worship. No wonder also that the veil of the temple was rent in the midst; for it was exactly this which his death secured—a way into the holiest through the rent veil of his flesh. And then, when the cry of desolation, that loud and bitter cry, "My God, my God, why hast thou forsaken me?" had given place to quiet assurance, and amid returning light the last cry from the cross went up to heaven, "Father, into thy hands I commend my spirit!" it was meet that he should quietly surrender his life and give up the ghost. There is much to encourage and strengthen us in this consummation on the cross.—R. M. E.

Vers. 47—56.—*The consequences of our Saviour's death.* Our Lord died in the light. The disappearance of the darkness before his decease was an outward symbol of the light and serenity which came across his spirit. His departure exercised a powerful influence upon all around the cross. Let us notice the consequences of the death, as detailed by Luke.

I. THE ROMAN CENTURION WAS CONVINCED OF CHRIST'S RIGHTEOUSNESS AND DIVINE SONSHIP. (Ver. 47.) In Matthew the exclamation of the centurion is given as, "Truly this was the Son of God;" while here in Luke it is, "Certainly this was a righteous Man." The one conclusion had reference to the Roman trial. His death was so glorious and triumphant as to vindicate his character from every aspersion. He was no malefactor, but a benefactor of mankind. The other conclusion had reference to the Jewish trial, which was on the ground of his claim of Sonship. Now, his last cry was in the light of Sonship, and "Father, into thy hands I commend my spirit!" was so tenderly and yet firmly uttered as to convince the centurion that the Lord's claim was real. In the same way, should not our death as believers constitute some vindication of our character and claims? It should show that our righteousness and sonship were not pretences, but glorious realities.

II. THE PEOPLE WERE CONVINCED OF THEIR SIN IN HAVING CLAMOURED FOR HIS CRUCIFIXION. (Ver. 48.) The smiting on the breast was a sign of perplexity and penitence. They were evidently humiliated that they had so treated One who could so nobly die. If the conviction of the centurion was an earnest of the conversion of the pagan world, this was an earnest of the conversion of the Jewish (cf. Godet, *in loc.*). The meek and quiet spirit with which Christ died broke down their hard-heartedness more than any other course could have done; so that its effect was a manifest preparation for the triumphs of the Pentecost. And should not a Christian's death strike alarm into the heart of unbelievers, suggesting to them the possibility of their being unable to meet death with becoming courage?

III. His acquaintance and the women from Galilee are petrified with astonishment. (Ver. 49.) "They stood," we are told, "afar off." They were so unmanned that they could not venture nigh. To them the death was inexplicable. It was apparently the defeat of all their hopes. It was a crushing blow. No mystery in providence had ever appeared to them exactly like this. They were ready to say, with Jacob, "All these things are against us." Is this not the position of God's people often? They have entertained bright hopes about the Master and his cause, but have found them fading away like summer flowers, so that they stand perplexed and afar off before God's providences. Is it not the dark hour before the dawn? Is it not the travail-hour before the jubilance of birth? The disciples experienced this, and so may we. Before apparent defeat, let us always exclaim by faith, "It is real victory."

IV. Joseph of Arimathæa is led by Christ's death to real decision. (Vers. 50—52.) Joseph, a good and just man, had been for some time, we know not how long, a "secret disciple" of Jesus. Nicodemus and he seemed to be in the same category, and perhaps they were led into faith about the same time. In the Sanhedrin they had done all that timid men could to prevent the crime of the Crucifixion; but popular feeling was always too strong for them. They had not as yet taken the bold step of professing to belong to Christ. But, strange to say, the death of Jesus, the apparent defeat of his cause, determined them both to be professors. Joseph accordingly goes and boldly begs the body from Pilate, that he may lay it in his own new tomb, while Nicodemus goes off to procure the needful spices. And here have we what seems a law in God's kingdom. Successors always appear to carry on his work. Christ's death induces two at least to join his cause at once. As the apparently important pass away, it is only to be succeeded by others, and perhaps a larger number, to take up the fallen banner and prove their faithfulness. Apparent calamities are splendid tests of character—they call forth the brave!

V. Christ's funeral could only be a temporary interment. (Vers. 53—56.) It was necessary that the body should be put away before the sabbath began. Now, if he died a little after three o'clock, there were less than three hours to complete the interment. There could not be the customary embalmment. All that was possible was to wrap the dear remains in linen with spices, and then, if nothing prevented, to complete the embalmment on the first day of the week. It was a hurried burial, therefore, and by compulsion a temporary one. Yet "with the rich was his tomb." It was in a virgin sepulchre, so to speak, he lay for a season, just as he had lain in the Virgin's womb. It was so far private also that none apparently but the immediate friends and acquaintances followed the funeral. All the circumstances combined to make the funeral and interment most singular. It was well known where they laid him; it was known that they intended completing the embalmment on the first day of the week; his enemies had every opportunity, therefore, to prevent any imposture about a resurrection. All was above-board, like everything in our Lord's life. Consequently there was in the burial of Jesus a noble foundation laid for that crowning hope of resurrection. We shall see that there was every advantage offered to those who wished to expose duplicity about his rising again. It was the most important burial and most hopeless, so far as the mourners were concerned. They above all others seemed oblivious of all promise of resurrection.—R. M. E.

EXPOSITION.

CHAPTER XXIV.

Vers. 1—49.—The Resurrection. All the four evangelists give an account of the Resurrection. None of the four, however, attempt to give a *history* of it simply from a human point of sight. Each Gospel probably reproduces the special points dwelt on in certain great centres of Christian teaching, in what we should now term different schools of thought. (Attempts have been made by theological scholars to *classify* these as Jewish, Gentile, Greek, Roman; but only with indifferent success).

The teaching which St. Matthew's Gospel represents, evidently in the Resurrection preaching dwelt with peculiar insistence on the great Galilæan appearance of the Risen. St. Luke confines himself exclusively to the appearance, in Judæa. St. John chooses for his Resurrection instruction scenes which had for their theatre both Galilee and Judæa. St. John, as his central or most detailed piece of teaching, dwells on a fishing scene on Gennesaret, the actors being the well-known inner circle of the apostles. While St. Luke chooses for his detailed Resurrection narrative a high-road in a Jerusalem suburb; and for actors, two devoted, but historically unknown, disciples.

Then there is no question of *discrepancies* in this portion of the great history. It is not easy to frame a perfectly satisfactory harmony of all the events related by the four, after the Lord had risen; for, in fact, we possess no detailed account or history of what took place in that eventful period in presence of the disciples. We simply have memoranda of eye-witnesses of certain *incidents* connected with the Resurrection selected by the great first teachers as specially adapted to their own preaching and instruction.

The events of the first Easter Day have been tabulated by Professor Westcott, in what he terms a provisional arrangement, as follows:—

Approx. time.	
Very early on Sunday	The Resurrection, followed by the earthquake, the descent of the angel, the opening of the tomb (Matt. xxviii. 2—4).
5 a.m.	Mary Magdalene, Mary the [mother] of James and Salome, probably with others, start for the sepulchre in the twilight. Mary Magdalene goes before the others, and returns at once to Peter and John (John xx. 1, etc.).
5.30 a.m.	Her companions reach the sepulchre when the sun had risen (Mark xvi. 2). A vision of an angel. Message to the disciples (Matt. xxviii. 5, etc.; Mark xvi. 5, etc.).
6 a.m.	Another party, among whom is Joanna, come a little later, but still in the early morning (ch. xxiv. 1, etc.; comp. Mark xvi. 1, note). A vision of "two young men." Words of comfort and instruction (ch. xxiv. 4, etc.).
6.30 a.m.	The visit of Peter and John (John xx. 3—10). A vision of two angels to Mary Magdalene (John xx. 11—13). About the same time the company of women carry their tidings to the apostles (ch. xxiv. 10, etc.).
7 a.m.	The Lord reveals himself to Mary Magdalene (John xx. 14—18; Mark xvi. 9). Not long after he reveals himself, as it appears, to the company of women who are returning to the sepulchre. Charge to the brethren to go to Galilee (Matt. xxviii. 9, etc.).
4—6 p.m.	The appearance to the two disciples on the way to Emmaus (ch. xxiv. 13, etc.; Mark xvi. 12).
After 4 p.m.	An appearance to St. Peter (ch. xxiv. 34; comp. 1 Cor. xv. 5).
8 p.m.	The appearance to the eleven and others (ch. xxiv. 36, etc.; Mark xvi. 14; John xx. 19, etc.).

In the above table one point must be specially noticed: *two companies* or separate groups of women are mentioned as going to the sepulchre with the same pious object of assisting in the final embalming of the sacred body.

If this be assumed to be the fact, there will be nothing improbable in the supposition that both these groups of women, all doubtless intimate friends belonging to the little company of the Master, but living probably some distance apart in Jerusalem, came together some time on the sabbath day, and then arranged to meet early on the first day at the sepulchre. Probably the spices purchased in some haste *just before the sabbath commenced* were judged inadequate.

(1) For in ch. xxiii. 56 we read of a company of women, most probably including all, *i.e.* both groups, of holy women, who, after beholding the sepulchre, "returned, and prepared spices and ointments; and *rested the sabbath day.*"

(2) In Mark xvi. 1 we read, "*When the sabbath was past*, Mary Magdalene, and Mary the mother of James, and Salome, bought [not '*had* bought'] sweet spices, that they might come and anoint him." This company (alluded to in Mark xvi. 1) arrives *the first* at the sepulchre, and sees the vision of one angel (Mark xvi. 5). The other company (alluded to in ch. xxiv. 1) arrives not long after at the sepulchre, and sees the vision of two angels (ch. xxiv. 4).

In considering the accounts of the Resurrection, the following memoranda will be found suggestive:—

(1) *The holy women* are the principal actors in all the four accounts of the circumstances connected with the tomb. But their assertions were not believed by the disciples until their statements were confirmed by the Lord's personal appearance.

(2) When St. Paul (1 Cor. xv. 5—8) sums up the great appearances of our Lord, the basis of our faith, he makes no reference to his appearance to Mary Magdalene (John xx. 14, etc.; Mark xvi. 9) or to the women (two Maries mentioned Matt. xxviii. 9, 10).

(3) No evangelist describes the Resurrection—no earthly being having been present. St. Matthew is the evangelist who, in his narrative, goes furthest back. He mentions the shock of the earthquake, the awful presence of the angel, the benumbing terror which seized the guards who were watching. Most probably these signs accompanied the Resurrection.

(4) The risen Lord appeared only to his own.

(5) That no future doubt should be thrown on the *reality* of the appearances of the Risen, he showed himself not only to solitary individuals, but to companies, *i.e.* to two, to the eleven (repeatedly), and to above five hundred brethren at once. And these manifestations took place (*a*) at different hours of the day; (*b*) in different localities—in Judæa, in Galilee, in rooms of houses, in the open air.

Vers. 1—12.—*The Resurrection. At the sepulchre.*

Ver. 1.—**Now upon the first day of the week, very early in the morning, they came unto the sepulchre, bringing the spices which they had prepared, and certain others with them.** In the foregoing general note on the Resurrection, the probability has been discussed of the holy women having been divided into two companies who separately came to the sepulchre. St. Luke's notice here refers to the party who arrived the second at the tomb.

Ver. 2.—**And they found the stone rolled away from the sepulchre.** The tomb in which the body of the "King's Son" was laid was in a garden close by the scene of the Crucifixion. It had been recently hewn out of a rock, the low ridge opposite the slight ascent of Calvary. "In front of a tomb belonging to a rich family there was generally a vestibule open to the air, then a low entrance sometimes, as in this case, on the side of a rock, leading into a square chamber of moderate dimensions, on one side of which was a place for the body, either cut some seven feet into the rock, or lengthways, three feet deep, with a low arch over it. . . . The tomb had been lately made, and the door which closed the entrance, the only aperture into the tomb, was a large stone" ('Speaker's Commentary,' on Matt. xxvii. 60). Recent investigations in Jerusalem serve to confirm the accuracy of the original traditional sites (comp. Williams, 'Holy City,' ii. 240; Professor Willis, 'Treatise on the Holy Sepulchre,' etc.). We find the following passage in the Bordeaux Pilgrim (A.D. 333): "On the left side (of the original Church of the Holy Sepulchre) is the hillock Golgotha, where the Lord was crucified. Thence about a stone-throw distance is the crypt where his body was deposited." St. Cyril of Jerusalem makes several references to the spot. In the days of Eusebius (first half of the fourth century) there was no doubt as to the site.

Ver. 4.—**And it came to pass, as they were much perplexed thereabout, behold, two men stood by them in shining garments.** To one company of women one angel appeared; to another, two. Mary Magdalene, a little later, saw two angels in white sitting, as it were keeping watch and ward over the sepulchre for a short time after the sacred form had left it. The words which these beings from another sphere spoke to the mourning women were slightly different, but the teaching was the same in each case: "He is not here, but is risen. Do you not remember what he told you when he was yet with you?" Van Oosterzee and Farrar repeat a beautiful passage from Lessing on this: "Cold discrepancy-mongers, do you not, then, see that the evangelists do not count the angels? . . . There were not only two angels—there were millions of them. They appeared not always one and the same, not always the same two; sometimes this one appeared, sometimes that; sometimes on this place, sometimes on that; sometimes alone, sometimes in company; sometimes they said this, sometimes they said that."

Vers. 6, 7.—**He is not here, but is risen.** These words were repeated in each of the angelic communications at the sepulchre. **Remember how he spake unto you when he was yet in Galilee, saying, The Son of man must be delivered into the hands of sinful men, and be crucified, and the third day rise again.** The angels here call to the women's memory the Master's former promises of the Resurrection. In SS. Matthew and Mark the angel bids them tell the disciples not to forget the appointed place of meeting in Galilee, referring to the Lord's words on the way from the "Last Supper" to Gethsemane (Matt. xxvi. 32; Mark xiv. 28).

Ver. 9.—**And told all these things unto the eleven, and to all the rest.** The account of the scenes at the sepulchre in St. Luke are the least vivid and detailed of the four evangelists. It must be remembered that Matthew, Mark (the amanuensis of Peter), and John relate their own memories here, as well as what they had heard from the holy women. Peter and John, we know, were present themselves at the sepulchre. St. Luke received his less detailed and more summarized account of that early morning, years after, most probably from the lips of one of the holy women who had formed part of one of the "two companies" who carried spices for the embalming.

Ver. 11.—**And their words seemed to them as idle tales, and they believed them not.** The utter incredulity of the friends of Jesus when these reports of his resurrection were brought to them is remarkable when contrasted with the evident dread of the Sanhedrin that *something of grave moment* would happen after three days had elapsed. The disciples were evidently amazed at their Master's rising from the dead. The chief priests and Jewish leaders would apparently have been surprised if something startling had not happened (see Matt. xxvii. 63, etc., where an account is given of the measures these able but unprincipled men took, in their short-sighted wisdom, to counteract any fulfilment of the Crucified One's word—a fulfilment *they* evidently looked forward to as to no improbable contingency). The utter surprise of the disciples at the Resurrection, which in their Gospels they truthfully acknowledge, is no small side-proof of the genuineness of these records of the event.

Ver. 12.—**Then arose Peter, and ran unto the sepulchre; and stooping down, he beheld the linen clothes laid by themselves, and departed, wondering in himself at that which was come to pass.** This verse is omitted in some of the ancient authorities. It is, however, no doubt genuine, and is, in fact, a condensed report (omitting all mention of John) of the narrative given at length in St. John's Gospel (xx. 3—10).

Vers. 13—35.—*The meeting with the risen Jesus on the way to Emmaus.*

Ver. 13.—**And, behold, two of them.** This long piece, which relates in a singularly vivid and picturesque manner one of the earliest appearances of the Risen, is peculiar to St. Luke. St. Mark (xvi. 12, 13) mentions it, but as it were only in passing. This Gospel, written probably after the Gospels of SS. Matthew and Mark, holds a middle place between the earliest apostolic memoirs represented by the first two Gospels and the last memoir, that of St. John, which was probably put out in its present form by the apostle "whom Jesus loved" some time in the last fifteen years of the first century. Writers of varied schools unite in expressions of admiration for this singularly beautiful "memory of the Lord." Godet styles it one of the most admirable pieces in St. Luke's Gospel. Renan, belonging to another, perhaps the most cheerless of all schools of religious thought, writes thus: "L'épisode des disciples d'Emmaus est un des récits les plus fins, les plus nuancés qu'il y ait dans aucune langue" ('Les Evangiles,' p. 282). Dean Plumptre speaks of "the long and singularly interesting narrative peculiar to St. Luke." He says, "It must be looked upon as among the 'gleaning of the grapes,' which rewarded his researches even after the full vintage had apparently been gathered in by others" (*i.e.* SS. Matthew and Mark). The "two of them," although doubtless well known in the apostolic age, seem to have held no distinguished place in early Christian history (see note on ver. 18, where Cleopas is mentioned). **That same day.** The first day of the week—the first Easter Day. The events of the early morning of the Resurrection have been already commented upon **To a village called Emmaus.** This Emmaus, the narrative tells us, was about sixty furlongs—some six miles and a half—from the holy city. It was situated east-south-east from Jerusalem. The name is connected with the modern Arabic term *Hammâm* (a bath), and indicates probably, like the Latin *Aquæ*, or the French *Aix*, and the English "Bath," or "Wells," the presence of medicinal springs; and this may possibly account for St. Luke the physician's attention having in the first instance been drawn to the spot. This Emmaus is now called *Kulonieh.* A curious Talmudical reference, quoted by Godet, belongs to this place Emmaus, now Kulonieh: "At Maûza they go to gather the green boughs for the Feast of Tabernacles" (Talmud, 'Succa,' iv. 5). Elsewhere it is said that "Maûza is Kulonieh."

Ver. 15.—**While they communed together and reasoned, Jesus himself drew near, and went with them.** One, if not the first, fulfilment of the comforting promise, "Where two or three are gathered together in my Name, there am I in the midst of them." Compare also the words of Malachi, "Then they that feared the Lord spake often one to another: and the Lord hearkened, and heard it" (iii. 16).

Ver. 16.—**But their eyes were holden, that they should not know him.** So Mary Magdalene looked on and failed to recognize at first the Person of her adored Master (John xx. 15). So by the lake-shore, as he stood and spoke to the tired fishermen, they who had been so long with him knew him not. Some mysterious change had been wrought in the Person of the Lord. Between the Resurrection and the Ascension, men and women now looked on him without a gleam of recognition, now gazed on him knowing well that it was the Lord. "It is vain," writes Dr. Westcott, "to give any simply natural explanation of the failure of the disciples to recognize Christ. After the Resurrection he was known as he pleased, and not necessarily at once. . . . Till they who gazed on him were placed in something of spiritual harmony with the Lord, they could not recognize him." The two on their walk to Emmaus, and Mary Magdalene in the garden, were preoccupied with their sorrow. The fisher-disciples on the lake were preoccupied with their work, so that the vision of the Divine was obscured. The risen Christ will surely fulfil his own words, "The pure in heart, they shall see God"—*but only the pure in heart.*

Ver. 17.—**What manner of communications are these that ye have one to another, as ye walk, and are sad?** The older authorities make the question stop at "as ye walk," and then add, "and they stood still, looking sad." This change is, of course, of no great importance, but it considerably adds to the vividness of the picture.

Ver. 18.—**And the one of them, whose name was Cleopas.** This name is a Greek contraction of *Cleopatros*, and points to Alexandrian antecedents. Dean Plumptre suggests that this may in part, perhaps, account for this Cleopas, not improbably a Jew of Alexandria, imparting to St. Luke what had not found its way into the current oral teaching of the Hebrew Church at Jerusalem, as embodied in the narratives of SS. Matthew and Mark. **Art thou only a stranger in Jerusalem?** better translated, *dost thou alone sojourn in Jerusalem, and not know*, etc.? That is to say, "Art thou the *only* stranger in Jerusalem who does not know about the wonderful events which have just taken place in the holy city?"

Ver. 19.—**And they said unto him, Concerning Jesus of Nazareth, which was a Prophet mighty in deed and word before God and all the people.** To the Stranger's question, "What things have so lately excited Jerusalem?" they both probably burst out with "the Name," then doubtless on all lips in the holy city, "Jesus of Nazareth," the hated and adored Name. And then they went on with a further explanation to One who seemed a stranger just arrived: they explained who this Jesus was supposed to have been. "He was a Prophet mighty in deed and word before God and all the people," which Lange happily paraphrases "equally great in secret contemplative holiness and in public acts of beneficence." But then the "two" explained, "*This he was;* for he is no more. Our chief priests and rulers have done him to death. They have crucified him."

Ver. 21.—**But we trusted that it had been he which should have redeemed Israel.** And *we* who were his friends and followers, we thought we had found in him the Redeemer of Israel, King Messiah! Think! the *Redeemer crucified!* Although the Redeemer, in the sense they probably understood the word, was something very different to the sense we give to it, the idea was still something very lofty and sublime. It included, no doubt, much of earthly glory and dominion for Israel, but in some definite sense the Gentile world, too, would share in the blessings of Messiah. And to think of the shameful cross putting an end to all these hopes! **And beside all this, to-day is the third day since these things were done.** But yet terrible and despairing as was the story of Cleopas and his friend, their tone was not quite hopeless; for they went on, "And now we have come to the third day since they crucified him." No doubt they dwelt a short space on the expression, "third day," telling the Stranger how their dead Master, when alive, had bade his friends watch for the third day from his death. The third day, he had told them, would be the day of his triumphant return to them; and, strangely enough, on the early morning of this third day, something *did* happen which had stirred, excited, and perplexed them. Certain women of their company, who had been early to the grave of the Master, meaning to embalm the corpse, found the sepulchre empty, and they came back reporting how they had seen a vision of angels there, who told them their Master lived. What did it all mean?

Ver. 24.—**And certain of them which were with us went to the sepulchre, and found it even so as the women had said: but him they saw not.** Tholuck writes, "Does not their word sound as the language of those in whose heart the smoking flax yet glimmers, though nigh to extinction?"

Ver. 25.—**Then he said unto them, O fools, and slow of heart to believe all that the prophets have spoken!** better translated, *O foolish men, and slow of heart to believe in all that the prophets have spoken!* The Stranger now replies to the confused story of sorrow and baffled hopes just lit up with one faint ray of hope, with a calm reference to that holy book so well known to, so deeply treasured by every Jew. "See," he seems to say, "in the pages of our prophets all this, over which you now so bitterly mourn, is plainly predicted: you must be blind and deaf not to have seen and heard this story of agony and patient suffering in those well-known, well-loved pages! When those great prophets spoke of the coming of Messiah, how came it about that you missed seeing that they pointed to days of suffering and death to be endured by him before his time of sovereignty and triumph could be entered on?"

Ver. 26.—**Ought not Christ to have suffered these things, and to enter into his glory?** better translated, *ought not the Christ*, etc.? "St. Luke dwells on the Resurrection as a spiritual necessity; St. Mark, as a great fact; St. Matthew, as a glorious and majestic manifestation; and St. John, in its effects on the members of the Church. . . . If this suffering and death were a necessity (οὐχ ἔδει), if it was in accordance with the will of God *that the Christ should suffer*, and so *enter into his glory*, and if we can be enabled to see this necessity, and see also the noble issues which flow from it, then we can understand how the same necessity must in due measure be laid upon his brethren" (Westcott). And so we obtain a key to some of the darkest problems of humanity. Thus the Stranger led the "two" to see the true meaning of the "prophets," whose burning words they had so often read and heard without grasping their real deep signification. Thus he led them to see that the Christ must be a *suffering* before he could be a *triumphing* Messiah; that the crucifixion of Jesus, over which they wailed with so bitter a wailing, was in fact an essential part of the counsels of God. Then he went on to show that, as his suffering is now fulfilled—for the Crucifixion and death were past—nothing remains of that which is written in the prophets, but the entering into his glory.

Ver. 27.—**And beginning at Moses and all the prophets, he expounded unto them in all the Scriptures the things concerning himself.** The three divisions, the Pentateuch (Moses), the prophets, and all the Scriptures, cover the whole Old Testament received then in the same words as we possess them now. The Lord's proofs of what he asserted he drew from the whole series of writings, rapidly glancing over the long many-coloured roll called the Old Testament. "Jesus had before him a grand field, from the Protevangelium, the first great Gospel of Genesis, down to Malachi. In studying the Scriptures for himself, he had found himself in them everywhere (John v. 39, 40)" (Godet). *The things concerning himself.* The Scriptures which the Lord probably referred to specially were the promise to Eve (Gen. iii. 15); the promise to Abraham (Gen. xxii. 18); the Paschal lamb (Exod. xii.); the scapegoat (Lev. xvi. 1—34); the brazen serpent (Numb. xxi. 9); the greater Prophet (Deut. xviii. 15); the star and sceptre (Numb. xxiv. 17); the smitten rock (Numb. xx. 11; 1 Cor. x. 4), etc.; Immanuel (Isa. vii. 14); "Unto us a Child is born," etc. (Isa. ix. 6, 7); the good Shepherd (Isa. xl. 10, 11); the meek Sufferer (Isa. l. 6); he who bore our griefs (Isa. liii. 4, 5); the Branch (Jer. xxiii. 5; xxxiii. 14, 15); the Heir of David (Ezek. xxxiv. 23); the Ruler from Bethlehem (Micah v. 2); the Branch (Zech. vi. 12); the lowly King (Zech. ix. 9); the pierced Victim (Zech. xii. 10); the smitten Shepherd (Zech. xiii. 7); the messenger of the covenant (Mal. iii. 1); the Sun of Righteousness (Mal iv. 2); and no doubt many other passages. Dr. Davison, in his book on prophecy, pp. 266—287, shows that there is not one of the prophets without some distinct reference to Christ, except Nahum, Jonah (who was himself a type and prophetic sign), and Habakkuk, who, however, uses the memorable words quoted in Rom. i. 17. To these we must add references to several of the psalms, notably to the sixteenth and twenty-second, where sufferings and death are spoken of as belonging to the perfect picture of the Servant of the Lord and the ideal King. His hearers would know well how strangely the agony of Calvary was foreshadowed in those vivid word-pictures he called before their memories in the course of that six-mile walk from Jerusalem to Emmaus.

Ver. 28.—**And they drew nigh unto the village, whither they went: and he made as though he would have gone further.** This was no feint or deception. The Lord would have left them then to themselves had they not prayed him with real earnestness to abide with them. "How many are there," says Stier, "*to* whom he has drawn near, but *with* whom he has not tarried, because they have suffered him to 'go away again,' in his living and heart-moving words! How comparatively rare is it for men to reach the full blessing they might receive (see, for example, the striking historical instance, 2 Kings xiii. 14, 19)!" But these were not content to let the unknown Teacher pass on, and see no more of him, and hear no more of his strange powerful teaching. It is the words of, and the thought contained in, this verse which suggested the idea of the well-known hymn—

"Abide with me; fast falls the eventide."

Ver. 29.—**And he went in to tarry with them.** Some have supposed that one at least of the two had a dwelling at Emmaus; but the position which the strange Teacher assumed as "Master of the household," in the solemn act recorded in ver. 30, seems to indicate that it was an inn where they sojourned.

Ver. 30.—**And it came to pass, as he sat at meat with them, he took bread, and blessed it, and brake, and gave to them.** There was a deep significance in the concluding act of this memorable appearance of the risen Lord. This taking the bread, and blessing it, and breaking it, and then giving it to them, was no ordinary act of courtesy, or welcome, or friendship, which, from a master or teacher might be shown to his disciples. It resembles too closely the great sacramental act in the upper room, when Jesus was alone with his apostles, for us to mistake its solemn sacramental character. The great teachers of the Church in different ages have generally so understood it. So Chrysostom in the Eastern, and Augustine in the Western Church; so Theophylact, and later Beza the Reformer all affirm that this meal was the sacrament. It taught men generally, even more plainly than did the first sacred institution teach the twelve, that in this solemn breaking of bread the Church would recognize their Master's presence. So generally, in fact, has this Emmaus "breaking of bread" been recognized by the Catholic Church as the sacrament, that later Romanist divines have even pressed it as a scriptural demonstration for the abuse which administered the elements under one form (compare, for instance, the 'Refutation of the Confession of Augsberg,' quoted by Stier, in his comment on this passage of Luke, 'Words of the Lord Jesus'). How unnecessary and forced such a construction is, Bishop Wordsworth points out in his note on ch. xxiv. 30, "It may be remembered that *bread* (ἄρτος) was to the Jews a general name for *food*, including drink as well as meat. . . . Thus *bread* became spiritually an expressive term for all the blessings received from communion in Christ's body and blood, and the κλάσις ἄρτου, or 'breaking of bread,' was suggestive of the source from which these blessings flow, (viz.) Christ's body (κλώμενον) broken (1 Cor. xi. 24); hence κλάσις ἄρτου in Acts ii. 42 is a general term for the Holy Eucharist."

Ver. 31.—**He vanished out of their sight.** Not *here*, not *now*, can we hope to understand the nature of the resurrection-body of the Lord; it is and must remain to us, in our present condition, a mystery. Certain facts have, however, been revealed to us: (1) The Resurrection was a reality, not an appearance; for on more than one occasion the Lord permitted the test of touch. He also ate before his disciples of their ordinary food. (2) Yet there was a manifest exemption from the common conditions of bodily (corporeal) existence; for he comes through a closed door; he could *withdraw himself* when he would from touch as well as from sight; he could vanish in a moment from those looking on him; he could, as men gazed on him, rise by the exertion of his own will into the clouds of heaven. (3) He was known just as he pleased and when he pleased; for at times during the "forty days" men and women looked on him without a gleam of recognition, at times they gazed at him, knowing well that it was the Lord. On the words, "he vanished out of their sight," Godet writes, "It must be remembered that Jesus, strictly speaking, *was* already *no more with them* (ver. 44), and that the miracle consisted rather in his appearing than in his disappearing." Dr. Westcott expresses the same truth in different language, "What was natural to him before was now miraculous, what was before miraculous is now natural."

Ver. 32.—**And they said one to another, Did not our heart burn within us, while he talked with us by the way?** better rendered, *was not our heart burning within us, while,* etc.?

Vers. 33, 34.—**And they rose up the same hour, and returned to Jerusalem.** "They fear no longer the night-journey from which they had dissuaded their unknown Companion" (Bengel). **And found the eleven gathered together, and them that were with them, saying, The Lord is risen indeed, and hath appeared to Simon.** Late that evening Cleopas and his friend arrived from Emmaus at Jerusalem. Hastening to the accustomed meeting-place of the disciples of Jesus, to tell their wondrous story of the meeting with the risen Master, they find the eleven together full of joy. Peter *had seen* and had no doubt conversed with his Master. What a meeting must that have been! The once eager and devoted apostle had probably not gazed on that form in life since he caught the sorrowful look bent on him in the court-yard, when Jesus, bound, passed through and heard his servant denying him with oaths and curses. This appearance to Peter is not recorded in the Gospels. It is, however, placed first of all by St. Paul in his records of the manifestation of the Risen (1 Cor. xv. 4—8).

Ver. 35.—**And they told what things were done in the way, and how he was known of them in breaking of bread.** The two travellers now relate to the eleven their wondrous story. The words used by Cleopas and his friend in their narration, ἐν τῇ κλάσει τοῦ ἄρτου, which should be rendered, "in the breaking of the bread," are significant. It is an expression which, at the time when St. Luke wrote his Gospel, had acquired a definite meaning in the language of the Christian Church, and was applied to breaking bread in the "Supper of the Lord" (see Acts ii. 42, 46; 1 Cor. x. 16). While they were speaking together, the personal appearance of the Lord was vouchsafed to them: for, of a sudden, he stood in the midst and spoke to them!

Vers. 36—49.—*The Lord appears to the apostles as they were gathered together on the evening of the first Easter Day.*

Ver. 36.—**And as they thus spake, Jesus himself stood in the midst of them.** St. John, who also gives an account of this appearance of the Risen, adds the detail, "when the doors were shut." The eleven and their friends were gathered together for counsel, probably too in hope that something more would happen after what had already taken place that Easter Day—the report of the holy women of the repeated vision of angels, their own verification of the empty sepulchre, and above all the testimony of Peter that he had seen the Lord. Into this anxious, waiting assembly the two "Emmaus" disciples enter with their wondrous story. In the act of their mentally comparing notes, *Jesus himself stood in the midst of them.* This sudden presence there is evidently supernatural. He "stood in the midst of them," though the doors were carefully closed and barred "for fear of the Jews." Rumours of the Resurrection, no doubt, had already spread through the city, and it was uncertain whether such rumours might not be followed by the arrest of the chief followers of the Crucified. **Peace be unto you.** This was the ordinary Jewish greeting, but on this occasion, spoken by the Lord, possessed more than the ordinary meaning. This "peace" was his solemn, comforting greeting to his own, just as "his peace" which he left with them on the sad Thursday eve was his solemn farewell to the eleven, spoken, perhaps, in the same "upper room" just before he went out to the garden of the agony.

Ver. 37.—**But they were terrified and affrighted.** They spoke one to another of the Master; they discussed the empty sepulchre, the angelic vision, the recital by Peter of his interview with the Risen, and were listening to the details of the quiet Emmaus meeting, all hoping for something more; but this sudden, mysterious appearance of their crucified Master in their midst was not, after all, what they had looked for. *It terrified them.* **And supposed that they had seen a spirit.** How else could they explain his presence in their midst, when the doors were shut? The evangelists make no attempt to explain his sudden appearance. *He was simply there* as they spoke of him. It is clear that his presence could be accounted for in no ordinary, natural way. His disciples felt that; hence their supposition that they were looking on a spirit. We can, with our present limited knowledge, form no adequate conception of this resurrection-body of the Lord. It was a reality, no phantasm or appearance; of that the scene about to be described gives us ample evidence. Still, it is clear that his resurrection-body was not bound by the present conditions of material existence of which we are conscious. Epiphanius ascribes to the body of the risen Lord λεπτότης πνευματική, "a spiritual subtilty." Euthymius uses similar language when he speaks of "his body being now subtile, thin, and unmixed." He could *come* into a closed, barred room. He could be visible or invisible, known or unknown, as he pleased and when he pleased.

Ver. 38.—**And he said unto them, Why are ye troubled? and why do thoughts arise in your hearts?** He had just given them his peace. He proceeds further to allay their fears. Before showing them his pierced hands and feet and side, before eating in their presence, he addresses these comforting words to them: "See," he seems to say, "I give you my peace. why are ye troubled? why do you allow perplexing, harassing thoughts to arise in your hearts?

The past is forgiven and forgotten." "I come not," as Stier beautifully sugests, "as a wrathful Judge to reckon with you for your unbelief and unfaithfulness. I bring to you (and all the world) from my sepulchre something very different from upbraidings."

Ver. 39.—**Behold my hands and my feet, that it is I myself.** "See," he says, inviting the terror-stricken disciples to a calm, unaffrighted contemplation—"see my hands and my feet pierced with the nails which fastened them to the cross; *it is I myself.*" **Handle me, and see; for a spirit hath not flesh and bones, as ye see me have.** The first words quietly told the awe-struck ones to look closely at him, and to ascertain from the dread marks he bore that what they looked upon was Jesus their Master. Then he proceeded to bid them *touch* him, handle him, and so assure themselves that it was no phantom, no bodiless spirit, that stood before them. These words of the Lord, and the invitation, "handle me, and see," made the deepest impression on the hearers. These, then, were proofs of the Resurrection that admitted of no shadow of doubt. These words, this sight, changed their lives. What cared they afterwards for men and men's threatenings? Death, life, to them were all one. They had *seen* the Lord, they had handled with their hands "that which was from the beginning" (see 1 John i. 1). Browning forcibly puts this thought which so influenced the first great teachers. The dying St. John is dwelling on the thought that when he is gone there will be none left with men who *saw* and *touched* the Lord.

"If I live yet, it is for good, more love
Through me to men: be nought but ashes here
That keep awhile my semblance, who was John.
Still, when they scatter, there is left on earth
No one alive who knew (consider this!),
Saw with his eyes, and handled with his hands,
That which was from the first, the Word of life.
How will it be when none more saith, 'I saw'?"

('A Death in the Desert.')

Ver. 40.—Some (but not the majority) of the older authorities omit this verse. **And when he had thus spoken, he showed them his hands and his feet.** It has been suggested that the Risen simply pointed to those parts of his body which were not covered with clothing, and invited the disciples to touch *these*, and so to assure themselves that he had actually flesh and bone. Von Gerlach has an interesting suggestion that the feet were especially referred to "because there was in the feet something more convincing and touching than even in the hands, on account of the wonder that One who had been so grievously wounded could move." The real reason, however, of the Lord calling attention to *the hands and feet* comes out from St. John's account of this appearance of the Risen, for he adds that Jesus also showed them *his side.* Thus he pointed to the *wounded members* of his blessed body to show that in the resurrection-body he retained these marks of his wounds. That he retained them now and for ever we know from the glorious vision of the Revelation, where the wounded humanity of the Lord appears throned and adored in the highest heaven: "Lo, in the midst of the throne and of the four beasts [living creatures], and in the midst of the elders, *stood a Lamb as it had been slain*" (Rev. v. 6). Our Master and God retains these as the glorious tokens of his victory and atonement. Augustine very strikingly deduces from this that perhaps we shall see the same with respect to the wounds of the martyrs ('De Civ. Dei,' lib. xxii. cap. 19).

Vers. 41, 42.—**And while they yet believed not for joy.** The awful joy of the disciples *now* was something too deep for words, even for calm belief. St. John records it, too, with simple pathos. "Then were the disciples glad, when they saw the Lord." This was the fulfilment of his promise to them, when, full of sadness, they were listening to him that last solemn Passover evening in the upper room. "Ye now therefore have sorrow: but I will see you again, and your heart shall rejoice, and your joy no man taketh from you" (John xvi. 22). In after-days, as John preached and taught in his old age, how the remembrance of *that hour* must have stirred in his heart when he thus wrote of it! **Have ye here any meat? And they gave him a piece of a broiled fish, and of an honeycomb.** The Master would not permit this state of wondering ecstasy to continue; so he changes the current of their thoughts by thus descending into the region of everyday life, at the same time powerfully demonstrating by this further proof that, though changed, his resurrection-body was no mere Docetic semblance, no phantom, but that he could eat if he chose. The next sentence (ver. 43) tells simply how he took the food, and ate before them. The fish and honeycomb which they gave him no doubt formed the staple of their evening meal. Fish was part of the common food of the disciples—we see this from the miracles of the five thousand and the four thousand, and also from the narrative of John xxi. 9. Honey, we know, in

Canaan, the land flowing with milk and honey, was common enough to enter into the diet of the poor (compare, among many passages, Exod. iii. 8, 17; Deut. xxvi. 9, 15; Jer. xi. 5; Isa. vii. 15, 22; Matt. iii. 4).

Vers. 44—49.—*A summary of some of the Lord's last words.* The next six verses do not record sayings uttered the same first Easter evening. They are, in fact, a very brief summary of instructions given by the Master on different occasions during the forty days which elapsed between the Resurrection and the Ascension.

In considering the reasons of the omission of any special reference to the Galilæan appearances of the risen Lord, two points must be borne in mind.

(1) Neither Luke nor Paul had any personal reminiscences, like Matthew, or Mark (who wrote down, we believe, St. Peter's memories), or St. John. Luke was dependent on other sources altogether.

(2) Luke, when he wrote the Gospel bearing his name, probably proposed to complete his recital of the close of the earthly ministry of the Lord in his second work, the Acts of the Apostles. His knowledge of what took place after the Resurrection was evidently derived from a source unfamiliar with the Galilæan manifestations of the risen Lord.

St. Luke's knowledge of the Ascension seems to have been most precise. He evidently lays great stress upon the importance of this last scene, both as a piece of evidence and as a theme of teaching; for he not only concludes his Gospel with it, but commences his book of the Acts with the same recital, accompanied with further details.

Ver. 44.—**And he said unto them, These are the words which I spake unto you, while I was yet with you, that all things must be fulfilled, which were written in the Law of Moses, and in the prophets, and in the Psalms, concerning me.** The words, "while I was yet with you," plainly show that, in the Master's mind, the period of his sojourn with men was, in the human sense of the expression, *past*. His abode now was elsewhere. This and the next verse (45) probably refer to what the Master said that first Easter evening to the assembled disciples, but the exact fixing the time in the forty days (the time specially mentioned by St. Luke in the Acts as elapsing between the Resurrection and the Ascension, Acts i. 3) is of comparatively small importance. What is, however, of real moment is the weight Jesus showed that he attached to Old Testament words and types and prophecies by this repeated mention. The remarks of Meyer and Van Oosterzee on this subject are well worthy of being quoted: "If the exegete should read the Old Testament Scriptures without knowing to whom and to what they everywhere point, the New Testament clearly directs his understanding, and places him under an obligation, if he would be a sound Christian teacher, to acknowledge its authority and interpret accordingly. Doubt as to the validity of our Lord and of his apostles' method of expounding, involves necessarily a renunciation of Christianity" (Meyer). "They who consult the teaching of Jesus and his apostles with respect to the prophecies concerning the Messiah, need not grope in uncertainty, but should, nevertheless, remember that the Lord probably directed the attention of the disciples, on this occasion (he is referring to the walk to Emmaus), less to isolated Scriptures than to the whole tenor of the Old Testament in its typical and symbolical character" (Van Oosterzee).

Ver. 45.—**Then opened he their understanding, that they might understand the Scriptures.** Assuming (as is most probably the case) that vers. 44 and 45 refer to words spoken by Jesus on the first Easter evening to the eleven and to Cleopas and his friend, then *the way* in which he opened their understanding is described by St. John (xx. 22) thus: "He breathed on *them*, and saith unto them, Receive ye the Holy Ghost." Among the new powers bestowed on them by this Divine gift, St. Luke especially dwells on the spiritual insight henceforth possessed by these men into the Scriptures of the Old Testament, hitherto only partly understood. This power was doubtless one of the great instruments of their success as preachers.

In the next four verses (46—49) St. Luke evidently briefly summarizes the Master's great sayings, some probably spoken in the course of the walk to Emmaus, some on that first Easter evening, some on other occasions during the forty days which elapsed between the Resurrection and the Ascension. The introductory words, "and said unto them" (ver. 46), seem the commencement of this summary.

Ver. 46.—**Thus it is written, and thus it behoved Christ to suffer, and to rise from the dead the third day.** The majority of the older authorities omit the words, "and thus it behoved." The verse should be read thus: "Thus it is written that Christ should suffer," etc. These words probably were spoken on that first Easter evening. They were apparently repeated on several occasions during the forty days. The Old Testament—they would see now with the new light cast upon it—showed the necessity of an *atoning* Redeemer, from the *sin* which it everywhere reveals, and of a *dying* Redeemer, from the *death* which it proclaims as the consequence. While the same Scriptures no less authoritatively proclaim that through this suffering the Redeemer-Messiah should attain to his glorification.

Ver. 47.—**And that repentance and remission of sins should be preached in his Name among all nations.** This is more definitely expressed in Matt. xxviii. 19 and Mark xvi. 15, where the universality of his message, here summarized, is found in the form of a definite command. **Beginning at Jerusalem.** St. Luke enlarges the thought contained in these words in his Acts (i. 8). Ps. cx. 2, contains the prophecy that from Zion should first proceed the proclamation.

Ver. 48.—**Ye are witnesses of these things.** This personal *witness* of the first preachers of Christianity was the secret of their great power over men's hearts. What Dr. Westcott wrote of St. John was true of the rest of the eleven. "*We have seen, and do testify.* He (John) had no laboured process to go through; he saw. He had no constructive proof to develop; he bore witness. His source of knowledge was direct, and his mode of bringing conviction was to affirm."

Ver. 49.—**And, behold, I send the promise of my Father upon you.** Promised on the last Passover evening (John xiv.—xvi; see especially John xiv. 16—26; xv. 26, 27; xvi. 7, etc.), and fulfilled partly on the first Easter evening, when he breathed on them (John xx. 22), and completely on the first Pentecost (Acts ii. 1, etc.). **But tarry ye in the city of Jerusalem, until ye be endued with power from on high.** These words apparently were spoken on the day of his ascension (see Acts i. 4).

Vers. 50—53.—The Ascension. In considering the questions which suggest themselves in connection with the ascension of our blessed Lord, we are met on the threshold with the fact that only St. Luke, in his Gospel in this place, and in the Acts (i.), has given us a detailed account of the scene. But the fact is referred to *plainly* by St. John (iii. 13; vi. 62; xx. 17) and by St. Paul (Eph. iv. 9, 10; 1 Tim. iii. 16). A vast number of passages besides, in the Epistles of SS. Paul, Peter, and James, and in the Revelation of St. John, presuppose the Ascension, when they describe the heavenly glory of Jesus and of his session at the right hand of God.

St. John's triple mention of the Ascension (see above) is exactly in accordance with his constant practice in his Gospel; he avoids rewriting a formal narrative of things which, when he wrote, were well known in the Churches; yet he alludes to these things in clear and unmistakable language, and draws from them his lessons and conclusions.

Notably this is the case in the Fourth Gospel with regard to the sacraments. "It contains," says Dr. Westcott, "no formal narrative of the institution of sacraments, and yet it presents most fully the idea of sacraments."

Neander writes with great force on this apparent omission of the Ascension: "We make the same remark upon the ascension of Christ as was before made upon his miraculous conception. In regard to neither is prominence given to the special and actual *fact* in the apostolic writings; in regard to both, such a fact is presupposed in the general conviction of the apostles, and in the connection of Christian consciousness. Thus the end of Christ's appearance on earth corresponds with its beginning. Christianity rests upon supernatural facts—stands or falls with them. By faith in them has the Divine life been generated from the beginning. Were this faith gone, there might indeed remain many of the *effects* of what Christianity has been; but as for Christianity in the true sense, as for a Christian Church, there could be none."

Ver. 50.—**And he led them out as far as to Bethany;** more accurately, *and he led them out until they were over against Bethany.* The scene of the Ascension could scarcely have been the central summit of the Mount of Olives (*Jebel-el-Tur*), according to ancient tradition; but it is more likely that it took place on one of the remoter uplands which lie above the village. "On the wild uplands which immediately overhang the village, he finally withdrew from the eyes of his disciples, in a seclusion which, perhaps, could nowhere else be found so near the stir of a mighty city; the long ridge of Olivet screening those hills, and those hills the village beneath them, from all sound or sight of the city behind; the view opening only on the wide waste of desert-rocks and ever-descending valleys, into the depths of the distant Jordan and its mysterious lake" (Dean Stanley, 'Sinai and Palestine,' ch. iii.). **He lifted up his hands, and blessed them.** In Acts i. 4 we read how Jesus, having assembled (συναλιζόμενος) the apostles, gave them some last commands before he left them. It is not expressly stated that only the eleven were present on this occasion. When he had finished speaking, "he lifted up his hands, and blessed them." There is *now* no laying on of hands. "Jam non imposuit manus," comments Bengel. Those hands, as they were lifted up, were already separated from them, the space between the Risen and those he was blessing grew greater every moment.

Ver. 51.—**And it came to pass, while he blessed them, he was parted from them, and carried up into heaven;** more accurately rendered, *while he blessed them, he parted from them, and was carried up into heaven.* The last clause, "was carried up into heaven," is absent from some, but not from the majority of the older authorities. The Acts (i. 9) describe the act of ascension thus: "As they were looking, he was taken up; and a cloud received him out of their sight." The eleven and those chosen to witness the last earthly scene of the Lord's ministry came together, in obedience probably to some command of their Master, to some meeting-place in Jerusalem, possibly the well-known upper room. Thence he led them forth from the sacred city, past the scene of the agony and the scene of the weeping, on to some quiet spot hard by loved Bethany, talking to them as they went; and as he spoke, suddenly he lifted up his pierced hands and blessed them; and in the very act of performing this deed of love, he rose, they still gazing on him—rose, as it appears, by the exercise of his own will into the air, and, while they still gazed, a cloud came and veiled him from their sight. *He was parted from them, and carried up into heaven.* Among the appearances of the Risen to his followers during the forty days (ten of these distinct appearances are related in the Gospels and Epistles), this last notably differs from all that preceded it. As at other times when he showed himself to his friends during these forty days, so on the "Ascension" day Jesus apparently came forth suddenly from the invisible world; but not, as on former occasions, did he suddenly vanish from sight, as if he might shortly return as he had done before. But on this fortieth day he withdrew in a different way; as they gazed he rose up into the air, and so he parted from them, thus solemnly suggesting to them that not only was he "no more with them" (ver. 44), but that even those occasional and supernatural appearances vouchsafed to them since the Resurrection were now at an end. Nor were they grieved at this final parting; for we read—

Ver. 52.—**And they worshipped him, and returned to Jerusalem with great joy.** This "great joy," on first thoughts, is singular till we read between the lines, and see how perfectly they *now* grasped the new mode of the Lord's connection with his own. They *knew* that henceforth, not for a little time as before the cross, not fitfully as since the Resurrection, but that for ever, though their eyes might not see him, would they feel his blessed presence near (see John xiv. 28; xvi. 7). One question more connected with the Ascension presses for an answer. Much modern criticism regards this last scene simply as one of the ordinary disappearances of the forty days, and declines to admit any external, visible fact in which the Ascension was manifested. But St. Luke's description, both in his Gospel and in the Acts, is plainly too circumstantial to admit of any hypothesis which limits the Ascension to a purely spiritual elevation. At the end of his earthly ministry, the evening before the cross, Jesus asked back his glory: "Now, O Father, glorify thou *me* with thine own self, with the glory which I had with thee before the world was" (John xvii. 5). The Ascension and consequent session at the right hand was the answer to the prayer of Christ. It was necessary for the training of the first teachers of Christianity that the great fact should be represented in some outward and visible form. "The physical elevation," writes Dr. Westcott, "was a speaking parable, an eloquent symbol, but not the truth to which it pointed, or the reality which it foreshadowed. The change which Christ revealed by the Ascension was not a change of place, but a change of state; not local, but spiritual. Still, from the necessities of our human condition, the spiritual change was represented sacramentally, so to speak, in an outward form. . . . He passed beyond the sphere of man's sensible existence to the open presence of God" ('The Revelation of the Risen Lord'). *The session at the right hand of God* (Mark xvi. 19) cannot designate any particular place. The ascension, then, of Jesus is not the exchange of one locality, *earth*, merely for another we term *heaven*. It is a change of state; it is a passing from all confinement within the limits of space to *omnipresence*.

Ver. 53.—**And were continually in the temple, praising and blessing God. Amen.** These last words of the Gospel just alluded to the life of the first teachers, which is dwelt upon with considerable detail in the Acts. In the early days which succeeded the Ascension, the temple and its courts were the principal resort of the teachers of the new "way." We know that in an extraordinarily short time the numbers of adherents to the crucified and risen Jesus, in Jerusalem only, were counted by thousands. The temple and its vast courts, from its storied past, from its having been the scene of much of the Master's last teaching, was the natural centre for these leaders of the new "way." When Luke wrote the words, "were continually in the temple," it is almost certain that he proposed continuing his great narrative in the book we know as the Acts of the Apostles, in which, guided by the Divine Spirit, he relates to us how the Lord Jesus continued to work on earth—in and by his Church—from his glory-throne in heaven. The early chapters of the Acts take up the thread of the gospel story, and describe the life and work of the friends of Jesus in the great Jerusalem temple, the dangers they had to encounter, and the splendid success which rewarded their brave, faithful toil. These same Acts, in the first lines of their thrilling story, take up again the Ascension scene, which is described with fresh and vivid details From these details we learn how, when the disciples' eyes were fixed on that cloud which veiled their ascending Master, they became aware of two stranger-forms with them, clad in white and glistening garments. They knew these belonged to no earthly company. They were two among the thousands of thousands of angels, possibly the angels of the Resurrection, who sat in the empty garden-tomb. These angels tell the awe-struck friends of the ascended Jesus that their adored Master will one day (Acts i. 2) come back to *earth* in like manner as they had seen him go to heaven. "O earth, thou grain of sand on the shore of the great ocean of the universe of God, thou Bethlehem among the princes of the regions of heaven, thou art and thou ever wilt be, among ten thousand times ten thousand suns and worlds, the loved one, the elect of the Lord; thee will he visit again; thou shalt provide him a throne, even as thou gavest him a manger; thou shalt rejoice in the splendour of his glory, even as thou drankest his blood and his tears, and mournedst at his death. On thee he hath a great work yet to accomplish" (Häfeli, quoted by Stier).

HOMILETICS.

Vers. 1—12.—*The Resurrection-morning.* Who are the witnesses to the Resurrection? What is the evidence on which it was believed by the first disciples?—on which it is received by all Christians still?

I. THE WITNESSES ARE THE HOLY WOMEN AND THE APOSTLES. It is (ver. 1) the very early morning: "while it was yet dark," says St. John; "as the day began to dawn," says St. Matthew; "at the rising of the sun," says St. Mark. Then the women hasten towards the sepulchre. How many formed the company, or, as seems to be implied, the two companies, of women we know not. The names of five are given, and the rest are grouped under the phrases, the "others that were with them," and "the others from Galilee." They quickly pass through the silent streets. Jerusalem is still asleep; neither memory of what had happened, nor fear of what might happen, has disturbed its repose. They have only one care (ver. 1)—the complete embalming of the body which had been hastily laid in the rock-hewn sepulchre of Joseph. There is no idea beyond this; there is no hope even against hope that, on this the third day, he would rise again. With the eagerness characteristic of woman's nature, they proceed, the question never suggesting itself until they near the tomb, "Who shall roll away the stone from the mouth of the cave?" It would seem that they did not know of the guard which had been commanded to watch or of the sealing of the stone, for that had been done on the sabbath morning; but some of them had observed the setting of the stone—a block three or four feet in height, and two or three in breadth, requiring several men to move it. "How shall it be moved? how shall we find an entrance?" is the question before them as they press towards the holy place. Now, what are the facts? In the dawn, half-clear and half-dark, as the east begins to lighten, Mary of Magdala, the foremost of the company, sees the cave standing wide open—the stone having been rolled aside. Horror-struck, she turns to her companions, and, yielding to the moment's impulse, she speeds back to the city to communicate her fears to Peter and John (John xx. 1, 2). In the mean time, her companions venture forward. Timidly they enter the tomb, or the vestibule of the tomb, to search for the body. Lo, there (Matt. xxviii. 2, 3), on the stone which had been pushed into a corner, sits one "whose countenance is like lightning, and his raiment white as snow," and prostrate on the ground are the Roman sentries. The women start, but the assuring word, "Fear not ye," is spoken, and the invitation (Matt. xxviii. 6) is given to "come and see the place where the Lord lay." Yes, guardians, and only guardians, are these—one where the head, another where the feet, of Jesus had been—token of the complete, protecting care of his Father. And these guardians ask (vers. 5—7), "Why do you seek the living among the dead?" and repeat the testimony, "He is not here: he is risen," bidding them remember his own words, and bear the news of the Resurrection to the sorrowing company. It is with fear and great joy that they depart, running to bring the disciples word. They encounter scepticism. Their hot, eager sentences (ver. 11) seem to the apostles "as idle tales, and they believe them not." Peter and John, however, have already obeyed the importunate pleading of Mary. And there, to be sure, as they reach the sepulchre, is the open door. John, who is first, looks in without entering; Peter, coming up, enters at once. "John," observes Matthew Henry, "could outrun Peter, but Peter could out-dare John." Undoubtedly the tomb is empty. Examining it, they discover (ver. 12) the linen clothes laid by themselves; and the napkin which had surrounded the head laid by itself. There had been no haste. Not thus would any have acted who had borne away the sacred form. Peter, after minute examination of the surroundings, "departed, wondering in himself at that which was come to pass." John, with the quick intuition of love, not only wondered, but believed—felt sure that these grave-clothes were the sign of a victory. Such is the account of that ever-memorable morning. The arrangement of its events may not be absolutely accurate; in the ignorance of all that occurred, it is impossible to supply every link in the chain of narrative. The evangelists are so filled with the one reality, "He is risen," that they are not careful as to the minutiæ of the circumstances. On the Resurrection, as personal, as real, the structure of Christian life and doctine is reared. By the effect of the Resurrection the apostles were transformed. The foolish and slow-hearted fishermen of the past became the princes of a new and heavenly kingdom. "With great power they gave witness to the resurrection of the Lord Jesus, and great grace was upon them all."

II. But WITHOUT FURTHER DWELLING ON THE EVIDENCES OF THE RESURRECTION AS AN HISTORICAL FACT, CONSIDER IT AS A MIGHTY SPIRITUAL FORCE. Consider what the apostle calls "the power of the Resurrection." What is the central truth of the forty days between the Resurrection and Ascension? Study the brief account of these forty days, and you see at once a change in the manner and conditions of the revelation of Christ. He shows himself only to chosen witnesses. St. Mark says that he appeared to the disciples "in another form." The eyes of the disciples are declared to be so held (ver. 16) that they do not know him. It is the same Jesus, but much is altered. "He came and he went as he pleased; material substances such as the fastened doors were no impediment to his coming; when he was present his disciples did not, as a matter of course, know him." These forty days were what the sunrise is to the day; they were the beginning of the relation in which he stands to his Church now. All his self-revelations are pictures of the way and truth of his presence as we are called to realize it. Men had seen him without knowing him; now they know him without seeing him. We behold him, as Newman has finely said, "passing from his hiding-place of sight without knowledge to that of knowledge without sight." As a transition-time, giving us intimations of the glory in which he is abiding and of the grace in which he is dealing with us, regard the period that was ushered in by the early morning of the first day of the week. It was a great day. Four appearances are noted. The first (John xx.), to Mary of Magdala, followed or preceded, perhaps, by an appearance to the other women (Matt. xxiii.); the second (vers. 13—35), to the two brethren journeying to Emmaus; the third, to Simon Peter (ver. 35); and the fourth (John xx. 19—23), to the disciples assembled at night when the doors were shut for fear of the Jews. Each of these appearances is significant. St. Luke relates the second. One remark only as to Mary of Magdala. Renan has asserted that the glory of the Resurrection belongs to her; that, "after Jesus, it is Mary who has done the most to the founding of Christianity." There can be nothing more contrary to the explicit statements of the evangelists than much that is contained in the brilliant Frenchman's statement. But the message of Mary is indeed the basis of the faith of the

Church, the basis of the faith of humanity. "If Christ is not risen, our hope is vain; we are yet in our sins." And the commandment which sent her to the disciples is the inspiration of all Christian hearts. "Go, tell my brethren." Tell the message of the risen Lord in the light with which the countenance is irradiated; tell it in the glad obedience by which the life is sanctified; tell it through all that you do and are; tell—let your teaching cease only with your breathing—that Christ has risen, that the imprisoning stone has been rolled away, and the kingdom of heaven is open to all believers, its gates being closed neither by day nor by night, for there is no night there.

Vers. 13—35.—*Emmaus.* (For a beautiful paraphrase of this Scripture, see the passage in Cowper's poem 'Conversation,' beginning, "It happened on a solemn eventide." The incident is presented by him as an illustration of converse "such as it behoves man to maintain, and such as God approves." And it is impossible to resist the appropriateness of the lesson which is enforced.) The time of the memorable appearance is the afternoon, probably between four and six; and its prominent persons are two disciples, not apostles, whom it is impossible to identify. The one is called Klopas or Cleophas, supposed by many to be Alphæus, the brother of Joseph of Nazareth, and father of James; but the name being a contraction of Cleopatrus, the supposition is scarcely admissible. The other is not mentioned by name, and many conjectures concerning him have been framed. A worthy German pastor once said, "The learned cannot come to any agreement who the other was, and I will give you this good counsel—let each of you take his place." Look at these two men as they journey. "The sun of the Resurrection was enveloped in thick clouds of despondency and sorrow, scarcely penetrated by a ray of light." It would seem that they had left the gathering of disciples before Mary had brought her tale. What they dwell on is, "True, the body was not in the tomb; but then he was not seen;" and one risen from the dead was a thought which they could scarcely credit. They are not sure even that the women really saw angels; it was, perhaps, only a vision of angels, and, having the notions of their time as to ghosts and apparitions, they incline to the belief that there was no reality in the presence of whom the Maries and Salome and others had spoken. No; he is dead, and the third day has come and gone, and he has not been seen. Let this state of mind be noted. There was no predisposition in Christ's followers to accept the Resurrection. Far from this, the evidence made way against doubtings, against scepticisms, we might say, of the most obstinate nature. These foolish and slow-hearted men were almost the last people likely to credit the tale. How was it that this temperament, incredulous, despondent, so quickly gave way to one full of worship and great joy? How was it that such men gave up all, travelled hither and thither with the one message ever on their lips, many of them suffering death because they would maintain that the Christ who was crucified did rise, had been seen by them, and is alive for evermore? I can find only one answer to the question—They witnessed to truth. "The Lord is risen indeed." But regard the incident in the light of the thought that the forty days in which Christ showed himself alive after his Passion were intended as a time of preparation for that new form of his presence which began when the day of Pentecost was fully come. Studying the forty-days' period, we can find many hints and suggestions as to the manner of Christ's intercourse with us, of his coming to us in the Comforter whom he promised until the end of the age. The special teaching of this journey to Emmaus, and all that befell the two, may be gathered under three points: (1) *Christ with us, but unrevealed;* (2) *Christ teaching, but personally unrecognized;* (3) *Christ revealed and recognized.*

I. Christ with us, but unrevealed. A Stranger asks the cause of the dejection of the two travellers, and, by his sympathy and courtesy, draws out their confidence. Two reasons for not discerning him are given. The one is (Mark xvi. 12), that "he appeared in another form" than that with which they were familiar. Not the form of the Shepherd going before them, but that of the Companion in walking and working clothes travelling by their side. But there is the other reason (ver. 16)—"Their eyes were holden that they should not know him." They were not at that time in spiritual light; their vision was narrowed by their great sorrow. Are not these still the reasons why so often we do not see the Christ who is with us as we travel along the thoroughfares of life? He is not in the form in which we expect him. Sometimes he hides himself, that he may get the more fully into our hearts. He is with us, wanting the halo, wanting all that would at once declare him, that he may be more intimately our Friend, "familiar, patient, condescending, free." And we miss or mistake him, because we cannot see beneath the form, because our minds are self-occupied, or, when intent on higher things, are wanting in the elevation, in the pure sweet light, of the spiritual mind. Only when the spiritual eyes are opened do we know who has been and is with us. But he is with us as we toil on our toilsome way, bearing the heat and burden of the afternoon. It is he who is touching the springs of our thought and action. It is he who is speaking to us. Fear not, thou weary and heart-sore disciple; when thy comforts seem to be gone, he, the Comforter, is close to thee. Thy tears are falling; he is nigh with his "Why weepest thou?" Thou art seeking thy God, but thy soul is unresting, because it cannot find the Rock; he is nigh with his "Whom seekest thou?" Thou hast left the city's din behind thee, and art alone with thyself; he is nigh, assuring thee that the fairest vineyards are those which are received from the valley of troubling. Thou art in communion with some kindred spirit, exchanging the fears and joys of the mind that turns to heaven; he is nigh, rejoicing to add himself to the two or three. The story of Emmaus is indeed a figure of the life-pilgrimage. Bear from it the pledge that whosoever is true to the light, is, though halting and uncertain may be his steps, the neighbour to Jesus Christ Jesus himself near and in fellowship with all communing and reasoning.

II. And how? TEACHING, ALTHOUGH PERSONALLY UNRECOGNIZED. What Christ was in his dealing with the two, he has been in his dealing with his Church. During the past centuries he has been "teaching and expounding the things concerning himself." Did he not promise that the Holy Ghost would be the Guide into all truth, through the glorifying of him, the receiving of his and showing it to his own? What is the witness for the fulfilment of this office? It is the history of the past eighteen centuries. The text from which the Holy Ghost has been preaching is that which Jesus sounded (ver. 26); and the way of the sermon is the very way of Christ (ver. 27). Moses and the prophets, apprehended in New Testament light, have, for these centuries, been read, opened up, as the treasury of the things of Christ. Thought and culture, devotion and obedience, stand to-day where they stood yesterday—before the mighty "Ought not Christ to have suffered these things, and to enter into his glory?" Is there not progressiveness in the teaching of the Holy Ghost? There is development in Christianity. It has its permanent, but it has its progressive, element also. It is only by little and little that the higher truth of the kingdom enters the hearts of men. Precept must be on precept, line on line, until the dispensation of the opening, when the Church, gathered fully into the house of the Lord, will receive from the pierced hand the bread of the eternal life. So in personal history and experience. There is One teaching us, even when we do not recognize who he is. Life is the school in which the Holy Ghost is the Instructor. Christ and Christ's love, and the meaning of our existence as interpreted in Christ's cross, is the lesson in which we are taught. We pass from standard up to standard, the book which regulates all the teaching being the Scriptures. Many are the forms which the Holy Ghost, the Teacher, assumes; many are the agencies through which he draws near. But if, with receptive minds, we are yielded to him, he is taking us step by step along the path of the manifold education meant for the disciple of Jesus; expounding as we are able to bear, stooping to our immaturities and weaknesses; a presence in us rather than external to us, stimulating thought and desire, enkindling into fuller flame the smoking flax; so that by-and-by we are able to say, "Did not our heart burn within us, while he talked with us by the way, and while he opened to us the Scriptures?" (ver. 32).

III. Behold CHRIST REVEALED AND RECOGNIZED. The village is reached. Must the delightful companionship end? Courteously saluting them, the Stranger apparently is going on. Nay, the sun is about to set; they entreat him not to leave them (ver. 29). He would have gone on if there had been no prayer. The personal desire is essential to the tarrying. But that desire never pleads in vain. How many never plead for the tarrying—indeed, do not want it! For the drawing near and journeying with us, no desire from us is needed. Christ does that of his own will. But the tarrying is another matter. He cannot force an entrance; he will be forced. "They constrained him." He receives sinners *for* salvation; their reception of him *is* salvation (Rev. iii. 20). At meat with them he is revealed. What it was that disclosed him we cannot exactly say. The whole manner is solemn and striking. At once he takes the head of the table. The Master's place is conceded to him. And that always prepares for revelation. When the heart is truly yielded to Christ, the moment of the showing of himself is near. He takes the bread; he blesses; he breaks, and gives it to the two. And their eyes are opened, and they know him. There is the voice, the blessing, and I think, the sight of the pierced hands—the sight that I expect to have in glory. The meal may not have been a full sacrament. But Christ's presence and blessing made, the meal sacramental; for that presence and that blessing elevate whatever is ordinary. And the action before us is a consecration of ordinance as well as Word as the means of revelation. The Word prepares for the ordinance; in the ordinance Christ is revealed. Is not this a forecast of the future? Is it not Christ's will to make himself known to those who sit at meat with him—they having first constrained him and being thus spiritually susceptible—in the breaking of bread? Observe the signs of the revelation. A new sight (ver. 31); a new energy (ver. 33); a new sympathy (vers. 33, 34); a new eloquence (ver. 35). Joy, joy to the disciples who have seen the Lord. But he has vanished out of their sight. He must not hinder, by his bodily presence, the lifting of the consciousness into the region of the spiritual presence. That on which afterwards they dwell is, not the glimpse they have had of face and hand, but the power of his Spirit, the life-giving force of his Word (ver. 32). The clouds were dispelled by the rising of the Day-star in the heart. That is the sign of Christ with us here. By that we know that it is he who has been talking with us. One day, but not in this present time, we shall see him as he is; he will bless and break and give to us himself, the Bread of life. And then he will not vanish out of our sight.

"Oh, then shall the veil be removed,
And round me thy brightness be poured;
I shall meet him whom absent I loved,
I shall see whom unseen I adored.'

Vers. 36—43.—*Christ and his Church.* I. THE CHURCH. It is found in miniature in the upper room—"The eleven, and them that were with them." 1. *Its separation.* It is isolated from the outer world. A new bond, a new manner, of union is already realized. It is not of the world, as Christ himself was not. There is a door shut between the little flock and the Jews. A supreme attraction to him whom the world sees not, an affiance of soul of which the world knows not, unites the company, and, in thus uniting, separates it. It has a secret with which the world does not intermeddle. 2. *Its unity.* (1) That stands in Christ, "Ye have not chosen me, but I have chosen you" (John xv. 16). The Church is not a mere voluntary association; it is a spiritual organism rooted and grounded in the Man Christ Jesus—in what he is and has done, in his Divine-human Person, and the offices which he executes as Redeemer. (2) It is realized through continuance in the apostles' doctrine and fellowship. "The eleven, and those with them." Christ had looked through the ages down to the end of the time, and thus had spoken: "I pray for those who shall believe on me through the word of the men whom thou didst give me." Here the eleven form the centre of the company. There is a definite word on which the Church is built. It has not a mere collection of "memoranda;" it is not an institution of "hazy outlines." It has a distinct testimony—that of the apostles and prophets. And there is a social life, a fellowship, by which it "makes increase to self-edifying in love"—the fellowship which continues that which is witnessed to in the assembly of the eleven and those with them. Remember, it is *fellowship*, all holding themselves to be fellows in Christ, exchanging their experiences, imparting the gift which each has received, that it may tend to quicken the faith and love of all. "As *they thus* spake, Jesus himself stood in the midst" (ver. 36).

II. CHRIST. He had promised, "I will not leave you comfortless: I will come to you." Behold the fulfilment and the way of the fulfilment of this promise. Behold him present in his Church. 1. *The sovereignty of the presence.* On a sudden he stands in the midst. They are not expecting him. He comes through barred doors. It is the day of his power. Christ prescribes means; he ordains channels of grace; and, where there is the obedience of faith in the use of the means, there is blessing. "Where two or three are gathered together, there am I in the midst of them." But in all that speaks of spiritual life, there is the witness for a spiritual sovereignty, for reserves of power in the hands of the Lord himself. The new birth is a secret and a surprise (John iii. 7, 8). 2. It is *the personal Jesus who is present to bless*—"*Jesus himself.*" (Ver. 36.) Above and beyond the mere teaching and fellowship, there is *the Lord.* Christianity is Christ. The full blessing, that which wholly fills the soul, is himself in felt relation with each self. "Of him are ye in Christ Jesus, who of God is made to us Wisdom, Righteousness, Sanctification, Redemption" (1 Cor. i. 30). 3. The *announcement of the presence is peace.* (Ver. 36.) One of the last words before he suffered was "peace." It was the legacy of the dying Saviour. The salutation of the risen Saviour is, "Peace *to* you!"—the customary salutation transformed and glorified. His immanence in the Church is evidenced by the breathing of peace over human souls. "Peace with God through the Lord Jesus Christ;" "The peace of God which passeth all understanding." 4. The *complete benediction of the presence.* (1) Fears and doubts are scattered. The disciples are terrified and affrighted (ver. 37). They are afraid at his tokens. Scepticisms reassert themselves. A Church, a Christian, wanting in spiritual enthusiasm, with a low spiritual temperature, is subject to the fogs of doubt. Its action is crippled by a subtle scepticism. When he is realized as truly in the midst, the fogs are dispelled. There is a counteracting *why* (ver. 38). In the psalms (Ps. xlii.) the soul, dark and doubtful, asks, "Why hast thou forgotten me?" Its questioning is dispelled through another *why:* "Why art thou cast down, O my soul?" The blessed Jesus-question to poor confused humanity is, "*Why* art thou troubled? and *why* do thoughts arise in thy heart?" As the Sun of Righteousness shines into the soul, the melancholy, perplexing thoughts scatter, the clouds whose banks lie so low on the heart's horizon flee away. (2) The *evidence of the sacrifice establishes the faith.* (Vers. 39, 40.) He shows the pierced hands and feet—the wounds whence comes the healing, the death whence has come the life. And, even in the glory into which he has entered, the print of the nails is seen. The gaze of the redeemed who share that glory is ever towards the Lamb that was slain. "Worthy is the Lamb!" (3) The *full revelation is the Divine humanity.* (Vers. 41—43.) While they believe, and yet can scarcely believe, for the joy seems too great and too wonderful, he eats the fish and honeycomb before them. It is no ghost who is in that room; it is very man of very man. And this is the abiding consciousness and strength of the Church. It presents the true humanity. It has the true humanitarianism. The Christ is he "who liveth and was dead, and is alive for evermore." And in him humanity is fulfilled, represented, and redeemed. This is the truth of the social life of th Church. The Church is not a mere institute for instruction and worship; it is a social state built up in the ever-abiding humanity of Jesus Christ. Thus, in the upper room at Jerusalem, on the first Easter night, there is an apocalypse of the great mystery, Christ and the Church.

Vers. 44—49.—*The instruction of the apostles.* The words contained in these verses are a summary of the instruction given by the risen Lord during the forty days in which he showed himself alive after his Passion. They are not to be regarded as the outline of only one discourse, following the appearance to the eleven recorded in the previous verses; they are rather the heads of the teaching which was imparted in the great period between the Resurrection and the Ascension. "We must suppose the evangelist to be hurrying to a close in this portion of his history, and to be giving us a brief sketch of the words and actions of our Lord which are summed up in the expression in the first chapter of the Book of Acts, "Jesus had given commandment unto the apostles." Note the points in this instruction.

I. The sword which his Church is to wield. (Vers. 44, 45.) As St. Paul afterwards said, "The sword of the Spirit, which is the Word of God." The Lord gives the treasury from which the Church is to draw—the Law, the prophets, the psalms, the Scriptures; but these writings, with the key to their inner meaning, to their saving force—"all things in them *concerning* me." The great word spelt through all the books—each book, as De Quincey put it, forming as it were a letter of the word—is

"Christ." And not only so; these Scriptures are to be expounded and enforced in the light and through the skill of the opened understanding. This is the secret of the effect; it is this that makes them the sword. Only when they are thus the weapon of the Spirit, illuminating the mind of the teacher, as well as acting on the conscience of the hearer, are they quick and powerful. The opening of the understanding is spoken of as a definite action at a definite time. "*Then* opened he their understanding." What a new light is then shed on the sacred page! What a blessed "Eureka!" is then realized! The foolish and slow in heart go forth with the sword of the Spirit, "conquering and to conquer."

II. THE MESSAGE WHICH THE CHURCH IS TO DELIVER. (Ver. 46.) The message is: the Christ whom God has sent, and the world needs—the *historical* Christ, incarnate, suffering, crucified, risen; and this Christ presented as the fulfilment of all Scripture, the consummation of Divine thought and purpose, "the Lamb slain from the foundation of the world," the Prophet, Priest, and King, by whom man is redeemed, in whom the nature and want, the hope and desire, of all nations are interpreted. The Church is called to teach that "thus it *behoved* Christ to suffer, and to rise from the dead the third day." Wide is the environment of truth, and the Church must sweep this environment in its vision; but this is the centre of all the circle.

III. THE CONDITIONS OF FELLOWSHIP IN THE KINGDOM OF GOD WHICH IT IS TO DECLARE. (Ver. 47.) The beginning of the gospel preached by Christ was the word "repent" (Matt. iv. 17). Now he solemnly and emphatically urges that repentance is to be the great fact in New Testament preaching. The end to be ever before the Church is "to open the eyes, and turn men from darkness to light, and from the power of Satan to God." And with this repentance is to be associated the blessing of the kingdom, "remission of sins;" *i.e.* the sending of the guilt and power of sin away from between the soul and God, and thus making the inner vision clear, inspiring with the consciousness of the spirit of adoption and the spirit of brotherhood, confirming in the liberty wherewith Christ makes free. In the name of Christ, all nations are to be summoned to repent, and receive this remission; the voice lifted up with strength, "There is none other Name given under heaven among men whereby we must be saved."

IV. THE WITNESS WHICH THE CHURCH IS TO REALIZE. (Ver. 48.) 1. Its *range.* "Among all nations." The universality and catholicity of the Christian word, of the Christian Church, are asserted, with regal authority, at the conference on the mountain in Galilee (Matt. xxviii. 18—20). 2. Its *course.* "Beginning at Jerusalem." There, where the Lord of glory was crucified, the first call to repentance is to be sounded, the first offer of the Christ for the remission of sins is to be made. So it was (Acts ii.). But, from Jerusalem, the course of the witness is ever outward—"to Judæa, Samaria, the uttermost parts of the earth." We are first to find our own; but the love which begins, is never to stop, at home. 3. Its *power.* (Ver. 49.) Not in the witnessing man or woman; not in the things witnessed to; not in word, ordinance, ministry; no, the power is from on high. Christ reasserts what he taught in the last discourse before he suffered. The great consolation then was the promise of the Father—that in which his Fatherly love and will are expressed, his great promise to his Son—the Holy Ghost. It is the Holy Ghost who testifies of him. He is not the accompaniment of the Church; the Church is his accompaniment. "He shall testify of me: and ye *also* shall bear witness" (John xv. 26, 27). Now, in the forty days' instruction, he repeats this word. He reminds us that *the* power of witnessing is a descent from on high, the anointing of the man by the Holy Spirit. Two things are said—the one, the declaration that the promise is imminent, "I am sending it;" and the other, the injunction to wait in the city, to attempt nothing, until the promise is made good, and they are endued with the power. Let the Church, let every Christian, remember the injunction; let eternal thanksgiving arise because the promise of the Father has been sent, and the Holy Spirit now dwells with the Church.

Vers. 50—53.—*The farewell and the Ascension.* Once more the old relation is resumed. The Shepherd of Israel goes before his little flock. They see him, as in the former time, at their head. The well-known route is taken, the well-known place is reached. And the crowning memory of Bethany is imprinted on their hearts. It is the scene of the last adieu, of the Ascension (ver. 50). In the earlier history of Israel (2 Kings ii.) there was a day when the sons of the prophets, referring to Elijah, said to Elisha, "Knowest thou that the Lord will take away thy master from thy head to-day?" And his answer was, "Yea, I know it; hold ye your peace." There were no sons of prophets thus speaking to the eleven. But whispers, no doubt, in their hearts raised shadows of some coming event. Something like the old amazement and fear (Mark x. 32) would be felt as, in silence, they followed their Leader. He is to be taken from their head; but better far than the mantle thrown on Elisha from the vanishing prophet is to be their portion. Observe Christ as he is revealed in the concluding verses of the Gospel; observe those whom he is to leave behind.

I. Observe Christ as he is here revealed. See: 1. *The action of the Lord towards them.* "He lifted up his hands" (ver. 50). Before he suffered he had lifted up his eyes to heaven, and the voice of intercession had been raised for them (John xvii.). As the high-priestly prayer closed, the voice had passed from the tones of earnest but humble pleading into those of the Sovereign expressing his will: "I will that they also whom thou hast given me, be with me where I am." Now the Priest, about to ascend to his throne, extends those hands in which is the print of the nails. It is the first time in which we are introduced to this attitude in the Gospels. The uplifted hands are the sign of the accepted sacrifice ever potent to cleanse. They are the sign of the righteousness ever ample to clothe. They are the sign of the protection ever sufficient to overshadow his Church. The uplifted hands constituted the last recollection of the Christ whom the disciples had seen; they mark the abiding truth of the Christ whom the eye sees not. And, as the hands are lifted, the lips are opened to bless. What were the words of the blessing? Perhaps the benediction (Numb. iv. 24) which the sons of Aaron were commanded to pronounce was included in it. But who can measure all that it comprehended—all the wealth of grace and truth with which it was charged? Let us say rather, with which it *is* charged for the Church until the end of the age. "Lo, I am with you alway, blessing and keeping, my face shining on you, my will gracious to you, the light of my countenance lifted on you, my peace possessing you." 2. *The ascending Lord.* "While blessing" (ver. 51). While the accents of his tenderness are flowing over the soul, lo! he moves from the soil on which he and his have been standing. Upward, ever upward, he is borne; they gaze in wonder as the form in which they have beheld him is sublimated and passes whither their adoring vision can no longer follow. The apostle who was "born out of due time" completes, as far as thought of mortal can, the account of the evangelist (Eph. i. 20—23), when he describes the ascent "far above all principality, and power, and might, and dominion, and every name that is named, not only in this world, but in that which is to come;" all things put under the feet of the glorified Man, "Head over all things to the Church, which is his body, the fulness of him that filleth all in all." He is "parted from them;" but only to be more nearly and entirely with them; only to bear with him the humanity through which Highest God is in touch with the whole life of man; only that, in the unchangeable Priesthood, he may ever live to make intercession; only to make good the word as to the promise of the Father. When ten more days have passed, the gates which had opened that the King of glory might enter, shall open again, and the Paraclete, Christ's other self, shall descend from the heaven into which he has gone, to fill the little company with his presence. And in that day they shall know that he is in the Father, and they in him, and he in them.

II. Observe the disciples. 1. *The new worship.* They had followed him, and had called him Master. His appearances during the forty days had prepared them for something higher still. Now, in deepest reverence, they kneel before the Lord. Thomas learns the whole reality of his answer, "My Lord and my God." Mary learns that which is higher and holier than the touch with which, on the resurrection-morning, she had sought to detain him. John learns the word which afterwards he wrote, "This is the true God, and the Eternal Life." Peter learns that which moves him to interpret the consciousness of faith, "Whom having not seen ye love." Then first sounds the music which burst forth, in later years, in the sublimest hymn of the Church: "We praise thee, O God; we acknowledge thee to be the Lord. . . . Thou art the King of glory, O Christ." And this worship is the true life of the Church. It is the outcome of the faith in the Resurrection. "Christ died, yea rather, is risen again, and is even at the right hand of God, making intercession for us." Wanting this, there may be such an apostrophe as that with which Renan concludes his 'Life of Jesus;' but worship full and adoring there cannot be. It is this worship which is the spring of all energy, the pledge of all victory, the bond of union between heaven and earth. "Salvation to our God who sitteth on the throne, and unto the Lamb for ever and ever." 2. *The new joy.* "They returned to Jerusalem" (ver. 25). But what a difference! They had left it dispirited, weighed down by many thoughts. Now "they come again rejoicing, bringing their sheaves with them." "Parted from them!" Might they not feel as sheep without a Shepherd? Nay; for they know that their Shepherd is with them. Their hope had been sealed and confirmed, and they are flushed with "a great joy." Should not this joy thrill the Church? Enthusiasm is essential to its vitality. To be strong, it must be sanguine, triumphant. Times of worshipful faith are always times of great joy. "We triumph in God through our Lord Jesus Christ, in whom we received the reconciliation." 3. *The new life.* "They were continually in the temple" (ver. 53). But the temple had a new meaning to them. Rite and offering, house of prayer and songs of praise, were all clothed with a new character. It was their Father's house, and he had given a new song to their lips. Continually are they "praising and blessing God." This is the life; for they are sitting in the heavenly places, and partaking of the heavenly things. "Day by day we magnify thee." Beautiful as the first days of summer is this picture of the waiting Church. Would that the impression of this life of praise and blessing were more evident in the Church, witnessing, working, and still waiting. May the Church be "found unto praise, and honour, and glory, at the appearing of Jesus Christ"!

HOMILIES BY VARIOUS AUTHORS.

Vers. 1—12.—*Side-lights from the Resurrection.* The simple, unpretending story of the Resurrection, as here narrated, brings into view other truths than that great and supreme fact of the rising of our Lord. We have our attention called to—

I. THE CONSTANCY AND THE EAGERNESS OF TRUE AFFECTION. (Ver. 1.) No thought had these women of deserting him whom they loved but whom the world hated and had now slain. On the contrary, the enmity of those that maligned and murdered him made their affection to cleave all the more firmly to him. It attended him right up to the very last; it followed him to the grave; it came to bestow those final ministries which only devoted affection would have cared to render. And it showed itself as eager as it was constant. "Very early in the morning they came unto the sepulchre." True love to our Lord will stand these tests. It will survive the enmities and oppositions of an indifferent or a hostile society; it will be unaffected by these except, indeed, to be strengthened and deepened by them; moreover, it will show its loyalty and its fervour by the eagerness of its service, not waiting for the last hour of necessity, but availing itself of the first hour of opportunity.

II. THE DISAPPEARANCE OF DIFFICULTIES AS WE GO ON OUR WAY OF FAITHFUL SERVICE. We know from Mark (xvi. 3) that these women were full of apprehension lest they should be unable to get the stone rolled away from the door. But they went on their way to do their sacred office; and when they reached the spot they found their difficulty vanished (ver. 2). This is the common experience of the seeker after God in Christ, of the man desirous of discharging his duty in the fear of God, of the Christian worker. "Who will roll away that intervening stone?" we ask timidly and apprehensively. "How shall we get over that insurmountable barrier? How will our weakness prevail against such solid obstacles?" Let us go on our way of faith, of duty, of loving service, and we shall find that, if some angel has not been on the scene, the hindrance has disappeared, the way is open, the goal within our reach, the service within the compass of our powers.

III. THE SURPRISES THAT AWAIT US AS WE PROCEED. These women found an empty grave, visitants from the unseen world, a most unexpected though most welcome message; instead of a mournful satisfaction, they found a new hope, far too good and far too great to be held all at once within their heart (vers. 4—7). Peter, too, found himself the subject of a great astonishment (ver. 12). God has his merciful surprises for us as we proceed on our Christian path. He may surprise us with a sudden fear or a sudden sorrow; but he also surprises us with an unanticipated peace; with an unlooked-for joy; with a new, strange hope; before long he will introduce us to the blessed surprise of the heavenly realities.

IV. THE NEARNESS OF THE HEAVENLY TO THE EARTHLY SPHERE. (Ver. 4.) Angels were always at hand to render service in the great redemptive work. Why should we think of heaven as "beyond the stars"? Why should we not think of it as encompassing us on every side, only separated from us by a thin veil, through which our mortal senses cannot pass to its glorious spectacles and its blessed harmonies?

V. THAT GOD HAS MUCH BETTER THINGS IN STORE FOR US THAN WE THINK POSSIBLE. Neither the wondering women nor the incredulous apostles could believe in such a happy issue as they were assured of, though they had been carefully prepared to expect it (ver. 11). In the feebleness of our faith we say to ourselves, "Surely God is not going to give me *that*, to place me *there*, to bestow on me such a heritage as *this!*" But why not? For him to make all grace, all power, all life, to abound, is for him to do what he has promised, and what he has been doing since he first opened his hand to create and to bestow.—C.

Vers. 5, 6.—*The Resurrection and the Life.* No smallest touch of censure can we trace in the words of these angels. On their errand of faithful love these women would not be greeted thus. It was but a strong, awakening appeal, calling them to consider that, while they had come in the right spirit, they had come on a superfluous mission, and were looking in the wrong place for their Lord. Not there in the tomb among the dead, but breathing the air of a life that would never be laid down, was he whom they sought. The words attest—

I. THE RESURRECTION OF OUR LORD. This was: 1. Here attested by the angels. It was, at the same time, indicated by the empty tomb. The latter, of course, would not of itself prove such a fact; but it strongly sustained the word of the heavenly visitants. But beyond this, weightier than this, was: 2. The repeated and unmistakable evidence of the apostles and the women. Ten several times, at least, the risen Saviour was seen by those who knew him best. These were so thoroughly assured of the fact of his rising again, that they not only testified it, but risked and even sacrificed their lives to propagate a faith of which it was the corner-stone. And they not only undoubtedly believed it themselves, but they spoke as men who could be and who were credited by those who heard them. Then we have here: 3. The twofold buttress of a *Divine promise* and of *human incredulity*. Jesus "spake, saying, . . . the third day he should rise again." This was the fulfilment of the promise of One who gave such convincing proof that he could do what he willed. Moreover, it was believed in spite of the strongest incredulity. The apostles ought to have expected it, but they did not; we might almost say that it was the last thing they were looking for. They had given up their Lord and their cause as utterly lost; and when the tidings came, they refused to believe (ver. 11). So far from the Resurrection being the figment of a diseased expectation, it was a fact forced upon minds strongly predisposed to discredit it. The second clause of the angels' sentence was as true as the first: he was not there; *he had risen.* He had kept his word; he who had commanded the winds and the waves, and who showed himself Master of the elements of nature, now proved that the keys of death were in his royal hand, and proved himself to be the Son of God, the Lord of life. And with his "glorious resurrection" comes the fact of—

II. OUR OWN IMMORTALITY. The resurrection of Jesus Christ is the sure sign, proof, forerunner, of our own life beyond the grave. Without that supreme and crowning fact, we could have had no certain hope, no assurance; without that he could not have been to us "the Resurrection and the Life." With that he can be and is. Now we have in him a *living Lord,* who can carry out his kindest promises and be to us all that, during his ministry, he undertook to be. Wherefore let us: 1. Seek and find spiritual life in the once-crucified and ever-living Saviour. "He that believeth in him, though he were [spiritually] dead, yet shall he live," live in very deed and truth, *i.e.* live before God, unto God, and in God—partake of the life which is spiritual and Divine. 2. Be assured, then, of a blessed immortality; for "whoso liveth [in him] and believeth in him shall never die." His outward, bodily dissolution will be a mere incident in his career; so far from its being a termination of it, it will prove to be the starting-point of another and nobler life than the present, one nearer to God and far fuller of power, of usefulness, of blessedness. 3. Realize this truth concerning the departed. We may go to the grave and weep there like the sorrowing sisters of Bethany; we may tend their tomb with the carefulness which is the simple prompting of pure and deep affection; but let us learn to dissociate our thoughts of our departed friends from the grave. *They* are not there; let us not be seeking the living among the dead. There rest their mortal remains, but they themselves are with God, with the Saviour whose presence and friendship are exceeding gladness, with the holy and the true who have passed into the skies. *They* are in the light and the love and the joy of home. Let us dwell on this, and comfort ourselves and comfort one another with these thoughts.—C.

Vers. 13—32.—*Privilege; unconscious companionship; incredulity.* In this most interesting narrative, beside a very pleasing and attractive picture, we have a variety of lessons. We may gather instruction respecting—

I. OUR LORD'S ELECTIVE LOVE. It was a very great favour he granted to these two men. Why, we ask, was it rendered *to them?* Of one we do not even know his name, and of the other nothing but his name. Why was so rare and high a privilege accorded to these obscure disciples, and not rather to those more prominent and active? In truth, we find ourselves quite unable to decide who are the fittest to receive special favours from the hand of God, or on what grounds he wills to manifest his presence and his power. His selections, we are sure, cannot be arbitrary or irrational. God must have not only a reason, but the best reason, for everything he does. But into the reasons for his choice we often may not enter; they lie beyond our reach. It is not to the acknowledged leaders of the Church that God often chooses to manifest especial privilege, but to those who are simple, unexpectant, unknown. He grants illuminations of his Spirit, peculiar joy and gladness of heart in him, remarkable success in the utterance of his truth, anticipatory glimpses of heavenly glory, to whom he will. And these are quite likely to be found amongst the humbler members of his Church. If there is any law which will guide our judgment it is this—that it is to the "pure in heart," to those who have most perfectly conquered the fleshly passions and are most freed from worldly ambitions and anxieties, who have the simplest and purest hope in him and desire toward him, that he vouchsafes his presence and grants the teaching and inspiration of his Spirit. But Christ's elective love is fully as much of a *fact* as it is of a *doctrine*.

II. UNCONSCIOUS COMPANIONSHIP WITH CHRIST. These two men were walking and talking with Christ, receiving his truth and responding to his appeal, their hearts "burning within them" as they held sweet and sacred intercourse with him; yet they did not recognize him; they had no idea that they were having fellowship with the Lord. There is much unconscious companionship with Jesus Christ now. Men are led into belief of the truth, are impressed with the sovereign claims of God upon their service, and of Jesus Christ upon their love; they ask, they inquire, they come to the feet of Christ to learn of him; they come to the cross of Christ to trust in him; they shun what they believe to be offensive, and pursue what they think is right and pleasing in his sight; and yet they are not at rest. They think they may be in a good way or in a fair way to find life; but they do not realize that they are *in* the *right* way. The fact is ofttimes that they are walking in the path of life with Christ, but "their eyes are holden that they do not know him." A Divine One has joined himself to them, as familiarly and unpretendingly as to these two disciples, ingratiating himself into their favour, wooing and winning their trust and their love; but because there has been no period of well-recognized revolution, no sudden remarkable convulsion, they have failed to perceive that the work wrought within them has been that of his own kind and holy hand. Such souls need to learn that oftenest it is not in the wind, or in the earthquake, or in the fire, but in the still small voice of familiar truth and gracious influence, that Christ comes to the soul in renewing power. If it is in Christ we are trusting, if it is in *his* service we are most willing to live, if it is *his* will we are most concerned to do, then it is *he* himself by whose side we are walking day by day.

III. **The strange incredulity of Christian discipleship.** Our Master, who was so gentle and so considerate, here employs a very strong expression (ver. 25). This is the language of serious reproach; it is a weighty rebuke. The disciples of Christ ought to have read their Scriptures better, and they ought to have heeded the reiterated warning and promise he had himself given them of his death and his rising again. But while we wonder at what seems to us their slowness to learn and to believe, are we not as obtuse and as incredulous as they were? Do we not fail to grasp the promises of God as they are written in his Word, as they were spoken by his Son our Saviour? When those things happen which we should expect to happen in connection with the teaching of Divine truth; when the Spirit of God works mightily and mercifully in the souls of men; when hard hearts are broken and stubborn wills are subdued to the obedience of Christ; when wrong and shameful lives are changed into pure and holy ones; when the kingdom of God comes amongst us;—are we not surprised, incredulous? Are we not tempted to ascribe these issues to other than heavenly sources? And yet *ought not* this very result to happen? Is it not precisely what we should have been looking for, and wondering that it did not occur? We shall probably find abundant illustrations of Christian incredulity to match anything of which we read in our New Testament. "Slow of heart" are we to believe all that the Master has said of the presence and the power and the promises of God.—C.

Vers. 13—32.—*Further lessons by the way.* Other lessons beside those already gleaned (see preceding homily) await our hand in this instructive story.

I. **The thread of trial which runs through the fabric of our life.** On one occasion our Lord asked a question of one of his disciples, and of that question it is said, "This he said to prove him" (John vi. 6). There were other occasions, *e.g.* that of the blind beggars by the wayside, and that of the Syro-phœnician woman, when Jesus said things to *prove* or to try those who came to him. We have the same thing here. He drew near to these two disciples in the guise of a stranger; he chose to remain unknown to them; he drew them out as if he were one unacquainted with the events which were filling their minds and hearts; he induced them to discover themselves freely and fully both to his own eyes and to theirs; moreover, he was in the act of passing on, and would have gone beyond Emmaus if they had not availed themselves of the opportunity of persuading him to remain. And thus he tried them. The "trial of our faith," and of our love and loyalty, forms a great part of our Master's dealing with ourselves. It explains many otherwise inexplicable things in our life. God appears to us other than the kind, gracious, pitiful, considerate Father that he is; Christ seems to be other than the present, strong, faith-rewarding Master that he is. Why does God let such things happen to us? Why does not Christ bring to pass that for which we labour and pray so earnestly? It may be that, in these cases, he is trying us, proving the sincerity and deepening the roots of our faith and love and zeal. We shall be the stronger, and our lives will be the more fruitful, for his action or his lingering, a little further on.

II. **The true way to make the sabbath a delight.** It was fitting that on the first sabbath of the Christian era there should be recorded an instance in which the day was spent as Christ would have it be. What a pleasant picture this of communion with Christ, of searching the Scriptures, of sitting down at the same table with him! We have here: 1. *Communion with our Lord.* About one-fourth of the whole day these favoured men were conversing with Christ, opening their minds and outpouring their hearts to him, telling him their hopes and their fears, and receiving kind and illuminating responses from his lips. So should our "fellowship be with the Father, and with his Son Jesus Christ," on the "day of the Lord." And as we may be sure that the way to Emmaus was marvellously shortened that afternoon, and the village houses showed themselves long before they were looked for, so will earnest and loving communion with our living Lord, so will our walking with Christ, make the hours go swiftly by on the wings of holy and elevated joy, and we shall "call the sabbath a delight." 2. *Sacred study.* (Vers. 27, 32.) How wonderful these Scriptures which contain the record of Divine revelation! So short as to be capable of being committed to the memory, and yet so full as to contain all that is needful for our enlightenment and enrichment, for guidance to God and heaven; so dull to the unquickened conscience, and so delightful to the awakened and renewed; holding mysteries insoluble to human learning, and yet intelligible and instructive from Genesis to Revelation to the earnest inquirer after truth and life; valueless in the market, and yet precious beyond all price to all who want to know how to live and how to die. As Christ and the two learners walked and talked, new light shone on the old passages, and the way was too short and the time too soon gone for their interest and their eagerness to be expended. 3. *Meeting the living Lord at his table.* (Ver. 30.) This was not, strictly speaking, a "sacramental" meal to which they sat down. It was not the "Lord's Supper" of which they partook. But there was about it so much of reverence, of religious earnestness, of holy communion, of sacred joy, that it may well suggest to us that most excellent way of spending some part of "the Lord's day."

III. The worth of all true Christian labour. Possibly those who teach may sometimes ask themselves whether it is worth their while to conduct so small a class, to preach to so poor a congregation. Here is the answer to that questioning. If the risen Lord of glory thought it worth his while to walk seven miles and spend two hours in enlightening the minds and comforting the hearts of two humble and obscure disciples; if he was content to spend a good part of his first sabbath in taking a class of two, and pouring from the rich treasury of his truth into their minds, we may not think it unworthy of us to spend time in enlightening or comforting *one* human heart that craves the succour it is in our power to give. The disciple is not above his Master.

IV. The secret of spiritual interest. Do we devoutly wish that we knew more of that sacred gladness of which these disciples were so happily conscious as he "talked with them by the way, and opened to them the Scriptures" (ver. 32)? Then: 1. Let us see that we are, as they were, earnestly desirous of knowing more of Jesus Christ. Let us go to our Bible and go up to the house of the Lord with that end *distinctly* and prominently in view. 2. Let us seek and gain the same Divine illumination. It is still to be had, though *that* voice is not now heard in our ear. The "Spirit of truth" is with us still, waiting to illumine and to enlarge our hearts; if we seek his aid and open our minds to his entrance, he will "guide us into all the truth" (John xvi. 13).—C.

Ver. 29.—*The exigency of old age.* The disciples "constrained" our Lord to abide with them; for, they said, "It is toward evening, and the day is far spent." This act of theirs and their words taken together are suggestive of the truth that those whose life is fast waning—with whom it is "toward evening," whose day is "far spent"—have urgent need that Jesus Christ should "abide with" them. We have before us the special spiritual necessities of old age. It has—

I. Its special responsibility. We look to advanced religious experience to set us a particularly blameless example, to show us most clearly the spirit and the complexion of a distinctly Christian life, to lead us in the direction of spirituality and purity. For this high service the near presence of the Saviour is needed, and the constant exercise of his gracious power.

II. Its special temptation. The temptation of age is to querulousness, to an illiberal criticism of the present and to an undue and partial preference of the past, to an unjust and unwise severity in judging the eccentricities and irregularities of the young, to a dissatisfaction with the comparative obscurity to which it is itself descending. To prevail against this temptation, and to preserve equanimity, sweetness, cheerfulness of spirit and hopefulness of heart, age has urgent need of a constant renewal from above.

III. Its special privations. There are a few who live to a "good old age" without any or without much consciousness of loss. But these are only a few. With old age usually comes privation. In respect of sight, of hearing, of power of locomotion, of facility in speaking, of memory, of intellectual grasp, the aged are painfully conscious that "they are not what they were; they speak with diminished fire, they act with a lessened force." Their life is lower, is narrowed; they are less to their contemporaries than they used to be. They need comfort under the sense of loss; they need another source of satisfaction and of joy. In whom, in what, shall they find it, but in the Person and the presence of the Divine Friend and Saviour?

IV. Its special loneliness. Age is often lonely. It misses the companions of its youth and its prime. Most of these, perhaps nearly all, have fallen, and they are as the last leaf upon the wintry bough. "They are all gone, the old familiar faces," is the plaintive strain of their discourse; and some who still live have drifted away from them in space or in spirit. There is no one left who can go back with them in thought and sympathy to the old times, the memory of which is so pleasant, and which they would fain revisit with the friends of youth and childhood. Age is apt to be very lonely, and it has great need of a Divine Companion who does not pass away, who "abides," who is "the same yesterday, and to-day, and for ever."

V. ITS SPECIAL LIMITATION. We all know that there *may* not be many days left in which we can bear witness for our Lord and his gospel. But the aged know that there *can* not be many more left to them. So much the more, therefore, as they see the night approaching when they can work no more for their Master, may they well desire to *be* and to *do* all that still lies in their power. Every hour is golden to him to whom but few remain. And because the opportunities of serving men here on earth are narrowing perceptibly day by day, the aged may earnestly entreat their Lord to be near to them, and to let his grace rest upon them, that their last days may be full of fruitfulness as well as of peace and hope.

VI. ITS NEARNESS TO DEATH. We wish not only to "*live* unto the Lord," but also to "*die* unto the Lord;" to honour him in the manner of our death as well as by the spirit of our life. They who feel that the evening shadows are gathering, and that the night of death is near, may well wish for the near presence of the upholding Saviour, with whom they will go tranquilly and hopefully through the last darkness. "Abide with us," they say; "be with us as we take the last steps of our earthly journey, go down with us into the deep waters, attend us till we reach the heavenly shore."

"Oh, meet us in the valley,
  When heart and flesh shall fail,
And softly, safely, lead us on,
  Until within the veil;
When faith shall turn to gladness,
  To find ourselves with thee,
And trembling Hope shall realize
  Her full felicity."

C.

Vers. 33—43.—*Sense and spirit: the Resurrection.* The story of the Resurrection in its relation to the disciples of our Lord suggests to us thoughts concerning—

I. THE TRIUMPH OF THE SPIRIT OVER THE FLESH. These two disciples who had walked from Jerusalem to Emmaus, and who persuaded the mysterious Stranger to remain because the day was far gone, and subsequently spent some time in earnest converse with him, now *hastened back to Jerusalem* (ver. 33). This was quite contrary to their intention when they set out from the city; it was not in the natural order of things to start out again on a long two-hours' walk after the fatigues of that eventful day. But their minds were so enlarged, their hearts so filled with joy, their souls so stirred with animating and vivifying hope, that they could not remain where they were; they must impart the transporting and transforming tidings to the crushed and sorrowing brethren they had left behind them that afternoon. It was late and dark, and (when they thought of it) they were tired. But what were these considerations? They were things not to be entertained for a moment, they were a mere feather's weight in the scale; and we may be certain that they set off to Jerusalem with a much lighter step in the evening, and far more alacrity of spirit, than they left that city in the afternoon of the day. In one sense "we are but dust and ashes," but "animated clay;" our soul is subject to certain limitations from its close connection with the body. Yet can the spirit triumph nobly over the flesh. Let but the kindling truth come down from heaven, let the Divine hand but touch the secret springs of the soul, and all our bodily sensations and our lower instincts go down and disappear. Fatigue, loss, danger, death itself, is nothing to a soul alight with the celestial fire. A new hope, a new faith, a new purpose, can carry the weary frame along the dusty road of duty, or up the steep ascent of arduous or dangerous achievement, better than angels' wings. Our true self is not the tabernacle of the flesh, but the indwelling and victorious spirit.

II. The essential service which the flesh renders to the spirit. Christianity is essentially spiritual. It makes its *appeal* to the spiritual nature; its *aim* is spiritual; and the *weapons* of its warfare are also spiritual—the efforts of the spirit of man and the energies of the Spirit of God. But it rests largely on a basis of facts attested by our senses—the fact of the Incarnation, "God manifested in the flesh," the "Word made flesh;" the fact of the miracles of Christ, miracles wrought before the eyes of men, and assured by their sensible observation of them; the fact of a blameless life lived in the bodily presence of eye-witnesses; the fact of the death at Calvary, borne witness to by those who actually beheld it; and the great crowning fact of the Resurrection, the return of Jesus Christ *in the flesh* to his disciples. The entire fabric of our religion rests upon the history of the Man Christ Jesus; and the acceptance of him as a Divine Teacher, whose word can be trusted and whose character can be honoured, stands or falls with the truth of the Resurrection. For if he did not rise again, he certainly was not the One he claimed to be. Of what service to us, then, these physical facts here recorded—his eating with the two at Emmaus; the sound of the familiar voice in many words of intercourse; the sight of his hands and feet with the imprint of the cruel nails; the sight and feeling of the "flesh and bones," which a spirit has not but which they found he had; and the act of sitting down at the table and eating of the fish and honeycomb before their eyes? The sight of his face, the sound of his voice, the style of his speech, the handling of his limbs ("handle me, and see," ver. 39), supplemented by his eating and drinking before them,—all this at length convinced their incredulity that it was indeed the risen Lord himself, returned according to his word. And all this accumulated evidence of all the senses is as good for us as it was for them. We are thankful for this multiplication of the material evidence, for, taken with other considerations, it substantiates the great fact of facts, and gives to us not only a marvellously original Thinker, but an unmistaken and faultless Exemplar, a Divine Lord and Master. The human senses never rendered to the human soul so great a service as when they attested the supreme fact of the resurrection of Jesus Christ. But they still do render very valuable service in every Christian life. 1. The control and regulation of our senses for Christ's sake and in obedience to his word is a continual tribute to the power of his truth. 2. Our feet can carry us forth on errands of Christian charity. 3. Our hands can be put daily to deeds of righteousness, of justice, of excellency. 4. Our lips can sing the praises of our Lord, and can speak words of kindness to the young, of sympathy to the suffering and sorrowing, of hope to the dying. 5. Our eye can read, our ears can hear, the truths which impart or which sustain the inner life of the spirit. Through our bodily senses God's own living truth, and with his truth himself also, comes continually into our soul; and through these same senses there go forth from us all healing, all helpful, all saving influences to the world; and thus we enrich and are enriched.—C.

Ver. 36.—*The peace of Christ.* It is true that these words, "Peace be unto you!" were the ordinary Jewish salutation. But remembering that our Lord used these words a second time in this interview (see John xx. 21), and having in mind the way in which he made these words his own, and gave to them not merely a formal but a profound significance (John xiv. 27), we may find much meaning in them. We recognize the fact that they were—

I. Specially appropriate to the circumstances. The minds of his apostles had passed through the deepest *distress*. They had lost their Lord and their Friend; and with him they had lost, as they thought, their cause and their hopes; they were, therefore, afflicted with an overwhelming grief. And now they were filled with the liveliest *agitation*. They were in a mental state in which blighted hopes were struggling with darkest fears; their soul was stirred to its very depths; and what, above all things, they needed was One that could come and say, "Peace be unto you!" It was the very word that was wanted to be breathed into their ear, to be spoken to their heart.

II. Admirably descriptive of his abiding mission. It is true that Jesus once said, "I came not to send peace, but a sword." But it will be found, on referring, that then he simply meant to say that division and strife would be an inevitable incident of the course of his gospel; he did not mean that this was its deep purpose or its long and last result. It was the back-water, and not the main current, of the truth he preached. Christ came to give peace to a world profoundly disturbed and disquieted by sin. "Come unto me," he said, "and I will give you rest." Not as the world gives rest or peace does he give. (1) Not mere comfort or gratification that is very short-lived; (2) nor satisfaction that is based on ignorance of ourselves, and must before long be exposed; (3) nor the quiet of indifference or unbelief that must soon be broken up. Not of this order is the peace of Christ. It is: 1. *Rest to the burdened conscience.* He shows us our sin and makes us ashamed of it; he fills our heart with a true and righteous sorrow for it; he awakes within us a just and honourable concern for the consequences of it. And then he offers himself as the One who bore the burden upon himself, through whom we may find forgiveness and acceptance. And "being justified by faith, we have peace with God through our Lord Jesus Christ." 2. *Abiding gladness to the hungering heart.* "In the world" is unsatisfiedness of soul, emptiness and heart-ache; a sense of disappointment. But in him is a true and lasting satisfaction. "How happily the days in his blest service fly!" To live heartily and wholly unto him who loved us and gave himself for us, to expend our powers in his praise and in his service,—this is the secret of lifelong peace. All the lower springs will fail, but this never. To "lose our life" *unto him* is to "find it" and to keep it for ever. 3. *Comfort to the troubled spirit.* When darkness falls upon the path, when losses come, when bereavement makes a gap in the home and in the heart, when some heavy disappointment blights the prospect,—then the felt presence, the realized sympathy, and the unfailing succour of that Divine Friend give a peace which is deeper than our disturbance, a thrice-blessed calm to the tempest-tossed soul. 4. *Peace in death.* For many centuries the dying have departed in peace because they have hoped for everything through the Divine Saviour; they have calmly "slept in Jesus;" and those who now look forward to death as a passage through which they will be passing can find no better wish or prayer than that "the music of his Name" may "refresh their soul in death."—C.

Ver. 45.—*The Divine Spirit and the human understanding.* It may be that we do not sufficiently recognize the very intimate connection between our human intelligence and the action of the Spirit of God. We may be seriously in danger of coming short in gratitude for all that God has wrought for us in this respect, and in prayer for his continued and especial help in the future.

I. The Divine endowment with which he starts us on our course. We receive from his creative hand a kind and a measure of intellectual power which may be said to vary with each individual of the human race. To one he giveth five talents, to another two, to another one. And it is not only difference in measure, but also in kind. The human spirit has many faculties, and one man has a large share of one and another a goodly share of another, "as it pleaseth him." Most happily for us, there is every possible variety of human understanding resulting from the different capacities and dispositions with which our Creator endows us.

II. The beneficent law of expansion he has ordained for us. The law under which we live, and under which our understanding grows, is this—"to him that hath is given." We observe, we hear and read, we reflect, we reason, we construct and produce; and as we do this, we grow—our intelligence is opened and enlarged. Thus by the operation of one of his wise and kind laws God is "opening our understanding" every day, but more particularly in the earlier days of curiosity and of study. Youth has but to do its rightful and proper work, and God will do his gracious, enlarging work; and thus he will "build up" a mind, well stored with knowledge and wisdom, capable of great and noble service.

III. The special illuminations he has granted and is willing to impart. 1. God has given to members of our race illumination or expansion of mind which we pronounce *miraculous*, i.e. not in accordance with known laws. Such was the inspiration he gave to Moses when he inspired him to write his books; or that he gave to Samuel, to Elijah, to Isaiah, to Zechariah, when he moved these prophets to remonstrate with or to exhort their contemporaries, or to write words that should live for all time on the sacred page; or that he gave to these two disciples when he opened *their* understanding that they might understand the Scriptures as they had never understood them before; or that he gave to the Apostles Peter and Paul and John when he prompted them to speak as they spoke and to write as they wrote. Here was an altogether unusual and supernatural enlightenment and enlargement of mind granted for the special purpose of making known his mind and will to the race of man. 2. God still imparts special illumination to us according to our need and in response to our prayer. The "age of miracles" may be past, but assuredly the age of Divine illumination is not passed. God remains, and will remain, in constant communication with his human children; he has, and ever will have, access to their understanding; he can touch and quicken us, can enlarge and equip our minds for special service in his Name and cause, can make clear to our minds those things which have been obscure, whether in his Word or in his providence, so that we can "understand the Scriptures," and also interpret his dealing with ourselves and his fashioning of our lives. Three things become us. (1) *A sense of our own insufficiency*—insufficiency both for *comprehending* what we are called upon both to consider and (as far as may be) to understand, and for *doing* the work of explanation and enforcement which is required of us. (2) *Faith in God*—in his observation of us; in his interest in our humble endeavours to take our part and do our work; in his power over us to "open our understanding" as well as to "open our heart" (Acts xvi. 44; see Eph. i. 18; 2 Tim. ii. 7). (3) *Prayer for Divine illumination.* Lacking wisdom, let us ask of God, "who giveth to all men liberally, and upbraideth not" (Jas. i. 5; see Col. i. 9; Eph. i. 16, 17). Whenever we read the Scriptures that we may learn the "mind of Christ," whenever we stand up to speak in his Name, whenever we set ourselves to any effort that requires spiritual wisdom, we do well to pray in the spirit, if not in the language, of our great poet—

> "Thou, O Spirit, that dost prefer
> Before all temples the upright heart and pure,
> Instruct me; for thou know'st: . . . What in me is dark,
> Illumine! What is low, raise and support!"

C.

Ver. 47.—*The solemn charge.* It is an allowable curiosity to wonder how the apostles of our Lord received this "their solemn charge." 1. They must have been greatly impressed by its extreme seriousness; they were to preach repentance and remission of sin "among *all nations.*" And although they did not know as we do what that meant, and how wide was the range of the Saviour's purpose, they could realize as we cannot how deep and bitter would be the enmity which a gospel of the crucified Nazarene would encounter, more especially in Jerusalem. 2. But they may have been powerfully sustained by the presence of the Lord himself. The "power of his resurrection" was then upon their souls; they were to go forth in *his* Name, who had just triumphed over man's last and greatest enemy—death. What could they not do through him? If we ask what was the message, in its fulness, which they were charged to deliver, we reply—

I. Repentance as Christ had preached it. They were to preach repentance *in his Name.* Therefore of the kind which he demanded. And this was no mere outward amendment; it was not found in the external habits of devotion; no amount of almsgiving, fasting, prayers, would constitute it. It meant: 1. *Self-condemnation.* Not necessarily the exhibition of overwhelming emotion, but the decided and deep conviction of our own unworthiness, and real regret for wrong done and for service withheld in the past. 2. *The return of the heart to God.* The coming back from the far country of estrangement, or forgetfulness, or denial and open enmity, and the seeking anew the Father's face and favour. 3. *The outcasting from the soul* of all tolerance of evil, so that sin is not only shunned but hated. 4. *The pursuit of all moral excellency;* to be attained by the study and the love of the great Exemplar himself. And this repentance, real and thorough, was to be *immediate.* There was to be no guilty and dangerous postponement; as soon as the soul recognized its duty it was to start on the true and right course.

II. Remission as Christ offered it. And this was: 1. *Full.* It was a forgiveness without reserve. The son (of the parable, ch. xv.) was not relegated to the servants' hall, though he had thought of asking for no more than that. He was admitted to the full honour of sonship; he was to wear the best robe and the ring, and he was to sit down to the table which was loaded in his honour. The mercy we receive through Christ, and which is to be offered "in his Name," is no imperfect thing;

it is full, entire, complete. All past transgressions are absolutely forgiven, so that they will never be alleged against us or stand between us and the love of God. We ourselves are taken into the gracious favour of our heavenly Father, admitted to his family, counted among his own children, constituted his heirs, having freest access to his presence, welcome to call him by the most endearing name. 2. *Immediate.* There is no probation or apprenticeship to be served; we have not to wait to approve ourselves; we are not sentenced to any form of expiation by menial service before we gain our childhood. At once, so soon as we return in spirit unto God, that moment we are welcomed to the side and to the home of our Father. 3. *In faith.* We are to seek and to find forgiveness "in Christ's Name," *i.e.* in the exercise of a simple but living faith in him as in our Divine Saviour. So the apostles evidently understood their Master (see Acts x. 43; xiii. 38, 39; 1 Pet. i. 8, 9; 1 John ii. 12). Thus the ascended Saviour instructed the "abortive-born apostle" (Acts xxvi. 18), and thus that faithful witness continually taught (see Acts xx. 21). Those who speak for Christ are to invite all sinful men to put their trust in him, the Saviour of mankind, the "Propitiation for the sins of the world," and, accepting him as such, to take the full, free mercy of God unto eternal life.

Such was the message which the apostles were solemnly charged to deliver. There was in this great instruction: 1. One charge which they were more particularly to observe—they were to begin at Jerusalem. It was right they should begin there, for it was there that all "these things" (ver. 48) were known and could be attested; and, beginning there, the grace and the magnanimity of the Crucified One would be more abundantly manifested. 2. Another, which more particularly affects ourselves—this message of mercy is to be carried to "all nations." It is "the common salvation," needed by all and fitted for all, to work out and send forth which the Lord Jesus lived and died.—C.

Ver. 48.—*Bearing witness.* These brief words, "Ye are witnesses," being among the very last which Jesus spoke to his apostles, must have lingered in their ear for the rest of their life. In moments of doubt, or of depression, or of danger, the remembrance that their Lord and Leader had charged them to be his witnesses may well have stirred and strengthened them to fresh courage and to renewed activity. They are words that may well stimulate us also to duty and self-sacrifice.

I. The unique service rendered by the apostles. They were witnesses of "those things," the greatest things that were ever seen and ever attested in the history of mankind; things they were on the full and true statement of which, on the cordial and practical acceptance of which, depended the life and the hope of the world. They could face all with whom they came in contact, and declare that they saw with their own eyes, heard with their own ears, witnessed in their own persons: 1. A perfectly beautiful, a spotless human life, in which, though they saw it under all possible circumstances and when under least constraint or reserve, they could find no flaw at all (1 Pet. ii. 22). 2. Works of power, which were invariably works of pity and of kindness, of such a nature that there was no possibility of mistake. 3. Words of truth and grace such as mortal lips had never spoken, and such as met the deepest wants of man's hungering heart, of his yearning and aspiring soul. 4. Sufferings and sorrows beyond what others knew, borne with a patience that was sublime. 5. A death undergone in shame and pain, amid natural wonders and with more than human nobility. 6. A glorious resurrection from the grave. 7. A message of mercy and hope to be delivered to all mankind in the name of this great Teacher, Healer, Sufferer, Conqueror.

II. The valuable service which is open to us all. 1. We also can testify, in word, to "these things." We leave, and are content to leave, some mysteries which belong to the Christian faith; we do not try, as we need not try, either to explain or to understand them. But "these things," which the world needs to know for its inward peace and its true prosperity, we can speak. We are familiar with the holy and beautiful life of Jesus Christ. We know the thought, we "have the mind of Christ" on all the deepest and highest subjects with which our character and our destiny are bound up. We are conversant with the sufferings and the sorrows of the Saviour; for the story of his Passion is better known by us than any other history whatsoever—it is not only in our memory, it is in our heart. We can speak of his death and of his triumph over the grave. We know well what is the message of truth and grace he desires to be declared to the whole world. We can speak of him and for him. 2. And we can find an audience. There are many who will not listen to us, but there are those who will. The *young*, who have a spirit of docility and inquiry; the *sick* and the *sad*, to whom "the consolation which is in Christ" is the one thing that heals and calms; the *poor*, to whom the pearl of great price is welcome, and who are willing to be made "rich toward God;" the *disappointed* and the *weary*, who are glad to know of One who can give "rest unto the soul;"—these will receive our testimony. 3. We can bear the best and truest witness of the life. What men want to be convinced of is that Christianity is a living power; that it not only has very fine sentiments to teach —these can be found elsewhere—but that it is a moral and spiritual power that can save the lost, can cleanse the foul, can soften the hard-hearted, can humble the proud, can arouse the indifferent and obtuse, can infuse cheerfulness and joy into the heart of the poor and lowly, can give rest of spirit to those who are encompassed by the cares of time, can fill the soul with tender sympathy and prompt to generous and self-denying succour, can substitute a forgiving for a vindictive spirit in the wronged, can enable its possessors to gain a victory over themselves and over the world and to crown a victorious life by a death of calm tranquillity and joyful hope. Here is scope for witness-bearing; and, as every Christian man has the truth of Christ on which to feed, the example of Christ to follow, and the Holy Spirit of Christ to whom to look for his indwelling power, it is open to every disciple to be a witness, whose testimony shall be valuable on earth and acceptable in heaven.—C.

Ver. 49.—*The secret of spiritual strength.* How came it to pass that the apostles of our Lord became such strong men and did such noble work for their Master and for mankind *so soon after* they manifested such weakness as they did? We consider—

I. THEIR INSUFFICIENCY UP TO THE TIME OF THE ASCENSION. They had been receiving for many months the inestimable advantage of Christ's own teaching for their mental enlightenment, and his own influence for their spiritual ennoblement. And this teaching and training cannot have been—we may confidently say *was not*—without very great value throughout their subsequent course. Yet they undoubtedly lacked something which would complete them for the great task before them. They showed but scant determination (Matt. xxvi. 41, 43), but feeble courage (Matt. xxvi. 56), but little understanding of their Master's aim (Acts i. 6); and this, too, at the very close of his ministry, when their great and special privilege was expiring. Something more they sadly needed to prepare them for their work.

II. THE PROMISED POWER. 1. Its announcement and its confirmation. It was first predicted by the prophets who preceded our Lord (Isa. xliv. 3); and more particularly Joel (ii. 28, 29). It was renewed and confirmed, at first more indefinitely, and here more definitely, by our Lord (John xiv. 16, 26; xv. 26, 27; xvi. 7; text). 2. Its historical fulfilment (Acts ii. 1—11). 3. Its permanent results. These men, whose character and whose fitness for their grand and lofty mission left much to be desired, "endued with power from on high," became wonderfully equipped for and admirably adapted to the noble mission to which Christ appointed them. They became strong (1) to stand in the evil hour of temptation, defying the authority of Jewish council and the sword of Roman ruler; they became strong (2) to suffer, rejoicing that they were "counted worthy to suffer shame" for the Master's sake and Name; they became strong (3) to testify, "with great power" giving witness to the Resurrection, and great grace being on them all; they became strong (4) to grasp the great central and saving truths of the gospel, making known to their own compeers by their speech, and to all time by their letters, the "mystery which was hidden from the generations," the great and gracious purpose of God to the whole race of men; they became strong (5) to build and work, to lay the foundation-stone of the gospel of Christ (Eph. ii. 26), of that Church of the future which has already endured for eighteen centuries, and is more than ever bent on the conversion and conquest of the world. We know what made these weak men strong, these failing men to triumph. It was the power of the Holy Ghost resting upon them, opening their eyes that they might see, quickening their souls that they might feel, nerving their hearts that they might stand, strengthening their hands that they might labour and achieve.

III. Its lasting lesson. It is this which, if anything does, will make us strong also. What the Christian workman wants is *the power which comes immediately from God*, the inspiration of the Divine Spirit; in truth, the same bestowal as that which the apostles were now promised and afterwards received. The miraculous endowments which accompanied the gift of the Holy Ghost were but the accidents of the bestowal. The power to heal without failure or to speak without error was nothing to the power to testify without fear and to live without reproach.

> "Though on our heads no tongues of fire
> Their wondrous powers impart,"

we need, as much as they did then, the illuminating, sanctifying, empowering influences of Heaven—"God's Spirit in our heart." Without that, our most heroic efforts will fail; with it, our humblest endeavours will succeed. To gain that we must have (1) purity of heart and aim; (2) earnest and believing prayer.—C.

Ver. 50.—*The Ascension.* Many thoughts offer themselves to us as we think upon this last scene.

I. The fitness of the place whence Jesus ascended. Not, indeed, that Jerusalem could claim to be worthy of such an honour—Jerusalem that had but lately dyed its hands in the blood of its Messiah. But as the ancient dwelling-place of God, as the seat and source of heavenly truth, as the metropolis of religion upon the earth, as the place that furnishes the name and type of the city of our hope, as the joyous gathering-place of the good,—it was well that, from without *its* walls, he whose presence makes the home and the joy and the glory of his people should pass to his throne. For from that moment "Jerusalem" meant another thing to mankind. Christ took up its meaning as he rose. All the associations of love and hope, of grandeur and gladness, which had belonged to the earthly are transferred to the heavenly city, where he dwells in glory, where he reigns in power. There is a transference, not formal but actual, of the centre and metropolis of religious thought from the Jerusalem below to the Jerusalem above.

II. The nature of the last scene. "They climb the hillside; they cross its summit; they are approaching Bethany. He stops; they gather round. He looks upon them; he lifts his hands; he begins to bless them. What love unutterable in that parting look! What untold riches in that blessing! His hands are uplifted, his lips engaged in blessing, when slowly he begins to rise. Earth has lost her power to keep him; the waiting up-drawing heavens claim him as their own. He rises, but still, as he floats upward through the yielding air, his eyes are bent on those uplooking men; his arms are stretched over them in the attitude of benediction, his voice is heard dying away in blessings as he ascends. Awe-struck, in silence they follow him with straining eyes as his body lessens to sight, till the commissioned cloud enfolds, cuts off all further vision, and closes the earthly and sensible communion between Jesus and his disciples" (Dr. Hanna).

III. The reception the Saviour had in heaven. There have been "triumphant entries" in this little world of ours, and in the history of our human race, the pouring forth in loud acclaim of the pride and joy of many thousands of hearts. But to what a vanishing point do they sink when placed by the side of this entry of the conquering Saviour into heaven! Though unable to form any conception that can approach the glorious reality, yet we may well love to linger in imagination over that blessed scene. His struggle over, his sorrows borne, his temptations met and mastered, his work finished, his great battle fought and his victory won,—the victorious Lord passes through all the ranks of the angelic host, amid their reverent worship and adoring acclamations, to his throne of power and glory.

> "Look, ye saints! the sight is glorious:
> See the Man of sorrows now
> From the fight returned victorious;
> Every knee to him shall bow."

IV. The effect immediately produced on the minds of the disciples. Blank dismay, inconsolable sorrow, should we think? So thinking, we should be wrong.

They "returned to Jerusalem with great joy." Yet their Master was gone from them to return no more till that uncertain and distant day of which the angels spoke (Acts i. 11). How do we account for this? The explanation is found here—they were *now perfectly assured of the Divine mission* of Jesus Christ. His death had cast a dark shadow of doubt and dread over their hearts. His resurrection had revived their confidence and their hope. But this final manifestation, this "sign in the heavens," this act of being taken up, like Elijah, into heaven, swept away the last fragment of doubt that may have been left behind; they were now absolutely sure, without any reserve or qualification whatever, that the Master they had loved and served was indeed their true Messiah, the Sent of God, worthy of their deepest veneration and their strongest attachment; so they "worshipped him" reverently, and went back to Jerusalem with the joy of faith and love filling their souls. There is no misery so unendurable as doubt, and there is no blessedness so sweet as rest of heart after spiritual disquietude.

V. ITS PERMANENT EFFECT ON THE APOSTLES' MINDS. This was unreservedly good. It *was* "expedient for them that he should go away." His bodily absence changed the complexion of their dependence upon him. It had been that of childhood; it was now to be that of manhood. With him by their side, as he had been, they would not have become the "men in him" they did become after he left them. The deeper and fuller knowledge of him they gained by his departure led to an enlargement of faith and to a deepening of love, and also to that fulness of attachment and consecration we recognize and rejoice in during their later life. They came to know him and love him and serve him as the Divine Saviour of mankind, and this made them worthier men and truer servants of their Lord. All earthly ambitions respecting the right and left hand of the throne were transformed into a noble consecration to the invisible Lord.

VI. ITS PRICELESS VALUE TO OURSELVES. 1. Christ is *accessible* to us all. Had he lived and reigned at Jerusalem, or some other sacred metropolis, he would only have been accessible to those who dwelt or journeyed there. But now he is "with us all." For heaven is everywhere; the throne of grace is within the reach of the faintest whisper that comes from every burdened heart, from every seeking soul, wheresoever it may be breathed. A living faith can now realize the constant nearness of its living Lord; it has not to take even a sabbath day's journey to find itself in his presence and to make known its request. 2. He is seated on the *throne of power*. To him who has passed into the heavens we can realize that "all power is given" (Matt. xxviii. 18). We can well believe that our Master in heaven can do for us what we ask of him; that his arm is one of glorious might; that his hand has plenteousness of bounty and of blessing. And in all our time of need we can go to him, with holy confidence, to ask of him the help, the guidance, the blessing, we require. 3. He has *all rightful authority*. If he still dwelt on earth, we might be dubious of this; but to the heavenly Saviour we unanimously and cordially ascribe all headship; to him we yield our willing and unquestioning obedience; and we rejoice to believe that he is ruling and governing the affairs of his Church, and reigning in the interests of the whole human race; that it is his hand that is at the helm, and that will safely guide the tempest-ridden vessel to the harbour. 4. He is our *constant and ever-living* Lord. With all that is earthly we associate change and death; with the heavenly we connect the thought of continuance and life. Of our heavenly Lord we can think, and we delight to think, that whoever changes he is evermore the same, "yesterday, and to-day, and for ever;" that while human ministers "are not suffered to continue by reason of death," he hath "an unchangeable priesthood," and is able to save *evermore* ("to the uttermost") all those "that come unto God by him." And as we look forward to the future, and realize our own mortality, we cherish the joyous thought that, if we do but "abide in him" until the evening shadows gather and "life's long day" passes into the darkness of death, we shall, in heaven's eternal morning, open our eyes to see the "King in his beauty," to "behold his glory," and shall "sit down with him on his throne," sharing for ever his own and his saints' everlasting rest.—C.

Vers. 1—12.—*The Resurrection discovered.* When the women and the other mourners left the Lord's tomb on the evening of the Crucifixion, it was with the intention, after the sabbath was past, of completing the embalmment. This office of love seems to have been left largely to the women; for it is they who make their way, in the early morning of the first day of the week, to the sepulchre. They seem to have had no knowledge, for they had no apprehension, of the Roman guard, which was manifestly placed at the sepulchre on the Jewish sabbath, when the disciples and the women were keeping the sad day in strictest privacy. Their one apprehension was how to roll away the stone; but, like so many apprehended difficulties, it was found to vanish away—some hands stronger than women's had been before them and had rolled away the stone, and left them no difficulty in *discovering* an empty tomb. The narrative of John about Mary Magdalene's visit is quite consistent with Luke's narrative; for, as Gilbert West has pointed out in his admirable analysis of the Resurrection-history, Mary rushes off alone to tell the disciples, "They have taken away the Lord out of the sepulchre, and *we* know not where they have laid him"—implying that others had been with her at the tomb. Without any misgivings, therefore, about the reliable character of the history, let us point out the instructive steps in the discovery of our Lord's resurrection.

I. THE WOMEN WITH THE SPICES DISCOVER AN EMPTY TOMB. (Vers. 1—3.) They had employed the evening after the sabbath was past in preparing all that was needful for embalming thoroughly and finally the Saviour's body. It was with this fragrant burden they made their way in the twilight towards the tomb, to find their fears groundless and the stone already removed. But a new fear now laid hold on them. There is no body in the tomb; it is empty. They do not appear to have taken in the significance of the grave-clothes carefully put aside because never to be needed more, as John did at his subsequent visit; their whole anxiety was about what had become of the dear body which they had come to embalm. The empty tomb was a discovery. The first impression, as indicated by Mary's message (John xx. 2), was that their enemies had seized the body and disposed of it to defeat all their ideas of embalming. One thing is certain from the history, that neither the women nor the disciples could have been parties to the removal of the body.

II. THE WOMEN THAT WAITED GOT EXPLANATIONS FROM THE ANGELS. (Vers. 4—7.) Mary Magdalene, acting on impulse, seems to have hurried off to tell Peter and John about the discovery of the empty tomb, while her companions wait longer to get some explanation, if possible, regarding it. And the waiting women are not disappointed. Angels appear in shining garments, and, as the women sink before them in terror, they proceed to reassure them with the glad tidings, "Why seek ye the living among the dead? He is not here, but is risen: remember how he spake unto you when he was yet in Galilee, saying, The Son of man must be delivered into the hands of sinful men, and be crucified, and the third day rise again." It was the angels that reminded them of the promise of resurrection, and how it was now fulfilled. This is the second stage, therefore, in the discovery of the Resurrection. The fear of the women had been that the Jews had got the body. But there could have been no such plot carried out, for the very simple reason that, if they had got the body and it had not risen, they could have produced such evidence at the Pentecost as would have overturned the apostolic testimony, and prevented the inauguration of the Christian society. The angelic explanation, based as it was on our Lord's previous promises, was the only satisfactory one. The Resurrection was the fulfilment of Christ's deliberate plan.

III. THE REPORT OF THE WOMEN TO THE ELEVEN AND THE REST. (Vers. 8—11.) It is quite reasonable to suppose that Mary Magdalene was the forerunner of the rest, and through her report induced Peter and John to start at once for the sepulchre, while the main body of the women, consisting of Joanna, Mary the mother of James, and others, returned more leisurely to make their report. At all events, the narrative of Luke implies all that is given by Matthew and by John. For the disciples who went to Emmaus distinctly say that certain of the disciples "went to the sepulchre, and found it even so as the women had said; but *him they saw not*" (ver. 24)—implying that the women, in their report, had spoken of having seen the Master.[1] The testimony of the women was based upon a threefold foundation—first, the assurance of the angels; secondly, the promise of resurrection given in Galilee by the Lord; thirdly, according to

[1] Cf. Gilbert West's 'Observations on the History and Evidences of the Resurrection of Jesus Christ'—a work which received favourable recognition from Lessing, in his remarks appended to the 'Wolfenbüttel Fragments.'

Matthew's account, an interview with the risen Lord himself (Matt. xxviii. 9, 10). It was a remarkable testimony certainly, but at the same time it had ample warrant.

IV. THE BEST-ATTESTED FACTS MAY SEEM, TO DAZED MINDS, THE IDLEST FANCIES. (Ver. 11.) The poor disciples are, however, so overpowered with grief and disappointment that they are utterly unprepared for the announcement of the Resurrection. Here the suppler mind of woman is revealed in contrast to the more plodding, sifting, logic-demanding mind of man. The women enjoy the consolations of the Resurrection much sooner than the men. They take in the evidence at a glance. They do not question. They simply accept. But the disciples will not believe in a hurry. And so the messengers of the best tidings ever related unto men are at first in the position of the Master himself, and constrained to cry, "Who hath believed our report?" And the unbelieving criticism of to-day is more unreasonable than the disciples were before the women. Because the resurrection of Christ may break in upon the ideas of nature's absolute uniformity which the critics have adopted, the whole evidence of resurrection-power continued through the ages is to be treated as an idle tale! Minds may be so dazed with grief or with success on certain lines as to discredit the completest evidence ever offered to the world. Before prejudice, the strongest facts get resolved into the idlest fancies. We should earnestly seek an impartial mind.

V. PETER'S FIRST ATTEMPT TO DEAL WITH THE EVIDENCE OF THE RESURRECTION. (Ver. 12.) Peter, as we learn from John's account, accompanied by John, rushes off to see the sepulchre. He reaches it after John, but pushes past him, and goes into the sepulchre. There he sees the linen clothes laid by themselves, yet departs without reaching anything but perplexity. To John's keener intellect the grave-clothes, so neatly deposited and the napkin laid in a place by itself, show that Jesus had risen, and laid aside his sleeping-clothes, as we do our night-dresses in the morning, because he had entered on the day of resurrection. John becomes a believer in the Resurrection on *circumstantial evidence.* Peter, it would seem, cannot make it out, and has to get a personal interview somewhat later on that day (cf. ver. 34), before he can take it in. It thus appears that one mind may handle the Resurrection evidence successfully, while another may only stumble through it into deeper perplexity. But when a soul like Peter is in earnest, the Lord will not leave him in the darkness, but will grant such further light as will dispel the gloom and dissipate all perplexity. Meanwhile the discovery of Christ's resurrection is but the interesting first stage in the remarkable evidence to part of which we have yet to proceed.—R. M. E.

Vers. 13—35.—*The risen Christ the best Escort on the pilgrimage of life.* We left Peter in perplexity, but he and John must have returned to the rest of the disciples, and reported the emptiness of the sepulchre, but that they had not seen the Risen One (ver. 24). John does not seem to have communicated his own convictions unto the others. Most likely he is turning the matter over in his mind, as contemplative and deep-thinking men will do before giving a public pronouncement. Meanwhile there is a dispersion of some of the disciples that very afternoon. Thomas seems to have gone away, and to have remained away that night. And two of them proceed seven or eight miles into the country to Emmaus, where their home seems to have been. It is these two pilgrims that we are now to follow. They leave the city, and their conversation is sad. They are discussing the bright hopes which have been so lately quenched by the crucifixion of their Lord. It is while so sad that Jesus joins them; for he who had been the "Man of sorrows" and "acquainted with grief" is ever breaking in upon men's troubles to relieve them. His treatment of these "unwilling sceptics," as they have been lately called, is most instructive.[1] He probes their sorrow, gets an insight into its cause, gets them to state their hopes, their disappointments, and the rumours they had heard of his resurrection. On this basis, although apparently an unknown Stranger, he proceeds to show them their error and slowness in not believing all that the prophets have spoken about Messiah. Beginning, therefore, at Moses, he expounds to them from all the prophets that Messiah must first suffer, and then enter into his glory. The exposition was so brilliant and interesting, that they felt their hearts burning within them during the process. Then, under compulsion, he enters their lodging at Emmaus, sits down as Guest, then proceeds as Host to distribute the food as

[1] Cf. Munger's 'Appeal to Life,' p. 25.

at the sacramental meal. Not till then did they recognize their risen Lord in the devout Being who graced their board. Once recognized, and thus dispelling all their doubt, he vanishes into the invisible. Such experience could not be quietly kept at Emmaus. They resolve to return that very night to Jerusalem, to report their interview, and how blessed an Escort Jesus had been in their pilgrimage. They are in time for the manifestation of the Risen One to the assembled disciples. We may learn from the narrative such lessons as these.

I. JESUS MAKES HIS ADVENT TO US WHEN OUR SOULS ARE SAD. This is the very spirit of the dispensation. Thus he cried, "Come unto me, all ye that labour and are heavy laden, and I will give you rest" (Matt. xi. 28). And as the risen Saviour he prefers, we may well believe, the house of mourning to the house of mirth. Not only so, but when souls are in sad perplexity, when they are "unwilling sceptics," it is his delight to come and be their Escort along life's way, and lead them out of gloom and difficulty into real peace and joy. Now, when we know how accessible he is through prayer, we should never undertake any pilgrimage without securing the companionship of Jesus.

II. WE LEARN THAT JESUS IS OFTEN WITH US WHILE WE KNOW IT NOT. Here was he with these two pilgrims, taking step by step with them to Emmaus, and yet their eyes were so holden that they did not know him. He was near them, but they did not know him. Is not this the case with all of us? He is at our side, he takes every step with us, but we are so blinded with care and preoccupation that we fail to see him or enjoy his society as we should. The omnipresence of Jesus should be the believer's constant consolation.

III. JESUS IS HIMSELF AT ONCE THE GREAT SUBJECT AND THE GREAT EXPOSITOR OF SCRIPTURE. Here we find him, after listening so sympathetically to all the difficulties of the disciples, proceeding to expound to them, "in all the Scriptures, the things concerning himself." "The testimony of Jesus is the spirit of prophecy." And here it is well to notice what is the substance of the whole revelation. It is put in these words of the risen Saviour, "Ought not Messiah to have suffered these things, and to have entered (εἰσελθεῖν) into his glory?" The Authorized and Revised Versions have alike failed to give the proper rendering here. Our Lord declares that he has entered already into his glory, just as he has already passed through his sufferings. We believe it can be made out from this and other passages that our Lord ascended—of course invisibly—without disciples as spectators, to heaven, and reported himself on high immediately after telling Mary, "I ascend [not 'will ascend'] unto my Father and your Father, to my God and your God" (John xx. 17; cf. also Bush on 'The Resurrection.') This supposition of an ascension on the very day of the Resurrection enables us to understand his movements during the rest of the day, and his bestowal of the Spirit, which was conditioned on his glorification, in the evening (John xx. 22; cf. John vii. 39). It also enables us to regard heaven as his head-quarters during the forty days before his *visible* ascension from Olivet. Upon this interesting subject we cannot now dwell, however; but we content ourselves by pointing it out, and emphasizing the fact of Jesus as the suffering and glorified Messiah being the Hero, the Substance, and the great Expositor of revelation. It is when we look for him in the Word that it becomes luminous and delightful.

IV. THE ENTERTAINMENT OF JESUS IS SURE TO LEAD TO SPECIAL BLESSING. These two men insisted on Jesus sojourning with them, because it was towards evening and the day was far spent. And as he sojourned, he was transmuted from Guest to Host, and gave them a sacramental instead of common feast. It is when devoutly asking a blessing on the bread that he is recognized, only, however, to vanish like a vision from their sight. Now we may pass through an analogous experience. Is not this what is meant by the Master when he says, "Behold, I stand at the door, and knock: if any man hear my voice, and open the door, I will come in to him, and will sup with him, and he with me" (Rev. iii. 20)? If we are open-hearted, and welcome Jesus, he will enter our hearts and sup with us, taking whatever we have to give him, and delighting in it, and enable us to sup with him. He will change into a *Host* from being our *Guest*. It was thus he acted at the marriage of Cana; it was thus he acted at Emmaus; it was thus he acted on the shore of the Galilæan lake. He may be Guest, but he will soon show himself to be our Host, and give us a feast of fat things.

V. Life is largely a living upon happy memories. As soon as the Risen One had vanished, they began to compare notes about the burning heart, and all the happy memories of their journey from Jerusalem. And as they plodded in that night through the dark to report their great discovery, they lived upon the happy memory. But, had they only known it, the risen Jesus was in some way making that return journey to Jerusalem too, making for the same upper room, to reveal himself to the disciples, and their fellowship with him might have been repeated. At all events, we need not live on happy *memories*, but may enjoy Christ's spiritual presence and his escort all through the pilgrimage of life. It is this which will make the present life a heaven, not by anticipation merely, but in actual enjoyment; for fellowship with Christ, even though he be unseen, is the chief element of heaven. May we have the great Escort with us all the way!—R. M. E.

Vers. 36—53.—*Infallible proofs and inevitable partings.* The Emmaus pilgrims have hardly entered the upper room and reported their interview with Jesus, receiving the intelligence that perplexed Peter has got his perplexity resolved, when, notwithstanding that the doors are barred for fear of the Jews, the Risen One appears in the midst of them, and says, "Peace be unto you!" They are at first terrified at such an advent, seeing that it sets aside the ordinary laws of matter, and shows all precaution unavailing when Jesus is determined to get in. But he soon disabuses their minds and dismisses their troubles. Although he can get through barred doors, he is not a disembodied spirit, but a Person with flesh and bones. This he proceeds to demonstrate to their sense-perceptions. Having given them infallible proofs, he next proceeds to expound the Scriptures in detail to them, just as he had done on the way to Emmaus. On these sure foundations he bases their faith, and sends them forth, commissioned to preach repentance and remission of sins. He concludes his interview with the promise of the Father, for which they were to wait at Jerusalem after his visible ascension. And so he is carried up to heaven from Bethany, and the disciples return to wait at Jerusalem in joy until they receive power from on high. And here we have to notice—

I. The message of the risen Saviour to distracted souls is peace. The salutation of the East received new depth and meaning when employed by the risen Saviour, when for the first time he appeared among his assembled disciples. He only could pacify them. He is the same "Peacemaker" still. It is his advent which drives away distractions, and secures a peace which passeth all understanding.

II. The risen Jesus supplies infallible proofs of his resurrection to the pacified disciples. When pacified by him, they were then fitted for judgment. To place the proofs before worldly, distracted souls would have been throwing pearls before swine.[1] It is before the disciples whose fears have been dispelled that he places the proofs. He urges calm investigation. Here are his hands and feet and side. Handle him, use sense-perception to the utmost. Make out that he has a body, and the same one which was crucified. Their joy at the proofs overpowered them for the moment, so that they could hardly credit it. Then he asked them for meat, and was content to eat before them a piece of a broiled fish. The honeycomb addition is not supported by the best manuscripts, and has been omitted in the Revised Version. The last doubt must depart before such proofs. It is the same Saviour who had been crucified, and he is among them in a body, able to partake of food, and perform all the functions assigned to a body dominated by a healthy spirit. Now, although we cannot see or handle the Risen One, we have yet the evidence of his Resurrection so set before us that only criminal partiality can resist it. Dr. Arnold, so accomplished an historian, declares that there is no fact of history sustained by better evidence.[2] If we made sure of impartial and fearful minds to begin with, the infallible proofs would be recognized in their full power.

III. The risen Saviour helps his servants to understand the Scriptures. We learn from John's account that "he breathed on them," and so conveyed to them the Holy Ghost. Along with the outward exposition, therefore, of the Scripture refer-

[1] Cf. on this important point a sermon by Bishop Reichel on 'The Necessary Limits of Christian Evidences.'

[2] 'Sermons on Christian Life: its Hopes, its Fears, and its Close,' 4th edit., pp. 15, 16.

ences to himself, there is given the inward inspiration. It is this which made these men such masters of the sacred oracles so far as they indicate Christ's mission. With opened understandings, with inspired hearts, the once sealed book became an open secret, and the fountain-head of missionary enterprise. And the witnesses need similar enlightenment still. By waiting on the Master prayerfully and studiously we shall obtain the key to interpretation, and have the fairy palaces unlocked for us.

IV. A GOSPEL OF REPENTANCE AND REMISSION OF SINS OF A UNIVERSAL CHARACTER IS TO BE PREACHED IN HIS NAME. For Christ comes to make men sorry for their sins, while at the same time they enjoy the sense of their pardon. As risen Saviour, he is the outward Guarantee of our justification from all things from which we could not be justified by the Law of Moses. He was "delivered for our offences, and raised again for our justification" (Rom. iv. 25). And to these benefits all nations are to have access. The proofs of resurrection, the understanding of the Scriptures, and the inspiration of the Holy Ghost, were with a view to a practical issue in the publication of glad tidings to all nations.

V. POWER IS GUARANTEED IF THEY WAIT PRAYERFULLY AT JERUSALEM. They had got the Spirit as zephyr-breath. They had still to get him in Pentecostal and fiery power. Hence they are encouraged by the Lord to wait for this at Jerusalem, for work without spiritual power would be useless. And they waited, and were made world-conquerors by the gift of power. So ought the Lord's people to wait for power still.

VI. THE ASCENSION WAS THE NECESSARY COMPLEMENT OF RESURRECTION, AND THE GUARANTEE OF ULTIMATE VICTORY. We have already seen reason for believing that, on the day of resurrection, Jesus *privately* ascended to the Father, reported himself there, and made heaven his head-quarters during "the great forty days." But a *public* ascension before the assembled disciples was necessary to establish their faith and joy. And so they were permitted to see their beloved Lord ascending, in spite of gravitation, up into the blue heavens, and speeding towards the centre of the universe at the right hand of God. Yet the inevitable separation did not prevent them from returning to Jerusalem with great joy, and continuing there until the Pentecost. They divided their time between the upper room and the temple. They waited in joyful anticipation of the promised power, and they got it in due season. And the Ascension ought to be to all believers a matter of definite experience. It is to this St. Paul refers when he speaks, in the Epistle to the Ephesians, of being "raised up together with Christ, and made to sit together in heavenly places in Christ Jesus." There is an ascension-experience as well as a resurrection-experience—an experience in which we feel that we have risen superior to all earthly attractions, and that we, setting our affections, indeed, on things above, are sitting by faith among them with our Lord. It is this ecstatic state which heralds the advent of spiritual power. May it belong to all of us!—R. M. E.

HOMILETICAL INDEX

TO

THE GOSPEL ACCORDING TO ST. LUKE.

VOLUME II.

CHAPTER XIII.

CHAPTER XIV.

CHAPTER XV.

CHAPTER XVI.

CHAPTER XVII.

CHAPTER XVIII.

CHAPTER XIX.

CHAPTER XX.

CHAPTER XXI.

CHAPTER XXII.

CHAPTER XXIII.

CHAPTER XXIV.